My friend Shane has written another terrific book. He is once again insightful and clever and has filled these pages with predictably kind and sometimes hard words. Shane is a voice I trust. I deeply value his insights, and I know you will as well.

—Bob Goff, *New York Times* bestselling author, *Love Does*, *Everybody Always*, and *Dream Big*

At a time of deep divisions, when religious faith is too often reduced to a marker of political allegiance and lines are too quickly drawn between friend and foe, Shane Claiborne offers a voice of resistance. Drawing on biblical teaching and church history, Claiborne invites readers to grapple with difficult issues with honesty, compassion, and courage. *Rethinking Life* is not just a book for progressive Christians but is for all Christians who seek to discern how to live faithfully in troubled times. This challenging, clear-eyed, and hope-filled book is a gift to the American church.

—Kristin Kobes Du Mez, author, *New York Times* bestseller *Jesus and John Wayne: How White Evangelicals Corrupted a Faith and Fractured a Nation*

Great truth is invariably simple, but not at all simplistic. It builds right on top of the very basics. Thus we have to forever relearn the basics—real well! Shane Claiborne does this almost naturally.

—Fr. Richard Rohr, Center for Action and Contemplation, Albuquerque

Rethinking Life is an intervention. In a moment when the politics of life is leading to death, master storyteller and public theologian Shane Claiborne leads followers of Jesus on a brave pilgrimage through the meaning, ethics, and politics of life—and death—and love. This is one of those books you will cherish and quote for the rest of your life.

—Lisa Sharon Harper, president and founder, FreedomRoad.us; author, *Fortune: How Race Broke My Family and the World and How to Repair It All*

I resonate with this book in the marrow of my bones! In *Rethinking Life*, Shane Claiborne shows us what a genuine pro-life theology, ethic, and practice demands of us and looks like in practice. Authentic Christianity has always been robustly pro-life, but it ̶̶̶̶̶̶̶̶̶̶ an selectively and narrowly applied. In *Ret* ̶̶̶̶̶̶̶̶̶̶ keen as his heart is compassionate. And b ̶̶̶̶̶̶̶̶̶̶ y page.

̶̶̶̶̶̶̶̶̶̶ *erything's on Fire*

Shane Claiborne is a force of gospel power. In this book he mobilizes his energy, wisdom, honesty, compassion, and practicality into a manifesto for transformation. As a truth teller, he does not flinch from the indices of our skewed public life, marked as they are by anti-neighborly violence. In the midst of this truth telling, however, Claiborne attests to the buoyancy of a gospel faith that can be acted out in any circumstance of our distorted life together. If readers follow his testimony, they will surely be led to life in a "contrast culture" that traffics in God's love and restorative justice, which are sure to create zones of well-being. This is a book that is wise in its exposé and fervent in its hope giving. What matters is to read attentively and then to act accordingly.

—Walter Brueggemann, Columbia Theological Seminary

Here is a book that courageously and effectively tackles several difficult issues around the ethics of life for those who wish to follow Jesus of Nazareth. Whether it is abortion, capital punishment, eugenics, war, or the historic culpability of the church, Shane Claiborne avoids oversimplification in any direction by focusing on the human element, offering provocative questions for both individuals and small groups to chew on.

—Most Rev. Michael B. Curry, Presiding Bishop of the Episcopal
Church; author, *Love Is the Way* and *The Power of Love*

When I am dismayed by how little Christians are turning to Jesus these days, along comes my dear younger brother in Christ, Shane Claiborne, with a new word or call, and now a new book! My students at Georgetown are deeply hungry for the "rethinking of life," and Shane is one of the best authors I know to help them do that. Despite their skepticism of religion, the young people I talk with every day are still deeply attracted to Jesus, and Shane offers them a real introduction to the one who most guides us to rethink everything.

—Jim Wallis, inaugural chair and founding director, Center
on Faith and Justice at Georgetown University

A calm but passionate defense of human life at every stage. Shane Claiborne reminds us that to be pro-life means to be pro all lives, not just pro some lives, from the innocent unborn child in the womb to the guilty inmate languishing on death row. Every life is sacred.

—James Martin, SJ, author, *Learning to Pray: A Guide for Everyone*

With theological savvy, historical insight, and uncommon wisdom, Shane Claiborne reminds us of the subversive power of telling the truth, being unafraid to follow wherever it leads. In summoning the followers of Jesus to become "midwives of a better world," Claiborne's prophetic voice has never been clearer—or more timely.

—Randall Balmer, author, *Bad Faith: Race and the Rise of the Religious Right*

Perhaps Shane Claiborne's most theologically significant work, *Rethinking Life* offers a profound articulation of a consistent pro-life Christian ethic, richly informed by Shane's on-the-ground experiences in activism and witness. Highly recommend!

—David Gushee, Distinguished University Professor of Christian Ethics, Mercer University; Chair in Christian Social Ethics, Vrije Universteit Amsterdam; senior research fellow, International Baptist Theological Study Centre; president emeritus, American Academy of Religion, Society of Christian Ethics

Shane Claiborne has once again offered the world a book that reorients our spiritual worldview toward compassion, justice, and humility. *Rethinking Life* dares the reader to embrace a sacred spiritual framework for life beyond hollow political talking points and shallow religious doctrine; we are called to witness the sacred in other people, cultures, traditions, faiths, classes, and racial classifications. This book pushes believers to fully live a Christ-centered life and challenges the nonbeliever to construct a moral philosophy rooted in compassion.

—Otis Moss III, author, *Dancing in the Darkness: Spiritual Lessons for Thriving in Turbulent Times*

What does love require of us? That is a question Christ followers need to be asking at every crossroads (and with every breath), and everyone else would benefit from asking it as well. This question and a variety of biblically rooted and profound answers are at the core of *Rethinking Life*. Shane Claiborne has a unique and powerful voice as he comments on the call of the church at this historic moment; he makes camp in the no-man's-land between the two sides of the cultural wars, exuding the winsome fragrance of Christ. You don't have to agree with all of his answers (not even his wife does, as Shane admits in the book), but there is no doubt that his questions matter, and his responses are provocative in all the best ways.

—Rev. Dr. Alexia Salvatierra, academic dean, Centro Latino; associate professor of mission and global transformation, Fuller Theological Seminary

In matters of life and death and of the heart of God, the stakes are too high to limit our conversation partners. Claiborne has given us a probing exploration of history, biblical themes, and personal experience that demands serious consideration for an expansive ethic of life.

—Walter Kim, president, National Association of Evangelicals

Shane's latest offering to the church, *Rethinking Life*, provides a useful juxtaposition of personal encounters and sacred text to guide us toward shaping a theologically sound Christian ethic informed by our lived experiences. While we may not arrive at the same conclusion in every circumstance, *Rethinking Life* sets a bountiful table of ideas and tools useful in reasoning together, when collective reasoning seems rare. I am certain I will return to this book often in the days and years to come.

—Rev. Traci D. Blackmon, associate general minister, Justice and Local Church Ministries, United Church of Christ

RETHINKING LIFE

Embracing the
Sacredness
of Every Person

SHANE CLAIBORNE

ZONDERVAN
BOOKS

ZONDERVAN BOOKS

Rethinking Life
Copyright © 2023 by Shane Claiborne

Requests for information should be addressed to:
Zondervan, *3900 Sparks Dr. SE, Grand Rapids, Michigan 49546*

Zondervan titles may be purchased in bulk for educational, business, fundraising, or sales
promotional use. For information, please email SpecialMarkets@Zondervan.com.

ISBN 978-0-310-36384-2 (softcover)
ISBN 978-0-310-36397-2 (audio)
ISBN 978-0-310-36391-0 (ebook)

Cover design: Spencer Fuller, Faceout Studio
Cover illustrations: blackred / iStock; Evannovostro / Shutterstock
Author photo: Katie Jo Brotherton
Interior design: Emily Ghattas

Printed in the United States of America

22 23 24 25 26 27 28 29 30 31 /LSC/ 15 14 13 12 11 10 9 8 7 6 5 4 3 2 1

To all the women of faith over the centuries, the midwives of a better world, and to the two most significant women in my life—my mom, Patricia, and my wife, Katie Jo

Contents

Introduction

An Invitation to Love Life

I grew up in the heart of the Bible Belt, in the foothills of the Smoky Mountains. I fell in love with Jesus there. Sunday school, youth group, Young Life, Fellowship of Christian Athletes (I wasn't even really an athlete)—I did it all. I am a child of the church. My grandparents were Southern Baptists, but Mom and I found a home among the Methodists. Before long, I wanted some of the Holy Ghost fire and the miracles and wonders of the Pentecostals, so I joined the charismatic movement. When that got a little funky, I leaned into the deep roots of Catholicism for a while. I guess you could say I'm a bit of a spiritual mutt, but all of it shaped who I am today.

My political and social imagination was also shaped by the culture wars of the 1980s. I helped lead the See You at the Pole campaign, where high school students gathered at their school's flagpole to pray for our nation before heading into classes. I was ready to go to jail if they (whoever "they" were) told us we couldn't pray in public school.

As my theology grew over the years, I learned to appreciate the treasures of many different traditions of Christianity, to savor the meat and spit out the bones. I also began to see some of the church's blind spots—both the theological ones and the practical ones—particularly when it came to our value for life.

I passionately embraced the label "pro-life," but my concept of what it meant to be pro-life revolved almost entirely around ending abortion. Ending abortion was as fundamental to my faith as being baptized or taking communion. I did not believe you could really be a Christian and not take a stand against the horror of abortion.

I distinctly remember learning to debate and loving the thrill of trying to argue someone into the ground. I can even recall, like it was yesterday, making the case in my twelfth-grade English class that abortion is murder and murderers deserve the death penalty, so why aren't we arresting abortion doctors and putting them on trial? I had all the Bible verses that I thought made the case crystal clear. I even thought about becoming a lawyer.

But my crystal-clear case started to crack a little bit when I realized I was justifying one form of violence (the death penalty) as punishment for another (abortion). And it wasn't too long before I began to see more contradictions, both in the church and in myself. For example, while I was learning to defend my faith with Lee Strobel's book *The Case for Christ*, I was also learning to defend guns, war, and the death penalty. The more I leaned into Jesus, read the Gospels, and reflected on the Sermon on the Mount, the more conflicted I felt about many of my political positions.

I began to realize that it would be more accurate for those of us who consider ourselves pro-life to call ourselves "pro-birth" or "anti-abortion." Sometimes we have been more concerned with life before birth than life after birth. It is a strange thing to live in a world where we can be pro-military, pro-guns, pro-executions, and still say we are pro-life so long as we stand against abortion. But, alas, that is where we find ourselves.

When I think back to those years in high school when abortion consumed so much of my energy, I realize that I had lots of ideologies, but few if any relationships with people whose lives were impacted by those ideologies. Ideologies alone don't require much of us, and mine hadn't required much of me.

I had a lot to say about abortion, but eventually it occurred to me that I couldn't think of a single person I knew who had actually had an abortion, or at least anyone who felt comfortable telling me about it. In retrospect, this is understandable since I had said out loud that I thought abortion doctors deserved the death penalty. As is too often the case, I was good at talking about issues, but not as good about having compassion for the people directly affected by the issues. Sometimes our theology or our political opinions become an obstacle to love rather than a conduit of love. And that is a problem.

We cannot talk about issues while avoiding the people who are affected by them. We cannot talk *at* each other; we must talk *with* each other.

A Lovely Question

This book is not just about issues. It is about people. It is about asking, What does love require of us? Ideologies do not demand much of us, but relationships do. "What does love require of us?" is a lovely question because it is a call to action.

Asking that question changed everything for me because what love required of me was more than a saying on a bumper sticker, a T-shirt, or a yard sign. It required proximity and relationships. It required drawing near and leaning in to those who had been impacted by the issues. In our neighborhood in North Philadelphia, gun violence is more than statistics; it has names and stories and tears. We have murals and memorials on nearly every corner to honor the lives lost to guns. Gun violence is about the three-year-old hit with a stray bullet on Malta Street. It's about the mother who collapsed onto the sidewalk when she got news her little boy had been killed. To me, gun violence is so much more than talking points because it affects neighbors whom I love. That's why I'm inviting you to join me in asking this question about every issue: What does love require of us?

It's the same with the death penalty. For me, the death penalty is not just a political issue, it's a reality that nearly took the life of Derrick Jamison, one of my close friends who was sentenced to die for a crime he had nothing to do with. He spent two decades on death row, had six execution dates, and was hours from execution when he was finally proved innocent. Listening to Derrick describe what it was like to watch his friends—more than fifty of them—be killed by the state, one by one, and to constantly wonder whether he would be next, does something to you. When you hear a mother say that the first time she kissed her son in thirty years was *after* his execution because they were not allowed to have contact visits, it does something to you.

When I think about war, it is no longer something I pontificate about in an abstract sense. It is about the children I held in the Al Monzer Pediatric Hospital in Baghdad. Their bodies were riddled with fragments from bombs dropped on them by the US during the 2003 invasion of Iraq. I'm still willing to talk about "just-war theory" with people who care about that, but what changed my heart was not just losing an argument, it was seeing the devastation of war firsthand. I became convinced that love doesn't do that to people.

What has changed me over the years is not slogans or rallying cries but listening to my immigrant neighbors, visiting refugee camps, sleeping on dirt floors, and biking along the US-Mexico border to talk with refugees and asylum seekers. These are the things—or to be accurate, these are the *people* who have caused me to wrestle with the question, What does love require of us? What does love require of *me*?

I am still a work in progress, and I don't pretend to have answers to all of the questions that will arise in the pages that follow, but this I know for certain: Being in proximity makes a difference. Relationships make issues real and complicated and personal. Relationships move us from ideology to compassion. We can't love our neighbors if we don't know them. And once we are proximate, love requires us to take action, to stand up for life in tangible ways.

Pro-Life for the Whole of Life

Back when I was trying to sort out the contradictions of what it means to be pro-life, I eventually bumped into this idea of a "consistent ethic of life," the conviction that all of life—from womb to tomb—matters. To have a consistent ethic of life is to be comprehensive in our advocacy for life and to refuse to think of issues in isolation from each other. It is a fundamental conviction that every person is sacred and made in the image of God. It requires pursuing whatever allows people to flourish and fighting everything that crushes life. That means that all these difficult issues—the military, guns, racism, the death penalty, poverty, and abortion—are connected, and we need a moral framework that integrates them. That's what it means to be pro-life for the whole of life.

For some, a consistent ethic of life is nothing new. Catholics have used the language of a "seamless garment" woven of all the issues. For centuries, Anabaptist Christians have maintained a commitment to life and a passion for nonviolence. The early Christians, as we will see, had a consistent ethic of life. They were a force to be reckoned with, speaking out against every manifestation of violence in their society. They spoke against war, domestic violence, capital punishment, and they spoke against abortion. They even spoke out against gladiator games, a popular form of entertainment in the Roman Empire and one of the particular ways our human infatuation with violence expressed itself in their culture.

Christianity's first three centuries were strikingly and wonderfully pro-life in the best and most encompassing sense of the word. And today, this idea of a consistent life ethic is resonating with a whole new generation that has grown tired of death in all of its ugly manifestations.

I want to invite us to love bigger, to extend the same passion that many of us have for one issue to all of the issues. We'll be building a broad, firm foundation that helps us be advocates for life comprehensively, without exceptions. We won't minimize the conversation about abortion, which we will address. Instead, we'll situate that conversation within an expansive, passionate ethic of life that includes other issues. We care about issues because behind the issues are real people.

I must confess that I wish some of my conservative friends cared as much about life after birth as they do life before birth. And I wish some of my progressive friends saw abortion not just as a rights issue but also as a life issue, a moral issue. Then we might do a better job at reducing the number of abortions.

So this is a book about life. And it's a book about love. We are asking the most important question of all: What does it look like to love God with our whole heart and mind and strength, and to love people as ourselves—without exceptions?

My primary ambition is not to reclaim the pro-life label. Instead, my hope is that you and I will embrace a robust ethic of life. I want this deep, heartfelt conviction that every person matters to God to impact how we think—theologically, politically, socially, morally—about a whole range of issues.

So let's get to it. This book is divided into three parts. Part 1 helps us build a foundation for a better ethic of life by looking to Scripture, Jesus, and the early Christians for inspiration. Part 2 is an honest look at where the foundation for life began to crack over the centuries. And I'll warn you, this part of the book is pretty heavy and heartbreaking, but the truth sets us free. So we'll take a closer look at the Crusades, slavery, colonization, and other ways Christians and the church have failed to be champions of life. Finally, in part 3, we'll explore what it will take to repair the cracks in the foundation of our ethic of life and how we can be a force for life and for love in the world. All along the way, we'll be asking, What does love require of us?

It's time to rethink how precious life is so we can reclaim the sacredness of every human being.

## PART 1

The Foundation
for Life

CHAPTER 1

Life Is Good

Our goal is to develop a comprehensive, all-encompassing ethic of life that compels us to be champions of life, to cherish life, and to defend it passionately. To do that, we need a foundation on which we can build, and one we can keep coming back to. And where better to start than at the beginning, with creation itself?

Here's how it all began, according to Genesis, the first book of the Bible. God took dirt and breathed life into it to make humanity. God created life and it was good.

It was good. That's the refrain in Genesis 1 as God creates the world.

Over and over, like the chorus of a song, the Bible says, "It was good."

God created the water. And it was good.

God created land and plants and trees and mountains and beaches. And it was good.

God created the moon and the sun and the stars in the sky. And it was good.

God created birds and fish and monkeys and butterflies and elephants and seahorses and the duck-billed platypus! And it was good.

Then God created humans in God's own image. And God saw all that had been made and declared it *very* good. After that sixth day, when God made the first human beings and looked at the whole of creation in all its wonder, that's when we get the addition of "very."

God's creation wasn't just good, it was *real* good. God was pumped. God was absolutely stoked.

And still is.

The Wonder Gap

Not many people are going to argue with the fact that life is good, but life is more than just good, it's miraculous! And yet we tend to lose a sense of wonder at the miracle of it all. That's why I love being around kids. They still have that sense of wonder.

Not long ago, I got a wonder wake-up call that started with a knock on my door. And it wasn't just any knock, it was the frantic kind, the pounding kind, what some of the kids on my block call the "cop knock." As I ran downstairs, I assumed there must have been an accident, a shooting, someone hit by a car, something bad. I took a deep breath to prepare myself for whatever might be next and opened the door. Standing there was eight-year-old Tysean, one of the neighborhood kids I've known since he was born. He grabbed my hand and began dragging me down the block. At this point, I could tell by his grin that it wasn't something bad, not a shooting or a car wreck. But what was it?

"You've got to see this," he said, pulling me like a dog on a leash. When we had gone about a hundred feet down the block, he pointed into the community garden. "What is that?" he asked. It was the first time he'd ever seen a firefly.

I thought for a moment and said the only thing I knew to say: "That was a really great day for God. God decided to make a bug whose butt glows in the dark."

Author Paul Hawken notes that Ralph Waldo Emerson once considered what we would do if the stars came out only once every thousand years. Commenting on Emerson's reflections, Hawken writes, "No one would sleep that night, of course. The world would become religious overnight. We would be ecstatic, delirious, made rapturous by the glory of God. Instead, the stars come out every night, and we watch television."[1] Or maybe today we miss it all because we are watching Netflix or scrolling through our socials.

One of my friends is an astronomer named Dr. David Bradstreet. Before he was a friend, he was my astronomy professor at Eastern University. He wrote a whole book about the heavens titled *Star Struck: Seeing the Creator in the Wonders of Our Cosmos*. He starts by sharing how excited he was as a child every time he saw the stars. As he got older, he decided to study astronomy and eventually became one of the leading astronomers in the country. He even has a comet named after him. When you have a comet named after you, that's beyond legit. Dr. Bradstreet is retired now, but he has never lost that sense of childlike wonder.

Some folks might suggest that the more you study the science of life, the less miraculous and wonder-full it seems. I know Christians who are scared of astronomy, fearful it might distract from the biblical narrative of creation. Others even see faith and science as opposing forces. But for Dr. Bradstreet, studying the science of creation has only increased his sense of wonder, deepened his faith, and further convinced him that there is a magnificent creator behind it all. All through his book, he drops spectacular facts, like the fact that the tail of Halley's comet is sixty million miles long.[2] Or check this one out: every second, the sun converts four million tons of material into energy, the equivalent of ten billion nuclear bombs.[3] Fortunately, the sun is the perfect distance away and all that heat loses at least a third of its radiant energy in the eight-minute journey it takes to reach the earth.[4] If the earth were any closer to the sun, we'd burn up. If the earth were any farther away, we'd freeze.

1. Paul Hawken, "Healing or Stealing? The Best Commencement Address Ever," in *A Sense of Wonder: The World's Best Writers on the Sacred, the Profane, and the Ordinary*, ed. Brian Doyle (Maryknoll, NY: Orbis, 2016), 191.
2. Dr. David Bradstreet and Steve Rabey, *Star Struck: Seeing the Creator in the Wonders of Our Cosmos* (Grand Rapids: Zondervan, 2016), 19.
3. Bradstreet and Rabey, *Star Struck*, 83.
4. To be exact, it takes 8.3 minutes to get here, traveling 186,000 miles a second over 93 trillion miles,

Okay, one more. Every day, the divinely constructed and scientifically sound protective shield around the earth—the atmosphere—saves us from being hit by one hundred tons of small rocks and other pieces of space debris that would otherwise destroy the earth.[5] Amazing! Sometimes we miss the fact that life itself is a miracle. It may very well take more faith to believe that all of this life "just happens" than it does to believe that there is a divine creator behind it all.

Dr. Bradstreet has helped me appreciate Scriptures like this one: "The heavens declare the glory of God; the skies proclaim the work of [God's] hands" (Ps. 19:1). And yet one of the questions Dr. Bradstreet raises is this: As the heavens cry out the glory of God, is anyone listening? He notes that some of his atheist peers in the scientific community have a deeper sense of wonder and awe about the universe than many of his Christian friends who are not scientists. He calls it the "wonder gap."[6]

Too many of us have a wonder gap when it comes to the miracle of life in the natural world. That's a problem because the more out of touch we are with the earth and the creatures of the earth, the easier it is to devalue or even destroy life.[7] When we are no longer awed by

---

which also means, if the sun stopped shining, it would take us 8.3 minutes to know that. The next closest star, Alpha Centauri, is so far away that it takes 4.3 years for its light to reach us over that 25-trillion-mile distance. *Whoa*. Bradstreet and Rabey, *Star Struck*, 249.

5. I could go on and on about the wonders I learned from Dr. Bradstreet in *Star Struck*. For example, did you know there are nineteen essential factors that not only make life on earth unique and miraculous but also provide the precise conditions for life to be possible at all? I won't go through all nineteen, but they are pretty spectacular. For example, the alignment of the earth's poles is off by exactly 23.5 degrees, creating the earth's tilt on its axis. That minor detail is why we have seasons and climates. Without the tilt, we would either burn up or freeze to death. The fact that the earth is 75 percent water is also clutch. Life on earth is possible because we have roughly 352,670,000,000,000,000,000 gallons of it, and because some of it evaporates and flows back to the earth as rain. The sun is just one of 100,000,000,000,000,000,000,000 stars. There are 200 billion stars in the Milky Way alone. But get this: in addition to ours, there are 200 billion more galaxies in the universe. The conditions for life on this little planet are truly a miracle. It makes you feel small and extremely special all at the same time. Bradstreet and Rabey, *Star Struck*, 58, 207.

6. Bradstreet and Rabey, *Star Struck*, 43.

7. Sometimes it's not even intentional destruction but a subtler apathy about things such as climate change. For example, did you know that the temperature of sand determines the sex of sea turtles? That means that because the sand has become warmer from climate change, male turtles have become almost extinct. More than 90 percent of the newborn turtles on the Great Barrier Reef are now female, which means the survival of the species is in grave danger. "Over 90% of Turtles Born Female Due to Climate Change," World Wild Fund for Nature, January 8, 2018, wwf.panda.org/wwf_news/?320295/90%2Dpercent%2Dfemale%2Dturtles.

the miracle of creation, it gets harder to believe in the goodness and beauty of life—and the good and beautiful creator behind it all. That's why gazing at fireflies and sunsets is a holy and spiritual practice. It not only fills us with wonder but also strengthens our foundation for life.

One of the ways we can bridge the wonder gap is by studying and contemplating how truly marvelous the world is. I've learned a lot about this from my wife, Katie Jo, who is one of the greatest nature lovers I've ever met. At one point, we had a spider who lived in the corner of the school-bus-turned-tiny-house we lived in for two years. When I went to remove it, she told me the spider's name was Gladys and we needed to keep her because she ate the bad bugs, like stink bugs and mosquitos, so she was now a pet. Later, Gladys got pregnant and I finally talked Katie into putting her outside. Spiders can have up to a thousand babies, and that is too many pets for a tiny house.

Katie doesn't have a wonder gap. She's always telling me nature facts. For example, that the male seahorse is the one that gives birth. And that a hummingbird's heart beats more than 1,200 times a minute and its wings flap sixty to eighty times a second. Katie is an aspiring beekeeper, and she taught me that bees have five eyes and that one hive can house around fifty thousand bees. Oh, and get this: the bees visit five million flowers to make one pint of honey. That makes you appreciate your honey, eh?

She's always marveling at how the octopus changes color or that there is a flamingo that makes its nest out of salt. She just told me starlings can learn multiple bird languages or song patterns and speak them. And here's a pigeon fact, which is important to know since pigeons can be challenging to love for those of us who live in the urban world. Even though they aren't mammals, pigeons apparently have a milk reservoir in their crop—a section of the lower esophagus. Their "crop milk" contains antioxidants to keep their little ones from dying. Those are just a few Katie Jo wonder facts for you.

One of the wonders of the natural world that always amazes me is the complex emotional lives of animals. Did you ever see that viral video of the mother whale circling and crying out over her dead calf? Whales mourn, loudly and visibly, when another whale dies. How wild is that?

I was also amazed at a video taken at an elephant refuge, where a lot of old circus elephants are taken when they are rescued from abuse. The video shows a new arrival running up to another elephant and the two ecstatically wrapping their trunks around each other in an elephant hug of sorts. Refuge staffers later discovered that the two elephants had been in a circus together years before. How about that?

We need to recapture the childlike sense of wonder that kids so often have, because our lives are bound up with the beauty and flourishing of the natural world. We also need to pay attention to it because creation itself has a lot to teach us about who God is. The apostle Paul wrote, "Ever since the world was created, people have seen the earth and sky. Through everything God made, they can clearly see his invisible qualities—his eternal power and divine nature. So they have no excuse for not knowing God" (Rom. 1:20 NLT).

And when it comes to having a foundation for life, one of the most important things we can learn about God is revealed within the miraculous diversity of life.

The Miraculous Diversity of Life

Did you know that there are roughly ten million forms of life on the planet? Among other things, that includes more than 300,000 different plants, 1.25 million animals, 900,000 insects, 10,000 birds, and 8,000 reptiles.[8] Those numbers are even more astounding when

---

8. I keep learning all the time. I just watched a documentary that said the three-toed sloth has eighty different species that live in its fur. Crazy!

you consider that 95 percent of the species that have ever existed on earth are now extinct. More specifically, one in eight birds, one in four mammals, and one in three amphibious creatures are now extinct. And we lose about one hundred species a day, which is twenty-seven thousand per year. Fortunately, we also discover several thousand new species of living creatures every year.

I learned a lot about the incredible diversity of life on earth when I visited my friend Claudio Oliver in Brazil. Claudio is part theologian, part veterinarian, and 100 percent nuts. He reminds me of the character Doc from *Back to the Future*—eccentric, wild, and full of passion and curiosity. When I visited, he woke me up at 5:00 a.m. and took me on an all-day adventure to show me what life is like running an urban homestead. We fed the rabbits, one of which would be dinner. We traded eggs for the milk of a neighbor's cow. We went to the shopping mall, as Claudio denounced the evils of capitalism, to pick up used coffee grounds from the food court for his worm compost. Then he took me to the holy of holies, the "gene bank" where he is helping preserve endangered species of chickens.

"Do you know how many kinds of chickens there are?" he asked. Naturally, I started rattling them off like Bubba rattled off kinds of shrimp in *Forrest Gump*. "Well, there is fried chicken. There's teriyaki chicken. Barbeque chicken. Chicken kababs."

"No, no!" Claudio belted out with a laugh. "How many *types* of chickens?"

I had no idea, so I kept going. "Chicken curry. Sweet and sour chicken. . . ."

And then he told me that there are more than four hundred kinds of chickens—species of chickens, that is. Heck, he added, there are also forty thousand different kinds of rice. And apparently twenty-nine thousand different fish. Then Claudio got on his biodiversity soapbox and brought it all home: "Monoculture is diabolical. Diversity is *divine*." He smiled and kept saying it louder and louder. "Monoculture is diabolical, but diversity is divine!"

Diversity is divine.

And diversity isn't limited to plants and animals. Did you know that human beings speak more than seven thousand living languages in the nearly two hundred countries of the world?[9] Not to mention that each human being has a unique fingerprint. Each of us also has our own DNA that is distinct from the other eight billion people on the planet.[10]

If my friend Claudio's theory sounds a bit out there to you, let me take you on a little Bible adventure to unpack this idea of monoculture and diversity. Think back to the Old Testament story of the Tower of Babel, one of the first major projects of human beings (Genesis 11). As the story goes, the whole human race was the same. There was one language, one culture, and the people were pretty impressed with themselves. They began an ambitious building project to bridge the heavens and the earth—the Tower of Babel. But God was not impressed. God scattered the people and had them speak different languages. Diversity was the way forward.

Flash forward to Pentecost in the New Testament, which is described in Acts 2. It is interesting to see what happens when the Holy Spirit falls on believers in the young church as they are gathered together in one room. The writer goes to great lengths to emphasize how diverse the people were. They were Parthians, Medes, Elamites, Cretans, and Arabs; they were residents of Mesopotamia, Judea, Cappadocia, Pontus, Asia, Phrygia, Pamphylia, Egypt, Libya near Cyrene, and Rome (Acts 2:9–11).

When the Holy Spirit falls on them, the people begin to speak in "other tongues" (v. 4). We often think of this event as when they got filled with the Holy Ghost fire and things got rowdy. While that's true, and they were in fact accused of having "too much wine" (v. 13), it's also true that we sometimes overlook the real miracle in this event.

9. "How Many Languages Are There in the World?" Ethnologue, www.ethnologue.com/guides/how-many-languages.
10. "Current World Population," Worldometer, www.worldometers.info/world-population/.

As they heard the gospel proclaimed, each one "heard their own language being spoken" (v. 6). Despite their diversity, they were "one in heart and mind" and began to share possessions radically, holding all things in common (4:32).

As we look at the juxtaposition of the Babel story and Pentecost, something is strikingly clear. Unity is not uniformity. Oneness is not sameness. This is the key difference between what happened at Babel and what happened at Pentecost. Babel is about the power of a monoculture—people impressed with themselves and the possibilities of uniformity. Pentecost is about the power of God to bring people together across all that divides them. Unity exists most powerfully when there is diversity. And the more diverse we are, the stronger we are when we unite, and the more clearly we see God's power at work to reconcile us.

Diversity is divine. Every human being is a reflection of God. And when we are surrounded by monoculture, by people who all look like us, we miss out not only on the full experience of God's wonderful and miraculous creation but also on who God is. To have a consistent ethic of life is to be awed by life in all its diversity and complexity. That's why I'm known to say from time to time, "If our community is all white, something's not quite right." And the same can be said of monoculture anywhere—it limits our vision, our perspective, our appreciation of the bigness of God's love for all people. We are all a reflection of God, and we are all made from the same dirt.

Breathing Life into Dirt

Dirt is an interesting contrast to the color-full, wonder-full creatures God made. And perhaps that is part of the point. God makes beautiful things out of dirt. And God continues to bring new life out of the compost of Christendom. There's a whole sermon there for sure, but we don't have time for that one right now.

The word *human* comes from the Latin *humus,* which literally means "dirt." It's also where we get the word for the chickpea side dish called hummus, which, some people contend, does look and taste a little like dirt. The *humus* of humanity hearkens back to the fact that God took dirt and breathed life into it to make us. It is also why on Ash Wednesday we remember the dirt from which we were made and the dirt to which we shall return. God sculpted human life from the raw material of creation itself. God made beautiful things out of dirt and continues to do so today. Maybe you've heard that Gungor song "Beautiful Things," which talks about how God makes beautiful things out of dust, and God makes beautiful things out of us. (I'm humming it now as I write.)

Adam, the name given to the first human being, comes from the Hebrew word *adamah,* which means "earth" or "the ground." Adam was made from the earth. And the name Eve simply means "life."[11] Isn't that beautiful? Life was made from the dirt as God breathed into it. The fact that we are all made from the dirt means none of us should think too highly of ourselves. But the fact that we are also made in the image of God means that none of us should think too lowly of ourselves either.

There is a fascinating lesson from the rabbis of old that explores another aspect of God's breath.[12] The rabbis suggest that the mysterious word for God in the Hebrew scriptures, YAHWEH, can actually be translated as "breath." The Hebrew word doesn't have vowels; vowels were added later to help the word make sense because

---

11. Don't read too much into the fact that Adam, the man, is dirt, and Eve, the woman, is life. I think it's enough to recognize that we are all equally fallen and equally holy. Maybe that's part of the point. As reformer Martin Luther put it, we all have a sinner and a saint at war within us, and each day, each moment, we get to choose which we will be. Just as original sin is a part of the story, so is original innocence. Good stuff comes from dirt. New life comes even out of compost.

12. To learn more about this, see Rabbi Arthur Waskow, "Why YAH/YHWH," The Shalom Center, April 14, 2004, https://theshalomcenter.org/content/why-yahyhwh.

YHWH is an odd word. But the rabbis suggest that this is part of the point. In the Hebrew alphabet, the vowels represent breathing sounds.

God is more glorious than we can wrap our heads around and doesn't need a name. That's why when Moses asks for God's name, God says, "I AM" or "I AM WHO I AM" (Ex. 3:14). God's response can also be translated "I am becoming who I am becoming." In similar fashion, YHWH has that reverent, mystical, transcendent quality that addressing God warrants. But here's the cool part: the rabbis suggest that YHWH is the sound of breath. Even as you listen to your breathing you can easily think of inhaling "YAH" and exhaling "WEH." On several occasions, I've been present when my friend Richard Rohr has led a group in a lovely prayer doing exactly that—breathing in YAH and breathing out WEH.

What if, just as God breathed life into the dirt, everything that has breath is praising God simply by existing, by breathing in and breathing out?[13] That is exactly what Scripture says: "Let everything that has breath praise the LORD" (Ps. 150:6). Jesus even said that if we don't praise God, the breathless rocks will cry out (Luke 19:40).

My friend Jason Gray is a musician who wrote a beautiful song about the breath of God called "The Sound of Our Breathing." When he introduces the song in a concert, he reflects on how wonderful it is to imagine that we are designed to say God's name simply by breathing in and out, which means that none of us can go very long without calling upon the name of the Lord. When babies are born, are they taking their first breath or are they calling out the name of the Lord? Do we die when we breathe our last breath, or are we no longer alive because the name of God is no longer on our lips?

---

13. This is all consistent with traditional rabbinical teaching, which is that life begins at our first breath, something I had a fascinating conversation about with Rabbi Danya Ruttenberg. I know it raises a potentially contentious issue about when life begins. We won't get into that here, but we will explore it in chapter 12. Just giving you a heads-up. For now, the point is to simply ponder the connection between breath and life, and God's breath giving us life.

Here are a few of Jason's lyrics.

> Everybody draws their very first breath
> With Your name upon their lips
> Every one of us is born of dust
> But come alive with heaven's kiss. . . .
> So breathe in
> Breathe out
> Breathe in
> Breathe out. . . .
> 'Cause the name of God
> Is the sound of our breathing

The deep conviction that life is good matters. Not only is life good, it is holy and wonder-full. It is a gift from God. Losing a sense of wonder and gratitude may be the first sign of a crack in a firm foundation for life. So protect your childlike wonder.

Creation is amazing. And the most sacred, beautiful thing God ever made is us. As incredible as all the creatures are, nothing is more sacred than human beings. Looking into the eyes of another person gives us one of our clearest glimpses of God. And the closest we can get to killing God is to kill or crush a child of God. Every single one of us bears the image of our creator. That's what we'll explore next.

RETHINKING LIFE

- When recently have you had an experience that snapped you out of the wonder gap, a moment in which you felt a sense of awe at the gift of life or the beauty of creation? What shifted in you as a result?
- What are some of the ways you routinely see God's fingerprint on creation? List some of your favorite animals, plants,

or people. Or maybe draw a picture of a place in which you have felt God's presence.

- How do you respond to Claudio Oliver's statement: "Monoculture is diabolical. Diversity is *divine*"? In what ways, if any, have you found this to be true in your experience?
- On a scale of one to ten, how would you characterize the diversity of your life and relationships right now? Consider factors such as race, culture, gender identity, age, language, sexual orientation, family status, income, and religion/ spirituality. On the following continuum, circle the number that best describes your response.

1   2   3   4   5   6   7   8   9   10

My life and relationships
are a monoculture.

My life and relationships
are diverse.

- In what areas is your life characterized primarily by mono-culture? Who would you say is on the outside of that monoculture? In what ways could your monoculture limit your vision, your perspective, or your appreciation of God's love for all people?
- In what areas is your life characterized primarily by diver-sity? Who is included in that diversity? In what ways has diversity expanded your vision, your perspective, or your appreciation of God's love for all people?

## CHAPTER 2

Every Person Bears
the Image of God

When I was growing up in the South, people often said to me, "You're the spitting image of your dad." I understood what they meant, but still, what's a "spitting" image? Someone later explained that it's slang for "spirit and image." It refers to more than just appearance. If you're someone's spitting image, you have their charisma or mannerisms, the same walk or laugh or smile. That's what people mean by spitting image—you remind them of someone.

Although I'm not 100 percent sure that's the origin of this southern phrase, I am convinced it offers insight into what it means to be made in the image of God. We might say that human beings are the spitting image of God. We remind the world of God. We are able, at our best, to act like God, to love like God, to create like God, and even to smell like God. I once heard someone say that saints are simply those who leave the fragrance of Jesus in the world. Their lives remind others of Jesus.

God created human beings in God's own image and then, over time, human beings decided they'd like to put their image on things too. Today, we call it branding. Think of millionaires or former presidents who build towers and plazas and casinos and put their names up in lights to spread their empires. Or think of Mount Rushmore or the faces of various presidents printed on our money. Every image is a reminder, an assertion of the image maker's power, position, or authority.

The kings and emperors of the ancient world were no different. For example, in Jesus' day, Caesar Augustus was obsessed with putting his image on everything. It was engraved on statues, on buildings, on war machines, on documents, and on coins. Augustus loved getting his name out there and branding everything he could with his imperial stamp.

But for Augustus and other caesars of old, stamping their image on things was more than just a narcissism complex. It was also about marking their turf and expanding their territory. Historians say that you can tell how far the power of a particular emperor reached by tracking the locations of the coins that had his image on it. As coins were used in commerce and war, they carried with them the influence of the person whose image they bore. Coins were a trail of crumbs that led back to those in power. They demonstrated how powerful the emperor was and how much territory his colonizing ambitions had amassed.

God's Coins

Perhaps you can see where this is going. God's image is too glorious to put on a coin or a statue, so God put the divine image on us. God chose to make us in God's image. We are the living currency of God. We are God's coins, bearing God's image, carrying God's influence wherever we go. And we can see how far God's kingdom extends—somebody say "amen"—wherever human beings find themselves. Where human beings are, God is. As the apostle John said, "No one has ever seen God; but if we love one another, God lives in us and [God's] love is made complete in us" (1 John 4:12). Wherever a human being is, God is; and whenever we crush a human being, we crush the image of God.

This is one of the big differences between Caesar and God. Caesar wanted to be seen but not known. And God wants to be known but cannot be seen. The image of God is too profound to carve into a stone or stamp onto a piece of metal. Perhaps the best illustration of this comes from the movie *Raiders of the Lost Ark* when the ark of the covenant is opened. As God's presence comes out of the ark, the skin of everyone present melts off their bones and their eyes pop out of their sockets.

When Moses asked to see God's glory, God said, "You cannot see my face, for no one may see me and live" (Ex. 33:20). Instead, God said he would shield Moses in the cleft of a rock and then pass by so Moses could see God's back. Maybe it was like wearing those special glasses that allow you to look at a solar eclipse without going blind. God wants to be known, so God appears in ways that are both mysterious and miraculous—to Moses in the burning bush (Ex. 3:1–5), to Elijah in the gentle whisper (1 Kings 19:11–13), to Abraham in the guise of three strangers (Gen. 18:1–2). In one encounter, God sends an angel to a woman named Hagar, Abraham's mistress, whom Abraham had banished into the desert with her son, Ishmael. Hagar names God as, get ready for this, "the One who sees me" (Gen. 16:13). That's what she names God: "You-Are-the-One-Who-Sees-Me." It's a stunning reflection of God's desire to know and be known. The God who saw Hagar and Ishmael is the God who sees us and longs to be known by us.

Finally, God puts on skin and comes to us with a name and a face in Jesus. But here's the part we sometimes forget. Just as we see God in Jesus, Jesus tells us that God lives in us (John 14:17). We are God's sanctuary. God does not dwell in temples made by human hands (Acts 17:24), but God lives in you and me (1 Cor. 3:16). Every person on the planet is the holy of holies. That should cause us to treat other people, every person, as if they are God's temple—because they are.

Caesar could reproduce his image in bronze or marble and mass produce his image on coins, but it was all lifeless. God chose to reproduce God's own image in us, in living human beings. Perhaps that is why we have the command to "be fruitful and multiply" (Gen. 1:28 NKJV). God is inviting us to broaden God's kingdom by filling the world with the currency of love. Wherever there are people loving one another, God is visible in the world.

One more thought here on the difference between the image of God and the image of Caesar. There's that time when the religious leaders used money as a pretext to trick Jesus (Matt. 22:15–22). As the story goes, the Pharisees and the Herodians came to entrap Jesus by asking him his opinion about paying imperial taxes. The Pharisees and Herodians were at odds on most things, but they loved money and were not big fans of Jesus. It is striking how a common enemy can create unlikely friends. So they asked Jesus if he thought it was right to pay taxes to Caesar.

It was a catch-22 situation. On the one hand, not paying taxes was a crime and sedition, an insult to Caesar. On the other hand, Jews considered treating the emperor as God to be idolatry. Even handling coins with the image of the emperor on them constituted idolatry, which may explain why Jesus asked them for a coin (because he didn't have any of Caesar's coins). They thought they could trap Jesus because there was no good answer to the question.

Here's what happened next.

They brought Jesus a coin and he asked them, "Whose image is this?" They replied, "Caesar's." And Jesus said, "Give back to Caesar what is Caesar's and to God what is God's" (Mark 12:16–17). In one version of the story, or perhaps it was another altercation altogether, when tax collectors asked whether Jesus paid his temple tax, Jesus sent Peter to catch a fish (Matt. 17:24–27). In the mouth of the fish was a coin to pay the temple tax. A bizarre and holy stunt. It's as if Jesus was saying, "Caesar can have his coin, but I made the fish."

With his characteristic combo of human winsomeness and divine flair, Jesus shines brilliantly. Instead of avoiding the question, he transcends it. His answer is more radical than "pay your taxes" or "don't pay your taxes." It is a teaching moment—a subversive one.

Sometimes people twist Jesus' statement, "Give back to Caesar what is Caesar's and to God what is God's," to support their view that we should never resist the powers of the empire. Always give Uncle Sam whatever he asks for. But Dorothy Day, a radical Catholic activist and founder of the Catholic Worker movement, offered this take: "Once we have given to God what is God's, there isn't much left for Caesar."

Jesus simultaneously reveals the true worth of Caesar's inflated coins and the immeasurable worth of life, which is too often devalued. Jesus raises the question, What is Caesar's and what is God's? Rabbi Arthur Waskow suggests that after Jesus asked whose image was on the coin, perhaps he took the face of a little child in his hands and said, "And whose image is on this coin?"

Coins are imprinted with Caesar's image. People are imprinted with God's image. Caesar can have his coins, but human life belongs to God. Caesar's coins are lifeless. And God's children are priceless.

Oh, and one more thing. Caesar's coins all looked the same. It is the way of empires and corporations to mass produce stuff. But God's coins are as wild and spectacular and diverse as God is. No DNA is the same. No fingerprint is the same. No "coin" is the same. But every human being bears the image of God—no exceptions.

God in Disguise

I had a powerful experience of what it means to recognize the image of God in another human being when I traveled to India in the late 1990s. I went to work with Mother Teresa and the Missionaries of Charity on the streets of Calcutta. It was incredible, holy work, which I've reflected on in other books. But one encounter especially left a mark on my soul.

I spent some time in a village of folks who had leprosy. One of the brothers who worked there had left for a week, and so there was an open bed—or an open spot on the floor, as it were, since the Missionaries of Charity choose to live very simply—and so I slept as they did, on a mat on the concrete floor.

I visited this "leper colony," as it was referred to by many locals, where more than 150 families lived on a little piece of land along the railroad tracks, which Mother Teresa helped acquire for them. Leprosy is a dreadful illness and exists only in the poorest parts of the world. Within the caste system of India, these families and their kids were "outcaste," shunned from their caste. That's where we get our word *outcast.* They were not allowed in any public space, including stores or restaurants. One of the men in the village explained that folks with leprosy often don't even know the words "thank you" because they have never needed to say them. They rarely experience an occasion when they can use the language of gratitude.

My experience there reminded me of something I'd read about lepers in the Middle Ages—that people with leprosy had to ring bells and call out "Unclean!" so that folks wouldn't accidently bump into one of them. But Mother Teresa knew better. She knew that these outcaste people were precious, that they were made in the image of God—no matter how badly the disease had distorted their faces, and no matter how much the world around them refused to recognize the divine image in them. So she helped them build this village called Gandhiji Prem Nivas, which literally means "Gandhi's new life."

Part of Mahatma Gandhi's philosophy was that we don't need to depend on systems that exploit us. We can make our own clothes and march to the sea to get our own salt. We can build a new world from the shell of the old one. His vision for a new world was on full display there in this little community. The residents of Gandhiji Prem Nivas grow their own food and make their own clothing. They make the blankets for the orphanages and the bandages for the clinic. They even make their own prosthetic arms and legs out of wood for those who have undergone amputation.

The village clinic was run by folks with leprosy who had been treated and were now the healers, caring for others afflicted by the disease. The caregivers would lay out a huge pile of cotton about four feet high, and my job was to roll cotton balls for them as they cared for one another. I watched the caregivers intently, fascinated by their love and compassion.

One afternoon as things were winding down, one of the caregivers had to leave early, but there were a few patients still waiting to be seen. The caregiver looked at me and emphatically said, "You know how this works; you have been watching. We need your help."

I came forward and sat in the caregiver's seat, gazed into the next patient's eyes, and began carefully dressing the man's wound. He stared back at me with such intensity that it felt like he was looking into my soul. Every once in a while, he slowly closed his eyes.

When I was finished wrapping his wound, he smiled, looked into my eyes again, and said, "Namaste." One of the men in the clinic that day explained to me the profound meaning of the word. He said that we don't have a good English translation that captures it, but it essentially means, "I see you. I love you. I recognize the image of God in you." In his words, "The Spirit of God in me loves the Spirit of God I see in you." In essence, "We are family."

I will never forget getting lost in that man's eyes as we sat together in that clinic by the railroad tracks. I knew I had looked into the eyes not just of some pitiful leper in Calcutta but of Jesus, and that he had seen not just some rich, do-gooder white kid from America but the image of God in me. We had seen Jesus in each other. I saw a clearer glimpse of Jesus in this man's eyes than any stained-glass window or religious icon could ever give me.

What would the world look like if we truly believed, as the apostle Paul figured out, that it is no longer we who live, but Christ who lives in us (Gal. 2:20)? Faith is not just about having new ideas. It is about having new eyes. We see the image of God in every person. We see our own brokenness and our own belovedness reflected in the eyes of those we meet.

In the murderers, we see our own hatred.

In the addicts, we see our own addictions.

In the saints, we catch glimpses of our own holiness.

We can see our own brokenness, our own violence, our own ability to destroy, and we can see our own sacredness, our own capacity to love and forgive. When we realize that we are both wretched and beautiful, we are freed up to see others the same way.

In his work *I and Thou*, the brilliant European philosopher Martin Buber speaks of how we can see a person in one of two ways. We can look *at* a person and see them as a material object, an "It;" or we can look *into* a person and enter the sacredness of their humanity so that they become a "Thou."[1] And as a Jewish man who immigrated to Palestine to advocate for Arab-Jewish cooperation, Buber knew all too well how easily we can objectify and demonize others.

Most of the time, we look *at* people—hot girls, beggars, pop stars, white folks, Black folks, people with suits or dreadlocks. But over time, we can develop new eyes and look *into* people. We can see them as sacred. We can enter the holiest of holies through their eyes. They can become a "Thou."

I experienced this when the man in the clinic whispered that sacred Hindi word *namaste*. I also witnessed it years later in Iraq when, after shaking hands in greeting, people put their right hand over their heart as a gesture of sincerity and respect. In South Africa, I learned about the philosophy of *ubuntu*, which conveys a similar idea. In the words of late Archbishop Desmond Tutu, *ubuntu* means, "My humanity is caught up, is inextricably bound up, in yours." Tutu goes on: "We belong in a bundle of life. We say, 'A person is a person through other persons.'"[2] This is what Dr. King talked about as the "inescapable network of mutuality; tied in a single garment of destiny."[3] As Dr. King put it, "Whatever affects one directly affects all indirectly. As long as there is poverty in this world, no man can be totally rich even if he has a billion dollars. . . . Strangely enough, I can never be what I ought to be until you are what you ought to be. You can never be what you ought to be until I am what I ought to

---

1. Martin Buber, *I and Thou* (Riverside, NJ: Free Press, 1971), 255.
2. Desmond Tutu, *No Future without Forgiveness* (New York: Doubleday, 1999), 31.
3. Martin Luther King, *A Testament of Hope: The Essential Writings and Speeches of Martin Luther King Jr.*, ed. James M. Washington, reprint (San Francisco: Harper, 2003), 210.

be." *Boom*. Or as Scripture says so poignantly, when one part of the body suffers we all suffer (1 Cor. 12:26). All of these are reflections of what it means to look into people, to affirm the sacred, to see the image of God in one another, and to see that we are all connected as God's children.

When we have new eyes, we can look into the eyes of those we don't even like and see the one we love. We can see God's image in everyone we encounter. As Henri Nouwen put it, "In the face of the oppressed I recognize my own face, and in the hands of the oppressor I recognize my own hands. Their flesh is my flesh; their blood is my blood; their pain is my pain; their smile is my smile."[4]

We are made of the same dust. We cry the same tears. We are all capable of the same evil. And we all have the same capacity to love. Every one of us is a reflection of God.

RETHINKING LIFE

- How do you respond to the idea that faith is not just about having new ideas, it's about having new eyes? What do you think it means to see your own brokenness or your own belovedness reflected in the eyes of another human being?

- Has there been a time when you have looked into the eyes of another person and felt as if you were looking into the face of God? Maybe it was seeing a newborn baby, a person with Down syndrome, or someone who was fighting cancer. Perhaps it happened when you encountered someone living on the streets or in an orphanage. Or maybe it was just looking into the mirror and realizing you are a child of God. Spend a few moments remembering when and where you have seen God in God's many disguises.

---

4. Henri J. M. Nouwen, *With Open Hands* (Notre Dame, IN: Ave Maria Press, 2006), 92.

- Dorothy Day once said, "I really only love God as much as the person I love the least." How would you describe what it's like to be a "least loved" person, someone in whom others fail to recognize the image of God? Conversely, what individual or group of people comes to mind when you consider those you love the least? In what ways do you see them as what Martin Buber called an "It"? What thoughts or emotions are you aware of when you try to see them as a "Thou" instead?

## CHAPTER 3

Sin Destroys Life

So God took dirt and breathed life into it to make humanity. God made human beings in God's own image and called the whole creation very good. But it wasn't long before things went haywire.

When we talk about "original sin," we tend to think about Adam and Eve eating the forbidden fruit in the garden of Eden. And that is when things begin to unravel, for sure. But the first time the word *sin* is used in the Bible isn't in connection with Adam and Eve. Instead, it's first used in the story of Cain and Abel. Let that sink in. The first time the word *sin* is used in the Bible is when Cain, a son of Adam and Eve, commits the Bible's first act of violence by taking the life of his own brother.

Murder is the first thing that happens outside the garden of Eden. The Lord confronts Cain, saying, "What have you done?" And then God utters one of the most profound statements in the entire Bible: "Your brother's blood cries out to me from the ground" (Gen. 4:10).

The Sound of Blood

What does it mean that the blood we shed cries out to God from the ground?

Some of my Jewish friends who are a little more polished in their Hebrew have taught me some profound insights hidden in this text.

Dam, the Hebrew word translated "blood," is plural. *Plural*. And the verb *sa'ak*, translated "cries," is in the present tense. It wasn't that the blood of Abel cried out just in that moment in the past, it cries out in the present. It *is* crying out to God. Anytime blood is shed, it cries out to God and continues crying out.

And the blood that cries out is not limited to the murder of Abel. God is making a statement that the blood of all people who are killed cries out. We miss this when we read "blood" as singular and limit it to the murder of Abel. The bloods of all individuals, tribes, and peoples who have been killed cry out to God from the earth. God's profound statement reflects the knowledge that this would not be humanity's only murder. This would not be the last of the shed blood. Killing and violence do not stop in Genesis 4. That's where they begin. The murder of Abel is simply a precursor to the murders and violence that will follow.

Abel's blood cries out to God. So does the blood of the martyrs, the saints, and all the freedom fighters over the centuries—it all cries out to God. The blood of Native Americans slaughtered on their own land cries out to God, and the blood of enslaved Africans who were whipped, raped, and lynched cries out to God. So does the blood of Michael Brown, Breonna Taylor, Tamir Rice, and Ahmaud Arbery. All the bloods cry out to God from the ground.

It is also interesting to note that although Abel does not utter a word in the biblical narrative, his blood speaks. His blood exerts power beyond his death as it cries out to God. It reminds me how, following the murder of George Floyd by a Minneapolis police officer, Floyd's then six-year-old daughter Gianna said, "Daddy changed the world." She wasn't romanticizing his murder or venerating him as a martyr but simply echoing the truth that a person's voice doesn't end when they are killed. It may just be the beginning, as their blood cries out to God.

By the sixth chapter of Genesis, the Bible says that the whole earth "was corrupt in God's sight and was full of violence" (Gen. 6:11). That's when God decided to send a flood, killing almost all the people and creatures still living, so he could start from scratch. It's impossible to avoid the paradox that a flood wiping out the earth is what was needed to protect life. But I invite you to think about it this way: humanity was essentially on a suicidal course and God intervened to save us from ourselves. I imagine it was sort of like divine chemotherapy, with God eradicating the cancer so that new life could flourish.

When the flood recedes and things start afresh with Noah and his descendants, God issues a new command, one we've never heard before: don't kill each other. God says, "And for your lifeblood I will surely demand an accounting. I will demand an accounting from every animal. And from each human being, too, I will demand an accounting for the life of another human being" (Gen. 9:5).

For the first time in human history, "thou shalt not kill" is a thing. And if perchance we decide not to listen to God and we do kill each other, God will demand an accounting.

So that's how a very good world started becoming a very broken world. Only a few chapters later in Genesis, humanity is engaged in full-on war, and the bloodshed continues to this day. But one of the core messages throughout the story of God is that God is good even when we are not. God is faithful even when we are not. God's love is bigger than our sins and mistakes.

It's a Love Story

Many years ago, a pastor friend of mine asked me, "Why does God hate sin?"

I thought about it for a minute and then said, "Because we are disobeying God."

He looked at me and shrugged his shoulders. He seemed unsatisfied by that answer, and he stared kindly back at me as he waited for me to dig deeper.

"Because we are breaking God's laws, disregarding God's commands," I said.

He smiled and held his stubborn silence.

I tried once more, "Because when we sin, it hurts God."

He seemed to like that answer and smiled big. I'll never forget what he said next. "Don't you think it hurts God because it hurts us?" He went on to give me one of the best lessons I've ever had about sin, and he did it in a way that wasn't patronizing or preachy at all.

God hates sin because God loves people. Sin hurts people. When we "miss the mark," which is the biblical definition of sin, it hurts us, it hurts others, and it hurts God's creation. God's commands are all meant to protect us—from ourselves.

It was one of those moments when it felt like God was speaking directly to me. My friend spoke in a tone of curiosity rather than certainty, and that was part of what made me lean in. I had never heard anyone talk about sin like this.

Incidentally, I use the word *sin* even though it may feel antiquated or weird to some of us. Although there are other ways of talking about it, I use the word *sin* because I want to reclaim some things that the televangelists and hell-obsessed pastors have distorted. We can't let the bad-news preachers hijack the good news. I love the picture Russian novelist Fyodor Dostoevsky paints of hell: "What is hell? . . . The suffering of being no longer able to love."[1]

What my pastor friend invited me to think about that day twenty-five years ago has shaped the way I've come to think about sin. God hates sin not because we are disobeying commands but because God cannot bear to see us hurt one another or ourselves. Commands about marriage, fidelity, and covenant are healthy for our souls. Divorce is awful not just because we break a promise but because it tears our hearts apart, it hurts us, it hurts our kids. Greed hurts people. Lust hurts people. Rage hurts people. Exploitation, war, drugs, and

1.   Fyodor Dostoevsky, *The Brothers Karamazov*, bicentennial edition, trans. Richard Pevear and Larissa Volokhonsky (1990; New York: Picador, 2021), 342.

promiscuity hurt people. Which is why sin is ultimately about love—God's love for us, our love for each other, and our love for ourselves. The whole law can be summed up in one word: love.

Remember the question I posed in the introduction: What does love require of us? We could say that sin is falling short of what love requires of us. Of course, we all fall short and that's why grace is so delicious. God's desire is for us to flourish, for love to reign. What happened in original sin is that human beings took their eyes off of love. Sin is narcissistic and self-centered, but love is sacrificial and others-centered. Sin is shortsighted, but love endures forever.

Sin at its core is the failure to love. Love always seeks the flourishing of every person and every creature. Sin values people for what they can give or produce or do, but love values people because they are made in the image of God—period. Sin sees the world and readily exploits it for selfish gain. The earth, nature, animals, even people are disposable when sin reigns. But love always protects, cherishes, and preserves life—that's what love does. Wherever sin destroys life, love heals the wounds.

I love these beautiful words from my friend Norman Wirzba. He's not the pastor who taught me about sin twenty-five years ago, but he has taught me much about it since: "God's love creates a beautiful world, but our distortion and denial of this love leads to life's degradation. God does not give up on us or any creature, and so God works to redirect our waywardness, so that we can participate with God in the healing of all life. The goal of God's love is for it to be fully active in the life of each and every creature. When that happens, life becomes heavenly."[2]

Growing up, I always heard that sin leads to death, but now I have a deeper understanding of what that really means. Sin is deadly. It destroys the sacred life God has created. It crushes the image of God that exists in every human being ever made. But God's love is bigger

---

2. Norman Wirzba, *Way of Love: Recovering the Heart of Christianity* (San Francisco: HarperOne, 2016), 42.

than sin and death. God's love heals all the wounds. That love should transform us so that we become a force for love and life in the world. We get to join the love story. If God is love, then hell is a loveless place and heaven is where love rules supreme. And if Scripture is true, we are not just to wait until we die to experience heaven but also to bring heaven to earth. We are to destroy every expression of hell and death on earth—with love.

In his letter to the church at Rome, the apostle Paul speaks of how immense and powerful God's love is. It's so powerful that there is nothing that can stop it—not death, not angels, not demons (Rom. 8:38–39). Nothing. And there's that place in the Gospels where Jesus says not even the gates of hell will prevail (Matt. 16:18–19). What if we choose to believe these aren't just promises for the afterlife but promises we can stand on right now? Hell doesn't stand a chance against love.

RETHINKING LIFE

- Reflect for a moment on your experiences with the concept of sin. Based on what you've been taught about sin, how might you have answered the question, "Why does God hate sin?"
- How do you feel about the idea that sin is a failure to love? In what ways, if any, does it change your understanding of sin?
- Love always seeks the flourishing of every person and every creature. How does this statement challenge you? How does it encourage you?
- In what ways does your current ethic of life reflect love? In what ways, if any, does it reflect a failure to love?

CHAPTER 4

God Is Like Jesus

Several years ago, a radio DJ in my home state of Tennessee was interviewing a friend of mine, Jim Wallis. This DJ was an interesting cacophony of things: he was a Jewish country music DJ who didn't seem to be very interested in religion. He confessed to Jim that he had read a lot of the Bible, and there were parts of it that he loved. Other parts he found confusing. And then he said, "But I've always liked the stuff in red," referring to Bibles that print the words of Jesus in red to set them apart. Then he said, "You all seem to like the red letters. You should call yourselves 'red-letter Christians.'" And it stuck. Red Letter Christians. It has turned into a movement, around the country and increasingly around the world, of people who aspire to live as if Jesus meant the stuff he said.

If we are honest, I think many of us can probably relate to the radio DJ. We love Jesus and the Gospels, but other parts of the Bible are harder to make sense of. Some parts of the Bible are even hard to reconcile with the things Jesus says in the red letters. Sometimes it's hard to know how to build a better foundation for life when the Bible itself does not always seem to demonstrate a consistent ethic of life.

Yeah, we're going there.

To get at this, let's start here: God is like Jesus. Jesus is like God. That's why Jesus himself said, "If you have seen me, you have seen the Father" (see John 14:9). Jesus is the full revelation of God. That's the claim made by both New Testament writers and the early Christians.

With Jesus, we don't just have God's Word on paper, we have God's Word made flesh. One of my pastor friends says it like this: "We believe in the authoritative, inerrant, infallible Word of God. His name is Jesus." There is nothing about God that contradicts Jesus. Jesus is the full revelation of God, and God is the same yesterday, today, and forever. When Scripture seems at odds with itself, Jesus becomes the referee, the sounding board, the litmus test. God is and always has been like Jesus.

Jesus is also the greatest champion of life who ever lived. He enters a world full of violence and exposes, absorbs, and subverts it at every turn. He is the Prince of Peace, living water, the narrow way that leads to life. On the cross, Jesus puts death on display and triumphs over it with love, grace, and an empty tomb. And yet, when it comes to having a consistent ethic of life, we still have to wrestle with some difficult questions about Jesus, God, and the Bible.

- How do we make sense of all the violence in the Bible, especially if we believe that all Scripture is "God-breathed" (2 Tim. 3:16)?
- If Jesus is a champion for life and the full revelation of God, why does he seem so different from the God of the Old Testament?
- What does it mean that a violent death lies at the center of our faith?
- Did God kill Jesus?
- Does God use violence, and is there ever a time Christians can use violence?

Although we aren't going to be able to get deep into the weeds of biblical interpretation, we can't have a book on life without at least acknowledging some of the confusing passages in the Bible that depict death and violence, especially when those confusing passages are sometimes used by Christians to justify really terrible things.

The Texts of Terror

Without a doubt, there are some brutal scenes in the Bible. Terrible violence. Entire passages are often called "the texts of terror." For example, Judges 19 describes the brutal gang rape of a nameless concubine. When she subsequently dies of her injuries, her master cuts her body into pieces and then distributes them among the twelve tribes of Israel.

Ugh.

Even more problematic are the stories in which violence seems to be orchestrated and blessed by God. When the Israelites flee from Egypt, God rescues them by drowning the army of Pharaoh in the Red Sea (Exodus 14). God destroys the people of Sodom and Gomorrah by raining down fire on them from heaven (Genesis 19). In the story of the flood, God destroys every human and animal that didn't have an all-access pass for Noah's ark (Genesis 6–9). My friend Greg Boyd tells the story of a kid he knows who asked, "What happened to the animals that didn't make it on the boat? Didn't God love them too?"

Other texts-of-terror passages detail how entire populations are wiped out, and the Bible depicts God as condoning or even ordering the bloodshed. In one passage, the Israelites are told to mercilessly slaughter anything that breathes, including animals and children (Deut. 20:16). We find variations of this "kill everything that breathes" command thirty-seven times in the Old Testament.[1] In Numbers 31, God is depicted as ordering every member of the Midianites to be slaughtered except for the virgin girls, whom the soldiers are told to "save for yourselves" as spoils of war.

Then there are the stories in which the violence just seems arbitrary. For example, I've always found it troubling that the ark of the covenant, which carried the presence of God, was deadly to anyone who touched it. A man named Uzzah, who simply tried to keep the

---

1. Greg Boyd, *Cross Vision: How the Crucifixion of Jesus Makes Sense of Old Testament Violence* (Minneapolis: Fortress, 2017), 9.

ark from falling off its cart, was struck dead for his efforts (2 Sam. 6:6–7). On another occasion, a bunch of people who just looked at the ark, without touching it at all, were struck dead (1 Sam. 6:19). I'd prefer to believe that people were brought to life rather than death by touching the container for God's presence.

Given all of this, it's not hard to see why some Christians have used such stories as justification for heinous violence, even to defend genocide and other atrocities. If we believe that God resorted to violence to solve problems, then it becomes much easier to justify resorting to violence ourselves.

So how do we make sense of violence in the Bible? The simplest answer is this: violence is the product of sin. It is always sinful. It began with Cain killing Abel in Genesis 4, and a few chapters later we have full-on wars. The blood of Abel and of every other person killed by violence still cries out to God from the ground.

We also have to acknowledge that, over the centuries, Christianity has accommodated itself to the logic of empires—specifically, to the idea that violence can bring peace, or that wealth will make us happy. It took only a few days for God's enslaved people to physically leave Pharaoh's empire, but we are still trying to get the empire out of us. Sometimes our bodies can be free but our imagination can still be enslaved. As Jesus told Peter at one point, we are still thinking with the mind of this world rather than having the mind of God (Matt. 16:23).

All you have to do is read the Sermon on the Mount (Matthew 5–7) to see how upside down and countercultural the revolution of Jesus really is. It reorients how we think about nearly everything—how we interact with evil, how we hold our possessions, how we respond to violence. The gospel confronts our human instincts: It is better to die than to kill. It is better to give than to receive. If we want to be rich, we must give away our possessions. If we want to find our lives, we must first lose them. God blesses all the people this world has crushed—the meek, the merciful, the poor, the peacemakers. All those who are last will be first and the first last. The mighty will be cast down and the lowly lifted up. That's the upside-down kingdom of God.

Another thing we need to be aware of is the human tendency to project onto God our own motives for violence and vengeance. We often do what makes sense to us and assume God would want the same thing. We assume God blesses whatever or whomever we bless and curses whatever or whomever we curse. As the old saying goes, "God created human beings in his own image and then human beings decided to return the favor." When we do things that hurt ourselves or others, we interpret the consequences as God's judgment. Or when we win the war or lose the war, we interpret the outcome as God's will rather than recognize that God didn't want a war at all. In the words of author Anne Lamott, "You can safely assume you've created God in your own image when it turns out that God hates all the same people you do."[2]

When we interpret inexplicable violence in the Bible as "justice" or "God's mysterious ways" rather than calling it what it is—a consequence of sin—we are projecting the human logic that makes sense to us onto God. But God is like Jesus, and Jesus rules by the law of love.

Love makes room for freedom, so God allows us to hurt ourselves and others. But God is always working through the cracks, healing us of our violence and showing us another way. Even in tragic events such as the flood, where God basically starts over because the world was "full of violence" (Gen. 6:11), we can see a God who is "grieved" by the suffering of the world (Gen. 6:6 NKJV).[3] We see a God who is working with us to make sure that life wins, that love wins, that death and violence don't destroy all the beauty God has made.

---

2. Anne Lamott, *Bird by Bird: Some Instructions on Writing and Life* (1994; New York: Anchor, 2019), 21.
3. Scholars point out that "acts of nature" in the Bible are often portrayed as the instruments of God. For example, when Egypt was beset by a series of plagues, the sea swallowed up Pharaoh's army, and the earth was destroyed by the flood. However, another way to view those peculiar events is as evidence that the entire world is out of whack, that creation itself is in upheaval when frogs, gnats, flies, locusts, and floods destroy the earth. The ancient Hebrews saw all of creation as connected, just as many Native American communities still do today. The Hebrew worldview saw human beings as connected to the rest of creation—that we were made from dirt itself—and that God's vision of shalom is a world in which everything is in good relationship with everything else. Noah's flood, the fire that rained down on Sodom and Gomorrah, and the plagues in Egypt are all evidence that things on earth are obviously not in a good way. We got way offtrack from shalom.

God Wants to Heal Us of Our Violence

The Bible is the book of life, not death, when we read it properly. For example, many view the wild, apocalyptic book of Revelation as a final act of divine vengeance. They see Jesus returning with a sword in his hand, though what Scripture describes is a sword that comes from his mouth, a very important poetic detail (Rev. 1:16; 19:15). And yet if we read Revelation properly, we discover it is about a restored creation, a new heaven and a new earth (Revelation 21). We see the new Jerusalem flourish, the Tree of Life in the middle of the city, the river of life running through it, the gates of the city left open because there is no longer any reason to fear. God is redeeming the world. That's why the gospel is called good news. It's a love story.

Here's what we know: God loves people. God loves life. God loves creation. The gospel of John has these wonderful words: "For God so loved the world." But we often forget the next verse: "For God did not send his Son into the world to condemn the world, but to save the world" (John 3:16–17). Not to condemn but to save. Say it again for the folks in the back: not to condemn but to save. The world was and is worth saving. You, me, all of us are worth saving. That's the good news of the gospel.

The problem is that some of the ways we learned to understand the Bible in Sunday school (for those of us who went to Sunday school) are wrong. For instance, I once heard a whole sermon about how Elisha called down a curse on a bunch of kids making fun of his bald head. It's such a bizarre story. A bunch of youth make fun of Elisha saying, "Get out of here, baldy!" When Elisha curses the boys "in the name of the LORD," two bears come out of the woods and maul forty-two of them (2 Kings 2:23–24).

According to the preacher who gave the sermon, the point of that story is, don't mess with God or the man of God. And the preacher was a bald man, of course. But I'm not so sure that is the point of the story. I'm pretty sure it is not. Perhaps the point of the story is that even a man of God who has been a powerful messenger and a prophet is not immune to violence and rage and is capable of misusing divine power in a terribly harmful way. Maybe Elisha even picked it up from his mentor, Elijah. For all the incredible and holy things he did, the prophet Elijah also called down fire from heaven to incinerate one hundred Samaritans, whom he mistakenly thought had come to harm him (2 Kings 1:9–12).

We might conclude that God approved of such behavior since the text doesn't condemn it. And yet, when Jesus' own disciples suggest doing the same thing to some Samaritans who didn't welcome Jesus, Jesus does not approve. James and John, known as the Sons of Thunder (which sounds like a pro-wrestling duo), ask Jesus, "Lord, do you want us to call fire down from heaven to destroy them?" (Luke 9:54). Instead of taking them up on their offer, Jesus steals their thunder (pun intended) and rebukes them in a way that makes it very clear God isn't a fan of bringing down fire on people. It is fascinating to realize that they actually had the ability to misuse their divinely given power.[4] That's exactly the temptation Satan had previously used against Jesus in the desert—to misuse his power.[5]

God is working through the cracks in everything. And ultimately, God's will is to heal us of our violence. Certainly, one of the deepest existential questions of faith is why God gives us the power and the freedom to heal or to kill in the first place.

---

4. I'm grateful for and riffing on the provocative work of my friend Greg Boyd and others here. Check out his book *Cross Vision: How the Crucifixion of Jesus Makes Sense of Old Testament Violence*. For an even deeper dive, check out his two-volume set *The Crucifixion of the Warrior God: Interpreting the Old Testament's Violent Portraits of God in Light of the Cross*.
5. Samson provides yet another example of misusing divine power. When Samson made and lost a foolish bet, he murdered thirty innocent people so he could steal their clothes to pay off his debt. When he got angry at the Philistines, he tied the tails of 150 pairs of foxes, attached a torch to each pair, and set them loose to burn down the Philistines' grain fields and vineyards. The Philistines retaliated by burning Samson's wife and her father. So he slaughtered them in return, killing another thousand people with the "jawbone of an ass." I'm quite sure none of that violence was God's most perfect will. Even people like Samson who have been endowed with exceptional miraculous gifts can misuse them.
   Samson succumbed to the temptation to misuse his power. His own strength and the misuse of it ultimately led to his death when he caused the temple to collapse, killing both himself and thousands of other people. Even here we can see the truth of Jesus' rebuke to Peter, "Put away your sword. . . . Those who use the sword will die by the sword" (Matt. 26:52 NLT).

Just as there are right and wrong ways to use a hammer or an ax, there are right and wrong ways to use supernatural gifts. We need to know this because it changes how we understand some of the events in the Bible, especially when kings and prophets engage in violence or misuse their power. Even Moses, it's worth noting, was vulnerable to his own anger and violence. He murdered a man (Exodus 2). At one point, Moses used his God-endowed supernatural power in a fit of rage and disobedience to smack a rock with his staff rather than speaking to the rock as God had commanded (Numbers 20). Water did indeed gush out of the rock, but God was not happy about Moses' tactics. God rebuked Moses and didn't allow him to enter the promised land as a result. It seems clear that divine power can be abused and misused in a way that is contrary to God even though God bestowed the power.

Just because characters in the Bible have God-given positions or gifts does not mean everything they do is ordained or blessed by God. Sometimes they rationalized or justified their own need for violence by projecting it onto God as if God were somehow responsible for their actions. For example, one way of understanding blood sacrifices and some of the violence attributed to God in the Hebrew Scriptures[6] is that it is humans, not God, who needed a way to atone for our sins. Animal sacrifice, then, became a kind of penance, another example of the misconception that violence can heal our violence, that blood will atone for bloodshed. It's similar to alcoholics who think they need more whiskey to deal with their drinking problem. Instead, God wants to wean us off our culturally conditioned belief that violence is going to heal our violence, that blood will atone for the bloodshed.

So even as Scripture and humanity move away from animal sacrifice to the final sacrifice to end all sacrifices, God persists in desiring "mercy, not sacrifice" (Hos. 6:6)! God blows up the sacrificial system once and for all in Jesus. Throughout the Bible, God is working through the cracks of broken humanity, moving us away from violence

---

6. I prefer "Hebrew Scriptures" or "Hebrew Bible" rather than "Old Testament" because the word *old* suggests it is irrelevant, and I don't think it is.

and the original sin of Cain killing Abel, and moving us toward that beautiful time when we will beat our swords into plows and our spears into pruning hooks (Isa. 2:4).

Centering Jesus

There are ways of reading the Bible that make a monster out of God—or at least portray a God who is easy to fear and hard to love. Which is why I want to spend some time thinking about Jesus, the full revelation of who God is, the great interrupter of violence. And yet even Jesus is vulnerable to being misunderstood. There are ways of understanding why Jesus died that can reinforce perceptions of a violent, bloodthirsty God. Some versions of why Jesus died portray a God who had a gun pointed at sinful humanity, ready to kill us, but then at the last minute aimed the gun at Jesus and killed him instead to save the world. We'll talk more about that in the next chapter.

Interestingly enough, some of the early Christians struggled to reconcile what they believed about Jesus with the God they read about in the Hebrew Scriptures. Some early Christians claimed that Jesus was a new and improved version of God. One of my friends jokes that it feels like somewhere between Malachi (the last book of the Old Testament) and Matthew (the first book of the New Testament) God got born again. Or at least went through some anger management classes.

It became more than just a debate for the early Christians; it was one of the first things they deemed heresy. The idea that Jesus was different and better than God, and not at all of the same character as the God of the Old Testament, was rejected as a heresy called Marcionism, named after its most avid proponent, Marcion of Sinope. But what's interesting is that the early Christians felt a tension many of us still feel today: trying to reconcile our deep love for Jesus with some of the harder to understand parts of the Bible.

Let's spend a little time reflecting on Jesus. I want to invite you to consider these three truths: Jesus is the lens through which we understand the Bible, Jesus is the fulfillment of a better ethic of life, and Jesus is the ultimate disrupter of violence and death. Jesus is consistently *for* life and consistently subverts death and violence.

Jesus Is the Lens through Which We Understand the Bible

In our community, we get a lot of food donations. I've learned the hard way that it's a bad idea to just dive full on into indulging donated food, especially when it comes to things like dairy and sushi. Before I put anything in my mouth, it first has to pass the sniff test. If it smells bad, I don't eat it.

I've adopted a similar principle when it comes to Christianity. There are lots of things that try to pass as Christianity, but they don't pass the sniff test. They don't smell like Jesus, so I don't want to indulge. Ultimately, the word *Christian* means "Christlike." If something doesn't smell like Jesus, sound like Jesus, and love like Jesus, it is not Christianity. And there have been lots of versions of Christianity over the centuries and even today that don't smell, sound, or love like Jesus. As with spoiled milk, if we consume them we'll probably get sick.

The whole Bible is God's Word to us, but Jesus is the sniff test through which we understand it all. Another way of saying it is that Jesus is the lens through which we interpret the Bible, and the lens through which we interpret the world and how to live in it. Again, whenever one passage of Scripture seems to conflict with another passage of Scripture, Jesus gets to be the referee. As my friend Brian Zahnd says, "I don't have a low view of Scripture; I have a high view of Christ. . . . Jesus is the only perfect theology, the only enduring foundation."[7] I agree with Brian.

The entire Bible and the whole narrative of God points to and centers Jesus. Don't just take my word for it, take his: "You study the

7. Brian Zahnd, *When Everything's on Fire: Faith Forged from the Ashes* (Downers Grove, IL: InterVarsity, 2021), 96, 100.

Scriptures diligently because you think that in them you have eternal life. These are the very Scriptures that testify about me, yet you refuse to come to me to have life" (John 5:39–40). Here, Jesus is telling us that we study the Bible thinking it gives us life, while missing the fact that the entire story points to him and that we are to come to him for life. The Bible is the menu not the meal.

The author of the book of Hebrews puts it this way: "In the past God spoke to our ancestors through the prophets at many times and in various ways, but in these last days he has spoken to us by his Son, whom he appointed heir of all things, and through whom also he made the universe. The Son is the radiance of God's glory and the exact representation of his being, sustaining all things by his powerful word. After he had provided purification for sins, he sat down at the right hand of the Majesty in heaven" (Heb. 1:1–3).

In his first letter to the church at Corinth, the apostle Paul says that we "see through a glass, darkly" (1 Cor. 13:12 KJV). Even with Jesus, we still have a hard time seeing everything. We see God only in part, sort of like we have spiritual cataracts. Or as Greg Boyd says, we see God through the clouds, like when you can't quite see the sun on an overcast day, but you know the sun is there. Jesus allows us to see the sun without the clouds and without blinding ourselves. Jesus comes to show us God in plain sight. Though we still have limited vision, Jesus helps us see a whole lot better.

By the way, I have terrible eyesight. When I don't have my glasses on, I can see shapes and forms and colors, but not much else. And that's sort of what I think it's like to look at God without Jesus. But when I look at God through the lens of Jesus, things become much clearer. In Christ, "the fullness of the Deity lives in bodily form" (Col. 2:9).

Jesus Is the Fulfillment of a Better Ethic of Life

Rather than seeing Jesus as the negation or abolition of the "old law," as some of the Marcionists did back in the day, let's consider what it means that Jesus is the fulfillment of the law, as he says in

Matthew 5:17–18. And let's start with one of the hardest ancient laws on the books: "An eye for an eye, a tooth for a tooth" (Ex. 21:24 NLT). It's one of many laws given to God's people through Moses after they left Egypt. It's also one of the most misunderstood and misused verses of the Bible.

The ancient idea was known as *lex talionis*, which means "law of retaliation." It is, quite literally, where we get our idea of retaliation. It allowed a person to return harm, the same harm done to them. It is sometimes called "parallel retaliatory justice" because you could reciprocate the injury inflicted on you to the person who did it. *Lex talionis* existed thousands of years before the compilation of the Bible, and as a guide to justice, it was a commonly accepted practice.

But here is what is clutch about *lex talionis*. It was never meant to be a license for violence. It was meant to limit the escalating cycle of violence. Another way of thinking of it is, "An eye for an eye, but no more than that." If someone gouges out your eye, you can gouge out their eye, but only one eye. If someone breaks your leg, you can break their leg. But it stops there.

Limiting violence is a good thing, and it's clear that's what the original law of retaliation was intended to do, stop the spiral of violence. You know how it goes: What starts as a tweet ends up turning into an argument. An argument turns into a fistfight. Fists turn into knives or bats or guns, and lives are lost.[8] There is all sorts of collateral damage.

With *lex talionis*, what was meant to limit violence has too often been used instead as a license for violence. The hope was to prevent the never-ending cycle of violence, to stop violence rather than validate or escalate it.

Enter Jesus.

Jesus knew the law, but he came to fulfill the law with a better ethic of life. He said to his followers, "You have heard that it was said,

---

8. And what's true of people is also true of nations. Think about the cycle of violence that began with the terrorist attacks on 9/11. Nearly three thousand people were killed on September 11, 2001—2,977 to be exact. Instead of stopping at 2,977 lives, the US government subsequently killed tens of thousands of people in Iraq and Afghanistan who were not even responsible for the 9/11 attacks.

'Eye for eye, and tooth for tooth.' But I tell you, do not resist an evil person. . . . You have heard that it was said, 'Love your neighbor and hate your enemy.' But I tell you, love your enemies and pray for those who persecute you" (Matt. 5:38–39, 43–44).

Jesus teaches a new way that transcends the law of *lex talionis*: his way is the law of love. As his followers, we should not hurt those who have hurt us. We can do better than mirroring the evil done to us. We don't poke out anyone else's eye, even if they poked out our eye. We do not repay evil with evil but seek to return evil with good. As my momma taught me, "Two wrongs don't make a right."

If we believe Jesus did not come to abolish the law but to fulfill the law, it all makes so much sense, right? Limiting violence was a good place to start; ending violence is where this whole thing is headed. And so Jesus expands our ideas of justice with the law of love. Just because we can retaliate doesn't mean we should. Just because something is legal doesn't make it right. Returning harm for harm is not the best we can do. Let the church say, "Amen."

Jesus challenged laws that got in the way of human flourishing in other ways too. He healed on the Sabbath, permitted his disciples to eat food the old law forbade eating, and blew away the legal and cultural norms of exclusion for women and other folks on the margins. For Jesus, everything boils down to this: Love God. Love people (Matt. 22:37–40). All the law is summed up in this: *love*.

Jesus healed on the Sabbath because that was what the law of love required. He said, "The Sabbath was made to meet the needs of people, and not people to meet the requirements of the Sabbath" (Mark 2:27 NLT). If laws get in the way of human flourishing, we choose love, not laws. In the words of author Barbara Brown Taylor, "The only clear line I draw these days is this: when my religion tries to come between me and my neighbor, I will choose my neighbor. . . . Jesus never commanded me to love my religion."[9]

---

9. Barbara Brown Taylor, *Holy Envy: Finding God in the Faith of Others* (San Francisco: HarperOne, 2019), 208.

Deep down, we know we can do better than returning harm for harm. If someone breaks your arm, not many of us are going to suggest you break that person's arm to get justice. If someone gouges out your eye, most of us are going to insist you can do better than gouging out the eye of the perpetrator. We don't rape those who rape to show that rape is wrong. And yet the ancient logic of *lex talionis* pervades our thinking. Especially when it comes to extreme crimes such as murder and war. We still cling to this dead-end logic that we can kill to show that killing is wrong, or kill to punish killing. In the end, we merely become the killers. We end up being the terrorists. In battling the beast, we become the beast.

The law of love is just one example of how Jesus, the Prince of Peace, challenged our logic of redemptive violence, the idea that violence can heal the wounds of violence. Jesus consistently emphasized life and mercy and redemption as key ingredients to a better ethic of life.

- "It is not the healthy who need a doctor, but the sick. I have not come to call the righteous, but sinners" (Mark 2:17).
- "Blessed are the merciful, for they will be shown mercy" (Matt. 5:7).
- "Forgive, and you will be forgiven" (Luke 6:37).
- "Do not judge, or you too will be judged" (Matt. 7:1).

Jesus is the full revelation of God—God with skin on. In Jesus, we see, unmistakably, that God is love. God is nonviolent. God is healing the wounds of violence and sin. God is showing us the narrow way that leads to life (Matt. 7:14). And that life is not just for us but for everybody else too, even our enemies.

Jesus Disrupts Violence and Death

Throughout his ministry, Jesus disrupts systems of death, disarms violent hearts, and casts out demons and powers that are hurting people. One of my favorite examples of this is when Jesus interrupts a mob execution.

A woman caught in adultery has been humiliated and dragged into the temple courts, where Jesus is teaching. (It's worth noting that, although it takes two to tango, the adulterous man is nowhere to be found.) Her all-male jury has condemned her to death, and they have their stones ready to carry out the execution. According to Jewish law, they have every legal right to kill her. She had committed a deathworthy crime. But as we've seen, just because it's legal doesn't make it right.

When the authorities bring her to Jesus for a verdict, hoping to trap him into defying the law so they can condemn him too, he interrupts the scene—with grace. He tells the men ready to kill the woman, "Let any one of you who is without sin be the first to throw a stone at her" (John 8:7). The stones drop and the men walk away. The story ends with Jesus standing alone with the woman, and this beautiful exchange between them:

> "Woman, where are they? Has no one condemned you?"
> "No one, sir" she said.
> "Then neither do I condemn you," Jesus declared. "Go now and leave your life of sin."
>
> —John 8:10–11

Not only does Jesus affirm the dignity of the woman but also he transforms that violent mob of men. He freed all of them from the demonic forces of violence and death. The only one left who has any right to throw a stone is Jesus, and he has absolutely no inclination to do so. In Jesus, we see that the closer we are to God, the less we want to throw stones at other people. That is good news because no one is above reproach, and no one is beyond redemption. We are all sinners in need of grace, and we are all made in the image of God.

The Way of Jesus Is Nonviolence

Perhaps the most stunning display we have of Jesus choosing God's redemptive love over violence is when Jesus interrupts the violence of one of his own disciples. Peter, one of Jesus' most devoted disciples, is faced with an existential crisis when armed soldiers come to arrest Jesus. Keep in mind that at this point Peter has walked with Jesus, side by side, for three years. He has heard the Sermon on the Mount *live* and in person. But when the soldiers come, his worst fears and insecurities take over and he grabs his sword. He stands his ground by cutting off an ear of one of the guys who had come to arrest Jesus.

Jesus' response is brilliant. First, Jesus scolds Peter, telling him to put his sword away: "Live by the sword, die by the sword." And then Jesus picks up the ear of the wounded man and puts it back on, healing the man Peter almost killed. The message is crystal clear: The way of Jesus is nonviolence, even toward those who are violent to us. We do not return harm for harm. We overcome evil with good.

The early Christians got it, as we will see in chapter 6. They understood that for Christ we may die, but we may not kill. Early church father Tertullian said, "When Jesus disarmed Peter, he disarmed every one of us." If ever there were a case to be made for justifiable violence, even to protect the innocent, Peter had it. There is no such thing as redemptive violence, even to protect the Messiah himself. Violence is the problem, not the solution. Violence is the disease, not the cure.

Jesus shows us another way—a way to interact with evil without becoming evil. It may cost us our lives, but we know that "to live is Christ and to die is gain" (Phil. 1:21). Ultimately, we have nothing to lose and nothing to fear. Many of the apostles were martyred, including Peter, who ended up being hung upside down on a cross. Many of the early Christians lost their lives as well. But they insisted that when we remain faithful to Jesus, even in death, God's love prevails. Love means being willing to die, but never to kill.

Peter learned, and any of us who dare follow Jesus must also learn, that we cannot carry a cross in one hand and a weapon in the other. We cannot serve two masters. Jesus teaches, and the whole New Testament affirms, that we should not return harm done to us.

There is no greater affirmation of life than the sweet Lord Jesus. And there is no greater enemy of death. Jesus, the way, the truth, *the life*. Jesus, the narrow way that leads to *life*. Jesus, the *living* water, the *living* bread, the source of life itself.

RETHINKING LIFE

- Growing up, how were you taught to understand the violence in the Bible? In what ways does this chapter challenge or affirm that understanding?
- What disconnects, if any, are there between how you think about God and how you think about Jesus?
- Which Scripture passages do you have a hard time making sense of, especially when it comes to having a consistent ethic of life?
- In what ways, if any, does it change your perspective to think of Jesus as the referee whenever Scripture is at odds with itself?
- What contemporary expressions of Christianity would you say don't pass the sniff test? They don't smell like Jesus, sound like Jesus, or love like Jesus?
- How do you respond to the idea that there is no such thing as redemptive violence? That love means being willing to die, but never to kill?

## CHAPTER 5

Jesus Died to Save Us from Death

Several years ago, a nineteen-year-old boy was shot in front of my house. I heard the gunshots, found him on the street, and held his hand as he died. His name was Papito.

It happened just before Easter, and we decided to do things a little different that year. We moved our services into the streets. On Good Friday, as Christians around the world remembered Jesus' death, we held our service in front of the neighborhood gun shop. And not just any gun shop but one among the 5 percent of gun shops responsible for 90 percent of guns used in crimes.

The young men in my neighborhood carried a giant wooden cross and set it up in front of the gun shop. We read the familiar story of Jesus' crucifixion and walked through the stations of the cross, each station focusing on one event from the day Jesus was condemned, tortured, brutally executed, and laid in a tomb. After reading the passage describing the women who were left weeping at the foot of the cross, we invited mothers who had lost a child to gun violence to share their stories. Something powerful—transcendent and supernatural—happened that Good Friday. The tears of women two thousand years ago met the tears of our mothers. The suffering of Calvary met the suffering of Kensington.

After the service, one of the mothers approached me, tears rolling down her face. "I get it. I get it," she said. I responded with a curious look, inviting her to say more. "God knows what it feels like," she said. "God knows what it feels like to lose your child. God knows what it feels like to be me." That's when I realized who she was: Papito's mom, the mother of the nineteen-year-old boy who had just been killed on our block.

God knows what it feels like to suffer violence. I've heard other powerful expressions of that same gospel truth over the years. The mother of a man on death row said it this way: "God knows what it's like to see your boy executed at the hands of the state."

The Paradox of an Executed Savior

At the very center of the Christian faith is the paradox of an executed Savior. In Jesus, we see a God who suffers with all who suffer. In Jesus, God leaves the comfort of heaven and joins the struggle here on earth. As the apostle Paul writes,

> Christ Jesus . . . who, being in very nature God,
> did not consider equality with God
> something to be used to his own advantage;
> rather, he made himself nothing
> by taking the very nature of a servant,
> being made in human likeness.
> And being found in appearance as a man,
> he humbled himself
> by becoming obedient to death—
> even death on a cross!
>
> —Philippians 2:5–8

I want to explore this strange paradox at the heart of Christianity: that Jesus died to save us from death. It is one of the greatest mysteries of our faith and one of the most misunderstood. And that's a problem, especially if we want to have a consistent ethic of life. When we misunderstand Jesus' death, we can end up missing the whole point and even justifying things that contradict the life and teachings of Jesus. For example, I regularly hear people say things like, "How can God be against the death penalty when God used the death penalty to redeem the world?"[1] In response, I ask, "Was Jesus' death God's ultimate endorsement of violence, or was it God's ultimate subversion of violence?" I believe it can't be both. It must be the latter.

As we ponder the mystery of what Jesus did on the cross, I want to keep us from getting too heady. The cross should do something not just in our heads but also in our hearts. What Jesus did on the cross is not just a theological puzzle to be figured out or a riddle to be solved but something that should reorient our whole lives, especially when it comes to how we think about violence. Because what's just as important as what we do with the crucifixion is what the crucifixion does with us.

For two thousand years, Christian thinkers and theologians have been trying to find language that best captures what Jesus did on the cross. Their ideas are often referred to as "theories of atonement." Atonement essentially means that God is healing the world, bringing back the shalom and human flourishing God intended from the beginning. All that was lost in Adam is restored in Christ—our relationship with God, with each other, and with creation itself.

When theologians describe what Jesus did on the cross, they use words such as penal substitution, ransom, sacrifice. As I mentioned earlier, some atonement theories make it sound as if God had a gun pointed at humanity but then shifted aim and instead killed Jesus to save the world. Some say there was a debt that had to be paid and Jesus paid it. I remember a preacher saying that just as a bank can forgive

---

1. A few years ago in my home state of Tennessee, the legislature voted to bring back the electric chair as a method of execution. Ironically, they did it on Maundy Thursday, the day the global church remembers Jesus preparing for his execution. It was one of the most poignant examples of theological dissonance I've ever seen. I wrote an op-ed suggesting Christian legislators in this Bible Belt state had forgotten the entire message of Easter, and that the only thing more offensive than reinstating the electric chair would be reinstating crucifixion.

your credit-card debt, "Jesus paid the bill." While it has a nice ring to it, I'd suggest Jesus did more than just pay the bill.

One of the kids on my block expressed how problematic this way of thinking is after he'd attended an outreach event at an evangelical church. He was just seven at the time, and I can only imagine the hellfire-and-brimstone sermon he'd heard that prompted this response: "I wish God didn't have to kill himself for me. I wouldn't have asked him to do that."

Lord, have mercy.

I want to invite us to think of Jesus' death—of atonement—in a fresh way, though I understand it may be a stretch. Let's think of it less as a puzzle to be solved and more of a wonder to be embraced. What Jesus accomplished on the cross is not just a mathematical equation with one right answer but something we can marvel at and be transformed by for the rest of our lives. We can learn more about it from scholars who analyze it just as we learn more about the stars from astronomers, but let's begin with a sense of wonder at the beauty of what Jesus did for us when he subverted death and sin on the cross.

Four Things Jesus Did on the Cross

Let me offer a few reflections as we explore a more robust and life-giving theology of the cross. Specifically, here are four things Jesus did on the cross: he joined the ranks of the despised and the marginalized, he made a spectacle of death, he reconciled all things, and he ended the sacrificial system.[2]

Jesus Joined the Ranks of the Despised and the Marginalized

Jesus is the most profound act of divine solidarity the world has ever seen. God left all the comfort of heaven to join the struggle here on earth.

---

2. This list of four things isn't meant to be exhaustive. It's just a starting point.

Think about it. Jesus came to us not in just any body but in a body with brown skin. He came from the badlands of Nazareth, a town from which people said nothing good could come (John 1:46). God entered the world as a brown-skinned Palestinian Jew. God was born a refugee, born in a manger because there was no room in the inn. As an adult, Jesus was homeless. He said of himself, "Foxes have dens and birds have nests, but the Son of Man has no place to lay his head" (Matt. 8:20). In every way imaginable, Jesus joined the ranks of those on the margins. Especially when he was hung on the cross.[3]

The word *crucifixion* is the root of the word *excruciating*, because crucifixion meant unimaginable pain and an agonizing, prolonged death. Crucifixion resulted in so much carnage and bloodshed that birds of prey often flew over the bodies looking to pick off pieces of meat and wild dogs gathered at the foot of the crosses to lap up the blood. One reason family members often chose to remain at the cross was to keep away the wild animals.

Crucifixion was also a shameful death. It was not unusual for executioners to amuse themselves by hanging people fully naked in a public place or to hang them in different positions, even upside down, as they did with the apostle Peter. Soldiers and passersby hurled insults at the condemned, as they did with Jesus, taunting him as "King of the Jews." His crown of thorns and purple robe were also intended as a mockery.

The actual cause of death from crucifixion was varied— dehydration, blood loss, shock, heart failure, and, more often than not, asphyxiation. "I can't breathe" was the cry of the cross just as it was the last cry of Eric Garner and George Floyd, both of whom were killed by police. It starts to make sense why protestors marching in our streets held signs with Jesus on the cross while chanting "Hands up" and "I can't breathe." One of the central messages of the cross is

---

3. I am grateful for and building on the work of theologians James Cone and Howard Thurman. To learn more about a better understanding of atonement and why Jesus died, see my book *Executing Grace: How the Death Penalty Killed Jesus and Why It's Killing Us.*

that God is with those who are being crushed by the systems of death and injustice.

Given the horror of crucifixion, it has been said that the cross could become a beloved religious symbol only a generation after anyone had seen a real one. In the ancient Roman world, the cross was something not to be adored but to be feared. It was a symbol not of victory and hope but of humiliation and defeat. The cross was an icon of imperial terror. In Jesus' day, it evoked the same feelings we might have today when we see a noose or an electric chair. It's not really something most people would have wanted to wear around their necks or get tattooed on their arms.

For centuries, crucifixion was a standard method of execution in the Roman Empire and often done *en masse*. For example, Roman general Marcus Crassus (115–52 BC) once crucified six thousand people all at once, erecting the crosses along a major roadway that led to Rome.[4] Crucifixion was a regular part of the empire's "liturgy" of death, to use a church word. I say liturgy because it was a kind of ritual—a violent and bloody one. Even Jesus was not crucified alone but with a person on his left and a person on his right.

As an object lesson, crucifixion was part of what my friend Mark Taylor calls "the theatrics of empire,"[5] a dramatic display of state power reserved for traitors, rebels, insurrectionists, agitators, failed messiahs. These were criminals the empire considered to be the worst kind—disruptors of the peace, dissenters, and revolutionaries. As such, crucifixion was also an effective means of instilling fear in the masses. Theologian James Cone called it the Roman Empire's public service announcement. The empire was making it clear that if you do what these people did, you too will hang on a cross.

---

4. Some historians have said there were often so many crosses on the horizon that you couldn't enjoy the sunset. That's how common it was. Mass crucifixions also happened in other ancient cultures. Alexander the Great (356–323 BC) had two thousand people crucified all at once, and Alexander Jannaeus (ca. 103–76 BC) executed eight hundred people by crucifixion in the middle of Jerusalem.
5. Mark Lewis Taylor, *The Executed God: The Way of the Cross in Lockdown America*, 2nd ed. (Minneapolis: Fortress, 2011), 101.

On the cross, Jesus joined "the crucified peoples of the world."[6] When enslaved Africans looked at the cross, they recognized one of their own, a Savior who had been lynched. Author Clarence Jordan, a New Testament Greek scholar, captured this idea when he wrote *The Cotton Patch Gospel*, a retelling of the gospel in the dialect and context of 1960s Georgia. In it, Jesus gets lynched by an angry white mob. Jordan writes, "There just isn't any word in our vocabulary which adequately translates the Greek word for 'crucifixion.' *Our* crosses are so shined, so polished, so respectable that to be impaled on one of them would seem to be a blessed experience. We have thus emptied the term 'crucifixion' of its original content of terrific emotion, of violence, of indignity and stigma, of defeat. I have translated it as 'lynching,' well aware that this is not technically correct."[7]

Remember what Papito's mom said? God knows what it feels like. God understands the grief of the mother whose son was executed by the state of Texas. In Jesus, God joined the ranks of all who have suffered across the centuries.

Not only does God know the pain but God also knows the loneliness, the sense of feeling abandoned in suffering. As Jesus was about to die, he cried out, "My God, my God, why have you forsaken me?" (Matt. 27:46). That's something we can contemplate for the rest of our lives: in Jesus, God felt the absence of God. So don't ever let anybody tell you it's not okay to have doubts or to feel despair or loneliness. Jesus is right there with you in the darkness.

So that's the first thing Jesus did on the cross: he joined the ranks of the despised, the disinherited people, the crucified peoples of the world.

Jesus Made a Spectacle of Death

Jesus made a spectacle of death when he triumphed over it with love, forgiveness, and an empty tomb. The apostle Paul states it plainly: "And

---

6. Psychologist John Neafsey has written a book about the relationship between the suffering of Christ and the suffering of people titled *Crucified People: The Suffering of the Tortured in Today's World.*
7. Clarence L. Jordan, *The Cotton Patch Version of Matthew and John* (New York: Association Press, 1970), 10–11.

having disarmed the powers and authorities, he made a public spectacle of them, triumphing over them by the cross" (Col. 2:15). Another translation says he "disarmed the spiritual rulers and authorities. He shamed them publicly by his victory over them on the cross" (NLT). As James Cone puts it, "The cross was God's critique of power . . . snatching victory out of defeat."[8] They thought they could kill God and crucify love, but God's love stole the show.

It was God's ultimate protest, God's rebuke of death.

Jesus' hanging on the cross was a fist held high in defiance of the deity of Rome. The empire set out to shame him, but it was the empire's violence and corruption that were exposed instead. As he hung naked, Jesus left the empire stripped naked. He laid bare all the machinery of death, and no one could miss it. At the moment of Jesus' death, the sun stood still, the sky split open, the earth shook, the veil of the temple was torn apart, and the entire system of death unraveled.

Jesus transformed one of the most horrific icons of evil, the cross, into a conduit of God's love. This should do something to us. When we center ourselves around a suffering Savior who died with mercy and forgiveness on his lips, it should make us sensitive to all who suffer violence—the victims of murder, the victims of execution, the victims of torture and bullying, and the victims of hatred. It should make us suspicious of state violence and of any religion that accommodates and legitimates that violence. What Jesus did on the cross should make us champions of life and mercy and love.

Jesus Reconciled All Things

Much of what we hear referred to as justice is really just revenge in disguise. As Dr. Martin Luther King Jr. spoke about the death penalty, he said, "What is capital punishment but society's final assertion that it is determined not to forgive?"[9] When we look at Christ on

---

8. James H. Cone, *The Cross and the Lynching Tree* (Maryknoll, NY: Orbis, 2011), 2.
9. Martin Luther King Jr., "Draft of Chapter IV, 'Love in Action,'" Martin Luther King Jr. Research and Education Institute, Stanford University, circa July 1, 1962 to March 1, 1963, https://kinginstitute.stanford.edu/king-papers/documents/draft-chapter-iv-love-action.

the cross, we see something entirely different. Jesus shows us how to combat evil without becoming evil. He shows us how to interact with violence without reciprocating that violence.

One way of breaking down the massive concept of atonement is to think of the word as *at-one-ment*—as being made one with. When Jesus died on the cross, he made it possible for us to be made one with him. Some use the shape of the cross to describe this. The vertical beam reminds us that our relationship with God is being restored; the horizontal beam reminds us that our relationship with each other is being restored. And the cross's being anchored in the ground reminds us that our relationship with the earth and all of creation is being restored. This is how Jesus reconciled, and continues to reconcile, all things.

Jesus is God's act of restorative justice. In contrast to punitive justice, restorative justice *restores*. It heals the wounds. It sets things right again. Scripture tells us that just as our innocence was lost in the garden of Eden with Adam, our sin is now atoned for through Christ. All that was lost in the garden of Eden is restored on Calvary.

When he died on the cross, Jesus took away the sting of death that began with the inaugural murder of Abel by his brother Cain. To rejoice in death or deem any form of death as justice is to undermine the reconciling and redemptive work of Jesus on the cross. Death has been defeated.

Jesus Ended the Sacrificial System

Jesus' death is like water poured on a live electric chair: it short-circuits the whole system of death. And yet if we aren't careful, this aspect of his death can end up making a monster out of God. It is important to get this right so we don't end up justifying the death penalty by effectively reinstating the sacrificial system, as if God had to use violence to save the world.

God did not *need* blood. God was willing to bleed.

Jesus was not obligated to die. Jesus was willing to die.

Jesus did not sin. He exposed our sin.

Jesus did not succumb to violence. He absorbed our violence.

In Jesus, God did not kill. God died—and rose again.

And those distinctions make all the difference in the world. Distinguishing between God's *needing* blood and God's being *willing* to shed God's own blood is not a nitpicky thing. There are serious ramifications when we choose to believe that God was the inventor of the electric chair rather than the one who poured water on it.

The cross is not about divine wrath but about divine mercy. The cross is not God's endorsement of the death penalty but God's rebuke of it. On the cross we see the full revelation of God's love on full display. And it is unmistakably clear: God would rather die than kill.

Taking some cues from French philosopher René Girard, I would say that Jesus is the end of the sacrificial system.[10] As Girard suggests, we needed a way to atone for our sins and to heal the harm we've done, so the sacrificial system was born. We shed the blood of animals to cover our sins and to inoculate ourselves against sinning again. But the vaccine didn't last and we needed to make sacrifices over and over. So much blood. Then Jesus, the sacrificial lamb, became the sacrifice to end all sacrifices. Some say he wasn't the ultimate sacrifice so much as the countersacrifice—the one who came not to legitimize the sacrificial system but to blow it up, to be like water on the electric chair. Through the prophet Hosea, God says, "I desire mercy, not sacrifice" (Hos. 6:6). And in Jesus' death, we see God's mercy and love on full display.

We cannot worship an executed Savior and seek to kill another person, however justified or righteous we think such an act might be. To do so is to disgrace the holy work of Jesus on the cross. Anytime we shed the blood of another person, we "are crucifying the Son of God all over again" (Heb. 6:6). We act as if Jesus' blood were not enough to cover the sins of the world. Just as the blood of Abel, the world's first murder victim, cries out to God from the ground, Jesus' blood is joined with all the blood that has been shed in the world throughout

---

10. René Girard (1923–2015) was one of the great thinkers of the past century whose writings reimagined new and better ways of understanding violence and Jesus' death. I build on some of his ideas. If you want to read more from Girard, a good place to start is his book *I See Satan Fall Like Lightning.*

history. His death on the cross is God's act of divine solidarity, a willing sacrifice to forever bring an end to our blood sacrifices.

Jesus was the sacrifice to end all sacrifices. No more blood is needed.

What Does the Crucifixion Do with Us?

Earlier, I stated that just as important as what we do with the crucifixion is what the crucifixion does with us. So now we must consider what all of this means for us.

What does it mean to have a Savior who suffered violence at the center of our faith? Hopefully, it gives us deep compassion for all victims of violence. As we drink the blood of Jesus and eat his broken body at communion, we are reminded of how much God loves us. Jesus on the cross is God's love on full display. And now we are to become what we eat. Like Jesus, we refuse to shed the blood of any other human being, but we are willing to shed our own. We embrace Jesus' teaching that there is no greater love than giving our life for another person (John 15:13). Just as Jesus died with mercy on his lips, forgiving even his executioners as they nailed him to the cross, we too are to love our enemies (Matt. 5:44). Jesus died not just for the victims of violence but also for the victimizers.

Jesus is the Prince of Peace, the great interrupter of violence. Jesus even presents Pontius Pilate with the evidence of his nonviolent followers, saying, "My kingdom is not of this world. If it were, my servants would fight to prevent my arrest by the Jewish leaders. But now my kingdom is from another place" (John 18:36).

For Christ we may die, but we may not kill. We are to live the way of the cross in a world that continues to trust in the sword.

Let us live as if Jesus meant the stuff he said, a "red letter" kind of faith. And let us dare to believe that God is as beautiful as the cross reveals God to be. Let us believe that God is as beautiful as Jesus and that all of Scripture is made flesh in Christ.

RETHINKING LIFE

- When you were growing up, what, if anything, were you taught about atonement, about what Jesus did on the cross?
- Overall, would you say that what you were taught about atonement portrays Christ's death more as a justification of violence or as a subversion of violence?
- The chapter describes four things Jesus did on the cross: he joined the ranks of the despised and the marginalized, he made a spectacle of death, he reconciled all things, and he ended the sacrificial system. Which of the four do you find most meaningful? Why?
- Which of the statements below do you find most compelling? How does that statement influence or reflect your view of atonement?
  - God did not *need* blood. God was willing to bleed.
  - Jesus was not obligated to die. Jesus was willing to die.
  - Jesus did not sin. He exposed our sin.
  - Jesus did not succumb to violence. He absorbed our violence.
  - In Jesus, God did not kill. God died—and rose again.
- We are to live the way of the cross in a world that continues to trust in the sword. In what ways does this statement challenge you? In what ways does it encourage you?

## CHAPTER 6

The Early Church Was a Force for Life

Christians have been subverting death since AD 33. And doing so routinely cost them their lives.

The first followers of Jesus experienced the empire's violent hand again and again. John the Baptist was beheaded. Stephen was stoned. Peter was hung upside down on a cross. Almost all of the apostles were executed. But all of the death only fueled their passion for life.

The early Christians were not just anti-death, they were comprehensively *for* life. Many of the things we are exploring in this book—being made in the image of God, overcoming evil with love, even transforming weapons into garden tools—all had their roots in the early church. They formed a foundation for a robust ethic of life.

For the first three hundred years, Christianity was a force for life. The early Christians were not perfect, in theology or in practice, but they had a firm foundation. That foundation cracked not all at once but slowly over the centuries. And while it is too simplistic to say, "Before Constantine, Christians were nonviolent, and after Constantine, they were violent," Christians spoke out consistently and passionately against violence and death in every form and often risked their lives in the process. No matter how hard the empire tried to kill them, they continued to multiply. As the old saying goes, "The blood of the martyrs is the seed of the saints." For every

Christian killed, ten new Christians seemed to arise. The martyrs were like apples: as they fell, they left behind seeds. One opponent of the early church described Christians as a "rank growth of weeds" because of how pervasive and persistent the movement proved to be. The more the empire persecuted and killed them, the greater their passion and their courage became, and the more committed they were to life and nonviolence.

Just as it is in our world, the world of the early Christians was one in which death and violence were all too common and familiar. There were wars and rumors of wars, there were plagues and pandemics. Their culture celebrated violence in both subtle and not-so-subtle ways. And it was within this culture of imperial crucifixions, gladiatorial games, and Roman military conquests that the early Christians developed their countercultural ethic of life, an ethic that led them to denounce death in all its ugly forms.

Jesus had radically reoriented how his followers thought about death. Following the executed and risen Savior meant that they were death's worst enemies. To be a follower of Jesus necessarily meant that you were a champion for life and for love, even enemy love. We know this in large part because of the documents the early Christians left behind. One of my favorite compilations is a big volume called *The Early Christians: In Their Own Words*.[1] It includes the edited writings, letters, poetry, and sermons of Christians who lived during the first two hundred years after Christ. One of the remarkable things about these texts is the early Christians' consistent passion for life and their consistent opposition to death.

I give their writings a lot of authority because these are the folks who were a part of things early on. Any movement or institution tends to forget the values it held dear in the early days, to drift from the original vision, to begin "majoring in the minors and minoring in the

---

1. *The Early Christians: In Their Own Words*, Eberhard Arnold, ed. (Rifton, NY: Plough, 2011). In 1920, the book's compiler founded the Bruderhof Community, an intentional Christian community that now includes twenty-nine settlements on nine continents. The book is available for free online at www .plough.com. And I bet if you visit a Bruderhof settlement, they'll also give you a hardcopy for free.

majors." The church has certainly suffered from that same dynamic over the centuries, which is why I love reading the writings of the early Christians. They provide one of the clearest visions of what the revolution of Jesus really was and what it means to follow him today.

It's remarkable how consistent the early Christians' ethic of life really was. They didn't hold back, compartmentalize, or accommodate their views to prevailing culture. They spoke passionately against all forms of violence consistently and comprehensively, covering everything from military service and abortion to capital punishment and the gladiatorial games.

Let's take a closer look at what they had to say. These are the early Christians in their own words!

For Christ We May Die, but We May Not Kill

No Christian writing before Constantine in the fourth century argues that there is any circumstance in which a Christian may kill. I have searched hard for an exception to that bold claim and have not found one. The early Christians simply did not believe there was an exception to the commandment, "Thou shalt not kill." Consider just a few statements made by early Christian scholars and theologians.

- Tertullian (ca. 155–220) sternly prohibited "every sort of man-killing."
- Minucius Felix (died ca. 250), a lawyer in Rome, said "to us it is not lawful either to see or to hear of human slaughter."
- Origen (ca. 185–253) said we must use the sword against no one: "He [Jesus] nowhere teaches that it is right for his own disciples to offer violence to anyone, however wicked. . . . For we no longer take up 'sword against nation,' nor do we 'learn war anymore,' having become children of peace, for the sake of Jesus."
- Cyprian (ca. 210–258) made the connection that we cannot

worship the Prince of Peace, the one who shed his blood even for his enemies, and then shed the blood of others. He said, "The hand that carries the Eucharist dare not be sullied by the blood-stained sword."

- Arnobius of Sicca (died ca. 330) insisted that "it is better to suffer wrong than to inflict it."
- Lactantius (ca. 250–325) said that we should "keep away from human blood" and be "ignorant of wars." (I love that one.) He states we should prefer "to perish than commit an injury." Christians would rather die than kill. He went on to say, "It is always unlawful to put to death a person who God willed to be a sacred creature."[2]

I think you see the point. They hated death. They abhorred violence.

Not many of us are going to argue with the idea that it is wrong for an individual to kill, but we have learned to extend a certain amount of license to the state to kill on our behalf, which is something the early church did not do. We allow the state to kill even though we do not give that permission to individuals, and we continue to do so despite the state's terrible track record of killing over the centuries.[3] We also grant exceptions, saying that it is wrong to kill except in war. Or it is wrong to kill except when it comes to executing the "worst of the worst" criminals. Or it is wrong to kill except in self-defense. But the early Christians insisted that it is always wrong to kill—no

---

2. Ronald J. Sider, *The Early Church on Killing: A Comprehensive Sourcebook on War, Abortion, and Capital Punishment* (Grand Rapids: Baker Academic, 2012). I ride the wave of Sider's thorough research throughout the discussion that follows. Quotes in this list can be found in his book as follows: Tertullian, 169; Minucius Felix, 169; Origen, 72, 74; Cyprian, 87; Arnobius of Sicca, 170; Lactantius, 110, 171.

3. Even now in the United States, for every eight executions that have been carried out, there is one exoneration. One out of nine persons sentenced to die have later been *proved* innocent. That's not a good track record. Can you imagine the response if one of every nine planes that took off crashed? We'd insist on stopping all planes. That terrible track record is why a growing movement of conservative-leaning leaders are calling for an end to the death penalty; it raises the question of how much we should entrust the irreversible power to kill to imperfect institutions. As my friend Sister Helen Prejean says, "Sometimes the question is not do *they* deserve to die, but do *we* deserve to kill?"

exceptions. It is wrong for a criminal to kill. And it is wrong for a king to kill or a governor to kill or a president to kill. If we build on the foundation of the early church, then those of us who seek to follow Christ, the Prince of Peace, must refuse to kill, even if we risk being killed or going to jail for that conviction.

To give you a sense of how robust and comprehensive the early Christians' ethic for life was, the following is an overview of what they had to say about three issues we continue to wrestle with today—military service, abortion, and capital punishment.

Military Service and Other Vocations

On military service, there was some debate among the early Christians. Interestingly enough, however, the debate was not about whether a Christian could kill. That much was clear: Christians, even Christians serving in the military, could not kill. Instead, the debate was whether a Christian could be in the military at all. Here's why that was up for discussion.

Some Christian leaders did not think the church should exclude folks who were already in the military as long as they made a commitment not to kill. If they agreed not to kill, they could remain in the military and still pursue Christian faith and baptism. Hippolytus of Rome (ca. 170–235) wrote, "A soldier in the sovereign's army should not kill, or if he is ordered to kill, he should refuse. If he stops, so be it; otherwise he should be excluded."[4]

In ancient Rome, the military was responsible for a lot more than just fighting wars. They built roads and aqueducts and much of the infrastructure for Roman society. It was conceivable that someone could enlist in the military and serve in a noncombatant role, though it often turned out to be more complicated than that, which led to the debate in the early church. Some church leaders held out the possibility that Christians could serve in the military, but all of them agreed that any Christian in the military must vow not to kill,

4. Hippolytus of Rome, quoted in Sider, *The Early Church on Killing*, 171.

even in combat. For Christ we may die, but we may not kill. Being a good Christian might make it difficult to be a good soldier. Or vice versa.

The early church leaders saw baptism as a holy rite of passage into Christian discipleship, and they took it seriously. They went so far as to say that any person seeking to be baptized should first consider how their new life in Christ might change their old way of life, including their occupation. The waters of baptism were almost literally about dying and being born again. The expectation was that one's entire life was wholly reoriented by Jesus. Following baptism, the Christian's life's mission became to "seek first the kingdom of God." So, among other considerations, candidates for baptism had to wrestle with some hard questions about their vocations. What did baptism mean for their jobs? Was their career compatible with their new life in Christ? What did it mean to be faithful to God and not serve "two masters"?

The early Christian leaders were specific about vocations that were incompatible with new life in Christ. For example, they stated that if someone worked for the brothels, they needed to find a new line of work. But they didn't stop at the brothels. If the person seeking baptism worked in the gladiatorial games, a wicked glorification of violence, that person needed to find a new job. As Hippolytus put it in AD 218, if a person seeking baptism wore "the purple robe" of the magistrate and carried out executions for the Roman government, they needed to leave their job. Likewise, if they were in a combat role in the military, they needed to lay down their weapons, to "exchange their swords for plowshares," as Justin Martyr put it.

All of this certainly raises the question of how seriously we take our faith and baptism today. What does following Jesus mean—not just if I work in a brothel or own a porn shop but if I work for a company that promotes death or profits from war or violence? What if I work for a corporation that exploits workers or is on the wrong side of life?

Abortion

Although the issue of abortion is virtually nonexistent in the Bible (even though it was common practice in biblical times), that is not the case with the writings of the early church. Of the prominent leaders and thinkers in the early church, eight mention abortion in eleven different writings (so some of them mention it multiple times). In every instance, they unequivocally condemn it.

- There are the blunt denunciations, such as this one from the *Didache*: "You shall not murder a child by abortion."[5]
- Another early text, the Epistle of Barnabas (ca. 100) puts it this way: "You shall love your neighbor more than your own soul. You shall not slay the child by procuring abortion; nor again, shall you destroy it after it is born."[6]
- Clement of Alexandria (ca. 150–215) and Tertullian (ca. 155–220) say that the unborn child has a soul from the moment of conception. Tertullian puts it like this: "In our case, murder being once for all forbidden, we may not destroy even the fetus in the womb."[7] He supports his argument by referring to the fact that John the Baptist leaped in Elizabeth's womb when Mary visited her.
- Athenagoras of Athens (ca. 133–190) says that the fetus is a "created being and therefore an object of God's care."[8] He goes on to denounce the use of drugs to bring on an abortion. Athenagoras also refutes the rumor that Christians are cannibals by arguing that Christians stand against all murder and bloodshed, even the gladiatorial games.

The most common reason for rejecting abortion is that taking the life of a human being is something no Christian should do. Some even

---

5. *Didache* 2, quoted in Sider, *The Early Church on Killing*, 19.
6. "Epistle of Barnabas," *Ante-Nicene Fathers*, vol. 1, quoted in David P. Gushee, *Introducing Christian Ethics: Core Convictions for Christians Today* (Canton, MI: Front Edge Publishing, 2022), 217.
7. Tertullian, quoted in Sider, *The Early Church on Killing*, 166.
8. Athenagoras, quoted in Sider, *The Early Church on Killing*, 166.

use extreme language to speak of the punishment coming for those who participate in abortion.

It's also very important to note that in the broader cultural context at the time of the early church, men carried most of the power and were primarily responsible for the decisions of who lived and died on almost all issues, including abortion. This meant that women did not have much control over their sexuality, childbearing, or their own autonomy.[9] Women did not usually have a choice about when to have sex, whether to have sex, or with whom to have sex. They didn't usually have much say in whether to have children or when or how many children to have. Men generally saw women and children as an extension of their own lineage, and it was they who decided if a child should die or live, in the womb or even after birth. Men often carried out the abortions themselves or would leave a child to die in the wilderness.

It's important to understand this broader cultural context so we don't conflate the way we think about abortion or birth control today with what it looked like two thousand years ago. Even the many facets of birth control we have today, such as the "day-after pill" or surgical procedures to have abortions, make it difficult to draw direct parallels to leaving a newborn child to die in the wilderness. One of the constants, however, is the early Christians' value for life, or even the potential for life, before, during, and after birth. The early Christians also recognized, as so many of us do today, how men essentially played God by controlling women and deciding whether a new life was allowed to come into the world.

While we can draw some conclusions and parallels about what it meant to have a consistent ethic of life in the early church, there are certainly other questions that are left unanswered. Where are the female voices in the early church? How might they have offered a different perspective? Is it fair to compare what people said two thousand

---

9. I'm grateful to David Gushee and Beverly Harrison for their insights and diving deeper into this issue. To learn more, check out David's book *Introducing Christian Ethics: Core Convictions for Christians Today* and Harrison's book *Our Right to Choose.*

years ago with what we now know about life in the womb and the opportunities given by science and technology?

The goal here is simply to offer a broad overview of the passion for life that was characteristic of the early Christians and to demonstrate how comprehensive they were in advocating for life. Not only was their value for life consistent and comprehensive, it was also specific and particular, and it included abortion. They made it clear that each of these issues that we might consider political were deeply spiritual.

Capital Punishment

The early Christians categorically denounced the death penalty.

- Tertullian (ca. 155–220) said that sitting in judgment over someone's life makes the list of things Christians should never do. For him, killing was wrong, even if it was done by the state: "Shall it be held lawful to make an occupation of the sword, when the Lord proclaims that he who uses the sword shall perish by the sword? . . . and shall he apply the chain, and the prison, and the torture, and the punishment, who is not an avenger even of his own wrongs? . . . The Creator puts his prohibition on every sort of man-killing by that one summary precept 'Thou shalt not kill.'"[10]
- Hippolytus of Rome (ca. 170–235) said Christians shouldn't even be judges if they would have to sentence people to death: "A proconsul or magistrate who wears the purple robe or governs by the sword, shall give it up or be rejected [for baptism]."[11] Those who worked for the empire's apparatus of death were to find new jobs before they were baptized.
- Origen (ca. 185–253) insists that all killing is wrong, even if it is legal: "The Christian lawgiver, Jesus, completely forbids putting

10. Tertullian, quoted in Sider, *The Early Church on Killing*, 47, 60.
11. Hippolytus, quoted in *The Early Christians: In Their Own Words*, 113.

people to death. . . . Christ nowhere teaches that it is right for his own disciples to offer violence to anyone, however wicked."[12]

- Athenagoras said, "We cannot bear to see a person put to death . . . even justly."[13]

- Lactantius (ca. 250–325) called for Christians to be noncompliant with the death-penalty system and insisted that we shouldn't cooperate with a system that can take someone's life. He said that Christians shouldn't even "accuse someone of a capital charge, because it makes no difference whether you put a person to death by word or rather by sword, since it is the act of putting to death itself which is prohibited."[14]

- Arnobius (died ca. 330) claimed that it is "better to suffer wrong than to inflict it."[15]

- Gregory Thaumaturgus (ca. 213–270) refers to those who execute their fellow human beings as "barbarians."[16]

- Cyprian (ca. 210–258) stated that when we execute, we not only commit a crime, we also teach our children to kill. He famously noted the hypocrisy of saying it is wrong for an individual to kill but then sanctifying killing and calling it justice when the state does it. He wrote, "The world is soaked with mutual blood, and when individuals commit homicide, it is a crime; it is called a virtue when it is done in the name of the state."[17] Cyprian knew that it was wrong to kill, regardless of whether the act was committed by an individual or the state.

It is clear that early Christians stood firmly against the death penalty, and it was not just because they were often the victims of

12. Origen, quoted in Sider, *The Early Church on Killing*, 124.
13. Athenagoras, quoted in Sider, *The Early Church on Killing*, 31.
14. Lactantius, quoted in Sider, *The Early Church on Killing*, 110.
15. Arnobius, quoted in Sider, *The Early Church on Killing*, 101.
16. Translated by S. D. F. Salmond, in *Ante-Nicene Fathers*, vol. 6, ed. Alexander Roberts, James Donaldson, and A. Cleveland Coxe (Buffalo: Christian Literature Publishing Co., 1886). Revised and edited for New Advent by Kevin Knight, www.newadvent.org/fathers/0603.htm.
17. Cyprian, quoted in Sider, *The Early Church on Killing*, 85.

it. They were against the death penalty because they were against killing, regardless of whether it was done by an individual or by the state. When governments killed, Christians were to be conscientious objectors, even if that meant going to jail or losing their lives. That's how passionately they believed in life.

. . .

Military service, abortion, and capital punishment are just three of the more prominent issues where the early Christians shine in their ethic of life. There are plenty of other areas in which they stood for life, including their opposition to the gladiatorial games, slavery, and mistreating workers. What you won't find, and I wish this were also true today, is a single prominent Christian defending violence in any form. They were pro-life, from womb to tomb.

Followers of Jesus Were a Contrast Culture

While it's clear the early Christians were a force for life, the fact is that many of them had not always been so committed to peace and nonviolence. Remember, there were several sword-wielding zealots who joined the movement, including the apostle Peter, who pulled a sword in the garden of Gethsemane in a misguided effort to protect Jesus.

Some of the early Christians had checkered pasts, but they were also being "made new," "born again" in Christ. All things can be made new. It is why the early Christians loved the prophetic image of beating swords into plows and spears into pruning hooks (Isa. 2:4; Mic. 4:3).

Moving from death to life, both spiritually and socially, was a visible sign of the kingdom and one of the recognizable marks of the Christian witness. In the blood-stained Roman Empire, Christians were, in the words of Clement of Alexandria, "the bloodless" people of peace.[18] Followers of Jesus were a contrast culture, a holy counterculture, who stood on the side of life. The Christians were to bear witness to love and grace. Anyone could love their friends, but Christians also loved their enemies. In a culture of death, they were the champions of life. In a culture of hatred, they were people of love. In a culture of fear, they were fearless. And that's why people paid attention to them. Christianity was not just a way of thinking, it was a way of living. It was not just taught, it was caught. In the New Testament, Christians referred to it as "the Way." Christianity was a lifestyle, a totally new and different way of living in the world.

Minucius Felix even said that Christians make a mockery of death. Just as Jesus exposed violence on the cross and subverted it with love, his followers, young and old, continued to courageously "mock" death, even when they faced the wrath of state execution. Check it out: "What a beautiful sight it is for God when a Christian . . . mocks at the clatter of the tools of death and the horror of the executioner; when he defends and upholds his liberty in the face of kings and princes, obeying God alone to whom he belongs. . . . Among us, boys and frail women laugh to scorn torture and the gallows cross, . . . and all the other horrors of execution!"[19]

Christians, according to church fathers such as Irenaeus (ca. 130–202), were to live in such a way that their witness caused a change in the nations—that swords became farm tools, hatred became love, and enemies became friends. Justin Martyr (100–167), one of the earliest Christian writers, argued that Jesus and the church were the fulfillment of this messianic prophecy of turning death to life: "We ourselves were well conversant with war, murder and everything evil, but all of us throughout the whole wide earth have traded in our weapons of war. We have exchanged our swords for plowshares, our spears for farm tools. Now we cultivate the fear of God, justice, kindness . . . , faith, and the expectation of the future given us . . . through

---

18. Clement of Alexandria, quoted in Sider, *The Early Church on Killing*, 35.
19. Minucius Felix, quoted in *The Early Christians: In Their Own Words*, 127–28.

the crucified one. . . . The more we are persecuted and martyred, the more do others in ever-increasing numbers become believers."[20]

We often see the swords-to-plows metaphor used when it comes to weapons of war, but the early Christians also used it with other forms of violence, such as the instruments of execution.[21] After all, transforming an instrument of execution is exactly what Christ did on the cross: he made a spectacle of death by turning something evil into something beautiful. In Christ, the cross, one of the ugliest symbols of death, was transformed into the icon of hope.

Tertullian takes it even farther, talking about the transformation of minds and tongues that are so prone to violence. He writes, "They shall change the dispositions of injurious minds, hostile tongues, blasphemy, and all kinds of evil into pursuits of moderation and peace."[22] Christ is not the prince of war but the prince of peace. God is transforming people. And God is also transforming the world.

The early Christians' rejection of death was comprehensive and so refreshing to see in a world with such an inconsistent ethic for life. They believed people were created by God, made in the image of God, and no mortal had the right to kill another person—not even Caesar, the head of state. And that conviction routinely cost them their lives. While the words of the early Christians might seem radical to us today, and they surely don't answer all our questions, we can still allow them to resonate in our souls. And also consider that it was not just their words that had so much power but their witness. They were willing to die but not kill for the convictions they held so deeply. They had no fear of death because Christ had already triumphed over it.

Let's let that do something to us. May the witness of the early Christians inspire us. And convict us. And may they dare us to take Jesus as seriously as they did, even if it costs us our lives.

---

20. Justin Martyr, quoted in *The Early Christians: In Their Own Words*, 81.
21. In addition to Justin Martyr, Irenaeus, Tertullian, Origen, and others latched onto the image of turning swords into plows. It seems to have been one of the go-to images of the early Christians.
22. Tertullian, quoted in Sider, *The Early Church on Killing*, 53.

A Revolutionary for Love

It's stunning how we lose the radical edge of some of the great saints over the centuries. They get domesticated and commercialized. Sometimes we even forget who they are. For instance, consider Valentine, from whom we get Valentine's Day.

As much as I like the chocolate—and I always hope my wife gets me some on February 14 (fair-trade organic chocolate, of course)—Valentine's Day wasn't always about chocolate, hearts, and roses. It wasn't about Cupid and romance. It was about a third-century priest named Valentine who was a champion of life, a war resister, a revolutionary for love. February 14 commemorates the day he was beheaded, executed by the state in AD 269.

Valentine lived in an age when Christians were persecuted and crushed by the state, and he was known for how he rescued many of them. But he was also known for something else. He lived under the terrible reign of Claudius II, a Roman emperor who declared war after war and needed many men to fight as soldiers. He believed that single men made better soldiers than married men, so he outlawed weddings. But Valentine wasn't having it. He stood up to the emperor and began to perform weddings throughout the empire. Not only was he saying yes to love, he was also saying no to war, because every young man who got married was disqualified from military service.

Now, you can imagine that didn't go over too well. Valentine was brutally beaten, arrested, and jailed. But even in jail he continued to return hatred with love, to overcome evil with good. One of the last stories we have of Valentine was that he got to know his jailer's daughter, who happened to be blind. Before his execution, Valentine healed her, restoring her vision, a dazzling act of enemy love.

As the story goes, on the day he was beheaded, he left the jailer's daughter a heartfelt note of love and friendship, and he signed it, "Your Valentine." That was the first love note on the first Valentine's Day. How about that?

RETHINKING LIFE

- What stands out most to you about the early Christians' comprehensive ethic of life?
- In contrast to the early Christians, how do contemporary Christians sometimes hold back, compartmentalize, or accommodate their views to prevailing culture when it comes to the sacredness of life?
- The chapter includes several quotes from early Christians affirming that for Christ we may die, but we may not kill (pages 71–72). Which quotes do you find most compelling or insightful? Which do you find most challenging?
- How do you respond to the early Christians' insistence that it is always wrong to kill—no exceptions?
- The early Christians' comprehensive advocacy for life often had serious consequences, sometimes even costing them their lives. What consequences do you think Christians today face when advocating for life? Share any stories or examples you're aware of in which being an advocate for life had serious consequences.

## PART 2

Cracks in the Foundation

CHAPTER 7

We Exchanged the Cross for the Sword

What started two thousand years ago with twelve disciples on the outskirts of the Roman Empire is now 2.4 billion Christians worldwide. Christianity is the largest religion in the world, making up nearly one-third of the global population.[1]

Describing the explosive growth of the early church, Scripture says that the Lord added to their number daily, sometimes in the hundreds and even the thousands, as the emerging Jesus movement spread through missionary journeys by land and by sea. Many of the New Testament books are letters written to these fledgling Christian communities, who were now navigating difficult issues about what it meant to be a unified body of believers.

As converts to Christianity began to come not just from the fringes and margins of society but also from the centers of wealth and power, the church faced several challenges. For example, could Roman soldiers, like the centurion in the book of Acts, become Christians and still be soldiers? What if they committed not to kill but still wanted to be soldiers? And what about tax collectors? Could they be

---

1. I love this quote, of which there are many variations, though the original tracks back to Richard Halverson, former chaplain of the United States Senate: "In the beginning the church was a fellowship of men and women centering on the living Christ. Then the church moved to Greece, where it became a philosophy. Then it moved to Rome, where it became an institution. Next, it moved to Europe, where it became a culture. And, finally, it moved to America, where it became an enterprise."

Christians, even if they didn't pay reparations in an act of repentance as Zacchaeus had done?

It's not hard to imagine that some in the early church would have wanted to be "seeker sensitive" to those who were on a spiritual journey. After all, Jesus' commands to love your enemy, to sell all that you have and give the money to the poor, and to take up your cross were no easier to follow then than they are now. The invitation to follow Christ and to be willing to die for him doesn't tend to draw a crowd, especially among folks who have a lot invested in the empire and a lot to give up.

As it is with any movement or organization, when the early church grew, they faced the challenge of mission drift—of compromising some of their core values and principles, one of which was their consistent ethic of life. But it didn't happen all at once. Rather remarkably, it took a few hundred years for the early Christians to budge on their consistent ethic of life.

The Constantinian Shift

The Christian movement started on the margins with a small group of renegade Jews who were a peculiar little sect within the vast terrain of the Roman Empire. By AD 100, there were roughly 7,500 Christians,[2] which is smaller than many of our megachurches today. A generation later, in AD 150, there were 40,000. But that was still only .07 percent of the population—not even a tenth of one percent of the empire. One hundred years after Christ was here in the flesh, there was roughly one Christian for every 1,430 people in the Roman world.

Then this little revolution began to spread beyond the periphery and to all sectors of society. Check this out. Historians estimate that between AD 100 and 300, the Christian movement grew from roughly

---

2. Rodney Stark, *The Rise of Christianity: How the Obscure, Marginal Jesus Movement Became the Dominant Religious Force in the Western World in a Few Centuries* (New York: HarperCollins, 1996), 7. Scholars vary on exact numbers, but Stark's estimates give a good overall sense of the rise of Christianity.

7,500 people to a whooping 6.3 million. By AD 300, Christians were 10 percent of the empire's population: one person in every ten was now a Christian. But with the growth came complexity, and it is at this point that Emperor Constantine entered the picture.

Constantine's reign is seen as a turning point for Christianity because it's when Christianity got the official stamp of approval from the Roman Empire. Given the persecution Christians had long endured, this might seem to have been a miraculous deliverance, and in many ways it was. However, the so-called Constantinian shift was also when the first cracks began to appear in the early Christians' ethic of life. Once they were in power, Christians went from being the persecuted to being the persecutors. They stopped loving their enemies and started killing them. They exchanged the cross for a sword.

Many scholars rightfully point out that Constantine was a symbol of something bigger happening in the culture, that he was the effect rather than the cause. Just as many of us point out that Donald Trump revealed America more than he changed America, perhaps the same can be said of Constantine. However, Constantine did crystalize some things that forever changed what it means to be a Christian. But before we get to that, it's important to understand more of the context that led up to Constantine's reign and how it shaped the early church.

Constantine's Backstory

Constantine came to power in the wake of horrific persecution of the church. To be sure, killing Christians had been a Roman pastime going all the way back to AD 33, but things had only gotten worse since. Historians point out that emperors such as Nero, who reigned in the generation after Jesus (AD 54–68), turned sadistic execution into a form of entertainment. There are reports of Christians being dressed in animal furs to be killed by dogs. They were crucified, even crucified upside down. Their bodies were often disfigured and contorted for the sake of dark appetites. According to the Roman historian Tacitus (ca. AD 56–120), Nero turned his own garden into a killing field, setting bodies on fire and using them as human torches.[3]

Then there was the persecution under Domitian, who reigned from AD 81–96. Domitian is the emperor who exiled John, the author of Revelation, to the island of Patmos. Persecution continued under Decius, who ruled from AD 249–51. Finally, there were the brutal, barbaric reigns of Diocletian (AD 284–305) and Galerius (AD 305–11), right before Constantine.

Most historians consider this era prior to Constantine to be the worst persecution Christianity had ever seen. Church buildings and property were destroyed. There were raids on churches in which sacred texts and relics were burned. Some Christians were demoted from places of honor if they would not renounce their faith. Some had their legal rights taken away, and others were forced into slavery if they refused to burn incense to Caesar (a loyalty test) or to recant their commitment to Christ. Under Diocletian, many were murdered during what historians call the "wholesale slaughter" of Christians.[4] This is when Constantine entered the scene, following the terrible reigns of terror under Diocletian and his son-in-law Galerius.

Constantine was the son of Constantius Chlorus, a lower-ranking emperor who ruled in the West (Britain, Gaul, and Spain) during the bloody reign of Diocletian. Although his father Constantius was not a Christian, he was quite tolerant of Christians and did not carry out vicious orders and persecutions. When Constantine became emperor after Constantius's death in 306, he took his dad's tolerance of Christians to a new level. And his devotion to the faith, even though some question its sincerity, became personal.

---

3. Tacitus wrote, "Mockery of every sort was added to their deaths. Covered with the skins of beasts, they were torn by dogs and perished, or were nailed to crosses, or were doomed to the flames and burnt, to serve as a nightly illumination, when daylight had expired. Nero offered his gardens for the spectacle, and was exhibiting a show in the circus, while he mingled with the people in the dress of a charioteer or stood aloft on a car." Cornelius Tacitus, "The Annals," *The Complete Works of Tacitus*, ed. Alfred John Church, Jackson Brodribb, Sara Bryant (New York: Random House, 1942), www.perseus.tufts .edu/hopper/text?doc=Perseus%3Atext%3A1999.02.0078%3Abook%3D15%3Achapter%3D44.
4. Kenneth Scott Latourette, *A History of Christianity*, vol. 1 (New York: Harper and Row, 1975), 91.

It's important to note that Constantine's ascension to the throne wasn't as simple as his father passing him the baton. The region historically had four regional emperors rather than one. When Diocletian stepped down in 305, there was a struggle to gain control of the empire as rival regional leaders fought for the throne. It wasn't until 312 that Constantine won the decisive Battle of Milvian Bridge that ended the civil war and secured his place on the throne. But this is what's so significant about that legendary battle against another aspiring emperor named Maxentius, especially with regard to our conversation about the sacredness of life. Prior to the battle, Constantine is said to have had a vision of the cross coming down from the sky in heavenly glory to bless him in the battle. Here's an account of the vision, written by a historian named Eusebius: "About the time of the midday sun, when day was just turning, he said he saw with his own eyes, up in the sky and resting over the sun, a cross-shaped trophy formed from light, and a text attached to it which said, 'By this conquer.'"[5]

"By this conquer." Kill in the name of Jesus.

Some question the credibility of the vision since it wasn't until ten years later and two years after Constantine died that we have any account of it.[6] It's also important to note that the account we do have was written not by Constantine but by Eusebius, whom Constantine, as he died, had appointed a bishop. Eusebius had previously written his classic *Ecclesiastical History*, published ten years into Constantine's reign, and he makes no mention of Constantine's vision in that work, which seems like a significant oversight.

Could Constantine's vision of the cross be imperial revisionist history? Totally possible, but it almost doesn't even matter. It became Roman legend, and eventually church legend. In the centuries that followed, this same theology is invoked and the cross continued to be

5. Eusebius, *Life of Constantine*, trans. Averil Cameron and Stuart G. Hall (Oxford: Clarendon, 1999), 81.
6. I'm grateful for the work of my friends Mark Charles and Soong-Chan Rah for pointing this out, and for their diligent work diving into the history of Constantinian Christianity. Mark Charles and Soong-Chan Rah, *Unsettling Truths: The Ongoing, Dehumanizing Legacy of the Doctrine of Discovery* (Downers Grove, IL: InterVarsity, 2019).

used as a symbol for battle and license for all sorts of atrocities. The cross, which had been such a powerful symbol of love and grace and redemption, would eventually be used in the Crusades and by colonizers doing the most unchristlike things imaginable.

Constantine was not a Christian when he became emperor in AD 306. He wasn't even baptized until just before he died. But one of his first acts after winning the Battle of Milvian Bridge and killing Maxentius was signing the Edict of Milan, which proclaimed religious tolerance throughout the Roman Empire. No doubt, the relatively peaceful reign of Constantine that followed, while providing temporarily relief from persecution, was a massive shift for Christians.

As the church entered this new season of peace, it faced a whole new set of challenges and tensions, many of which were consequences of centuries of persecution. One of those tensions was that some Christians had begun to make compromises with the empire. To avoid becoming fodder for the empire's fires, they essentially denied their faith with their fingers crossed behind their backs. They burned a little incense to Caesar to avoid being burned alive. As one ancient proverb aptly put it, they would "bow before the emperor and fart." They paid only enough homage to avoid getting killed.

It's understandable, right? To be a Christian at the time of Constantine meant you and everyone you knew had, for generations, lost friends and family members to the brutal persecution of the Roman Empire, the same empire that had killed your Messiah. It's hard enough to gather the faith and courage to die for Jesus but harder still to sustain that fervor decade after decade and century after century while the empire is killing you, your kids, your parents, and the poor and vulnerable everywhere. So if you had the option to make a small compromise in exchange for your life, it probably seemed like a worthwhile trade. And the temptation to acquire or align yourself with power and resources to stop the oppression would be hard to resist. It was one of the temptations Satan posed to Jesus in the desert. And it is a temptation we face in America today. So that should give us some grace for the early Christians who, just a few hundred years in, made some regrettable, even if understandable, compromises.

Even so, not all of them compromised. Some felt more convicted than ever, believing that a willingness to die for Christ was the ultimate test of discipleship. Persecution had only stiffened their spines and solidified their resolve. And herein lies one of the most significant crossroads of the early church. Those who refused to compromise excommunicated many of those who did, including leaders, for making concessions and assimilating within the empire. The early Christians knew they could not serve two masters. There was a choice to be made: would they serve Jesus or Caesar? Excommunication has a bad vibe for many of us today, but the early Christians saw it as preserving the radical call of Christ and not compromising the cost of discipleship. There was no room for "cheap grace," as Dietrich Bonhoeffer called it centuries later before he himself was martyred.

There's an old saying we often hear in social movements today: "We have nothing to lose but our chains." And while that was true of many of the early followers of Jesus who were poor or otherwise disenfranchised, it had become less unilaterally true a few centuries later. By this time, many new converts had a whole lot to lose. They wanted to hold on to their possessions and even stay in careers that earlier generations had deemed incompatible with Christian discipleship. Could you be a politician, much less the leader of the Roman Empire, and still be a follower of Christ? I think you see the source of the tension, which is one we still face today.

Constantine's Impact

There is a lot we could say about Constantine and the evident contradictions in his faith and leadership, but there is no denying that he radically parted ways with previous emperors and initiated welcome reforms. The reforms he instituted throughout society and the church were significant and leave a mark to this day—for better and for worse. In addition to proclaiming religious tolerance, he banned the gladiatorial games. He made it harder to kill babies by banning the Roman practice called exposure. He also banned the branding of criminals, which was done on the face.

Constantine explicitly acknowledged that human beings are made in the image of God.[7] He funded the mission of the church, rebuilt church buildings, and reproduced copies of the Bible. He established the Sunday as a Sabbath day and ordered that the holy days of the Christian calendar be recognized by all. He even provided tax exemption for clergy and church property. I suppose he could be credited with setting up the first 501(c)(3) tax exemptions for the church, for better or for worse.

He also ended the practice of crucifixion. Unfortunately, he didn't end capital punishment, just execution by crucifixion. He ended up killing his own wife and son, so let there be no mistake, I'm not trying to defend him.[8] I just want to be honest about the complexities and contradictions of a man many Christians today recognize as a saint, especially regarding the sanctity of life. Certainly, there are questions to be raised about his motives for all of these reforms, whether they came from an authentic respect for the Christian faith, political pragmatism, or some messy combo of both.

While scholars may debate how much Constantine himself actually changed the church, one thing is clear: the church was changing and the reign of Constantine certainly was a manifestation of that change. And Constantine took a role not only in initiating social reforms but also in shaping and solidifying the theology of the church.

By the time Constantine came to power, there were serious divisions in the church, many of which stemmed from the rapid growth

---

7. David P. Gushee, *The Sacredness of Human Life: Why an Ancient Biblical Vision Is Key to the World's Future* (Grand Rapids: Eerdmans, 2013), 149.

8. I am grateful, however, for the work of Peter Leithart in helping us more fully understand Constantine in all of his complexity and contradictions, and how this Constantinian shift was less of a moment and more of a movement. Peter J. Leithart, *Defending Constantine: The Twilight of an Empire and the Dawn of Christendom* (Downers Grove, IL: InterVarsity, 2010).

of Christianity and its proximity to the power and wealth of Rome. Christians under Constantine began asking questions we still ask today. Does God want Christians to use worldly power to transform the world? Should Christians impose their values on others? Can Christians be political without losing their souls? Other contentious issues were more theological, such as disagreement about the full divinity and humanity of Christ and the nature of the Trinity.

In an effort to create unity and restore peace, Constantine tried to bring church leaders together. He hosted a summit of bishops in 314 at Arles in southern Gaul. And in 325, he convened one of the most significant ecumenical councils in the history of Christianity, the Council of Nicaea. There he brought together bishops and church leaders in an attempt to resolve differences and establish some norms and procedures within the church.

The rapidly growing church needed clarity about the structures of leadership as well as what church discipline looked like with heretics and lapsed Christians. What were the dignity standards for clergy? What did real repentance look like, and could someone be reinstated after they fell from grace? There were also questions about organizational structure and liturgical practice. One of the most pressing issues before the Nicean council was how to understand the relationship between God and Jesus. The council produced the Nicene Creed, a defining statement of belief, which is still recited today, 1,700 years later, by Christians all over the world.

While the councils addressed various heresies and defined orthodox belief in the Nicene Creed, the message of Christianity itself did not change much. What did change, however, was how Christians lived out the message of Jesus in the world. The early church was called "the Way" and was known for its countercultural way of living. However, over the centuries and in response to persecution, Christianity gradually became primarily a way of believing rather than a way of living. During the era of Constantine and in the years that followed, much more energy was spent on defining how Christians are to think rather than how Christians are to live. The theological conversations progressively moved from the heart to the head, focusing more on doctrines and less on actions.

From Christianity's earliest days, friends and foes alike had described how radically different Christians were. Jesus had said that the world would know we are Christians by our love, and that is exactly what happened in those first few centuries. The onlooking world marveled that Christians fed the pagan poor as well as their own. They turned enemies into friends and loved even those who hated them. They would rather die than kill. Sadly, however, it was not these ways of living that were codified during the councils Constantine convened. What was debated and crystallized were doctrinal beliefs. To be clear, some important clarifications were needed. And yet you can't help but wonder what might have happened if it hadn't been just doctrine that was set into stone but also an ethic of life, lifestyle commitments, and a strong stance against violence.

What if the creed millions of Christians still recite every Sunday in worship also stated a commitment to life and affirmed the dignity of every person—the *imago dei*? Maybe it's time to write a few new creeds today.

Historically, Christianity has always affirmed orthodoxy, meaning "right belief," from which we get doctrine. But it has also held orthodoxy together with orthopraxis, meaning "right practice" or "right living." Like the two blades of scissors or the two oars of a rowboat, orthodoxy and orthopraxis go together.

Faith without works is dead (James 2:14–26). They will know we are Christians by our love (John 13:35). We can't say that we love God and ignore our neighbor in need (1 John 3:16–17). Even as we look at Jesus, we do not see him teaching doctrines and theology alone but also teaching us and showing us how to live. Welcome the stranger (Matt. 25:35). Feed the hungry (Matt. 25:35). Visit those in prison (Matt. 25:36). Love your enemies (Matt. 5:43–44). Give your money to the poor (Mark 10:21). He put flesh on doctrine by becoming the Word made flesh (John 1:14). Jesus was not just inviting people to sign a doctrinal statement, he was inviting people to join a revolution, and he still is. But that's what began to give way during Constantine—the revolutionary, countercultural way of life of early Christianity.

Some point out, and rightly so, the irony that Constantine wasn't even a baptized Christian as he oversaw these historic gatherings. Many contend that his primary interests were political more than they were religious: a divided church meant a divided empire and a weaker base. Perhaps he did have a deathbed conversion and got baptized before he died, as many believe. But in all those years before his death, he was quite a paradox and ultimately did much damage to our understanding of what it means to be a disciple of Jesus.

A tree is known by its fruit, as Jesus said. In the end, if Christianity was more than just a political endorsement for Constantine, it is hard to see how that really translated into his own life. The year after he hosted the Council of Nicaea, he killed his own son Crispus. And a month or so later, he killed his wife Fausta by having her basically boiled to death in hot water. Not very befitting of any man of God, if I might be so pretentious as to say. And yet to this day, Constantine is recognized by many Christians as a saint. The Orthodox Church calls him *isapostolos*—equal to the apostles. And that is part of the problem.

What had fundamentally changed was the church's proximity to power, and now the church faced decisions about how to use its power. Specifically, should it use the power of the state to enforce the doctrines of the church? And by "enforce," it's important to know that the church now had the authority not just to excommunicate heretics but to kill them.

It was also during Constantine's reign that we begin to see the seeds of Christian colonization, which we'll dig into in chapter 8. The words of Constantine's vision, "By this conquer," echoed throughout the ages to conquistadors and colonizers, providing holy cover for unholy missions.[9]

Constantine's reign is where we recognize the first cracks in the steadfast commitment to life that characterized the early Jesus movement. It's also when we begin to see what a compromised Christian faith can look like, more generally speaking. I guess some would call it the evolution of Christianity. I would call it the dissolution. Some would call it progress. I would call it digress, especially when it comes to how we value life.

The Post-Constantine Era

By AD 350, just more than a decade after the death of Constantine, there were thirty-three million Christians in the Roman Empire. They were now more than half the Roman population: 56 percent. Christians outnumbered non-Christians for the first time. Let that sink in. In a mere seventy years, Christianity went from being a persecuted revolutionary movement to an accepted minority religion, and then to the established religion of the entire Roman Empire.

While Constantine had made Christianity the majority religion in the empire, it was the next emperor, Theodosius (AD 379–95), who made it the official religion of the Roman Empire. Theodosius was the emperor who began to aggressively Christianize the empire. He used his power to ban both unorthodox Christians and pagans. He destroyed pagan temples and incited mob violence alongside the violence wielded by the state. At one point, undoubtedly provoked and emboldened by the emperor, the archbishop of Alexandria rounded up a group of monks to destroy the serapeum, one of the shrines to the

9. Here's an interesting connection between Constantine and fifteenth-century colonization. Among the many things Constantine did was to build the Church of the Holy Sepulchre in Jerusalem, which still stands today. It is a spectacular building, built on top of what is believed to be Jesus' tomb. However, centuries later, this same church eventually became a conquest goal for Christopher Columbus (1451–1506).

Egyptian god Serapis. And Theodosius congratulated the Christians who tore it down. This was his decree: "It is our will that all the peoples who are ruled by . . . our Clemency shall practice that religion which the divine Peter the Apostle transmitted to the Romans. . . . We command that those persons who follow this rule shall embrace the name of Catholic Christians. . . . The rest, however, whom we adjudge demented and insane, shall sustain the infamy of heretical dogmas, . . . and they shall be smitten first by divine vengeance and secondly by the retribution of our own initiative, which we shall assume in accordance with divine judgement."[10]

Obviously, that didn't go over well with many people, especially the formerly pagan majority that was now quickly becoming a minority both in numbers and in access to power. At one point, there were riots, and Theodosius was brutal, slaughtering thousands of men, women, and children. On another occasion, he killed seven thousand people in three hours. Theodosius was so relentlessly violent that he was temporarily excommunicated by one of the bishops of the church, Bishop Ambrose of Milan. He was not permitted to take the Eucharist because he had betrayed Christ by spilling blood. You may recall the statement of the third-century bishop Cyprian, that the hand that takes the Eucharist should not be "sullied by the blood-stained sword!"[11]

Shortly after the rule of Theodosius, fifteen years later to be precise, the Roman Empire collapsed, sacked by Visigoths in AD 410. For the first time in eight hundred years, Rome was unable to defend itself from outside invasion. The Roman Empire fell, but the church lived on.

Other emperors would come and go. Some, such as Justinian in AD 527, considered themselves to be what historian Susan Wise Bauer describes as "the representative of Christ on earth."[12] As a

---

10. Theodosius, quoted in Robert Bruce Mullin, *A Short World History of Christianity* (Louisville: Westminster John Knox, 2008), 56.

11. Ronald J. Sider, *The Early Church on Killing: A Comprehensive Sourcebook on War, Abortion, and Capital Punishment* (Grand Rapids: Baker Academic, 2012), 87.

12. Susan Wise Bauer, *The History of the Medieval World: From the Conversion of Constantine to the First Crusade* (New York: Norton, 2010), 200–201.

Byzantine emperor and professing Christian, Justinian began the ambitious mission known as *renovation imperii*, or "the restoration of the empire." In the service of his cause, Justinian slaughtered thirty thousand people in one week to put down what came to be called the Nika Riots in Constantinople. It is unclear whether he saw himself representing God or the state—or both—as he killed these men, women, and children. It is hard to know where the emperor's reign ended and God's kingdom began. The marriage of church and state had begun.

Christians began to kill other Christians whom they considered to be heretics. And Christians began to kill people of other faiths, along with native peoples and pagans. Those who had been tortured and jailed became the ones who tortured and jailed others. The ones who had seen their books burned and their buildings torched became the ones who burned the books and destroyed the buildings of others. The persecuted became the persecutors. Those who had been the victims of state power now wielded that power. Those who had suffered from military occupation now served in the military. The executed became the executioners. After three hundred years of steadfast commitment to life and standing up against death and violence in all of its manifestations, Christians became the empire and exchanged the cross for a sword.

The brilliant Danish theologian Søren Kierkegaard insisted that where everything is Christian nothing is Christian. We lose our essence, the distinctive, countercultural witness of the upside-down kingdom.

We can say that we are a Christian empire, but the question is, How much do we remind the world of Jesus? As history shows, Christian empires, if there is such a thing, usually lose their souls.

A wise man once said, "What good is it to gain the whole world but lose your soul?"

RETHINKING LIFE

- What stands out most to you about what Christians gained and what they lost once they had proximity to power?
- How would you respond to some of the same questions the early Christians faced?
    - Does God want Christians to use worldly power to transform the world?
    - Should Christians impose their values on others?
    - Can Christians be political without losing their souls?
- How do you make sense of the complications and contradictions of Constantine, a man who ushered in welcome reforms but who also killed his own wife and son? Was he an authentic Christian, a political pragmatist, or a messy combination of both? Do you believe God used him, or that Constantine used God?
- Do you believe Christians at the time should have supported and aligned themselves with Constantine or challenged him? What about contemporary leaders who exhibit complications and contradictions as Constantine did? Should Christians support and align themselves with such leaders today? Share the reasons for your response.
- The councils Constantine convened codified doctrinal beliefs. Do you wish the councils had also codified an ethic of life, such as a strong stand against violence and lifestyle commitments? What do you imagine might have happened if they had?
- What parallels do you recognize between the church's proximity to power in Constantine's era and the church's proximity to power today? Should Christians try to use their political power to enforce Christian beliefs and doctrines? Why or why not?

- It is during the reign of Constantine that we begin to see what compromised Christian faith can look like. Some Christians compromised to align themselves with power and resources, others did so to protect their livelihoods or to save their lives. In what ways might Christians today be tempted to make similar compromises? What motivates those compromises?
- How do you respond to Søren Kierkegaard's idea that where everything is Christian nothing is Christian? How would you describe the difference between working to bring God's kingdom to earth (Matt. 6:10) and establishing a Christian government or empire?

## CHAPTER 8

We Spread the Gospel through Force

One of my favorite punk rock bands in my younger years was Bad Religion. They were controversial because they often had an upside-down cross on their T-shirts and merchandise. But the more I began to listen to the lyrics of Bad Religion and other punk bands, the more I resonated with much of their rejection of "bad religion."[1]

Fortunately, there's also good religion. Some of the most life-giving things in the world have been done by people who were inspired by good religion: hospitals, shelters, legal clinics, adoption agencies, reentry programs, social-reform movements, recovery communities, libraries, economic development organizations, just to name a few. But if we're honest, we also have to acknowledge the flip side: that some of the most life-crushing things in the world have been done by people who are driven by bad religion, and I'm not talking about the band.

No one kills with more zeal than someone who believes God is on their side. That may sound crass, but history repeatedly proves

---

1. Incidentally, while I'm talking music, there's a beautiful song called "Have You Got Good Religion?" It's a call-and-response hymn with the refrain "Certainly, Lord." The song leader asks, "Have you got good religion?" And the people respond, "Certainly, Lord." The leader asks, "Do you love everybody?" And the people respond, "Certainly, Lord, certainly Lord. Certainly, certainly, certainly, Lord!" It is a declaration that good religion loves everybody. Sing that one next Sunday!

it true. To be fair, every major religion has its own version of religious extremists, haters who distort and exploit the faith, using it as a weapon. In recent years, we are all too familiar with "Muslim"[2] extremists who have carried out suicide bombings and terrorist attacks. If you visit the Al Ibrahimi Mosque in Hebron, which houses the tomb of Abraham and Sarah, you can still see bullet holes in the walls from a "Jewish" terrorist who, in 1994, opened fire on Muslims during a prayer service, killing twenty-nine people and injuring dozens more.

As Christians, we have our own share of terrorists and extremists of the worst kind. I can think of "Christians" who have bombed abortion clinics and those who rioted at the US Capitol on January 6, 2020. To this day, the Ku Klux Klan devotes a section of their website to making the case that they are a Christian organization.

Unfortunately, the centuries are full of people who profess to be Christians but do very unchristlike things. Some of the most brutal violence in history has been committed by Christians:

- The Crusades (1095–1291)
- The Inquisition, which began in the twelfth century and lasted hundreds of years, resulted in some thirty-two thousand executions.[3]
- The Trans-Atlantic slave trade (1526–1867). Though slavery had existed for thousands of years, between 1526 and 1867, some 12.5 million enslaved people were taken from Arica, and 10.7 million arrived in the Americas.
- The conquest of the Americas (roughly 1492–1800)

---

2. I use quotation marks when referring to the faith of religious extremists to distinguish them from the larger community of the faith they misrepresent. There are global movements of Muslims, Jews, and Christians standing against such violence and denouncing it as an illegitimate expression of their faith. Even as folks who kill may claim a particular faith, a tree is known by its fruit, and so I see no reason to affirm extremist violence as a legitimate expression of faith. Hence, the quotation marks.
3. History.com Editors, "Inquisition," *History*, November 17, 2017, updated August 21, 2018, www.history.com/topics/religion/inquisition#:~:text=Beginning%20in%20the%2012th%20 century,resulting%20in%20some%2032%2C000%20executions.

- Lynching and Jim Crow laws (1882–1968)
- Apartheid in South Africa (1948–1994)
- The Rwandan genocide (1994)

Although there have always been saints and heroic movements that stood for life and resisted bad religion, violence in the name of Christ still has a long history.[4] And some of the worst "bads" in our history are the ways we have tried to spread the gospel by force, to justify violence and war as a means of spreading the gospel of love.

From "Just War" to "Holy War"

As the church struggled to find its way in the post-Constantinian era, the vision of Christianity as a countercultural lifestyle began to dissolve. Over time, characteristic values such as rejecting violence and practicing enemy love became minority movements within the larger world of Christendom.[5]

What emerged were factions and competing narratives of what Christians really believed and, more important, how Christians were to live in the midst of the empire. Many of the challenges had to do with differing views on how the church should use its power—state power and ecclesial power.

One of the great thinkers of the church who tried to help navigate the tensions and build unity was a theologian named Augustine (AD 354–430). He is undoubtedly one of the most influential leaders in

---

4. I know I've given him several shout-outs already, but I am deeply indebted to the work of David Gushee. He's one of the smartest Christian ethicists out there and does a deep dive into the best and worst of Christian witness over the centuries. I'm building on much of his work here. He was also one of my earliest expert readers helping to sharpen this book. I still have a hunch he thinks I'm too hard on just-war theory in this chapter and too easy on violence in the Bible. Grateful for friends who sharpen us.
5. In the wake of Constantine, some Christians felt compelled to leave what they considered to be corrupt centers of Christian power. In the spirit of John the Baptist and other desert prophets, many of them went to the desert to call people to repent. They viewed the desert, ironically, as fertile ground on which to build a new world from the shell of the old one.

the history of the church. However, among his many contributions to Christian thought is a regrettable one called "just-war theory." It was Augustine's attempt to construct the moral criteria for when war could be considered a faithful response for Christians and for governments in general. As part of that attempt, Augustine justified some terrible things—or he at least paved the way for others to justify terrible things using his ideas. Consider this statement: "It is indeed better (as no one ever could deny) that men should be led to worship God by teaching, than that they should be driven to it by fear of punishment or pain; but it does not follow that because the former course produces the better men, therefore those who do not yield to it should be neglected. For many have found advantage (as we have proved, and are daily proving by actual experiment), in being first compelled by fear or pain, so that they might afterwards be influenced by teaching, or might follow out in act what they had already learned in word."[6] If peaceful means of persuading someone to the faith does not work, it is permissible to compel them through "fear of punishment and pain."

You can see how this idea sowed the theological seeds that later yielded disastrous consequences. In the words of my friends Soong-Chan Rah and Mark Charles, "Augustine's theological acceptance of Christian empire, his collusion through just war theory, and his justification of imperial power to enforce church doctrine set the stage for the Crusades in the eleventh century."[7]

Although the original intent of just-war theory may have been to limit violence by creating a moral framework for it, it ultimately became a license for violence instead. Christian ethicist David Gushee writes, "In large stretches of Christian history, 'just wars' that were supposed to be fought with Augustinian mournfulness and careful limits became crusades fought with zealous piety and without

---

6. Saint Augustine of Hippo, "Treatise on the Correction of the Donatists," *The Political Writings of Saint Augustine*, ed. Henry Paolucci (Washington, DC: Regnery, 1962), 214.
7. Mark Charles and Soong-Chan Rah, *Unsettling Truths: The Ongoing, Dehumanizing Legacy of the Doctrine of Discovery* (Downers Grove, IL: InterVarsity, 2019), 62.

restraint. Just-war theory has been pristine only in theory, not where the bodies pile up."[8]

Every generation since Augustine has violated the limits of just-war theory as they have twisted it to justify their violence. Everything from the Crusades to the most recent "war on terror" in Iraq and Afghanistan have explicitly appealed to Augustine's theory in service of their cause. In response to the 9/11 attacks, President Bush used the word *crusade* as he declared war on terrorism.[9] American Christians used just-war theory to justify dropping nine hundred bombs a day on Iraq,[10] killing thousands of civilians who had nothing to do with the 9/11 attacks.

I'd like to believe that Augustine would be appalled by how Christians over the centuries have used his ideas to justify violence and that he would protest how easily we baptize bombs today, but there's no denying that he big-time missed the mark with just-war theory.[11]

Over the centuries, as Christian theology increasingly accommodated itself to using violence, war became not only permissible but blessed. The church went from condoning "just war" to condoning "holy war." Instead of seeing it as a necessary evil, the church began to view war as a divine mandate. We see this most clearly in the Crusades.

In the thirteenth century, it was Thomas Aquinas (1225–74),

---

8. David P. Gushee, *The Sacredness of Human Life: Why an Ancient Biblical Vision Is Key to the World's Future* (Grand Rapids: Eerdmans, 2013), 166.

9. Peter Waldman and Hugh Pope, "'Crusade' Reference Reinforces Fears War on Terrorism Is against Muslims," *Wall Street Journal*, September 21, 2001, www.wsj.com/articles/SB1001020294332922160.

10. I witnessed the horror of this firsthand as I was in Baghdad in March 2003, when the war began.

11. I am grateful that Pope Francis has directly challenged just-war theory. He writes, "We can no longer think of war as a solution, because its risks will probably always be greater than its supposed benefits. In view of this, it is very difficult nowadays to invoke the rational criteria elaborated in earlier centuries to speak of the possibility of a 'just war.' Never again war!" These words are from the pope's wonderful encyclical *Fratelli Tutti* (meaning "all brothers," a phrase Francis of Assisi used), which is a passionate affirmation of life. He offered this statement as he visited Assisi, home of St. Francis, from whom the pope takes his name. In 2020, he signed the encyclical on October 3, and it was made public on October 4, the day the church celebrates St. Francis each year. Pope Francis wanted to make sure no one would miss his love for St. Francis! "Encyclical Letter *Fratelli Tutti* of the Holy Father Francis on Fraternity and Social Friendship," *Holy See* (daily bulletin of the Holy See Press Office), October 3, 2020, www.vatican.va/content/francesco/en/encyclicals/documents/papa-francesco_20201003_enciclica -fratelli-tutti.html.

another great theologian of the church, who built on Augustine's ideas to reconcile the power of the state with the strengthening force of Christendom. In his seminal work *Summa Theologica*, he penned a chapter titled "Whether heretics ought to be tolerated?" In it, he made this scary assertion: "They [heretics] deserve not only to be to be separated from the Church by excommunication, but also to be severed from the world by death."[12]

Aquinas went on to say that just as the state uses the death penalty for "forgers of money and other evil-doers," all the more should the church condemn heretics "to be not only excommunicated but even put to death." And so it goes.

Christians now had theological justification for killing enemies, whom Jesus called us to love. That is perhaps the ultimate of heresies: killing those with whom we disagree. And over the centuries, Christians have killed not only "pagans" and Indigenous people and Muslims and nonbelievers but also other Christians, often in the cruelest of ways. Though Thomas Aquinas is not solely to blame, he definitely has some of that blood on his hands.

And Aquinas is not alone. Bernard of Clairvaux (ca. 1090–1153), one of the most influential clerics of his time, passionately promoted the Crusades a century before Aquinas. Clairvaux wrote, "The Christian glories in the death of the pagan, because Christ is glorified."[13] I actually got sick to my stomach as I typed that.

An honest assessment of history leaves us with the conclusion that the church has, paradoxically, been one of the greatest champions of life *and* one of the greatest champions of death, sometimes simultaneously. Some of the most horrendous exploits in history have been committed by Christians with Bibles in their hands. And some of the most beautiful movements resisting the forces of death have also seen

---

12. St. Thomas Aquinas, *The "Summa Theologica" of St. Thomas Aquinas*, trans. Fathers of the English Dominican Province (London: R&T Washbourne, 1920), 154.
13. Bernard of Clairvaux, *In Praise of the New Knighthood: A Treatise on the Knights Exemplar and the Holy Places of Jerusalem*, quoted in Gushee, *The Sacredness of Human Life*, 164.

Christians on the frontlines. This was true even during the worst years of the Crusades.

I want to briefly step away from the history of bad religion to share a good-religion story. It's about St. Francis, one of my favorite revolutionaries for life. His life is a beautiful example of what it means to have good religion in the midst of a lot of bad religion.

A Good-Religion Hero in a Bad-Religion Time

Francis of Assisi lived a countercultural faith that stood in stark contrast to the militant Christianity of the thirteenth century. He was born in 1182 and lived during the Crusades. As the son of a wealthy Italian businessman, he had a privileged upbringing and went off to war with dreams of becoming a knight.

Among the reasons Francis ultimately abandoned both materialism and militarism was the connection he saw between war and the corruption of wealth and power within the church.[14] These are Francis's own words: "If we had any possessions we should also be forced to have arms to protect them, since possessions are a cause of disputes and strife."[15] My paraphrase: "The more stuff you have, the more weapons you need to protect it." And the church at the time had a lot of stuff to protect. Francis was no doubt familiar with the teaching of the apostle James: "What causes fights and quarrels among you? Don't they come from your desires that battle within you? You desire but do not have, so you kill. You covet but you cannot get what you want, so you quarrel and fight. You do not have because you do not ask God" (James 4:1–2).

We've seen the truth of these words repeatedly throughout history

---

14. Dr. Martin Luther King Jr. later made this same connection between what he called the interlocking "triplets of evil": racism, materialism, and militarism.

15. St. Francis, quoted in Paul Moses, *The Saint and the Sultan: The Crusades, Islam and Francis of Assisi's Mission of Peace* (New York: Doubleday, 2009), 38.

and into the present day. What creates wars and violence among us? Greed. Selfishness. A desire for what is not ours.

One of my favorite stories about Francis took place when he decided to meet with a Muslim sultan during the Fifth Crusade (1217–21). It was a tumultuous time. The Crusades had been raging for two hundred years and were still going strong. One of the primary motivations for the Crusades was to take back the Holy Land from Muslims. Pope Urban II, one of the earliest champions of the Crusades, described Muslims as "an accursed race, a race utterly alienated from God," and he claimed it was the church's duty to "exterminate this vile race from our lands."[16]

Think about that. Christians were fighting to reclaim the land that Jesus walked while missing the whole point of Jesus' message. How much more bizarre can it get than that—killing Muslims so we could own the land where Jesus preached about enemy love?

Yikes.

Francis had been sent off as a soldier, but when he could not reconcile the violence of war with the grace of Christ, he got off his warhorse and put down his sword. Then he did something crazy: he went back to the battlefield unarmed. In 1219, Francis headed to Egypt, one of the most hostile areas, where he was among forty thousand Crusade soldiers. It was a bloodbath. In the port city of Damietta, which had been home to eighty thousand people, only three thousand residents survived. One historian notes, "So many Muslims were decapitated that the Christians set to hurling their heads into Damietta with their siege engines."[17] Christians did that, and Francis witnessed that kind of barbaric hatred.

Francis pleaded with the military commander, Cardinal Pelagius Galvani, to end the fighting. Pelagius refused. He more than refused. He renewed his commitment to kill Muslims in the name of Christ. Pelagius was convinced that God was blessing their violence. He even

---

16. Pope Urban II, quoted in Karen Armstrong, *Holy War: The Crusades and Their Impact on Today's World* (1988; New York: Anchor, 2001), 3.
17. Moses, *The Saint and the Sultan*, 88.

used a relic thought to be a sliver of the real cross of Christ to rally the troops and to invite Christ's blessing. He prayed that they would "be able to convert the perfidious and worthless people, so that they ought duly to believe with us in the Holy Trinity and in Your Nativity and in Your Passion and death and resurrection."[18] This is what bad religion looks like, and Francis knew it.

The war raged. Pelagius broke off all diplomatic relations with the sultan of Egypt, al-Malik al-Kamil. The sultan in turn decreed that anyone who brought him the head of a Christian would be rewarded with a Byzantine gold piece. Undeterred, Francis traveled through fierce fighting and surmounted all dangers on his journey to see the sultan. He was inevitably met by soldiers of the sultan's army, who beat him savagely, put him in chains, and dragged him before the sultan himself.

When Francis spoke of God's love and grace, the sultan listened intensely and was so moved that he offered Francis gifts and money. Francis, of course, had no desire for the money, but he gladly accepted one gift, an ivory horn used in the Muslim call to prayer. Francis took it back with him and used it to summon his own community for prayer. Both Francis and the sultan were transformed by their encounter.[19] Francis knew what the church still needs to learn: the gospel spreads not by force or by violence but by love.

Francis and Pelagius give us two different pictures of Christianity: one of a believer who is willing to die for the cause of Christ, and the other of a believer who is willing to kill for it. Good religion and bad religion. These convictions have been at odds for centuries, and both still try to make their case today. In the words of British historian R. H. Tawney, "War is either a crime or a crusade."[20] It is something so costly to human life that it can be seen only as evil or as divinely ordained.

Hang on to the hope and inspiration of our hero Francis, because

---

18. Moses, *The Saint and the Sultan*, 89.
19. I've actually seen the horn, which is on display in Assisi.
20. R. H. Tawney, quoted in Roland Bainton, *Christian Attitudes toward War and Peace: A Historical Survey and Critical Re-evaluation* (1960; Eugene, OR: Wipf and Stock, 2008), 242.

we've got more bad religion to cover. Also keep in mind that knowing our history and telling it accurately is an expression of good religion, because what Jesus said is true: the truth does set us free (John 8:32).

We're not doing a full investigation of history here—that's more than you or I signed up for in this particular book—but I do want to make a few important dives into history so that we can see how the hairline fractures in the ethic of life start to turn into full-on fault lines that have caused many people to question the foundation of Christianity. For the next stop on our bad-religion tour, we'll time warp a couple of hundred years into the future after the death of St. Francis. That's when we encounter yet another glaring crack in our foundation for life: church-sanctioned colonization of non-Christian lands.

Colonizing for Christ

Let's start with the dictionary definition of colonization, which is "the action or process of settling among and establishing control over the Indigenous people of an area." Colonization is taking land from people who live on that land. As my friend Mark Charles says, "You can't discover land that people already live on." He often follows up by inviting people to hold out their phones so he can "discover them."

There are many ways we look back at history and attempt to justify colonization. We even use theological terms such as *manifest destiny* to try to explain why we were able to do something so obviously wrong. And this is why colonization by Christians reveals one of the most tragic cracks in the foundation of our ethic of life.

In the fifteenth and sixteenth centuries, the Roman Catholic Church issued a series of documents known as the "papal bulls," which were a kind of public announcement from the pope. The term comes from the old Latin *bulla*, which means "a round seal," a reference to the official stamp the pope used to seal and authenticate documents. Papal bulls might cover anything from the canonization of a saint to doctrinal statements. However, during this era, they were also used to pave the way for both the slave trade and the colonization of native lands.

In 1452, Pope Nicholas V released a papal bull titled *Dum Diversas*, which granted permission to King Alfonso V of Portugal to "invade, search out, capture, vanquish, and subdue all Saracens [Muslims] and pagans whatsoever, and other enemies of Christ wheresoever placed . . . and to reduce their persons to perpetual slavery . . . and to convert them to his and their use and profit."[21]

As we read this and other documents six centuries later, it is nearly impossible to comprehend how anyone thought this was okay. But that's how history and hindsight work. Nearly every generation looks back in horror and shame at what previous generations did in the name of God.

Two years later, in January 1454, Pope Nicholas V authored another papal bull, *Romanus Pontifex*, also on behalf of the kingdom of Portugal. It allowed, even sanctioned, European Catholic nations to expand their dominion over "discovered" land. In what became known as the Doctrine of Discovery, this pronouncement justified the possession of non-Christian lands as well as the enslavement of native peoples. Cloaked in religious language, it cast a missional vision for reaching the "pagan" world for Christ. The pope spoke of seeking "salvation" for all people and expressed a longing for the church to "bring the sheep entrusted to him by God into the single divine fold, . . . [to] acquire for them the reward of eternal felicity, and obtain pardon for their souls."[22]

Romanus Pontifex also conferred divine ordination or "noble personage" to Prince Henry, the uncle of King Alfonso. With this stamp of approval from the pope, Prince Henry and other Christian "missionaries" were considered to be agents of God. Sadly, but unsurprisingly,

---

21. Pope Nicholas V, "*Dum Diversas*," June 18, 1452, Doctrine of Discovery Project, July 23, 2018, https://doctrineofdiscovery.org/dum-diversas.
22. Pope Nicholas V, "*Romanus Pontifex*," January 8, 1454, Doctrine of Discovery Project, July 23, 2018, https://doctrineofdiscovery.org/the-bull-romanus-pontifex-nicholas-v/.

Prince Henry would become one of the earliest proponents of the African slave trade.[23]

It is worth noting that Portuguese explorers had captured and brought back to Portugal the first twelve enslaved people in 1441, several years before the papal bulls were released. The church had an opportunity then to be a moral force against slavery. But in at least some of the most prominent places of power and influence, the church instead provided moral cover and theological justification for slavery.[24] In the decades and centuries to come, millions of people were captured and enslaved, with the first African slaves arriving on the American continent in 1502. The direct passage was later established in 1525, which created a pipeline for human trafficking to the rest of the world.[25]

Theologian Willie Jennings emphasizes how "deeply Christian" the foundations for the slave trade were. The practice of slavery was so entrenched in Christian theology that Prince Henry ordered a human tithe be given to God through the church. That tithe was two Black boys.[26] Human beings became currency, even for the church.[27]

Christ, have mercy on us.

Tragically, this sanctification of evil was the case in the conquest of the Americas as well. In the United States, many of us learned a rhyme in elementary school: "In 1492, Columbus sailed the ocean blue." What many of us did not learn is that on May 4, 1493—one year later—Pope Alexander VI issued a papal bull titled *Inter Caetera*,

---

23. Charles and Rah, *Unsettling Truths*, 17.
24. For more on the continued attempts to justify colonization theologically, I highly recommend the book *Unsettling Truths* by my friends Mark Charles and Soong-Chan Rah.
25. Charles and Rah, *Unsettling Truths*, 18.
26. Willie James Jennings, *The Christian Imagination: Theology and the Origins of Race* (New Haven, CT: Yale Univ. Press, 2010), 16.
27. One of Prince Henry's closest companions, a man named Zurara, saw through the religious language being used to sanctify such evil, at least initially. Zurara served as Prince Henry's historian at the onset of the transatlantic slave trade. Willie Jennings notes that Zurara was troubled by what he saw because he "recognizes their humanity, their common ancestry with Adam." Sadly, the church propaganda eventually overwhelmed Zurara's conscience and he accepted the narrative of slavery being a road to salvation: "We, the Portuguese, will save them. They will become Christians" (Jennings, *The Christian Imagination*, 16–22). I wish this story had a better ending, but we have to tell the bad stories as well as the good ones.

offering a blessing for the conquest of the Americas. It was addressed to the king and queen of Spain, whom the pope referred to as "our very dear son in Christ, Ferdinand, king, and our very dear daughter in Christ, Isabella." It shared the pope's hope "that in our times especially the Catholic faith and the Christian religion be exalted and be everywhere increased and spread, that the health of souls be cared for and that barbarous nations be overthrown and brought to the faith itself."[28]

Inter Caetera also pronounced the official blessing of the church over the state-sanctioned conquests of Christopher Columbus, who was mentioned by name as a "beloved son" of the church and "a man assuredly worthy and of the highest recommendations and fitted for so great an undertaking." That undertaking included this charge to Columbus: "to bring under your sway" the lands and the inhabitants and to bring the people "to the Catholic faith. . . . to embrace the Christian religion." Colonization was baptized and sanctified by the church. Columbus even traveled with priests. Bad religion, to be sure.

Many of us have been taught to romanticize explorers such as Columbus. I can remember having to memorize their names, even their ship's names, and the routes they took on their voyages. What most of us did not learn in school is that Christopher Columbus considered himself a missionary on a church-sanctioned expedition to bring the "barbarous nations" (in the words of *Inter Caetera*) to Christ and into submission to "the Crown." Once again, we see the toxic cocktail of church and state power.

Columbus carried a cross in one hand and a sword in the other. Wooden crosses were used to "put a stake in the ground" and claim land for the crown. And with evangelical zeal, Columbus and the Spanish conquerors confronted native Americans with an "invitation" to convert. They did this by reading aloud *El Requerimiento*

---

28. Alexander VI, *Inter Caetera*, May 4, 1493, Doctrine of Discovery Project, July 23, 2018, https://doctrineofdiscovery.org/inter-caetera.

(in English, "The Requirement"). Every conquistador carried a copy of it in their pocket. It included this: "I implore you to recognize the Church as a lady and in the name of the Pope take the King as lord of this land and obey his mandates. If you do not do it, I tell you that with the help of God I will enter powerfully against you all. I will make war everywhere and every way that I can. I will subject you to the yoke and obedience to the Church and to his majesty. I will take your women and children and make them slaves. . . . The deaths and injuries that you will receive from here on will be your own fault and not that of his majesty nor of the gentlemen that accompany me."[29]

Upon meeting the native people, Columbus noted how easy it would be to enslave them. In his journal, he wrote, "They are so ingenuous and so liberal with all their possessions that no one who has not seen them would believe it. If one asks for anything they have, they never say no. On the contrary, they offer a share to anyone. . . . They should be good servants. . . . With fifty men they can all be subjugated and made to do what is required of them."[30]

These are haunting words. He essentially says, "They are so kind and free and open it will be easy to make them our slaves." And this is a man who not only is celebrated but who, to this day, even has his own holiday in some US cities (though that is changing). Christopher Columbus may have been a daring adventurer, but he is not someone we want our kids to think of as a role model, much less an exemplary Christian.

However, there was another man who lived during this era that we can look up to and learn from. His name was Bartolomé de Las Casas. Just as St. Francis and others were a part of the resistance to death during the Crusades, there were good-religion Christians of conscience during the era of colonization as well.

---

29. "The Requirement," quoted in James W. Loewen, *Lies My Teacher Told Me: Everything Your American History Textbook Got Wrong* (1995; New York: Touchstone, 2007), 36–37. To learn more, I recommend Loewen's book as well as Howard Zinn's *A People's History of the United States*.

30. Christopher Columbus, *The Four Voyages of Christopher Columbus: Being His Own Log-Book, Letters, and Dispatches with Connecting Narratives*, rev. ed. (1969; New York: Penguin Classics, 1992), 117, 56, 59.

Another Christian with a Conscience

Bartolomé de Las Casas was among the first settlers of the Americas. We know his story because he kept careful journals of the colonizers' conquests and later became a moral voice against the atrocities he saw, and in which he was arguably complicit. He was twenty-eight years old when he traveled with Columbus to an island Columbus named Hispaniola (it was known as Guanahani by the native peoples), which included modern day Haiti and the Dominican Republic.

Like many settlers at the time, Las Casas had embarked on the adventure thinking God had chosen Columbus to bring the gospel to the New World. He became the keeper of Columbus's diaries, copying and summarizing them. But Las Casas, who was also a slaveowner, over time experienced some massive shifts in his heart. And fortunately for us, he was prolific in capturing his thoughts in writing.

Las Casas was influenced by a Dominican missionary friar named Antonio de Montesinos, who did not hold back in denouncing the atrocities of the conquistadors and the complicity of the church in their evils: "With what right and with what justice do you keep these poor Indians in such cruel and horrible servitude? By what authority have you made such detestable wars against these people who lived peacefully and gently on their own lands? Are these not men? Do they not have rational souls? Are you not obliged to love them as yourselves?"[31]

So the Dominicans became a community of resistance to the slave trade and to colonization. Las Casas formally joined them in 1510, becoming a priest, but his transformation was neither immediate nor complete. Even after becoming a priest, he still owned slaves and traveled with the conquistadors for several years. But it was during these travels

---

31. Antonio de Montesinos, quoted in Anthony Pagden's introduction to Bartolomé de Las Casas, *A Short Account of the Destruction of the Indies*, trans. Nigel Griffin (London: Penguin, 1992), xxi. Montesinos's words "Are they not men?" strike me as particularly relevant as we declare every human life is equally sacred and made in the image of God. His words also bring to mind the signs carried by striking sanitation workers in Memphis in 1968 that read, "I am a man." It was a declaration and a demand to be seen and respected.

that his writings took a more aggressive stand against the horrors he witnessed. Eventually, he began to call colonialism what it was: theft and murder. "Everything which had been done to the Indians in the Indies was unjust and tyrannical," he wrote. He said only he had been willing to break "the conspiracy of silence about what has really been happening."[32]

And he did a pretty good job at that. He named the bad religion at the heart of it all, saying it was done by "those pretending to be Christians." Whoa, he called it what it was: people pretending to be Christians. He wrote, "This whole region, once teeming with human beings, is now deserted over a distance of more than two thousand leagues. . . . At a conservative estimate, the despotic and diabolic behaviour of the Christians has, over the last forty years, led to the unjust and totally unwarranted deaths of more than twelve million souls, women and children among them."[33]

Las Casas saw it all firsthand. He listed the atrocities in a four-page summary before going into more detail. Here are a few of those "despotic and diabolical" things he witnessed: "The mass slaughter of men, women and children; mass enslavement; torture; rape; verbal mockery of the suffering of those dying; gamesmanship and wagers among the conquerors related to their skills in torture and murder; smashing babies against rocks, the slow roasting of men and women in groups as a form of torture-execution; the use of dogs to track those trying to escape and to kill them; and the execution of one hundred natives for every one European killed in self-defense."[34]

The offenses were evil enough. What added even more horror to an already horrific situation was the twisting of the Christian faith

---

32. Las Casas, *A Short Account of the Destruction of the Indies*, 127.
33. Las Casas, *A Short Account of the Destruction of the Indies*, 12.
34. It's important to note that it was not just Christopher Columbus who committed these atrocities. Of the conquest of Guatemala by conquistador Pedro de Alvarado, Las Casas had this to say: "Oh if one were to catalogue all those orphaned by him, all those whose children he stole, all those whose wives he took, all the women he widowed, and all the adultery, violence and rape that could be laid at his door, as well as all those he deprived of liberty and all the torment and calamity countless people suffered because of him! If one could calculate how many tears were shed and how many sighs and anguished groans were caused by his actions, how much grief he occasioned in his life, and how many souls he consigned to eternal damnation in the life hereafter." Las Casas, *A Short Account of the Destruction of the Indies*, 14–17, 64.

to justify them. In the same spirit and tone that Frederick Douglass later used to decry "Christian" justifications for slavery, Las Casas denounced the unchristlike religion of the conquistadors pretending to be Christian: "Having abandoned all Christian sense of right and wrong [they have] been totally given over to a reprobate mind. . . . The longer they spent in the region the more ingenious were the torments, each crueler than the last."[35]

Las Casas scoffed at the idea that they had any intentions other than acquiring gold and power, saying of the conquistadors that they "have taken no more trouble to preach the Christian faith to these peoples than if they had been dealing with dogs."[36]

In the end, Las Casas grieved the millions of lives lost because of sinful greed and conquest. He could not believe the devastation, writing, "Who in future generations will believe this? I myself writing it as a knowledgeable eyewitness can hardly believe it."[37]

One of Las Casas's core convictions was that every life is equally precious and sacred. He declared that natives are "created in God's image."[38] He pointed to the cross as a reminder that these people mattered enough that Jesus died for them. He noted that all the law is summed up into one thing: love. And what he was seeing was not love; it was not Christlike; it was not Christian. It did not pass the sniff test.

Unbelievably, there were those who not only disagreed with Las Casas but argued against him and other prophetic voices. Over the course of two years, Las Casas debated a Spanish theologian named Juan Gines de Sepulveda, who passionately argued—theologically—that some lives matter more than others. The debate had been commissioned by the king of Spain, and it was deemed important enough that all conquests were halted until the debate was finished. Las Casas recounts the debate in his work *In Defense of the Indians*.

---

35. Las Casas, *A Short Account of the Destruction of the Indies*, 69, 80.
36. Las Casas, *A Short Account of the Destruction of the Indies*, 126.
37. Bartolomé de Las Casas, *Brief Account of the Devastation of the Indies*, vol. 1542, cited in Milton W. Taylor, *Viruses and Man: A History of Interactions* (New York: Springer, 2014), 271.
38. Las Casas, *A Short Account of the Destruction of the Indies*, 74.

The arguments Juan Gines de Sepulveda used against Las Casas were not new. He built on ideas that went all the way back to Plato and Aristotle. Sepulveda's basic argument, according to Las Casas, was that the natives were barbarians, of limited capacity, and incapable of learning beyond certain basic skills. As such, Sepulveda argued they were unable to govern themselves and were naturally cruel, violent, and immoral. Drawing on Aristotle's logic, Sepulveda suggested they were natural slaves who needed to submit to their intellectual and moral superiors. He also argued that there was a parallel calling between the conquest of the promised land and the conquest of the New World,[39] that there was theological justification. Just as God ordained Israel to take land from the Canaanites, so God ordained the church to take land from natives. At the heart of the argument was the belief that some people were naturally, even divinely, appointed to conquer and rule. To be clear, he meant that God had appointed them to kill, torture, and enslave other human beings.

In response, Las Casas argued that there can be no lesser and greater human beings. We are all sacred in the eyes of God. We are all equally made in the image of God, no exceptions. In a long history of bad religion, it is beautiful to see Las Casas, five hundred years ago, arguing that native lives not only matter to God but are infinitely precious.

Pretending to Be Christians

The argument that native peoples are made in the image of God no doubt seems like a no-brainer to us today. But it was not and is not (even today) something we can take for granted. Five hundred years ago, Las Casas did not hold back: "Now if Christians unsettle everything by wars, burnings, fury, rashness, fierceness, sedition, plunder, and insurrection . . . where are the holy deeds that should move the

---

39. I'm grateful again here to David Gushee's work for putting this on my radar.

hearts of pagans to glorify God?"[40] We can't kill people in the name of Christ. The gospel does not spread by force but by love. Christ came not with a sword but with a cross.

Christopher Columbus saw himself as a man of God on a mission in large part because the church had reinforced the idea. In his diary, he records his desire to find enough wealth in the Americas to fund an expedition "to conquer the Holy Sepulchre"—to fund another Crusade against the Muslims. He had some bad end-times notions that he would help create the conditions for the second coming of Christ, in part by recapturing Jerusalem.[41] I know it sounds nuts, like some wild mix of Indiana Jones and the Left Behind films, or some of the end-times-prepper theology we see today, but this triumphalist, conquering bad religion produced all sorts of bitter fruit all over the world that is still making us sick today. As Columbus was sailing to the New World, Christians were killing Muslims in the Iberian Peninsula and Christians were kicking Jews out of Spain. It is all connected, and it is all bad religion, or as Las Casas put it, people "pretending to be Christians."

It's easy for us to look back with disgust at the Christian colonizers and deem ourselves morally and theologically superior. But let's resist that temptation and ask some deeper questions: How does the colonizing mindset still affect us today? In what ways might the legacy of colonization still be active in our missions and evangelism? What might it look like to heal the wounds of history by reimagining what it means to "go into all the world" with the good news of Jesus?

As we wrestle with these questions, let us also commit ourselves to living out a better version of the faith. Let us spread the gospel not by force but by fascination. The answer to bad religion is not no religion but good religion. Let's live out a version of Christianity that looks like Jesus and that champions life rather than destroys it.

---

40. Bartolomé de Las Casas, quoted in Gushee, *The Sacredness of Human Life*, 194. Bartolomé Las Casas, *In Defense of the Indians*, trans. Stafford Poole (De Kalb, IL: Northern Illinois Univ. Press, 1992), chapters 42–48.

41. Jonathan Phillips, *Holy Warriors: A Modern History of the Crusades* (New York: Random House, 2009), 305.

RETHINKING LIFE

- Growing up, what were you taught to believe about war? In what ways, if any, has your view of war changed over the years?
- How do you respond to the ideas of "just war" and "holy war"? Do you believe that there are times when war can be just? Or when war can be a divine mandate? Why or why not?
- St. Francis and Cardinal Pelagius Galvani give us two different pictures of Christianity: one of a believer willing to die for the cause of Christ, and the other of a believer willing to kill for it. In what ways do you recognize these perspectives in Christian life, thought, or politics today?
- Nearly every generation looks back in horror and shame at what previous generations did in the name of God. How do you imagine future generations might one day view this generation? What might they look back on in horror and shame that this generation did in the name of God?
- Bartolomé de Las Casas was a Christian with a conscience who denounced the atrocities of the conquistadors and the complicity of the church in their evils. If he were alive today, which of the following statements do you imagine he might make about the American church? Share the reasons for your response.
  - The American church today is no longer complicit in evil.
  - The American church today is sometimes complicit in evil.
  - The American church today continues to be complicit in evil.
  - Other:
- How do you respond to the three questions posed at the end of the chapter?

— How does the colonizing mindset still affect us today?
— In what ways might the legacy of colonization still be active in our missions and evangelism?
— What might it look like to heal the wounds of history by reimagining what it means to "go into all the world" with the good news of Jesus?

- What do you think it means to spread the gospel not by force but by fascination? In what ways, if any, have you experienced the gospel by force? By fascination?

CHAPTER 9

We Theologized Hate

We all have prejudices, ways we "pre-judge" people based on anything from how they look to their religion, their culture or language, their sexuality, or the color of their skin. We are comfortable around people who are like us and we are uncomfortable around people who aren't. Even when we work hard to be fair and unbiased, too often we treat people who aren't like us differently than we treat people who are like us.

When our prejudice leads us to treat others unjustly, it's called discrimination. To discriminate, we need a certain degree of power.[1] For example, the power to create a welcoming or a hostile environment, to include or exclude, to give or refuse service in a restaurant, to hire or not hire, to rent or not rent housing, to worship or not worship together. The more power we have, the more we can discriminate; and the more we discriminate, the more harm we can cause. With enough power, we can discriminate not just against individuals but entire people groups. That's what happens when prejudice moves from the small scale to the large scale: organizations and governments paint an entire people group with a broad brush of inferiority and systemize prejudice into laws and policies.

Certainly, many of us are working hard to purge ourselves of our prejudices and to learn to love as God loves, but one of the worst things we can do is ignore that our history has shaped how we see people today, sometimes in ways we may not even realize. While some prejudices are

---

1. My friend Jemar Tisby puts it plainly: "Racism is prejudice plus power." Jemar Tisby (@jemartisby). Instagram, May 31, 2022, www.instagram.com/p/CeOTKGtOn_8/.

based on our experiences, others are not. Instead, they are transmitted through cultural biases, inherited directly or indirectly from others, or taught as truth. Sadly, this has happened even in the church. Over the course of history and into the present, the church has actually theologized prejudice and hatred, sometimes even to the point of supporting genocide, which is what happened in Nazi Germany.

Some historians consider anti-Semitism the original sin of Christianity because we see the roots of it from the very beginning. Following Jesus' crucifixion, there were some who said it was the Jews rather than our own sins that killed Jesus. This anti-Jewish prejudice began to take root in Christian theology early on, but it took centuries for the power dynamic to shift in such a way that prejudice could turn into large-scale discrimination and ultimately genocide.

Hate Escalates

We need to understand how hate becomes policy because the kind of resentment that leads to genocide doesn't happen in a vacuum. It follows a predictable pattern that begins with biased attitudes and progresses to acts of bias, discrimination, bias-motivated violence, and then genocide.[2] What's important to note is that the seeds of genocide are first sown as biased attitudes, which include stereotypes, fear of differences, and believing negative information about others—all of which are abundantly evident in our current climate.

The Holocaust in Nazi Germany followed this pattern of hate. It didn't spring up overnight. There were social conditions, policies, and, yes, theology, that made Hitler's Germany fertile ground for genocide. Holocaust scholar and Christian ethicist David Gushee traces the long history of anti-Semitism as evidenced in anti-Jewish laws over the centuries. Take a look.

---

2. "Pyramid of Hate," Anti-Defamation League, 2021, www.adl.org/sites/default/files/pyramid-of-hate
-web-english_1.pdf.

- Prohibition of intermarriage and sexual intercourse between Jews and Christians (306)
- Jews and Christians not permitted to eat together (306)
- Jews not allowed to hold public office (535)
- Jews not allowed to employ Christian servants (538)
- The Talmud and other Jewish books burned (681)
- Jews obliged to pay taxes to support the church (1078)
- Jews not permitted to be plaintiffs or witnesses against Christians (1179)
- Jewish clothes marked with special badges (1215)
- Construction of new synagogues prohibited (1222)
- Compulsory ghettos mandated (1267)
- Adoption of Judaism by a Christian banned (1310)
- Jews not permitted to obtain academic degrees (1434)[3]

One of the striking things the list demonstrates is how persistently these laws appear across the centuries. Hate is a resilient thing. It's also important to note that such laws are rarely one-offs but reflect deeper hostilities and prejudice that can eventually manifest themselves in full-blown violence. Sometimes policy violence is the precursor to physical violence. It's like a warning light on the dashboard of a car: it signals trouble ahead. It was the same with Black codes or Jim Crow laws in the US, and it has many other expressions across time and around the world.[4] We can all think of people who face discrimination today. That's why a pursuit of equality and justice in policies is a way not only of affirming human life and dignity but also of nipping hatred in the bud.

We're going to take a closer look at anti-Semitism in the church

---

3. David P. Gushee, *The Sacredness of Human Life: Why an Ancient Biblical Vision Is Key to the World's Future* (Grand Rapids: Eerdmans, 2013), 207–8.

4. Lest we think anti-Semitism is on its way out, we need only look to recent events to see how alive the fires of hatred still are. When white supremacists with tiki torches marched in Charlottesville during the Unite the Right rally in 2017, one of their chants was, "Jews will not replace us." Just a year later in my home state of Pennsylvania, a man armed with multiple guns, including an AR-15, entered the Tree of Life Synagogue in Pittsburgh and opened fire during their morning Shabbat service. He killed eleven people and wounded six. A subsequent review of his social media posts found them full of anti-Semitic hatred and conspiracy theories as well as photos of his guns.

because it is one of the earliest cracks in our foundation when it comes to affirming the sacredness of every person, and it is a crack that persists to this day. Understanding our history of anti-Semitism can also help us think critically about other forms of discrimination, help us combat it in other forms, and keep us from repeating the mistakes of history. The devil may be a liar, but he often keeps telling the same lies over and over, just in new ways.

A Brief History of Anti-Semitism in the Church

Christians have had a complicated relationship with our Jewish cousins pretty much from the beginning, ever since folks 2,200 years ago started proclaiming that the long-awaited Messiah had come to us as a Jewish carpenter from Galilee. As much as some folks might prefer to believe otherwise, it's impossible to erase Jesus' Jewishness. He went to synagogue. He observed Passover. He knew the law, and he knew when to break it. He expanded his followers' imagination and blew their minds by showing how big God's dream for the world is, and how big God's grace is—for the Jewish people, but also for non-Jewish people.

Remember, as more and more non-Jews became recipients of grace, one of the debates in the early church was what it meant for a gentile to become a Christian. Did they need to become Jewish in order to become Christian—for instance, did they need to get circumcised and eat kosher? What about when someone converted, such as a centurion in the Roman army? This was a question Peter really wrestled with (Acts 10), and much of the tension in the early church formed around how Christians related to Jews. You can see why it was a legitimate question, and the early church did a pretty great job navigating these waters, for at least a few centuries.

Then came the Constantinian shift. Anti-Jewish sentiment certainly existed in the Christian community before Constantine, but, as we have seen, what changed was proximity to power. Before Constantine,

Christians didn't have the power to overtly discriminate against Jews or anyone else in any systematic way. But that changed once Christianity became the majority religion and then the official religion of the empire.

Over time, we developed some toxic ways of twisting Scripture that fueled anti-Semitism. Some Christian leaders blamed the Jews for killing Jesus, rather than rightfully seeing all of humanity—including Romans officials, Jewish religious leaders, and the sins of you and me—as being responsible for Christ's death. We were all culpable. Many Christians, then and now, interpreted the destruction of Jerusalem and all the lives that were lost as God's judgment on the Jews for rejecting Jesus, the Messiah. In support of their view, they referred to verses such as this one from the apostle Paul: "You suffered from your own people the same things those churches suffered from the Jews who killed the Lord Jesus and the prophets and also drove us out. They displease God and are hostile to everyone" (1 Thess. 2:14–15). Some now saw "the Jews" as the culprit and made them a scapegoat.

While many Christians clung to their ancestors in the faith, including the ancient prophets and sacred texts, they rejected their Jewish roots and origins. It became known as supersessionism—the idea that the Jewish story ended with the birth of Christ and the church has superseded Israel as God's chosen people. There is even an entire theology known as *adversus Judaeos*, meaning "against the Jews." This theology can be traced all the way back to the fourth century and is especially evident in the teachings of John Chrysostom (ca. AD 347–407), who is sometimes referred to as the "golden mouthed," which is what *chrysostom* means in Greek but was also a reference to how eloquent his sermons were. However, his writings reveal a not so golden theology of contempt that portrayed Jews as heretics, blasphemers, and prophet killers. As we attempt to be honest about some of these iconic church thinkers, many of whom are now revered as saints, it is helpful to see that someone can be brilliant on some things and still be blind on others. Some of the things Chrysostom said were gold, and others were fool's gold.

Chrysostom called Jews dogs, goats, and pigs. He characterized them as fat and lazy drunkards, and called their synagogues "haunts of demons." He called them "assassins of Christ," held them responsible for the crucifixion, and considered them guilty of "deicide": they were God-killers.[5] More subtle anti-Jewish themes also can be seen in several writings of other early Christians, including Justin Martyr, Tertullian, Cyprian, and Origen.

Dangerous Words

It is vitally important for Christians, and for everyone who believes in life, to stand against hatred in all its forms. And a good place to start is with our rhetoric. As we've seen in history, we sow deadly seeds the moment we use or even tolerate dehumanizing language, such as calling any group of people cockroaches, dogs, or vermin. Not too long ago, there was a president of the United States whose rhetoric and policies sowed many of those dangerous seeds on a global scale. He referred to Mexican immigrants as "rapists and murderers." He referred to entire countries as "shitholes." Those are dangerous words, the kind of words that led to a surge in hate crimes and acts of overt racism.[6] All the while, he insisted that he did not have "a racist bone" in his body.[7] Out of the overflow of the heart, the mouth speaks.

Words have consequences, whether they're spoken by a school bully, a politician, or a preacher. We can all be interrupters of hateful and dangerous words by standing against language that tears people down and denies the image of God in them. One way we can do that is simply to ask the speaker, "Don't you think they are made in the image of God, just like you are?"

---

5. John Chrysostom, "Homily 1," *Against the Jews*, Tertullian Project, www.tertullian.org/fathers/chrysostom_adversus_judaeos_01_homily1.htm. St. John Chrysostom, *The Fathers of the Church: A New Translation*, vol. 72, trans. Paul W. Harkins (Washington, DC: Catholic Univ. of America Press, 1979), 39.

6. Ayal Feinberg, Regina Branton, and Valerie Martinez-Ebers, "Counties That Hosted a 2016 Trump Rally Saw a 226 Percent Increase in Hate Crimes," *Washington Post*, March 22, 2019, www.washingtonpost.com/politics/2019/03/22/trumps-rhetoric-does-inspire-more-hate-crimes/.

7. I particularly like how many people pointed out that it was not his bones that were racist but his heart, his words, his actions, and his policies.

Fast-forward to the sixteenth century and the Protestant Reformation. Martin Luther began with some sympathy and compassion for Jewish people, speaking against the anti-Semitism of the Roman Catholic Church. He even wrote an essay in 1523 titled "That Jesus Was a Jew," in which he condemned the fact that the church had "dealt with the Jews as if they were dogs rather than human beings."[8] He was clearly right to condemn that. However, just twenty years later in 1543, he published "The Jews and Their Lies," a sixty-five-thousand-word manifesto calling for a litany of horrors, including the destruction of synagogues, Jewish schools, and homes.[9] I cringe as I type his words: "We are at fault in not slaying them."[10] He called them a "whoring people" with a law that "must be accounted as filth."

Ugh.

It's not hard to see how his hateful rhetoric ultimately provided a theological foundation for the outright slaughter of Jews under the Nazis. From its earliest days, the Nazi regime used Luther's writing to fuel their movement. Martin Sasse, a Lutheran bishop in the German state of Thuringia, is just one example. Following Kristallnacht, two days of Nazi-incited mob violence that is now seen as the beginning of the systematic destruction of Jews,[11] Bishop Sasse wrote and distributed a pamphlet titled *Martin Luther on the Jews: Away with Them!* In it, he defended and justified the mass slaughter that would soon unfold.[12]

Some who defend Luther are quick to point out that he was old and starting to lose it as he wrote his anti-Semitic work. But that

---

8. Eric W. Gritsch, "Was Luther Anti-Semitic?" *Christian History* 39, 1993, www.christianitytoday.com /history/issues/issue-39/was-luther-anti-semitic.html.

9. Michael Coren, "The Reformation at 500: Grappling with Martin Luther's Anti-Semitic Legacy," *Maclean's*, October 25, 2017, www.macleans.ca/opinion/the-reformation-at-500-grappling-with-martin -luthers-anti-semitic-legacy/.

10. Martin Luther, "On the Jews and Their Lies," in *Luther's Works*, vol. 47, ed. Franklin Sherman (Philadelphia: Fortress, 1971), 267.

11. According to the United States Holocaust Memorial Museum, approximately 7,500 Jewish-owned businesses, homes, and schools were destroyed; 91 Jews were murdered; and 30,000 Jewish men were sent to concentration camps. "Kristallnacht was a turning point in the history of the Third Reich, marking the shift from antisemitic rhetoric and legislation to the violent, aggressive anti-Jewish measures that would culminate with the Holocaust." "Kristallnacht," United States Holocaust Memorial Museum, undated, www.ushmm.org/collections/bibliography/kristallnacht.

12. Coren, "The Reformation at 500."

defense skirts the fact that he was nevertheless capable of having Jews expelled from Saxony and other areas of Germany in 1537, just six years before writing his anti-Semitic manifesto. And he didn't die until 1546, three years after writing those sickening words. I wish I could say that there was universal outrage when he published his remarks, but that would be a stretch. Although Christians did eventually condemn Luther's words, it took centuries.

Unfortunately, anti-Semitism in the church didn't end with Luther. In 1555, on the other side of the Reformation and a decade after Luther died, Pope Paul IV issued a papal bull removing the rights of Jews. And it wasn't until Vatican II in 1965 that the Roman Catholic Church formally rejected its doctrinal anti-Semitism.

In the case of Nazi Germany, it's important to acknowledge that some Christians were part of the resistance and many of those ended up being killed alongside their Jewish neighbors. We'll consider their example next. However, it would be hard to imagine Hitler coming to power without the twisted theology and moral defense of the church. He did it all with a Bible in his hand, even likening himself to Jesus. He said that just as Jesus cleansed the temple of the Jews, he, Hitler, was cleansing the world of Jews.[13]

All you have to do is twist the cross to get a swastika.

The Genocide in Rwanda

For some of us, the Holocaust might feel like distant history even though we are just a generation or two removed from it. We might be tempted to think we would never allow something like that to happen now. That's why it's important to remember that another atrocity of history took place in Rwanda in 1994. We need to remember this history so we don't repeat it.

At the time of the genocide, Rwanda had one of the highest

---

13. Hitler makes this connection in *Mein Kampf*, but he avoids using the name of Jesus, referring to him only as "the Founder of Christianity." Adolf Hitler, *Mein Kampf* (1925; Boston: Houghton Mifflin, 1971), 254. He makes the temple comparison on p. 307.

concentrations of Christians of any country in Africa, and really of nearly any country in the world. Some estimate that up to 90 percent of the population was Christian, at least nominally. It does raise the question of how one of the worst atrocities of our generation happened when nine out of ten people involved were Christians.

In his brilliant book *Mirror to the Church*, Ugandan theologian and priest Emmanuel Katongole shows exactly how it happened. Certainly, there were demonic forces at work, but there was also a propaganda machine. In a country comprised of approximately 85 percent Hutus and 14 percent Tutsis, Tutsis were routinely dehumanized. There was also a complex historical backdrop of inequality that led to the propaganda and the narrative of hatred that became so deadly. Among other things, the Tutsis were called cockroaches and their lives equated with bugs, just waiting to be crushed.

The Rwandan genocide claimed some 800,000 lives in 100 days.[14] About 10,000 people were killed each day, mostly by machetes, in one of the most sickening events in my lifetime. I can remember it—I was in my first year of college. Years later, I got to visit Rwanda. Almost everywhere we went there were memorials, markers indicating mass graves, and in some places even the bones of those who died were left in place so we dare not forget.

On one of the monuments I visited were the words, "If you had known me, you would not have killed me." It is a powerful quote, a reminder that it is harder to kill people when you know them. But it is also a complicated quote because many of the people in Rwanda *did* know the people they killed. Many of them slaughtered their neighbors.

It was the same with slavery and lynching in the United States. Theologian and civil rights leader Howard Thurman spoke poignantly about this, naming the fact that proximity alone didn't

---

14. "Rwanda Genocide: 100 Days of Slaughter," BBC, April 4, 2019, www.bbc.com/news/world-africa -26875506.

guarantee compassion and respect. Black folks and white folks were living in proximity to each other even as Black folks were abused, tortured, raped, and sold on street corners. White folks did not really see Black folks, certainly not in an I-Thou kind of way.

Being a Christian, perhaps also just being a decent human being, means having more than just new ideas. It means having new eyes. Lots of smart people throughout history have also been racist. They had big ideas, but they did not have the eyes to see, as Jesus said (Matt. 13:16). When we say, "I see you," we are affirming not just that we are looking at someone but that we notice them, feel with them, and stand in solidarity with them.

It's easy for us to look back at this horrific event with disbelief or even a sense of moral superiority, thinking, "We would never do that," or, "We would never let that happen again." And yet I bet that's what every generation says as it looks back on the horrors of the past. Nearly every new generation has its own genocide, and, as we will soon see, the twentieth century was the bloodiest century in the history of the world. We must never take progress for granted. And it is worth noting that this genocide happened primarily with knives. How much more damage could have been done with nuclear bombs and weapons of mass destruction?

Faithful Resisters

When it comes to anti-Semitism, we can grieve the failures of the church even as we celebrate its faithfulness. In Nazi Germany, heroes such as Dietrich Bonhoeffer and members of the Confessing Church movement stood against hatred and fascism, and it cost many of them their lives. There were also many underground movements of subversive love and hospitality, and courageous individuals who risked their lives to save Jewish lives.

Certainly, one of the most well-known Christian resisters was

Corrie ten Boom, daughter of a Dutch watchmaker, who rescued hundreds of Jewish people before she and her family were arrested and sent to concentration camps. After surviving the war, she wrote a book about her story in which she recounts a conversation with a pastor who had come to her father's watch shop for a repair. Hoping to enlist the pastor's help, she went to another room and came back with a little baby who, with his mother, needed to be rescued. The pastor leaned over and looked at the baby, initially moved as anyone would be. But then he pulled back. "We could lose our lives for that Jewish child!" he said. Corrie's father overheard the comment, took the child in his arms, and then said to the pastor, "You say we could lose our lives for this child. I would consider that the greatest honor that could come to my family."[15] Courage is contagious. And so is fear.

There were also courageous youth movements that resisted Hitler's theology and policies. The White Rose was a youth movement sparked by a few dozen university students whose faith and idealism inspired them to act. At the center of the group were two siblings, Hans and Sophie Scholl. Hans was twenty-four and Sophie was twenty-one. They illegally printed and distributed hundreds of leaflets, doing all they could to counter the narrative of hatred. They were convicted of treason, sentenced to death, and beheaded on February 22, 1943, just four days after their arrest.

Other Christians, such as Franz Jägerstätter, a conscientious objector who refused to fight for the Nazi regime, met a similar fate for their courageous witness.[16] That's what faithful Christianity—good religion—looks like. Their courage and faithfulness can inspire us today as we stand up for life and resist the forces of death and hatred.

In the years since the Holocaust, the work of faithful resisters has continued through courageous and noble endeavors to heal the wounds and repair the cracks in our ethic of life. While such resistance

---

15. Corrie ten Boom, *The Hiding Place*, 35th anniv. ed. (1971; Grand Rapids: Chosen, 1984), 115.

16. My coauthors and I celebrate also sorts of courageous champions of life in our book, *Common Prayer: A Liturgy for Ordinary Radicals*. I also recommend the wonderful work of my friend Robert Ellsberg in his books *Blessed among Us* and *All Saints*. We need new heroes.

may not be like resisting the Nazi regime, it does show us other versions of courage and repair. Sometimes faithful resistance can be as simple as building a new relationship, one in which we speak truth to one another in love and try to heal some of the wounds of history.

Rabbi Lawrence Kushner tells a powerful story of a healing friendship with an Episcopal priest that began about forty-five years ago. The two men had decided to meet once a month for a meal together so they could share about their faith and deepen mutual understanding. Eventually, they decided to share their thoughts about Jesus, which they first wrote out and then read to one another as they ate. These are some of the words Rabbi Kushner wrote to his Episcopal friend:

> I am wary of Jesus. Not because of anything he taught or even because of anything his disciples taught about him. . . .
>
> I am wary of Jesus because of history and what so many of those who said they believed in him have done to my people. Christianity, you could say, has ruined Jesus for me. Somehow through the ages the suffering Jesus has become confused with the suffering of the Jewish people, my people. That is the key to my problem with him. His death has even become causally linked with some denial on *my* part. And this in turn has been used as a justification for my suffering.
>
> In this way Jesus means for me not the one who suffered for the world's sins but the one on account of whom I must suffer.[17]

Rabbi Kushner then relayed what happened next. He looked up at his Episcopal friend, whose face was "ashen." "I winced," he said, "fearing that I had crossed some line, that with my smug bluntness I had injured my new friend." But then the priest responded with a tearful whisper, "Please forgive me, forgive us. It could not have been Jesus *those* Christians served." Rabbi Kushner described it as a transformative moment. Their conversation continued.

---

17. Lawrence Kushner, "My Lunch with Jesus," in *Jesus through Jewish Eyes: Rabbis and Scholars Engage an Ancient Brother in a New Conversation*, ed. Beatrice Bruteau (New York: Orbis, 2001), 120.

"Your religion," I said, "wants you to care about me that much?"

"Oh yes," he said. "Don't you see, I must continuously seek to find God in every person. Jesus is only the beginning. You, Larry, are easy. But the ultimate goal is to find my Lord within everyone—even people I like a lot less than you, even people I dislike, even ones I despise."

And then it dawned on me: So that's what it means to say that God can take the form of a human being.[18]

To heal some of the wounds of the past, we need that kind of honest cross-faith dialogue today, that sort of deep mutual understanding and trust.

These are a few glimpses of what courage in the face of hate can look like. Resistance has many different forms. Sometimes it looks like risking our lives and sometimes it looks like building a friendship with someone who is different from us. I guess the real question is, What does courage in the face of hate look like for us today?

Love Overcomes

I have had several wonderful opportunities over the years to visit Israel and Palestine. It is an incredible thing to walk the land that Jesus and our Jewish ancestors walked. One of the people I spend a lot of time with when I am in Israel and the West Bank is my friend Sami Awad. Sami comes from a long line of Palestinian Christians who are also advocates for peace and champions of life. On one of my first visits, Sami told me his story as we walked along the Israeli West Bank wall that separates Israel and Palestine.[19]

18. Kushner, "My Lunch with Jesus," 121.

19. Israel has erected one of the largest separation walls ever built, and one many consider the most sophisticated apartheid system the world has ever seen. Approximately 441 miles in length, it separates Israel from Palestine and makes life exceedingly difficult for Palestinians. It is important to remember the historic backdrop of centuries of anti-Semitism that have contributed to Israel's actions in the West Bank. While it doesn't justify their actions, it does help us understand them. It is not uncommon for groups who have been oppressed to become oppressors, especially as they gain access to power. It is the story of our faith as Christians, and of other faiths as well. The corrupting influence of power is a part of the human story, and no religion is immune to it.

Growing up in Palestine, he had seen so much hatred that he knew it was a dead end. I guess you could say, as Dr. King put it, Sami had "seen too much hate to hate," and he chose love because hate is too heavy of a burden. As an adult, he ended up taking a pilgrimage to Germany to study and, more important, to experience the history of what his Jewish neighbors suffered in the Holocaust. He visited concentration camps, a Holocaust museum, and memorials. His heart ached because of what was done to them. The experience gave him new eyes. It enabled him to grieve and to be outraged about what has happened to the Jews over the centuries, and especially in the Holocaust.

Sami's grief and compassion for his Jewish neighbors doesn't prevent him from also being grieved by and outraged at what the state of Israel is doing to his neighbors in the West Bank and Gaza, but it does change what he sees. "I used to look at the wall and see hatred," he said. "Now I look at the wall and I see fear." That understanding doesn't justify the injustices he witnesses every day, but it does help him understand the fear behind the wall. It is love that fuels his desire for the wall to come down and for both Jews and Palestinians, Muslims and Christians, and all people, to be honored equally as beautiful and made in the image of God.

Sami's willingness to see and love his enemies—to affirm their humanity—makes me want to advocate for those on all sides of the Israeli-Palestinian conflict. It makes me want to be pro-Israel, pro-Palestine, pro-peace. It makes me want to advocate that schools and healthcare in Gaza should be as good as schools and healthcare in Jerusalem. And just as we can see throughout history why it is important to say "Jewish lives matter," the injustice and violence in Israel and Palestine should also compel all of us to say with equal conviction, "Palestinian lives matter." We cannot be quiet when someone is hurting our brothers and sisters, no matter what language they speak, what religion they practice, or what side of the wall they live on.

Believing and living out a consistent ethic of life always leads to compassion rather than hate. I got to witness a beautiful example of that several years ago following an act of hate that could have been explosive. Amid rising anti-Muslim tensions in our city and around the country in 2015, someone dumped the head of a pig in front of a mosque in Philadelphia, a gross display of hatred against Muslims, for whom pork is forbidden. But what happened next is where the light of life shines.

Leaders from multiple faith traditions, including many Christian and Jewish communities, gathered outside the mosque as our Muslim neighbors went to prayer, to stand in solidarity with them and as an expression of love.

A couple of years after the incident at the mosque, there was another act of hatred in our state. Someone went into a Jewish cemetery in Philadelphia and defaced the tombs, vandalizing them with symbols of hate. In an immediate act of solidarity and love, the Muslim community in Philly started a campaign that ultimately raised thousands and thousands of dollars to repair the Jewish cemetery.

We need more of that kind of love. The kind of love that repairs the cracks in our foundation for life. The kind of love that affirms the dignity of every person—and not only affirms it but also celebrates it. The kind of love that heals the violence of hatred. The kind of love that refuses to be enemies. While it is true that we have theologized hate over the centuries, the answer to hateful theology is not no theology but a theology of love. For God is love.

I am convinced that love and fear are enemies. They cannot coexist. And while the biblical promise is true that "perfect love casts out fear," fear also has the power to cast out love. They are like opposing magnets. Too often, it is fear rather than love that motivates us in both our personal lives and in our local and national policies. We are driven by fear of scarcity, fear of being replaced by immigrants, fear of people who are different from us. So the question we need to grapple with is this: What might it look like for us to be driven by love rather than fear? What does love require?

RETHINKING LIFE

- We all have some prejudices. Some are based on our experiences and others are transmitted through cultural biases,
  inherited directly or indirectly from others, or actually taught
  as truth. What prejudices do you now recognize in the culture
  or church in which you were raised? In what ways did they
  shape how you see people today?
- Hate escalates. It follows a predictable pattern that begins
  with biased attitudes and progresses to acts of bias, discrimination, bias-motivated violence, and then genocide.
  What social conditions, policies, or theology would you say
  are escalating hate in our current climate?
- What stands out most to you about the history of anti-
  Semitism in the church?
- We looked closely at the history of anti-Semitism, but hate
  also targets other marginalized communities. What other
  marginalized communities today are victims of similar patterns of discrimination and hate, particularly in the US?
- This chapter describes several faithful resisters who stood
  against hatred and fascism, as well as whole communities
  that overcame hatred with acts of love. In what ways do
  these examples inspire or encourage you? In what ways do
  they challenge you?
- What do you think it means in practical terms to be a faithful
  resister in our context today? How do you hope you might
  respond the next time you encounter anti-Semitism or other
  forms of hate or discrimination in your community?

## CHAPTER 10

We Decided Some Lives Matter More Than Others

God looked at all that had been made and called it "good." All of it was good. I suppose that included even the mosquitos, the hornets, and the stink bugs. It was all God's creation, and it was all good.

After God made the first two humans, God called all of creation "very good." One human was not better than the other. They were both very good, and they were both created in the image of God. And yet, ever since that inaugural murder when Cain killed Abel, we have been trying to create a hierarchy of life—to deem some lives better than others. Or we have been trying to make the case that some of us bear the image of God a little more than others. Sure, all lives matter, but some lives matter just a little more. Or a lot more.

While the compulsion to value some lives more than others is as old as time, it certainly reached a pinnacle in the movement that became known as "eugenics" beginning in the mid-1800s. *Eugenics* literally means "good creation," and it is the idea that the human species can be improved by selectively mating people with desirable hereditary traits.

The so-called father of eugenics was Francis Galton, who happened to be the cousin of Charles Darwin. Darwin is famous for his theory of natural selection and his contributions to evolutionary biology, so you might well imagine how he and Galton swapped ideas about the survival of the fittest and engineering the perfect human species. And it should come as no surprise that their ideas were later used by the Nazis, who started measuring people's noses to determine who should be thrown into the gas chambers. We'll talk more about how eugenics paved the way for horrific attempts to breed the perfect human race shortly. But first, let's travel back a little farther in time, to four hundred years before Christ and the ancient philosopher Plato (428–348 BC). While we're not going to go into all the nitty-gritty of history, it is important to understand the ancient origins of the philosophies and theologies that have undermined our ethic of life.

The Ancient Origins of Eugenics

Plato didn't coin the word *eugenics* but he would have known the Greek words from which it is derived: *eu*, which translates to "good," and *genos*, which means "birth." Together, they convey the idea of being "well born," of "good stock," or of "noble race."[1] Even before Plato, the historian Herodotus (ca. 484–425 BC), who is known by the grandiose titles "Father of History" and "Father of Ethnography," used the word *genos* to denote nobility.

In *The Republic*, Plato wrote about creating a superior society by encouraging the best and brightest humans to reproduce and by discouraging the lesser humans from reproducing. He even suggested that humans can be ranked like metals into gold, silver, and bronze, sort of like the Olympics, only it was his way of ranking *people*. He came up with a bunch of different rules he thought would bring about a supreme society. While the knowledge of DNA or genes did not yet exist, the idea that some people were superior to others very much did exist. And Plato thought it was all about breeding more of the good people and less of the bad ones.

---

1. *Online Etymology Dictionary*, s.v. "eugenics (n.)," updated September 25, 2018, www.etymonline.com /word/eugenics.

Plato also thought it was right for the "superior" to rule over the "inferior." He wrote, "Nature herself intimates that it is just for the better to have more than the worse, the more powerful than the weaker; and in many ways she shows, among men as well as among animals, and indeed among whole cities and races, that justice consists in the superior ruling over and having more than the inferior."[2]

The idea of racial superiority was not yet fully developed, but what Plato so tragically put words to is the notion that some people are superior and some are inferior, and that it is not only right and natural but better for the inferior to be ruled and dominated by the superior.[3] Like cattle or sheep or dogs, the idea is to breed the best genes. Perhaps you can see where this is headed.

Philosophizing Slavery

Aristotle was a student of Plato. Their lives overlapped for several decades and Aristotle spent about twenty years (from the age of eighteen to thirty-seven) learning from Plato in Athens.[4] It was Aristotle who came up with the terrible notion of "natural slavery"—the idea that slavery is an organic condition and that human beings come in two types, slaves and nonslaves. He wrote, "For that some should rule and others be ruled is a thing not only necessary, but expedient; from the hour of their birth, some are marked out for subjection, others for rule."[5]

According to Aristotle, some people were born to be slaves, to be treated as property; and others were made to be masters. But he didn't stop there. He went on to say that those who were born to be slaves

---

2. Plato, "Gorgias," *Early Platonic Dialogues Collection: Apology, Charmides, Crito, Euthyphro, Gorgias, Hippias Minor, Ion, Laches, Lysis, Protagoras*, trans. Benjamin Jowett (Independently published, 2021), 115.

3. Note the stark contrast between this idea and the words Jesus taught four hundred years later: "The last will be first, and the first will be last" (Matt. 20:16), and the gospel proclamation that "he has put down the mighty from their thrones, and exalted the lowly" (Luke 1:52 NKJV). You certainly get the sense that the kingdom of God is upside down and is flipping this world on its head. All those deemed inferior will be lifted up, and all those deemed superior will be brought down.

4. Plato lived from 428–348 BC and Aristotle lived from 384–322 BC. Aristotle lived about twenty-six years after Plato died at age eighty.

5. Aristotle, *Politics*, trans. Benjamin Jowett (Overland Park, KS: Digireads Publishing, 2017), 9.

did not have fully developed souls. They lacked certain abilities, such as how to think properly and how to conduct themselves. For this reason, they needed masters. Without masters, slaves wouldn't be able to make it. They were like domesticated animals, fit only for physical labor and incapable of full human thought and potential. He wrote, "And indeed the use made of slaves and of tame animals is not very different; for both with their bodies minister to the needs of life."[6] Aristotle went on to argue that some people "are as different from others as body is from soul or beast from human."[7] He says that some people are more like animals than humans.

Whoa.

For the record, Aristotle did differentiate between "natural slaves" and "legal slaves." Legal slaves were not born to be slaves but ended up becoming slaves through bad luck, such as becoming a prisoner in war. Aristotle suggests that in a just world, the legal slaves would be free, and any natural slaves that were free would be made slaves. Don't miss that: his vision for an ideal world was not the abolition of slavery but what he considered a just use of it.

The whole point here is for us to recognize how far back the lie of human hierarchy goes. The idea that some lives matter more than others is nothing new, even though every generation produces fresh expressions of this age-old idea. It is also just one of the many dehumanizing ideas Jesus defied when he flipped the whole world upside down with the gospel. Seeing how deep the roots of human hierarchy go gives us a better appreciation of how radical Jesus' teaching really was—and is.

Jesus arrived on the scene four hundred years after Plato, and the revolution he sparked interrupted the ancient philosophers' flawed hierarchy of life to offer us a new way of seeing the world. However,

---

6. Aristotle, *Politics*, quoted in "Philosophers Justifying Slavery," BBC, undated, www.bbc.co.uk/ethics /slavery/ethics/philosophers_1.shtml#:~:text=In%20fact%20Aristotle%20seems%20to,to%20 the%20needs%20of%20life.

7. Dan Lowe, "Aristotle's Defense of Slavery," 1000-Word Philosophy, September 10, 2019, https:// 1000wordphilosophy.com/2019/09/10/aristotles-defense-of-slavery/.

in the centuries after Jesus, the seeds planted by Plato and Aristotle continue to bear terrible fruit—and not just in the wider world but within the church itself.

Theologizing Slavery

The ideas Plato and his student Aristotle had about slavery and human hierarchy later influenced some of the most influential thinkers in the church, most notably Augustine (354–430) and Thomas Aquinas (1225–74).

Augustine lived and wrote in the fourth and fifth centuries, in the post-Constantinian era when the church was crystallizing its theology around all sorts of things. He offered a new theological angle on slavery, albeit a troubling angle, especially as we can now see how it was used to justify slavery for generations to come.

Augustine viewed slavery as part of the divine order, though not as the result of natural law, as Plato and Aristotle had. Augustine saw it as the result of sin. In a perfect world, he reasoned, slavery would not exist, but this is not a perfect world and human sin has led to slavery. He also assumed that it was the enslaved person, rather than the master, who had sinned. He put it this way: "The prime cause, then, of slavery is sin, which brings man under the dominion of his fellow— that which does not happen save by the judgment of God, with whom is no unrighteousness, and who knows how to award fit punishments to every variety of offense."[8]

Eight centuries later, Thomas Aquinas, a Dominican friar and priest who lived during the Crusades, began to synthesize Aristotle's ideas with Christianity. And, of course, that included Aristotle's messed-up idea of natural slavery. Although Aquinas agreed with Augustine that slavery was a result of sin, he also agreed with Aristotle that the universe had a natural order that gave some people power over others. He wrote, "For men of outstanding intelligence naturally

---

8. Augustine, *The City of God*, trans. Marcus Dods (Overland Park, KS: Digireads Publishing, 2017), 578.

take command, while those who are less intelligent but of more robust physique, seem intended by nature to act as servants."[9]

To his credit, Aquinas did have a somewhat higher view of enslaved people than Aristotle did. He argued that they should be treated with a certain degree of dignity and offered some restricted rights.[10] But he still held to the disturbing argument that there is a natural order in which some people are less valuable than other people. He tried to make sense of this by using the analogy of a father and a son: "A son, as such, belongs to his father, and a slave, as such, belongs to his master; yet each, considered as a man is something having separate existence and distinct from others. Hence in so far as each of them is a man, there is justice towards them in a way: and for this reason too there are certain laws regulating the relations of father to his son, and of a master to his slave."[11]

These words are so hard to read.

Aquinas and Augustine were both learned men who made invaluable contributions to the theology of the church. And yet they both engaged in theological gymnastics to argue that some people were made to be slaves. While some might try to excuse them as products of their times, that's not an excuse that would satisfy anyone who's been enslaved. Slavery was as wrong then as it is now and always has been.

I say all of this with a heavy heart, knowing that these two men made immeasurably important contributions on myriad other fronts. We are more than our worst idea, but perhaps we are more than our best idea as well. Humans are complex, especially when we dare to put words to a transcendent God. Their bad ideas do not discredit their

---

9. Thomas Aquinas, *Summa Contra Gentiles*, quoted in "Philosophers Justifying Slavery."
10. Here's one example of Aquinas advocating fairer treatment of enslaved people, though it is important to be clear he was not even close to being an abolitionist. I still find these words deeply troubling and in conflict with everything I believe as a Christian: "And while it was perfectly acceptable for a master to hit a slave, it might be better to be merciful since the child is subject to the power of the parent, and the slave to the power of his master. . . . The command that masters should forbear from threatening their slaves may be understood in two ways. First that they should be slow to threaten. . . . secondly, that they should not always carry out their threats." Aquinas, *Summa Theologica*, quoted in "Philosophers Justifying Slavery."
11. Aquinas, *Summa Theologica*, quoted in "Philosophers Justifying Slavery."

good ideas, but neither does their brilliance erase or excuse the errors in their thinking. These ideas became much more than pontification; eventually real lives were lost as these ideas evolved into practical theology. My goal here is not to defend or discredit these Christian thinkers but simply to tell the truth and to let the truth set us free. I also want to highlight the dangers of allowing theology to trickle down rather than bubble up. By that I mean that the best theology often comes from those who have been oppressed and crushed rather than from those who reside at the top of our social hierarchies.

Many of our famous theologians and philosophers contemplated ideas in ivory towers rather than in the trenches of life. Where we sit affects what we see, including how we understand God and our own place in the world. To get a feel for this, imagine you could travel back in time to the days of Augustine or Aquinas and sit in a room with theologians on one side and enslaved people on the other. You pose this question to both groups: "Is the hierarchy of human value something that came from God or from the devil?" It's not hard to imagine which group is going to give the right answer—the answer Jesus would have given. That's why I say the church's best theology has comes from the bottom, from those whom Howard Thurman calls "the disinherited," James Cone calls "the despised," liberation theologians call "the crucified peoples" of the world, and Derrick Bell describes as "the faces at the bottom of the well."

We allow theology to bubble up when we center and amplify the voices who are at the bottom of the social hierarchy and join them in building a better theology and a better spiritual foundation. Imagine how the work of Augustine and Aquinas might have changed if they had listened to and come alongside those who were enslaved, genuinely entering into their world. After all, according to the apostle Paul, that is exactly what God did in Jesus: "He gave up his divine privileges; he took the humble position of a slave and was born as a human being. When he appeared in human form, he humbled himself in obedience to God and died a criminal's death on a cross" (Phil. 2:5–8 NLT).

This is what it looks like for theology—and love—to bubble up from the bottom. In Jesus, God joined those at the bottom. And God has been casting down the mighty and lifting up the lowly since the beginning of time. The only hierarchies we see in the Gospels are the last becoming first, the first becoming last, mountains being leveled, and valleys being lifted up. In the eyes of God, we are all equally precious. And it is time for us to treat each other like we believe that.

Now that we understand some of the trickle-down philosophy and theology that led even Christians to justify a hierarchical view of life, let's circle back to the more recent story of eugenics and its deadly consequences.

The Terrible Consequences of Tampering with Creation

The word *eugenics* was coined in 1883 by Sir Francis Galton. (Of course he was a "Sir," knighted by King Edward VIII of the United Kingdom.) Galton was an anthropologist and, as I mentioned, the cousin of Charles Darwin. Eugenics was essentially the terrible idea that we can engineer a superior human race by selectively mating people with "desirable" hereditary traits. You can see how Galton's idea, which had catastrophic repercussions, was rooted in the ideas of Plato and Aristotle. But Galton took those ideas to a whole new level.

Early proponents of eugenics believed that things such as mental illness, criminal behavior, and even poverty could be passed down through the gene pool. Hence, they reasoned, such conditions could also be eliminated from the gene pool. They believed they could "breed out" disease, racial impurities, disabilities, mental illness, and any other characteristics deemed undesirable.

Eugenics became popular in the United States during the first half of the twentieth century. In 1911, John Harvey Kellogg, the same guy who made great cereals, started "a pedigree registry" with a foundation called the Race Betterment Foundation that hosted conferences on eugenics.[12] There was also the agricultural and farming side of all of this, which is mostly what we think of today when we hear "genetic engineering." But early on, eugenics was focused primarily on human engineering.

Eventually, prominent citizens, funders, and scientists established a Eugenics Record Office in Cold Spring Harbor, New York. I know this sounds really Orwellian, like a dystopian sci-fi movie. I wish it were fiction, but it's not. From 1910–39, the Eugenics Record Office tracked families and their genetic traits with the hope of limiting reproduction within less desirable people groups such as immigrants, poor folks, and pretty much everyone who wasn't white. The office maintained that there was clear scientific evidence that negative traits were caused by bad genes.[13]

Eugenics was a factor that contributed to reinforcing and broadening restrictive marriage laws in the United States, especially when it came to "race mixing." To be clear, there were other factors that played a role in controlling reproduction and interracial relationships. For example, slave owners claimed as their property the children born to enslaved people, so forced breeding of enslaved people was a common practice. Laws forbidding interracial romantic relationships go back hundreds of years and are among the first laws passed in the US colonies. From the birth of America, white folks were not to intermarry with Black folks. All interracial romantic relationships were prohibited, at least on the books. Lynchings of African Americans often stemmed from the real or perceived belief that Black folks were trying to intermingle romantically with white folks. But eugenics was applied to more than just race. The perceived hierarchy of human value also

---

12. History.com Editors, "Eugenics," *History*, updated October 28, 2019, www.history.com/topics/germany/eugenics.

13. These same ideas continue to be promoted to this day in the United States. For example, Donald Trump has regularly mentioned having "good genes" and even referenced "racehorse theory" about breeding thoroughbreds. Gregory J. Wallance, "Trump's 'Good Genes' Speech Echoes Racial Eugenics," *Hill*, September 25, 2020, https://thehill.com/opinion/civil-rights/518031-trumps-good-genes-speech-echoes-racial-eugenics/.

extended to other groups, such as those with physical or mental disabilities. For example, in 1896, Connecticut made it illegal for people with epilepsy or the "feeble minded" to marry.[14]

Racism combined with patriarchy and the eugenics ideology became a deadly cocktail in the United States. One of the most horrific consequences was the forced sterilization of women of color and other marginalized people. From 1909 to 1979, around twenty thousand sterilizations occurred in California mental institutions alone,[15] all under the guise of protecting society by keeping people with mental illness from producing offspring. Thirty-two states eventually allowed involuntary sterilization of whomever lawmakers deemed unworthy to reproduce, sterilizing more than sixty thousand people.[16] Federally funded sterilization programs took place in thirty-two states throughout the twentieth century.

In 1927, the US Supreme Court ruled that the forced sterilization of handicapped people did not violate the US Constitution. Supreme Court Justice Oliver Wendell Holmes Jr. used these terrible words in explaining the decision: "Three generations of imbeciles are enough."[17] The decision also stated, "Experience has shown that heredity plays an important part in the transmission of insanity, imbecility, etc."[18] The decision was overturned in 1942, but not before thousands of people underwent forced sterilization.[19]

According to scholar Katherine Andrews, "Between the 1930s and

---

14. History.com Editors, "Eugenics."

15. History.com Editors, "Eugenics."

16. History.com Editors, "Eugenics." Alexandra Minna Stern, "Forced Sterilization Policies in the US Targeted Minorities and Those with Disabilities—and Lasted into the Twenty-First Century," Institute for Healthcare Policy and Innovation, University of Michigan, September 23, 2020, https://ihpi.umich .edu/news/forced-sterilization-policies-us-targeted-minorities-and-those-disabilities-and-lasted-21st.

17. "BUCK v. BELL, Superintendent of State Colony Epileptics and Feeble Minded," 274 US 200 (1927), Legal Information Institute, Cornell Law School, www.law.cornell.edu/supremecourt/text/274/200.

18. It also included this haunting paragraph: "We have seen more than once that the public welfare may call upon the best citizens for their lives. It would be strange if it could not call upon those who already sap the strength of the State for these lesser sacrifices, often not felt to be such by those concerned, in order to prevent our being swamped with incompetence. It is better for all the world, if instead of waiting to execute degenerate offspring for crime, or to let them starve for their imbecility, society can prevent those who are manifestly unfit from continuing their kind." "BUCK v. BELL, Superintendent of State Colony Epileptics and Feeble Minded."

19. History.com Editors, "Eugenics."

1970s, approximately one-third of the female population of Puerto Rico was sterilized, making it the highest rate of sterilization in the world."[20] And of course, as a US territory, this was done with the complicity and cooperation of the US government. Menendez Ramos, the governor of Puerto Rico who initiated the involuntary sterilizations in the 1930s, claimed it was all to combat poverty, but it was certainly fueled by the eugenics movement, which was really just the most recent weapon used against vulnerable bodies and populations by those in power.[21]

In the words of eugenics expert and author of *Eugenic Nation*, Alex Stern, "Many sterilization advocates viewed reproductive surgery as a necessary public health intervention that would protect society from deleterious genes and the social and economic costs of managing 'degenerate stock.'"[22]

Those of us who care about life cannot help but be appalled. This is what happens when we value some lives more than others and lose sight of the image of God in every human being. And again, it's not hard to see where all of this is going.

The "Master" Race

Certainly, efforts to establish and enforce a hierarchy of life hit a chilling climax as Hitler attempted the ultimate eugenics venture: to create a superior Aryan race. Hitler himself referred to the eugenics movement, and specifically to some of the experiments being done in the United States, in his book *Mein Kampf.* He declared that non-Aryan races such as Jews and gypsies were inferior. His pursuit of racial purity was also why he wanted to exterminate gay folks and people with disabilities. Hitler believed he should do everything possible, including

20. Katherine Andrews, "The Dark History of Forced Sterilization of Latina Women," *Panoramas*, Center for Latin American Studies at the University of Pittsburgh, October 30, 2017, www.panoramas.pitt .edu/health-and-society/dark-history-forced-sterilization-latina-women.

21. Lisa Ko, "Unwanted Sterilization and Eugenics Programs in the United States," PBS, January 29, 2016, www .pbs.org/independentlens/blog/unwanted-sterilization-and-eugenics-programs-in-the-united-states/.

22. Alex Stern, quoted in Ko, "Unwanted Sterilization and Eugenics Programs."

genocide, to create a pure gene pool. And in 1933, during the same period the US was carrying out forced sterilizations, the Nazis created the Law for the Prevention of Hereditarily Diseased Offspring, which resulted in thousands of forced sterilizations in Germany. By 1940, hundreds of thousands of Germans with mental and physical disabilities were euthanized by gas or lethal injection. This was human engineering at its worst.

The Nazis also conducted evil science experiments in their attempts to engineer the master race. The efforts were led by Josef Mengele, an SS doctor who oversaw countless gruesome experiments on human beings under the guise of helping Hitler produce perfect humans. Mengele used chemical eye drops to try to create blue eyes. He injected people with diseases and performed surgeries without anesthesia, all of which later earned him the title Angel of Death. It was pure evil.

By the time Hitler killed himself in 1945, millions upon millions of people—each one of them a child of God, made in the image of God—had been murdered.[23] And their blood cries out to God. Most of them died because Hitler and many others who enabled him believed they could and should be like God; they should be the ones to engineer the perfect human race and to rid the world of anyone they deemed inferior.

The Nazi version of white supremacy was a disease that infected every part of German society—philosophy, science, history, industry, education, economics, religion, and more. It's also important to remember that Hitler was using not just twisted science but also twisted philosophy—with the help of Plato, Aristotle, and later Nietzsche and the enlightened humanists—as well as twisted theology. Remember, all that's needed to get a swastika is to twist the cross. And that is exactly what Hitler did, both literally and theologically. Hitler was convinced he was on a mission from God, and many "Christians" at the time reassured him that he was right.

---

23. So many millions were killed that it is hard to get the exact number, but we know that six million Jews were murdered in the Holocaust, and millions more non-Jewish people were murdered as well, most of them members of other marginalized communities.

Getting Our History Right So We Can Get Our Future Right

Given the horrors of the Holocaust, we might expect that the appeal and influence of eugenics in the United States came to a swift and decisive end in the years after the war, but that is sadly not the case. To this day, we are still learning more about our history, including the evil ways human beings tried to manipulate life and control births through sterilization. For example, it wasn't until 1976, a year after I was born, that we learned the tragic fact that somewhere between 25 and 50 percent of Native Americans had been sterilized from 1970–76.[24] Some of these procedures were coerced and others happened without consent during other medical procedures such as appendectomies.[25] And that's not according to conspiracy theories but according to a 1976 report from the US government's own Government Accounting Office.

Restrictions on marriage also continued. Keep in mind, we did not have a federal law legalizing interracial marriage in the United States until 1967 (*Loving v. Virginia*). Even in my youth, I remember hearing someone argue against interracial relationships using birds as a metaphor: "Bluebirds and cardinals don't crossbreed; neither should we." Bob Jones University, which we will take a closer look at in chapter 12, held out against interracial marriage until the turn of the twenty-first century. It wasn't until March 2000 that they dropped their ban on interracial dating.[26]

All of this is to say that we have to remember our history—all of it—so we don't repeat it. Until we get our past right, we are never going to get our future right. And one of the clear lessons of history

---

24. History.com Editors, "Eugenics."

25. Gregory W. Rutecki, "Forced Sterilization of Native Americans: Late Twentieth Century Physician Cooperation with National Eugenic Policies," Center for Bioethics and Human Dignity, October 8, 2010, https://cbhd.org/content/forced-sterilization-native-americans-late-twentieth-century-physician-cooperation-national-#_edn6%20.

26. Evangelical Press, "Bob Jones University Drops Interracial Dating Ban," *Christianity Today*, March 1, 2000, www.christianitytoday.com/ct/2000/marchweb-only/53.0.html.

is how important it is to be specific in affirming life. The atrocities of history have been perpetuated not against all lives indiscriminately but against specific lives. The forces of evil have targeted Jewish lives, women's lives,[27] brown lives, Black lives, and more. That's why we must affirm what history has denied. Until we can affirm every life specifically, we cannot say we truly believe that all lives matter. What does that mean for us today? It means we should be able to say Palestinian lives matter. Indigenous lives matter. Ukrainian lives matter. Haitian lives matter. Muslim lives matter. Transgender lives matter. The lives of those with disabilities matter. Black lives matter.

Do All Lives Really Matter?

The United States is at a crossroads when it comes to racial justice, reckoning with our history, and dismantling the myth of racial hierarchy. As we talk about how precious every life is, we have to acknowledge that our history includes four hundred years of slavery and racism that have desecrated Black lives.

Our country was built with stolen labor on stolen land. We ripped African women, men, and children from their families and communities, trafficked them across oceans in horrific conditions, and sold Black bodies on street corners, contradicting any conviction that Black bodies are as much God's temples as white bodies are.

In landmark cases such as *Dred Scott v. Sandford*, in which an enslaved man named Dred Scott sued for his family's freedom and was ultimately denied by the Supreme Court, we repeatedly denied the fact that Black men and women have any rights that white people are required to recognize. Even the founding documents of our country

---

27. It's important to understand that such wicked manipulations of people's bodies provides the historic backdrop that fuels many people today who advocate for women's rights and bodily autonomy. Even those who have reservations about the movement for reproductive rights need to understand how those in power have manipulated and exploited vulnerable bodies, especially those of women and people of color.

consider Black folks three-fifths human and refer to Native Americans as "savages." The same forefathers who penned the words "All men are created equal" also owned Black people as property.

So again, there is something to be said about the particularity of God's love given our history in America. To say that "Black lives matter" is simply to affirm what four hundred years of history has denied. And to say that Black lives matter is not to say that white lives don't matter. It's not to say Black lives matter more, but it is certainly to affirm that they do not matter less. If we cannot emphatically say that Black lives matter, it is hard to believe we really mean it when we say, "All lives matter." I heard a comedian named Michael Che put it like this: "When your wife asks, 'Honey, do you love me?' you don't respond, 'Baby, I love everybody.'" At least, you better not respond that way.

Just as God so loved the world, God also loves you and me in a personal way. And certainly, when Jesus names those who are blessed by God—the poor, the meek, the merciful, those who mourn, the peacemakers—he is naming particular people who have been crushed by the world in which they live. He is putting the spotlight on those the world has pushed to the margins. I honestly believe if Jesus were to make that same proclamation today, "Blessed are the poor," someone would probably try to correct him by saying, "God also wants to bless the rich. God loves everybody. Why should we focus only on the poor or those who mourn? Rich lives matter."

Our country is at a critical juncture. Those of us who are white need to understand that our Black and brown brothers and sisters are in the streets asking us to affirm their lives and their dignity. They are asking us, "Do you love me? Does my life matter?" One thing we can be sure of is that Black lives matter to God. The question is, How much do they matter to us?

In Jesus' manifesto, the Sermon on the Mount, there's that part we call the Beatitudes, where Jesus blesses the poor, the meek, the merciful, the pure in heart, those who mourn, the peacemakers (Matt.

5:1–12). Jesus basically blesses all the people this world has crushed. He centers the people this world has marginalized. He celebrates the people this world forgets. He validates, in specific ways, the people this world invalidates. Think about it: you can't come up with a list that is much more countercultural than the people Jesus blesses.

- *The poor?* Our world blesses the rich and praises the productive.
- *Those who mourn?* Mourning can feel like weakness, or like we are ashamed of our past.
- *The meek?* Our culture scoffs at the meek, adores what it deems the bold, the strong, and the ambitious.
- *Those who hunger for justice?* Even among those of us who want justice it is hard to imagine feeling hungry or starved for it.
- *The merciful?* Our society idolizes systems of law and order and scoffs at mercy.
- *The pure in heart?* To be pure in heart is to be without deceit or hypocrisy, a trait considered quaint at best in a culture that values acquiring affluence and influence by any means possible.
- *The peacemakers?* Our world dismisses any talk of peace as naïve.
- *Those who are persecuted?* Our culture is obsessed over comfort and safety and avoids persecution at any cost, even the cost of our integrity and convictions.

God's Affirmative Action

God's affirmative action. That's what my friend Alexia Salvatierra calls it when God gives special honor to the parts of the body of Christ that have been dishonored. I've found it to be a helpful take on the "all lives matter" versus "Black lives matter" debate.

The backdrop is this beautiful passage written by the apostle Paul about how we are one body with many parts: "Just as a body, though one, has many parts, but all its many parts form one body, so it is with Christ. For we were all baptized by one Spirit so as to form one body—whether Jews or Gentiles, slave or free—and we were all given the one Spirit to drink. Even so the body is not made up of one part but of many" (1 Cor. 12:12–14).

We often focus on the diversity Paul celebrates in this part of the chapter but miss the point he makes near the end of it. It is lovely that Paul begins with the powerful recognition that there is neither Jew nor gentile, slave nor free, but we are all part of one body in Christ. He makes it clear that the body works because the ear has a different role to play than the nose, and the hand doesn't think of itself as better than the foot. I often say that a symphony is beautiful because it includes so many different instruments (and a bunch of French horns on their own are not that fun to listen to). But Paul really brings it home near the end of the chapter, and this is what we sometimes miss: "Those parts of the body that seem to be weaker are indispensable, and *the parts that we think are less honorable we treat with special honor*. And the parts that are unpresentable are treated with special modesty, while our presentable parts need no special treatment. But God has put the body together, giving greater honor to the parts that lacked it, so that there should be no division in the body, but that its parts should have equal concern for each other. If one part suffers, every part suffers with it; if one part is honored, every part rejoices with it" (1 Cor. 12:22–26, emphasis added).

The text teaches us to give special honor to the parts of the body that have been dishonored. That's what Alexia Salvatierra means by "God's affirmative action."

History has not been colorblind. Our systems continue to discriminate. We cannot simply be post-race or colorblind; we need to undo the harm that has been done by hundreds of years of racism. Injustice and oppression have disproportionately affected people of color and other marginalized groups, and it is our holy duty to give special honor to those parts of our family that this world, for hundreds of years, has dishonored.

RETHINKING LIFE

- What, if anything, surprises you about the human history of valuing some lives more than others?
- As you think of the ways different groups of people have been crushed or desecrated throughout history, who would you say is being crushed or desecrated today? Consider those within your own community as well as those across the country and around the world.
- In what ways are the ancient philosophies about a hierarchy of life still evident in the world today? In what ways might the ancient theologies about a hierarchy of life be evident in the Christian community today, both within your community and the church at large?
- How do you respond to the idea that the best theology bubbles up from the bottom (p. 147–48)? In what ways, if any, have your beliefs been shaped by your experience as a person on the margins or by being in relationship with those who are?
- What, if anything, makes it difficult for you to affirm life in the particular—to say that specific lives matter rather than just that all lives matter?

CHAPTER 11

We Believed America
Was Exceptional

I grew up in a small town in East Tennessee that was still segregated. I spent most of my childhood on the white side of town, except for maybe when my church did a mission trip with the youth group on the other side of town or my school played a football game there. (And we'd be sure to dip out before it got too late.) I attended Maryville High School and we were the Rebels. The Confederate flag was on everything, including our lunchroom trays, our hallways, and our football field.[1]

It wasn't until I went to college in Philadelphia that I acquired eyes to see things differently. As I moved into my dorm room and put my high school yearbook on the shelf, one of my new friends noticed the Confederate flag on it and was horrified. He quickly let me know that the Confederate flag was "not cool" and was "not about sports or team spirit." That flag was about racism.

To this day, there are people who try to manipulate the narrative about the Confederate flag, saying it is about "heritage, not hate." But it is increasingly clear to most people that it is about a heritage of hate, of seeing Black folks as less than human, or at least as less than white folks. I'm horrified when I see photos of armed militia marching

---

1. I was recently invited back to my high school to speak and was encouraged that I did not encounter any Confederate flags at my alma mater.

with the Confederate flag in white supremacist rallies like the one in Charlottesville in 2017, when a young woman named Heather Heyer was killed by a man who intentionally drove a car into a crowd of counterprotesters. And then that same flag of hate was carried into the halls of the US Capitol during the January 6 insurrection in 2021, when more lives were lost.

Dolly Parton, a childhood hero of mine who grew up around the corner from my grandparents in the Smoky Mountains, understands this heritage of hate. She changed the name of her Dixie Stampede dinner theater show to get rid of the Dixie, recognizing that it represents the Confederacy and racist ideology. She did that right after the 2017 white supremacist rally in Charlottesville and got plenty of pushback for her decision. When in a 2020 interview *Billboard* magazine asked for her views about Black lives mattering, she quipped in classic Dolly Parton style, "Of course Black lives matter. Do we think our little white asses are the only ones that matter? No!" She also said, "I understand people having to make themselves known and felt and seen."[2]

Dolly then went on to say, "As soon as you realize that [something] is a problem, you should fix it. Don't be a dumbass. That's where my heart is." I've always liked Dolly because she doesn't hold back and tells it like it is. But what I also like is that she didn't just make a statement about Black lives mattering, she took action and made some changes.

Unfortunately, not everyone has the courage to change things, especially things that have been connected to traditional narratives about our history or our heritage. For example, it wasn't until July 2021 that Tennessee state legislators removed a statue of Nathan Bedford Forrest from their capitol building. Forrest was a Confederate general who also served as the first Grand Wizard of the Ku Klux Klan from 1867 to 1869. The proposal to remove the statue came after the 2015

---

2. Dolly Parton, quoted in Camila Domonoske, "'Of Course Black Lives Matter,' Dolly Parton Tells Billboard," NPR, August 14, 2020, www.npr.org/2020/08/14/902506007/of-course-black-lives-matter-dolly-parton-tells-billboard.

massacre in Mother Emanuel African Methodist Episcopal Church in Charleston. The mass shooting was an act of racially motivated terrorism by Dylann Roof, who had posed with the Confederate flag for which Nathan Bedford Forrest fought. Even after the decision to remove the statue was affirmed by both Republican and Democratic state legislators and had the full support of the governor, it still took six years of struggling with bureaucratic barriers to actually get it taken out of the state capitol. And that's just one example of where some Americans' hearts are: more committed to protecting Confederate monuments than they are Black lives. Sadly, there are still many more monuments all over the South that commemorate people who were on the wrong side of justice and equality.

There is a reason you won't see any monuments to Hitler or the Nazis in Germany. The way we honor history is by remembering those who suffered or overcame injustices, not those who perpetrated them. We don't remember 9/11 by setting up statues to the seventeen terrorists responsible for the attack. We remember the names of all the people who lost their lives. And yet all over the US we have statues honoring the victimizers rather than the victims. Such monuments are just the most visible manifestation of how deeply embedded our reductionist history runs. And to be clear, one of the great tragedies is not just that we memorialize those who were on the wrong side of history but that we have also erased the memory of so many people whose lives were crushed. And we don't need just monuments to honor Black and Indigenous victims, we also need to remember and celebrate their dignity, their courage, and their countless contributions to society. Their brilliance. Their art. Their resilience. Their joy. Their faith.

America is far from alone when it comes to having a painful history. Lots of countries enslaved people and massacred indigenous people. And lots of countries have since tried to do the hard work to tell the truth about what they did and heal the wounds of their history. But that truth-telling part is where America is different, exceptional. Here's how scholar and commentator Eddie Glaude put it: "America is not unique in its sins as a country. We're not unique in our evils. I think where we may be singular is our refusal to acknowledge them. And the legends and myths we tell about our inherent goodness, to hide and cover and conceal so that we can maintain a kind of willful ignorance that protects our innocence."[3]

Whoa. Talk about a mic-drop moment.

It's time to tell the truth about America, and to bust the myth of American exceptionalism. It's also time to tell the truth about America's "heroes," those whom we continue to honor as role models even though they were not champions of life. And one of the most prominent American heroes who needs to be busted is none other than "honest" Abe Lincoln.

Abraham Lincoln: America's Hero?

Abraham Lincoln consistently polls as one of America's heroes and favorite presidents. His face is engraved on Mount Rushmore. His birthday is when America celebrates Presidents' Day, and even Black History Month was set in February in part because of Lincoln's birthday. One of the most iconic American statues is the Lincoln Memorial in Washington, DC. President Obama, America's first Black president, took his oath of office on Lincoln's Bible. If there were such a thing as sainthood in American politics, Lincoln would no doubt be among the beatified. And yet there are some troubling parts of his legacy that are routinely overlooked, particularly when it comes to enslaved and Indigenous peoples.

Lincoln and Slavery

Consider this statement Lincoln made in 1858 during the first of seven debates with Stephen Douglas, his incumbent opponent for a US

---

3. Eddie Glaude, "Blaming Trump Is Too Easy: This Is Us," *Deadline: White House*, MSNBC, August 5, 2019, www.msnbc.com/deadline-white-house/watch/blaming-trump-is-too-easy-this-is-us-65354309615.

Senate seat: "I have no purpose, directly or indirectly, to interfere with the institution of slavery in the States where it exists. . . . I have no purpose to introduce political and social equality between the white and black races. There is a physical difference between the two, which, in my judgment, will probably forever forbid their living together upon the footing of perfect equality. . . . I, as well as Judge Douglas, am in favor of the race to which I belong having the superior position."[4]

Several weeks later, in the fourth debate, he doubled down:

> I am not, nor ever have been, in favor of bringing about in any way the social and political equality of the white and black races [interrupted by applause] that I am not nor ever have been in favor of making voters or jurors of negroes, nor of qualifying them to hold office, nor to intermarry with white people. . . . There is a physical difference between the white and black races which I believe will forever forbid the two races living together on terms of social and political equality. . . . There must be the position of superior and inferior, and I as much as any other man am in favor of having the superior position assigned to the white race.[5]

It is clear that believing in the superiority of the white race was a regular talking point for Lincoln. Even after being elected president, he said this in his 1861 inaugural address: "I have no purpose, directly or indirectly, to interfere with the institution of slavery in the States where it exists. I believe I have no lawful right to do so, and I have no inclination to do so."[6]

Lincoln was a complex person, a man of contradictions, and a

---

4. Abraham Lincoln in "First Debate: Ottawa, Illinois," August 21, 1858, debate transcript, National Park Service, Lincoln Home, updated April 10, 2015, https://home.nps.gov/liho/learn/historyculture/debate1.htm.

5. Abraham Lincoln in "Fourth Debate, Charleston, Illinois," September 18, 1858, debate transcript, National Park Service, Lincoln Home, updated April 10, 2015, www.nps.gov/liho/learn/historyculture/debate4.htm.

6. Abraham Lincoln, "First Inaugural Address," March 4, 1861, National Park Service, Lincoln Home, updated September 26, 2016, www.nps.gov/liho/learn/historyculture/firstinaugural.htm.

man who was navigating a complex world. I'm not giving him an excuse, just naming a reality. Although many of us were taught in school that Lincoln was the president who freed the slaves by signing the 1863 Emancipation Proclamation, most of us weren't taught that he also pushed for the Corwin Amendment. The proposed Corwin Amendment was the Hail Mary attempt of Congress to avert secession of the Southern states and civil war by giving constitutional protection to the institution of slavery. Lincoln sent letters to all thirty-four state governors asking them to ratify the Corwin Amendment.[7] These are Lincoln's famous words: "My paramount object in this struggle is to save the Union, and is not either to save or to destroy slavery. If I could save the Union without freeing any slave I would do it, and if I could save it by freeing all the slaves I would do it; and if I could save it by freeing some and by leaving others alone I would also do that."[8]

Lincoln was far from a revolutionary abolitionist. He was a pragmatist. He was more interested in what was politically expedient than what was moral and right.

Lincoln and Native Americans

Lincoln's pragmatism is also evident in his treatment of Native Americans. In addition to nullifying treaties with Native tribes, he also signed into law the Homestead Act of 1862, which allowed any adult citizen who had never borne arms against the US government to claim 160 acres of surveyed government land. When settlers met with resistance from Dakota Indians in Minnesota, Lincoln oversaw the military tribunals in which more than three hundred Dakota were condemned to death. On December 26, 1862, Lincoln ordered one of the largest mass executions in US history. With nearly four thousand

---

7. Daniel W. Crofts, *Lincoln and the Politics of Slavery: The Other Thirteenth Amendment and the Struggle to Save the Union* (Chapel Hill, NC: Univ. of North Carolina Press, 2016), 287.
8. Abraham Lincoln, "Abraham Lincoln Papers: Series 2. General Correspondence. 1858–1864: Abraham Lincoln to Horace Greeley, Friday, August 22, 1862 (Clipping from Aug. 23, 1862 *Daily National Intelligencer*, Washington, D.C.)," Library of Congress, http://hdl.loc.gov/loc.mss/ms000001 .mss30189a.4233400.

white Americans looking on, thirty-eight Dakota men were simultaneously executed by hanging. And that's not all.[9]

Under Lincoln's presidency, militias were sent out to hunt down Native Americans. Colonel Henry Sibley paid the hunters $1.50 per day and $25 per scalp. And the price was even higher for vigilantes who were not affiliated with a militia: they collected $75 per scalp. The prices went up to $2 per day and up to $200 per scalp for killing a Dakota Indian. Coincidentally, in October 1863, President Lincoln issued a proclamation for the final Thursday in November to be commemorated as a national day of thanksgiving.

The more we learn about American heroes such as Lincoln, it's not hard to see why there is a racial justice reckoning happening in the US and why people might want to shield their kids from the truth about history. The kids might not want to celebrate Thanksgiving if they knew the truth about what our country did to Native Americans in the weeks leading up to that first Thanksgiving. If we knew the truth about Lincoln, we might not want his head engraved on Mount Rushmore, the sacred mountain of the Dakota people he terrorized. We might not want to put the portraits of presidents who owned slaves on our money or anything else.

As an icon of American history, Abraham Lincoln represents more than just himself. So does Christopher Columbus, as we will see shortly. They represent the narrative of American exceptionalism— the notion that America is exceptionally good, even holy, and blessed by God in ways other nations are not. Lincoln and Columbus are seen as having had divine vocations in ending slavery and in the conquest of America. They represent a narrative of America that imagines our history as we wish it had been, rather than as it really was. And if we are going to get our future right, we have to get our history right.

---

9. I've previously mentioned how grateful I am for the work of my friends Soong-Chan Rah and Mark Charles in *Unsettling Truths*. They do a deeper dive on Lincoln, and I am indebted to their scholarship. The whole book is great, and there are two chapters dedicated to Lincoln: chapter 9, "Abraham Lincoln and the Narrative of White Messiahship," and chapter 10, "Abraham Lincoln and Native Genocide."

Rediscovering Columbus

In our book *Common Prayer*, my coauthors and I wrote liturgies for each day of the year. Our entry for Columbus Day on October 12 begins, "In 1492, the indigenous peoples of the Americas discovered Christopher Columbus." We celebrate that many today are reclaiming October 12 as Indigenous People's Day and using it as an opportunity to tell the dark truth about Columbus. The way Americans have lauded Columbus is yet another reminder of how we have believed a myth that makes heroes of people who did terrible things and failed to honor those whose lives they crushed.

When Christopher Columbus arrived in the Americas in 1492, the Native population of North America ranged between 1.2 million and 20 million. Scholars I respect use the median of 9.4 million. Subtracting the 3–4 million who lived in what is now Canada and Alaska, we can estimate the Native population in 1500 to be about 6 million. Between 1492 and 1900, the estimated population of Indigenous peoples in the continental US had plummeted to 237,000. That is a 96 percent rate of genocide. If we narrow the focus to a hundred-year period, 1800–1900, we discover that the Native population declined from 600,000 to 237,000. And if we focus in on just one ten-year period—1860–1870, the decade in which Lincoln was president—the number in the US census of tax-paying, assimilated American Indians living off the reservation fell from 44,000 to 25,713.[10]

My friends Mark Charles and Soong-Chan Rah offer this metaphor to summarize how the US treated Native peoples:

> It feels like our indigenous peoples are an old grandmother who lives in a very large house. It is a beautiful place with plenty of rooms and comfortable furniture. But years ago, some people came into her house and locked her upstairs in the bedroom. Today her

---

10. Mark Charles and Soong-Chan Rah, *Unsettling Truths: The Ongoing, Dehumanizing Legacy of the Doctrine of Discovery* (Downers Grove, IL: InterVarsity, 2019), 162.

home is full of people. They are sitting on her furniture. They are eating her food. They are having a party in her house. They have since come upstairs and unlocked the door to her bedroom, but now it is much later, and she is tired, old, weak, and sick; so she can't or doesn't want to come out. And the most hurtful part is that virtually no one from the party ever goes upstairs to visit the grandmother in the bedroom. No one sits down next to her, to take her hand and simply say, "Thank you. Thank you for letting us be in your house."[11]

"Our nation was born in genocide when it embraced the doctrine that the original American, the Indian, was an inferior race." Dr. King said that. And we did not stop there. We created a mythology of racial hierarchy from the very beginning of the American experiment, even as our founding documents directly contradicted that hierarchy.

While the Declaration of Independence does assert that "all men are created equal," a few paragraphs later it refers to Indigenous people as "merciless Indian savages." In the US Constitution, Black folks are counted as only three-fifths of a person.[12] And women are not mentioned in the Constitution at all. All fifty-one gender-specific pronouns in the Constitution are male.

When it comes to rights and human dignity, landmark cases such as the 1823 Supreme Court case *Johnson v. M'Intosh* made it clear that Native Americans also did not have rights as citizens, and even invoked the bygone Doctrine of Discovery. The Supreme Court said that when European, Christian nations discovered new lands, the discovering country automatically gained sovereign and property rights over the lands of non-European, non-Christian peoples, even though, obviously, the native peoples already owned, occupied, and used those lands.

---

11. Charles and Rah, *Unsettling Truths*, 194.
12. A recent *Washington Post* article laid it all out there: more than 1,800 congressmen participated in enslaving Black people. More than *1,800*. Julie Zauzmer Weil, Adrian Blanco, Leo Dominguez, "More Than 1,800 Congressmen Once Enslaved Black People. This Is Who They Were, and How They Shaped the Nation," *Washington Post*, May 15, 2022, www.washingtonpost.com/history/interactive/2022/congress-slaveowners-names-list/.

When gold was discovered in California, more than 300,000 people flooded the state, devastating the Indigenous population. California's Native American population was estimated at 150,000 in 1848, and in less than three decades that number was fewer than 30,000.[13] Native people could be traded in for cash by anyone willing to capture or kill them, and Mark and Soong-Chan document how little those lives were worth. In 1851 in Shasta City, officials offered a bounty of $5 for each Native American head turned in. The Pechanga Band of Luiseno Indians, one of California's original tribes, has documentation of a $1 million California state fund created to pay militias who captured and killed Native Americans. The payment ranged from 25 cents for a scalp and $5 for a severed head. Four-thousand Native-American children were sold into slavery in the late nineteenth century, and the prices ranged from $60 for a boy to $200 for a girl.[14]

Over and over, we have treated Native Americans as less than human. In 1890, three hundred Lakota men, women, and children were slaughtered by the US Army at Wounded Knee. Eighteen medals of honor were given to the soldiers who participated in the massacre. The US Army website lists 425 Congressional Medals of Honor that were given to US soldiers between 1839 and 1898 for fighting Native Americans. During the nineteenth century, the US population grew from 5.3 million to 76.2 million, and during that same period, the Native population dwindled from 600,000 to 237,196. As Native peoples were displaced from their land in movements such as the Trail of Tears, as many as one out of four of them died.[15]

Indian children were allowed to be auctioned off to white settlers. Laws such as the Indian Indenture Act of 1850 codified injustice, establishing a "form of legal slavery for the native peoples of the state

13. Benjamin Madley, *An American Genocide: The United States and the California Indian Catastrophe, 1846–1873* (New Haven, CT: Yale Univ. Press, 2016), 3.

14. "Native American Adversity in California," Pechanga Band of Luiseno Indians, www.pechanga-nsn .gov/index.php/history/facts-or-myths/pechanga-history-fact-or-myth/native-american-adversity -in-california.

15. Charles and Rah, *Unsettling Truths*, 115.

by allowing whites to declare them vagrant and auction off their services for up to four months."[16]

In America, we have worked hard not just to ignore but also to defend, justify, and theologize away the terrible things we did to Native Americans. This tragic legacy is why it is important for us to be able to say today, "Indigenous lives matter." Our history has constantly contradicted that truth, and it is time to change that if we are going to get our future right. And I believe the church could play a vital role in that—if we are willing to rise to the occasion.

The Sins and Responsibility of the American Church

I believe the church, the body of Jesus-followers across our country and around the world, has a central role to play in repairing the cracks in our foundation for life. We are to heal the wounds of violence and sin, just as Christ did. And that process must include confession, truth telling, repentance, and repair—both personally and socially. In 1970, Reverend Calvin B. Marshall III, chairman of the National Black Economic Development Conference, was asked why he and others singled out the church as having a responsibility to heal the wounds of racism, and he responded with this brilliant line: "Because the church is the only institution claiming to be in the business of salvation, resurrection and the giving and restoring of life. . . . General Motors has never made that kind of claim."[17]

As we saw in other places and periods of church history, the full story of the American church is one of both faithfulness and faithlessness, often at the same time. In the struggle for racial equality in America, we see the faithfulness of Christians in the historic Black

---

16. Indian Indenture Act of 1850, cited in Charles and Rah, *Unsettling Truths*, 113.
17. Thomas A. Johnson, "Blacks Press Reparations Demands," *New York Times*, June 10, 1970, www.nytimes.com/1970/06/10/archives/blacks-press-reparations-demands-blacks-press-demands-for.html.

church when they heard the liberating Word of God, illegally learned to read it, preached it, and baptized people in secret gatherings. Beyond the Black church, Mennonites and other Anabaptist communities banned slavery as early as 1663. Groups such the American Anti-Slavery Society were faithful in their work to win over hearts and minds to abolition and to prophetically call slavery evil.[18] In 1838, there were 1,346 local antislavery associations with a membership of more than 100,000 people, and many of them were Christians.[19] This is the church at its best. Everywhere I go, I hear new stories of this kind of courage and faithfulness.

Faithful Christians and other people of conscience, of all shades of skin, took tremendous risks and were often beaten and jailed for their courageous witness against racism and slavery. Many of them were firmly grounded in the fundamental ethic of life at the heart of this book, believing as abolitionist Theodore Dwight Weld did that, "No condition of birth, no shade of color, no mere misfortune of circumstance can annul the birth-right charter, which God has bequeathed to every being upon whom he has stamped his own image."[20]

However, Christians were also part of the problem. In the words of abolitionist Albert Barnes, "There is no power *out* of the church that could sustain slavery an hour if it were not sustained *in* it."[21] The National Committee of Black Churchmen declared that white Christians have been "the moral cement" for racism in the United States. This has had many different iterations over the years.

A shameful number of Christians were slaveowners. In 1855, abolitionist minister John Fee estimated that members of Protestant

---

18. Duke L. Kwon and Gregory Thompson note how active and persistent groups such as the Anti-Slavery Society were in preaching, debating, and printing materials for the cause of abolition. In 1834, they distributed 122,000 pieces of literature, and by 1840, that number shot up to three million. Duke L. Kwon and Gregory Thompson, *Reparations: A Christian Call for Repentance and Repair* (Grand Rapids: Brazos, 2021), 112. See also David Brion Davis, *The Problem of Slavery in the Age of Emancipation* (New York: Vintage, 2014), 260.

19. David Brion Davis, *Inhuman Bondage: The Rise and Fall of Slavery in the New World* (Oxford: Oxford Univ. Press, 2006), 260.

20. Theodore Dwight Weld, quoted in Kwon and Thompson, *Reparations*, 112.

21. Kwon and Thompson, *Reparations*, 116.

churches, including pastors, owned 660,563 slaves, representing a total market value of $264 million. Adjusted for inflation, that would be about $8 billion today.[22] And check this out. In addition to individual Christians who owned slaves, there were entire congregations that collectively owned slaves.[23] Congregations purchased enslaved people who were then hired out on an annual basis, and the compensation for the leased labor often went to pay the minister's salary. In one example, Briery Presbyterian Church in Virginia bought five enslaved people. Over about eighty years, that number increased to thirty-five enslaved people—without purchasing another person. Church trustees hired out nine-year-old Spencer for $4 for an entire year. They auctioned off a ten-year-old for $2.50. Adult spouses were often separated and hired out to different families.

Scholars point out that church-owned slavery was especially cruel. In contrast to slave masters who had a vested interest in keeping families together and an incentive to provide some basic healthcare for the sake of productivity, enslaved people owned and hired out by churches suffered from an even deeper form of exploitation, as those who kept them skimped on all provisions to get as much from them in a year as possible. This is why scholars such as Jennifer Oast call church-based slavery "the worst kind" of slavery.

The church not only profited from slavery but also provided theological cover for it, twisting Scripture to justify such evil. One of the clearest examples is "Slave Bibles," in which texts were removed that affirmed the dignity of Black folks and could fuel the fire for the abolition of slavery. Verses such as the apostle Paul's statement in Galatians 3:28 that "there is neither Jew nor Gentile, neither slave nor free" were trimmed. And large portions of the Hebrew Scriptures were excised, including Joseph's escape from slavery and Israel's liberation from bondage in Egypt.

---

22. Kwon and Thompson, *Reparations*, 117.
23. Jennifer Oast, "'The Worst Kind of Slavery': Slave-Owning Presbyterian Churches in Prince Edward County, VA," *Journal of Southern History* 76, no. 4 (2010): 867–900.

Enslaved people were also indoctrinated with what my friend Jonathan Wilson-Hartgrove calls "slaveholder religion." Here's one example of an Episcopalian slave catechism from Charleston, South Carolina:

Q: Who gave you a master and a mistress?
A: God gave them to me.
Q: Who says that you must obey them?
A: God says that I must.
Q: What book tells you all these things?
A: The Bible. . . .
Q: What does God say about your work?
A: He that will not work shall not eat.
Q: Did Adam and Eve have to work?
A: Yes, they were to keep the garden.
Q: Was it hard to keep that garden?
A: No, it was very easy.
Q: What makes the crops so hard to grow now?
A: Sin makes it.
Q: What makes you lazy?
A: My own wicked heart.[24]

Sweet Jesus. We did that. "Christians" did that. The deeper I dive into history, what breaks my heart is not just the evil things we did but the ways we have covered them up—defending them, denying them, willfully forgetting them—and often done so under the mantle of "American exceptionalism."

As much as we might like to believe that America is exceptional—a beacon of light, freedom, and equality in the world—our own history tells a different story. It is clear that Christians in America, and white Christians in particular, went to great lengths to create a

---

24. Rev. J. R. Balme, *American States, Churches, and Slavery*, 3rd ed. (London: Hamilton, Adams and Co., 1864), 39.

theology and a mythology that bury the truth. So when we think of healing the wounds of racism, this is another reason Christians have to take responsibility: because we contributed to so much harm. We twisted Scripture to justify evil and all sorts of violence, using it as a weapon to crush the image of God in our fellow human beings.

One of the most powerful insights of Duke Kwon and Gregory Thompson in their book *Reparations* is what all this violence has also done to white people, past and present. They suggest that until we acknowledge the sins the American church and Christians have committed, there can be no pardon, repentance, or restitution—only insecurity, fear, and shame. Denying the past not only hurts those who were wronged in the past, it also hurts those of us in the present whose ancestors and spiritual forebearers participated in the wrong-doing. So long as we refuse to acknowledge our wrong, we will be haunted by fear and insecurity. But the truth will set us free.

The Racial Terror of Lynching

Perhaps nothing more clearly reveals the lie behind the myth of America's inherent goodness and innocence than the racial terror of lynching. Lynching is the killing of a person, often by hanging, for an alleged offense, usually without a legal trial. It is what Bryan Stevenson calls "racialized terror." Lynching claimed the lives of thousands of men, women, and children in the United States, especially in the late 1800s and early 1900s.

I didn't hear much about lynching growing up in Tennessee, even though it had taken place all over that region and the KKK was founded in my state. I can't remember hearing much about lynching in my high-school history classes or even in my college political-science classes. I can't remember anyone mentioning it at all when I was growing up in the Bible Belt. But I later learned about a horror that happened in 1917 in Dyersburg, Tennessee, just a couple of hours away from where I grew up. A white mob tortured a Black man named Lation Scott with a blazing-hot poker iron for more than three hours. They gouged out his eyes, shoved the hot poker iron down his throat, and pressed the poker iron all over his body before castrating him and then burning him alive over a fire. This was not ISIS in Iraq; this was white folks in the Bible Belt.[25]

The circumstances leading up to lynching murders varied. Some of the lynched resisted mistreatment or refused to work for free. Many tried to intervene when another person was falsely accused or abused. Others were said to have looked at a white person the wrong way, spoken inappropriately, or sat where they were not allowed to sit. Nearly a quarter of lynchings were sexual in origin—for example, a Black person accused of sexually assaulting or even consensually dating a white person.

One hundred years later, most Americans are ashamed of this part of our history, but in its heyday, the lynching of Black Americans was often a public spectacle, announced in advance in newspapers and over radios. Thousands showed up to watch these public displays.[26] The atmosphere was often more like a circus or carnival than a murder. Ambitious business folks would set up stalls to sell merchandise, postcards, souvenirs, and snacks. Kids were dismissed early from school so they could watch. Cameras clicked everywhere.[27] Children were

---

25. Until recently, it was estimated that nearly 3,500 African Americans and 1,300 whites were lynched in the United States between 1882 and 1968, mostly from 1882 to 1920. However, in 2017, the most thorough study of lynching to date revealed that the extent of the killing was even worse. The information on lynching cited here is from that 2017 report done by Bryan Stevenson and the Equal Justice Initiative (EJI). The full report is *Lynching in America: Confronting the Legacy of Racial Terror*. You'll find it and other important info at EJI's website: www.eji.org.

According to EJI's 2017 report, in the twelve most active lynching states—Alabama, Arkansas, Florida, Georgia, Kentucky, Louisiana, Mississippi, North Carolina, South Carolina, Tennessee, Texas, and Virginia—there were 4,084 documented lynchings of African Americans alone between the years 1877 and 1950. Future studies may reveal even more. Equal Justice Initiative, *Lynching in America: Confronting the Legacy of Racial Terror*, 3rd ed. (Montgomery, AL: Equal Justice Initiative, 2017), https://eji.org/reports/lynching-in-america/.

26. I am indebted to James Cone for his work naming the theological and spiritual forces behind lynching, especially his book *The Cross and the Lynching Tree*.

27. The following description of the 1915 lynching of a Black man named Thomas Brooks in Fayette County, Tennessee, is an on-the-spot report of the party atmosphere that prevailed: "Hundreds of Kodaks clicked all morning at the scene of the lynching. People in automobiles and carriages came

sometimes given the chance to cut off pieces of the lynched person's flesh—fingers, toes, ears, even genitals—to take home as souvenirs.[28]

There is no other word but evil to describe the mindset that not only justified lynching but made it entertainment.

And lest we think that lynching was the preserve of isolated racists or hooded KKK members, it's important to note that many of the tens of thousands of folks who participated in and celebrated lynching were well-respected white folks who sat in church pews every Sunday morning. The practice of lynching cannot be blamed on a small cohort of fanatics.

Of the 4,084 lynchings studied by the Equal Justice Initiative, not a single white person was convicted of murder. And of all the lynchings committed after 1900, only 1 percent resulted in a lyncher being convicted of a criminal offense.[29]

And here's just one reason why this history remains important for us today. Where lynchings happened one hundred years ago is where state executions are still happening today. The states that held on to slavery the longest are also the ones that continue to hold on to the death penalty. What's more, as the incidence of illegal lynching decreased, "legal" lynching increased in the form of public executions. "Perhaps the most important reason that lynching declined is that it was replaced by a more palatable form of violence," according to *Lynching in America*, a report by the Equal Justice Initiative.[30] By 1915, court-ordered executions outnumbered lynchings in the former slave states for the first time.

Two-thirds of those executed in the 1930s were Black. In 1950, African Americans made up about 10 percent of the US population,

---

from miles around to view the corpse dangling from the end of a rope. . . . Picture cards photographers installed a portable printing plant at the bridge and reaped a harvest in selling the postcard showing a photograph of the lynched Negro. Women and children were there by the score. At a number of country schools the day's routine was delayed until boy and girl pupils could get back from viewing the lynched man." *The Crisis* 10, no. 2, June 1915, quoted in James Cone, *The Cross and the Lynching Tree* (Maryknoll, NY: Orbis, 2011), 1.

28. Equal Justice Initiative, *Lynching in America*, 33.

29. Equal Justice Initiative, *Lynching in America*, 48.

30. Equal Justice Initiative, *Lynching in America*, 62.

but they accounted for 75 percent of the executions. Fast-forward to today when African Americans are about 12 percent of the US population but still account for nearly half of those on death row and about a third of executions.

This is yet another of many reasons why we need to be able to say that Black lives matter. We must face the racial violence of both our past and our present, especially if we dare to call ourselves pro-life.

America's Exceptional Violence

When some people speak of American exceptionalism, they are referring to the belief that America is not just one nation among many but that God has a special destiny for America. Some contend our founding documents were inspired by God. Others say America has a unique role to play in the history of the world or the unfolding of biblical prophecy. But I think there is a different way to understand American exceptionalism, which is America's exceptional reliance on violence.

Dr. Martin Luther King Jr. called America the "greatest purveyor of violence in the world today." While it's not his most famous quote and you probably won't hear it quoted by a politician on MLK day, the speech in which he gave it is golden:

> As I have walked among the desperate, rejected, and angry young men, I have told them that Molotov cocktails and rifles would not solve their problems. . . . But they asked, and rightly so, "What about Vietnam?" They asked if our own nation wasn't using massive doses of violence to solve its problems, to bring about the changes it wanted. Their questions hit home, and I knew that I could never again raise my voice against the violence of the oppressed in the ghettos without having first spoken clearly to the greatest purveyor of violence in the world today: my own government.[31]

---

31. Martin Luther King Jr., "Beyond Vietnam: A Time to Break Silence," speech delivered April 4, 1967,

If that seems a little harsh or hyperbolic, consider this: The United States today has more guns than people. And we produce more guns than any other country in the world: 9.5 million guns per year, 26,000 per day, one gun every three seconds.[32]

We also lead the world when it comes to weapons of mass destruction. Of the 15,000 nuclear bombs in the world, 93 percent are owned by two countries, the USA and Russia.[33] We have approximately 7,000 of them. Some of these bombs are 3,000 times stronger than Little Boy, the code name for the bomb used in Hiroshima. Our 7,000 nuclear bombs have the capacity of more than 50,000 Hiroshima bombs.[34] Not only do we have the most weapons of mass destruction, we are also the world's biggest arms dealer, boasting weapons contracts with more than 150 countries. We export weapons around the world, sometimes to countries that are at war with each other, profiting off of death. And perhaps what makes us most exceptional of all, we are the only country that has ever actually used a nuclear weapon, and we did it twice in one week.[35]

Another unique marker of our penchant for violence is capital punishment. The United States consistently makes the list of the deadliest countries when it comes to executions. The United States is always in the top ten and usually in the top five executing countries in the world, a list which also includes China, Iran, Iraq, and Saudi Arabia. In 1975, the year I was born, only fifteen countries had abolished the death penalty. Today, two-thirds of the world—more than 150 countries—have abolished it. Only a handful of countries still carry out executions, and the US is one of them.

at Riverside Church, New York City, American Rhetoric Online Speech Bank, www.americanrhetoric .com/speeches/mlkatimetobreaksilence.htm.

32. Irina Ivanova, "Number of Guns Made in the US Nearly Tripled Since 2000," CBS News, May 18, 2022, www.cbsnews.com/news/guns-us-manufacturing-nearly-tripled-since-2000/.

33. "Status of World Nuclear Forces," Federation of American Scientists," n.d., https://fas.org/issues /nuclear-weapons/status-world-nuclear-forces/.

34. This incredible video gives a sense of the terrifying scale of our nuclear weaponry. Real Life Lore, "The Terrifying True Scale of Nuclear Weapons," YouTube, October 7, 2016, www.youtube.com /watch?v=fs1CIrwg5zU.

35. At the end of World War II, the US dropped both bombs on Japan: in Hiroshima on August 6, 1945, and in Nagasaki on August 9, 1945.

My point is not to ignore the good things about the United States but to tell the truth about the bad ones. And the truth is that we have a problem. We are addicted to violence. *Addicted.* I've spent quite a bit of time in communities of folks recovering from addiction, and the first step of the Twelve Step program is admitting we have a problem. There are many other steps to recovery, but when it comes to healing our addiction to violence, we must start with acknowledging the harm we've done as a nation.

Dr. King was not wrong when he called America the greatest purveyor of violence in the world. We have a problem. We continue to trust in our chariots and our horses, our bombs and our guns. We continue to believe we can live by the sword but not die by the sword. We continue to choose vengeance over love as the force that will bring peace to the world. And in the face of all that, we even have the pretension to call ourselves a Christian nation.

The word *Christian* means "Christlike," but there are many things about America's past and present that are not Christlike at all. When we conflate Christianity with nationalism, it does a lot of damage to the Christian faith. I think of these iconic words of abolitionist Frederick Douglass: "Between the Christianity of this land, and the Christianity of Christ, I recognize the widest possible difference—so wide, that to receive the one as good, pure, and holy is of necessity to reject the other as bad, corrupt, and wicked. . . . I love the pure, peaceable, and impartial Christianity of Christ: I therefore hate the corrupt, slaveholding, women-whipping, cradle-plundering, partial and hypocritical Christianity of this land. Indeed, I can see no reason, but the most deceitful one, for calling the religion of this land Christianity."[36]

Over and over, we hear, "God bless America," even as many of our policies crush the people Jesus blessed in the Beatitudes. In the end, the truest test of our nation and our faith is not our might but how we care for the "least of these."

---

36. Frederick Douglass, *Narrative of the Life of Frederick Douglass, an American Slave* (Hollywood, FL: Simon and Brown, 2012), 90.

The Ongoing Legacy of Racism

It is important to challenge the myths about America with the truth about America. In the words of my friends Duke Kwon and Gregory Thompson, "The truth, however, is that White supremacy, rather than being an unfortunate and aberrant weed in the garden of democracy, was in fact a native species that grew into and flowered out of every institution that the American founders created, in every region of the nation."[37]

Even some moments in history that we point to as milestones of progress are more complicated than we would like to remember. For example, the passage of the Thirteenth Amendment, which abolished slavery in 1864. It states that neither slavery nor involuntary servitude is permissible "except as a punishment for crime whereof the party shall have been duly convicted." The United States has about 5 percent of the world's population, but we have 25 percent of the world's prison population: one in every four prisoners in the world is here in the USA, the land of the free. Slavery did not end. It evolved into mass incarceration.

One-third of African American men between the ages of eighteen and thirty are in jail or prison, or on parole or some form of judicial constraint. One in every three African American boys born today can expect to go to prison. *One in three.* We have more African Americans in prison than the number of people enslaved in 1850. In 1972, America had roughly three hundred thousand people in prison, but we now have more than 2.3 million.[38] In my lifetime! Racism evolved.

The US criminal justice system is one of the institutions least impacted by the ongoing fight for civil rights and equality. To this day, African Americans are eleven times more likely than white defendants

---

37. Kwon and Thompson, *Reparations*, 63.
38. Bryan Stevenson, "We Need to Talk about an Injustice," TED, March 2012, www.ted.com/talks/bryan_stevenson_we_need_to_talk_about_an_injustice?language=en.

to receive the death penalty, and twenty-two times more likely if the victim is white. Hundreds of years of racism and slavery continue to affect nearly every aspect of our society: housing, education, healthcare, policing, employment, transportation, banking, wages, and even voting. For example, in Alabama, 34 percent of African Americans have lost the right to vote. The current number of disenfranchised African Americans is estimated to be higher than before the passage of the Voting Rights Act of 1965.[39] If we truly believe that all lives matter and that every person is equally made in the image of God, we have repair work to do.

It's also important to note that these ongoing legacies of slavery are not so much about the racist behavior of individuals but about the toxic residue of hundreds of years of anti-life policies and systems.[40]

An Allegiance Deeper Than Nationalism

Some of us were taught in school that Lincoln, Columbus, and the founding fathers of America were heroes. Today, some Americans think that our country's founding documents are equal to the Word of God and that America can do no wrong. But history tells a different, more complicated story.

The good news is that those of us who follow Jesus have an

---

39. These statistics about the death penalty and voting are from my friend Bryan Stevenson's TED Talk "We Need to Talk about an Injustice."

40. A Freakonomics Radio episode described "audit studies" in which researchers sent out identical resumes to employers with the only difference being the first name on the resume: one sounded like a white name and the other sounded like a Black name. Over and over, the studies found that the apparently white name was 50 percent more likely to receive a callback than the apparently Black name. So Jason gets a callback, but Jacquil doesn't. Shannon gets a callback, but Chanequa doesn't. Mark gets a callback, but Mohammad doesn't. Or you may have seen the story of a Black family who had their house appraised at $472,000, but when a white family switched places with them, it appraised at $750,000 (www .nytimes.com/2022/08/18/realestate/housing-discrimination-maryland.html). Racism still has a toxic residue today.

   Racism affects our hearts and it also affects our systems and institutions. It has left cracks throughout every sector of our society, especially when it comes to honoring the life of every person as equally precious and made in the image of God. Freakonomics Radio, "How Much Does Your Name Matter?" epi. 122, August 7, 2019, https://freakonomics.com/podcast/how-much-does-your-name-matter-ep -122-rebroadcast/.

allegiance that runs far deeper than ethnicity or nationality. To be born again means that we love beyond our own families and cultures and borders. The Bible does not say, "For God so loved America." It says, "For God so loved the world." My friend Bernice King puts it this way: "Christ is not American. The church is global. Our neighbors are all of humanity. The national anthem is not a gospel song."[41]

Our allegiance is to God, the author of life. And that means that we do not need to be afraid to tell the truth about our national history.[42] As citizens of God's kingdom, truth is never something we need to fear; it's something that sets us free. If we truly want our country to be exceptional, we can reclaim what that means by telling the truth, dispelling the myth of our inherent goodness and innocence, and deconstructing the legacies of slaveholder theology. Those are the first steps for reconstructing our faith and repairing the cracks in our ethic of life.

RETHINKING LIFE

- Some of us grew up not realizing that certain words (such as *Dixie*) or symbols (such as the Confederate flag) are racist. What racist words or images, if any, did you grow up not knowing are racist? How did you eventually acquire eyes to see them differently?
- Commentator Eddie Glaude describes the "legends and myths we tell about our inherent goodness, to hide and cover and conceal so that we can maintain a kind of willful ignorance that protects our innocence."
  — What are some of the legends and myths you were taught about America's inherent goodness?

---

41. Bernice King (@BerniceKing), Twitter, September 6, 2020, https://twitter.com/berniceking/status/1302610541362454528?lang=en.
42. For a deeper dive into nationalism and allegiance, check out the book I coauthored with Chris Haw, *Jesus for President: Politics for Ordinary Radicals*.

- — What examples come to mind of willful ignorance today? What, specifically, do you think people are unwilling or afraid to acknowledge about our country? Why?
- What, if anything, surprises you about Abraham Lincoln—as a person or his positions on slavery and Native Americans?
- What, if anything, were you taught in school about the history of Native Americans in this country? How does what you read in the chapter support or contradict what you were taught in school?
- When asked why the church has a responsibility to heal the wounds of racism, Rev. Calvin Marshall said, "Because the church is the only institution claiming to be in the business of salvation, resurrection, and the giving and restoring of life." How do you respond to Reverend Marshall's statement? Do you agree or disagree? Share the reasons for your response.
- The American church not only profited from slavery but also provided theological cover for it. In what ways, if any, do you think the American church might still be providing theological cover for racism today?
- What stands out most to you about the history of lynching and its ongoing connection to the disproportionate use of the death penalty and the incarceration of Black people today? In what ways does it challenge or support your views of capital punishment and the justice system?
- Do you agree that America is addicted to violence? Why or why not? Share the reasons for your response.
- In what ways would you like America to become truly exceptional? What's your vision for what might happen if we could be set free by telling the truth about America?

CHAPTER 12

We Chose Pro-Birth over Pro-Life

I want to be very clear: abortion matters. And yet it is also an exceedingly complicated moral issue, one that may not be as straightforward as many of us believe it to be. One of the things that makes it especially complicated for American Christians is that most of us are unaware of how abortion not only became the single issue that has eclipsed all other issues but became the litmus test for whether we are pro-life—or even whether we are considered Christians at all.

We need to understand how the cultural wars around abortion became a crack in the foundation for life, especially for Christians who want to be champions of life from womb to tomb. Today, it would be more accurate for many people who say they are pro-life to say instead that they are pro-birth or anti-abortion. Their commitment to life is limited to ending abortion. However, if we want to repair the foundation for life, we must continue to pursue a comprehensive ethic of life, one that includes advocating for all lives in every circumstance. Part of that requires having a better conversation about abortion, one that is rooted in facts, in history, and in relationships. And yet even having a conversation about abortion remains a difficult and complicated prospect for most of us.

It's Complicated

Abortion is complicated in part because there are some major questions at the heart of the debate. For example, when does life begin—at conception, at the first heartbeat, at quickening (when the baby moves in the womb), at viability (when the fetus can live outside of the womb), or when the child takes its first breath? What happens when the rights of the unborn child collide with the rights of the mother? Can we be champions of both the unborn child and of women? Who do we trust most to make abortion decisions, the government or the parents—especially in tragic situations such as rape, incest, or medical complications?

Abortion is also complicated because the culture wars around abortion have obliterated common ground, making it nearly impossible for us to even discuss these questions. Instead, people have chosen sides, developed strong opinions, dug in their heels, and doubled down, leaving little room for nuance, much less for meaningful dialogue.

Then there's the complicated historical backdrop, as we have seen in previous chapters, of men manipulating women's bodies. Even in the early church, it was men who controlled when women would have children and how many they would have. In the era of American slavery, white men manipulated women's bodies, especially those of Black women who were forced to breed children for the value they had as slaveholder property. And women were sometimes forcibly sterilized to control who could reproduce and who could not. We can't disregard the dark backdrop of history when addressing the thorny issue of abortion today.

One of the first cases that made the news after the Supreme Court's reversal of *Roe v. Wade* in 2022 was that of a ten-year-old girl who had been raped and become pregnant. The state of Ohio denied her the right to have an abortion. What a terrible, complex situation. Regardless of what our opinion might be, we must be willing to grieve for the young girl in this case. Even if we feel strongly that we would go through with the pregnancy if we or our daughter were in her place, we still have to wrestle with some difficult questions. Could we not have the grace to allow her to make a different decision than we would? Should this little girl or her family face criminal charges for choosing to have an abortion? What about the doctors, nurses, social workers, or any others who assisted her? It's complicated, right?

When I think of complications, I also think of people like my friend Patrick O'Neill, who together with his wife, Mary, gave birth to a daughter who has Down syndrome. Patrick has written beautifully about the gift his daughter Mary Evelyn, the youngest of eight kids, is to the world.[1] With few social boundaries, she regularly waves at people, dances uninhibited when she hears music, and hugs complete strangers who often say she made their day. He told me one story of how Mary Evelyn visited a nursing home and pretended to be a doctor, going door to door visiting patients.

Patrick grieves the fact that the population of folks with Down syndrome worldwide has declined by 30 percent since the onset of prenatal testing. It's hard to get an exact number on how many women receiving a prenatal diagnosis for Down syndrome opt for abortion, but Patrick believes it's certainly more than 50 percent. One of the few studies we do have is from Denmark, where 95 percent of parents choose to have an abortion when receiving a prenatal Down syndrome diagnosis.[2] In the support group Patrick runs for parents with kids who have Down syndrome, expectant mothers often break down in tears because of the pressure they feel to have an abortion.

Again, we need to sit and wrestle with the complexity of these situations and be willing to extend grace and to find some common ground. We also need to listen to those whose lives are directly affected by any policy decisions we make. One of those is Heidi Crowter, a Down syndrome activist in the UK. There is a viral video of Heidi, who has Down

---

1. Patrick O'Neill, "The Joys of a Down Syndrome Child," *News and Observer*, January 28, 2017, www .newsobserver.com/opinion/op-ed/article129404459.html.
2. Sarah Zhang, "The Last Children of Down Syndrome," *Atlantic*, December 2020, www.theatlantic .com/magazine/archive/2020/12/the-last-children-of-down-syndrome/616928/.

syndrome and is now in her twenties, saying, "At the moment, the law [in the UK] is that a typical baby can be aborted up to twenty-four weeks [but] then a baby with Down syndrome can be aborted up to full term. As someone with Down syndrome, I find it deeply offensive, and it makes me really upset and cry because it reminds me that no one loves me. And yet they do." She goes on to say her life is "full of adventure and a life of opportunity" and admonishes us "to see the person behind the extra chromosome, and see their inner beauty."[3]

While we're not going to resolve all the complicated questions surrounding abortion, my hope is that we can begin to lay the groundwork for a better conversation about abortion. If we are really honest, can't we all think of horrifying situations in which abortion might be necessary, even late in pregnancy, perhaps because of medical concerns for the mother or the child? Or in cases of rape and incest? Or shouldn't it at least be a legal option, even if it is not the decision we would make? Do we really think all abortion should always be illegal and always have criminal consequences?

On the flip side, can't we imagine commonsense abortion laws that would prohibit some abortions, such as those in the last trimester that are not directly related to medical concerns? Can't we reason with one another? And beyond the legal concerns, regardless of whether we consider ourselves pro-life or pro-choice, can't we find a way to be pro-active and pro-love and pro-compassion? Can't we put our heads and hearts together to find ways to reduce the number of abortions and address the root causes that lead to abortion? And shouldn't we be willing to at least listen, not only to those with whom we disagree but also to those whose lives are directly impacted?

As we consider what it might mean to have a better conversation about abortion, perhaps the best place to begin is to find common ground by getting the facts, particularly about the incidence of abortion and who has abortions.

---

3. Heidi Crowter, in an interview with Channel 5 News, UK, May 13, 2020, https://twitter.com/5_news /status/1232654146970537989?lang=en.

Getting a Pulse on Things

In 2020, my friend Lisa Sharon Harper and I cohosted a couple of town-hall-style gatherings online in the hope of starting some new conversations about abortion. Leading up to those gatherings, I tossed out a poll on Twitter to get a sense of where folks were. I asked, "When does life begin?" There were four response options: conception, heartbeat (five to ten weeks), fetal viability (twenty-two weeks or more), or birth (first breath). About six thousand people responded. Here are the results:

- Conception: 50.9 percent
- Heartbeat: 15.5 percent
- Fetal viability: 18.3 percent
- Birth: 15.2 percent

I also asked, "What's your view on abortion?" Here's how people responded to four options:

- Illegal, reverse *Roe v. Wade*: 14.4 percent
- Legal, safe, and rare: 67.9 percent
- Legal, no restrictions: 8.9 percent
- Other: 8.8 percent

Several things struck me when I saw these results. First, and no surprise, we are pretty divided on the issue of abortion and people have strong opinions. However, the fact that 68 percent thought abortion should be legal, safe, and rare is potentially a large piece of common ground. Many of us who want to reduce the number of abortions do not think legislation—making abortion illegal—is the only approach or even the best approach. Most of us think there are cases when abortion should be a legal option, which is why our nation was in turmoil following the Supreme Court's

2022 decision to overturn *Roe v. Wade.* But many of us also think there should be some reasonable restrictions. Just as we think of commonsense gun laws that limit the capacity of magazines or the number of handguns any one person is allowed to own, there are many of us who would like to have commonsense abortion laws that place some limits on it, such as prohibiting abortions in the third trimester except in cases where the life of the mother or child is at stake.

Fundamental Facts

While there are many things on which we might disagree when it comes to abortion and some things we may not know about abortion, foundational facts about abortion can give us a good place to start. So before we do anything else, I want to lay out a few things that we do know about abortion in the US. As the cliché goes, we are entitled to have our own opinions but not our own facts.

According to the Guttmacher Institute, a research organization that studies sexual activity, contraception, abortion, and childrearing, this is what we know about abortion in the US:

- The number of abortions in the US steadily dropped in the fifty years since the *Roe v. Wade* decision in 1973, and it has dropped under both Republican and Democratic presidents.[4]
- Ninety-one percent of abortions happen before thirteen weeks, during the first trimester.
- Abortion in the US is a common experience. One in four

---

4. With the *Roe v. Wade* decision in 1973, women no longer had to go underground or to Mexico to have an abortion. In the 1980s, researchers began tracking the numbers of abortions in the US. It was easy at that point for anti-abortion activists to say that abortion numbers were "the highest they've ever been" because it was the first data tracking we had done. The numbers have steadily dropped over the fifty years since *Roe v. Wade.*

women has had an abortion by the age of forty-five. The primary reason given for having an abortion is financial viability.[5]

- Late-term abortions, though rare, account for 1.3 percent of abortions, around six thousand cases per year. The primary reason given for an abortion late in pregnancy is medical, usually to address a threat to the mother's health.[6]

The *New York Times* featured an article based on Guttmacher Institute research that summarizes what we know about women who have abortions, and some of us might be surprised at what it reveals. The article starts like this:

The typical patient . . .
> Is already a mother.
> Is in her late twenties.
> Attended some college.
> Has a low income.
> Is unmarried.
> Is in her first six weeks of pregnancy.
> Is having her first abortion.
> Lives in a blue state.[7]

We also know—and this is important—that there is a direct correlation between poverty and abortion. Study after study shows that finances and lack of access to healthcare or affordable childcare are the top reasons listed for having an abortion.[8] Even if we can't all agree on

---

5. "Abortion Is a Common Experience for US Women, Despite Dramatic Declines in Rates," news release, Guttmacher Institute, October 19, 2017, www.guttmacher.org/news-release/2017/abortion-common-experience-us-women-despite-dramatic-declines-rates.

6. The Centers for Disease Control and Prevention also provides additional information here: www.cdc.gov/mmwr/volumes/67/ss/ss6713a1.htm.

7. Margot Sanger-Katz, Claire Cain Miller, Quoctrung Bui, "Who Gets Abortions in America?" *New York Times*, December 14, 2021, www.nytimes.com/interactive/2021/12/14/upshot/who-gets-abortions-in-america.html.

8. Teresa Ghilarducci, "Fifty-Nine Percent of Women Seeking Abortions Are Mothers Facing High Poverty Risk," *Forbes*, December 24, 2021, www.forbes.com/sites/teresaghilarducci/2021/12/24/59-of-women-seeking-abortions-are-mothers-facing-high-poverty-risk/?sh=1710548f264f.

abortion laws, we know without a doubt that access to affordable child-care and healthcare would save the lives of both the unborn and the already born. Don't we want to work together to champion those things?

It's important to know the facts so we don't get caught up in the extremes of culture-war rhetoric. Constantly emphasizing the extremes has stalled progress we might otherwise have made in reducing abortions had we focused instead on finding common ground. By extreme rhetoric, I mean use of such language as "baby killers" and "murderers" while disregarding the difference between having an abortion just after fertilization (using the "day-after pill") and having a late-term abortion. No matter how passionate we are about our side of the cause, extreme rhetoric is not our ally. It inevitably deteriorates into a pointless shouting match with folks on one side shouting "baby killers" and folks on the other side shouting "hands off my uterus." There's no progress in that either way.

Here are the facts when it comes to late-term abortions. Abortions in the third trimester are devastating situations that account for 1.3 percent of abortions in the United States, approximately six thousand per year. I have never met a single person who has chosen to terminate a pregnancy in the third trimester when it was not a life-threatening medical emergency. And I have tried to find those people! Yet it is not uncommon to hear people speak as if a mother sometimes just randomly decides eight months into a pregnancy that she doesn't want the baby. Or, in the bizarre scenario laid out by a former president, a baby is born, wrapped in a blanket, and the mother and doctor then decide whether to kill the baby.[9] That does not happen. And if it were to happen, it is what we would refer to as murder.

So let's have a better conversation about those 1.3 percent of abortions late in pregnancy and hopefully find some guardrails that can save and protect lives even in those wrenching situations when people

---

9.   Jon Greenberg, "Donald Trump Repeats, Falsely, That Doctors, Mothers Decide to Execute Live Babies after Birth," PolitiFact, Poynter Institute, April 29, 2019, www.politifact.com/factchecks/2019/apr/29/donald-trump/donald-trump-repeats-falsely-doctors-mothers-decid/.

are faced with a choice between their life or the life in their womb. And let's also try to have a better conversation about the other 99 percent of abortions.

For all of the same reasons it's important to know the facts about abortion, we also need to be clear about what the Bible says—and doesn't say—about abortion.

Better Conversations Begin with Relationships Rather Than Opinions

It was only when I carved out space for people to have a better conversation on abortion and on what it means to be a champion for life that I heard stories from women who had had an abortion. One of those women is my mom. Another is my wife.

I am a momma's boy—an only child and an only grandchild on both sides. My dad died when I was nine, so Mom and I are tight. We've been through a divorce together, and she has been a single mom for most of my life. We are best friends. And yet as I began hosting conversations about abortion on social media and mentioning the possibility of this book, I picked up on an uneasiness from my mom. This was unusual because my mom is my biggest fan. She has all of my books on her shelf and comes to every event she can even though she's heard me preach hundreds of times. I couldn't quite get it.

Then she told me she wanted to talk. She needed to tell me something. And the floodgates opened: Mom had had an abortion. It happened when I was one, and in forty-five years of life together she had never told me. My dad was sick with multiple sclerosis, and my mom was already raising a wild toddler (me!) and had a full-time teaching job, and she just didn't feel like she could add one more kid. She is a woman of great faith and looks back now saying, "I know God would have helped me through it, but then I just couldn't imagine adding more. I am sorry every day of my life."

And of course she followed that up by saying how thankful she is for God's grace. We processed the shame, the guilt, the weight of not knowing how to talk about it. Of course, when I even considered including her story in the book, I asked her about it. Without any hesitation she said, "I want you to include it. I want to be able to be honest about it. I want people to know." But it took hosting a town hall on abortion and writing a book about life to create the space for my mom to be able to share it with me.

Chances are there are people in your life who have had an abortion. One in four women is a lot. They are in our churches, in our workplaces, in our families. Until we choose to love the people in our lives more than we love our opinions, some of that pain will remain buried. I've also found that not every person who's had an abortion processes that decision in the same way. While some feel deeply grieved and full of regret, others feel ambivalent and don't really think about it that much. Still others feel strongly that the decision to have an abortion was the right one, and they'd do it again in a minute. There are so many ways people process their decision. As long as we continue to debate abortion as if it were just some issue without centering those most impacted by it, we will continue to hurt the people around us.[1]

What the Bible Says—and Doesn't Say—about Abortion

One of the things that makes the issue of abortion especially challenging for Christians is that Jesus doesn't mention it. Not only does Jesus not mention abortion, the Bible hardly mentions it at all, even though, as we've noted, it was a common practice in ancient times. Of course,

---

1. For further reading about folks who have faced the complicated decision of whether to terminate a pregnancy, Katey Zeh has compiled a powerful book called *A Complicated Choice.*

while Jesus and the Bible don't provide direct counsel on the issue of abortion, neither do they mention guns or nuclear weapons, and yet we still derive guidelines about those issues based on biblical teaching and the life and words of Jesus.[10]

So what does the Bible actually say about abortion? There are a few verses that are sometimes used to make a case against abortion, such as this one from the prophet Jeremiah: "Before I formed you in the womb I knew you" (Jer. 1:5). But there is only one specific verse in Exodus 21 that has implications for how we might approach abortion and life in the womb. This text sits right in the middle of the Hebrew laws and is specifically about people who are fighting and cause harm to a woman or her child: "If people are fighting and hit a pregnant woman and she gives birth prematurely but there is no serious injury, the offender must be fined whatever the woman's husband demands and the court allows. But if there is serious injury, you are to take life for life, eye for eye, tooth for tooth, hand for hand, foot for foot, burn for burn, wound for wound, bruise for bruise" (Ex. 21:22–25).

Scholars have consistently interpreted this verse to affirm the life of the mother and acknowledged a lack of clarity when it comes to the life of the child. The only verse of Scripture that has moral implications for abortion has not only been contested but generally used to show that an unborn child is not considered equal to a fully developed human. And it's not just liberal scholars and teachers who have come to this conclusion but even the most conservative ones.

Consider this quote from a book published by an evangelical publishing house in 1973:

> There are sharp differences among Christians with regard to abortion. Some consider it murder; others say the operation might be an act of mercy. Some believe that the soul enters the fetus at

---

10. It is also worth noting that we do have direct counsel from the early Christians, as we learned in chapter 6. While they were human and mostly male—which means they had their blind spots and limitations—their commitment to life was comprehensive and clear.

conception. Others feel that the zygote (fertilized ovum) is just a cell that may become a potential human being but is not yet one at the moment, and hence its removal is not "murder." The Bible is silent on the subject, although some Christians believe Exodus 21:22–23 may indicate a developing embryo or fetus was not regarded as a full human being, since inflicting an injury on a pregnant woman which resulted in its loss was to be punished by a fine rather than by death, under the "life for life" law.[11]

The quote is from a book called *Sex Is a Parent Affair* by Letha Scanzoni, and get this: it has a foreword written by none other than Dr. James Dobson, founder of Focus on the Family. Let that sink in. Dr. Dobson—in 1973, the same year as *Roe v. Wade*—endorsed a book that rightly says the Bible is silent on abortion except for one text in Exodus that seems to suggest an unborn child was not yet regarded as a full human being.

Certainly, there are other Bible passages that affirm the sanctity of life, even the potential for life in the womb, but they are more poetry than law. For example, Psalm 139 is a beautiful description about God knitting us together in the womb and having plans for us even as we develop in the belly of our mother. And there's that magnificent moment in the Gospels when Mary, pregnant with Jesus, visits Elizabeth, who is pregnant with John the Baptist, and the baby leaps for joy in Elizabeth's womb. These verses shaped my theological imagination as a young man and continue to fuel my passion for life in the womb to this day.

But Exodus stands alone in helping us navigate the complexities of abortion in the contemporary world. The passage in Exodus 21 states plainly that if anyone hurts or kills a woman, there are serious consequences—eye-for-eye, tooth-for-tooth consequences. And if a woman is killed, the law stipulates taking a life for a life. But with the

---

11. Letha Scanzoni, *Sex Is a Parent Affair: Help for Parents in Teaching Their Children about Sex* (Ventura, CA: Regal, 1973), 147.

unborn child, the law sets a fine instead. It is clear there is a different standard for the death of the mother, a fully grown human being, than for the unborn child. That's what many of the most influential evangelical leaders were saying in 1973. Based on what they wrote and said at the time, the dominant view was that there is a distinction between a mother and her unborn child, and that the Bible has a different ethic of life for each.

The point here is simply to demonstrate that abortion is complicated even for those who see the Bible as their primary authority. Even James Dobson and other evangelical leaders seem unclear on how they felt about it, at least in the 1970s. But one thing is for sure: it was not a central, definitive issue for people of faith, nothing like it is today. Of course, many of them changed their minds over the years, but in the 1970s many evangelicals saw abortion as a Catholic issue. As we will see, even Jerry Falwell by his own admission did not preach his first anti-abortion sermon until February 26, 1978—more than five years after *Roe*.

Fast-forward fifty years to today, when abortion, something the Bible barely even mentions, has become the single most important issue for many Christians. How did this happen? How did abortion, something Jesus never mentioned and something the Bible only barely addresses, become the most important issue for so many American Christians? For many white evangelicals over fifty, it is the only political issue they want to talk about, preach on, or vote on. What changed? How did abortion become the issue that eclipses all other issues related to life? How did it come to define what it means to be pro-life in America?

It warrants a deeper dive.

The Pivot from Segregation to Abortion

While we might assume that it was a careful reading of the Bible or adherence to the teachings of Jesus that has created our singular focus on abortion, that is not the case. Nor is it the case that it was the *Roe v. Wade* decision that catalyzed the anti-abortion movement we see today. As we dig into the history, particularly of evangelical Christianity in America, what we find is something else entirely, something really disturbing. And it is this history that reveals how and why we chose pro-birth over pro-life.

When my friend Lisa Sharon Harper and I hosted those Instagram town-hall discussions on abortion, one of our guests was a man named Randall Balmer, a Dartmouth College historian who has written extensively about how abortion took center stage for American evangelicals. In his book *Bad Faith*, Balmer describes the moment that redirected the course of his scholarship.[12] The year was 1990, and he was invited to a closed-door conference in Washington, DC, where he found himself in a room with "luminaries of the Religious Right," including Paul Weyrich, Ralph Reed, Richard Land, Carl F. H. Henry, Ed Dobson, and others.[13] Balmer describes hearing Weyrich, the architect of the Religious Right, deliver an impassioned talk in which "he declared that abortion had nothing whatsoever to do with the emergence of the Religious Right. [Ed] Dobson quickly concurred."[14]

Weyrich went on to explain that since the Goldwater campaign in 1964, he had been trying to mobilize evangelical voters, raising issues such as pornography, school prayer, the Equal Rights Amendment, and abortion but nothing was rallying them together—nothing, that is, until the Internal Revenue Service began to challenge the tax-exempt status of racially segregated schools.

Whoa.

It wasn't until 1979—six years after *Roe v. Wade*—that evangelical leaders rallied together in what became known as the Religious

---

12. Much of this chapter builds on the work of Randall Balmer, a friend and leader in the Red Letter Christians movement. I highly recommend all of his books, but related to this conversation, I especially recommend *Bad Faith: Race and the Rise of the Religious Right*.
13. Randall Balmer, *Bad Faith: Race and the Rise of the Religious Right* (Grand Rapids: Eerdmans, 2021), xi.
14. Balmer, *Bad Faith*, xii.

Right. But it wasn't abortion that brought them together; it was segregation. And it wasn't the need to eliminate segregation that united them but the need to keep it.

As a side note, it's unclear how much the Rev. Billy Graham foresaw the damaging impact ahead, but consider these words spoken just two years later in 1981 by one of America's most influential evangelical leaders: "I don't want to see religious bigotry in any form. It would disturb me if there was a wedding between the religious fundamentalists and the political right. The hard right has no interest in religion except to manipulate it."[15]

Also consider this: the Southern Baptist Convention, which is the largest and arguably among the most conservative Christian denominations in the US, passed a resolution in 1971 encouraging "Southern Baptists to work for legislation that will allow the possibility of abortion under such conditions as rape, incest, clear evidence of severe fetal deformity, and carefully ascertained evidence of the likelihood of damage to the emotional, mental, and physical health of the mother."[16] That was the Southern Baptists in 1971! Not only that, but they reaffirmed that position in 1974, one year after *Roe v. Wade*, and then again in 1976. The point is, abortion, even following *Roe v. Wade*, was not a rallying cry for the Southern Baptist Convention, or for many white Christians, but segregation was.

One of the most famous fundamentalists at the time, W. A. Criswell, pastor of First Baptist Church of Dallas, Texas, where Robert Jeffress is now pastor, had this to say: "I have always felt that it was only after a child was born and had a life separate from its mother that it became an individual person, and it has always, therefore, seemed to me that what is best for the mother and for the future should be allowed."[17] Criswell, however, was a segregationist.

15. Billy Graham said this in an interview with *Parade* magazine published February 1, 1981. Quoted in Richard A. Kauffman, "Faith and Freedom: Quotations to Stir the Heart and Mind," *Christianity Today*, July 11, 2005, www.christianitytoday.com/ct/2005/july/24.48.html.
16. Balmer, *Bad Faith*, 34.
17. W. A. Criswell quoted in "Abortion Decision: A Death Blow?" *Christianity Today*, February 16, 1973, www.christianitytoday.com/ct/1973/february-16/abortion-decision-death-blow.html.

Again, keep in mind that the backdrop at the time was segregation and the civil rights movement, which had climaxed in the late 1960s. After some major victories in the struggle for racial justice, such as the passing of the Civil Rights Act in 1964 and the Voting Rights Act of 1965, society began to shift toward racial equality. White folks in the South were especially upset about the shift. Just as many prominent white legislators had, for overtly racist reasons, left the Democratic Party to start the Dixiecrats in 1948, prominent white leaders in the 1970s were not happy about changes brought about by the civil rights movement. So while *Roe v. Wade* was in 1973, it closely followed the end of legal segregation.

As we look at American history, one thing that is disturbingly consistent is that the priorities of many white Christians seem to have been shaped more by racism than by Jesus. Our priorities have been shaped more by our pursuit of power than by a close reading of Scripture or faithful discipleship of our Savior. What ultimately made abortion a front-and-center issue began as a political strategy of the Religious Right. The goal was to unite evangelicals around an issue—any issue—to build a voting bloc for conservative causes and political candidates. The leaders of the Religious Right wanted political power, and they exploited religious belief to get that power.[18] The challenge, however, was that segregation—the cause that galvanized conservative voters—was proving difficult to champion.

Defending Segregation at Bob Jones University

In 1971, there was another Supreme Court case that is not as well known but just as significant historically as *Roe v. Wade*: *Green v. Connally*. In it, the Supreme Court ruled that a private school that practiced racial discrimination was ineligible for tax-exempt status. This had massive implications for "Christian" institutions that wanted

---

18. Kelley McDaniel, "Maine Voices: Anti-abortion Movement's History Shows How Faith Was Exploited for Votes," *Portland Press Herald*, May 13, 2022, www.pressherald.com/2022/05/13/maine -voices-anti-abortion-movements-history-shows-how-a-political-cause-became-a-religious-one/.

to continue to practice racial segregation, and Bob Jones University is where everything eventually came to a head. Bob Jones Jr., the school's founder, argued that racial segregation was mandated by the Bible, which obviously collided with recent changes in the law brought about by the civil rights movement.

When the IRS sent a letter informing Bob Jones University that it would lose its tax-exempt status if it continued to practice racial segregation, the university tried to appease the IRS by admitting one African American—a man who worked in the campus radio station—as a part-time student. He dropped out a month later. In 1975, again to placate the IRS, the school began admitting African Americans to the student body, but only if they were married. The fear was that allowing single African American students to attend could result in interracial marriage. The school had a strict policy on interracial dating. Anyone who decided to date interracially or who was even associated with organizations that advocated for interracial dating would be expelled.

One of my friends, pastor David Gibbons, attended Bob Jones in the 1980s. Dave's father was believed to be white, and his mother is Korean. And get this: when he applied to the school, he had to declare a race so he would not be guilty of interracial dating. He laughed when he told me that there were not a lot of Korean women at Bob Jones, so he declared his race as white to have some options. And, happily, he met and was able to date Becca, the woman who became his wonderful bride. God works through the cracks of everything.

Unsurprisingly, the administration at Bob Jones University failed in its efforts to hide its racism from anyone, much less the IRS. In January 1976, after years of warnings, the IRS rescinded the school's tax-exempt status. It wasn't until they realized defending racial discrimination was not a winnable platform that Bob Jones University began to pivot. What could they rally around to achieve similar goals? As Weyrich had discovered, pornography, school prayer, the Equal Rights Amendment, and many other issues garnered support from many Christians, but nothing provided the united front they needed to fortify a conservative political movement—at least, not yet.

It became disturbingly clear that white evangelicals and fundamentalists were desperately looking for a common rallying cry, something to unite them politically. Once they had political power, they could pursue all the causes that mattered most to them, regardless of how unpalatable some of them, such as segregation, might be to the wider public. The challenge was that many evangelicals at the time wanted nothing to do with politics. They preferred to avoid most political issues and to focus instead on spiritual issues: personal salvation and life after death rather than life before death.

Back in the 1970s, there were not a lot of political issues evangelical Christians could rally around other than segregation. Remember, up to this point, abortion wasn't even on the radar.[19] But it soon would be.

Lawyers and activists who wanted to uphold segregation agreed that they did not have a case based on race, given the recent victory of the 1964 Civil Rights Act. And "separate but equal" no longer stood a chance since the 1954 decision in *Brown v. Board of Education*. They could not discriminate based on race, so what were they to do? That's when Paul Weyrich and other prominent white activists initiated some of their most strategic organizing—especially among evangelical Christians—since the 1925 Scopes Monkey Trials about teaching evolution in public schools. Up to this point with Bob Jones University, there was no real unifying force other than racism, and no one wanted to admit to or overtly organize around that, if for no other reason than racial discrimination did not stand a chance in court. But religious liberty did.

For some Christian institutions like Bob Jones, the cause of religious liberty initially became a strategic way to posture the right to

---

19. According to Randall Balmer, "One of the most durable myths in recent history is that the Religious Right, the coalition of conservative evangelicals and fundamentalists, emerged as a political movement in response to the US Supreme Court's 1973 *Roe v. Wade* ruling legalizing abortion." Randall Balmer, quoted in "Abortion Is a Common Experience for US Women."

discriminate. The decision to fight on the grounds of religious liberty rather than racial discrimination was a strategic, legal, and pragmatic choice. The fight would be about the freedom to practice religion as a constitutional right, even if the strategy was deeply rooted in racism. However, some were ready to move on from the issue of race altogether and focusing on abortion provided an exit strategy.

In 1983, Bob Jones lost the case defending their right to discriminate, and when they did, they flew the American flag at half-mast. Even so, Bob Jones kept fighting for their right to discriminate for another seventeen years. The university did not change its segregated dating policy until 2000. That's not a typo: *2000*. It cannot be overstated that racism and money—not faithful discipleship, biblical values, moral courage, or Christian conscience—were the primary forces at work.

What happened at Bob Jones University came to represent some of the worst forms of racism baptized in theological language, so much so that many leaders, including Billy Graham, who had attended Bob Jones in the 1960s, distanced themselves from it, referring to themselves as evangelicals rather than fundamentalists.[20]

When it became apparent that defending racism and segregation was neither politically expedient nor financially advantageous, abortion became the strategic issue around which the Religious Right chose to rally. While there are concerns today that are worthy of respect and engagement by conservative Christians, this at least is clear. The Religious Right, the forerunner of the Christian conservative movement today, was birthed in service not of biblical values but of racial segregation and the defense of white superiority. Or as my friend Lisa Sharon Harper puts it, "The contemporary pro-life movement was gestated in the womb of segregation."

---

20. Bob Jones Jr. and Billy Graham continued to have a tense relationship. In March of 1966, Bob Jones Jr. said Graham was "doing more harm to the cause of Jesus Christ than any living man." Paul Hyde, "Billy Graham Had a Rocky Relationship with Bob Jones University and Its Past Presidents," *Greenville News*, February 21, 2018, www.greenvilleonline.com/story/news/2018/02/21/billy-graham-had-rocky-relationship-bob-jones-university-and-its-past-presidents/360074002/.

It was also around this time that the Religious Right began to focus on the power of the Supreme Court, another shift that continues to leave its mark. Remember, in the 2016 presidential election, many white evangelicals chose to support a candidate who openly violated some of their deepest moral convictions, hoping he would deliver on his promise to appoint pro-life federal judges and pro-life justices to the nation's highest court. Judas betrayed Jesus with a kiss for a few pieces of silver, and many evangelicals betrayed Jesus for a few seats on the Supreme Court and a bunch of federal judges. But let's not get too far offtrack.

Abortion Takes the Stage

It took several years and a lot of theological gymnastics, but abortion eventually became the Religious Right's definitive moral issue, along with sexuality. Later there were banners, bumper stickers, and even people carrying a jarred fetus outside abortion clinics, but all that took time.

The fact is, evangelicals were initially hard to persuade that abortion was a central issue. Even Jerry Falwell issued no public statement on abortion until 1975, and by his own admission did not preach against it until 1978, more than five years after the *Roe v. Wade* decision.[21] Ed Dobson, who was then Falwell's assistant and who ended up being a key leader in the Moral Majority, put it plainly: "The Religious New Right did not start because of a concern about abortion." He goes on, "I sat in the non-smoke-filled back room with the Moral Majority, and I frankly do not remember abortion being mentioned as a reason why we ought to do something."[22]

When *Conservative Digest* documented evangelical discontent with President Jimmy Carter in 1979, it was IRS regulations that

---

21. Falwell is often quoted for these strong words: "The Supreme Court had just made a decision by a seven-to-two margin that would legalize the killing of millions of unborn children." But it is noteworthy that this statement was made fourteen years *after Roe v. Wade,* yet another indicator of how low on the priority list this issue was. Balmer, *Bad Faith,* 31.
22. Balmer, *Bad Faith,* 46.

topped their list of concerns; his stance on abortion wasn't even mentioned. By 1980, even though Jimmy Carter, a self-professing born-again Christian, had sought to reduce the incidence of abortion, he was ousted by his Republican opponent, Ronald Reagan. This despite the fact that Reagan, as governor of California, had in 1967 signed into law the most liberal abortion bill in the country.

One of the pivotal moments in Reagan's presidential campaign was when he spoke to a packed house of fifteen to twenty thousand evangelical Christians in Reunion Arena in Dallas on August 22, 1980. While Reagan called out the "unconstitutional regulatory agenda" directed by the Internal Revenue Service "against independent schools," he made no mention at all of abortion.[23] In the words of Randall Balmer, "Although abortion had begun to emerge as a rallying cry late in the 1980 campaign, the real roots of the Religious Right lay not in the defense of the fetus but in the defense of racial segregation."[24]

Many evangelicals saw abortion as a "Catholic issue," not something central to Scripture, which evangelicals consider their primary moral authority. In 1968, five years before *Roe v. Wade*, twenty-five leading evangelical theologians were convened by the flagship evangelical magazine *Christianity Today*. Their purpose was to find common ground on abortion. After several days of deliberations, they issued a statement acknowledging that they could not agree on any one position, and that the ambiguities of the issue allowed for many different approaches. "Whether or not the performance of an induced abortion is sinful we are not agreed," the statement read, "but about the necessity and permissibility for it under certain circumstances we are in accord."[25]

The statement went on to list possible justifications for abortion

---

23. Balmer, *Bad Faith*, 62.
24. Balmer, *Bad Faith*, 65.
25. "A Protestant Affirmation on the Control of Human Reproduction," a consensus of twenty-five evangelical scholars, *Christianity Today*, November 8, 1968, www.christianitytoday.com/ct/1968/november-8/protestant-affirmation-on-control-of-human-reproduction.html.

that included "individual health, family welfare, and social responsibilities."[26] It even noted that there are instances when fetal life "may have to be abandoned to maintain full and secure family life."[27] So it is safe to say that abortion was not a defining issue of evangelicalism in the 1960s or 1970s.

Without diminishing the passion many people, including myself, feel to eradicate abortion today, we need to understand and reckon with the history of how abortion became the single issue that eclipsed all others. So much so that now when many people think "pro-life" they think about one thing only: abortion. Our history shows that the singular focus many Christians have on abortion did not originate with devotion to Jesus or to Scripture but with the social and political tensions that arose during and after the civil rights movement. It was less about *Roe v. Wade* and more about *Brown v. Board of Education*. It was less about the pursuit of life and more about the pursuit of power.

Broadly speaking, Christians in America today have a wide array of moral issues they care about, and issues such as poverty, immigration, the environment, and healthcare all make the list for various Christian demographics. However, white Christians in America are the only demographic that consistently view abortion as either their only priority or their top priority; they also view it as a binary issue that one is either for or against. That's why some consider it a litmus test of authentic Christian faith.

Abortion is much farther down the priority list for most born-again Christians of color. Many other issues, such as welcoming immigrants, providing affordable healthcare, and caring for the poor and most vulnerable among us are often in the forefront for Christians who have roots outside white evangelicalism. And while issues such as

---

26. This phrasing comes from a revised version of the 1968 statement issued in 1970 by the Christian Medical Society. Christian Medical Society, "A Protestant Affirmation on the Control of Human Reproduction," with responses by Claude Stipe, Richard H. Bube, Earl J. Reeves, and Russell L. Mixter, *Journal of the American Scientific Affiliation* 22 (June 1970): 46–47, www.asa3.org/ASA/PSCF/1970/JASA6-70Christian.html.

27. Christian Medical Society, "A Protestant Affirmation."

abortion and same-sex marriage matter to them, they consider other issues to be more firmly rooted in the core teachings of Christ and in the whole of the Bible. After all, there are more than two thousand verses that talk about caring for the poor, only about seven that mention same-sex relationships,[28] and only one or two that can be interpreted to address abortion.

I am hopeful that we can still find common ground, not on ideologies and not even on questions such as when life begins but on how we might better address why many people choose not to carry a pregnancy to term. If we really want to reduce the number of abortions, then we must use our advocacy and our votes to support strategies that address those reasons: affordable childcare, universal healthcare, early childhood education, paid parental leave, raising the minimum wage, and more. Measures such as these could substantially reduce abortions and enhance the lives of both the born and unborn.

No matter how strongly we feel about abortion or any other issue, I hope we can agree that we must also be committed to loving those who disagree with us, even those who might consider us to be their enemies. And let us agree to show special love for those who have been directly impacted by the issues we care about, many of whom may be closer to us than we know. "We cannot love issues," wrote Henri Nouwen, "but we can love people, and the love of people reveals to us the way to deal with issues."[29]

Katie Jo's Story

Katie and I talked and prayed about how she wanted to be involved with this book. Throughout my writing process, she has been so gracious as my partner, my best friend, and my sounding board. She read

---

28. See Genesis 9; Genesis 19; Leviticus 18:22; 20:13; Deuteronomy 23:17–18; Romans 1:26–27; 1 Corinthians 6:9; 1 Timothy 1:10.

29. Henri Nouwen, *Peacework: Prayer, Resistance, Community* (Maryknoll, NY: Orbis, 2005, 2014), 78.

portions of this book repeatedly to help me get it right. But I had concerns about whether to share her story. While I believe those who have experienced abortion need to be front and center anytime we have a conversation about it, I also wanted to be careful not to exploit her experience. Ultimately, we decided that the best approach was for Katie to put things in her own words, so here you go.

From Katie Jo:

This is the chapter I was most nervous about. Shane and I don't completely agree on everything surrounding abortion and, to be honest, I haven't liked everything he has ever written. I hope that's not a shocker. But I really wanted to like this one.

When I read an early draft of this chapter and got to the part where Shane told my story, I didn't like it, so we took it out. It's hard to read someone else's retelling of your life. While I trust him completely and asked him to write my story, he still didn't get it right. (This was hard for him because he's a perfectionist.) And it's not for lack of trying. He has heard me talk about and process the many emotions of my abortion for more than twelve years. That alone should tell you how nuanced and personal having an abortion is: no one else can fully understand what it's like.

When I had my abortion seventeen years ago, I was engaged to someone I was looking forward to spending my life with. When I found out I was pregnant, I called him right away. He was not excited and quickly arranged for me to have an abortion. He was ashamed. He didn't want his family to know he was having premarital sex. Feeling like there were no other options, we decided to have an abortion.

When we drove up to the clinic, I was met by an escort after we parked. We needed an escort because there was a crowd of protestors surrounding the clinic, all of them hurling a barrage of insults. "You're a terrible mother!" "You're a terrible father!" Those are the only ones I remember. I also remember seeing only white men protesting. There were so many people that we had to push our way through them to get inside. It was awful.

Once we got inside, I was taken to a counselor who made sure this was a decision I wanted. We waited. Eventually, I was called back and given an ultrasound. There was some discussion that I was too far along because I was at the end of twelve weeks and abortions going into the thirteenth week could not be performed there. The next thing I remember is waking up in a recovery room with my fiancé sitting next to me.

We drove home. I was sad. Then I felt guilty for being sad because I knew I was supposed to feel relief. The emotions I experienced after my abortion were complex, and they're still complex. Sometimes I feel sad, angry, sad again, relief sometimes but not often, happy, guilty, that I'm a bad mom, acceptance, and the list goes on. Any time I reflect on that day or find myself in a discussion about abortion, the one thing I almost never feel is love.

Let's love big. Let's extend our concern for life beyond the womb to all of life. Let's build a movement of Christians that is truly pro-life, not just pro-birth, a movement that advocates for life comprehensively and without exceptions. Let's recommit ourselves to love the people affected by issues such as abortion. After all, we are called to love our neighbors, not our ideologies.

It will be interesting to see what happens in the next era of the experiment we call America, especially as abortion continues to take center stage. It will also be interesting to see what role Christians play as advocates, peacemakers, and reconcilers. As we have seen over the centuries, Christians have too often been on the wrong side of history on issues of life and racial justice. I hope the next generation will look back and see that we were more faithful to Christ than some of the generations before us. May it be so.

RETHINKING LIFE

- Abortion is complicated for many reasons. What makes abortion especially complicated for you?
- How do you respond to the idea that, regardless of our position on abortion, we should be pro-active, pro-love, and pro-compassion? What do you think that means in practical terms?
- Which of the following four options best describes your view on abortion? Share the reasons for your response.
  — Abortion should be illegal.
  — Abortion should be legal, safe, and rare.
  — Abortion should be legal, with no restrictions.
  — Other:
- Which, if any, of the facts about abortion (pp. 188–91) surprise you?
- What's your view about what the Bible says and does not say about abortion?
- How do you respond to Lisa Sharon Harper's statement, "The contemporary pro-life movement was gestated in the womb of segregation"? In what ways, if any, does this influence your view of abortion or of the pro-life movement?
- What do you think it means to be a bridge builder or a force for good when it comes to the deeply divisive issue of abortion?
- Though we may not all agree on everything, we can avoid extreme rhetoric and seek common ground. What are some ways people on both sides of abortion could take action together?

## PART 3

Repairing the Foundation

## CHAPTER 13

Be a Truth Teller

Throughout this book, I've attempted to tell the truth about our history, especially the parts that are hard to hear. I know it isn't easy to read some of the things written by theological giants such as Augustine, Thomas Aquinas, John Chrysostom, Martin Luther, and others. And yet I hope you feel, as I do, that we can embrace the truth they spoke while simultaneously rejecting the untruth they spoke. Truth is from God, always, no matter who the messenger is. And the devil is a liar, a liar who can at times confuse even the brightest of our theologians and preachers and saints. It is so important to acknowledge that the church can be both a force for good and a force for evil—sometimes simultaneously. As we now consider what it might mean to repair the cracks in our foundation for life, to once again become a force for life, we begin by committing ourselves to be truth tellers.

Truth telling is the beginning, the first step toward healing. After truth telling and confession, we can then move toward healing, repair, and reconciliation. But truth is where we start. And the truth is what sets us free! Hiding the truth only keeps us captive to shame, fear, guilt, and other life-sucking things.

We need to tell the truth about ourselves. We need to tell the truth about history. We need to tell the truth about the sins of our past, even if we were not directly responsible. And we need to tell the truth about the church's complicity with evil, even if it wasn't all the church all the time, even if the church was simultaneously faithful and unfaithful.

Telling the truth means celebrating the good things and confessing the bad things. And it is always liberating, even when it is hard.

We need to be truth tellers in all things, but one of the issues I propose we tackle first is that of our own history as a country. As we explored in chapter 11, instead of telling the truth about our national history, we have created a mythology about our inherent goodness, and even a theology that not only justifies and defends the sins of our past but also denies or minimizes the toxic legacy of those sins that continues to compromise our foundation for life in the present. I'm speaking specifically about the sin of slavery and its legacy of racism.

Festering Wounds

We all want to move on from the mistakes of our national past, but we can't heal the festering wounds of slavery and racism without first acknowledging the truth about them. Festering wounds are life threatening. Ask me how I know.

For two years, Katie and I temporarily relocated from Philadelphia to the South to be closer to both of our families. (Katie's family is in North Carolina and mine is in Tennessee.) We lived on a "skoolie," a school bus that had been converted into a solar-powered mobile tiny home (with a composting toilet). It was a pretty great experience, and Katie mentioned she may write a book about it titled *Living Our Bus Life Now*. In case you missed it, that was a wink at the smiling preacher Joel Osteen, who wrote *Your Best Life Now*. As great as it was, there were also some downsides to the bus life, one of which was the spiders. At one point, I got bit by one on the foot.

To be honest, both Katie and I had already had a few spider bites at that point, and they weren't a big deal. So when this spider bit me, as per usual, I simply monitored it to see how it looked. Two days in, the bite wound was pretty red and starting to feel warm. I didn't have a fever or anything, so I continued to wait it out, and it continued to get more and more sore. Then one day when I got out of bed, I could barely walk on it. So off to urgent care we went.

I was a little embarrassed to go if I'm perfectly honest. I sort of shrugged it off when I met the doctor, using the "I just wanted to be safe" line. But when the doctor examined my foot, he seemed pretty concerned, and the more he looked, the more concerned he got. I told the doctor how I kept thinking it would go away, and also explained that I didn't really feel much different now than I had when I first got the bite. It didn't seem like the poison was making me sick.

That's when he said this: "It probably was a poisonous spider, but it's not the poison that got you. What got you is the residue, the bacteria left from not treating it." My first thought was, *There's a sermon in that. That'll preach.* He went on to tell me that the infection could get into my bloodstream, and that could be serious. It could end me. I asked him to help me not die. And he did.

All that's to say, the original sin of America's past may be over in the sense of chattel slavery, and the poison of what was done may be diluted now. But the toxic residue remains. And it will be deadly if we don't attend to it.

"Like a boil that can never be cured as long as it is covered up . . . injustice must be exposed . . . before it can be cured." That's how Dr. King put it. If we ignore or minimize the sins of our past, they become festering wounds.

As Christians, we don't have the option of willful ignorance, of pretending the brutal history of slavery hasn't left a scar. Not only is there a scar, there is an infected wound that is poisoning the bloodstream that gives us all life. Injustice must be exposed before it can be healed. We cannot have racial reconciliation until we have truth. As my friend Jemar Tisby says, "History and Scripture teach us there can be no reconciliation without repentance. There can be no repentance without confession. And there can be no confession without truth."[1]

Amen to that.

---

1. Jemar Tisby, *The Color of Compromise: The Truth about the American Church's Complicity in Racism* (Grand Rapids: Zondervan, 2019), 15.

No Distractions

Being a truth teller about slavery and colonization requires taking a painfully honest look at America's past misdeeds, but it also requires telling the truth about how racism continues to plague our country today. While we need to tell the truth about Jim Crow and lynching in the past, we also need to tell the truth about issues such as mass incarceration and systemic racism in the present. And yet at a time when the need to confront racism has been front-page news, many of us have been preoccupied with a distraction instead, which is the culture war debate about critical race theory (CRT). To be clear, CRT is an important topic, but it has also been used by some to create a distraction so we don't have to talk about the things we really should be talking about, including telling the truth about our history.

I know a thing or two about distractions. Back in the day (the late 1900s), I went to circus school, and among the many skills I picked up was magic tricks. I tend to keep that on the down-low because once folks find out you know how to do a little magic or that you know how to juggle knives—much less that you know how to breathe fire—you are always on call for entertainment. So I only bust out my magic skills when I want to. But one of the important things I learned about magic is the core principle of distraction. The goal is to distract people into looking at one hand so you can get away with something else in the other hand. And that's a pretty good analogy for much of the debate around CRT: it's a way of distracting us from what we should really be looking at. Because what we should be looking at is the painful truth of slavery and the persistence of racism in American culture and institutions.

Here are just a few examples of how the distraction dynamic has played out with CRT. In 2021, the state of Texas proposed and passed measures that play down references to slavery in schools, to the point of keeping words such as *slavery* from even appearing in textbooks. That same year, states such as Louisiana, New Hampshire, and Tennessee introduced bills that would "ban teaching about the enduring legacies of slavery and segregationist laws, or that any state or country is inherently racist or sexist."[1] Some politicians said they didn't want our kids to be taught about slavery because it could make white kids feel bad about themselves or ashamed because of the sins of our ancestors. This line of thinking is not an option for Christians. What our faith teaches is truth telling. In a culture saturated by lies and willful ignorance, we are called to be champions of truth. And we can be champions of truth while simultaneously being champions of hope, redemption, and reconciliation.

No distractions.

Experiments in Public Truth Telling

My friend Bryan Stevenson says, "We can't get our future right until we get our history right." Bryan is the founder of the Equal Justice Initiative (EJI), a nonprofit based in Montgomery, Alabama, that provides legal representation to people who may have been wrongly convicted and people who can't afford effective representation. EJI also founded the National Memorial for Peace and Justice, sometimes informally referred to as the National Lynching Memorial. The memorial is an ambitious project in truth telling about racial terrorism and its legacy.

One of the exhibits at the memorial features glass jars containing soil gathered from the sites where Black people were lynched. It's a powerful way to remember the thousands of lives lost to acts of racially motivated terror. I had the heavy, holy experience of filling one of the jars with dirt to help tell one of those stories.

The memorial also features 805 steel monuments, each a six-foot tall rectangular column that hangs from the roof of an open-air structure. The columns are inscribed with the names of more than four thousand victims of lynching in America. Not only are those names preserved and memorialized there in Montgomery but the memorial also created a monument for each county in the US where those lynchings occurred, also inscribed with the names of the victims and the dates they were lynched. These additional 805 monuments lie on the ground out in the open air. Each county has been invited to claim their monument, to own their history, and then to honor the lives of victims by establishing a memorial in their county. There's no excuse for ignoring the truth of the past. While some counties have claimed their historic markers, many others remain unclaimed.

Sadly, there are also many other monuments in our country that honor not the victims of injustice but those who perpetrated it. To this day, there are monuments to the Confederacy across the South. As I mentioned earlier, the Tennessee Capitol building displayed a statue of Nathan Bedford Forrest, one of the founders of the Ku Klux Klan, until 2021. *Until 2021.* It is clear that some people are more committed to preserving Confederate monuments than they are to honoring and protecting Black lives. It is time to change that.

I've started making it a habit to research the history behind the names of places, especially of the places where I grew up. For example, who is William Blount, the namesake of a high school I attended for one year? I've also started researching the backgrounds of people who are honored with historic monuments, and I am often embarrassed by the people we honor and the people we erase. Not long ago, I went on a pilgrimage to the mountains—on the border between what is now Tennessee and North Carolina—where it is believed the Trail of Tears (1837–39) began. The federal government forced tens of thousands of Native Americans off their ancestral lands in Georgia, Tennessee, Alabama, North Carolina, and Florida.[2] They were forced to walk hundreds of miles and many of them died from exposure, disease, and

---

2. History.com Editors, "Trail of Tears," *History*, July 7, 2020, www.history.com/topics/native-american-history/trail-of-tears.

starvation. The name Trail of Tears comes from a Cherokee phrase meaning "the trail where we cried." I couldn't find a single historic marker to memorialize the tens of thousands of Native peoples who were forcibly removed, terrorized, and tortured.

It's important to note that honoring those on the wrong side of history doesn't happen only in the South. In Philadelphia, the school where my wife has taught initiated a name change in 2022. Sheridan Elementary School was named after Union General Philip Sheridan, a man well-known for his brutal campaigns against Native Americans. He's also known for his infamous quote, "The only good Indian is a dead Indian." The school conducted a vote to choose a new name, and the winner was Gloria Casarez, the city of Philadelphia's first director of LGBTQ affairs and a fierce advocate for the LGBTQ equality. She had also been a student at the school. It's pretty powerful to think about who we honor and remember, isn't it?

Monuments, memorials, and place names that honor those who enslaved, brutalized, and slaughtered other human beings are just one of the ways we have distorted the truth of our history. All of them must be replaced, but that is just the beginning of what it means to remember history accurately and to celebrate those who are truly worthy of honor.

One country that's ahead of us when it comes to telling the truth with monuments is Germany. When I traveled through Germany, I saw memorials to the lives lost in the Holocaust almost everywhere I went. Germany's historic markers, museums, and memorials to the victims of World War II serve as a constant reminder of what happened in their Nazi past, and Germans have passed laws that prohibit publicly denying the Holocaust. They ensure that we don't forget, and that we don't repeat that evil.

After September 11, we constantly heard the refrain, "Never forget." Memorials were established to remember the names of the people who lost their lives in those horrific, evil attacks and to honor the bravery and sacrifice of firefighters and first responders who gave their lives. It would be unthinkable to erect statues honoring the terrorists as a way of remembering 9/11. And yet that is exactly what we have done with other parts of our history. When it comes to the Civil War, we created monuments honoring the folks who were on the wrong side of history, those who fought against equality and freedom and the dignity of every person. We honored the victimizers rather than the victims. There is an old proverb that puts it like this: "Until the lions have their own historians, the history of the hunt will always glorify the hunter."

Thankfully, we live in an age when those whose lives have been historically marginalized are telling the truth and it is setting us all free. The truth not only sets the oppressed free but it also paves the way to freedom for those who have done the oppressing.

The American Church Can Be a Moral Force for Life

An essential part of telling the truth about our national past is telling the truth about the American church, both the good and the bad, as we've attempted to do throughout this book. That truth is that the American church has been both a moral force and a moral failure when it comes to protecting life. Many of our denominations formed because some white Christians were more committed to defending slavery than defending Black lives. But that doesn't have to be our legacy as we turn our attention to repairing the cracks in our foundation for life.

The church has an essential role to play in leading with moral courage and creating innovative restorative projects. To start, churches can begin by learning the history of the land in which their people live and on which their buildings are located. Who were the original inhabitants? If they were Native tribes, what happened to them? Every church and region can do an audit of their land history to seek and tell the truth. Once we know our history, we can ask what true repentance and repair might look like—or as we've been asking in this book, what love requires of us. Repair might look different in Tulsa, Oklahoma, than it does in Selma, Alabama. Repair might look different for the Catholic Church than it does for the Southern Baptist Convention. The important thing is that truth telling should always lead to repair and concrete restorative actions.

Princeton Theological Seminary is one recent example of a Christian institution taking restorative action to repair the wounds of its role in slavery. "We did not want to shy away from the uncomfortable part of our history and the difficult conversations that revealing the truth would produce," said seminary president M. Craig Barnes.[3]

After a year-long dive into its role in doing harm, the seminary announced a $27.6 million reparations initiative. And many students and alumni wanted to do more, suggesting at least 15 percent of the seminary's $986 million endowment, approximately $147 million. While there were competing visions for what should be done with the money, the seminary committed to multiple initiatives, including full-tuition and cash scholarships for students descended from slaves or from underrepresented groups, renaming the seminary library for its first African-American graduate, and hiring a full-time director for their Center for Black Church Studies. While students and alumni are asking the seminary to do more, it's a start. It also demonstrates the importance of beginning with truth and following through with repentance and repair.[4]

Another thing the church can do is to think about how we use our buildings to tell the truth and to honor life. I've teamed up with

---

3. Valerie Russ, "Princeton Theological Seminary Pledges $27 Million Reparations Plan," *Philadelphia Inquirer*, October 22, 2019, www.inquirer.com/news/reparations-princeton-theological-seminary-slavery-repent-27-million-20191022.html.

4. Georgetown University has also embarked on a multi-million-dollar reparations effort to create scholarships for the descendants of those who were enslaved. Rachel L. Swarns, "Is Georgetown's $400,000-a-Year Plan to Aid Slave Descendants Enough?" *New York Times*, October 30, 2019, www.nytimes.com/2019/10/30/us/georgetown-slavery-reparations.html.

friends in Philadelphia around a project called Memorials to the Lost that helps places of worship create a space to honor the lives of people lost to gun violence.[5] We display T-shirts with the names and ages of everyone killed by guns in our city or state in the past year. As folks go to worship, they see the truth about the crisis of gun violence, and they leave with a sense of urgency to stop it.

Another project I've been part of is writing *Common Prayer*, a collection of daily prayers that invites faith communities from around the world to pray together for the most pressing issues of the day. Throughout the year, we pray for the ongoing tragedies of life, and we also remember some of the great champions for life and allow them to inspire us in our work for life today.[6]

These are just a few examples of public truth telling and how the church can take the lead in being a moral force for life. This is the kind of truth telling that leads to repair and social change. We need more of it.

The Sacrament of Confession

Not only do we need to tell the truth about the sins of our nation and the sins of the church, we also need to do some personal truth telling as well. As Jesus said, we need to get the log out of our own eye first. To varying degrees, we have all been complicit with the desecration of human life. We are all equally capable of the same evil and of the same compassion. That's why humility and confession have been so central to Christian spirituality throughout the centuries.

Scripture repeatedly speaks of how we should confess our sins to God and to one another. Confession, which is a form of truth telling, is the first step toward healing. Confession paves the way for

---

5. To learn more, see "Memorials to the Lost," Heeding God's Call to End Gun Violence, www.heedinggodscall.org/memorials-to-the-lost.
6. To find out more about *Common Prayer*, visit our website: www.CommonPrayer.net.

repentance and reconciliation. That's why it is so important for us to confess when we fall short of what love requires of us.

Confession is countercultural. Not many of us make a habit of voluntarily, preemptively saying "I am sorry" or "I was wrong," but those are some powerful words. In a world where any confession of wrong stirs fears getting canceled or inviting the wrath of social-media opportunists ready to pounce on vulnerable prey, confession is an endangered art.

For many Christians, confession is considered a sacrament, meaning it is a holy, healing, and transcendent practice that imparts divine grace. *Mysterion*, the Greek word for sacrament, means "holy mystery." I am convinced that there is something holy that happens when we admit we are wrong. I don't just think that's true, I know it's true. The world is not looking for Christians who are perfect. It is looking for Christians who are honest.

When people say to me, "The church is full of hypocrites," I tell them, "No, it's not, we've always got room for more." I learned that from my friend Tony Campolo, with whom I started Red Letter Christians. He told me many years ago that we all have internal struggles, contradictions, and hypocrisies. The goal is to tell the truth about them as best we can so that tomorrow we are less of a hypocrite than we are today.

Before Jesus was crucified, he had a profound encounter with Pontius Pilate, in which Jesus said, "Everyone on the side of truth listens to me" (John 18:37). Pilate then tried to diminish the importance of truth itself, retorting, "What is truth?" It's an exchange that continues to resonate in our context. There are lots of folks in the world today who are truth deniers, and it is doing a lot of damage to the world, especially as we seek to repair the cracks in our foundation for the sacredness of life. As we endeavor to tell the truth, there will continue to be those who try to diminish it, who ask with Pilate, "What is truth?" But let us listen to Jesus and stand with him on the side of truth. Let us tell the truth about our past, the truth about the church, and the truth about ourselves.

RETHINKING LIFE

- Telling the truth about our national history requires difficult conversations. How would you characterize your experience of having such conversations? For example, have you tended to avoid them, initiated them, gotten caught up instead in distraction issues, or something else?
- How do you respond to the idea that truth telling should always lead to repair and concrete restorative actions? In what ways does it challenge you? In what ways does it encourage you?
- Monuments can be examples of both public truth hiding and public truth telling. What experiences have you had of both? For example, what monuments have you encountered that honor victimizers? Who should have been honored instead? What monuments have you encountered that honor victims? How did the experience impact you?
- In what ways, if any, has your church been a moral force for life? In what other ways would you like to see your church lead with moral courage and create restoration or reparation projects?
- What do you know about the history of your context and place? Are there things that have happened in the past that might need to be confessed and healed? What might truth telling look like where you are?
- Jesus said that the truth will set us free. When have you seen the truth set people free? For example, can you think of a story of forgiveness or confession that led to restoration, in your own life or in the life of someone you know? What insights from that experience might help you to be a truth teller repairing the foundation for life?

## CHAPTER 14

Practice Proximity

Proximity to the suffering of the world is essential if we are going to be champions of life. Proximity to those impacted by injustice gives us a sense of urgency, a constant reminder of what is at stake and how important it is to get in the way of injustice. Proximity is exactly what Jesus did when he left all the comforts of heaven to join the human struggle here on earth. He could have chosen to be born to earthly power and wealth. Instead, he was born as a brown-skinned refugee baby. As an adult, he was homeless and executed on a cross as a wrongfully convicted criminal. Jesus lived a marginalized existence in every way from the day he was born until the day he was killed.

Jesus chose proximity. And he offers us the countercultural invitation to live as he lived by making the same choice: to lean into the suffering of the world. While nearly every force in our society compels us to move away from suffering—out of high-crime neighborhoods and away from people who don't look like us—the gravity of the gospel pulls us in the opposite direction: toward the suffering, toward the pain, toward those on the margins, and away from centers of wealth and power, hipness and comfort.

Having said that, I want to acknowledge one other dynamic here. For those among us who are from communities that have been historically marginalized, being proximate to pain is not a choice. Many people do not get to choose whether to be near to suffering because they are born into it. Those who are marginalized do not get to choose which issues they care about; the issues choose them. Gun violence chooses them. Police brutality chooses them. Immigration chooses them. They are born into struggle.

We need to understand that the option to choose proximity is itself a privilege. One way of defining privilege is that we have the freedom to choose which issues we care about and which ones we don't. It is a privilege to opt out of some justice issues because they either don't interest us or don't directly affect us. That's why proximity—being in relationship with folks whose survival is at stake—is so clutch. When it comes to repairing the foundation for life, nothing puts a fire in our bones like proximity. The urgency we feel on any given issue is often proportionate to how it impacts us or people we know and love.

On almost every issue of life we've addressed, what moved my soul and changed my thinking was connected to being in relationship with people who had been impacted by the injustices. And I think that's how change happens for most of us. I don't know too many people who changed their minds because they lost an argument. I don't know many people who have been talked into thinking differently or even preached into thinking differently. But I do know tons of people who have been moved in their hearts, and then their heads followed. I know many people who have been "storied in" to new thinking, and even more who have been moved by relationships, especially with those whose lives are affected by issues of life and death or injustice and racism.

When it comes to repairing the foundation for life, one of the biggest challenges too many of us face is a lack of proximity. We have a relationship problem and a geography problem more than a theology problem. For example, it's not that we don't care about poor people but that we don't know many poor people. It's impossible to love our neighbors as ourselves if we don't know them.

We can talk about immigrants and have strong opinions without knowing any immigrants. We can share our views about abortion, but not with those who have had one. We can talk about the LGBTQ community and still exclude them from the conversation. We can make policies around affordable housing without inviting people who need homes to the table.

Mother Teresa was one of my early role models in practicing proximity. She used to say, "It may be very fashionable to talk about the poor, but not as fashionable to talk to them." She knew all too well that we can talk about justice and have all the right bumper stickers on our cars and books on our shelves but still not be in close relationship with those affected by the issues we say we care about.

So what exactly does it look like to choose proximity? Before I answer that question, I want to share two snapshots of how proximity shaped my activism. One happened on death row and the other happened at the US-Mexico border. As you read each story, I invite you to imagine you are in the scenes with me, experiencing the same things I am and having face-to-face conversations with the same people. How might proximity to this person challenge your views on capital punishment or immigration? What might love require of you in each situation?

Life on Death Row

For ten years, I've been visiting the Riverbend Maximum Security Institution and spending time with the guys on unit 2, Tennessee's death row. I go every chance I get and often take others with me, including my mom; my wife, Katie Jo; and several friends. Every visit has an impact on me, but the experience that stands out most happened on one of my very first visits.

I had just spoken at a conference in Nashville, where I talked about grace, redemption, and my hope for ending the death penalty. On my way out, as I was headed to Riverbend, I bumped into the then-governor of Tennessee, Bill Haslam, who was also speaking at the conference. He had just set the dates for the first few executions to take place after nearly ten years without one in the state of Tennessee.

Honestly, I wasn't sure what to say, but I knew I wanted to say something. I've found that talking to governors who single-handedly have the power over life and death is a delicate thing. You don't want to say anything that could harden their hearts or shut down the possibility of stopping an execution. As we were talking, I recalled that Mother Teresa, in a similar encounter with a governor, had said, "Do what Jesus would have you do." So that's pretty much what I said to Governor Haslam, whom I knew to be a regular church-attender—do what Jesus would do. I appealed to his Christian faith, reminding him that Jesus blessed the merciful.

Then I made my way to Riverbend, still rehearsing in my head what I could have said to the governor to try to convince him to abandon the death penalty. After going through the clunky process of getting into the prison—metal detectors, pat downs, and one slamming metal door after another—I arrived at unit 2. It's a unique facility where I was able to spend time face to face with a group of men who were all sentenced to die.

Unlike many other states, Tennessee allows contact visits. The men were not shackled or even handcuffed. When I arrived, I received an enthusiastic and warm welcome: smiles, hugs, updates on life. And then I mentioned my encounter with the governor. I asked them what they would have said to the governor if they had bumped into him. I knew some of them were among those whose execution dates the governor had just set. I leaned in, curious about what they would say.

After a brief pause, one of the guys, Kevin Burns, spoke up. "I'd invite the governor to come pray with us," he said. The other guys enthusiastically agreed. Some went on to explain how much it would mean to them, and could mean to the governor, if they could share with him what Jesus had done in their lives and how God's love had transformed them.

Eventually, our conversation led the residents of unit 2 to extend a formal invitation. More than half of the men on Tennessee's death row wrote a letter to the governor asking him to visit them and pray with them.

Kevin Burns, the young man who spoke up, has since become a dear friend. A few years ago he was ordained, and I got to be there. His ordination service took place right there on death row, with corrections officers all around us. He shared his testimony, his love for Jesus, and the power of God's grace to redeem and transform. And then his first act as an ordained minister was to serve us all communion. We had communion on death row, served to us by a newly ordained pastor who was still facing execution. It was one of the most profound gospel experiences I've ever had.

Governor Haslam never did accept the invitation to visit unit 2, but he did start executing people. Now there is a new governor in Tennessee, Bill Lee. Although he too professes to be a Christian, he has continued to execute people. As of this writing, Governor Lee has not yet accepted the invitation to visit the men on unit 2, to pray with them and hear their testimonies. I wish he would, because proximity changes everything.

Some of the men I know on death row are innocent. Some of them have been proven innocent since I've known them. Others are guilty of the horrific crimes for which they have been convicted, but I have seen how God has transformed their lives over the years. As my friend Bryan Stevenson says, "We are all more than the worst thing we've ever done."

One of the transformed men I got to know on death row was Donnie Johnson. He was sentenced to death for the terrible murder of his wife, the details of which made me sick to my stomach when I heard them. Over the years, I spent many hours with Donnie. I learned more about how hard his life had been, with years of abuse and unimaginable pain. While none of that was an excuse for what he did, knowing his history did help me understand it more.

I also got to know Donnie's daughter, Cynthia, who was initially the poster child for his execution. She was quoted in the press as saying, "I want the freak to fry." She told me how she hated him and wanted him to die. After thirty years without speaking with him, she paid him a visit, intending to tell him off once and for all. But as she poured out her anger and pain, he listened. He did not defend himself or try to justify himself. He listened. She thought it would be the last time she would ever see him. But then something happened in her. She realized her hatred was not hurting him, but it was destroying her. It has been said that resentment is like eating rat poison and hoping the rat will die. In the end, she forgave him—not so he could sleep at night but so she could sleep at night. To this day, she is one of my heroes. Relationships change us, especially the hard ones.

Shortly after Donnie and Cynthia got a fresh start and began the hard work of healing, Donnie received his execution date. I was with him the week of his execution. We prayed together and sang together. He insisted he was "too blessed to be stressed." As the dark liturgy of state killing goes, he was offered a last meal. Donnie decided to fast instead. He forfeited his last meal and asked that the money be donated to a soup kitchen.

While he was being strapped to a gurney, he asked forgiveness for what he had done, and he extended forgiveness to those who were killing him. He asked the warden if he could sing as they killed him. He had told me that no matter what happened, he wanted his last words to be words that honored God. He died singing the song "Soon and Very Soon."

> Soon and very soon,
> We are going to see the King. . . .
> No more crying there,
> We are going to see the King. . . .
> No more dying there,
> We are going to see the King.

And he breathed his last.

I honestly believe if Governor Bill Lee had met Donnie, it would have been next to impossible for him to carry out the execution. Proximity changes us. It changed me. And many of my friends have shifted how they feel about the death penalty because they have built relationships with folks who are impacted by it. It is relationships, not debates or arguments, that change us.

On my desk, I have a few visual reminders that help me feel connected to my friends on death row even when I can't be with them. One is a twelve-inch wooden lighthouse that Donnie made me. Then there is the origami butterfly made by my friend John Ramirez, who is facing execution within a few months. He's become quite skilled at origami and includes a new creation in each letter he sends me. I also have a letter that I keep prominently displayed. It's from one of the guys who is no longer on death row. The letter closes with this P.S.: "Shane, just as I started to seal this letter up, I was moved off death row after thirty years. I walked on grass a few seconds ago for the first time in thirty years! God is great!"

Proximity.

Life on the Border

Not long ago, my friend Doug Pagitt organized a 3,200-mile bike ride along the US-Mexico border. Riders dipped their tires in the Pacific Ocean and then headed east, where they ended the ride sixty-six days later by dipping their tires in the Atlantic Ocean. I wish I could say I rode the whole thing, but I didn't. Maybe next time. I did, however, ride two hundred miles or so, which is not too shabby for me. The whole point of the We the People Ride was to get proximate with immigrants at the border and to share the stories of those we met.

One of the folks we met had just been captured by border patrol. To protect his identity, I'll call him Julio. Julio is a father in his twenties. He is from a small village in Honduras that relied on income from cruise ships that stopped in his town. When COVID hit, no more cruise ships came and Julio no longer had any income. His daughter had a medical condition that required treatment and he could no longer afford to pay for it. Without treatment, his daughter was in a lot of pain. Desperate to help her, Julio decided to make the risky trip to the US border to find a better future, or at least to earn some money to help his daughter. "Wouldn't you do the same thing for your daughter?" he asked us through tears.

Many of those with whom he traveled died on the journey. He had almost made it to the border when he became dangerously dehydrated. At one point, he could see a gas station where he could get water, but it was swarming with border patrol, so he kept moving. Eventually, he fainted of exhaustion and dehydration. That's when border patrol agents found him and brought him to a mission in Mexico, which is where we met him. He was glad to be alive, but also devastated that he had done all of that for his daughter without success. He could not apply for asylum in the US unless he made it across the border. He wasn't sure what he was going to do next.

Sitting next to Julio was an elderly woman in a wheelchair. I'll call her Rosa. She had fallen from the border wall and shattered her hip as she risked her life to find freedom. These were the people we met at the border, and hundreds more like them, each with their own stories of desperation, courage, and hope.

When I think about the issues of immigration and border security, I think of Julio and Rosa, just two of the hundreds of people we met. Immigrants are not just an issue to debate. They are neighbors seeking our love and compassion. Lots of people have opinions about immigrants, but opinions don't mean much when you have an undocumented person in your life. That's when immigration goes from being a political debate to an existential crisis that needs immediate attention. What we do for those Jesus called "the least of these brothers and sisters of mine," we do for Christ (Matt. 25:40).

Leaning into the pain of the world moves us closer to our

neighbors. It also moves us closer to God. It's what puts a fire in our bones to repair the foundation for life by changing the things that are crushing our brothers and sisters.

An Invitation to Choose Proximity

Based on what you've just read, how would you answer the question raised at the beginning of the chapter: What does it look like to choose proximity? What comes to mind when you think about drawing near to those on death row or to those on the US-Mexico border? What might it look like to lean into the suffering near you? Mother Teresa famously said, "Calcuttas are everywhere, if we will only have eyes to see." Sometimes we think about people on the other side of the world but forget the people on the other side of town. One of the things each of us can do is ask, Who around me is invisible in their suffering? Who is alone or vulnerable? Then we can ask the question we've been asking throughout this book: What does love require of me?

One of the other things I've learned about proximity is that the first steps are often the hardest ones. There's that old saying, "The hardest part about running a marathon is not getting to the finish line, it's getting to the start line." When it comes to proximity, it is uncomfortable and challenging to build relationships with folks who are different from us, especially when that might mean entering a prison for the first time. I've found it really helpful to join others who are already proximate, who have cracked open a door that I can follow them through. Rather than starting something brand new, I encourage people to join what others are already doing. Learn from their mistakes and listen to their wisdom. And if you are among those who are already living in places of vulnerability because proximity to suffering has chosen you, thank you for opening your life to people who have a lot to learn from your faith, resilience, and experience.

We are stronger together than we are on our own.

RETHINKING LIFE

- How do you respond to the idea that the gravity of the gospel pulls us toward those on the margins and away from centers of wealth and power, hipness and comfort?
- In what ways, if any, do you have the privilege of choosing which issues to care about? In what ways, if any, have the issues chosen you? What role has privilege or marginalization played in the issues you care about?
- What thoughts and emotions were you aware of as you imagined yourself in the room with those living on death row and on the US-Mexico border? In what ways did these stories challenge you or make you uncomfortable? In what ways did they encourage or motivate you?
- In what ways, if any, has proximity to a suffering person changed your perspective on a social issue? How did your relationship with that person make the issue personal?
- What might practicing proximity look like for you? Specifically, how would you like to lean into the struggle of others a little more, and what might it look like to get to the start line?
- Who comes to mind when you consider building closer relationships with people affected by an injustice we've reflected on in this book? For example, maybe it's becoming a pen pal with someone in prison or on death row, volunteering in a crisis pregnancy clinic, or getting involved with a group that welcomes immigrants and asylum seekers.

CHAPTER 15

Be a Force for Life

I am convinced we are at a critical moment in history, both in our country and in the world. Our country is fragile and fractured, as are countries in so many other parts of the world.

I was on a Zoom call recently that put in stark terms just how dangerous fragility at a national and global scale can be. The call featured scholars who study the factors that precipitate wars and revolutions. In a recent assessment of democracies around the world, they'd identified some of the red flags that often occur before violent uprisings. They were careful to state that they did not want to be alarmists, but that many of the warning signs that precede eras of war and upheaval are currently present in America. Here are a few of those signs:

- *Limited political options.* We are polarized between two parties that are increasingly divided. Many countries have a dozen or more political parties, but the United States has only two, and the only thing worse than having only two is having only one political party.
- *Access to lots of guns.* We have a heavily armed population. We have more guns than people in the US, which makes the outbreak of widespread violence a real possibility, especially when many people also hold conspiracy theories and consider their own government a potential threat.
- *Distrust of democratic process and institutions.* An alarming

portion of our population questions our democratic process, election results, the media, and the government, all of which contribute to a potentially explosive environment. Citing examples of violent revolutions in other countries, one of the experts suggested that all that's needed is a catalytic event, such as an assassination or a refusal to concede a national election. Another scholar described how difficult it may be for the United States to maintain the impossible tensions between the federal government and states on issues such as gun laws, abortion, and immigration. He suggested that states attempting to secede from the United States may be a real problem, not just a fringe movement.

Yikes. That's a lot to take in on a one-hour Zoom call.

I'm not a doomsayer. I am a relentlessly hopeful person. But as one who cares deeply about life, I sure do not want to see another civil war or a violent uprising in our country. Nevertheless, we must acknowledge that our country and our world are fragile right now. We need to prepare ourselves, and by that I don't mean building bunkers and hoarding supplies. I mean we need to train ourselves in love and ground ourselves in nonviolence. In the days to come, we are going to need people who know how to be peacemakers, because that's what it will take to be a force for life, no matter how tumultuous the days ahead turn out to be. And the starting point for peacemaking is humility.

Start with Humility

If we are going to be a force for life, even advocating for the lives and dignity of those who disagree with us, we must start with humility. Humility is always a virtue, but too many of us have lost sight of it in recent years, especially when it comes to public discourse and advocacy. Instead of humility, we're caught up in the rightness—or self-righteousness—of whatever our political views may be. But as important as it may be to be right, it is also important to be loving.

My friend Kirsten Powers wrote a beautiful book titled *Saving Grace*. It includes lots of good tips about how to be humble and loving without compromising our convictions, but she also points out some alarming statistics about how polarized we are as a country. For example, she cites a More in Common study that revealed the following:

- 86 percent of Republicans described Democrats as brainwashed, and 84 percent said Democrats were hateful.
- 88 percent of Democrats described Republicans as brainwashed, and 87 percent said Republicans are hateful.[1]

These findings may not be all that surprising, but it is disturbing to think that not only do those of us in both parties see things differently, we also make value judgments that the other side is full of hate. What's more, another study found that more than 40 percent of each party view the opposing party as "downright evil." And 20 percent of Democrats and 15 percent of Republicans agreed with the statement, "We'd be better off as a country if large numbers of the opposing party in the public just died."[2]

Whoa.

That's a stunning number of both Republicans and Democrats who view the other as evil and believe the world would be better off without them.[3] It's also a stunning lack of humility.

1. Daniel Yudkin, Stephen Hawkins, and Tim Dixon, *The Perception Gap: How False Impressions Are Pulling Americans Apart*, More in Common, June 2019, https://perceptiongap.us/media/zaslaroc/perception-gap-report-1-0-3.pdf.
2. Nathan P. Kalmoe and Lilliana Mason, "Lethal Mass Partisanship: Prevalence, Correlates, and Electoral Contingencies," paper presented at the January 2019 NCAPSA American Politics Meeting, www.dannyhayes.org/uploads/6/9/8/5/69858539/kalmoe___mason_ncapsa_2019_-_lethal_partisanship_-_final_lmedit.pdf.
3. One encouraging finding was that more than 80 percent of Americans know someone from the other party whom they like and respect. Those in this group show signs of hope, grace, and depolarization. It also relates back to how much relationships matter and change how we think beyond issues, categories, and labels and think about *people*.

We must take our moral convictions seriously, but we must also beware of viewing our rightness as a contrast to another person's wrongness. Jesus did not come to make bad people good. Jesus came to bring dead people to life. Jesus came not to give us guilt but to give us life. Jesus came not to make us judgmental but to make us loving.

I'd rather hang out with a humble conservative than a self-righteous liberal. And I'd rather hang out with a humble liberal than a self-righteous conservative. Self-righteousness is always toxic, but humility is life giving. And when it comes to being a force for life, humility starts by being honest about our own "stuff."

English writer G. K. Chesterton was once asked, "What's wrong with the world today?" With characteristic wit, he responded, "I am." Gandhi put it like this, "Be the change you want to see in the world." The wisdom of both Chesterton and Gandhi reflect the principle Jesus taught: "First get rid of the log in your own eye; then you will see well enough to deal with the speck in your friend's eye" (Matt. 7:5 NLT).

Jesus also told a remarkable story that demonstrates both the danger of self-righteousness and the power of humble honesty about our own sinful condition. It's a story about two folks praying.

> "Two men went up to the temple to pray, one a Pharisee and the other a tax collector. The Pharisee stood by himself and prayed: 'God, I thank you that I am not like other people—robbers, evildoers, adulterers—or even like this tax collector. I fast twice a week and give a tenth of all I get.'
>
> "But the tax collector stood at a distance. He would not even look up to heaven, but beat his breast and said, 'God, have mercy on me, a sinner.'
>
> "I tell you that this man, rather than the other, went home justified before God."
>
> —Luke 18:10–14

The Pharisee, a member of the Jewish religious elite in Rome's empire, boasts of his religious devotion and moral obedience, thanking God that he is not like the "evildoers." Then there is the tax collector, a Jew who worked for the empire and was despised for it, who stands at a distance and prays, "God, have mercy on me, a sinner." Jesus no doubt shocked all his listeners when he stated it was the humbly honest tax collector rather than the self-righteous Pharisee who went home justified before God.

The world is looking not for elite Christians who are perfectly righteous but for Christians who are humbly honest about their spiritual condition. Instead, too many of us have gone the way of the Pharisee, ignoring the logs in our own eyes while making a show of pointing out specks in the eyes of others.

Self-righteousness was among the things Jesus warned us to beware of when he said, "Be on your guard against the yeast of the Pharisees and Sadducees" (Matt. 16:6). At the time, yeast was a common symbol of evil. Just as yeast permeates dough, Jesus wanted his followers to understand how easily evil can embed itself in what is good. Unfortunately, the yeast of self-righteousness thrives today in the camps of both liberals and conservatives, and it undermines our ability to be a force for life.

So we humbly begin with ourselves, because being a force for life starts with some internal spiritual work. Then it extends beyond us into the world, where we can speak life, preach with our lives, and vote for life.

Speak Life

As we consider what it means to be a force for life in this world, we've spent some necessary time on how to address the big issues, as we should. But it's just as important to also reflect on the ways we can bring life in smaller, everyday ways. And one of those has to do with how we use our words.

Several years ago, I got a beautiful lesson in using life-giving words from the Reverend Doctor Otis Moss III, or OM3, as he's known on Twitter and to his friends. We were both speaking at the prestigious Chautauqua Institution in New York. I think it may have been the first time we met, and I'm grateful that it was also the beginning of a wonderful friendship. His sermon was titled "Speak Life," and it was one of the best sermons I've ever heard on the power of words to give or take life.

He started by reminding us that speech is created with breath. He noted the biblical descriptions of God as *ruah*, which is Hebrew for "wind," and *pneuma*, which is Greek for "spirit." He said that when the Spirit merges with human speech, life happens.

To demonstrate his point, he complimented one of his friends in the audience, saying how nice he looked, how smooth he is, how much goodness his friend brings into the world. Then he busted out some science about what he calls "neurology theology": "As I spoke, the words floated out into the air, and they made their way from his outer ear to the tympanic membrane, and then his cochlear nerve and the hair cells began to move back and forth to determine the frequency of the speech that I gave him. That frequency then sent a signal to the cerebral cortex. The cerebral cortex began to release dopamine in his system. When it released that dopamine it increased his immune system, and I just gave thirty seconds more life to him for living as a result of the speech that I just gave. There is power in speech."[4]

He went on to explain that good memories in our brains are coated by dopamine, a type of neurotransmitter and hormone. Dopamine is released in our brains when we have a good experience. Even a taste or a smell that reminds us of a game or movie we loved as a kid can release dopamine in the brain. He also pointed to a study that found

---

4. Otis Moss III, "Speak Life," Chautauqua Institution, July 5, 2013. You can listen to the talk for free on the Chautauqua Institution website: https://programarchive.chq.org/ci/sessions/8137/view.

when seniors are around children and hear the sound of their laughter, it triggers a similar life-giving force. When old folks hang out with kids, it can extend their lives and strengthen their immune systems.

But there is also another neurological force at work in the world. When we hear destructive words, something is released in our system known as cortisol. Cortisol is a stress hormone. Although it plays many important roles in the body, too much cortisol has the opposite effect of bringing life and strengthening our immune system. The brain releases cortisol when we experience stress, anxiety, fear, or sadness, and it can even make us feel physically sore. It can also compromise our immune system, making it easier for us to get sick.

Reverend Moss said, "I'm here to let you know that there are some cortisol Christians around. . . . They will give you the kind of speech that will create stress in your life, and you don't feel better when you've been around them." Such speech does not bring life. It is toxic. Then he brought it home when he said, "But I believe that there is some dopamine that God wants to release within us neurologically that will increase our immune system so that we can change our republic and do what God calls us to do. It is all through speech. You can change the atmosphere with your speech." Let's just say I was sitting on the back row with some serious dopamine flowing through my brain during his sermon.

So to riff off my friend Otis Moss III, we need to constantly remember that we can speak life, every day, in every moment. We can breathe life into the world with kind words even when it takes a little effort or feels uncomfortable. If my brother OM3 is right with his neurotheology, and I'm pretty sure he is, maybe kind words can even prolong someone's life. Make it a habit to produce some dopamine in somebody today. Don't be a cortisol Christian. Let us be the kind of people who bring life with every word we speak.

Oh, and OM3 ended his sermon by taking back the pro-life language, of course. He said when people ask us if there are only two issues in America (abortion and sexuality), we can just say we break it down differently: "I'm pro-life. I'm pro-education. I'm pro-healthcare.

Pro-accountability. . . . Pro-love. Pro-faith. Pro-equality. Pro-grace. Pro-redemption. Pro-peace. Pro-family, whatever combination that family may be . . . Speak life! Speak life! Speak life!"

These are certainly days when we really need to speak life into the world—and grace and love and tenderness. And all beautiful things. Here are several principles I try to practice for speaking life into the world:

- *Communicate directly, one-on-one.* I try not to talk at people or around them but to talk with them directly, even people who have hurt or offended me—actually, especially people who have hurt or offended me.[5] This is difficult in our social-media age, when it is so much easier to jump on social media and rally a Twitter storm when someone upsets us. Even when I confront people in public for things they have done or said in public, I start by communicating with them in private, one-on-one, to see if we can talk or pray together.

- *Affirm the best in others.* And not just those we like but also—and especially—those who frustrate us. This doesn't mean ignoring our convictions or the real disagreements we have with other people, but there is something about affirming the goodness in even the people we find it most difficult to get along with. When we show kindness to someone it's hard to be kind to, studies show that it has the potential not only to do good things for them but also to do good things for us.

- *Be quick to confess.* I want to be quick to confess when I have done something wrong because, remember, confession is a sacrament, a holy mystery, and it heals. "I'm sorry" is one of the holiest phrases in the world. Let's say it more. Repentance also means repairing harm, but lots of healing and redemptive stuff begins with a heartfelt confession.

- *Mute negativity.* I love the mute button on Twitter. We also may

---

5. This is also how Jesus says to go about things in Matthew 18.

need to "redefine the relationship" with folks who speak a lot of negativity in our lives. St. Benedict called such negativity "murmuring" and he said it is poisonous. Talking negatively about people doesn't help them, or us, and reduces the dopamine in the world. Remember, we don't want to be cortisol Christians or hang out with those who are.

- *Surround yourself with life-giving people.* I often describe community as surrounding ourselves with people who remind us of Jesus and help us become more like him. We tend to become like the people we hang out with. When we are teenagers, we often hear about peer pressure as a bad thing, and it can be. But there's another side to it. When we hang out with hopeful people, their hope rubs off on us. Courage is contagious. So is generosity. If you want to be more courageous, hang out with courageous people and their daring will rub off on you. If you want to be more generous, hang out with generous people.

- *Protect your joy.* My wife and I like the circus so much we joined it! Well, almost. We are jugglers, unicyclers, and fire breathers! The world needs more joy. Which is why I've always liked the circus arts, and they have come in handy in protests, especially when tensions are high in our neighborhood. While you may not want to take up fire breathing, you could consider learning a skill or fine-tuning a skill that brings joy to the world. I have always liked twentieth-century activist Emma Goldman's declaration, "If I can't dance, then it's not my revolution." And I love that old song: "This joy that I have, the world didn't give it to me, and the world can't take it away."

- *Do a content audit.* Each of us can do a personal audit of the content we are digesting. That includes everything from music and social media to films, books, games, podcasts, and anything else contained on a digital device. Is the content we're consuming giving us life? Bringing life into the world? Does it produce more dopamine or cortisol?

Preach with Your Life

When I think of what it means to be a force for life, Mother Teresa is one of the people who comes to mind. She's often known for her passion on the issue of abortion, but like Dr. King, her passion for life wasn't limited to just one issue.[6] It encompassed all the issues, and her life showed it. One of my favorite quotes from Mother Teresa is, "Our best sermon is our life."

Mother Teresa didn't just say she was pro-life, she showed us she was pro-life. She took in fourteen-year-old moms and picked up orphans abandoned in the train stations of Calcutta. I had the privilege of working with her in India. While I was there, I met a young man, about thirty years old, who said to me, "You know why we call her Mother Teresa, right?" I shook my head. "Because she's our mom," he said. Then he showed me things Mother Teresa had given him over the years, just as any mom would give her kids. That's the sort of integrity the pro-life movement needs today: not just talking points but a lifestyle. To be truly pro-life is a way of life. It requires a daily commitment to living into that question we've asked all through this book: What does love require of us?

I want to be pro-life like Mother Teresa was pro-life, and that means taking action. It means taking in teenage mothers and walking alongside families in poverty. It means creating support groups for people who have chosen to have abortions and are living with

---

6. Like Mother Teresa, Dr. Martin Luther King Jr. is a brilliant example of what it looks like to embody a consistent ethic of life. Dr. King spoke out against the war in Vietnam, but he also grieved the violence and riots in our streets. As a gun owner, he became convinced that even owning a gun was to be unfaithful to his Savior and to his vision for a world free of violence. He believed the means had to reflect the ends, that he couldn't use violence to achieve peace and justice. On the death penalty, he became a passionate voice for abolition, saying it was "society's final assertion that we will not forgive."

Dr. King was a champion for life. He was one of those rare leaders who embodied a consistent ethic of life to his core. He went to India to spend some time with Mohandas Gandhi to learn more about nonviolence. He became convinced that we cannot use the weapons of war to bring peace. Hatred cannot drive out hatred, only love can do that. Violence cannot drive out violence.

And we have to remember it was Jesus who inspired Dr. King, Mother Teresa, and so many other champions for life throughout history. We follow in their footsteps when we allow Jesus to shape and form us as a force for love and life in the world.

the complicated emotions of that decision. It means welcoming refugees and getting in the way of militarism and war. It means getting involved in the lives of folks facing execution and standing against all killing, both legal and illegal.

Mother Teresa didn't picket abortion clinics. She didn't wear an "Abortion is murder" T-shirt. She didn't shame or condemn people. Instead, she provided for young people with such love that they called her Mother.

Mother Teresa knew that abortion was not the only life issue. She was just as passionate in her opposition to the death penalty and other forms of violence. She personally phoned governors in the US, asking them to stop executions. She told them, "Do what Jesus would do." Mother Teresa spoke out consistently and courageously for life. She's a great model for us today as we seek to be pro-life for the whole life— and not just in word but in deed.

Nearly every day, I hear new stories about the creative ways people take action to be fully pro-life. Recently, a pastor friend of mine, Joel Simpson, shared a letter he saw about an organ donation. It was written by the person who received a ligament, to the family of the deceased person who donated it.[7]

Dear Donor Family,

I am writing to express my gratitude for the gift of a ligament in my knee. I am a mother of four children. I am a lifelong athlete who loves to be active and play sports. I had to have my MPFL ligament in my knee reconstructed after an accident while sledding with my church youth group.

I am so grateful for this gift of the new ligament so that I have the ability to be active once again with my family. The gift to be

---

7. This letter prompted me to search "letters from organ donors" online. Talk about life-giving content! I got totally absorbed and even shed a lot of tears. I also thought of my friend Chris Lahr who donated a kidney to a friend here in Philly who really needed one, an incredible life-giving act. And I think of one of the guys on death row whose execution we fought hard to stop. He insisted that if the execution went forward, he wanted to donate his organs so that renewed life could come from his own death. *Whoa.*

able to walk is not one that I take lightly and feel gratitude each day for it.

My love and condolences to your family at the loss of your loved one. I have prayed many times for you and am thankful to have this gift. May you have peace knowing that a mom in California is able to be active with her family because of your family's gift. My whole family is now on the donor registry in your family's honor.

Thank you,
Leslie

My uncle recently passed away, and it turns out that he was a registered organ donor. My grandmother got this letter in the mail – it gave our family some much needed solace

Love is contagious. One pro-life action can sow the seeds of many more. That's how we preach with our lives.

So let us reimagine the pro-life movement today as a movement that stands consistently for life and against death. And let us move beyond stale rhetoric and ideologies to action. What's just as important as whether we are pro-life or pro-choice is how we are pro-active. What does it look like to be a champion of life? What does it look like to proclaim the sacredness of every person not just with our words but with our lives?

Maybe that means volunteering in a prison. Maybe it means opening your home to a refugee family. Maybe it means fostering a child. We can't do everything, but each of us can do something. One more thing Mother Teresa taught me is this: "What's important is not how much we do, but how much love we put into doing it." We are called to do not great things but "small things with great love." And enough small things done with great love can transform the world.

Vote for Life

Fatigue with politics is nothing new for sure. Way back in the 1990s, one of my favorite punk-rock songs talked about "politics schmolitics," which expressed a similar sentiment. But the exhaustion and discontentment with political divisions and inertia has reached an all-time high in our day. Polls show that our satisfaction with nearly every aspect of our democracy is plummeting. The Supreme Court. The president. Congress. No one seems to get much done, especially on issues such as commonsense gun laws, where 90 percent of Americans want to see changes.[8] A lot of young people are no longer willing to accept the standard arguments defending institutions such as the electoral college. One article in the *Atlantic* was titled "The Outsiders: How Can Millennials Change Washington If They Hate It?"[9]

Politics schmolitics.

I'm the first to confess that I've got some serious anti-establishment leanings, as you might have guessed given my fondness for punk-rock music. I pull from the wisdom of the Catholic worker movement, the base community movements in Latin America, the revolutionary anti-imperial faith of the early Christians, and the radical reformers of the Anabaptist traditions. Many of these movements share a deep skepticism about how much we can rely on governments and politicians to change the world. I get that.

I have also spent the last ten years in close relationship with Black and brown leaders whose ancestors were enslaved and oppressed, and they tend to have a different angle on politics and voting. As the saying goes, "Where we sit determines what we see." I also find that while

---

8. In 2022, President Biden did sign the most significant gun legislation bill in more than thirty years, and I got to be there at the White House to celebrate it. But even this bill only scratches the surface. During the ceremony, one father who lost his son in the 2018 mass shooting at Stoneman Douglas High School in Parkland, Florida, stood and interrupted President Biden, saying the bill was not enough. We still have much work to do.

9. Ron Fournier, "The Outsiders: How Can Millennials Change Washington If They Hate It?" *Atlantic*, August 26, 2013, www.theatlantic.com/politics/archive/2013/08/the-outsiders-how-can-millennials-change-washington-if-they-hate-it/278920/.

many of my friends in these communities are passionate about voting rights and holding politicians accountable, they are also able to protect their hope, even when politicians fail them. They embody the lyrics of the old hymn: "My hope is built on nothing less than Jesus' blood and righteousness. . . . On Christ the solid rock I stand, all other ground is sinking sand."

When it comes to being a force for life, I want to suggest that we view voting as just one tool in our toolbox, even if we consider it, as I do, damage control. When we vote, we aren't trying to elect a savior; we've found our Savior. What we are trying to do is to stand against the principalities and powers that are hurting our people. That may sound cynical, over-spiritualized, or both, but it has helped me and others to navigate political engagement without feeling like we're losing our souls. Instead, we're simply using every tool in our toolbox.

The word *politics* has its root in the Greek word *polis*, which means "city." This is why we have cities to this day that end in *polis*, such as Indianapolis and Minneapolis. *Metropolis* means "mother city." *Cosmopolitan* is "world city." And the Greek term *polites* means "citizen." That means politics has to do with how people relate and live together in society. So when we think about politics, it's helpful to think about people.

No one has much love for politics, but most of us do care about people. And I want to suggest that loving our neighbors as ourselves means we cannot ignore the local and national policies that affect their lives and their ability to thrive.

All of us, especially those of us trying to follow Jesus, are called to love our neighbors—the *polites*, our fellow citizens. Loving our neighbors requires thinking about how we live together well, how we organize our shared life, how we protect our most vulnerable citizens, and how we protect life and the common good of all.

Policies don't solve everything. No law can change a human heart. We cannot legislate love or compassion. But policies can contribute to the flourishing of life, or to the crushing of it. Dr. King recognized both the importance of laws and the limitations of laws when he wrote,

> The law does not seek to change one's internal feelings, it seeks to control the external effects of those internal feelings. For instance, the law cannot make a man love me—religion and education must do that . . . but it can keep him from lynching me. The law cannot make an employer have compassion for me, but it can keep him from refusing to hire me because of the color of my skin. Religion and education must change one's internal feelings, but it is scarcely a moral act to encourage others to patiently accept injustice until a man's heart gets right. All that we seek through legislation is to control the external effects of one's internal feelings.[10]

On nearly every policy that requires casting a vote, we can ask two questions: How can I use my vote to best protect life? What does it look like for love (rather than fear) to be the compelling force shaping our policies?

Think about cars. Cars are not designed to kill, but they can be deadly. So we have done all sorts of things, including passing laws, in order to save lives. We've added seat belts. We require driver's licenses and set minimum age requirements. You have to pass a driving test. And if you abuse your license, you can lose it. There's a limit to the alcohol you can consume while operating a car. We have speed limits. And it's not laws alone that we use to protect people. We also develop new technology such as airbags to help save lives. When new challenges arise, such as texting while driving, we adapt and create new policies to keep people safe—hands-free technology or even laws against texting and driving. All of it to protect life. One person's

---

10. Martin Luther King Jr., "The 'New Negro' of the South: Behind the Montgomery Story," *Socialist Call* 24 (June 1956), Martin Luther King Jr. Research and Education Institute, Stanford University, https://kinginstitute.stanford.edu/king-papers/documents/new-negro-south-behind-montgomery-story.

freedom—to text and drive or to drink and drive—is limited because it impacts another person's safety.

Policies are never perfect, but we can ask ourselves whether the policies and politicians we support with our votes free people up or hold people down. Do they lock people out or invite people in? Do they allow people to flourish or crush people's dignity? Are they driven by love or by fear?

Dr. Cornel West has said, "Tenderness is what love looks like in private; justice is what love looks like in public." That's why I keep asking, What does love require? One of the questions we can ask as citizens is what our country would look like if our policies were driven by love rather than fear. So much of our rhetoric, especially around politics, is driven by fear. But as Christians, we know the promise of Scripture that "perfect love casts out fear" (1 John 4:18 NKJV). Love and fear are enemies. Much like opposing magnets, they can't occupy the same space. Fear casts out love, and love casts out fear. The invitation is to imagine what America could look like if love shaped our policies—on immigration, guns, abortion, the death penalty, poverty, healthcare, racial justice, and every other issue. And I would suggest that Christians have a leading role to play in making that vision a reality.

Dr. King had a beautiful way of naming our calling as a church. He said that we are not meant to be the master of the state or the servant of the state. Instead, the church is to be the conscience of the state. And it is vitally important that we claim that calling today.

When I mentioned earlier that voting is one way to stand against principalities and powers, I meant it. In the past few years, we have seen some of the darkest demonic forces of white supremacy and hatred manifest themselves in terrible ways. And as we noted in the beginning of this chapter, our nation is at a crossroads. While casting a vote for a policy that promotes life may not by itself defeat demonic forces, voting and political engagement can facilitate harm reduction or damage control. We can limit the reach of principalities and powers. Remember, when we vote, we are not looking for a political savior; we are trying to protect life and control damage. And it is reasonable to expect that our government, our elected leaders, and our policies do both.

I want to vote for policies that will do the least harm and the most good, and alleviate the suffering of as many people as possible. I steer away from endorsing candidates because I have offered my ultimate allegiance to Jesus. Many politicians are pro-life on one issue and not on another, so I tend to think more about what policies are life giving and work with anyone on those policies, regardless of party affiliation.

One way of thinking about what it means to allow love to lead our politics is to consider how closely the policies we vote for support those whom Jesus blesses in the Beatitudes: the poor, the meek, the merciful, those who mourn, the peacemakers. The word *vote* shares the same root as *voice*, and voting is about using our voices to advocate for the most vulnerable people in our society. In a real way, we are voting *for them*. We are voting for the poor, those whom Jesus called "the least of these."

What if, when we vote to fund programs that provide food stamps and housing to needy families, we imagine that we are doing that for Christ?

What if, when we discover that the water system in a predominantly Black city, such as Flint, Michigan, is polluted with lead, we move swiftly to fix it because it is Christ drinking that water?

What if, when we vote to provide affordable healthcare to millions of people that need it, we imagine that we are providing affordable healthcare for Christ?

What if, when we welcome immigrants, we do so imagining it is Jesus himself we are welcoming?

Christians have always had a subversive political imagination. Every time the early Christians said "Jesus is Lord," they were declaring "Caesar is not." Today, our hope is not in the donkey or the elephant but in the Lamb. It is not the government but the body of

Christ, the church, that is God's primary instrument for transforming the world.

So let us be a force for life. Let us vote for life not every four years but every single day. Let us vote not just with our ballots but with our love. Let us breathe life into the world by speaking life to each other. Let us embody the good news of Jesus with our words and with our lives.

The early Christians were a force for life. They were not just antideath but comprehensively *for* life. And we can be that same force for life today if we want to be. Wouldn't it be incredible if five hundred years from now, the world looked at the Christians of today in wonder because of how passionately and comprehensively we were champions of life?

We can do this.

RETHINKING LIFE

- Studies have found that Republicans and Democrats both view the other as "brainwashed," "hateful," and even "evil." In what ways, if any, do you relate to these views?
- What do you think it looks like to be humble and loving without compromising convictions? When have you seen someone do this well?
- When G. K. Chesterton was asked, "What's wrong with the world today?" he responded, "I am." What might it look like for Christians on both sides of the political aisle to say something similar today? What do you imagine the response might be, from both allies and opponents?
- If being a force for life starts with doing our own internal spiritual work, what might that work include for you? In what ways might you be humbly honest about your own spiritual condition?

- As we considered several practices we can use to speak life into the world (communicating directly, affirming the best in others, being quick to confess, etc.), which one stood out most to you? Share the reasons for your response. What other practices would you add to the list?
- Who is someone you admire for how they have preached with their life by putting words into action? What have you learned from them about what love requires of us?
- How do you respond to the idea that when we vote, we aren't trying to elect a savior, we're simply using every tool in our toolbox to protect life? Do you agree or disagree? Share the reasons for your response.
- In what ways, if any, would you say your politics have been driven by fear rather than love? What makes it difficult to ask what love requires when it comes to politics?
- What comes to mind when you imagine voting for the poor and the vulnerable? How might it shape your vote to imagine that every vote represents something you do to Christ?
- Beyond election day, in what ways do you feel drawn to advocate for life-giving policies?

CHAPTER 16

Protestify

One of Jesus' best-known stories is the parable of the Good Samaritan. In it, a person gets beat up and left unconscious on the side of the Jericho Road. The religious folks who travel the road avoid the man in the ditch and pass by on the other side. And then comes the Samaritan, a member of a community that is shunned and despised, and he becomes the compassionate hero of the story. He takes care of the man in the ditch and demonstrates what it means to love our neighbors as ourselves.

I love this parable and I preach on it all the time. There are lots of solid lessons to pull out of it. I especially love the spin Martin Luther King Jr. put on the story. Dr. King pointed out that we are all called to be the Good Samaritan, but there comes a point when we have lifted so many people out of the same ditch that we say, "We need to do something about the whole road to Jericho." Here are King's words, delivered at Riverside Church in New York City in 1967: "We are called to play the Good Samaritan on life's roadside, but that will be only an initial act. One day we must come to see that the whole Jericho Road must be transformed so that men and women will not be constantly beaten and robbed as they make their journey on life's highway. True compassion is more than flinging a coin to a beggar. It comes to see that an edifice which produces beggars needs restructuring."[1]

---

1. Martin Luther King Jr., "Beyond Vietnam: A Time to Break Silence," transcript of a sermon delivered April 4, 1967, Riverside Church, New York City, www.americanrhetoric.com/speeches/mlkatimetobreaksilence.htm.

Repairing the cracks in the foundation of our ethic of life requires both compassion and justice. Compassion is about lifting our neighbor out of the ditch; justice is doing something about why they ended up in the ditch to begin with.

The late Archbishop Desmond Tutu, one of our great champions for life, put it this way: "There comes a point when we need to stop pulling people out of the river. We need to go upstream and find out why they are falling in." And these are the words of Dietrich Bonhoeffer, who was executed for his opposition to the Nazis: "We are not to simply bandage the wounds of the victims beneath the wheels of injustice, we are to drive a spoke into the wheel itself."

My mentor John Perkins has a great take on the saying "If you give someone a fish, they will eat for a day. But if you teach them to fish, they will eat for the rest of their lives." He adds, "But we also have to do something about who owns the pond." Feeding people is compassion work, but making sure people have equal access to the pond is justice work. Figuring out why the pond is polluted is justice work. Asking why a fishing license costs so much is justice work. Tearing down the walls around the pond so everyone can fish for themselves is justice work. Compassion is important, but so is justice.

Justice work requires being a prophetic force for life. It's about going beyond just lifting people out of the ditch and reimagining the whole road to Jericho. It is about what theologian Walter Brueggemann called "prophetic imagination." Or, as I like to say, we are called not just to protest but to protestify.[2]

We Are Called to Protestify

Public protests are important. I go to a lot of them. I believe it is part of our calling as people of faith and conscience to protest the things

---

2. I think I first heard the word *protestify* used by my friend Brian McLaren, and I've loved it ever since.

that are wrong in the world. We need to get in the streets and put our bodies in the way of injustice. But I want to invite us to go even farther. We can do more than just name things that are wrong. We can proclaim how they can be made right. We can declare a vision for a better world. We can protestify.

This is prophetic work, and Christians are called to be the prophets of a new and better world, not just the chaplains of empire and defenders of the status quo.

The word *prophet* means "mouthpiece of God." The prophets of the Hebrew Scriptures were appointed to be God's emcees, ambassadors of the Holy One—to speak the words of God and to convey the heart and mind of God to the people. The prophets lived with a profound sense of good and evil. They felt with God, saw with God, and heard with God. The closer they got to God, the more deeply they felt the agonizing consequences of sin—the failure of God's people to do what love required of them. One of the great Jewish thinkers of the twentieth century, Rabbi Abraham Heschel, said it well: "To us a single act of injustice—cheating in business, exploitation of the poor—is slight; to the prophets, a disaster. To us injustice is injurious to the welfare of the people; to the prophets it is a deathblow to existence: to us, an episode; to them, a catastrophe, a threat to the world."[3]

Perhaps this is why the prophets were also seen as weird and extreme. To be honest, they did some pretty odd things to get people to pay attention and to obey God. Moses turned his staff into a snake. Elijah smacked a rock and fire came out. Jeremiah wore a yoke on his back to symbolize the heavy weight of oppression. Ezekiel held a protest in the nude and even cooked poop to make a point. John the Baptist wore camel skin, ate locusts, and lived in the desert wilderness where he called people to repent and be baptized in the fresh water of the Jordan. No doubt, the prophets were a little odd. But they were

---

3. Abraham J. Heschel, *The Prophets* (1962; New York: HarperCollins, 2001), 4.

odd because they saw how messed up the world was and they wanted people to pay attention and do something about it.

The prophets' nearness to God and their proximity to injustice, especially injustice committed against the poor, put a fire in their bones. Prophet Jeremiah said, "His word burns in my heart like a fire. It's like a fire in my bones! I am worn out trying to hold it in! I can't do it!" (Jer. 20:9 NLT). The prophets could not stay silent about injustice. And for that they were routinely ostracized, jailed, tortured, and killed.

In his book *The Prophetic Imagination*, Walter Brueggemann points out that we often misunderstand the biblical prophets, imagining them as fortune tellers who predict the future. But Walter suggests that's not quite it. The prophets were not fortune tellers but truth tellers. And they were trying not to predict the future but to change the future. They wanted to wake us up to the present and invited us to imagine a different future than the one we're headed toward.

That's what it means to protestify.

Exposing Injustice

There's an old saying, "I used to protest in order to change the world. But now I protest to keep the world from changing me." Part of protesting is about keeping ourselves from becoming numb to the suffering of others. But I want to invite us to dream about what it could look like to protest, or protestify, in new ways, ways that move people to join us in advocating for the life and dignity of every person. Banners, yard signs, and T-shirts may have a place in our work, but let's not stop there. Let's go beyond slogans and consider what it looks like to bear prophetic witness for life to the world today.

One of the things we must do is expose injustice. Just as the Hebrew prophets did, we want injustice to make people so uncomfortable that they can't ignore it. That's what happened in the civil rights movement and other social movements throughout history: prophetic witness exposed injustice and made it impossible for anyone to ignore it. As police beat Black folks in the streets, knocked them down with fire hoses, and set dogs on them, protestifyers exposed injustice. As Memphis sanitation workers marched with signs that said, "I am a man," they protestified inhumane conditions and low wages and exposed injustice. I've seen peaceful protestors hold up mirrors to militarized police, inviting them simply to look at themselves. That's what prophetic actions do: they force us to look at ourselves truthfully, to face injustice, and to do something about it. And as we work to repair the foundation for life, we get to imagine what such prophetic action looks like for us today.

In chapter 14, we discussed the power of proximity, how we can draw near to those who are marginalized and suffering. But here's another way to think about what it means to practice proximity: we can bring the pain of the marginalized and suffering to those who have the power to change things. We bring the cries of the oppressed to the powers that be. And we do this by amplifying the voices of those who are hurting, by putting those who have been impacted by injustice at center stage.

Remember that line from Dr. King? "The church must be reminded that it is not the master or the servant of the state, but rather the conscience of the state." We have seen throughout history the abuses that happen when the church becomes the master of the state, and also how impotent the church becomes when it is the servant of the state—and both are catastrophic. We have also seen what happens when the church lives into its vocation of being the prophetic conscience of the state.

As we consider what love might require of us, I want to share a few snapshots of what it looks like to be a prophetic conscience, especially when it comes to issues of life. Each snapshot is a sort of experiment in subverting death and advocating for life.

Protestifying the Opioid Crisis

During the opioid crisis in Philadelphia, as our city was seeing more than a thousand lives each year lost to heroin, my friends and neighbors in North Philly had an idea. Moved by the kids in our neighborhood who had grown tired of seeing heroin needles everywhere,[4] we launched a campaign we called Need a Little Help (pun intended). We gathered hundreds of heroin needles from our streets, put them into glass jars, and delivered them to our city officials as a plea for help. Almost immediately, they responded. Before long, our mayor declared a state of emergency and provided funding and a strategic plan to address it. Among other things, the plan provided needle drop boxes where people could safely discard needles. I still have city officials tell me all the time that they kept the jar of needles in their office as a constant reminder of the urgency of this crisis and the lives that were at stake.

SHANE CLAIBORNE

4. We routinely find used needles everywhere in our neighborhood. The final straw came one winter when kids were playing in the snow and were worried they might get hurt on needles buried under the fresh snow as they made a snowman.

SHANE CLAIBORNE

COE BURCHFIELD

COE BURCHFIELD

Protestifying for Immigration Reform

I joined hundreds of other activists from around the country, including my close friends at the Christian Community Development Association, in holding a prayer vigil in the Capitol. To put a face on the issue, every speaker was accompanied by a DREAMer, a young immigrant activist who shared their story. We had collected the dreams of more than three thousand immigrant families, each written on a little piece of paper, and delivered them to the Capitol, demanding immigration reform and a path to citizenship. We prayed and read the dreams aloud in the halls of Congress until we were arrested. One of the officers arresting us quietly said, "I'm with you. Thank you for what you are doing."

STEVE SCHAPIRO

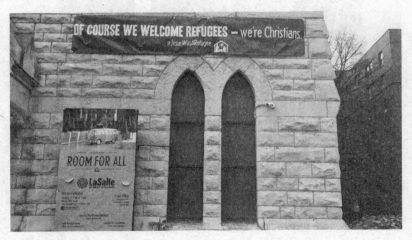

KRISTEN METZ

Protestifying the Death Penalty

In 2016, people from across the country fighting for alternatives to the death penalty gathered at the Supreme Court in Washington, DC. Together with families of murder victims and with families of those who had been executed, they declared that violence was the problem, not the solution. We carried roses in two colors, one red and one yellow, insisting we wanted to remember both the victims of violent crimes and the victims of execution. We held forty posters, one for each year, with the names of the more than fifteen hundred people who have been executed since 1976, when the Supreme Court allowed executions to resume. We were arrested for holding a banner that said "Stop Executions" on the steps of the Supreme Court, just as the State of Virginia carried out another execution. One of the things that made the event so powerful was having the families of the murdered together with the families of the executed as we declared that killing is wrong, always wrong.

COE BURCHFIELD

COE BURCHFIELD

Protestifying Guns

One of the most powerful experiences of protestifying I've been a part of recently is transforming guns into garden tools. Inspired by the biblical prophets Micah and Isaiah, who cast a vision of "beating swords into plowshares and spears into pruning hooks," my friend Mike Martin and I take donated guns to public demonstrations and turn them into shovels and plows on stage. Mike is the founder of RAWtools and coauthor with me of *Beating Guns*, and we've now traveled to more than forty cities transforming guns into garden tools.

One of the things that has made these events so powerful is centering the voices of those who have been victims of gun violence. We've featured folks who survived mass shootings, police officers, activists, pastors, gun owners, veterans, mothers, grandmothers, children. All of them get to take the hammer and beat on a gun to transform it. It is more than a merely symbolic act. It is a sacramental act. Some share that they have killed someone. Others share their trauma of surviving gun violence. Allowing them to have a voice honors their pain and makes space for their grief. It also gives everyone hope that things can change.

THEOPHILUS DONOGHUE

KATIE JO BROTHERTON

KATIE JO BROTHERTON

I watched with tears rolling down my face as Rev. Sharon Risher beat on a gun at one of our events. Her mother had been killed in the 2015 mass shooting at Emanuel AME church in Charleston, South Carolina. She named all nine of those who had been killed that day as she beat on the gun. Afterward, she tried to explain to me what that act of protestifying did for her, and did in her. She smiled and said that all the anger she had for Dylann Roof, the shooter, she had taken out on that gun.

These are just a few snapshots of protestifying—of exposing injustice, amplifying the people impacted, and casting an alternative vision for the future. They are meant not to prescribe but to provoke, not to tell you what to do but to motivate you to do your own protestifying. Each of us needs to ask, in our particular context, What are the things that are crushing people's lives and how might we creatively move people's hearts to respond?

Protestify Where You Are

Public actions are powerful and we need more of them. But we can also protestify in our spaces at home and at work, as well as in our places of worship. We can use our prophetic imagination in wild and wondrous ways when we protestify right where we are.

Prophetic imagination has many different expressions today, just as it did for the prophets of old. Jesus taught us to seek first the kingdom of God, and that means asking ourselves some prophetic questions. What would it look like for God's dream to come on earth as it is in heaven? What would it look like for God's dream to come to my block, my neighborhood, my city? Or maybe we can ask the opposite: What does *not* look like God's dream for the world? God's dream is for us to welcome immigrants as if they are our own flesh and blood (Lev. 19:34). God's dream is for mercy to triumph over judgment. God's dream is for us to transform our swords into plows and our guns into garden tools. God's dream is *not* for more than one hundred lives to be lost to guns every day in America. The question is, How can we participate in announcing and in ushering in God's dream?

Let us begin as the prophets did, by drawing near to God and by being proximate to those who are suffering. Let us pray that our hearts would be broken by the things that break the heart of God. May we feel the anger, the hope, and the love of God. May we see with God the people others choose not to see: the invisible ones, the hidden ones, the marginalized ones. May we hear the blood that still cries out from the ground and the voices of those crying out, "I can't breathe." And let us raise our voices in unison with them. May we become the prophetic conscience of our day, the mouthpieces of God for our time and place.

Let's do this. Let's reimagine the Jericho Road together.

RETHINKING LIFE

- What are the Jericho Roads in your community, the issues and dangers that consistently put people in a ditch of suffering? What's the compassion work that needs to be done to address that Jericho Road? What's the justice work that needs to be done?
- We can do more than just name things that are wrong; we can proclaim how they can be made right. What do you think it means in practical terms to do both of these? Draw on any examples you can think of from history or recent events.
- In what ways does the weird and extreme behavior of the Hebrew prophets challenge you? In what ways does it encourage or motivate you?
- How do you feel about the idea of protestifying to make people uncomfortable with injustice? Is that something you are willing to do? Why or why not?

- What stood out most to you about the four snapshots of pro-testifying (pp. 258–62)? Share the reasons for your response.
- We tend to view the Hebrew prophets as weird and extreme, but we could also see them as creatives—those who used their prophetic imagination to draw attention to injustice and to imagine a different future. What are some ways, large or small, that you have seen people being creative in exposing injustice or declaring God's love?
- What comes to mind when you think of using your own pro-phetic imagination? How might you use your creativity to address injustices where you are? What might it look like to protestify in your own way?

## CHAPTER 17

Give Birth to a Better World

A survey of history makes it pretty clear that it is men who have been responsible for mass violence and death. Consider this list of atrocities that have happened in just the last century alone, the bloodiest century in the history of the world. It's worth noting that these are just the fourteen largest massacres, and the estimates of lives lost include noncombatant casualties only, not military ones.

- Mao Zedong (China and Tibet, 1949–69): 49–78 million
- Joseph Stalin (USSR, 1932–39): 23 million
- Adolf Hitler (Nazi Germany, 1939–45): 12 million
- Leopold II (Belgian Congo, 1886–1908): 8 million
- Hideki Tojo (Japan, 1941–44): 5 million
- Ismail Enver (Turkey, 1915–20): 2.5 million
- Pol Pot (Cambodia, 1975–79): 1.7 million
- Kim Il-Sung (North Korea, 1948–94): 1.6 million
- Mengistu (Ethiopia, 1975–78): 1.5 million
- Leonid Brezhnev (Afghanistan, 1979–82): 800,000
- Jean Kambanda (Rwanda, 1994): 800,000
- Suharto (East Timor/West Papua, 1966–98): 800,000
- Saddam Hussein (Iraq, Iran, and Kurdistan, 1980–90): 600,000
- Tito (Yugoslavia, 1945–87): 570,000[1]

---

1. David P. Gushee, *The Sacredness of Human Life: Why an Ancient Biblical Vision Is Key to the World's Future* (Grand Rapids: Eerdmans, 2013), 305.

The total exceeds 107 million, and almost all of these atrocities are the result of decisions made by men with access to immense power. To be clear, human beings are all equally sinful. We are all capable of terrible evil and likewise of heroic compassion. However, while wars, guns, and terrorism are broadly human problems, there is also a striking dynamic of male aggression and toxic masculinity at work when it comes to the many manifestations of violence, going all the way back to Cain and Abel. Without a doubt, violence is more about power than gender. The problem is not men per se but patriarchy—a social system in which men hold power and women are largely excluded from power. Patriarchy has been crushing people for hundreds of years, as we have seen. And it is still crushing us.

Today in the United States, men are responsible for 90 percent of all homicides.[2] As we think of the mass shooters, terrorists, white supremacists, tyrants, and dictators who have massacred people, both recently and over the centuries, the violence has come disproportionately from men with a distorted sense of power, what my friend Kristin Du Mez has named "militant masculinity." I believe a lot of the reason for that has to do with social constructs, or what Scripture refers to as "principalities and powers."[3] That's why it's important to remind ourselves that this is not a battle of "flesh and blood" but is much bigger than that. It is a battle of principalities and powers, of evil at work in the world.

There is a case to be made that in patriarchal societies it is simply men's proximity to power that allows us to do such destructive things. If women had the same access to power, the argument goes, they might do the same terrible things. While that may be true, there remains an

---

2. For a deeper dive into male aggression, take a look at the book I wrote with Michael Martin, *Beating Guns*—specifically chapter 9, "Dudes and Their Guns."

3. In Ephesians, the apostle Paul writes, "For we do not wrestle against flesh and blood, but against principalities, against powers, against the rulers of the darkness of this age, against spiritual hosts of wickedness in the heavenly places" (Eph. 6:12 NKJV). He uses "principalities" and "powers" to describe the forces of evil that destroy life. It is a reminder that the devil does not have a red tail and a pitchfork but works through human systems and structures, and even "rulers of the darkness," as the apostle Paul put it.

unmistakable thread throughout history in which male aggression and female conscience are at odds—where male aggression has nearly destroyed us, and female conscience (with the help of God) has saved us.

In the current state of America, men have been the steady base of support for some of our most hurtful policies, and women—Black women in particular—have been our prophetic conscience. That's why, as we consider what it will take to repair the cracks in our foundation for life, I believe we need to listen to and learn from women—and especially women (and other folks) who have been historically marginalized. These voices are our conscience, our spiritual and moral lifeline back to a consistent ethic of life. We need to sit at the feet of those who have lived on the margins of power because where we sit determines what we see.

Dear Church

As our entire country and the church continue reckoning with the legacies of patriarchy—as we have seen in the #MeToo and #ChurchToo movements—what is clear is that the more institutions exclude women at all levels of leadership, the more space they make for the demonic forces of abuse and exploitation. We've seen that prove itself true from the Catholic Church and the Southern Baptist Convention to the Boy Scouts of America. It is time, long past time, that we listen to women and follow their lead. In my community, we speak of spaces that are not racially diverse by saying, "If it's all white, something's not right." And we might also say, "If it's all guys, something's awry," even though it doesn't rhyme as well. In the words of my pal Carlos Rodriguez:

> Dear Church,
> Jesus believed women.
> Protected women.
> Empowered women.

Honored women publicly.

Released the voice of women.

Confided in women.

Was funded by women.

Celebrated women by name.

Learned from women.

Respected women.

And spoke of women as examples to follow.

Your turn.[4]

Militant Masculinity versus Female Conscience

While it's true that sin transcends gender, it is stunning to contrast militant masculinity and female conscience throughout history. Consider just a few examples.

When Pharaoh feared revolt among the enslaved Israelites in Egypt, he commanded the Hebrew midwives, Shiphrah and Puah, "If you see that the baby is a boy, kill him; but if it is a girl, let her live" (Ex. 1:16). The midwives, however, engaged in subversive acts of civil disobedience and let the boys live. Likewise, Moses' mother, Jochebed, defied imperial terror when she put Moses in a basket and floated him downriver, where he was rescued and raised by Pharaoh's own daughter. Shiphrah, Puah, and Jochebed chose life, subverted the powers of death, and thwarted a patriarchal genocide.

Rahab fearlessly defied the powers that be when she risked her life taking in the Hebrew spies in the city of Jericho.

It was the women who remained at the foot of the cross when all the men in Jesus' life had betrayed, fled, or denied him.

---

4. Carlos A. Rodriguez (@CarlosHappyNPO), Twitter, February 11, 2019, https://twitter.com/carlos happynpo/status/1095117168805437440.

It was women such as Perpetua and Felicity in the third century who showed us what fierce love looks like in the face of persecution and martyrdom.

It was Sojourner Truth who stood against oppression, declaring in 1852, "Ain't I a woman?"

During the 1900s, when the gun manufacturer Winchester launched an aggressive ad campaign aimed to reach 3.4 million boys, it was the moms who thwarted their success. When Winchester advertised that "every real boy needs a gun," the boys took the bait, but the moms didn't. One retailer complained, "I could sell a thousand rifles to boys if it weren't for their parents." Those moms were the resistance to the proliferation of guns, even as Moms Demand Action (which now has more members than the NRA) is a force for life today.[5]

Over and over, women in Scripture and throughout history subvert the violence of men in powerful positions. These mothers of our faith and of our conscience are our standard bearers, teaching us to resist evil with boldness, to lead with wisdom, and to heal the wounds of violence.

As I dive into Scripture and church history, I keep finding new heroes of faith and new champions for life. Some of them are women I never heard about in Sunday school, such as Rizpah, a concubine of King Saul.

Rizpah's story is told in 2 Samuel. The backstory is that King Saul

---

5. There are countless other examples of this collision between male aggression and female conscience throughout history and across the globe. In recent years we can see that those who have been most marginalized historically, namely Black women, have risen up as a prophetic conscience in our nation. In so many ways, Donald Trump's presidency was not just about flesh and blood but the principalities and powers: he surfaced some of our worst demons. And it was Black women and people of color who were the resistance.

White evangelical support for Trump held steady around 75 percent or higher during his presidency. While white women were divided almost down the middle in their support for Trump, 88 percent of Black voters and 94 percent of Black women did not support him. Roughly eight in ten white evangelical Protestants supported Trump, and roughly eight in ten Black Christians opposed him. As we have surveyed history, this is no surprise. Some folks want to "make America great again," and it has become clear that what they mean is, "Make America white again."

Gregory A. Smith, "Among White Evangelicals, Regular Churchgoers Are the Most Supportive of Trump," Pew Research Center, April 26, 2017, www.pewresearch.org/fact-tank/2017/04/26/among -white-evangelicals-regular-churchgoers-are-the-most-supportive-of-trump/; Amanda Becker, "White Women Had Doubts. They Voted for Trump Anyway," 19th News, November 7, 2020, https://19thnews.org /2020/11/white-women-had-doubts-they-voted-for-trump-anyway/.

had been doing what kings do: declaring war and shedding blood. And as we know, the blood of those killed cries out to God. As a consequence, there had been three years of famine in the land. When David, who was now king, prayed for guidance, the Lord said, "It is on account of Saul and his blood-stained house; it is because he put the Gibeonites to death" (2 Sam. 21:1).

In an effort to end the famine, David struck a deal with the Gibeonites, using human lives as currency. To make amends for lives taken by Saul, David agreed to give seven of Saul's descendants, including the two sons of Rizpah, as a blood offering. More blood to pay off the blood already shed. He handed over the sons of Rizpah and five others to be massacred. Scripture says that they were "killed and their bodies exposed before the LORD" (v. 6).

It's sickening to think how numb human beings can become to evil. As I read the story of Rizpah again, I thought of eighteen-year-old Michael Brown, who was killed by police in Ferguson, Missouri, in 2014. After police shot him, his body was left in the street for four hours.

In the case of Rizpah, not only were her children killed, their bodies were also left out in the open on a hill and without a proper burial. They were left exposed for birds of prey and wild animals. The bodies of human beings made in the image of God were left outside as animal food.

But Rizpah wasn't numb and she wouldn't stand for it.

With the reckless love and courage of a grieving mother, she set up camp. She spread sackcloth on a rock beside the bodies and stayed there from the "beginning of the harvest till the rain poured down from the heavens on the bodies," suggesting that she was there for the season (v. 10). Day after day, perhaps week after week, she kept vigil and protected the bodies from the animals. She protestified. Instead of hiding her grief, she chose to go public. And it was her public display of lament that became a wake-up call of conscience for her country.

Word of Rizpah's vigil spread all over the land, eventually making it all the way to King David. And it stirred something in David. When he heard of Rizpah's courage, he was moved to gather up the bones of all the dead and bury them. Rizpah pricked the conscience of a king who had become way too comfortable with killing. Rizpah also helped wake up a culture that had become so dehumanized, it never questioned the exchange of human lives as currency.

Rizpah's story reminds me of another mother, Mamie Till. Emmett Till, Mamie's fourteen-year-old son, a Black boy, was tortured and lynched by white men in Mississippi in 1955. Mamie demonstrated Rizpah's motherly courage and prophetic fire when she insisted on having an open-casket funeral for her young son. She wanted everyone to see what had really happened to him. She protestified, and it was her prophetic lament that shook our nation.

That's what a woman of conscience can do, and it's what public lament in the face of violence can do. Such acts of prophetic resistance wake us up to our violence so that we can be set free from it. A mother's conscience can move militant rulers to honor life again. A woman's tears have the power to heal our blood-stained land. Neither Rizpah or Mamie Till got their sons back, but they transformed the evil and death they suffered into life with their courage.

The God Who Comforts

These examples of female conscience stand in stark contrast to male ambition and militant masculinity. They can also help us better understand God, especially since we know that women are made in the image of God just as much as men are. And yet most of the metaphors used to describe God reflect traditionally masculine images of power: king, warrior, Lion of Judah, father, lord. When those are the only images we focus on, we're missing out on a whole part of God's character.

Many adjectives and metaphors for God in Scripture are feminine, and certainly the Holy Spirit, the Comforter, has been understood as a feminine or maternal part of God. I relate to this because I was raised by a single mom who taught me by example what love, compassion, hospitality, and grace look like. It's natural for me to see a reflection of God in my mother or a reflection of my mother's love in God. My mother has helped me understand and experience God's love in the absence of a father for most of my life.

My friend Lauren Winner often points out how the names of many churches reflect a male bias. You've probably seen a Church of the Good Shepherd and a Church of the Redeemer, but have you ever seen a Church of the Mother Hen? That, too, is a part of God's character. Speaking of the people of Jerusalem who rejected him, Jesus said, "How often I have longed to gather your children together, as a hen gathers her chicks under her wings" (Luke 13:34). One of the Hebrew names for God, El Shaddai, which is usually translated as "God Almighty," can also be translated as the "Breasted One." We also have images in Scripture of God as a mother bear, as an eagle hovering over her nest, and as a woman in labor.[6] Speaking through the prophet Isaiah, God says, "For a long time I have kept silent, I have been quiet and held myself back. But now, like a woman in childbirth, I cry out, I gasp and pant" (Isa. 42:14).

Certainly, the Bible also portrays God as a father. In Gethsemane, Jesus called out to God as "Abba," which is Aramaic for "Daddy." As someone who was raised by a single mother, I've always felt comforted by the verse that God is a "father to the fatherless" (Ps. 68:5). But none of the traditionally male images of God in Scripture are more important than the female images that portray God as a comforter, a nurturer, a caregiver. These characteristics actually transcend gender.

---

6. See Hosea 13:8, Deuteronomy 32:10–11 (NLT), and Isaiah 42:14. My friend Mimi Haddad has done great work on this. For a quick read, check out her piece "Is God Male?" *Mutuality*, Autumn 2012, www.cbeinternational.org/sites/default/files/god_male_haddad.pdf.

The point is this: we have a God who comforts. Some of us have felt love from a mother; some of us have felt love from a father. Some of us have felt love from both parents, and some of us have felt love from neither. But God is here for all of us, to show us the love of mother and father, and even to provide the love some of us might never have felt at home. This is why Scripture gives us so many images and metaphors for God: wherever we have felt love and comfort, we have experienced God. God *is* love. And where love is, God is.

Midwives of a Better World

I want to close this book on life by inviting us to think of ourselves as midwives. We are to be midwives of a better world. We are to help God give birth to something new, to assist God in bringing new life into the world.

It's a metaphor that might be a stretch for some of us dudes, but it is firmly biblical. When I was in India working with Mother Teresa, she asked me to read a Scripture verse during one of our morning prayer services. The verse that day was from the book of Romans, and it has become one of my favorites: "We know that the whole creation has been groaning as in the pains of childbirth right up to the present time" (Rom. 8:22). The next verse goes on to say that we find ourselves groaning along with it.

There is a lot of groaning in our world today, and yet this biblical vision is not of a dying world but of a pregnant world. Even as the age in which we live is filled with death, anxiety, and grief, it is also a time that is pregnant with hope and the promise of new life. If you find yourself saddened by the state of the world, I pray that you will be reminded and reassured that there is life on the other side of this.

Being a man with no biological kids, I can't write with any authority about giving birth, but I understand that before there is the beautiful new life, there is pain, yelling, sweat, tears, and even a choice word or two that gets dropped. We call it labor for a reason. It involves groaning, weeping, and blood. It feels like that's where our country is right now: in pain.

I'm told by those who have given birth that there are times during labor when they felt like they couldn't breathe. It makes me think of all those in our streets who have cried out, "I can't breathe," in solidarity with George Floyd, Eric Garner, Breonna Taylor, and all those whose lives and dignity are being crushed. Our country is hurting. Our world is aching. But maybe, just maybe, death doesn't get the last word.

The image of a world in labor reminds me of the truth spoken by my sister Valarie Kaur, a Sikh activist and lawyer, when she offered a prophetic reflection on the present darkness in which we find ourselves.[7] She raised this very issue: Could it be that America is not dying, but being born? Is this the darkness of the tomb, or is this the darkness of the womb?

Valarie ended her powerful talk by inviting us all to participate, to labor, to breathe and push. Inspired her vision, I leave you with this invitation.

Breathe.

And push.

Breathe in the Spirit of the living God.

Push back against the forces of death.

Breathe in life.

Push back against the darkness.

Breathe in Jesus.

Push back against the principalities and powers that crush life.

Breathe.

And push.

In this present darkness, with all the groaning and pain, the world is pregnant with hope.

---

7. Valarie's speech is epic, and you can watch or read it here. Valarie Kaur, "'Breathe! Push!' Watch This Sikh Activist's Powerful Prayer for America," *Washington Post*, March 6, 2017, www.washingtonpost.com/news/acts-of-faith/wp/2017/03/06/breathe-push-watch-this-sikh-activists-powerful-prayer-for-america/.

A new world is waiting to be born.
And we get to be the midwives.
Breathe in.
And push.

RETHINKING LIFE

- Given what you've read about violence throughout human history, would you say that the primary factor is gender, proximity to power, or social constructs such as patriarchy? Share the reasons for your response.
- In what ways do you recognize female conscience at work in your community and in the larger world today? Or, more broadly, where have you seen moral courage standing against aggression and violence? Who are some of your heroes and sheroes?
- What insights or principles might you discern in the story of Rizpah about what it means to be a voice of conscience? What did love require of her?
- Overall, would you say you tend to think of God primarily in terms of male or female images? What images do you find most meaningful?
- How might our view of God as male or female help or hurt us when it comes to protecting and advocating for life?
- How would you answer Valarie Kaur's questions: Could it be that America is not dying but being born? Is this the darkness of the tomb, or is this the darkness of the womb?
- How do you respond to the metaphor of being midwives of a better world? What does love require of midwives? How might that translate into what love requires of you as you colabor with God to be an advocate for life?

Node.js in Practice

ALEX YOUNG
MARC HARTER

For online information and ordering of this and other Manning books, please visit
www.manning.com. The publisher offers discounts on this book when ordered in quantity.
For more information, please contact

    Special Sales Department
    Manning Publications Co.
    20 Baldwin Road
    PO Box 761
    Shelter Island, NY 11964
    Email: orders@manning.com

Manning Publications Co.
20 Baldwin Road
PO Box 761
Shelter Island, NY 11964

Development editor: Cynthia Kane
Technical development editor: Jose Maria Alvarez Rodriguez
Copyeditor: Benjamin Berg
Proofreader: Katie Tennant
Typesetter: Gordan Salinovic
Cover designer: Marija Tudor

3 9547 00398 3306

ISBN 9781617290930
Printed in the United States of America
1 2 3 4 5 6 7 8 9 10 – EBM – 19 18 17 16 15 14

brief contents

iii

contents

v

foreword

You have in your hands a book that will take you on an in-depth tour of Node.js. In the pages to come, Alex Young and Marc Harter will help you grasp Node's core in a deep way: from modules to real, networked applications.

Networked applications are, of course, an area where Node.js shines. You, dear reader, are likely well aware of that; I daresay it is your main reason for purchasing this tome! For the few of you who actually read the foreword, let me tell you the story of how it all began.

In the beginning, there was the C10K problem. And the C10K problem raised this question: if you want to handle 10,000 concurrent network connections on contemporary hardware, how do you go about that?

You see, for the longest time operating systems were terrible at dealing with large numbers of network connections. The hardware was terrible in many ways, the software was terrible in other ways, and when it came to the interaction between hardware and software … linguists had a field day coming up with proper neologisms; plain *terrible* doesn't do it justice. Fortunately, technology is a story of progress; hardware gets better, software saner. Operating systems improved at managing large numbers of network connections, as did user software.

We conquered the C10K problem a long time ago, moved the goal posts, and now we've set our sights on the C100K, C500K, and C1M problems. Once we've comfortably crossed those frontiers, I fully expect that the C10M problem will be next.

Node.js is part of this story of ever-increasing concurrency, and its future is bright: we live in an increasingly connected world and that world needs a power tool to connect everything. I believe Node.js is that power tool, and I hope that, after reading this book, you will feel the same way.

BEN NOORDHUIS
COFOUNDER, STRONGLOOP, INC.

preface

When Node.js arrived in 2009, we knew something was different. JavaScript on the server wasn't anything new. In fact, server-side JavaScript has existed almost as long as client-side JavaScript. With Node, the speed of the JavaScript runtimes, coupled with the event-based parallelism that many JavaScript programmers were already familiar with, were indeed compelling. And not just for client-side JavaScript developers, which was our background—Node attracted developers from the systems level to various server-side backgrounds, PHP to Ruby to Java. We all found ourselves inside this movement.

At that time, Node was changing a lot, but we stuck with it and learned a whole lot in the process. From the start, Node focused on making a small, low-level core library that would provide enough functionality for a large, diverse user space to grow. Thankfully, this large and diverse user space exists today because of these design decisions early on. Node is a lot more stable now and used in production for numerous startups as well as established enterprises.

When Manning approached us about writing an intermediate-level book on Node, we looked at the lessons we had learned as well as common pitfalls and struggles we saw in the Node community. Although we loved the huge number of truly excellent third-party modules available to developers, we noticed many developers were getting less and less education on the core foundations of Node. So we set out to write *Node in Practice* to journey into the roots and foundations of Node in a deep and thorough manner, as well as tackle many issues we personally have faced and have seen others wrestle with.

acknowledgments

We have many people to thank, without whose help and support this book would not have been possible.

Thanks to the Manning Early Access Program (MEAP) readers who posted comments and corrections in the Author Online forum.

Thanks to the technical reviewers who provided invaluable feedback on the manuscript at various stages of its development: Alex Garrett, Brian Falk, Chris Joakim, Christoph Walcher, Daniel Bretoi, Dominic Pettifer, Dylan Scott, Fernando Monteiro Kobayashi, Gavin Whyte, Gregor Zurowski, Haytham Samad, JT Marshall, Kevin Baister, Luis Gutierrez, Michael Piscatello, Philippe Charrière, Rock Lee, Shiju Varghese, and Todd Williams.

Thanks to the entire Manning team for helping us every step of the way, especially our development editor Cynthia Kane, our copyeditor Benjamin Berg, our proofreader Katie Tennant, and everyone else who worked behind the scenes.

Special thanks to Ben Noordhuis for writing the foreword to our book, and to Valentin Crettaz and Michael Levin for their careful technical proofread of the book shortly before it went into production.

Alex Young

I couldn't have written this book without the encouragement and support of the DailyJS community. Thanks to everyone who has shared modules and libraries with me over the last few years: keeping up to date with the Node.js community would have been impossible without you. Thank you also to my colleagues at Papers who have allowed me to use my Node.js skills in production. Finally, thanks to Yuka for making me believe I can do crazy things like start companies and write books.

Marc Harter

I would like thank Ben Noordhuis, Isaac Schlueter, and Timothy Fontaine for all the IRC talks over Node; you know the underlying systems that support Node in such a deep way that learning from you makes Node even richer. Also, I want to thank my coauthor Alex; it seems rare to have such a similar approach to writing a book as I did with Alex, plus it was fun for a Midwestern US guy to talk shop with an English chap. Ultimately my heart goes out to my wife, who really made this whole thing possible, if I'm honest. Hannah, you are loved; thank you.

about this book

Node.js in Practice exists to provide readers a deeper understanding of Node's core modules and packaging system. We believe this is foundational to being a productive and confident Node developer. Unfortunately, this small core is easily missed for the huge and vibrant third-party ecosystem with modules prebuilt for almost any task. In this book we go beyond regurgitating the official Node documentation in order to get practical and thorough. We want the reader to be able to dissect the inner workings of the third-party modules they include as well as the projects they write.

This book is not an entry-level Node book. For that, we recommend reading Manning's *Node.js In Action*. This book is targeted at readers who already have experience working with Node and are looking to take it up a notch. Intermediate knowledge of JavaScript is recommended. Familiarity with the Windows, OS X, or Linux command line is also recommended.

In addition, we're aware that many Node developers have come from a client-side JavaScript background. For that reason, we spend some time explaining less-familiar concepts such as working with binary data, how underlying networking and file systems work, and interacting with the host operating system—all using Node as a teaching guide.

Chapter roadmap

This book is organized into three parts.

Part 1 covers Node's core fundamentals, where we focus our attention on what's possible using only Node's core modules (no third-party modules). Chapter 1 recaps

Node.js's purpose and function. Then chapters 2 through 8 each cover in depth a different core aspect of Node from buffers to streams, networking to child processes.

Part 2 focuses on real-world development recipes. Chapters 9 through 12 will help you master four highly applicable skills—testing, web development, debugging, and running Node in production. In addition to Node core modules, these sections include the use of various third-party modules.

Part 3 guides you through creating your own Node modules in a straightforward manner that ties in all kinds of ways to use npm commands for packaging, running, testing, benchmarking, and sharing modules. It also includes helpful tips on versioning projects effectively.

There are 115 techniques in the book, each module covering a specific Node.js topic or task, and each divided into practical Problem/Solution/Discussion sections.

Code conventions and downloads

All source code in the book is in a `fixed-width font like this`, which sets it off from the surrounding text. In many listings, the code is annotated to point out the key concepts, and numbered bullets are sometimes used in the text to provide additional information about the code.

This book's coding style is based on the Google JavaScript Style Guide.[1] That means we've put `var` statements on their own lines, used `camelCase` to format function and variable names, and we always use semicolons. Our style is a composite of the various JavaScript styles used in the Node community.

Most of the code shown in the book can be found in various forms in the sample source code that accompanies it. The sample code can be downloaded free of charge from the Manning website at www.manning.com/Node.jsinPractice, as well as from GitHub at the following link: https://github.com/alexyoung/nodeinpractice.

Author Online forum

Purchase of *Node.js in Practice* includes free access to a private web forum run by Manning Publications where you can make comments about the book, ask technical questions, and receive help from the authors and from other users. To access the forum and subscribe to it, point your web browser to www.manning.com/Node.jsinPractice. This page provides information on how to get on the forum once you're registered, what kind of help is available, and the rules of conduct on the forum.

The Author Online forum and the archives of previous discussions will be accessible from the publisher's website as long as the book is in print.

You can also contact the authors at the following Google Group URL: https://groups.google.com/forum/#!forum/nodejsinpractice.

---

[1] https://google-styleguide.googlecode.com/svn/trunk/javascriptguide.xml

about the cover illustration

The caption for the illustration on the cover of *Node.js in Practice* is "Young Man from Ayvalik," a town in Turkey on the Aegean Coast. The illustration is taken from a collection of costumes of the Ottoman Empire published on January 1, 1802, by William Miller of Old Bond Street, London. The title page is missing from the collection and we have been unable to track it down to date. The book's table of contents identifies the figures in both English and French, and each illustration bears the names of two artists who worked on it, both of whom would no doubt be surprised to find their art gracing the front cover of a computer programming book ... two hundred years later.

The collection was purchased by a Manning editor at an antiquarian flea market in the "Garage" on West 26th Street in Manhattan. The seller was an American based in Ankara, Turkey, and the transaction took place just as he was packing up his stand for the day. The Manning editor didn't have on his person the substantial amount of cash that was required for the purchase, and a credit card and check were both politely turned down. With the seller flying back to Ankara that evening, the situation was getting hopeless. What was the solution? It turned out to be nothing more than an old-fashioned verbal agreement sealed with a handshake. The seller simply proposed that the money be transferred to him by wire, and the editor walked out with the bank information on a piece of paper and the portfolio of images under his arm. Needless to say, we transferred the funds the next day, and we remain grateful and impressed by this unknown person's trust in one of us. It recalls something that might have happened a long time ago.

We at Manning celebrate the inventiveness, the initiative, and, yes, the fun of the computer business with book covers based on the rich diversity of regional life of two centuries ago, brought back to life by the pictures from this collection.

Part 1

Node fundamentals

Node has an extremely small standard library intended to provide the lowest-level API for module developers to build on. Even though it's relatively easy to find third-party modules, many tasks can be accomplished without them. In the chapters to follow, we'll take a deep dive into a number of core modules and explore how to put them to practical use.

By strengthening your understanding of these modules, you'll in turn become a more well-rounded Node programmer. You'll also be able to dissect third-party modules with more confidence and understanding.

Getting started

Node has quickly become established as a viable and indeed efficient web development platform. Before Node, not only was JavaScript on the server a novelty, but non-blocking I/O was something that required special libraries for other scripting languages. With Node, this has all changed.

The combination of non-blocking I/O and JavaScript is immensely powerful: we can handle reading and writing files, network sockets, and more, all asynchronously *in the same process*, with the natural and expressive features of JavaScript callbacks.

This book is geared toward intermediate Node developers, so this chapter is a quick refresher. If you want a thorough treatment of Node's basics, then see our companion book, *Node.js in Action* (by Mike Cantelon, Marc Harter, TJ Holowaychuk, and Nathan Rajlich; Manning Publications, 2013).

In this chapter we'll introduce Node, what it is, how it works, and why it's something you can't live without. In chapter 2 you'll get to try out some techniques by looking at Node's globals—the objects and methods available to every Node process.

Preflight check

Node In Practice is a recipe-style book, aimed at intermediate and advanced Node developers. Although this chapter covers some introductory material, later chapters advance quickly. For a beginner's introduction to Node, see our companion book, *Node.js in Action*.

1.1   Getting to know Node

Node is a *platform* for developing network applications. It's built on V8, Google's JavaScript runtime engine. Node isn't just V8, though. An important part of the Node platform is its core library. This encompasses everything from TCP servers to asynchronous and synchronous file management. This book will teach you how to use these modules properly.

But first: why use Node, and when should you use it? Let's look into that question by seeing what kinds of scenarios Node excels at.

1.1.1   Why Node?

Let's say you're building an advertising server and distributing millions of adverts per minute. Node's non-blocking I/O would be an extremely cost-effective solution for this, because the server could make the best use of available I/O without you needing to write special low-level code. Also, if you already have a web team that can write JavaScript, then they should be able to contribute to the Node project. A typical, heavier web platform wouldn't have these advantages, which is why companies like Microsoft are contributing to Node despite having excellent technology stacks like .NET. Visual Studio users can install Node-specific tools[1] that add support for IntelliSense, profiling, and even npm. Microsoft also developed WebMatrix (http://www.microsoft.com/web/webmatrix/), which directly supports Node and can also be used to deploy Node projects.

Node embraces non-blocking I/O as a way to improve performance in certain types of applications. JavaScript's traditional event-based implementation means it has a relatively convenient and well-understood syntax that suits asynchronous programming. In a typical programming language, an I/O operation blocks execution until it completes. Node's asynchronous file and network APIs mean processing can still occur while these relatively slow I/O operations finish. Figure 1.1 illustrates how different tasks can be performed using asynchronous network and file system APIs.

In figure 1.1, a new HTTP request has been received and parsed by Node's `http` module ❶. The ad server's application code then makes a database query, using an asynchronous API—a callback passed to a database read function ❷. While Node waits for this to finish, the ad server is able to read a template file from the disk ❸.

---

[1] See https://nodejstools.codeplex.com/.

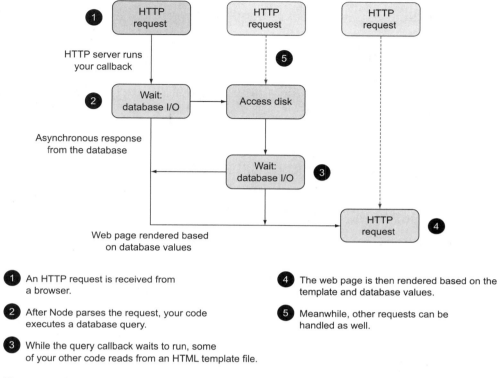

1. An HTTP request is received from a browser.

2. After Node parses the request, your code executes a database query.

3. While the query callback waits to run, some of your other code reads from an HTML template file.

4. The web page is then rendered based on the template and database values.

5. Meanwhile, other requests can be handled as well.

Figure 1.1 An advertising server built with Node

This template will be used to display a suitable web page. Once the database request has finished, the template and database results are used to render the response ④.

While this is happening, other requests could also be hitting the ad server, and they'll be handled based on the available resources ⑤. Without having to think about threads when developing the ad server, you're able to push Node to use the server's I/O resources very efficiently, just by using standard JavaScript programming techniques.

Other scenarios where Node excels are web APIs and web scraping. If you're downloading and extracting content from web pages, then Node is perfect because it can be coaxed into simulating the DOM and running client-side JavaScript. Again, Node has a performance benefit here, because scrapers and web spiders are costly in terms of network and file I/O.

If you're producing or consuming JSON APIs, Node is an excellent choice because it makes working with JavaScript objects easy. Node's web frameworks (like Express, http://expressjs.com) make creating JSON APIs fast and friendly. We have full details on this in chapter 9.

Node isn't limited to web development. You can create any kind of TCP/IP server that you like. For example, a network game server that broadcasts the game's state to

When to use Node

To get you thinking like a true Nodeist, the table below has examples of applications where Node is a good fit.

Node's strengths

Scenario	Node's strengths
Advertising distribution	■ Efficiently distributes small pieces of information ■ Handles potentially slow network connections ■ Easily scales up to multiple processors or servers
Game server	■ Uses the accessible language of JavaScript to model business logic ■ Programs a server catering to specific networking requirements without using C
Content management system, blog	■ Good for a team with client-side JavaScript experience ■ Easy to make RESTful JSON APIs ■ Lightweight server, complex browser JavaScript

various players over TCP/IP sockets can perform background tasks, perhaps maintaining the game world, while it sends data to the players. Chapter 7 explores Node's networking APIs.

1.1.2   *Node's main features*

Node's main features are its standard library, module system, and npm. Of course, there's more to it than that, but in this book we'll focus on teaching you how to use these parts of Node. We'll use third-party libraries where it's considered best practice, but you'll see a lot of Node's built-in features.

In fact, Node's strongest and most powerful feature is its standard library. This is really two parts: a set of binary libraries and the core modules. The binary libraries include libuv, which provides a fast run loop and non-blocking I/O for networking and the file system. It also has an HTTP library, so you can be sure your HTTP clients and servers are fast.

Figure 1.2 is a high-level overview of Node's internals that shows how everything fits into place.

Node's core modules are mostly written in JavaScript. That means if there's anything you either don't understand or want to understand in more detail, then you can read Node's source code. This includes features like networking, high-level file system operations, the module system, and streams. It also includes Node-specific features like running multiple Node processes at once with the cluster module, and wrapping sections of code in event-based error handlers, known as *domains*.

The next few sections focus on each core module in more detail, starting with the events API.

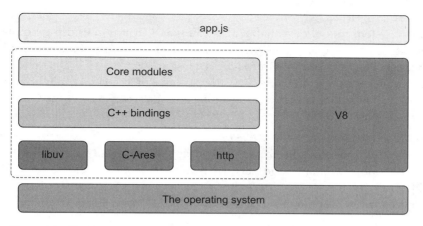

Figure 1.2 Node's key parts in context

EVENTEMITTER: AN API FOR EVENTS

Sooner or later every Node developer runs into `EventEmitter`. At first it seems like something only library authors would need to use, but it's actually the basis for most of Node's core modules. The streams, networking, and file system APIs derive from it.

You can inherit from `EventEmitter` to make your own event-based APIs. Let's say you're working on a PayPal payment-processing module. You could make it event-based, so instances of `Payment` objects emit events like `paid` and `refund`. By designing the class this way, you decouple it from your application logic, so you can reuse it in more than one project.

We have a whole chapter dedicated to events: see chapter 4 for more. Another interesting part of `EventEmitter` is that it's used as the basis for the `stream` module.

STREAM: THE BASIS FOR SCALABLE I/O

Streams inherit from `EventEmitter` and can be used to model data with unpredictable throughput—like a network connection where data speeds can vary depending on what other users on the network are doing. Using Node's `stream` API allows you to create an object that receives events about the connection: `data` for when new data comes in, `end` when there's no more data, and `error` when errors occur.

Rather than passing lots of callbacks to a readable stream constructor function, which would be messy, you subscribe to the events you're interested in. Streams can be piped together, so you could have one stream class that reads data from the network and then pipe it to a stream that transforms the data into something else. This could be data from an XML API that's transformed into JSON, making it easier to work with in JavaScript.

We love streams, so we've dedicated a whole chapter to them. Skip to chapter 5 to dive right in. You might think that events and streams sound abstract, and though that's true, it's also interesting to note that they're used as a basis for I/O modules, like `fs` and `net`.

FS: WORKING WITH FILES

Node's file system module is capable of reading and writing files using non-blocking I/O, but it also has synchronous methods. You can get information about files with `fs.stat`, and the synchronous equivalent is `fs.statSync`.

If you want to use streams to process the contents of a file in a super-efficient manner, then use `fs.createReadStream` to return a `ReadableStream` object. There's more about this in chapter 6.

NET: CREATE NETWORK CLIENTS AND SERVERS

The networking module is the basis for the `http` module and can be used to create generalized network clients and servers. Although Node development is typically thought of as web-based, chapter 7 shows you how to create TCP and UDP servers, which means you're not limited to HTTP.

GLOBAL OBJECTS AND OTHER MODULES

If you have some experience making web applications with Node, perhaps with the Express framework, then you've already been using the `http`, `net`, and `fs` core modules without necessarily realizing it. Other built-in features aren't headline-grabbing, but are critical to creating programs with Node.

One example is the idea of global objects and methods. The `process` object, for example, allows you to pipe data into and out of a Node program by accessing the standard I/O streams. Much like Unix and Windows scripting, you can `cat` data to a Node program. The ubiquitous `console` object, beloved by JavaScript developers everywhere, is also considered a global object.

Node's module system is also part of this global functionality. Chapter 2 is packed with techniques that show you how to use these features.

Now that you've seen some of the core modules, it's time to see them in action. The example will use the `stream` module to generate statistics on streams of text, and you'll be able to use it with files and HTTP connections. If you want to learn more about the basics behind streams or HTTP in Node, refer to *Node.js in Action*.

1.2   *Building a Node application*

Instead of wading through more theory, we'll show you how to build a Node application. It's not just any application, though: it uses some of Node's key features, like modules and streams. This will be a fast and intense tour of Node, so start up your favorite text editor and terminal and get ready.

Here's what you'll learn over the next 10 minutes:

- How to create a new Node project
- How to write your own stream class
- How to write a simple test and run it

Streams are great for processing data, whether you're reading, writing, or transforming it. Imagine you want to convert data from a database into another format, like CSV. You could create a stream class that accepts input from a database and outputs it as a stream of CSV. The output of this new CSV stream could be connected to an HTTP request, so you could stream CSV directly to a browser. The same class could even be connected to a writable file stream—you could even fork the stream to create a file *and* send it to a web browser.

In this example, the stream class will accept text input, count word matches based on a regular expression, and then emit the results in an event when the stream has finished being sent. You could use this to count word matches in a text file, or pipe data from a web page and count the number of paragraph tags—it's up to you. First we need to create a new project.

1.2.1 Creating a new Node project

You might be wondering how a professional Node developer creates a new project. This is a straightforward process, thanks to npm. Though you could create a JavaScript file and run `node file.js`, we'll use `npm init` to make a new project with a package.json file. Create a new directory ❶, cd ❷ into it, and then run `npm init` ❸:

Get used to typing these commands: you'll be doing it often! You can press Return to accept the defaults when prompted by npm. Before you've written a line of JavaScript, you've already seen how cool one of Node's major features—npm—is. It's not just for installing modules, but also for managing projects.

> **When to use a package.json file**
>
> You may have an idea for a small script, and may be wondering if a package.json file is really necessary. It isn't always necessary, but in general you should create them as often as possible.
>
> Node developers prefer small modules, and expressing dependencies in package .json means your project, no matter how small, is super-easy to install in the future, or on another person's machine.

Now it's time to write some JavaScript. In the next section you'll create a new JavaScript file that implements a stream.

1.2.2 Making a stream class

Create a new file called countstream.js and use `util.inherits` to derive from `stream.Writable` and implement the required `_write` method. Too fast? Let's slow down. The full source is in the following listing.

Listing 1.1   A writable stream that counts

```
var Writable = require('stream').Writable;
var util = require('util');

module.exports = CountStream;

util.inherits(CountStream, Writable);          ❶ Inherit from the
                                                  Writable stream.

function CountStream(matchText, options) {
  Writable.call(this, options);
  this.count = 0;                              ❷ Create a RegExp object that
  this.matcher = new RegExp(matchText, 'ig');     matches globally and ignores case.
}

CountStream.prototype._write = function(chunk, encoding, cb) {
  var matches = chunk.toString().match(this.matcher);   ◄── Convert the current
  if (matches) {                                            chunk of input into
    this.count += matches.length;                          a string and use it
  }                                                      ❸ to count matches.
  cb();
};

CountStream.prototype.end = function() {
  this.emit('total', this.count);              ◄── When the stream has
};                                                 ended, "publish" the total
                                               ❹ number of matches.
```

This example illustrates how subsequent examples in this book work. We present a snippet of code, annotated with hints on the underlying code. For example, the first part of the class uses the `util.inherits` method to inherit from the `Writable` base class ❶. This example won't be fully fleshed-out here—for more on writing your own streams, see technique 30 in chapter 5. For now, just focus on how regular expressions are passed to the constructor ❷ and used to count text as it flows into instances of the class ❸. Node's `Writable` class calls `_write` for us, so we don't need to worry about that yet.

> **STREAMS AND EVENTS**   In listing 1.1 there was an event, `total`. This is one we made up—you can make up your own as well. Streams inherit from `EventEmitter`, so they have the same `emit` and `on` methods.

Node's `Writable` base class will also call `end` when there's no more data ❹. This stream can be instantiated and piped as required. In the next section you'll see how to connect it using `pipe`.

1.2.3   Using a stream

Now that you've seen how to make a stream class, you're probably dying to try it out. Make another file, index.js, and add the code shown in the next listing.

Listing 1.2   Using the `CountStream` class

Instantiate a CountStream class that counts text matching "book." ❷

Download www.manning.com. ❸

```
var CountStream = require('./countstream');   ◁
var countStream = new CountStream('book');
var http = require('http');

http.get('http://www.manning.com', function(res) {
    res.pipe(countStream);                     ◁
});

countStream.on('total', function(count) {
    console.log('Total matches:', count);
});
```

Load the countstream.js file. ❶

Pipe the data from the website to countStream, thereby counting the text matching "book." ❹

You can run this example by typing `node index.js`. It should display something like `Total matches: 24`. You can experiment with it by changing the URL that it fetches.

This example loads the module from listing 1.1 ❶ and then instantiates it with the text `'book'` ❷. It also downloads the text from a website using Node's standard `http` module ❸ and then pipes the result through our `CountStream` class ❹.

The significant thing here is `res.pipe(countStream)`. When you pipe data, it doesn't matter how big it is or if the network is slow: the `CountStream` class will dutifully count matches until the data has been processed. This Node program *does not* download the entire file first! It takes the file—piece by piece—and processes it. That's the big thing here, and a critical aspect to Node development.

To recap, figure 1.3 summarizes what you've done so far to create a new Node project. First you created a new directory, and ran `npm init` ❶, then you created some JavaScript files ❷, and finally you ran the code ❸.

Another important part of Node development is testing. The next section wraps up this example by testing `CountStream`.

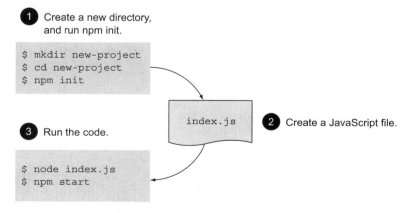

❶ Create a new directory, and run npm init.

```
$ mkdir new-project
$ cd new-project
$ npm init
```

`index.js`

❷ Create a JavaScript file.

❸ Run the code.

```
$ node index.js
$ npm start
```

Figure 1.3   The three steps to creating a new Node project

1.2.4 *Writing a test*

We can write a short test for `CountStream` without using any third-party modules. Node comes with a built-in `assert` module, so we can use that for a quick test. Open test.js and add the code shown next.

Listing 1.3   Using the `CountStream` class

The 'total' event will be emitted when the stream is finished. **❶**

Create a **❸** readable stream of the current file, and pipe the data through CountStream.

❷ Assert the count is the expected amount.

```
var assert = require('assert');
var CountStream = require('./countstream');
var countStream = new CountStream('example');
var fs = require('fs');
var passed = 0;

countStream.on('total', function(count) {
  assert.equal(count, 1);
  passed++;
});

fs.createReadStream(__filename).pipe(countStream);

process.on('exit', function() {
  console.log('Assertions passed:', passed);
});
```

❹ Just before the program is about to exit, display how many assertions have been run.

This test can be run with `node test.js`, and you should see `Assertions passed: 1` printed in the console. The test actually reads the current file and passes the data through `CountStream`. It might invoke Ouroboros, but it's a useful example because it gives us content that we know something about—we can always be sure there is one match for the word *example*.

> **ASSERTIONS** Node comes with an assertion library called `assert`. A basic test can be made by calling the module directly – `assert(expression)`.

The first thing the test does is listen for the `total` event, which is emitted by instances of `CountStream` ❶. This is a good place to assert that the number of matches should be the same as what is expected ❷. A readable stream that represents the current file is opened and piped through our class ❸. Just before the end of the program, we print out how many assertions were hit ❹.

This is important because if the `total` event never fires, then `assert.equal` won't run at all. We have no way of knowing whether tests in callbacks are run, so a simple counter has been used to illustrate how Node programming can require patterns from the other programming languages and platforms that you might be familiar with.

If you're getting tired, you can rest here, but there's a bit of sugar to finish off our project. Node developers like to run tests and other scripts using npm on the command line. Open package.json and change the `"test"` property to look like this:

```
"scripts": {
    "test": "node test.js"
},
```

Now you can run tests just by typing `npm test`. This comes in handy when you have lots of tests and running them is more complicated. Running tests, test runners, and asynchronous testing issues are all covered in chapter 10.

> **npm scripts**
>
> The `npm test` and `npm start` commands can be configured by editing package.json. You can also run arbitrary commands, which are invoked with `npm run command`. All you need to do is set a property under `scripts`, just like listing 1.4.
>
> This is useful for specific types of tests or housekeeping routines—for example `npm run integration-tests`, or maybe even `npm run seed-data`.

Depending on your previous experience with Node, this example might have been intense, but it captures how Node developers think and take advantage of the powerful resources that come with Node.

Now that you've seen how a Node project is put together, we're done with the refresher course on Node. The next chapter introduces our first set of techniques, which is the bulk of this book's format. It covers ways of working with the global features that are available to all Node programs.

1.3   Summary

In this chapter you've learned about *Node.js in Practice*—what it covers and how it focuses on Node's impressive built-in core modules like the networking module and file system modules.

You've also learned about what makes Node tick, and how to use it. Some of the main points we covered were

- When to use Node, and how Node builds on non-blocking I/O, allowing you to write standard JavaScript but get great performance benefits.
- Node's standard library is referred to as its *core modules*.
- What the core modules do—I/O tasks like network protocols, and work with files and more generic features like streams.
- How to quickly start a new Node project, complete with a package.json file so dependencies and scripts can be added.
- How to use Node's powerful `stream` API to process data.
- Streams inherit from `EventEmitter`, so you can emit and respond to any events that you want to use in your application.
- How to write small tests just by using npm and the `assert` module—you can test out ideas without installing any third-party libraries.

Finally, we hope you learned something from our introductory application. Using event-based APIs, non-blocking I/O, and streams is really what Node is all about, but it's also important to take advantage of Node's unique tools like the package.json file and npm.

Now it's time for techniques. The next chapter introduces the features that you don't even have to load to use: the global objects.

Globals:
Node's environment

2

This chapter covers

- Using modules
- What you can do without requiring a single module
- The process and console objects
- Timers

Global objects are available in all modules. They're universal. Whether you're writing network programs, command-line scripts, or web applications, your program will have access to these objects. That means you can always depend on features like console.log and __dirname—both are explained in detail in this chapter.

The goal of this chapter is to introduce Node's global objects and methods to help you learn what functionality is available to all Node processes. This will help you better understand Node and its relationship to the operating system, and how it compares with other JavaScript environments like browsers.

Node provides some important functionality out of the box, even without loading any modules. In addition to the features provided by the ECMAScript language, Node has several *host objects*—objects supplied by Node to help programs to execute.

A key global object is `process`, which is used to communicate with the operating system. Unix programmers will be familiar with standard I/O streams, and these are accessible through the `process` object using Node's streaming API.

Another important global is the `Buffer` class. This is included because JavaScript has traditionally lacked support for binary data. As the ECMAScript standards evolve, this is being addressed, but for now most Node developers rely on the `Buffer` class. For more about buffers, see chapter 3.

Some globals are a separate instance for each module. For example, `module` is available in every Node program, but is local to the current module. Since Node programs may consist of several modules, that means a given program has several different `module` objects—they behave like globals, but are in *module scope*.

In the next section you'll learn how to load modules. The objects and methods relating to modules are globals, and as such are always available and ready to be used.

2.1 Modules

Modules can be used to organize larger programs and distribute Node projects, so it's important to be familiar with the basic techniques required to install and create them.

TECHNIQUE 1   Installing and loading modules

Whether you're using a core module provided by Node or a third-party module from npm, support for modules is baked right into Node and is always available.

PROBLEM

You want to load a third-party module from npm.

SOLUTION

Install the module with the command-line tool, npm, and then load the module using `require`. The following listing shows an example of installing the express module.

Listing 2.1   Using npm

```
$ npm search express
express                    Sinatra inspired web development framework
$ npm install express
express@x.x.x ./node_modules/express
└── methods@x.x.x
└── (Several more dependencies appear here)

$ node
> var express = require('express');
> typeof express
'function'
```

Search for a module based on keywords. ❶

❷ **Load the module using the require method.**

DISCUSSION

The npm command-line tool is distributed with Node, and can be used to search, install, and manage packages. The website https://npmjs.org provides another interface for searching modules, and each module has its own page that displays the associated readme file and dependencies.

Once you know the name of a module, installation is easy: type npm install module-name ❶ and it will be installed into ./node_modules. Modules can also be "globally" installed—running npm install -g module_name will install it into a global folder. This is usually /usr/local/lib/node_modules on Unix systems. In Windows it should be wherever the node.exe binary is located.

After a module has been installed, it can be loaded with require('module-name') ❷. The require method usually returns an object or a method, depending on how the module has been set up.

Searching npm

By default, npm searches across several fields in each module's package.json file. This includes the module's name, description, maintainers, URL, and keywords. That means a simple search like npm search express yields hundreds of results.

You can reduce the number of matches by searching with a regular expression. Wrap a search term in slashes to trigger npm's regular expression matching: npm search /^express$/

However, this is still limited. Fortunately, there are open source modules that improve on the built-in search command. For example, npmsearch by Gorgi Kosev will order results using its own relevance rankings.

The question of whether to install a module globally is critical to developing maintainable projects. If other people need to work on your project, then you should consider adding modules as dependencies to your project's package.json file. Keeping project dependencies tightly managed will make it easier to maintain them in the future when new versions of dependencies are released.

TECHNIQUE 2   Creating and managing modules

In addition to installing and distributing open source modules, "local" modules can be used to organize projects.

PROBLEM

You want to break a project up into separate files.

SOLUTION

Use the exports object.

DISCUSSION

Node's module system provides a solution to splitting code across multiple files. It's very different from include in C, or even require in Ruby and Python. The main difference is that require in Node returns an object rather than loading code into the current namespace, as would occur with a C preprocessor.

In technique 1 you saw how npm can be used to install modules, and how require is used to load them. npm isn't the only thing that manages modules, though—Node has a built-in module system based on the CommonJS Modules/1.1 specification (http://wiki.commonjs.org/wiki/Modules/1.1).

This allows objects, functions, and variables to be exported from a file and used elsewhere. The `exports` object is always present and, although this chapter specifically explores global objects, it's not really a global. It's more accurate to say that the exports object is in module scope.

When a module is focused around a single class, then users of the module will prefer to type `var MyClass = require('myclass');` rather than `var MyClass = require('myclass').MyClass`, so you should use `modules.export`. Listing 2.2 shows how this works. This is different from using the `exports` object, which requires that you set a property to export something.

Listing 2.2   Exporting modules

```
function MyClass() {
}

MyClass.prototype = {
  method: function() {
    return 'Hello';
  }
};

var myClass = new MyClass();

module.exports = myClass;
```

Objects can be exported, including other objects, methods, and properties.

Listing 2.3 shows how to export multiple objects, methods, or values, a technique that would typically be used for utility libraries that export multiple things.

Listing 2.3   Exporting multiple objects, methods, and values

```
exports.method = function() {
  return 'Hello';
};

exports.method2 = function() {
  return 'Hello again';
};
```

Finally, listing 2.4 shows how to load these modules with `require`, and how to use the functionality they provide.

Listing 2.4   Loading modules with require

```
var myClass = require('./myclass');      ①  Load myclass.js.
var module2 = require('./module-2');
                                         ②  Load module-2.js.

console.log(myClass.method());
console.log(module2.method());
console.log(module2.method2());
```

Note that loading a local module always requires a path name—in these examples the path is just ./. Without it, Node will attempt to find a matching module in $NODE _PATH, and then ./node_modules, $HOME/.node_modules, $HOME/.node_libraries, or $PREFIX/lib/node.

In listing 2.4 notice that ./myclass is automatically expanded to ./myclass.js **❶**, and ./module-2 is expanded to ./module-2.js **❷**.

The output from this program would be as follows:

```
Hello
Hello
Hello again
```

Which module?

To determine the exact module Node will load, use `require.resolve(id)`. This will return a fully expanded filename.

Once a module is loaded, it'll be cached. That means that loading it multiple times will return the cached copy. This is generally efficient, and helps you heavily reuse modules within a project without worrying about incurring an overhead when using `require`. Rather than centrally loading all of the dependencies, you can safely call `require` on the same module.

Unloading modules

Although automatically caching modules fits many use cases in Node development, there may be rare occasions when you want to unload a module. The `require.cache` object makes this possible.

To remove a module from the cache, use the `delete` keyword. The full path of the module is required, which you can obtain with `require.resolve`. For example:

```
delete require.cache[require.resolve('./myclass')];
```

This should return `true`, which means the module was unloaded.

In the next technique you'll learn how to group related modules together and load them in one go.

TECHNIQUE 3 **Loading a group of related modules**

Node can treat directories as modules, offering opportunities for logically grouping related modules together.

PROBLEM

You want to group related files together under a directory, and only have to load it with one call to `require`.

SOLUTION

Create a file called index.js to load each module and export them as a group, or add a package.json file to the directory.

DISCUSSION

Sometimes a module is logically self-contained, but it still makes sense to separate it into several files. Most of the modules you'll find on npm will be written this way. Node's module system supports this by allowing directories to act as modules. The easiest way to do this is to create a file called index.js that has a `require` statement to load each file. The following listing demonstrates how this works.

Listing 2.5 The group/index.js file

```
module.exports = {
  one: require('./one'),
  two: require('./two')
};
```

❶ A module is exported that points to each file in the directory.

The group/one.js and group/two.js files can then export values or methods ❶ as required. The next listing shows an example of such a file.

Listing 2.6 The group/one.js file

```
module.exports = function() {
  console.log('one');
};
```

Code that needs to use a folder as a module can then use a single `require` statement to load everything in one go. The following listing demonstrates this.

Listing 2.7 A file loading the group of modules

```
var group = require('./group');

group.one();
group.two();
```

The call to require doesn't need any special handling to work with a directory of modules.

The output of listing 2.7 should look like this:

```
one
two
```

This approach is often used as an architectural technique to structure web applications. Related items, like controllers, models, and views, can be kept in separate folders to help separate concerns within the application. Figure 2.1 shows how to structure applications following this style.

Node also offers an alternative technique that supports this pattern. Adding a package.json file to a directory can help the module system figure out how to load all of the files in the directory at once. The JSON file should include a `main` property to point to a JavaScript file. This is actually the default file Node looks for when loading

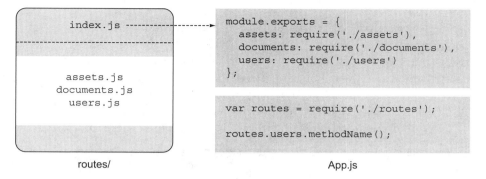

Figure 2.1 Folders as modules

modules—if no package.json is present, it'll then look for index.js. The next listing shows an example of a package.json file.

Listing 2.8   A package.json file for a directory containing a module

```
{ "name" : "group",
  "main" : "./index.js" }        ⟵—— This could point to any file.
```

File extensions

When loading a file, Node is configured to search for files with the .js, .json, and .node extensions. The `require.extensions` array can be used to tell `require` to load files with other extensions. Node's module system will take this into account when treating directories as modules, as well.

This feature is marked as deprecated in Node's documentation, but the module system is also marked as "locked" so it shouldn't go away. If you want to use it, you should check Node's documentation first.[1] If you're just trying to load a JavaScript file from a legacy system that has an unusual extension, then it might be suitable for experimentation.

The `require` API provides many ways to manage files. But what about when you want to load something relative to the current module, or the directory where the module is saved? Read on for an explanation in technique 4.

TECHNIQUE 4   Working with paths

Sometimes you need to open files based on the relative location. Node provides tools for determining the path to the current file, directory, and module.

PROBLEM

You want to access a file that isn't handled by the module system.

---
[1] See http://nodejs.org/api/globals.html#globals_require_extensions.

SOLUTION

Use __dirname or __filename to determine the location of the file.

DISCUSSION

Sometimes you need to load data from a file that clearly shouldn't be handled by Node's module system, but you need to take the path of the current script into account—for example, a template in a web application. The __dirname and __filename variables are extremely useful in such cases.

Running the following listing will print the output of these values.

Listing 2.9   Path variables

```
console.log('__dirname:', __dirname);
console.log('__filename:', __filename);
```
⟵ **These variables point to the fully resolved locations of the current script.**

Most developers join these variables with path fragments using simple string concatenation: var view = __dirname + '/views/view.html';. This works with both Windows and Unix—the Windows APIs are clever enough to automatically switch the slashes to the native format, so you don't need special handling to support both operating systems.

If you really want to ensure paths are joined correctly, you can use the path.join method from Node's path module: path.join(__dirname, 'views', 'view.html');.

Apart from module management, there are globally available objects for writing to the standard I/O streams. The next set of techniques explores process.stdout and the console object.

2.2   Standard I/O and the console object

Text can be piped to a Node process by using command-line tools in Unix or Windows. This section includes techniques for working with these standard I/O streams, and also how to correctly use the console object for a wide range of logging-related tasks.

TECHNIQUE 5   **Reading and writing to standard I/O**

Whenever you need to get data into and out of a program, one useful technique is using the process object to read and write to standard I/O streams.

PROBLEM

You want to pipe data to and from a Node program.

SOLUTION

Use process.stdout and process.stdin.

DISCUSSION

The process.stdout object is a writable stream to stdout. We'll look at streams in more detail in chapter 5, but for now you just need to know it's part of the process object that every Node program has access to, and is helpful for displaying and receiving text input.

The next listing shows how to pipe text from another command, process it, and output it again.

Listing 2.10   Path variables

```
// Run with:
//   cat file.txt | node process.js

process.stdin.resume();
process.stdin.setEncoding('utf8');

process.stdin.on('data', function(text) {
  process.stdout.write(text.toUpperCase());
});
```

Tell the stream we're ready to start reading.

This callback transforms the data in chunks when they're available.

Every time a chunk of text is read from the input stream, it'll be transformed with toUpperCase() and then written to the output stream. Figure 2.2 shows how data flows from one operating system process, through your Node program, and then out through another program. In the terminal, these programs would be linked together with the pipe (|) symbol.

This *pipe*-based approach works well when dealing with input in Unix, because many other commands are designed to work this way. That brings a LEGO-like modularity to Node programs that facilitates reuse.

If you just want to print out messages or errors, Node provides an easier API specifically tailored for this purpose through the console object. The next technique explains how to use it, and some of its less obvious features.

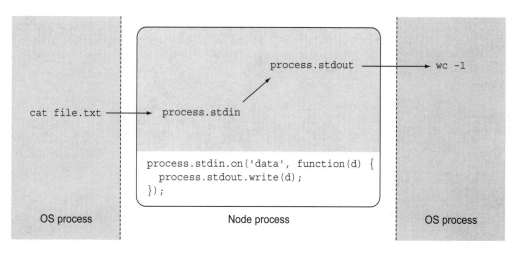

Figure 2.2   Data flows in a simple program that uses stdio.

| TECHNIQUE 6 | **Logging messages** |

The easiest way to log information and errors from a program is by using the `console` object.

PROBLEM

You want to log different types of messages to the console.

SOLUTION

Use `console.log`, `console.info`, `console.error`, and `console.warn`. Be sure to take advantage of the built-in formatting facilities provided by these methods.

DISCUSSION

The `console` object has several methods that can be used to output different types of messages. They'll be written to the relevant output stream, which means you can pipe them accordingly on a Unix system.

Although the basic usage is `console.log('message')`, more functionality is packed in. Variables can be interpolated, or simply appended alongside string literals. This makes it extremely easy to log messages that display the contents of primitive values or objects. The following listing demonstrates these features.

Listing 2.11 Path variables

```
var name = 'alex';
var user = { name: 'alex' };

console.log('Hello');
console.log('Hello %s', name);
console.log('Hello:', name);
console.log('Hello:', user);

console.error('Error, bad user:', user);
```

Simple variable interpolation can be used with strings or numbers.

A space will automatically be added after the colon.

The output of listing 2.11 looks like this:

```
Hello
Hello alex
Hello: alex
Hello: { name: "alex" } //
 Error, bad user: { name: 'alex' }
```

The user object is internally formatted using util.inspect.

When message strings are formatted, `util.format` is used. Table 2.1 shows the supported formatting placeholders.

Table 2.1 Formatting placeholders

Placeholder	Type	Example
%s	String	'%s', 'value'
%d	Number	'%f', 3.14
%j	JSON	'%j', { name: 'alex' }

These formatting placeholders are convenient, but just being able to simply include objects in `console.log` messages without manually appending strings is a handy way to log messages.

The `info` and `warn` methods are synonyms for `log` and `error`. The difference between `log` and `error` is the output stream used. In technique 5, you saw how Node makes standard input and output streams available to all programs. It also exposes the standard error stream through `process.stderr`. The `console.error` method will write to this stream, rather than `process.stdout`. This means you can redirect a Node process's `error` messages in the terminal or in a shell script.

If you ran the previous listing with `2> error-file.log`, the error messages would be redirected to `error-file.log`. The other messages would be printed to the console as usual:

```
node listings/globals/console-1.js 2> errors-file.log
```

The `2` handle refers to the error stream; `1` is standard output. That means you could redirect errors to a log file without having to open files within your Node program, or use a specific logging module. Good old-fashioned shell redirection is good enough for many projects.

> **Standard streams**
>
> Standard streams come in three flavors: stdin, stdout, and stderr. In Unix terminals, these are referred to with numbers. `0` is used for standard input, `1` is standard output, and `2` is standard error.
>
> The same applies to Windows: running a program from the command prompt and adding `2> errors-file.log` will send the error messages to `errors-file.log`, just like Unix.

Stack traces

Another feature of the `console` object is `console.trace()`. This method generates a stack trace at the current point of execution. The generated stack trace includes line numbers for the code that invokes asynchronous callbacks, which can help when reporting errors that would otherwise be difficult to track down. For example, a trace generated inside an event listener will show where the event was triggered from. Technique 28 in chapter 5 explores this in more detail.

Another slightly more advanced use of `console` is its benchmarking feature. Continue reading for a detailed look.

TECHNIQUE 7   Benchmarking a program

Node makes it possible to benchmark programs without any additional tools.

PROBLEM

You need to benchmark a slow operation.

SOLUTION

Use `console.time()` and `console.timeEnd()`.

DISCUSSION

In your career as a Node programmer, there will come a time when you're trying to determine why a particular operation is slow. Fortunately, the `console` object comes with some built-in benchmarking features.

Invoking `console.time('label')` records the current time in milliseconds, and then later calling `console.timeEnd('label')` displays the duration from that point. The time in milliseconds will be automatically printed alongside the label, so you don't have to make a separate call to `console.log` to print a label.

Listing 2.12 is a short program that accepts command-line arguments (see technique 9 for more on handling arguments), with benchmarking to see how fast the file input is read.

Listing 2.12 Benchmarking a function

```
var args = {
  '-h': displayHelp,
  '-r': readFile
};

function displayHelp() {
  console.log('Argument processor:', args);
}

function readFile(file) {
  if (file && file.length) {
    console.log('Reading:', file);
    console.time('read');
    var stream = require('fs').createReadStream(file)
    stream.on('end', function() {
      console.timeEnd('read');
    });
    stream.pipe(process.stdout);
  } else {
    console.error('A file must be provided with the -r option');
    process.exit(1);
  }
}

if (process.argv.length > 0) {
  process.argv.forEach(function(arg, index) {
    args[arg].apply(this, process.argv.slice(index + 1));
  });
}
```

Calling console.timeEnd() will cause the benchmark to be displayed.

Using several interleaved calls to `console.time` with different labels allows multiple benchmarks to be performed, which is perfect for exploring the performance of complex, nested asynchronous programs.

These functions calculate duration based on `Date.now()`, which gives accuracy in milliseconds. To get more accurate benchmarks, the third-party `benchmark` module (https://npmjs.org/package/benchmark) can be used in conjunction with micro-time (https://npmjs.org/package/microtime).

The process object is used for working with standard I/O streams, and used correctly, console handles many of the tasks that the uninitiated may tackle with third-party modules. In the next section we'll further explore the process object to look at how it helps integrate with the wider operating system.

2.3 *Operating system and command-line integration*

The process object can be used to obtain information about the operating system, and also communicate with other processes using exit codes and signal listeners. This section contains some more-advanced techniques for using these features.

TECHNIQUE 8 Getting platform information

Node has some built-in methods for querying operating system functionality.

PROBLEM

You need to run platform-specific code based on the operating system or processor architecture.

SOLUTION

Use the process.arch and process.platform properties.

DISCUSSION

Node JavaScript is generally portable, so it's unlikely that you'll need to branch based on the operating system or process architecture. But you may want to tailor projects to take advantage of operating system–specific features, or simply collect statistics on what systems a script is executing on. Certain Windows-based modules that include bindings to binary libraries could switch between running a 32- or 64-bit version of a binary. The next listing shows how this could be supported.

Listing 2.13 Branching based on architecture

```
switch (process.arch) {
  case 'x64':
    require('./lib.x64.node');
    break;
  case 'ia32':
    require('./lib.Win32.node');
    break;
  default:
    throw new Error('Unsupported process.arch:', process.arch);
}
```

Other information from the system can also be gleaned through the process module. One such method is process.memoryUsage()—it returns an object with three properties that describe the process's current memory usage:

- rss—The *resident set size*, which is the portion of the process's memory that is held in RAM

- heapTotal—Available memory for dynamic allocations
- heapUsed—Amount of heap used

The next technique explores handling command-line arguments in more detail.

TECHNIQUE 9   Passing command-line arguments

Node provides a simple API to command-line arguments that you can use to pass options to programs.

PROBLEM
You're writing a program that needs to receive simple arguments from the command line.

SOLUTION
Use process.argv.

DISCUSSION
The process.argv array allows you to check if any arguments were passed to your script. Because it's an array, you can use it to see how many arguments were passed, if any. The first two arguments are node and the name of the script.

Listing 2.14 shows just one way of working with process.argv. This example loops over process.argv and then slices it to "parse" argument flags with options. You could run this script with node arguments.js -r arguments.js and it would print out its own source.

Listing 2.14   Manipulating command-line arguments

```
var args = {                         ◁──┐   This is a simple object
  '-h': displayHelp,                      used to model the
  '-r': readFile                     ❶    valid arguments.
};

function displayHelp() {
  console.log('Argument processor:', args);
}
                                                    ❷  Pipe out a file
function readFile(file) {                               through the
  console.log('Reading:', file);                       standard
  require('fs').createReadStream(file).pipe(process.stdout);   ◁──┘  output stream.
}
                                                    Call a matching method
if (process.argv.length > 0) {                      from the arg parameter
  process.argv.forEach(function(arg, index) {       model, and slice the full
    args[arg].apply(this, process.argv.slice(index + 1));  ◁──  list of arguments to
  });                                               effectively support
}                                                   passing options from
                                                  ❸  command-line flags.
```

The args object ❶ holds each switch that the script supports. Then createReadStream is used ❷ to pipe the file to the standard output stream. Finally, the function referenced by the command-line switch in args is executed using Function.prototype.apply ❸.

Although this is a toy example, it illustrates how handy `process.argv` can be without relying on a third-party module. Since it's a JavaScript `Array`, it's extremely easy to work with: you can use methods like `map`, `forEach`, and `slice` to process arguments with little effort.

> ### Complex arguments
>
> For more complex programs, use an option parsing module. The two most popular are `optimist` (https://npmjs.org/package/optimist) and `commander` (https://npmjs.org/package/commander). `optimist` converts arguments into an `Object`, which makes them easier to manipulate. It also supports default values, automatic usage generation, and simple validation to ensure certain arguments have been provided. `commander` is slightly different: it uses an abstracted notion of a *program* that allows you to specify your program's accepted arguments using a chainable API.

Good Unix programs handle arguments when needed, and they also exit by returning a suitable status code. The next technique presents how and when to use `process.exit` to signal the successful—or unsuccessful—completion of a program.

TECHNIQUE 10 Exiting a program

Node allows you to specify an exit code when a program terminates.

PROBLEM

Your Node program needs to exit with specific status codes.

SOLUTION

Use `process.exit()`.

DISCUSSION

Exit status codes are significant in both Windows and Unix. Other programs will examine the exit status to determine whether a program ran correctly. This becomes more important when writing Node programs that take part in larger systems, and helps with monitoring and debugging later on.

By default, a Node program returns a `0` exit status. This means the program ran and terminated correctly. Any non-zero status is considered an error. In Unix, this status code is generally accessed by using `$?` in a shell. The Windows equivalent is `%errorlevel%`.

Listing 2.15 shows a modification to listing 2.14 that causes the program to exit cleanly with a relevant status code when no filename is specified with the `-r` option.

Listing 2.15 Returning meaningful exit status codes

```
var args = {
  '-h': displayHelp,
  '-r': readFile
};

function displayHelp() {
```

```
    console.log('Argument processor:', args);
}

function readFile(file) {
  if (file && file.length) {
    console.log('Reading:', file);
    require('fs').createReadStream(file).pipe(process.stdout);
  } else {
    console.error('A file must be provided with the -r option');
    process.exit(1);
  }
}

if (process.argv.length > 0) {
  process.argv.forEach(function(arg, index) {
    args[arg].apply(this, process.argv.slice(index + 1));
  });
}
```

Both console.error and process.exit are used to correctly ❶ indicate an error occurred.

After running listing 2.15, typing `echo $?` in a Unix terminal will display 1. Also note that `console.error` ❶ is used to output an error message. This will cause the message to be written to `process.stderr`, which allows users of the script to easily pipe error messages somewhere.

Exit codes with special meanings

In the Advanced Bash-Scripting Guide (http://tldp.org/LDP/abs/html/index.html), a page is dedicated to status codes called Exit Codes With Special Meanings (http://tldp.org/LDP/abs/html/exitcodes.html). This attempts to generalize error codes, although there's no standard list of status codes for scripting languages, outside of non-zero indicating an error occurred.

Because many Node programs are asynchronous, there are times when you may need to specifically call `process.exit()` or close down an I/O connection to cause the Node process to end gracefully. For example, scripts that use the Mongoose database library (http://mongoosejs.com/) need to call `mongoose.connection.close()` before the Node process will be able to exit.

You may need to track the number of pending asynchronous operations in order to determine when it's safe to call `mongoose.connection.close()`, or the equivalent for another database module. Most people do this using a simple counter variable, incrementing it just before asynchronous operations start, and then decrementing it once their callbacks fire. Once it reaches 0, it'll be safe to close the connection.

Another important facet to developing correct programs is creating signal handlers. Continue reading to learn how Node implements signal handlers and when to use them.

Responding to signals

Node programs can respond to signals sent by other processes.

PROBLEM

You need to respond to signals sent by other processes.

SOLUTION

Use the signal events that are sent to the `process` object.

DISCUSSION

Most modern operating systems use signals as a way of sending a simple message to a program. Signal handlers are typically used in programs that run in the background, because it might be the only way of communicating with them. There are other cases where they can be useful in the kinds of programs you're most likely write—consider a web application that cleanly closes its connection to a database when it receives `SIGTERM`.

The `process` object is an `EventEmitter`, which means you can add event listeners to it. Adding a listener for a POSIX signal name should work—on a Unix system, you can type `man sigaction` to see the names of all of the signals.

Signal listeners enable you to cater to the expected behavior of Unix programs. For example, many servers and daemons will reload configuration files when they receive a `SIGHUP` signal. The next listing shows how to attach a listener to `SIGHUP`.

Listing 2.16   Adding a listener for a POSIX signal

**Binding a
listener to the
SIGHUP signal. ❷**

```
process.stdin.resume();
process.on('SIGHUP', function () {
    console.log('Reloading configuration...');
});

console.log('PID:', process.pid);
```

**❶ Read from stdin so the
program will run until
CTRL-C is pressed or
it's killed.**

**❸ The PID is displayed so you can
use it to send signals using the
kill command.**

Before doing anything with standard input, `resume` should be called ❶ to prevent Node from exiting straight away. Next, a listener is added to the `SIGHUP` event on the process object ❷. Finally, the PID is displayed for the current process ❸.

Once the program in listing 2.16 is running, it'll display the process's PID. The PID can be used with the `kill` command to send the process signals. For example, `kill -HUP 94962` will send the `HUP` signal to PID `94962`. If you send another signal, or just type `kill 94962`, then the process will exit.

It's important to realize that signals can be sent from any process to any other, permissions notwithstanding. Your Node process can send another process a signal by using `process.kill(pid, [signal])`—in this case `kill` doesn't mean the process will be "killed," but simply sent a given signal. The method is named `kill` after the C standard library function in `signal.h`.

Figure 2.3 shows a broad overview of how signals originate from any process in an operating system and can be received by your Node processes.

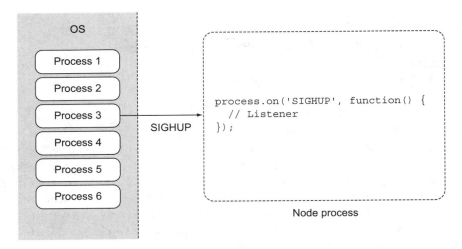

Figure 2.3   Signals originate from a process, and are handled with an event listener.

You don't have to respond to signals in your Node programs, but if you're writing a long-running network server, then signal listeners can be extremely useful. Supporting signals like SIGHUP will make your program fit into existing systems more naturally.

A large part of Node's appeal is its asynchronous APIs and non-blocking I/O features. Sometimes it's desirable to fake this behavior—perhaps in automated tests—or simply to just force code to execute later on. In the next section we'll look at how Node implements JavaScript timers, which support this type of functionality.

2.4 *Delaying execution with timers*

Node implements the JavaScript timer functions setTimeout, setInterval, clear-Timeout, and clearInterval. These functions are globally available. Although they're part of JavaScript as defined by Mozilla, they're not defined in the ECMAScript standard. Instead, timers are part of the HTML DOM Level 0 specification.

TECHNIQUE 12   **Executing functions after a delay with setTimeout**

It's possible to run code once after a delay using Node's setTimeout global method.

PROBLEM

You want to execute a function after a delay.

SOLUTION

Use setTimeout, and use Function.prototype.bind if necessary.

DISCUSSION

The most basic usage of setTimeout is simple: pass it a function to execute and a delay in milliseconds:

```
setTimeout(function() {
  console.log('Hello from the past!');
}, 1000);
```

This seems simple and contrived, but you'll see it used most commonly in tests where asynchronous APIs are being tested and a small delay is necessary to simulate real-world behavior. Node supports JavaScript timers for just such cases.

Methods can also easily be passed to `setTimeout` by using `Function.prototype`
`.bind`. This can be used to bind the first argument to `this`, or more often the object that the method belongs to. The following listing shows how `bind` can be used with a simple object.

Listing 2.17   Combining `setTimeout` with `Function.prototype.bind`

```
function Bomb() {
  this.message = 'Boom!';
}

Bomb.prototype.explode = function() {
  console.log(this.message);
};

var bomb = new Bomb();

setTimeout(bomb.explode.bind(bomb), 1000);
```

Call .bind to ensure the method is bound correctly so it can access internal properties.

Binding ensures that the code inside the method can access the object's internal properties. Otherwise, `setTimeout` would cause the method to run with `this` bound to the global object. Binding a method can be more readable than creating a new anonymous function.

To cancel scheduled functions, retain a reference to the `timeoutId` returned by `setTimeout` and then call `clearTimeout(timeoutId)` **❶**. The next listing demonstrates `clearTimeout`.

Listing 2.18   Using `clearTimeout` to prevent scheduled functions

```
function Bomb() {
  this.message = 'Boom!';
}

Bomb.prototype.explode = function() {
  console.log(this.message);
};

var bomb = new Bomb();

var timeoutId = setTimeout(bomb.explode.bind(bomb), 1000);

clearTimeout(timeoutId);
```

Defuse the bomb by calling clearTimeout to prevent bomb.expode from running. **❶**

When exactly does the callback run?

Although you can specify when a callback runs in milliseconds, Node isn't quite *that* precise. It can guarantee that the callback will run *after* the specified time, but it may be slightly late.

As well as delaying execution, you can also call functions periodically. The next technique discusses how to achieve this by using setInterval.

TECHNIQUE 13 **Running callbacks periodically with timers**

Node can also run callbacks at regular intervals using setInterval, which works in a fashion similar to setTimeout.

PROBLEM

You want to run a callback at a regular interval.

SOLUTION

Use setInterval, and clearInterval to stop the timer.

DISCUSSION

The setInterval method has been around for years in browsers, and it behaves in Node much like the client-side counterparts. The callback will be executed on or just after the specified delay, and will run in the event loop just after I/O (and any calls to setImmediate, as detailed in technique 14).

The next listing shows how to combine setInterval with setTimeout to schedule two functions to execute in a sequence.

Listing 2.19 Using setInterval and setTimeout together

```
function tick() {
  console.log('tick:', Date.now());
}

function tock() {
  console.log('tock:', Date.now());
}

setInterval(tick, 1000);

setTimeout(function() {                    ❶ Run another setInterval
  setInterval(tock, 1000);                    after the first one.
}, 500);
```

The setInterval method itself returns a reference to the timer, which can be stopped by calling clearInterval and passing the reference. Listing 2.19 uses a second call to setTimeout ❶ to trigger a second interval timer that runs 500 milliseconds after the first.

Because setInterval prevents a program from exiting, there are cases where you might want to exit a program if it isn't doing anything else. For example, let's say you're running a program that should exit when a complex operation has finished, and you'd like to monitor it at regular intervals using setInterval. Once the complex operation has finished, you don't want to monitor it any more.

Rather than calling clearInterval, Node 0.10 allows you to call timerRef.unref() at any time before the complex operation has finished. This means you can use setTimeout or setInterval with operations that don't signal their completion.

Listing 2.20 uses `setTimeout` to simulate a long-running operation that will keep the program running while the timer displays the process's memory usage. Once the timeout's delay has been reached, the program will exit *without* calling `clearTimeout`.

Listing 2.20   Keeping a timer alive until the program cleanly exits

```
function monitor() {
  console.log(process.memoryUsage());
}

var id = setInterval(monitor, 1000);
id.unref();                              ◁——— Tell Node to stop the
                                              interval when the program
setTimeout(function() {                       has finished the long-
  console.log('Done!');                       running operation.
}, 5000);
```

This is extremely useful in situations where there isn't a good place to call `clear-Interval`.

Once you've mastered timers, you'll encounter cases where it's useful to run a callback after the briefest possible delay. Using `setTimeout` with a delay of zero isn't the optimum solution, even though it seems like the obvious strategy. In the next technique you'll see how to do this correctly in Node by using `process.nextTick`.

TECHNIQUE 14   Safely managing asynchronous APIs

Sometimes you want to delay an operation just slightly. In traditional JavaScript, it might be acceptable to use `setTimeout` with a small delay value. Node provides a more efficient solution: `process.nextTick`.

PROBLEM
You want to write a method that returns an instance of `EventEmitter` or accepts a callback that *sometimes* makes an asynchronous API call, but not in all cases.

SOLUTION
Use `process.nextTick` to wrap the synchronous operation.

DISCUSSION
The `process.nextTick` method allows you to place a callback at the head of the next cycle of the run loop. That means it's a way of *slightly* delaying something, and as a result it's more efficient than just using `setTimeout` with a zero delay argument.

It can be difficult to visualize why this is useful, but consider the following example. Listing 2.21 shows a function that returns an `EventEmitter`. The idea is to provide an event-oriented API, allowing users of the API to subscribe to events as needed, while being able to run asynchronous calls internally.

Listing 2.21   Incorrectly triggering asynchronous methods with events

```
var EventEmitter = require('events').EventEmitter;

function complexOperations() {
```

```
    var events = new EventEmitter();

    events.emit('success'); 1((callout-globals-nexttick-1))

    return events;
}

complexOperations().on('success', function() {
    console.log('success!');
});
```

❶ This is an event that is triggered outside of any asynchronous callbacks.

Running this example will fail to trigger the success listener ❶ at the end of the example. Why is this the case? Well, the event is emitted before the listener has been subscribed. In most cases, events would be emitted inside callbacks for some asynchronous operation or another, but there are times when it makes sense to emit events early—perhaps in cases where arguments are validated and found to contain errors, so error can be emitted very quickly.

To correct this subtle flaw, any sections of code that emit events can be wrapped in process.nextTick. The following listing demonstrates this by using a function that returns an instance of EventEmitter, and then emits an event.

Listing 2.22   Triggering events inside process.nextTick

```
var EventEmitter = require('events').EventEmitter;

function complexOperations() {
    var events = new EventEmitter();

    process.nextTick(function() {
        events.emit('success');
    });

    return events;
}

complexOperations().on('success', function() {
    console.log('success!');
});
```

The event will now be emitted when the listener is ready.

Node's documentation recommends that APIs should always be 100% asynchronous or synchronous. That means if you have a method that accepts a callback and *may* call it asynchronously, then you should wrap the synchronous case in process.nextTick so users can rely on the order of execution.

Listing 2.23 uses an asynchronous call to read a file from the disk. Once it has read the file, it'll keep a cached version in memory. Subsequent calls will return the cached version. When returning the cached version, process.nextTick is used so the API still behaves asynchronously. That makes the output in the terminal read in the expected order.

Listing 2.23   Creating the illusion of an always asynchronous API

```
var EventEmitter = require('events').EventEmitter;
var fs = require('fs');
var content;

function readFileIfRequired(cb) {
  if (!content) {
    fs.readFile(__filename, 'utf8', function(err, data) {
      content = data;
      console.log('readFileIfRequired: readFile');
      cb(err, content);
    });
  } else {
    process.nextTick(function() {
      console.log('readFileIfRequired: cached');
      cb(null, content);
    });
  }
}

readFileIfRequired(function(err, data) {
  console.log('1. Length:', data.length);

  readFileIfRequired(function(err, data2) {
    console.log('2. Length:', data2.length);
  });

  console.log('Reading file again...');
});

console.log('Reading file...');
```

❶ **If the content hasn't been read into memory, read it asynchronously.**

❷ **If the content has been read, pass the cached version to the callback, but first use process.nextTick to ensure the callback is executed later.**

❸ **Make subsequent calls to the asynchronous operation to ensure it behaves as expected.**

In this example, a file is cached to memory by using `fs.readFile` to read it ❶, and then return a copy of it ❷ for every subsequent call. This is wrapped in a process that's called multiple times ❸ so you can compare the behavior of the non-blocking file system operation to `process.nextTick`.

Visualizing the event loop: setImmediate and process.maxTickDepth

The `setImmediate` and `clearImmediate` global functions accept a callback and optional arguments, and will run *after* any upcoming I/O events but *before* `setTimeout` and `setInterval`.

Callbacks added this way are pushed onto a queue, and one callback will be executed per run loop. This is different from `process.nextTick`, which causes `process.maxTickDepth` callbacks to run per iteration of the run loop.

The callbacks that have been passed with `process.nextTick` are usually run at the end of the current event loop. The number of callbacks that can be safely run is controlled by `process.maxTickDepth`, which is 1000 by default to allow I/O operations to continue to be handled.

Figure 2.4 illustrates how each of the timer functions is positioned within a single iteration of the event loop.

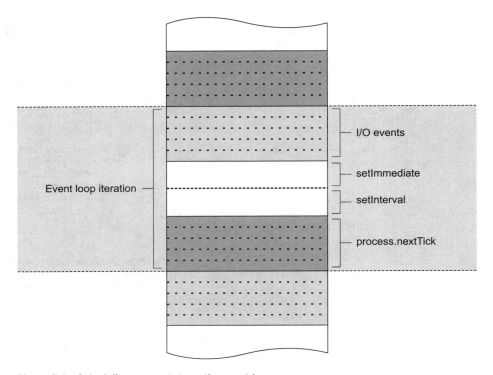

Figure 2.4   Scheduling `nextTick` **on the event loop**

When you're creating your own classes and methods that behave asynchronously, keep behavior consistent and predictable by using `process.nextTick`.

Node's implementation of the standard browser-based JavaScript timers fits in well with its event loop and non-blocking I/O. Although these functions are typically used for testing asynchronous code, a deep understanding of when `setTimeout`, `setImmediate`, and `process.nextTick` will be executed provides mastery over the event loop.

2.5   Summary

In this chapter you've seen some of the surprisingly powerful things that are built into Node programs without going to the trouble of loading a module. The next time you want to group related modules together, you can create an index.js file, as described in technique 3. And if you need to read standard input, you can use the `process` object's `stdin` property (technique 5).

In addition to the `process` object, there's also the often overlooked `console` object, which will help you debug and maintain programs (technique 6).

In the next chapter you'll learn about buffers. Buffers are great for working with binary data, which has traditionally been seen as a weakness of JavaScript. Buffers also underpin some of Node's powerful features such as streams.

Buffers: Working with bits, bytes, and encodings

This chapter covers

- Introduction to the Buffer data type
- Changing data encodings
- Converting binary files to JSON
- Creating your own binary protocol

JavaScript has historically had subpar binary support. Typically, parsing binary data would involve various tricks with strings to extract the data you want. Not having a good mechanism to work with raw memory in JavaScript was one of the problems Node core developers had to tackle when the project started getting traction. This was mostly for performance reasons. All of the raw memory accumulated in the `Buffer` data type.

Buffers are raw allocations of the heap, exposed to JavaScript in an array-like manner. They're exposed globally and therefore don't need to be required, and can be thought of as just another JavaScript type (like `String` or `Number`):

Allocate 255 bytes. ——▷
```
var buf = new Buffer(255);
buf[0] = 23;                    ◀—— Write integer 23 to the first byte.
```

If you haven't worked much with binary data, don't worry; this chapter is designed to be friendly to newcomers but also equip those who are more familiar with the concept. We'll cover simple and more advanced techniques:

- Converting a `Buffer` to different encodings
- Using the `Buffer` API to transform a binary file to JSON
- Encoding and decoding your own binary protocol

Let's look first at changing encodings for buffers.

3.1   Changing data encodings

If no encoding is given, file operations and many network operations will return data as a `Buffer`. Take this `fs.readFile` as an example:

```
var fs = require('fs');
fs.readFile('./names.txt', function (er, buf) {      isBuffer returns
  Buffer.isBuffer(buf); // true      ◀——      true if it's a Buffer.
});
```

But many times you already know a file's encoding, and it's more useful to get the data as an encoded string instead. We'll look at converting between `Buffer`s and other formats in this section.

TECHNIQUE 15   **Converting buffers into other formats**

By default, Node's core APIs return a buffer unless an encoding is specified. But buffers easily convert to other formats. In this next technique we'll look at how to convert buffers.

PROBLEM

You want to turn a `Buffer` into plain text.

SOLUTION

The `Buffer` API allows you to convert a `Buffer` into a string value.

DISCUSSION

Let's say we have a file that we know is just plain text. For our purposes we'll call this file names.txt and it will include a person's name on each line of the file:

```
Janet
Wookie
Alex
Marc
```

If we were to load the file using a method from the file system (`fs`) API, we'd get a `Buffer` (buf) by default

```
var fs = require('fs');
fs.readFile('./names.txt', function (er, buf) {
  console.log(buf);
});
```

which, when logged out, is shown as a list of octets (using hex notation):

```
<Buffer 4a 61 6e 65 74 0a 57 6f 6f 6b 69 65 0a 41 6c 65 78 0a
        4d 61 72 63 0a>
```

This isn't very useful since we know that the file is plain text. The `Buffer` class provides a method called `toString` to convert our data into a UTF-8 encoded string:

```
var fs = require('fs');
fs.readFile('./names.txt', function (er, buf) {
  console.log(buf.toString());
});
```

> **toString by default will convert data into a UTF-8 encoded string.**

This will yield the same output as our original file:

```
Janet
Wookie
Alex
Marc
```

But since we know that this data is only comprised of ASCII characters,[1] we could also get a performance benefit by changing the encoding to ASCII rather than UTF-8. To do this, we provide the type of encoding as the first argument for `toString`:

```
var fs = require('fs');
fs.readFile('./names.txt', function (er, buf) {
  console.log(buf.toString('ascii'));
});
```

> **toString accepts an encoding as the first argument.**

The `Buffer` API provides other encodings such as `utf16le`, `base64`, and `hex`, which you can learn more about by viewing the `Buffer` API online documentation.[2]

TECHNIQUE 16 Changing string encodings using buffers

In addition to converting buffers, you can also utilize buffers to turn one string encoding into another.

PROBLEM
You want to change from one string encoding to another.

SOLUTION
The Node `Buffer` API provides a mechanism to change encodings.

DISCUSSION
Example 1: Creating a Basic authentication header
Sometimes it's helpful to build a string of data and then change its encoding. For example, if you wanted to request data from a server that uses Basic authentication,[3] you'd need to send the username and password encoded using Base64:

```
Authorization: Basic am9obm550mMtYmFk
```

> **am9obm550mMtYmFk is encoded credentials**

---

[1] See http://en.wikipedia.org/wiki/ASCII.
[2] See http://nodejs.org/api/buffer.html.
[3] See http://en.wikipedia.org/wiki/Basic_access_authentication.

Before Base64 encoding is applied, Basic authentication credentials combine the username and password, separating the two using a : (colon). For our example, we'll use johnny as the username and c-bad as the password:

```
var user = 'johnny';
var pass = 'c-bad';                              username and
                                                 password are
var authstring = user + ':' + pass;  ◁———        separated using colon
```

Now we have to convert this into a Buffer in order to change it into another encoding. Buffers can be allocated by bytes, as we've seen already by simply passing in a number (for example, new Buffer(255)). They also can be allocated by passing in string data:

```
                                                 String data converted
var buf = new Buffer(authstring);    ◁———        to a Buffer
```

Specifying an encoding

When strings are used to allocate a Buffer, they're assumed to be UTF-8 strings, which is typically what you want. But you can specify the encoding of the incoming data using a second, optional, encoding argument:

```
new Buffer('am9obm550mMtYmFk', 'base64')
```

Now that we have our data as a Buffer, we can turn it back into a Base64-encoded string by using toString('base64'):

```
                                                 Result:
var encoded = buf.toString('base64');  ◁———      am9obm550mMtYmFk
```

This process can be compacted as well, since instance methods can be called on the returned Buffer instance right away and the new keyword can be omitted:

```
var encoded = Buffer(user + ':' + pass).toString('base64');
```

Example 2: Working with data URIs

Data URIs[4] are another example of when using the Buffer API can be helpful. Data URIs allow a resource to be embedded inline on a web page using the following scheme:

```
data:[MIME-type][;charset=<encoding>[;base64],<data>
```

For example, this PNG image of a monkey can be represented as a data URI:

```
data:image/png;base64,iVBORw0KGgoAAAANSUhEUgAAACsAAAAoCAYAAABny...
```

And when read in the browser, the data URI will display our primate as shown in figure 3.1.

Let's look at how we can create a data URI using the Buffer API. In our primate example, we were using a PNG image that has the MIME type of image/png:

Figure 3.1   Data URI read in a browser displays the monkey as an image

```
var mime = 'image/png';
```

---

[4] See http://en.wikipedia.org/wiki/Data_URI_scheme.

Binary files can be represented in data URIs using Base64 encoding, so let's set up a variable for that:

```
var encoding = 'base64';
```

With our MIME type and encoding, we can construct the start of our data URI:

```
var mime = 'image/png';
var encoding = 'base64';
var uri = 'data:' + mime + ';' + encoding + ',';
```

We need to add the actual data next. We can use `fs.readFileSync` to read in our data synchronously and return the data inline. `fs.readFileSync` will return a `Buffer`, so we can then convert that to a Base64 string:

```
var encoding = 'base64';
var data = fs.readFileSync('./monkey.png').toString(encoding);
```

Let's put this all together and make a program that will output our data URI:

```
var fs = require('fs');                                          ◁──┐ Require fs module to
var mime = 'image/png';                                               use fs.readFileSync
var encoding = 'base64';
var data = fs.readFileSync('./monkey.png').toString(encoding);
var uri = 'data:' + mime + ';' + encoding + ',' + data;          ◁──┐
console.log(uri);                                                      Construct data URI
```

Output data URI → `console.log(uri);`

The output of this program will be

```
data:image/png;base64,iVBORw0KGgoAAAANSUhEUgAAACsAAAAoCAYAAAABny...
```

Let's flip the scenario around. What if you have a data URI but you want to write it out to an actual file? Again, we'll work with our monkey example. First, we `split` the array to grab only the data:[5]

```
var uri = 'data:image/png;base64,iVBORw0KGgoAAAANSUhEUgAAACsAAAAo...';
var data = uri.split(',')[1];
```

We can then create a `Buffer` using our `data` string and specifying the encoding:

```
var buf = Buffer(data, 'base64');
```

Next, we use `fs.writeFileSync` to write this synchronously to disk, giving it a file name and the `Buffer`:

```
fs.writeFileSync('./secondmonkey.png', buf);
```

Putting this example all together looks like this:

```
var fs = require('fs');                                          ◁──┐ Require fs module to
var uri = 'data:image/png;base64,iVBORw0KGgoAAAANSUhEUgAAACsAAAAo...';  use fs.writeFileSync
var data = uri.split(',')[1];
var buf = Buffer(data, 'base64');
fs.writeFileSync('./secondmonkey.png', buf);
```

---

[5] This is not prescriptive for all data URIs, as commas could appear elsewhere.

When opened in our default image viewer, this gives us our monkey, as shown in figure 3.2.

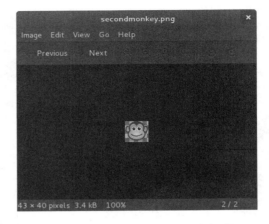

Most of the time, when you deal with `Buffer` objects in Node, it will be to convert them to other formats, and sometimes you'll change encodings. But you may find yourself having to deal with a binary file format, and the `Buffer` API—which we'll look at next—provides a rich set of tools to work with that as well.

3.2   *Converting binary files to JSON*

Working with binary data is kind of like solving a puzzle. You're given clues by

Figure 3.2   Generated secondmonkey.png file from a data URI

reading a specification of what the data means and then you have to go out and turn that data into something usable in your application.

TECHNIQUE 17   Using buffers to convert raw data

What if you could utilize a binary format to do something useful in your Node program? In this technique we'll cover, in depth, working with binary data to convert a common file format into JSON.

PROBLEM

You want to convert a binary file into a more usable format.

SOLUTION

The Node API extends JavaScript with a `Buffer` class, exposing an API for raw binary data access and tools for dealing more easily with binary data.

DISCUSSION

For the purposes of our example, namely, file conversion, you can think of the process in terms of figure 3.3.

Binary data is read, processed, and written out in a more usable format using the binary specification as a guide and the binary API as the mechanism for accomplishing the transformation. This is not the only use of binary data. For example, you could do processing on a binary protocol to pass messages back and forth and the diagram would look different.

For our technique, the binary file format we'll work with is DBase 5.0 (.dbf). That format may sound obscure, but (to put it into context) it was a popular database format that's still heavily in use for attribution of geospatial data. You could think of it as a simplified Excel spreadsheet. The sample we'll work with is located at buffers/world.dbf.

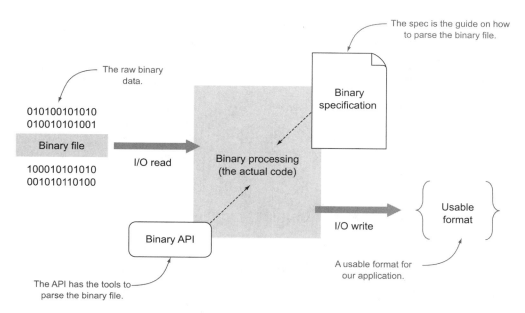

Figure 3.3 The transformation of binary data into a more usable/programmable format

The file contains geospatial information for the countries of the world. Unfortunately, if you were to open it in your text editor, it wouldn't be very useful.

WHY ARE WE COVERING IN DEPTH A BINARY FORMAT THAT I MAY NEVER USE? Although we could've picked a number of binary formats, DBase 5.0 is one that will teach you a lot of different ways of approaching problems with reading binary files that are common to many other formats. In addition, binary formats are unfamiliar to many coming from a web development background, so we're taking some time to focus on reading binary specifications. Please feel free to skim if you're already familiar.

Since we want to use it in our Node application, JSON would be a good format choice because it can be natively parsed in JavaScript and resembles native JavaScript objects. This is illustrated in figure 3.4.

Figure 3.5 shows an example of the transformation we want to make: on the left is the raw binary opened in a text editor, and on the right is the converted JSON format.

The header

Before we can start tackling this problem, we'll need to do some research to find out the specification for the binary format we want to deal with. In our case, a number of similar specifications were found online from search engine queries. For DBase 5.0, the primary specification we'll use for this example is found at http://mng.bz/i7K4.

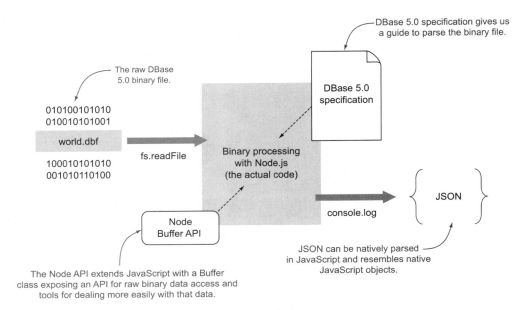

Figure 3.4   Binary data is read using `FileSystem` API into Node.js, transformed using the `Buffer` API into an easier-to-use JSON format.

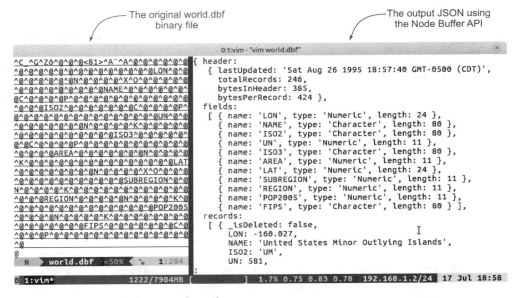

Figure 3.5   Final result of our transformation

The first portion of the specification is called the *header*. Many binary formats will use a header as a place to store metadata about the file; table 3.1 shows what the specification looks like for DBase 5.0.

Table 3.1 DBase 5.0 header specification

Byte	Contents	Description
0	1 byte	Valid dBASE for Windows table file; bits 0-2 indicate version number ...
1-3	3 bytes	Date of last update; in YYMMDD format
4-7	32-bit number	Number of records in the table
8-9	16-bit number	Number of bytes in the header
10-11	16-bit number	Number of bytes in the record
...	...	...
32-n each	32 bytes	Field descriptor array
n+1	1 byte	0Dh stored as the field terminator

Let's take a peek at the first row.

Byte	Contents	Description
0	1 byte	Valid dBASE for Windows table file; bits 0-2 indicate version number ...

This row tells us the byte located at position 0 contains the information specified in the description. So how do we access the byte at position 0? Thankfully, this is really simple with buffers.

In Node, *unless you specify a particular encoding* for the data you're reading in, you'll get back a Node `Buffer`, as seen in this example:

```
var fs = require('fs');

fs.readFile('./world.dbf', function (er, buf) {
  Buffer.isBuffer(buf); // true
});
```

`fs.readFile` isn't the only way to get back a buffer but, for the sake of simplicity, we'll use that method so we get the entire buffer back as an object after it's read. This method may not be ideal for large binary files where you wouldn't want to load the whole buffer into memory at once. In that case, you could stream the data with `fs.createRead-Stream` or manually read in parts of the file at a time with `fs.read`. It should also be noted that buffers aren't available only for files; they exist pretty much anywhere you can get streams of data (for example, post data on an HTTP request).

If you wanted to view a string representation of a buffer, a simple `buf.toString()` call would suffice (this defaults to UTF-8 encoding). This is nice if you're pulling in data that you know is just text:

```
var fs = require('fs');

fs.readFile('./world.dbf', function (er, buf) {
  console.log(buf.toString());
});
```

Returns a UTF-8 string by default

In our case, `buf.toString()` would be just as bad as opening up the world.dbf file in a text editor: unusable. We need to make sense of the binary data first.

NOTE From here forward, whenever you see our variable `buf`, it refers to an instance of a `Buffer`, therefore part of the Node `Buffer` API.

In the table we talked about byte position 0. Buffers in Node act very similar to JavaScript arrays *but the indices are byte positions in memory*. So byte position 0 is `buf[0]`. In `Buffer` syntax, `buf[0]` is synonymous with the byte, the octet, the unsigned 8-bit integer, or positive signed 8-bit integer at position 0.

For this example, we don't really care about storing information about this particular byte. Let's move on to the next byte definition.

Byte	Contents	Description
1-3	3 bytes	Date of last update; in YYMMDD format

Here's something interesting: the date of the last update. But this spec doesn't tell us anything more than that it's 3 bytes and in YYMMDD format. All this is to say that you may not find all you're looking for in one spot. Subsequent web searches landed this information:

> *Each byte contains the number as a binary. YY is added to a base of 1900 decimal to determine the actual year. Therefore, YY has possible values from 0x00-0xFF, which allows for a range from 1900-2155.*[6]

That's more helpful. Let's look at parsing this in Node:

```
var header = {};

var date = new Date();
date.setUTCFullYear(1900 + buf[1]);
date.setUTCMonth(buf[2]);
date.setUTCDate(buf[3]);
header.lastUpdated = date.toUTCString();
```

Result: "Sat Aug 26 1995 ..."

Here we use a JavaScript `Date` object and set its year to 1900 plus the integer we pulled out of `buf[1]`. We use integers at positions 2 and 3 to set the month and date. Since JSON doesn't store JavaScript `Date` types, we'll store it as a UTC `Date` string.

---

[6] See http://www.dbase.com/Knowledgebase/INT/db7_file_fmt.htm.

Let's pause to recap. "Sat Aug 26 1995..." as shown here is the result of parsing a portion of world.dbf binary data into a JavaScript string. We'll see more examples of this as we continue.

Byte	Contents	Description
4-7	32-bit number	Number of records in the table

This next definition gives us two clues. We know the byte starts at offset 4 and it's a 32-bit number with the least significant byte first. Since we know the number shouldn't be negative, we can assume either a positive signed integer or an unsigned integer. Both are accessed the same way in the `Buffer` API:

```
header.totalRecords = buf.readUInt32LE(4);    ◁—— Result: 246
```

`buf.readUInt32LE` will read an unsigned 32-bit integer with little-endian format from the offset of 4, which matches our description from earlier.

The next two definitions follow a similar pattern except they're 16-bit integers. Following are their definitions.

Byte	Contents	Description
8-9	16-bit number	Number of bytes in the header
10-11	16-bit number	Number of bytes in the record

And here's the corresponding code:

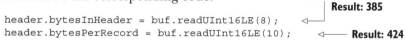

```
                                                     Result: 385
header.bytesInHeader = buf.readUInt16LE(8);    ◁—┘
header.bytesPerRecord = buf.readUInt16LE(10);  ◁—— Result: 424
```

The transformation that has taken place between the specification and the code for this header section is illustrated in figure 3.6.

The field descriptor array

Only one more relevant piece of information for this example remains in the header of the world.dbf file. It's the definitions for the fields, including type and name information, seen in the following lines.

Byte	Contents	Description
32-n each	32 bytes	Field descriptor array
n+1	1 byte	0Dh stored as the field terminator

From this we know that each field description is stored as 32 bytes of information. Since this database could have one or more fields for data, we'll know it's finished

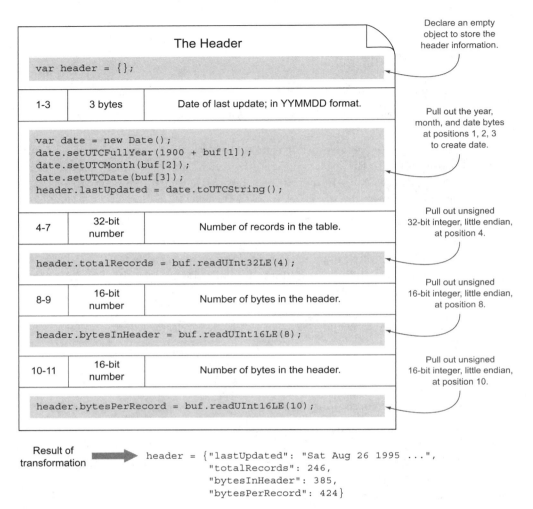

Figure 3.6   The header: transformation from the specification to code using the Node `Buffer` API

when we hit the 1 byte field terminator (0Dh) shown in the second row. Let's write a structure to handle this:

```
var fields = [];
var fieldOffset = 32;
var fieldTerminator = 0x0D;

while (buf[fieldOffset] != fieldTerminator) {
  // here is where we parse each field
  fieldOffset += 32;
}
```

JavaScript hex literal notation to represent 0Dh

Here we loop through the buffer 32 bytes at a time until we hit the `fieldTerminator`, which is represented in hexadecimal notation.

Now we need to handle the information concerning each field descriptor. The specification has another table specifically for this; the relevant information for our example is shown in table 3.2.

Table 3.2   DBase 5.0 field descriptor array specification

Byte	Contents	Description
0-10	11 bytes	Field name in ASCII (zero-filled)
11	1 byte	Field type in ASCII (C, N, ...)
...	...	...
16	1 byte	Field length in binary

Note that the indexing for the bytes starts over at 0, even though we're well past byte position 0 in our reading of the file. It would be nice to start over at each record so we could follow the specification more closely. `Buffer` provides a `slice` method for us to do just that:

```
var fields = [];
var fieldOffset = 32;
var fieldTerminator = 0x0D;

while (buf[fieldOffset] != fieldTerminator) {
  var fieldBuf = buf.slice(fieldOffset, fieldOffset+32);
  // here is where we parse each field
  fieldOffset += 32;
}
```

`buf.slice(start,end)` is very similar to a standard array slice method in that it returns a buffer indexed at `start` to `end`. But it differs in that it doesn't return a new copy of the data. It returns just a snapshot of the data at those points. So if you manipulate the data in the sliced buffer in any way, *it will also be manipulated in the original buffer.*

With our new `fieldBuf` indexed at zero for each iteration, we can approach the specification without doing extra math in our heads. Let's look at the first line.

Byte	Contents	Description
0-10	11 bytes	Field name in ASCII (zero-filled)

Here's the code to extract the field name:

```
var field = {};

field.name = fieldBuf.toString('ascii', 0, 11).replace(/\u0000/g,'');
```
Result, such as "LON" (longitude)

By default, `buf.toString()` assumes `utf8`, but Node `Buffers` support other encodings as well,[7] including `ascii`, which is what our spec calls for. `buf.toString()` also

---

[7] See http://nodejs.org/api/buffer.html#buffer_buffer.

allows you to pass in the range that you want converted. We also have to replace() the zero-filled characters with empty strings if the field was shorter than 11 bytes so we don't end up with zero-filled characters (\u0000) in our names.

The next relevant field is a field data type.

Byte	Contents	Description
11	1 byte	Field type in ASCII (C, N, ...)

But the characters C and N don't really mean anything to us yet. Further down the specification, we get definitions for these types, as shown in table 3.3.

Table 3.3 Field types specification

Data type	Data input
C (Character)	All OEM code page characters
N (Numeric)	- . 0 1 2 3 4 5 6 7 8 9

It would be nice to convert this data to relevant types for our application. JavaScript doesn't use the language *character* or *numeric*, but it does have *String* and *Number*, let's keep that in mind when we parse the actual records. For now we can store this in a little lookup object to do the conversion later:

```
var FIELD_TYPES = {
  C: 'Character',
  N: 'Numeric'
}
```

Now that we have a lookup table, we can pull out the relevant information as we continue converting the binary data:

Result: will be "Character or "Numeric"

```
field.type = FIELD_TYPES[fieldBuf.toString('ascii', 11, 12)];
```

buf.toString() will give us our one ASCII character that we then look up in the hash to get the full type name.

There's only one other bit of information we need to parse the remaining file from each field description—the field size.

Byte	Contents	Description
16	1 byte	Field length in binary

We write this now-familiar code:

```
field.length = fieldBuf[16];
```
⟵——— **Result, such as 435**

The transformation that has taken place between the specification and the code for this field descriptor array section is illustrated in figure 3.7.

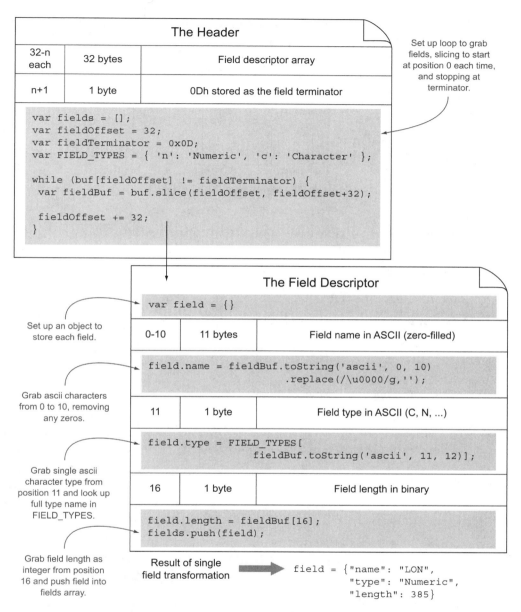

Figure 3.7   The field descriptor array: transformation from the specification to code using the Node `Buffer` API

The records

Now that we've parsed the header, including the field descriptors, we have one more part to process: the actual record data. The specification tells us this:

The records follow the header in the table file. Data records are preceded by one byte, that is, a space (20h) if the record is not deleted, an asterisk (2Ah) if the record is deleted. Fields are packed into records without field separators or record terminators. The end of the file is marked by a single byte, with the end-of-file marker, an OEM code page character value of 26 (1Ah).

Let's break this down for discussion:

The records follow the header in the table file.

Although we could've kept track of the byte position after the `fieldOffset`, the header had a field for number of bytes in the header, which we stored as `header.bytesInHeader`. So we know we need to start there:

```
var startingRecordOffset = header.bytesInHeader;
```

We also learned a couple other things from our parsing of the header. The first is how many records exist in the data, which we stored as `header.totalRecords`. The second is how many bytes are allocated for each record, which was stored as `header.bytes-PerRecord`. Knowing where to start, how many to iterate, and how much of a jump per iteration helps us set up a nice `for` loop for handling each record:

```
for (var i = 0; i < header.totalRecords; i++) {
    var recordOffset = startingRecordOffset +
                        (i * header.bytesPerRecord);
    // here is where we parse each record
}
```

Now, at the beginning of each iteration, we know the byte position we want to start at is stored as `recordOffset`. Let's continue reading the specification:

Data records are preceded by one byte, that is, a space (20h) if the record is not deleted, an asterisk (2Ah) if the record is deleted.

Next we have to check that first byte to see if the record was deleted:

```
var record = {};
record._isDel = buf.readUInt8(recordOffset) == 0x2A;    ◄─
recordOffset++;
```

Note: We could've also used buf[recordOffset]

Similar to when we tested for the `fieldTerminator` in our header file, here we test to see if the integer matches `0x2A` or the ASCII "asterisk" character. Let's continue reading:

Fields are packed into records without field separators or record terminators.

Lastly, we can pull in the actual record data. This pulls in the information we learned from parsing the field descriptor array. We stored a `field.type`, `field.name`, and `field.length` (in bytes) for each field. We want to store the name as a key in the record where the value is the data for that length of bytes converted to the correct type. Let's look at it in simple pseudo code:

```
record[name] = cast type for (characters from length)
e.g.
record['pop2005'] = Number("13119679")
```

We also want to do this type conversion for every field per record, so we use another `for` loop:

```
for (var j = 0; j < fields.length; j++) {
  var field = fields[j];
  var Type = field.type == 'Numeric' ? Number : String;
  record[field.name] = Type(buf.toString('ascii', recordOffset,
                             recordOffset+field.length).trim());
  recordOffset += field.length;
}
```

We loop through each of the fields:

1 First, we find out which JavaScript type we want to cast the value to and store it in a variable `Type`.

2 Then, we use `buf.toString` to pull out the characters from `recordOffset` to the next `field.length`. We also have to `trim()` the data because we don't know if all the bytes were used to store relevant data or just filled with spaces.

3 Lastly, we increment the `recordOffset` with the `field.length` so that we keep the location to start at for the next field when we go around the `for` loop again.

The transformation that has taken place between the specification and the code for this records section is illustrated in figure 3.8.

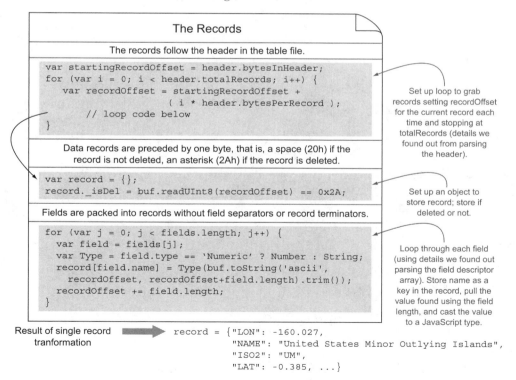

Figure 3.8   The records: transformation from the specification to code using the Node `Buffer` API

Still with me? I hope so. The complete code sample is shown in figure 3.9.

Reading in world.dbf
and receiving a
buffer object

The Header
(metadata on
how to read
the file)

The Field
Descriptor Array
(part of the
header that
deals with field
metadata)

The Records
(read from
information
learned from
parsing
metadata)

Writing out JSON
data to console
(STDOUT)

```
var fs = require('fs');

fs.readFile('./world.dbf', function (err, buf) {
  var header = {};

  var date = new Date();
  date.setFullYear(1900 + buf[1]);
  date.setMonth(buf[2]);
  date.setDate(buf[3]);
  header.lastUpdated = date.toString();

  header.totalRecords = buf.readUInt32LE(4);
  header.bytesInHeader = buf.readUInt16LE(8);
  header.bytesPerRecord = buf.readUInt16LE(10);

  var fields = [];
  var fieldOffset = 32;
  var fieldTerminator = 0x0D;

  var FIELD_TYPES = {
    C: 'Character',
    N: 'Numeric'
  };

  while (buf[fieldOffset] != fieldTerminator) {
    var fieldBuf = buf.slice(fieldOffset, fieldOffset+32);
    var field = {};
    field.name = fieldBuf.toString('ascii', 0, 11).replace(/\u0000/g,'');
    field.type = FIELD_TYPES[fieldBuf.toString('ascii', 11, 12)];
    field.length = fieldBuf[16];

    fields.push(field);
    fieldOffset += 32;
  }

  var startingRecordOffset = header.bytesInHeader;
  var records = [];

  for (var i = 0; i < header.totalRecords; i++) {
    var recordOffset = startingRecordOffset + (i * header.bytesPerRecord);
    var record = {};

    record._isDel = buf.readUInt8(recordOffset) == 0x2A;
    recordOffset++;

    for (var j = 0; j < fields.length; j++) {
      field = fields[j];
      var Type = field.type === 'Numeric' ? Number : String;
      record[field.name] = Type(buf.toString('utf8',recordOffset,
                                    recordOffset+field.length).trim());
      recordOffset += field.length;
    }

    records.push(record);
  }

  console.log({ header: header, fields: fields, records: records });
})
```

Figure 3.9   The full set of code for parsing a DBF file into JSON

Using the Node `Buffer` API, we were able to turn a binary file into a usable JSON format. The output of running this application is shown next:

```
{ header:
   { lastUpdated: 'Sat Aug 26 1995 21:55:03 GMT-0500 (CDT)',
     totalRecords: 246,
     bytesInHeader: 385,
     bytesPerRecord: 424 },
  fields:
   [ { name: 'LON', type: 'Numeric', length: 24 },
     { name: 'NAME', type: 'Character', length: 80 },
     { name: 'ISO2', type: 'Character', length: 80 },
     { name: 'UN', type: 'Numeric', length: 11 },
     { name: 'ISO3', type: 'Character', length: 80 },
     { name: 'AREA', type: 'Numeric', length: 11 },
     { name: 'LAT', type: 'Numeric', length: 24 },
     { name: 'SUBREGION', type: 'Numeric', length: 11 },
     { name: 'REGION', type: 'Numeric', length: 11 },
     { name: 'POP2005', type: 'Numeric', length: 11 },
     { name: 'FIPS', type: 'Character', length: 80 } ],
  records:
   [ { _isDel: false,
       LON: -160.027,
       NAME: 'United States Minor Outlying Islands',
       ISO2: 'UM',
       UN: 581,
       ISO3: 'UMI',
       AREA: 0,
       LAT: -0.385,
       SUBREGION: 0,
       REGION: 0,
       POP2005: 0,
       FIPS: '' },
     { _isDel: false,
       LON: 35.278,
       NAME: 'Palestine',
       ISO2: 'PS',
       UN: 275,
       ISO3: 'PSE',
       AREA: 0,
       LAT: 32.037,
       SUBREGION: 145,
       REGION: 142,
       POP2005: 3762005,
       FIPS: '' },
     ...
}
```

And almost magically a binary file that wasn't human-readable is turned into, not only a readable format, but also a usable data format to work with and do more transformations with. Of course, it isn't magic, but rather investing the time to learn a binary format and using the tools available to do a conversion. The `Buffer` API provides good tools to do this.

Using fs methods

We could've also chosen to write the resulting code out to a file using `fs.writeFile` and friends.[a] Just like most APIs in Node can read in a buffer object, most also can write out a buffer object. In our case we didn't end up with a buffer but rather a JSON object, so we could've used `JSON.stringify` in conjunction with `fs.writeFile` to write that data out:

```
fs.writeFile('world.json', JSON.stringify(result), ...
```

[a.]See http://nodejs.org/api/fs.html.

Binary file formats can be a lot of fun to crack. Another fun but practical use for `Buffers` is working binary protocols, which we'll tackle next.

3.3   *Creating your own binary protocol*

It feels like you've cracked a code when you read a binary file and make sense out of it. It can be just as fun to write your own puzzles and decode them. Of course, this isn't just for fun. Using a well-defined binary protocol can be a compact and efficient way to transfer data.

TECHNIQUE 18   **Creating your own network protocol**

In this technique we'll cover some additional aspects of working with binary data, like bit masks and protocol design. We'll also look into compressing binary data.

PROBLEM

You want create an efficient transport of messages across the network or in process.

SOLUTION

JavaScript and the Node `Buffer` API give you tools to create your own binary protocol.

DISCUSSION

To create a binary protocol, you first have to define what kind of information you want to send across the wire and how you'll represent that information. Like you learned in the last technique, a specification provides a good roadmap for this.

For this technique, we'll develop a simple and compact database protocol. Our protocol will involve

- Using a bitmask to determine which database(s) to store the message in
- Writing data to a particular key that will be an unsigned integer between 0-255 (one byte)
- Storing a message that is compressed data of any length using zlib

Table 3.4 shows how we could write the specification.

Table 3.4 Simple key-value database protocol

Byte	Contents	Description
0	1 byte	Determines which database(s) to write the data to based on which bits are toggled on. Each bit position represents a database from 1–8.
1	1 byte	An unsigned integer of one byte (0–255) used as the database key to store the data in.
2-n	0-n bytes	The data to store, which can be any amount of bytes that have been compressed using `deflate` (zlib).

Playing with bits to select databases

Our protocol states that the first byte will be used to represent which databases should record the information transferred. On the receiving end, our main database will be a simple multidimensional array that will hold spots for eight databases (since there are eight bits in a byte). This can be simply represented using array literals in JavaScript:

```
var database = [ [], [], [], [], [], [], [], [] ];
```

Whatever bits are turned on will indicate which database or databases will store the message received. For example, the number 8 is represented as `00001000` in binary. In this case we'd store the information in database 4, since the fourth bit is on (bits are read from right to left).

> **ZERO-INDEXED ARRAYS** Arrays are zero-indexed in JavaScript, so database 4 is in array position 3, but to avoid complicating things, we're intentionally calling our databases 1 through 8 instead of 0 through 7 to match our language more closely when talking about bits in a byte.

If you're ever curious about a number's binary representation in JavaScript, you can use the built-in `toString` method, giving it a base 2 as the first argument:

```
8..toString(2) // '1000'
```

> **Two dots (..) are needed to call a method on a number, since the first is parsed as a decimal point.**

Numbers can have more than one bit turned on as well; for example, 20 is `00010100` in binary, and for our application that would mean we wanted to store the message in databases 3 and 5.

So how do we test to see which bits are turned on for any given number? To solve this, we can use a *bitmask*. A bitmask represents the bit pattern we're interested in testing. For example, if we were interested in finding out whether we should store some data in database 5, we could create a bitmask that has the fifth bit turned on. In binary, this would look like `00010000`, which is the number 32 (or `0x20` in hex notation).

We then have to test our bitmask against a value, and JavaScript includes various bitwise operators[8] to do this. One is the `&` (bitwise AND) operator. The `&` operator

---

[8] See https://developer.mozilla.org/en-US/docs/JavaScript/Reference/Operators/Bitwise_Operators.

behaves similarly to the && operator, but instead of testing for two conditions to be true, it tests for two bits to be on (have ones and not zeros) and keeps the bits on (or one) where that's the case:

```
  000101000
& 000100000
-----------
  000100000
```

Bit position 5 was on for both values, so it remains when using &. Armed with this knowledge, we can see that a value compared with the bitmask *will be the bitmask* if it has the same bit or bits turned on. With this information, we can set up a simple conditional to test:

```
if ( (value & bitmask) === bitmask) { .. }
```

It's important that the & expression be surrounded by parentheses; otherwise, the equality of the bitmasks would be checked first because of operator precedence.[9]

To test the first byte received in our binary protocol, we'll want to set up a list of bitmasks that correspond with the indexes of our databases. If the bitmask matches, we know the database at that index will need the data written to it. The "on" bits for every position are an array

```
var bitmasks = [ 1, 2, 4, 8, 16, 32, 64, 128 ]
```

which corresponds to this:

```
1        2        4        8        16       32       64       128
-----------------------------------------------------------------------
00000001 00000010 00000100 00001000 00010000 00100000 01000000 10000000
```

Now we know that if a byte matches 1 in our bitmasks array, it will match database 1 or array position 0. We can set up a simple loop to test each bitmask against the value of the first byte:

```
var database = [ [], [], [], [], [], [], [], [] ];
var bitmasks = [ 1, 2, 4, 8, 16, 32, 64, 128 ];

function store (buf) {
  var db = buf[0];                                          ◁─── Grabbing the byte
  bitmasks.forEach(function (bitmask, index) {                   from position 0
    if ( (db & bitmask) === bitmask) {
      // found a match for database[index]
    }
  });
}
```

Working with bits can be tricky at first, but once you understand more about how they work, they become more manageable. So far all of what we've covered is available not only in Node, but in browser JavaScript too. We've made it far enough to determine

---

[9] See https://developer.mozilla.org/en-US/docs/JavaScript/Reference/Operators/Operator_Precedence.

which database we should put our incoming data in; we still have to find out which key to store the data in.

Looking up the key to store the data

This is the easiest part of our example, because you've already learned this from the previous technique. Before we begin, let's look at the relevant part of the specification defined earlier in table 3.4.

Byte	Contents	Description
1	1 byte	An unsigned integer of one byte (0–255) used as the database key to store the data in.

We know we'll be receiving at byte position 1 an unsigned integer of one byte (0-255) that will be used as a database key to store the data in. We purposely set up the database to be a multidimensional array where the first dimension is the databases. Now we can use the second dimension as a place to store the keys and values, and since the keys are numbers, an array will work.[10] Let's illustrate to make this more concrete. Here's what storing the value `'foo'` inside the first and third databases at key 0 would look like:

```
[
  ['foo'],
  [],
  ['foo'],
  [],
  [],
  [],
  [],
  []
]
```

To get the key value out of position 1, we can use the hopefully now familiar `readUInt8` method:

```
var key = buf.readUInt8(1);
```
Note that buf[1] does the same thing

Let's add that to our previous main code sample we're building:

```
var database = [ [], [], [], [], [], [], [], [] ];
var bitmasks = [ 1, 2, 4, 8, 16, 32, 64, 128 ];

function store (buf) {
  var db = buf[0];
  var key = buf.readUInt8(1);

  bitmasks.forEach(function (bitmask, index) {
    if ( (db & bitmask) === bitmask) {
```

---

[10] Although there are more-ideal alternatives coming in ECMAScript 6.

```
        database[index][key] = 'some data';
    }
  });
}
```

'some data' is a
placeholder for now.

Now that we're able to parse the database(s) and the keys within those database(s), we can get to parsing the actual data to store.

Inflating data with zlib

It's a smart idea to compress string/ASCII/UTF-8 data when sending it across the wire, as compression can really cut down on bandwidth usage. In our simple database protocol, we assume that the data we get to store has been compressed; let's look at the specification to see the relevant description.

Node includes a built-in `zlib` module that exposes `deflate` (compress) and `inflate` (uncompress) methods. It also includes gzip compression. To avoid getting malformed messages, we can check that the received message was indeed properly compressed, and if not, we'll refuse to inflate it. Typically, the first byte of zlib "deflated" data is `0x78`,[11] so we can test for that accordingly:

Remember, we start at byte position 2
because the previous were the key (1) and
the database byte (0) we covered earlier.

```
if (buf[2] === 0x78) { .. }
```

Now that we know that we're most likely dealing with deflated data, we can inflate it using `zlib.inflate`. We'll also need to use `buf.slice()` to get just the data portion of our message (since leaving the first two bytes would cause an error):

zlib.inflate
returns a
buffer, so
we convert
it into a
UTF-8 string
to store.

```
var zlib = require('zlib');
...
if (buf[2] === 0x78) {
  zlib.inflate(buf.slice(2), function (er, inflatedBuf) {
    if (er) return console.error(er);

    var data = inflatedBuf.toString();
  })
}
```

Even though we checked,
something else could have
failed; if so, we log it out
and don't continue.

We have everything we need to store some data in our database using our simple database protocol. Let's put all the components together:

```
var zlib = require('zlib');
var database = [ [], [], [], [], [], [], [], [] ];
var bitmasks = [ 1, 2, 4, 8, 16, 32, 64, 128 ];

function store (buf) {
  var db = buf[0];
  var key = buf.readUInt8(1);

  if (buf[2] === 0x78) {
    zlib.inflate(buf.slice(2), function (er, inflatedBuf) {
      if (er) return console.error(er);
```

---

[11] A more robust implementation should do more checks; see http://tools.ietf.org/html/rfc6713.

```
      var data = inflatedBuf.toString();

      bitmasks.forEach(function (bitmask, index) {
        if ( (db & bitmask) === bitmask) {
          database[index][key] = data;
        }
      });
    });
  }
}
```

The actual data is stored in the key of every database that matched.

Now we have the code in place to store some data. We could generate a message by using the following:

```
      var zlib = require('zlib');
      var header = new Buffer(2);

      header[0] = 8;
      header[1] = 0;
```

Store in key 0

Store in database 4 (8 = 00001000)

```
      zlib.deflate('my message', function (er, deflateBuf) {
        if (er) return console.error(er);
        var message = Buffer.concat([header, deflateBuf]);
        store(message);
      })
```

Concat header and data into one message

Deflate the data 'my message'

Store message

We could write an example that sends messages over TCP and do more error handling. But let's leave that as an exercise for you to tackle as you learn about networking in Node in a later chapter.

3.4 Summary

In this chapter you learned about buffers and how to turn buffers into different encoded strings using the toString method. We dove into the complicated task of turning a binary file into something more usable using the Buffer API. Lastly, we had some fun creating our own protocol and learning about bitmasks and compression.

We covered some common uses of buffers in Node, varying in difficulty to hopefully make you more comfortable using them and making the most of them. Go forth and tackle a binary format conversion and publish your work on NPM, or maybe a protocol that better fits your business needs is waiting to be written.

In the next chapter we'll look at another core part of Node—events.

Events: Mastering
EventEmitter and beyond

This chapter covers

- Using Node's EventEmitter module
- Managing errors
- How third-party modules use EventEmitter
- How to use domains with events
- Alternatives to EventEmitter

Node's events module currently includes just a single class: EventEmitter. This class is used throughout both Node's built-in modules and third-party modules. It contributes to the overall architecture of many Node programs. Therefore it's important to understand EventEmitter and how to use it.

It's a simple class, and if you're familiar with DOM or jQuery events, then you shouldn't have much trouble understanding it. The major consideration when using Node is in error handling, and we'll look at this in technique 21.

EventEmitter can be used in various ways—it's generally used as a base class for solving a wide range of problems, from building network servers to architecting application logic. In view of the fact that it's used as the basis for key classes in popular Node modules like Express, learning how it works can be useful for writing idiomatic code that plays well alongside existing modules.

In this chapter you'll learn how to use EventEmitter to make custom classes, and how it's used within Node and open source modules. You'll also learn how to solve problems found when using EventEmitter, and see some alternatives to it.

4.1 Basic usage

To use EventEmitter, the base class must be inherited from. This section includes techniques for inheriting from EventEmitter and mixing it into other classes that already inherit from another base class.

TECHNIQUE 19   Inheriting from EventEmitter

This technique demonstrates how to create custom classes based on EventEmitter. By understanding the principles in this technique, you'll learn how to use EventEmitter, and how to better use modules that are built with it.

PROBLEM

You want to use an event-based approach to solve a problem. You have a class that you'd like to operate when asynchronous events occur.

Web, desktop, and mobile user interfaces have one thing in common: they're event-based. Events are a great paradigm for dealing with something inherently asynchronous: the input from human beings. To show how EventEmitter works, we'll use a music player as an example. It won't really play music, but the underlying concept is a great way to learn how to use events.

SOLUTION

The canonical example of using events in Node is inheriting from EventEmitter. This can be done by using a simple prototype class—just remember to call EventEmitter's constructor from within your new constructor.

The first listing shows how to inherit from EventEmitter.

Listing 4.1   Inheriting from EventEmitter

```
var util = require('util');
var events = require('events');

function MusicPlayer() {
  events.EventEmitter.call(this);
}

util.inherits(MusicPlayer, events.EventEmitter);
```
Using util.inherits is the idiomatic Node way to inherit from prototype classes.

DISCUSSION

The combination of a simple constructor function and util.inherits is the easiest and most common way to create customized event-based classes. The next listing extends the previous listing to show how to emit and bind listeners using on.

Listing 4.2   Inheriting from EventEmitter

```
var util = require('util');
var events = require('events');
var AudioDevice = {
  play: function(track) {
    // Stub: Trigger playback through iTunes, mpg123, etc.
  },

  stop: function() {
  }
};

function MusicPlayer() {
  this.playing = false;
  events.EventEmitter.call(this);
}

util.inherits(MusicPlayer, events.EventEmitter);

var musicPlayer = new MusicPlayer();

musicPlayer.on('play', function(track) {
  this.playing = true;
  AudioDevice.play(track);
});

musicPlayer.on('stop', function() {
  this.playing = false;
  AudioDevice.stop();
});

musicPlayer.emit('play', 'The Roots - The Fire');

setTimeout(function() {
  musicPlayer.emit('stop');
}, 1000);
```

The class's state can be configured, and then EventEmitter's constructor can be called as required.

The inherits method copies the methods from one prototype into another—this is the general pattern for creating classes based on EventEmitter.

The emit method is used to trigger events.

This might not seem like much, but suppose we need to do something else when play is triggered—perhaps the user interface needs to be updated. This can be supported simply by adding another listener to the play event. The following listing shows how to add more listeners.

Listing 4.3   Adding multiple listeners

```
var util = require('util');
var events = require('events');

function MusicPlayer() {
  this.playing = false;
  events.EventEmitter.call(this);
}

util.inherits(MusicPlayer, events.EventEmitter);
```

```
var musicPlayer = new MusicPlayer();

musicPlayer.on('play', function(track) {
  this.playing = true;
});

musicPlayer.on('stop', function() {
  this.playing = false;
});

musicPlayer.on('play', function(track) {       ◁─┐  New listeners can be
  console.log('Track now playing:', track);          added as needed.
});

musicPlayer.emit('play', 'The Roots - The Fire');

setTimeout(function() {
  musicPlayer.emit('stop');
}, 1000);
```

Listeners can be removed as well. `emitter.removeListener` removes a listener for a specific event, whereas `emitter.removeAllListeners` removes all of them. You'll need to store the listener in a variable to be able to reference it when removing a specific listener, which is similar to removing timers with `clearTimeout`. The next listing shows this in action.

Listing 4.4 Removing listeners

```
function play(track) {        ◁─┐  A reference to the
  this.playing = true;              listener is required to
}                                   be able to remove it.

musicPlayer.on('play', play);

musicPlayer.removeListener('play', play);
```

`util.inherits` works by wrapping around the ES5 method `Object.create`, which inherits the properties from one prototype into another. Node's implementation also sets the superconstructor in the `super_` property. This makes accessing the original constructor a lot easier—after using `util.inherits`, your prototype class will have access to `EventEmitter` through `YourClass.super_`.

You can also respond to an event once, rather than every time it fires. To do that, attach a listener with the `once` method. This is useful where an event can be emitted multiple times, but you only care about it happening a single time. For example, you could update listing 4.3 to track if the play event has ever been triggered:

```
musicPlayer.once('play', {
  this.audioFirstStarted = new Date();
});
```

When inheriting from `EventEmitter`, it's a good idea to use `events.EventEmitter` `.call(this)` in your constructor to run `EventEmitter`'s constructor. The reason for this is because it'll attach the instance to a `domain` if domains are being used. To learn more about domains, see technique 22.

The methods we've covered here—`on`, `emit`, and `removeListener`—are fundamental to Node development. Once you've mastered `EventEmitter`, you'll find it cropping up everywhere: in Node's built-in modules and beyond. Creating TCP/IP servers with `net.createServer` will return a server based on `EventEmitter`, and even the `process` global object is an instance of `EventEmitter`. In addition, popular modules like Express are based around `EventEmitter`—you can actually create an Express app object and call `app.emit` to send messages around an Express project.

TECHNIQUE 20   **Mixing in EventEmitter**

Sometimes inheritance isn't the right way to use `EventEmitter`. In these cases, mixing in `EventEmitter` may work.

PROBLEM

This is an alternative option to technique 19. Rather than using `EventEmitter` as a base class, it's possible to copy its methods into another class. This is useful when you have an existing class and can't easily rework it to inherit directly from `EventEmitter`.

SOLUTION

Using a for-in loop is sufficient for copying the properties from one `prototype` to another. In this way you can copy the necessary properties from `EventEmitter`.

DISCUSSION

This example might seem a little contrived, but sometimes it really is useful to copy `EventEmitter`'s properties rather than inherit from it in the usual way. This approach is more akin to a mixin, or multiple inheritance; see this demonstrated in the following listing.

Listing 4.5   Mixing in `EventEmitter`

```
var EventEmitter = require('events').EventEmitter;

function MusicPlayer(track) {
  this.track = track;
  this.playing = false;

  for (var methodName in EventEmitter.prototype) {        ⟵  This is the for-in loop
    this[methodName] = EventEmitter.prototype[methodName];     that copies the relevant
  }                                                             properties.
}

MusicPlayer.prototype = {
  toString: function() {
    if (this.playing) {
      return 'Now playing: ' + this.track;
    } else {
      return 'Stopped';
```

```
      }
    }
};

var musicPlayer = new MusicPlayer('Girl Talk - Still Here');

musicPlayer.on('play', function() {
  this.playing = true;
  console.log(this.toString());
});

musicPlayer.emit('play');
```

One example of multiple inheritance in the wild is the Connect framework.[1] The core `Server` class inherits from multiple sources, and in this case the Connect authors have decided to make their own property copying method, shown in the next listing.

Listing 4.6 `utils.merge` **from Connect**

```
exports.merge = function(a, b){
  if (a && b) {
    for (var key in b) {
      a[key] = b[key];
    }
  }
  return a;
};
```

This technique may be useful when you already have a well-established class that could benefit from events, but can't easily be a direct descendant of `EventEmitter`.

Once you've inherited from `EventEmitter` you'll need to handle errors. The next section explores techniques for handling errors generated by `EventEmitter` classes.

4.2 *Error handling*

Although most events are treated equally, `error` events are a special case and are therefore treated differently. This section looks at two ways of handling errors: one attaches a listener to the `error` event, and the other uses domains to collect errors from groups of `EventEmitter` instances.

TECHNIQUE 21 **Managing errors**

Error handling with `EventEmitter` has its own special rules that must be adhered to. This technique explains how error handling works.

PROBLEM
You're using an `EventEmitter` and want to gracefully handle when errors occur, but it keeps raising exceptions.

---

[1] See http://www.senchalabs.org/connect/.

SOLUTION

To prevent `EventEmitter` from throwing exceptions whenever an `error` event is emitted, add a listener to the `error` event. This can be done with custom classes or any standard class that inherits from `EventEmitter`.

DISCUSSION

To handle errors, bind a listener to the `error` event. The following listing demonstrates this by building on the music player example.

Listing 4.7   Event-based errors

```
var util = require('util');
var events = require('events');

function MusicPlayer() {
  events.EventEmitter.call(this);
}

util.inherits(MusicPlayer, events.EventEmitter);

var musicPlayer = new MusicPlayer();

musicPlayer.on('play', function(track) {
  this.emit('error', 'unable to play!');
});

musicPlayer.on('error', function(err) {            ◁─┐  Listening for
  console.error('Error:', err);                        an error event
});

setTimeout(function() {
  musicPlayer.emit('play', 'Little Comets - Jennifer');
}, 1000);
```

This example is perhaps simple, but it's useful because it should help you realize how `EventEmitter` handles errors. It feels like a special case, and that's because it is. The following excerpt is from the Node documentation:

> When an `EventEmitter` instance experiences an error, the typical action is to emit an *error* event. Error events are treated as a special case in Node. If there is no listener for it, then the default action is to print a stack trace and exit the program.

You can try this out by removing the `'error'` handler from listing 4.7. A stack trace should be displayed in the console.

This makes sense semantically—otherwise the absence of an error handler would lead to potentially dangerous activity going unnoticed. The event name, or *type* as it's referred to internally, has to appear exactly as `error`—extra spaces, punctuation, or uppercase letters won't be considered an `error` event.

This convention means there's a great deal of consistency across event-based error-handling code. It might be a special case, but it's one worth paying attention to.

TECHNIQUE 22   **Managing errors with domains**

Dealing with errors from multiple instances of EventEmitter can feel like hard work ... unless domains are used!

PROBLEM

You're dealing with multiple non-blocking APIs, but are struggling to effectively handle errors.

SOLUTION

Node's domain module can be used to centralize error handling for a set of asynchronous operations, and this includes EventEmitter instances that emit unhandled error events.

DISCUSSION

Node's domain API provides a way of wrapping existing non-blocking APIs and exceptions with error handlers. This helps centralize error handling, and is particularly useful in cases where multiple interdependent I/O operations are being used.

Listing 4.8 builds on the music player example by using two EventEmitter descendants to show how a single error handler can be used to handle errors for separate objects.

Listing 4.8   Managing errors with domain

```
var util = require('util');
var domain = require('domain');          ⊲─┐ The Domain module must be
var events = require('events');            │ loaded, and then a suitable instance
var audioDomain = domain.create();         │ created with the create method.

function AudioDevice() {
  events.EventEmitter.call(this);
  this.on('play', this.play.bind(this));
}

util.inherits(AudioDevice, events.EventEmitter);

AudioDevice.prototype.play = function() {
  this.emit('error', 'not implemented yet');
};

function MusicPlayer() {
  events.EventEmitter.call(this);

  this.audioDevice = new AudioDevice();
  this.on('play', this.play.bind(this));          This error and any
                                                  other errors will be
  this.emit('error', 'No audio tracks are available');   ⊲─┘ caught by the same
}                                                        error handler.

util.inherits(MusicPlayer, events.EventEmitter);
```

```
MusicPlayer.prototype.play = function() {
  this.audioDevice.emit('play');
  console.log('Now playing');
};

audioDomain.on('error', function(err) {
  console.log('audioDomain error:', err);
});

audioDomain.run(function() {
  var musicPlayer = new MusicPlayer();
  musicPlayer.play();
});
```

Any code that raises errors inside this callback will be covered by the domain.

Domains can be used with EventEmitter descendants, networking code, and also the asynchronous file system methods.

To visualize how domains work, imagine that the domain.run callback wraps around your code, even when the code inside the callback triggers events that occur outside of it. Any errors that are thrown will still be caught by the domain. Figure 4.1 illustrates this process.

Without a domain, any errors raised using throw could potentially place the interpreter in an unknown state. Domains avoid this and help you handle errors more gracefully.

Now that you know how to inherit from EventEmitter and handle errors, you should be starting to see all kinds of useful ways that it can be used. The next section broadens these techniques by introducing some advanced usage patterns and higher-level solutions to program structure issues relating to events.

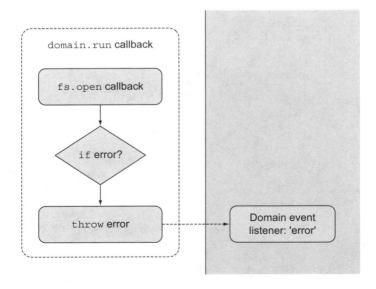

Figure 4.1 Domains help catch errors and handle them with an EventEmitter-style API.

4.3 Advanced patterns

This section offers some best practice techniques for solving structural issues found when using EventEmitter.

TECHNIQUE 23   **Reflection**

Sometimes you need to dynamically respond to changes to an instance of an EventEmitter, or query its listeners. This technique explains how to do this.

PROBLEM

You need to either catch when a listener has been added to an emitter, or query the existing listeners.

SOLUTION

To track when listeners are added, EventEmitter emits a special event called new-Listener. Listeners added to this event will receive the event name and the listener function.

DISCUSSION

In some ways, the difference between writing good Node code and *great* Node code comes down to a deep understanding of EventEmitter. Being able to correctly reflect on EventEmitter objects gives rise to a whole range of opportunities for creating more flexible and intuitive APIs. One dynamic way of doing this is through the new-Listener event, emitted when listeners are added using the on method. Interestingly, this event is emitted by using EventEmitter itself—it's implemented by using emit.

The next listing shows how to track newListener events.

Listing 4.9   Keeping tabs on new listeners

```
var util = require('util');
var events = require('events');

function EventTracker() {
  events.EventEmitter.call(this);
}

util.inherits(EventTracker, events.EventEmitter);

var eventTracker = new EventTracker();

eventTracker.on('newListener', function(name, listener) {     ◁─┤ Track whenever new
  console.log('Event name added:', name);                          listeners are added.
});

eventTracker.on('a listener', function() {
  // This will cause 'newListener' to fire
});
```

Even though 'a listener' is never explicitly emitted in this example, the newLis-tener event will still fire. Since the listener's callback function is passed as well as the event name, this is a great way to create simplified public APIs for things that require access to the original listener function. Listing 4.10 demonstrates this concept by automatically starting a timer when listeners for `pulse` events are added.

Listing 4.10   Automatically triggering events based on new listeners

```
var util = require('util');
var events = require('events');

function Pulsar(speed, times) {
  events.EventEmitter.call(this);

  var self = this;
  this.speed = speed;
  this.times = times;

  this.on('newListener', function(eventName, listener) {
    if (eventName === 'pulse') {
      self.start();
    }
  });
}

util.inherits(Pulsar, events.EventEmitter);

Pulsar.prototype.start = function() {
  var self = this;
  var id = setInterval(function() {
    self.emit('pulse');
    self.times--;
    if (self.times === 0) {
      clearInterval(id);
    }
  }, this.speed);
};

var pulsar = new Pulsar(500, 5);

pulsar.on('pulse', function() {
  console.log('.');
});
```

Display a dot for each pulse.

We can go a step further and query `EventEmitter` objects about their listeners by calling `emitter.listeners(event)`. A list of *all* listeners can't be returned in one go, though. The entire list is technically available within the `this._events` object, but this property should be considered private. The `listeners` method currently returns an `Array` instance. This could be used to iterate over multiple listeners if several have been added to a given event—perhaps to remove them at the end of an asynchronous process, or simply to check if any listeners have been added.

In cases where an array of events is available, the `listeners` method will effectively return `this._events[type].slice(0)`. Calling `slice` on an array is a JavaScript shortcut for creating a *copy* of an array. The documentation states that this behavior may change in the future, so if you really want to create a copy of attached listeners, then call slice yourself to ensure you really get a copy and not a reference to a data structure within the emitter instance.

Listing 4.11 adds a stop method to the Pulsar class. When stop is called, it checks to see if there are any listeners; otherwise, it raises an error. Checking for listeners is a good way to prevent incorrect usage, but you don't have to do this in your own code.

Listing 4.11   Querying listeners

```
Pulsar.prototype.stop = function() {
  if (this.listeners('pulse').length === 0) {
    throw new Error('No listeners have been added!');
  }
};

var pulsar = new Pulsar(500, 5);

pulsar.stop();
```

TECHNIQUE 24   **Detecting and exploiting EventEmitter**

A lot of successful open source Node modules are built on EventEmitter. It's useful to spot where EventEmitter is being used and to know how to take advantage of it.

PROBLEM

You're working on a large project with several components and want to communicate between them.

SOLUTION

Look for the emit and on methods whenever you're using either Node's standard modules or open source libraries. For example, the Express app object has these methods, and they're great for sending messages within an application.

DISCUSSION

Usually when you're working on a large project, there's a major component that's central to your problem domain. If you're building a web application with Express, then the app object is one such component. A quick check of the source shows that this object mixes in EventEmitter, so you can take advantage of events to communicate between the disparate components within your project.

Listing 4.12 shows an Express-based example where a listener is bound to an event, and then the event is emitted when a specific route is accessed.

Listing 4.12   Reusing EventEmitter in Express

```
var express = require('express');
var app = express();

app.on('hello-alert', function() {
  console.warn('Warning!');
});
```

```
app.get('/', function(req, res){
  res.app.emit('hello-alert');
  res.send('hello world');
});
```
⟵ **The app object is also available in res.app.**

```
app.listen(3000);
```

This might seem contrived, but what if the route were defined in another file? In this case, you wouldn't have access to the app object, unless it was defined as a global.

Another example of a popular project built on EventEmitter is the Node Redis client (https://npmjs.org/package/redis). Instances of RedisClient inherit from EventEmitter. This allows you to hook into useful events, like the error event, as shown in the next listing.

Listing 4.13   Reusing EventEmitter in the redis module

```
var redis = require('redis'),
var client = redis.createClient();

client.on('error', function(err) {
  console.error('Error:', err);
});

client.on('monitor', function(timestamp, args) {
  console.log('Time:', timestamp, 'arguments:', args);
});

client.on('ready', function() {
  // Start app here
});
```
⟵ **The monitor event emitted by the redis module for tracking when various internal activities occur**

In cases where the route separation technique has been used to store routes in several files, you can actually send events by calling res.app.emit(event). This allows route handlers to communicate back to the app object itself.

This might seem like a highly specific Express example, but other popular open source modules are also built on EventEmitter—just look for the emit and on methods. Remember that Node's internal modules like the process object and net.create-Server inherit from EventEmitter, and well-written open source modules tend to inherit from these modules as well. This means there's a huge amount of scope for event-based solutions to architectural problems.

This example also highlights another benefit of building projects around EventEmitter—asynchronous processes can respond as soon as possible. If the hello-alert event performs a very slow operation like sending an email, the person browsing the page might not want to wait for this process to finish. In this case, you can render the requested page while effectively performing a slower operation in the background.

The Node Redis client makes excellent use of EventEmitter and the author has written documentation for what each of the methods do. This is a good idea—if somebody joins your project, they may find it hard to get an overall picture of the events that are being used.

TECHNIQUE 25   Categorizing event names

Some projects just have too many events. This technique shows how to deal with bugs caused by mistyped event names.

PROBLEM

You're losing track of the events in your program, and are concerned that it may be too easy to write an incorrect event name somewhere causing a difficult-to-track bug.

SOLUTION

The easiest way to solve this problem is to use an object to act as a central dictionary for all of the event names. This creates a centralized location of each event in the project.

DISCUSSION

It's hard to keep track of event names littered throughout a project. One way to manage this is to keep each event name in one place. Listing 4.14 demonstrates using an object to categorize event names, based on the previous examples in this chapter.

Listing 4.14   Categorizing event names using an object

```
var util = require('util');
var events = require('events');

function MusicPlayer() {
  events.EventEmitter.call(this);
  this.on(MusicPlayer.events.play, this.play.bind(this));
}

var e = MusicPlayer.events = {          ◁——    The object used to store
  play: 'play',                                 the event list is aliased
  pause: 'pause',                               for convenience.
  stop: 'stop',
  ff: 'ff',
  rw: 'rw',
  addTrack: 'add-track'
};

util.inherits(MusicPlayer, events.EventEmitter);

MusicPlayer.prototype.play = function() {
  this.playing = true;
};

var musicPlayer = new MusicPlayer();

musicPlayer.on(e.play, function() {    ◁——    When adding new listeners, users
  console.log('Now playing');                 of the class can refer to the events
});                                            list rather than writing the event
                                               names as strings.
musicPlayer.emit(e.play);
```

Although `EventEmitter` is an integral part of Node's standard library, and an elegant solution to many problems, it can be the source of a lot of bugs in larger projects where people may forget the name of a given event. One way around this is to avoid writing events as strings. Instead, an object can be used with properties that refer to the event name strings.

If you're writing a reusable, open source module, you should consider making this part of the public API so it's easy for people to get a centralized list of event names.

There are other observer pattern implementations that avoid using string event names to effectively type check events. In the next technique we'll look at a few that are available through npm.

Although `EventEmitter` provides a wide array of solutions when working on Node projects, there are alternative implementations out there. The next section includes some popular alternatives.

4.4   *Third-party modules and extensions*

`EventEmitter` is essentially an *observer pattern* implementation. There are other interpretations of this pattern, which can help scale Node programs to run across several processes or over a network. The next technique introduces some of the more popular alternatives created by the Node community.

TECHNIQUE 26   **Alternatives to EventEmitter**

`EventEmitter` has a great API and works well in Node programs, but sometimes a problem requires a slightly different solution. This technique explores some alternatives to `EventEmitter`.

PROBLEM

You're trying to solve a problem that doesn't quite fit `EventEmitter`.

SOLUTION

Depending on the exact nature of the problem you're trying to solve, there are several alternatives to `EventEmitter`: publish/subscribe, AMQP, and `js-signals` are some popular alternatives with good support in Node.

DISCUSSION

The `EventEmitter` class is an implementation of the *observer pattern*. A related pattern is publish/subscribe, where publishers send messages that are characterized into classes to subscribers without knowing the details of the subscribers themselves.

The publish/subscribe pattern is often useful in cases where horizontal scaling is required. If you need to run multiple Node processes on multiple servers, then technologies like AMQP and ØMQ can help implement this. They're both specifically designed to solve this class of problem, but may not be as convenient as using the Redis publish/subscribe API if you're already using Redis.

If you need to horizontally scale across a distributed cluster, then an AMQP implementation like RabbitMQ (http://www.rabbitmq.com/) will work well. The `rabbitmq-nodejs-client` (https://github.com/adrai/rabbitmq-nodejs-client) module has a publish/subscribe API. The following listing shows a simple example of RabbitMQ in Node.

Listing 4.15   Using RabbitMQ with Node

```
var rabbitHub = require('rabbitmq-nodejs-client');
var subHub = rabbitHub.create( { task: 'sub', channel: 'myChannel' } );
var pubHub = rabbitHub.create( { task: 'pub', channel: 'myChannel' } );

subHub.on('connection', function(hub) {
  hub.on('message', function(msg) {              ◁─────┐  Print the message
    console.log(msg);                                  │  when it's received.
  }.bind(this));
});
subHub.connect();

pubHub.on('connection', function(hub) {
  hub.send('Hello World!');
});
pubHub.connect();
```

ØMQ (http://www.zeromq.org/) is more popular in the Node community. Justin Tulloss and TJ Holowaychuk's `zeromq.node` module (https://github.com/JustinTulloss/zeromq.node) is a popular binding. The next listing shows just how simple this API is.

Listing 4.16   Using ØMQ with Node

```
var zmq = require('zmq');
var push = zmq.socket('push');
var pull = zmq.socket('pull');

push.bindSync('tcp://127.0.0.1:3000');
pull.connect('tcp://127.0.0.1:3000');
console.log('Producer bound to port 3000');

setInterval(function() {
  console.log('sending work');
  push.send('some work');
}, 500);

pull.on('message', function(msg) {
  console.log('work: %s', msg.toString());
});
```

If you're already using Redis with Node, then it's worth trying out the Pub/Sub API (http://redis.io/topics/pubsub). Listing 4.17 shows an example of this using the Node Redis client (https://github.com/mranney/node_redis).

Listing 4.17   Using Redis Pub/Sub with Node

```
var redis = require('redis');
var client1 = redis.createClient();
var client2 = redis.createClient();
```

```
var msg_count = 0;

client1.on('subscribe', function(channel, count) {
  client2.publish('channel', 'Hello world.');
});

client1.on('message', function(channel, message) {
  console.log('client1 channel ' + channel + ': ' + message);
  client1.unsubscribe();
  client1.end();          ◁────┐   Be sure to close client connections
  client2.end();                   when using the Redis module.
});

client1.subscribe('channel');
```

Finally, if publish/subscribe isn't what you're looking for, then you may want to take a look at js-signals (https://github.com/millermedeiros/js-signals). This module is a messaging system that doesn't use strings for the signal names, and dispatching or listening to events that don't yet exist will raise errors.

Listing 4.18 shows how js-signals sends and receives messages. Notice how signals are properties of an object, rather than strings, and that listeners can receive an arbitrary number of arguments.

Listing 4.18   Using Redis Pub/Sub with Node

```
var signals = require('signals');
var myObject = {
  started: new signals.Signal()
};

function onStarted(param1, param2){
  console.log(param1, param2);
}
                                                              Dispatching the
Binding a                                                     signal using two
listener to the  ┌──▷ myObject.started.add(onStarted);        parameters
started signal   └─   myObject.started.dispatch('hello', 'world');  ◁───┘
```

js-signals provides a way of using properties for signal names, as mentioned in technique 25, but in this case the module will raise an error if an unregistered listener is dispatched or bound to. This approach is more like "strongly typed" events, and is very different from most publish/subscribe and event observer implementations.

4.5   Summary

In this chapter you've learned how EventEmitter is used through inheritance and multiple inheritance, and how to manage errors with and without domains. You've also seen how to centralize event names, how open source modules build on EventEmitter, and some alternative solutions.

What you should take away from this chapter is that although EventEmitter is usually used as a base class for inheritance, it's also possible to mix it into existing classes. Also, although EventEmitter is a great solution to many problems and used throughout

Node's internals, sometimes other solutions are more optimal. For example, if you're using Redis, then you can take advantage of its publish/subscribe implementation. Finally, `EventEmitter` isn't without its problems; managing large amounts of event names can cause bugs, and now you know how to avoid this by using an object with properties that act as event names.

In the next chapter we'll look at a related topic: streams. Streams are built around an event-based API, so you'll be able to use some of these `EventEmitter` techniques there as well.

5

Streams: Node's most powerful and misunderstood feature

This chapter covers

- What streams are and how to use them
- How to use Node's built-in streaming APIs
- The stream API used in Node 0.8 and below
- The stream primitive classes bundled since Node 0.10
- Strategies for testing streams

Streams are an event-based API for managing and modeling data, and are wonderfully efficient. By leveraging EventEmitter and Node's non-blocking I/O libraries, the stream module allows data to be dynamically processed when it's available, and then released when it's no longer needed.

The idea of a stream of data isn't new, but it's an important concept and integral to Node. After chapter 4, mastering streams is the next step on the path to becoming truly competent at Node development.

The `stream` core module provides abstract tools for building event-based stream classes. It's likely that you'll use modules that implement streams, rather than creating your own. But to exploit streams to their fullest, it's important to understand how they really work. This chapter has been designed with that goal in mind: understanding streams, working with Node's built-in streaming APIs, and finally creating and testing your own streams. Despite the conceptually abstract nature of the `stream` module, once you've mastered the major concepts, you'll start to see uses for streams everywhere.

The next section provides a high-level overview of streams and addresses the two APIs that Node supports as of Node 0.10.

5.1 Introduction to streams

In Node, streams are an *abstract interface* adhered to by several different objects. When we talk about streams, we're referring to a way of doing things—in a sense, they're a protocol. Streams can be readable or writable, and are implemented with instances of `EventEmitter`—see chapter 4 for more on events. Streams provide the means for creating data flows between objects, and can be composed with LEGO-like modularity.

5.1.1 Types of streams

Streams always involve I/O of some kind, and they can be classified into groups based on the type of I/O they deal with. The following types of streams were taken from James Halliday's `stream-handbook` (https://github.com/substack/stream-handbook/), and will give you an idea of the wide array of things you can do with streams:

- *Built-in*—Many of Node's core modules implement streaming interfaces; for example, `fs.createReadStream`.
- *HTTP*—Although technically network streams, there are streaming modules designed to work with various web technologies.
- *Parsers*—Historically parsers have been implemented using streams. Popular third-party modules for Node include XML and JSON parsers.
- *Browser*—Node's event-based streams have been extended to work in browsers, offering some unique opportunities for interfacing with client-side code.
- *Audio*—James Halliday has written some novel audio modules that have streamable interfaces.
- *RPC (Remote Procedure Call)*—Sending streams over the network is a useful way to implement interprocess communication.
- *Test*—There are stream-friendly test libraries, and tools for testing streams themselves.
- *Control, meta, and state*—There are also more abstract uses of streams, and modules designed purely for manipulating and managing other streams.

The best way to understand why streams are important is to first consider what happens when data is processed without them. Let's look at this in more detail by comparing Node's asynchronous, synchronous, and stream-based APIs.

5.1.2   *When to use streams*

When reading a file synchronously with `fs.readFileSync`, the program will block, and all of the data will be read to memory. Using `fs.readFile` will prevent the program from blocking because it's an asynchronous method, but it'll still read the entire file into memory.

What if there were a way to tell `fs.readFile` to read a chunk of data into memory, process it, and then ask for more data? That's where streams come in.

Memory becomes an issue when working with large files—compressed backup archives, media files, large log files, and so on. Instead of reading the entire file into memory, you could use `fs.read` with a suitable buffer, reading in a specific length at a time. Or, preferably, you could use the streams API provided by `fs.createReadStream`. Figure 5.1 illustrates how only a chunk of a file is read at a time with `fs.createReadStream`, compared to the entire file with `fs.readFile`.

Streams are asynchronous by design. Rather than reading that entire file into memory, a buffer's worth will be read, the desired operations will be performed, and then the result will be written to the output stream. This approach is as close to idiomatic Node as you can get. What's more, streams are implemented with plain old JavaScript. Take `fs.createReadStream`—it offers a more scalable solution, but ultimately just wraps simple file system operations with a better API.

Node's streaming APIs feel idiomatic, yet streams have been around in computer science for a long time. This history is examined briefly in the next section to give you some background on where streams come from and where they're used.

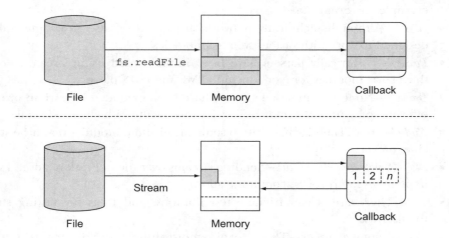

Figure 5.1   Using streamable APIs means I/O operations potentially use less memory.

5.1.3 History

So where did streams originate? Historically, streams in computer science have been used to solve problems similar to streams in Node. For example, in C the standard way to represent a file is by using a stream. When a C program starts, it has access to the standard I/O streams. The standard I/O streams are also available in Node, and can be used to allow programs to work well with large amounts of data in the shell.

Traditionally, streams have been used to implement efficient parsers. This has also been the case in Node: the `node-formidable` module (https://github.com/felixge/node-formidable) is used by Connect to efficiently parse form data with streams, and database modules like the Node `redis` module (https://npmjs.org/package/redis) use streams to represent the connection to the server and respond by parsing on demand.

If you're familiar with Unix, you're probably already aware of streams. If you've used pipes or I/O redirection, then you've used streams. You can literally think about Node streams as you would Unix pipes—except data is filtered through functions instead of command-line programs. The next section explains how streams have evolved in Node, up until version 0.10 when they changed significantly.

STREAMS OLD AND NEW

Streams are part of Node's core modules, and as such remain backward compatible with earlier versions. As of this writing, Node is at version 0.10, which has seen significant changes in the streams API. Though it remains backward compatible, the new streams syntax is in some ways stricter than earlier versions, yet ultimately more flexible. This boils down to the behavior of `pipe`—pipes must now originate from a `Readable` stream and end at a `Writable` stream. The `util.pump` method, found in earlier versions of Node, has now been deprecated in favor of the new `pipe` semantics.

The evolution of streams in Node came from a desire to use the event-based APIs to solve non-blocking I/O problems in an efficient way. Older solutions like `util.pump` sought to find efficiency in intelligent uses of "drain" events—this is emitted when a writable stream has emptied and it's safe to write again. This sounds a lot like pausing a stream, and the handling of paused streams was something the pre-0.10 streams API couldn't handle effectively.

Now Node has reached a point where the core developers have seen the types of problems people are tackling with streams, so the new API is richer thanks to the new stream primitive classes. Table 5.1 shows a summary of the classes available from Node 0.10 onward.

Learning to take advantage of streams will pay dividends when it comes to working with third-party modules that implement streams. In the next section, a selection of popular stream-oriented modules is examined.

5.1.4 Streams in third-party modules

The main use of streams in Node is for creating event-based APIs for I/O-like sources; parsers, network protocols, and database modules are the key examples. A network

Table 5.1   A summary of the classes available in *streams2*

Name	User methods	Description
stream.Readable	_read(size)	Used for I/O sources that generate data
stream.Writable	_write(chunk, encoding, callback)	Used to write to an underlying output destination
stream.Duplex	_read(size), _write(chunk, encoding, callback)	A readable *and* writable stream, like a network connection
stream.Transform	_flush(size), _transform(chunk, encoding, callback)	A duplex stream that changes data in some way, with no limitation on matching input data size with the output

protocol implemented with streams can be convenient when composition is desired—think about how easy it would be to add data compression to a network protocol if the data could be passed through the gzip module with a single call to pipe.

Similarly, database libraries that stream data can handle large result sets more efficiently; rather than collecting all results into an array, a single item at a time can be streamed.

The Mongoose MongoDB module (http://mongoosejs.com/) has an object called QueryStream that can be used to stream documents. The mysql module (https://npmjs.org/package/mysql) can also stream query results, although this implementation doesn't currently implement the stream.Readable class.

You can also find more creative uses of streams out there. The baudio module (see figure 5.2) by James Halliday can be used to generate audio streams that behave just like any other stream—audio data can be routed to other streams with pipe, and recorded for playback by standard audio software:

Figure 5.2   The baudio module by James Halliday (substack) supports the generation of audio streams (from https://github.com/substack/baudio).

```
var baudio = require('baudio');

var n = 0;
var b = baudio(function (t) {
  var x = Math.sin(t * 262 + Math.sin(n));
  n += Math.sin(t);
  return x;
});
b.play();
```

When selecting a network or database library for your Node projects, we strongly recommend ensuring it has a streamable API, because it'll help you write more elegant code while also potentially offering performance benefits.

One thing all stream classes have in common is they inherit from `EventEmitter`. The significance of this is investigated in the next section.

5.1.5 *Streams inherit from EventEmitter*

Each of the `stream` module base classes emits various events, which depend on whether the base class is readable, writable, or both. The fact that streams inherit from `EventEmitter` means you can bind to various standard events to manage streams, or create your own custom events to represent more domain-specific behavior.

When working with `stream.Readable` instances (see table 5.2 for guidance on selecting a stream base class), the `readable` event is important because it signifies that the stream is ready for calls to `stream.read()`.

Attaching a listener to `data` will cause the stream to behave like the old streams API, where data is passed to `data` listeners when it's available, rather than through calls to `stream.read()`.

The `error` event is covered in detail in technique 28. It'll be emitted if the stream encounters an error when receiving data.

The `end` event signifies that the stream has received an equivalent of the end-of-file character, and won't receive more data. There's also a `close` event that represents the case where the underlying resource has been closed, which is distinct from `end`, and the Node API documentation notes that not all streams will emit this event, so a rule of thumb is to bind to `end`.

The `stream.Writable` class changes the semantics for signifying the end of a stream to `close` and `finish`. The distinction between the two is that `finish` is emitted when `writable.end()` is called, whereas `close` means the underlying I/O resource has been closed, which isn't always required, depending on the nature of the underlying stream.

The `pipe` and `unpipe` events are emitted when passing a stream to the `stream.Readable.prototype.pipe` method. This can be used to adapt the way a stream behaves when it's piped. The listener receives the destination stream as the first argument, so this value could be inspected to change the behavior of the stream. This is a more advanced technique that's covered in technique 37.

> **About the techniques in this chapter**
>
> The techniques in this chapter all use the *streams2* API. This is the nickname of the newer API style found in Node 0.10 and 0.12. If you're using Node 0.8, forward compatibility is supported through the `readable-stream` module (https://github.com/isaacs/readable-stream).

In the next section you'll learn how to solve real-world problems using streams. First we'll discuss some of Node's built-in streams, and then we'll move on to creating entirely new streams and testing them.

5.2 *Built-in streams*

Node's core modules themselves are implemented using the stream module, so it's easy to start using streams without having to build your own classes. The next technique introduces some of this functionality through file system and network streaming APIs.

TECHNIQUE 27   Using built-in streams to make a static web server

Node's core modules often have streamable interfaces. They can be used to solve many problems more efficiently than their synchronous alternatives.

PROBLEM

You want to send a file from a web server to a client in an efficient manner that will scale up to large files.

SOLUTION

Use fs.createReadStream to open a file and *stream* it to the client. Optionally, pipe the resulting stream.Readable through another stream to handle features like compression.

DISCUSSION

Node's core modules for file system and network operations, fs and net, both provide streamable interfaces. The fs module has helper methods to automatically create instances of the streamable classes. This makes using streams for some I/O-based problems fairly straightforward.

To understand why streams are important and compare them to nonstreaming code, consider the following example of a simple static file web server made with Node's core modules:

```
var http = require('http');
var fs = require('fs');

http.createServer(function(req, res) {
  fs.readFile(__dirname + '/index.html', function(err, data) { //
    if (err) {
      res.statusCode = 500;
      res.end(String(err));
    } else {
      res.end(data);
    }
  });
}).listen(8000);
```

Even though this code uses the fs.readFile method, which is non-blocking, it can easily be improved on by using fs.createReadStream. The reason is because it'll read the entire file into memory. This might seem acceptable with small files, but what if you don't know how large the file is? Static web servers often have to serve up potentially large binary assets, so a more adaptable solution is desirable.

The following listing demonstrates a streaming static web server.

Listing 5.1 A simple static web server that uses streams

```
var http = require('http');
var fs = require('fs');

http.createServer(function(req, res) {
  fs.createReadStream(__dirname + '/index.html').pipe(res);
}).listen(8000);
```

Data is piped from a file to Node's HTTP Response object.

This example uses less code than the first version, and improves its efficiency. Now instead of reading the entire file into memory, a buffer's worth will be read at a time and sent to the client. If the client is on a slow connection, the network stream will signal this by requesting that the I/O source pauses until the client is ready for more data. This is known as *backpressure*, and is one of the additional benefits using streams brings to your Node programs.

We can take this example a step further. Streams aren't just efficient and potentially more syntactically elegant, they're also extensible. Static web servers often compress files with gzip. The next listing adds that to the previous example, using streams.

Listing 5.2 A static web server with gzip

```
var http = require('http');
var fs = require('fs');
var zlib = require('zlib');

http.createServer(function(req, res) {
  res.writeHead(200, { 'content-encoding': 'gzip' });
  fs.createReadStream(__dirname + '/index.html')
    .pipe(zlib.createGzip())
    .pipe(res);
}).listen(8000);
```

Set the header so the browser knows gzip compression has been used.

Use two calls to pipe, compress, and stream the file back to the client.

Now if you open http://localhost:8000 in a browser and use its debugging tools to look at the network operations, you should see that the content was transferred using gzip. Figure 5.3 shows what our browser reported after running the example.

This could be expanded in several other ways—you can use as many calls to pipe as required. For example, the file could be piped through an HTML templating engine and then compressed. Just remember that the general pattern is readable.pipe(writable).

Note that this example is simplified to illustrate how streams work and isn't sufficient for implementing a production HTTP asset server.

Now that you've seen a fleshed-out example of how streams are used to solve a common problem, it's time to look at another piece of the puzzle: error handling.

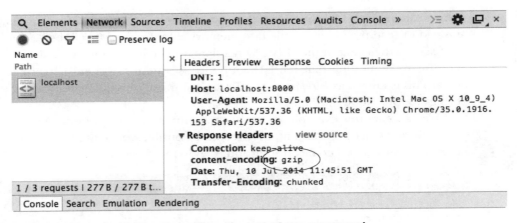

Figure 5.3   The network inspector confirms the content was compressed.

TECHNIQUE 28   Stream error handling

The stream classes inherit from EventEmitter, which means sane error handling comes as standard. This technique explains how to handle errors generated by a stream.

PROBLEM

You want to catch errors generated by a stream.

SOLUTION

Add an error listener.

DISCUSSION

The standard behavior of EventEmitter is to throw an exception when an error event is emitted—unless there's a listener attached to the error event. The first argument to the listener will be the error that was raised, a descendent of the Error object.

The following listing shows an example of an intentionally generated error with a suitable error listener.

Listing 5.3   Catching errors during streaming

Cause an error to be generated by trying to open a file that doesn't exist. ❶

Use the events API to attach an error handler. ❷

```
var fs = require('fs');
var stream = fs.createReadStream('not-found');

stream.on('error', function(err) {
  console.trace();
  console.error('Stack:', err.stack);
  console.error('The error raised was:', err);
});
```

Here we attempt to open a file that doesn't exist ❶, causing an 'error' event to be triggered. The error object passed to the handler ❷ will usually have extra information to aid in tracking down the error. For example, the stack property may have line number information, and console.trace() can be called to generate a full stack trace. In listing 5.3 console.trace() will show a trace up to the ReadStream implementation in Node's events.js core module. That means you can see exactly where the error was originally emitted.

Now that you've seen how some of Node's core modules use streams, the next section explores how third-party modules use them.

5.3   Third-party modules and streams

Streams are about as idiomatic Node as you can get, so it's no surprise that streamable interfaces crop up all over the open source Node landscape. In the next technique you'll learn how to use streamable interfaces found in some popular Node modules.

TECHNIQUE 29   Using streams from third-party modules

Many open source developers have recognized the importance of streams and incorporated streamable interfaces into their modules. In this technique you'll learn how to identify such implementations and use them to solve problems more efficiently.

PROBLEM

You want to know how to use streams with a popular third-party module that you've downloaded with npm.

SOLUTION

Look at the module's documentation or source code to figure out if it implements a streamable API, and if so, how to use it.

DISCUSSION

We've picked three popular modules as examples of third-party modules that implement streamable interfaces. This guided tour of streams in the wild should give you a good idea of how developers are using streams, and how you can exploit streams in your own projects.

In the next section you'll discover some key ways to use streams with the popular web framework, Express.

Using streams with Express

The Express web framework (http://expressjs.com/) actually provides a relatively lightweight wrapper around Node's core HTTP module. This includes the Request and `Response` objects. Express decorates these objects with some of its own methods and values, but the underlying objects are the same. That means everything you learned about streaming data to browsers in technique 27 can be reused here.

A simple example of an Express *route*—a callback that runs for a given HTTP method and URL—uses `res.send` to respond with some data:

```
var express = require('express');
var app = express();

app.get('/', function(req, res) {
  res.send('hello world');
});

app.listen(3000);
```

The `res` object is actually a *response* object, and inherits from Node's `http.Server-Response`. In technique 27 you saw that HTTP requests can be streamed to by using the `pipe` method. Express is built in a way that allows buffers and objects to work with the `res.send` method, and for streams you can still use the `pipe` method.

Listing 5.4 is an Express web application that will run with Express 3 and streams content from a custom-readable stream by using `pipe`.

Listing 5.4   An Express application that uses streams

```
var stream = require('stream');
var util = require('util');
var express = require('express');
var app = express();

util.inherits(StatStream, stream.Readable);

function StatStream(limit) {
  stream.Readable.call(this);
  this.limit = limit;
}

StatStream.prototype._read = function(size) {
  if (this.limit === 0) {
    // Done
    this.push();
  } else {
    this.push(util.inspect(process.memoryUsage()));
    this.push('n');
    this.limit--;
  }
};

app.get('/', function(req, res) {
  var statStream = new StatStream(10);
  statStream.pipe(res);
});

app.listen(3000);
```

❶ Create a readable stream by inheriting from stream.Readable and calling the parent's constructor.

❷ Respond with some data—this sends a string representation of the Node process's memory usage.

❸ Use the standard readable.pipe(writable) pattern to send data back to the browser.

Our custom readable stream, StatStream, inherits from stream.Readable ❶ and implements the _read method, which just sends memory usage data ❷. The _read method must be implemented whenever you want to make a readable stream. When sending the response back to the browser, the stream can be piped to the res object ❸ provided by Express without any extra work.

The implementation of the send module that comes with Express 3 uses fs.createReadStream, as described in technique 27. The following sample code is taken from the source to send:

```
SendStream.prototype.stream = function(path, options){
  TODO: this is all lame, refactor meeee
  var self = this;
  var res = this.res;
  var req = this.req;

  pipe
  var stream = fs.createReadStream(path, options);
  this.emit('stream', stream);
  stream.pipe(res);
```

It takes a lot more work to correctly deal with things like HTTP Content-Range headers, but this snippet demonstrates that leveraging the built-in streaming APIs like fs.createReadStream can lead to solutions powerful enough to underpin major open source projects.

Using streams with Mongoose

The Mongoose module (http://mongoosejs.com/) for the MongoDB database server (http://www.mongodb.org/) has an interface called QueryStream that provides Node 0.8-style streams for query results. This class is used internally to allow query results to be streamed using the stream method. The following code shows a query that has its results piped through a hypothetical writable stream:

```
User
  .where('role')
  .equals('admin')
  .stream()
  .pipe(writeStream);
```

This pattern—using a class to wrap an external I/O source's streamable behavior, and then exposing streams through simple method calls—is the style employed by Node's core modules, and is popular with third-party module authors. This has been made clearer by the streams2 API's use of simple abstract classes that can be inherited from.

Using streams with MySQL

The third-party mysql module (https://npmjs.org/package/mysql) is often seen by Node developers as something low-level that should be built on with more complex libraries, like the Sequelize (http://www.sequelizejs.com/) object-relational mapper (ORM). But the mysql module itself shouldn't be underestimated, and supports streaming results with pause and resume. Here's an example of the basic API style:

```
var query = connection.query('SELECT * FROM posts');
query
.on('result', function(row) {
  connection.pause();
  processRow(row, function() {
    connection.resume();
  });
});
```

This streaming API uses domain-specific event names—there's also a `'fields'` event. To pause the result stream, `connection.pause` must be called. This signals to the underlying connection to MySQL that results should stop briefly until the receiver is ready for more data.

SUMMARY

In this technique you've seen how some popular third-party modules use streams. They're all characterized by the fact they deal with I/O—both HTTP and database connections are network- or file-based protocols, and both can involve network connections and file system operations. In general, it's a good idea to look for Node network and database modules that implement streamable interfaces, because they help scale programs and also write them in a readable, idiomatic style.

Now that you've seen how to use streams, you're probably itching to learn how to create your own. The next section has a technique for using each base stream class, and also shows how to correctly inherit from them.

5.4   *Using the stream base classes*

Node's base stream classes provide templates for solving the kinds of problems that streams are best at. For example, `stream.Transform` is great for parsing data, and `stream.Readable` is perfect for wrapping lower-level APIs with a streamable interface.

The next technique explains how to inherit from the stream base classes, and then further techniques go into detail about how to use each base class.

TECHNIQUE 30   Correctly inheriting from the stream base classes

Node's base classes for streams can be used as a starting point for new modules and subclasses. It's important to understand what problems each solves, and how to correctly inherit from them.

PROBLEM

You want to solve a problem by creating a streamable API, but you're not sure which base class to use and how to use it.

SOLUTION

Decide on which base class closely matches the problem at hand, and inherit from it using `Object.prototype.call` and `util.inherits`.

DISCUSSION

Node's base classes for streams, already summarized in table 5.1, should be used as the basis for your own streamable classes or modules. They're *abstract classes*, which means they're methods that you must implement before they can be used. This is usually done through inheritance.

All of the stream base classes are found in the `stream` core module. The five base classes are `Readable`, `Writable`, `Duplex`, `Transform`, and `PassThrough`. Fundamentally, streams are either readable or writable, but `Duplex` streams are both. This makes sense if you consider the behavior of I/O interfaces—a network connection can be both readable and writable. It wouldn't be particularly useful, for example, if `ssh` were only able to send data.

`Transform` streams build on `Duplex` streams, but also change the data in some way. Some of Node's built-in modules use `Transform` streams, so they're fundamentally important. An example of this is the `crypto` module.

Table 5.2 offers some hints to help you choose which base class to use.

Table 5.2   Selecting a streams base class

Problem	Solution
You want to wrap around an underlying I/O source with a streamable API.	`Readable`
You want to get output from a program to use elsewhere, or send data elsewhere within a program.	`Writable`
You want to change data in some way by parsing it.	`Transform`
You want to wrap a data source that can also receive messages.	`Duplex`
You want to extract data from streams without changing it, from testing to analysis.	`PassThrough`

Inheriting from the base classes

If you've learned about inheritance in JavaScript, you might be tempted to inherit from the stream base classes by using `MyStream.prototype = new stream.Readable();`. This is considered bad practice, and it's better to use the ECMAScript 5 `Object.create` pattern instead. Also, the base class's constructor must be run, because it provides essential setup code. The pattern for this is shown next.

Listing 5.5   Inheriting from the `stream.Readable` base class

```
var Readable = require('stream').Readable;

function MyStream(options) {
  Readable.call(this, options);
}

MyStream.prototype = Object.create(Readable.prototype, {
  constructor: { value: MyStream }
});
```

❶ Call the parent constructor, and be sure to pass any options to it as well.

❷ Use Object.create to correctly set up the prototype chain.

Node includes a utility method called `util.inherits` that can be used instead of `Object.create`, but both approaches are widely used by Node developers. This example uses the `Object.create` method **❶** instead so you can see what `util.inherits` does.

Note that in listing 5.5 the `options` argument ❷ is passed to the original `Readable` constructor. This is important because there's a standard set of options that Node supports for configuring streams. In the case of `Readable`, the options are as follows:

- *highWaterMark*—The number of bytes to store in the internal buffer before pausing reading from the underlying data source.
- *encoding*—Causes the buffer to be automatically decoded. Possible values include `utf8` and `ascii`.
- *objectMode*—Allows the stream to behave as a stream of objects, rather than bytes.

The `objectMode` option allows JavaScript objects to be handled by streams. An example of this has been provided in technique 31.

SUMMARY

In this technique you've seen how to use Node's stream base classes to create your own stream implementations. This involves using `util.inherits` to set up the class, and then `.call` to call the original constructor. We also covered some of the options that these base classes use.

Properly inheriting from the base classes is one thing, but what about actually implementing a stream class? Technique 31 explains this in more detail for the `Readable` base class, but in that specific case it involves implementing a method called `_read` to read data from the underlying data source and `push` it onto an internal queue managed by the base class itself.

TECHNIQUE 31   Implementing a readable stream

Readable streams can be used to provide a flexible API around I/O sources, and can also act as parsers.

PROBLEM

You'd like to wrap an I/O source with a streamable API that provides a higher-level interface than would otherwise be possible with the underlying data.

SOLUTION

Implement a readable stream by inheriting from the `stream.Readable` class and creating a `_read(size)` method.

DISCUSSION

Implementing a custom `stream.Readable` class can be useful when a higher level of abstraction around an underlying data source is required. For example, I (Alex) was working on a project where the client had sent in JSON files that contained millions of records separated by newlines. I decided to write a quick `stream.Readable` class that read a buffer's worth of data, and whenever a newline was encountered, `JSON.parse` was used to parse the record.

One way of using `stream.Readable` to parse newline-separated JSON records is shown next.

Listing 5.6   A JSON line parser

```
var stream = require('stream');
var util = require('util');
var fs = require('fs');

function JSONLineReader(source) {
  stream.Readable.call(this);
  this._source = source;
  this._foundLineEnd = false;
  this._buffer = '';

  source.on('readable', function() {
    this.read();
  }.bind(this));
}

util.inherits(JSONLineReader, stream.Readable);

JSONLineReader.prototype._read = function(size) {
  var chunk;
  var line;
  var lineIndex;
  var result;

  if (this._buffer.length === 0) {
    chunk = this._source.read();
    this._buffer += chunk;
  }

  lineIndex = this._buffer.indexOf('n');

  if (lineIndex !== -1) {
    line = this._buffer.slice(0, lineIndex);
    if (line) {
      result = JSON.parse(line);
      this._buffer = this._buffer.slice(lineIndex + 1);
      this.emit('object', result);
      this.push(util.inspect(result));
    } else {
      this._buffer = this._buffer.slice(1);
    }
  }
};

var input = fs.createReadStream(__dirname + '/json-lines.txt', {
  encoding: 'utf8'
});
var jsonLineReader = new JSONLineReader(input);

jsonLineReader.on('object', function(obj) {
  console.log('pos:', obj.position, '- letter:', obj.letter);
});
```

1 Always ensure the constructor's parent is called.

2 Call read() when the source is ready to trigger subsequent reads.

3 Inherit from stream.Readable to create a new class that can be customized.

4 All custom stream.Readable classes must implement the _read() method.

5 When the class is ready for more data, call read() on the source.

6 Slice from the start of the buffer to the first newline to grab some text to parse.

7 Emitting an "object" event whenever a JSON record has been parsed is unique to this class and isn't necessarily required.

8 Send the parsed JSON back to the internal queue.

9 Create an instance of JSONLineReader and give it a file stream to process.

Listing 5.6 uses a constructor function, `JSONLineReader` ❶, that inherits from `stream.Readable` ❸ to read and parse lines of JSON from a file. The source for `JSON-LineReader` will be a readable stream as well, so a listener for the `readable` event is bound to, so instances of `JSONLineReader` know when to start reading data ❷.

The `_read` method ❹ checks whether the buffer is empty ❺ and, if so, reads more data from the source and adds it to the internal buffer. Then the current line index is incremented, and if a line ending is found, the first line is sliced from the buffer ❻. Once a complete line has been found, it's parsed and emitted using the `object` event ❼—users of the class can bind to this event to receive each line of JSON that's found in the source stream.

When this example is run, data from a file will flow through an instance of the class. Internally, data will be queued. Whenever `source.read` is executed, the latest "chunk" of data will be returned, so it can be processed when `JSONLineReader` is ready for it. Once enough data has been read and a newline has been found, the data will be split *up to the first newline*, and then the result will be collected by calling `this.push` ❽.

Once `this.push` is called, `stream.Readable` will queue the result and forward it on to a consuming stream. This allows the stream to be further processed by a writable stream using `pipe`. In this example JSON objects are emitted using a custom `object` event. The last few lines of this example attach an event listener for this event and process the results ❾.

The `size` argument to `Readable.prototype._read` is *advisory*. That means the underlying implementation can use it to know how much data to fetch—this isn't always needed so you don't always implement it. In the previous example we parsed the entire line, but some data formats could be parsed in chunks, in which case the size argument would be useful.

In the original code that I based this example on, I used the resulting JSON objects to populate a database. The data was also redirected and gzipped into another file. Using streams made this both easy to write and easy to read in the final project.

The example in listing 5.6 used strings, but what about objects? Most streams that deal directly with I/O—files, network protocols, and so on—will use raw bytes or strings of characters. But sometimes it's useful to create streams of JavaScript objects. Listing 5.7 shows how to safely inherit from `stream.Readable` and pass the `object-Mode` option to set up a stream that deals with JavaScript objects.

Listing 5.7   A stream configured to use `objectMode`

```
var stream = require('stream');
var util = require('util');

util.inherits(MemoryStream, stream.Readable);

function MemoryStream(options) {
  options = options || {};
  options.objectMode = true;
  stream.Readable.call(this, options);
}
```

❶ This stream should always use objectMode, so set it here and pass the rest of the options to the stream.Readable constructor.

```
MemoryStream.prototype._read = function(size) {
  this.push(process.memoryUsage());
};
```

② **Generate an object by calling Node's built-in process.memoryUsage() method.**

```
var memoryStream = new MemoryStream();
memoryStream.on('readable', function() {
  var output = memoryStream.read();
  console.log('Type: %s, value: %j', typeof output, output);
});
```

Attach a listener to readable to track when the stream is ready to output data; then call stream.read() to fetch recent values. **③**

The `MemoryStream` example in listing 5.7 uses objects for data, so `objectMode` is passed to the `Readable` constructor as an option **①**. Then `process.memoryUsage` is used to generate some suitable data **②**. When an instance of this class emits `readable` **③**, indicating that it's ready to be read from, then the memory usage data is logged to the console.

When using `objectMode`, the underlying behavior of the stream is changed to remove the internal buffer merge and length checks, and to ignore the size argument when reading and writing.

TECHNIQUE 32 **Implementing a writable stream**

Writable streams can be used to output data to underlying I/O sinks.

PROBLEM

You want to output data from a program using an I/O destination that you want to wrap with a streamable interface.

SOLUTION

Inherit from `stream.Writable` and implement a `_write` method to send data to the underlying resource.

DISCUSSION

As you saw in technique 29, many third-party modules offer streamable interfaces for network services and databases. Following this trend is advantageous because it allows your classes to be used with the `pipe` API, which helps keep chunks of code reusable and decoupled.

You might be simply looking to implement a writable stream to act as the destination of a `pipe` chain, or to implement an unsupported I/O resource. In general, all you need to do is correctly inherit from `stream.Writable`—for more on the recommended way to do this, see technique 30—and then add a `_write` method.

All the `_write` method needs to do is call a supplied callback when the data has been written. The following code shows the method's arguments and the overall structure of a sample `_write` implementation:

The chunk argument is an instance of Buffer or a String. **①**

```
MyWritable.prototype._write = function(chunk, encoding, callback) {
  this.customWriteOperation(chunk, function(err) {
    callback(err); //
  });
};
```

The callback provided by Node's internal code is called with an error if one was generated. **③**

customWriteOperation is your class's custom write operation. It can be asynchronous, so the callback can be safely called later. **②**

A _write method supplies a callback **❶** that you can call when writing has finished. This allows _write to be asynchronous. This customWriteOperation method **❷** is simply used as an example here—in a real implementation it would perform the underlying I/O. This could involve talking to a database using sockets, or writing to a file. The first argument provided to the callback should be an error **❸**, allowing _write to propagate errors if needed.

Node's stream.Writable base class doesn't need to know *how* the data was written, it just cares whether the operation succeeded or failed. Failures can be reported by passing an Error object to callback. This will cause an error event to be emitted. Remember that these stream base classes descend from EventEmitter, so you should usually add a listener to error to catch and gracefully handle any errors.

The next listing shows a complete implementation of a stream.Writable class.

Listing 5.8   An example implementation of a writable stream

```
var stream = require('stream');
GreenStream.prototype = Object.create(stream.Writable.prototype, {
    constructor: { value: GreenStream }                          ◁──── Use the usual inheritance
});                                                                     pattern to create a new
                                                                        writable stream class.
function GreenStream(options) {
    stream.Writable.call(this, options);
}

GreenStream.prototype._write = function(chunk, encoding, callback) {
    process.stdout.write('u001b[32m' + chunk + 'u001b[39m');
    callback();                      ◁──── Call the callback once the text
};                                         has been sent to stdout.

process.stdin.pipe(new GreenStream());      ◁──── Pipe stdin through
                                                   stdout to transform
                                                   text into green text.
```

Decorate the chunk with the ANSI escape sequences for green text.

This short example changes input text into green text. It can be used by running it with node writable.js, or by piping text through it with cat file.txt | node writable.js.

Although this is a trivial example, it illustrates how easy it is to implement streamable classes, so you should consider doing this the next time you want to make something that stores data work with pipe.

Chunks and encodings

The encoding argument to write is only relevant when strings are being used instead of buffers. Strings can be used by setting decodeStrings to false in the options that are passed when instantiating a writable stream.

Streams don't always deal with Buffer objects because some implementations have optimized handling for strings, so dealing directly with strings can be more efficient in certain cases.

TECHNIQUE 33 **Transmitting and receiving data with duplex streams**

Duplex streams allow data to be transmitted and received. This technique shows you how to create your own duplex streams.

PROBLEM

You want to create a streamable interface to an I/O source that needs to be both readable *and* writable.

SOLUTION

Inherit from `stream.Duplex` and implement _read and _write methods.

DISCUSSION

Duplex streams are a combination of the `Writable` and `Readable` streams, which are explained in techniques 31 and 32. As such, Duplex streams require inheriting from `stream.Duplex` and implementations for the _read and _write methods. Refer to technique 30 for an explanation of how to inherit from the stream base classes.

Listing 5.9 shows a small `stream.Duplex` class that reads and writes data from `stdin` and `stdout`. It prompts for data and then writes it back out with ANSI escape codes for colors.

Listing 5.9 A duplex stream

```
var stream = require('stream');

HungryStream.prototype = Object.create(stream.Duplex.prototype, {
  constructor: { value: HungryStream }
});

function HungryStream(options) {
  stream.Duplex.call(this, options);
  this.waiting = false;
}

HungryStream.prototype._write = function(chunk, encoding, callback) {
  this.waiting = false;
  this.push('u001b[32m' + chunk + 'u001b[39m');
  callback();
};

HungryStream.prototype._read = function(size) {
  if (!this.waiting) {
    this.push('Feed me data! > ');
    this.waiting = true;
  }
};

var hungryStream = new HungryStream();
process.stdin.pipe(hungryStream).pipe(process.stdout);
```

1 This property tracks if the prompt is being displayed.

2 This _write implementation pushes data onto the internal queue and then calls the supplied callback.

3 Display a prompt when waiting for data.

4 Pipe the standard input through the duplex stream, and then back out to standard output.

The HungryStream class in listing 5.9 will display a prompt, wait for input, and then return the input with ANSI color codes. To track the state of the prompt, an internal property called waiting ❶ is used. The _write method, which will be called by Node automatically, sets the waiting property to false, indicating that input has been received, and then the data is pushed to the internal buffer with color codes attached. Finally, the callback that gets automatically passed to _write is executed ❷.

When the class is waiting for data, the _read method pushes a message that acts as the prompt ❸. This can be made interactive by piping the standard input stream through an instance of HungryStream and then back out through the standard output stream ❹.

The great thing about duplex streams is they can sit in the middle of pipes. A simpler way to do this is to use the stream.PassThrough base class, which only relays data, allowing you to plug into the middle of a pipe and track data as it flows through it. The diagram in figure 5.4 shows how chunks of data flow through the duplex stream object, from the input to the output stream.

Several stream.Duplex implementations in the wild implement a _write method but keep the _read method as a blank stub. This is purely to take advantage of duplex streams as something that can enhance the behavior of other streams through pipes. For example, hiccup by Naomi Kyoto (https://github.com/naomik/hiccup) can be used to simulate slow or sporadic behavior of underlying I/O sources. This novel use of streams comes in handy when you're writing automated tests.

Duplex streams are useful for piping readable streams to writable streams and analyzing the data. Transform streams are specifically designed for changing data; the next technique introduces stream.Transform and the _transform method.

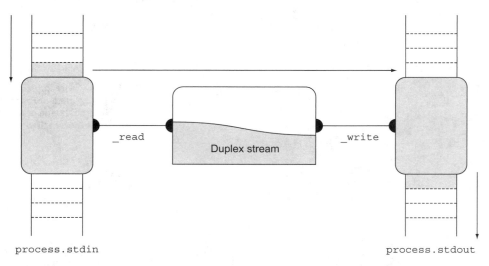

Figure 5.4   A duplex stream

Parsing data with transform streams

Streams have long been used as a way to create efficient parsers. The `stream.Transform` base class can be used to do this in Node.

PROBLEM

You want to use streams to change data into another format in a memory-efficient manner.

SOLUTION

Inherit from `stream.Transform` and implement the `_transform` method.

DISCUSSION

On the surface, transform streams sound a little bit like duplex streams. They can also sit in the middle of a pipe chain. The difference is that they're expected to transform data, and they're implemented by writing a `_transform` method. This method's signature is similar to `_write`—it takes three arguments, chunk, encoding, and `callback`. The callback should be executed when the data has been transformed, which allows transform streams to parse data asynchronously.

Listing 5.10 shows a transform stream that parses (albeit simplified) CSV data. The CSV is expected to contain comma-separated values without extra spaces or quotes, and should use Unix line endings.

Listing 5.10   A CSV parser implemented using a transform stream

```
var fs = require('fs');
var stream = require('stream');

CSVParser.prototype = Object.create(stream.Transform.prototype, {
  constructor: { value: CSVParser }
});

function CSVParser(options) {
  stream.Transform.call(this, options);

  this.value = '';              These properties are
  this.headers = [];            used to track the
  this.values = [];           ❶ state of the parser.
  this.line = 0;
}                                                          The _transform ❷
                                                           implementation.
CSVParser.prototype._transform = function(chunk, encoding, done) {
  var c;
  var i;

  chunk = chunk.toString();             ❸ The input data is turned into a
                                           string and then iterated over,
  for (i = 0; i < chunk.length; i++) {     character by character.
    c = chunk.charAt(i);
                              ❹ If the character is a comma,
    if (c === ',') {            add the previously collected
      this.addValue();          data to the internal list of
                                headers or values.
```

```
    } else if (c === 'n') {
      this.addValue();
      if (this.line > 0) {
        this.push(JSON.stringify(this.toObject()));
      }
      this.values = [];
      this.line++;
    } else {
      this.value += c;
    }
  }
  done();
};
```

⑤ If the character is a line ending, record the previously collected header or field, and then use push to send a JSON version of the data fields to the internal queue.

⑥ When processing has finished, call the callback provided by Node.

⑦ Convert the internal array of headers and the most recent line of fields into an object that can be converted to JSON.

```
CSVParser.prototype.toObject = function() {
  var i;
  var obj = {};
  for (i = 0; i < this.headers.length; i++) {
    obj[this.headers[i]] = this.values[i];
  }
  return obj;
};

CSVParser.prototype.addValue = function() {
  if (this.line === 0) {
    this.headers.push(this.value);
  } else {
    this.values.push(this.value);
  }
  this.value = '';
};
```

Headers are assumed to be on the first line; otherwise the most recently collected data is ⑧ assumed to be a data value.

```
var parser = new CSVParser();
fs.createReadStream(__dirname + '/sample.csv')
  .pipe(parser)
  .pipe(process.stdout);
```

Parsing CSV involves tracking several variables—the current value, the headers for the file, and the current line number ❶. To do this, a stream.Transform descendent with suitable properties can be used. The _transform implementation ❷ is the most complex part of this example. It receives a chunk of data, which is iterated over one character at a time using a for loop ❸. If the character is a comma, the current value is saved ❹ (if there is one). If the current character is a newline, the line is transformed into a JSON representation ❺. This example is synchronous, so it's safe to execute the callback supplied to _transform at the end of the method ❻. A toObject method has been included to make it easier to change the internal representation of the headers and values into a JavaScript object ❼.

The last line in the example creates a readable file stream of CSV data and pipes it through the CSV parser, and that output is piped again back through stdout so the results can be viewed ❽. This could also be piped through a compression module to directly support compressed CSV files, or anything else you can think of doing with `pipe` and streams.

This example doesn't implement all of the things real-world CSV files can contain, but it does show that building streaming parsers with `stream.Transform` isn't too complicated, depending on the file format or protocol.

Now that you've learned how to use the base classes, you're probably wondering what the `options` argument in listing 5.10 was used for. The next section includes some details on how to use options to optimize stream throughput, and details some more advanced techniques.

5.5   *Advanced patterns and optimization*

The stream base classes accept various options for tailoring their behavior, and some of these options can be used to tune performance. This section has techniques for optimizing streams, using the older streams API, adapting streams based on input, and testing streams.

TECHNIQUE 35   **Optimizing streams**

Built-in streams and the classes used to build custom streams allow the internal buffer size to be configured. It's useful to know how to optimize this value to attain the desired performance characteristics.

PROBLEM

You want to read data from a file, but are concerned about either speed or memory performance.

SOLUTION

Optimize the stream's buffer size to suit your application's requirements.

DISCUSSION

The built-in stream functions take a buffer size parameter, which allows the performance characteristics to be tailored to a given application. The `fs.createReadStream` method takes an `options` argument that can include a `bufferSize` property. This option is passed to `stream.Readable`, so it'll control the internal buffer used to temporarily store file data before it's used elsewhere.

The stream created by `zlib.createGzip` is an instance of `streams.Transform`, and the `Zlib` class creates its own internal buffer object for storing data. Controlling the size of this buffer is also possible, but this time the options property is `chunkSize`. Node's documentation has a section on optimizing the memory usage of zlib,[1] based on the documentation in the zlib/zconf.h header file, which is part of the low-level source code used to implement zlib itself.

In practice it's quite difficult to push Node's streams to exhibit different CPU performance characteristics based on buffer size. But to illustrate the concept, we've included a small benchmarking script that includes some interesting ideas about measuring stream performance. The next listing attempts to gather statistics on memory and elapsed time.

---

[1]   See "Memory Usage Tuning"—http://nodejs.org/docs/latest/api/all.html#all_process_memoryusage.

Listing 5.11   Benchmarking streams

```
var fs = require('fs');
var zlib = require('zlib');

function benchStream(inSize, outSize) {
  var time = process.hrtime();
  var watermark = process.memoryUsage().rss;
  var input = fs.createReadStream('/usr/share/dict/words', {
    bufferSize: inSize
  });
  var gzip = zlib.createGzip({ chunkSize: outSize });
  var output = fs.createWriteStream('out.gz', { bufferSize: inSize });

  var memoryCheck = setInterval(function() {
    var rss = process.memoryUsage().rss;

    if (rss > watermark) {
      watermark = rss;
    }
  }, 50);

  input.on('end', function() {
    var memoryEnd = process.memoryUsage();
    clearInterval(memoryCheck);

    var diff = process.hrtime(time);
    console.log([
      inSize,
      outSize,
      (diff[0] * 1e9 + diff[1]) / 1000000,
      watermark / 1024].join(', ')
    );
  });

  input.pipe(gzip).pipe(output);

  return input;
}

console.log('file size, gzip size, ms, RSS');

var fileSize = 128;
var zipSize = 5024;

function run(times) {
  benchStream(fileSize, zipSize).on('end', function() {
    times--;
    fileSize *= 2;
    zipSize *= 2;

    if (times > 0) {
      run(times);
    }
  });
```

1 hrtime is used to get precise nanosecond measurements of the current time.

2 A timer callback is used to periodically check on memory usage and record the highest usage for the current benchmark.

3 When the input has ended, gather the statistics.

4 Log the results of the memory usage and time, converting the nanosecond measurements into milliseconds.

5 Stream the input file through the gzip instance and back out to a file.

6 A callback that will run when each benchmark finishes.

7 Recursively call the benchmark function.

```
}

run(10); 8((callout-streams-buffer-size-8))
```
◁─── ⑧ **Initially call the benchmark function with the number of times we want it to run.**

This is a long example, but it just uses some of Node's built-in functionality to gather memory statistics over time for streams designed to use different buffer sizes. The bench-Stream function performs most of the work and is executed several times. It records the current time using `hrtime` ❶, which returns more precise measurements than `Date.now()` would. The input stream is the Unix dictionary file, which is piped through a gzip stream and then out to a file ❺. Then benchStream uses `setInterval` to run a periodic check on the memory usage ❷. When the input stream ends ❸, the memory usage is calculated based on the values before and after the input file was gzipped.

The `run` function doubles the input file's buffer and gzip buffer ❻ to show the impact on memory and the time taken to read the streams over time. When the reading of the input file completes, the memory usage and elapsed time will be printed ❹. The input file is returned by the benchStream function so run can easily be called when benchmarking has finished. The `run` function will be called repeatedly ❼, depending on the first argument passed to it ❽.

Note that `process.hrtime` has been used to accurately benchmark the elapsed time. This method can be used for benchmarking because it's precise, and also accepts a `time` argument for automatically calculating the elapsed time.

I (Alex) ran this program with a 20 MB file to try to generate more interesting results than /usr/share/dict/words, and I've included a graph of the results in figure 5.5.

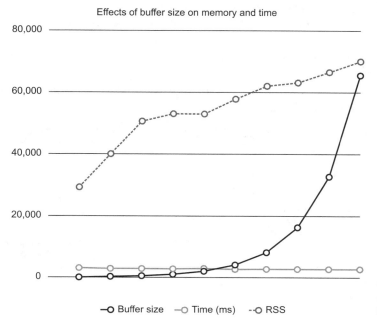

Figure 5.5 A graphical representation of the memory usage of streams

I found when I experimented with various files that the results indicated that elapsed time was far less affected than the memory usage. That indicates that it's generally desirable to use smaller buffers and be more conservative about memory usage, although this test should be repeated with a load-testing benchmark to really see how long it takes Node to process those buffers.

Node had an older API for streams that had different semantics for pausing a stream. Although the newer API should be used where possible, it's possible to use the older API alongside the newer one. The next technique demonstrates how to use modules written with the older API.

TECHNIQUE 36   ## Using the old streams API

Before Node 0.10 (and technically 0.9.4), streams had a different API. Code written using that API can be used with the newer APIs by wrapping it to behave like the newer `stream.Readable` class.

PROBLEM

You want to use a module that implements the old-style streaming API with classes that use the newer APIs.

SOLUTION

Use `Readable.prototype.wrap`.

DISCUSSION

The older stream API had readable and writable streams, but pausing a stream was "advisory" only. This led to a different API design that wasn't based around the newer streams2 classes. As people gradually realized how useful streamable classes are, a wealth of modules appeared on npm. Although the newer API solves key problems with the older design, there are still useful modules that haven't been updated.

Fortunately, older classes can be wrapped using the `Readable.prototype.wrap` method provided by the `stream` module. It literally wraps the older interface to make it behave like the newer `stream.Readable` class—it effectively creates a `Readable` instance that uses the older class as its data source.

Listing 5.12 shows an example of a stream implemented with the older API that has been wrapped with the newer `Readable` class.

Listing 5.12   An old-style stream that has been wrapped

The older API required that classes inherited from the stream module and set the readable property to true. ➊

```
var stream = require('stream');
var Readable = stream.Readable;
var util = require('util');

util.inherits(MemoryStream, stream);

function MemoryStream(interval) {
  this.readable = true;

  setInterval(function() {
    var data = process.memoryUsage();
    data.date = new Date();
    this.emit('data', JSON.stringify(data) + 'n');
```

The data event is emitted with some example values. Make sure strings or Buffer instances are used. ➋

Here the new ❹
stream is piped to
a writable stream
that is compatible
with the newer
streams API.

```
        }.bind(this), interval);
    }

    var memoryStream = new MemoryStream(250);
    var wrappedStream = new Readable().wrap(memoryStream);

    wrappedStream.pipe(process.stdout);
```

An instance of the original stream must ❸
be wrapped to become an instance of the
newer class.

The example in listing 5.12 presents a simple class that inherits from the Node 0.8
stream module. The `readable` property ❶ is part of the old API, and signifies that this
is a readable stream. Another indicator that this is a legacy stream is the `data` event ❷.
The newer `Readable.prototype.wrap` method ❸ is what translates all of this to make
it compatible with the streams2 API style. At the end, the wrapped stream is piped to a
Node 0.10 stream ❹.

Now you should be able to use older streams with the newer APIs!

Sometimes streams need to change their behavior depending on the type of input
that has been provided. The next technique looks at ways of doing just that.

TECHNIQUE 37   **Adapting streams based on their destination**

Stream classes are typically designed to solve a specific problem, but there's also
potential for customizing their behavior by detecting how the stream is being used.

PROBLEM

You want to make a stream behave differently when it's piped to the TTY (the user's
shell).

SOLUTION

Bind a listener to the `pipe` event, and then use `stream.isTTY` to check if the stream is
bound to a terminal.

DISCUSSION

This technique is a specific example of adapting a stream's behavior to its environment, but the general approach could be adapted to other problems as well. Sometimes it's useful to detect whether a stream is writing output to a TTY or something
else—perhaps a file—because different behavior in each is desirable. For example,
when printing to a TTY, some commands will use ANSI colors, but this isn't usually
advisable when writing files because strange characters would clutter the results.

Node makes detecting whether the current process is connected to a TTY simple—
just use `process.stdout.isTTY` and `process.stdin.isTTY`. These are Boolean properties that are derived from OS-level bindings in Node's source (in lib/tty.js).

The strategy to use for adapting a stream's output is to create a new `stream.Writable`
class and set an internal property based on `isTTY`. Then add a listener to the `pipe` event,
which changes `isTTY` based on the newly piped stream that's passed as the first argument
to the listener callback.

Listing 5.13 demonstrates this by using two classes. The first, `MemoryStream`, inherits from `stream.Readable` and generates data based on Node's memory usage. The

second, OutputStream, monitors the stream it's bound to so it can tell the readable stream about what kind of output it expects.

Listing 5.13   Using `isTTY` to adapt stream behavior

```
var stream = require('stream');
var util = require('util');

util.inherits(MemoryStream, stream.Readable);
util.inherits(OutputStream, stream.Writable);

function MemoryStream() {
  this.isTTY = process.stdout.isTTY;
  stream.Readable.call(this);
}

MemoryStream.prototype._read = function() {
  var text = JSON.stringify(process.memoryUsage()) + 'n';
  if (this.isTTY) {
    this.push('u001b[32m' + text + 'u001b[39m');
  } else {
    this.push(text);
  }
};

// A simple writable stream
function OutputStream() {
  stream.Writable.call(this);
  this.on('pipe', function(dest) {
    dest.isTTY = this.isTTY;
  }.bind(this));
}

OutputStream.prototype._write = function(chunk, encoding, cb) {
  util.print(chunk.toString());
  cb();
};

var memoryStream = new MemoryStream();

// Switch the desired output stream by commenting one of these lines:
//memoryStream.pipe(new OutputStream);
memoryStream.pipe(process.stdout);
```

① Set an internal flag to record what kind of output is expected.

② Use ANSI colors when printing to a terminal.

③ When the writable stream is bound with a pipe, change the destination's isTTY state.

Internally, Node uses `isTTY` to adapt the behavior of the `repl` module and the `readline` interface. The example in listing 5.13 tracks the state of `process.stdout.isTTY` **①** to determine what the original output stream was, and then copies that value to subsequent destinations **③**. When the terminal is a TTY, colors are used **②**; otherwise plain text is output instead.

Streams, like anything else, should be tested. The next technique presents a method for writing unit tests for your own stream classes.

TECHNIQUE 38 **Testing streams**

Just like anything else you write, it's strongly recommended that you test your streams. This technique explains how to use Node's built-in `assert` module to test a class that inherits from `stream.Readable`.

PROBLEM

You've written your own stream class and you want to write a unit test for it.

SOLUTION

Use some suitable sample data to drive your stream class, and then call `read()` or `write()` to gather the results and compare them to the expected output.

DISCUSSION

The common pattern for testing streams, used in Node's source itself and by many open source developers, is to drive the stream being tested using sample data and then compare the end results against expected values.

The most difficult part of this can be coming up with suitable data to test. Sometimes it's easy to create a text file, or a *fixture* in testing nomenclature, that can be used to drive the stream by piping it. If you're testing a network-oriented stream, then you should consider using Node's `net` or `http` modules to create "mock" servers that generate suitable test data.

Listing 5.14 is a modified version of the CSV parser from technique 34; it has been turned into a module so we can easily test it. Listing 5.15 is the associated test that creates an instance of `CSVParser` and then pushes some values through it.

Listing 5.14   The `CSVParser` stream

```
var stream = require('stream');

module.exports = CSVParser;

CSVParser.prototype = Object.create(stream.Transform.prototype, {
  constructor: { value: CSVParser }
});

function CSVParser(options) {
  options = options || {};
  options.objectMode = true;
  stream.Transform.call(this, options);

  this.value = '';
  this.headers = [];
  this.values = [];
  this.line = 0;
}

CSVParser.prototype._transform = function(chunk, encoding, done) {
  var c;
  var i;
```

❶ **Export the class so it can be easily tested.**

❷ **We can test this method by calling .push() on an instance of the class.**

```
      chunk = chunk.toString();

      for (i = 0; i < chunk.length; i++) {
        c = chunk.charAt(i);

        if (c === ',') {
          this.addValue();
        } else if (c === 'n') {
          this.addValue();
          if (this.line > 0) {
            this.push(this.toObject());
          }
          this.values = [];
          this.line++;
        } else {
          this.value += c;
        }
      }

      done();
    };

    CSVParser.prototype.toObject = function() {
      var i;
      var obj = {};
      for (i = 0; i < this.headers.length; i++) {
        obj[this.headers[i]] = this.values[i];
      }
      return obj;
    };

    CSVParser.prototype.addValue = function() {
      if (this.line === 0) {
        this.headers.push(this.value);
      } else {
        this.values.push(this.value);
      }
      this.value = '';
    };
```

The CSVParser class is exported using module.exports so it can be loaded by the unit test ❶. The _transform method ❷ will run later when push is called on an instance of this class. Next up is a simple unit test for this class.

Listing 5.15   Testing the CSVParser stream

```
var assert = require('assert');
var fs = require('fs');
var CSVParser = require('./csvparser');

var parser = new CSVParser();
var actual = [];

fs.createReadStream(__dirname + '/sample.csv')
```

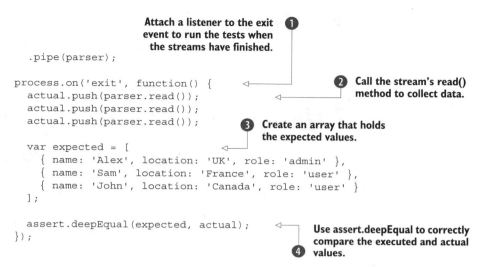

```
    .pipe(parser);

process.on('exit', function() {
  actual.push(parser.read());
  actual.push(parser.read());
  actual.push(parser.read());

  var expected = [
    { name: 'Alex', location: 'UK', role: 'admin' },
    { name: 'Sam', location: 'France', role: 'user' },
    { name: 'John', location: 'Canada', role: 'user' }
  ];

  assert.deepEqual(expected, actual);
});
```

Attach a listener to the exit event to run the tests when the streams have finished. ❶

❷ **Call the stream's read() method to collect data.**

❸ **Create an array that holds the expected values.**

Use assert.deepEqual to correctly compare the executed and actual values. ❹

A fixture file, sample.csv, has been used to pipe data to the CSVParser instance. Then the assert.deepEqual method has been used to make it easy to compare the expected array with the actual array.

A listener is attached to exit ❶ because we want to wait for the streams to finish processing the data before running the assertion. Then data is read ❷ from the parser and pushed to an array to examine with assertions ❹—the expected values are defined first ❸. This pattern is used in Node's own streams tests, and is a lightweight version of what test frameworks like Mocha and node-tap provide.

5.6   Summary

In this chapter you've seen how the built-in streamable APIs work, how to create new and novel streams using the base classes provided by Node, and how to use some more advanced techniques to structure programs with streams. As you saw in technique 36, building new streams starts with correctly inheriting from the base classes—and don't forget to test those streams! For more on testing, refer back to technique 38.

As you saw, there are some novel uses of streams, like substack's baudio module (https://github.com/substack/baudio) that speaks in streams of sound waves. There are also *two* streams APIs: the original Node 0.8 and below API, and the newer streams2 API. Forward compatibility is supported through the readable-stream module (https://github.com/isaacs/readable-stream), and backward compatibility is made possible by wrapping streams (technique 36).

A big part of working with streams is handling files. In the next chapter we'll look at Node's file system handling in detail.

File system: Synchronous and asynchronous approaches to files

This chapter covers

- Understanding the `fs` module and its components
- Working with configuration files and file descriptors
- Using file-locking techniques
- Recursive file operations
- Writing a file database
- Watching files and directories

As we've noted in previous chapters, Node's core modules typically stick to a low-level API. This allows for various (even competing) ideas and implementations of higher-level concepts like web frameworks, file parsers, and command-line tools to exist as third-party modules. The `fs` (or file system) module is no different.

The `fs` module allows the developer to interact with the file system by providing

- POSIX file I/O primitives
- File streaming
- Bulk file I/O
- File watching

The `fs` module is unique compared with other I/O modules (like `net` and `http`) in that it has both asynchronous and synchronous APIs. That means that it provides a mechanism to perform blocking I/O. The reason the file system also has a synchronous API is largely because of the internal workings of Node itself, namely, the module system and the synchronous behavior of `require`.

The goal of this chapter is to show you a number of techniques, of varying complexity, to use when working with the file system module. We'll look at

- Asynchronous and synchronous approaches for loading configuration files
- Working with the file descriptors
- Advisory file-locking techniques
- Recursive file operations
- Writing a file database
- Watching for file and directory changes

But before we get to the techniques, let's first take a high-level view of all you can do with the file system API in order to capture the functionality and provide some insight into what tool may be the best for the job.

6.1 An overview of the fs module

The fs module includes wrappers for common POSIX file operations, as well as bulk, stream, and watching operations. It also has synchronous APIs for many of the operations. Let's take a high-level walk through the different components.

6.1.1 POSIX file I/O wrappers

At a bird's-eye view, the majority of methods in the file system API are wrappers around standard POSIX file I/O calls (http://mng.bz/7EKM). These methods will have a similar name. For example, the `readdir` call (http://linux.die.net/man/3/readdir) has an `fs.readdir` counterpart in Node:

```
var fs = require('fs');
fs.readdir('/path/to/dir', function (err, files) {
  console.log(files); // [ 'fileA', 'fileB', 'fileC', 'dirA', 'etc' ]
});
```

Table 6.1 shows a list of the supported POSIX file methods in Node, including a description of their functionality.

Table 6.1   Supported POSIX file methods in Node

POSIX method	fs method	Description
rename(2)	fs.rename	Changes the name of a file
truncate(2)	fs.truncate	Truncates or extends a file to a specified length
ftruncate(2)	fs.ftruncate	Same as truncate but takes a file descriptor
chown(2)	fs.chown	Changes file owner and group
fchown(2)	fs.fchown	Same as chown but takes a file descriptor
lchown(2)	fs.lchown	Same as chown but doesn't follow symbolic links
chmod(2)	fs.chmod	Changes file permissions
fchmod(2)	fs.fchmod	Same as chmod but takes a file descriptor
lchmod(2)	fs.lchmod	Same as chmod but doesn't follow symbolic links
stat(2)	fs.stat	Gets file status
lstat(2)	fs.lstat	Same as stat but returns information about link if provided rather than what the link points to
fstat(2)	fs.fstat	Same as stat but takes a file descriptor
link(2)	fs.link	Makes a hard file link
symlink(2)	fs.symlink	Makes a symbolic link to a file
readlink(2)	fs.readlink	Reads value of a symbolic link
realpath(2)	fs.realpath	Returns the canonicalized absolute pathname
unlink(2)	fs.unlink	Removes directory entry
rmdir(2)	fs.rmdir	Removes directory
mkdir(2)	fs.mkdir	Makes directory
readdir(2)	fs.readdir	Reads contents of a directory
close(2)	fs.close	Deletes a file descriptor
open(2)	fs.open	Opens or creates a file for reading or writing
utimes(2)	fs.utimes	Sets file access and modification times
futimes(2)	fs.futimes	Same as utimes but takes a file descriptor
fsync(2)	fs.fsync	Synchronizes file data with disk
write(2)	fs.write	Writes data to a file
read(2)	fs.read	Reads data from a file

The POSIX methods provide a low-level API to many common file operations. For example, here we use a number of synchronous POSIX methods to write data to a file and then retrieve that data:

Create a buffer with data to write.

Write the buffer to the file.

Fill the read buffer with the data stored in the file.

Open or create file.txt for writing and reading (w+).

Create an empty read buffer the same size as what was written.

Close the file.

Assert the written and read data are indeed the same.

```
var fs = require('fs');
var assert = require('assert');

var fd = fs.openSync('./file.txt', 'w+');
var writeBuf = new Buffer('some data to write');
fs.writeSync(fd, writeBuf, 0, writeBuf.length, 0);

var readBuf = new Buffer(writeBuf.length);
fs.readSync(fd, readBuf, 0, writeBuf.length, 0);
assert.equal(writeBuf.toString(), readBuf.toString());

fs.closeSync(fd);
```

When it comes to reading and writing files, typically you won't need a level this low, but rather can use a streaming or bulk approach.

6.1.2 Streaming

The fs module provides a streaming API with fs.createReadStream and fs.create-WriteStream. fs.createReadStream is a Readable stream, whereas fs.createWrit-eStream is a Writeable. The streaming APIs can connect to other streams with pipe. For example, here's a simple application that copies a file using streams:

Create or overwrite copy.txt with new data.

Open original.txt to start reading.

While reading in original.txt, write it out to copy.txt.

```
var fs = require('fs');
var readable = fs.createReadStream('./original.txt');
var writeable = fs.createWriteStream('./copy.txt');
readable.pipe(writeable);
```

File streaming is beneficial when you want to deal with bits and pieces of data at a time or want to chain data sources together. For a more in-depth look at streams, check out chapter 5.

6.1.3 Bulk file I/O

The file system API also includes a few bulk methods for reading (fs.readFile), writing (fs.writeFile), or appending (fs.appendFile).

The bulk methods are good when you want to load a file into memory or write one out completely in one shot:

Entire file is buffered and provided in the buf variable

```
var fs = require('fs');
fs.readFile('/path/to/file', function (err, buf) {
  console.log(buf.toString());
});
```

6.1.4   *File watching*

The fs module also provides a couple of mechanisms for watching files (fs.watch and fs.watchFile). This is useful when you want to know if a file has changed in some way. fs.watch uses the underlying operating system's notifications, making it very efficient. But fs.watch can be finicky or simply not work on network drives. For those situations, the less-efficient fs.watchFile method, which uses stat polling, can be used.

We'll look more at file watching later on in this chapter.

6.1.5   *Synchronous alternatives*

Node's synchronous file system API sticks out like a sore thumb. With a big Sync tacked onto the end of each synchronous method, it's hard to miss its purpose. Synchronous methods are available for all the POSIX and bulk API calls. Some examples include readFileSync, statSync, and readdirSync. Sync tells you that this method will block your single-threaded Node process until it has finished. As a general rule, synchronous methods should be used when first setting up your application, and not within a callback:

```
var fs = require('fs');
var http = require('http');
fs.readFileSync('./output.dat');

http.createServer(function (req, res) {
  fs.readFileSync('./output.dat');
}).listen(3000);
```

A good spot for a synchronous method, top level, gets called on initialization of the application

A bad spot for a synchronous method, halts the server until the file is read on every request

Of course there are exceptions to the rule, but what's important is understanding the performance implications of using synchronous methods.

Testing server performance

How do we know synchronous execution within the request handling of a web server is slower? A great way to test this is using ApacheBench (http://en.wikipedia.org/wiki/ApacheBench). Our earlier example showed a ~2x drop in performance when serving a 10 MB file synchronously on every request rather than cached during application setup. Here's the command used in this test:

```
ab -n 1000 -c 100 "http://localhost:3000"
```

With our quick overview out of the way, we're now ready to get into some of the techniques you'll use when working with the file system.

TECHNIQUE 39   **Loading configuration files**

Keeping configuration in a separate file can be handy, especially for applications that run in multiple environments (like development, staging, and production). In this technique, you'll learn the ins and outs of how to load configuration files.

PROBLEM

Your application stores configuration in a separate file and it depends on having that configuration when it starts up.

SOLUTION

Use a synchronous file system method to pull in the configuration on initial setup of your application.

DISCUSSION

A common use of synchronous APIs is for loading configuration or other data used in the application on startup. Let's say we have a simple configuration file stored as JSON that looks like the following:

```
{
  "site title": "My Site",
  "site base url": "http://mysite.com",
  "google maps key": "92asdfase8230232138asdfasd",
  "site aliases": [ "http://www.mysite.com", "http://mysite.net" ]
}
```

Let's first look at how we could do this asynchronously so you can see the difference. For example, say doThisThing depends on information from our configuration file. Asynchronously we could write it this way:

```
var fs = require('fs');
fs.readFile('./config.json', function (err, buf) {
  if (err) throw er;                                  ◁────  Since the application can't run
  var config = JSON.parse(buf.toString());   ◁──           without this config file, we'll just
  doThisThing(config);                                       throw the error so the Node
})                                                           process will exit with a stack trace.
```

We get a Buffer back, convert to a string, and then parse the JSON.

This will work and may be desirable for some setups, but will also have the effect of having everything that depends on the configuration nested in one level. This can get ugly. By using a synchronous version, we can handle things more succinctly:

```
var fs = require('fs');
var config = JSON.parse(fs.readFileSync('./config.json').toString());   ◁────
doThisThing(config);
```

Synchronous methods will automatically throw if there's an error.

One of the characteristics of using Sync methods is that whenever an error occurs, it will be thrown:

```
var fs = require('fs');
try {                                    ◁────   Synchronous errors can
  fs.readFileSync('./some-file');                be caught using a
                                                 standard try/catch block.
```

```
}
catch (err) {                          Handle
  console.error(err);        ◄─┘       the error.
}
```

> **A note about require**
>
> We can `require` JSON files as modules in Node, so our code could even be short-ened further:
>
> ```
> var config = require('./config.json');
> doThisThing(config);
> ```
>
> But there's one caveat with this approach. Modules are cached globally in Node, so if we have another file that also requires `config.json` and we modify it, it's modified everywhere that module is used in our application. Therefore, using `readFileSync` is recommended when you want to tamper with the objects. If you choose to use `require` instead, treat the object as frozen (read-only); otherwise you can end up with hard-to-track bugs. You can explicitly freeze an object by using `Object.freeze`.

This is different from asynchronous methods, which use an error argument as the first parameter of the callback:

```
fs.readFile('./some-file', function (err, data) {   ◄─   Asynchronous errors are
  if (err) {                                              handled as the first parameter
    console.error(err);   ◄─┐                             in the callback function.
  }                         Handle
});                         the error.
```

In our example of loading a configuration file, we prefer to crash the application since it can't function without that file, but sometimes you may want to handle synchronous errors.

TECHNIQUE 40   Using file descriptors

Working with file descriptors can be confusing at first if you haven't dealt with them. This technique serves as an introduction and shows some examples of how you use them in Node.

PROBLEM
You want to access a file descriptor to do writes or reads.

SOLUTION
Use Node's `fs` file descriptor methods.

DISCUSSION
File descriptors (FDs) are integers (indexes) associated with open files within a process managed by the operating system. As a process opens files, the operating system keeps track of these open files by assigning each a unique integer that it can then use to look up more information about the file.

Although it has *file* in the name, it covers more than just regular files. File descriptors can point to directories, pipes, network sockets, and regular files, to name a few.

Node can get at these low-level bits. Most processes have a standard set of file descriptors, as shown in table 6.2.

Table 6.2   Common file descriptors

Stream	File descriptor	Description
stdin	0	Standard input
stdout	1	Standard output
stderr	2	Standard error

In Node, we typically are used to the `console.log` sugar when we want to write to stdout:

```
console.log('Logging to stdout')
```

If we use the stream objects available on the `process` global, we can accomplish the same thing more explicitly:

```
process.stdout.write('Logging to stdout')
```

But there's another, far less used way to write to stdout using the `fs` module. The `fs` module contains a number of methods that take an FD as its first argument. We can write to file descriptor 1 (or stdout) using `fs.writeSync`:

```
fs.writeSync(1, 'Logging to stdout')
```

> **SYNCHRONOUS LOGGING**   `console.log` and `process.stdout.write` are actually synchronous methods under the hood, provided the TTY is a file stream

A file descriptor is returned from the `open` and `openSync` calls as a number:

```
var fd = fs.openSync('myfile','a');
console.log(typeof fd == 'number');    ⟵——— Returns true
```

There are a variety of methods that deal with file descriptors specified in the file system documentation.

Typically more interesting uses of file descriptors happen when you're inheriting from a parent process or spawning a child process where descriptors are shared or passed. We'll discuss this more when we look at child processes in a later chapter.

TECHNIQUE 41   Working with file locking

File locking is helpful when cooperating processes need access to a common file where the integrity of the file is maintained and data isn't lost. In this technique, we'll explore how to write your own file locking module.

PROBLEM

You want to lock a file to prevent processes from tampering with it.

SOLUTION

Set up a file-locking mechanism using Node's built-ins.

DISCUSSION

In a single-threaded Node process, file locking is typically something you won't need to worry about. But you may have situations where other processes are accessing the same file, or a cluster of Node processes are accessing the same file.

In these cases, there's the possibility that races and data loss may occur (more about this at http://mng.bz/yTLV). Most operating systems provide mandatory locks (those enforced at a kernel level) and advisory locks (not enforced; these only work if processes involved subscribe to the same locking scheme). Advisory locks are generally preferred if possible, as mandatory locks are heavy handed and may be difficult to unlock (https://kernel.org/doc/Documentation/filesystems/mandatory-locking.txt).

> **FILE LOCKING WITH THIRD-PARTY MODULES** Node has no built-in support for locking a file directly (either mandatory or advisory). But advisory locking of files can be done using syscalls such as `flock` (http://linux.die.net/man/2/flock), which is available in a third-party module (http://github.com/baudehlo/node-fs-ext).

Instead of locking a file directly with something like `flock`, you can use a *lockfile*. Lockfiles are ordinary files or directories whose *existence* indicates some other resource is currently in use and not to be tampered with. The creation of a lockfile needs to be atomic (no races) to avoid collisions. Being advisory, all the participating processes would have to play by the same rules agreed on when the lockfile is present. This is illustrated in figure 6.1.

Let's say we had a file called config.json that could potentially be updated by any number of processes at any time. To avoid data loss or corruption, a `config.lock` file could be created by the process making the updates and removed when the process is finished. Each process would agree to check for the existence of the lockfile before making any updates.

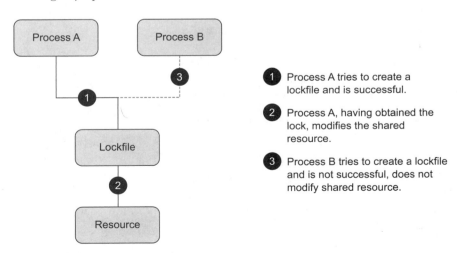

Figure 6.1   Advisory locking using a lockfile between cooperating processes

Node provides a few ways to perform this out of the box. We'll look at a couple of options:

- Creating a lockfile using the exclusive flag
- Creating a lockfile using `mkdir`

Let's look at using the exclusive flag first.

Creating lockfiles using the exclusive flag

The `fs` module provides an `x` flag for any methods that involve opening a file (like `fs.writeFile`, `fs.createWriteStream`, and `fs.open`). This flag tells the operating system the file should be opened in an exclusive mode (`O_EXCL`). When used, the file will fail to open if it already exists:

```
fs.open('config.lock', 'wx', function (err) {          ← Open in an exclusive
    if (err) return console.error(err);      ←              write mode.
                                               Any failure including
});           ←      Safely modify             if file exists.
                     config.json.
```

> **FLAG COMBINATIONS WHEN OPENING FILES** There are a variety of flag combinations you can pass when opening files; for a list of all of them consult the `fs.open` documentation: http://nodejs.org/api/fs.html#fs_fs_open_path _flags_mode_callback.

We want to fail if another process has already created a lockfile. We fail because we don't want to tamper with the resource behind the lockfile while another process is using it. Thus, having the exclusive flag mechanism turns out to be useful in our case. But instead of writing an empty file, it's a good idea to throw the PID (process ID) inside of this file so if something bad happens, we'll know what process had the lock last:

```
Any failure │   fs.writeFile('config.lock', process.pid, { flags: 'wx' },
including if │       function (err) {                    ←
file exists. └──→       if (err) return console.error(err);   Write PID to lockfile
                                                              if it doesn't exist.
                    });     ←      Safely modify
                                   config.json.
```

Creating lockfiles with mkdir

Exclusive mode may not work well if the lockfile exists on a network drive, since some systems don't honor the `O_EXCL` flag on network drives. To circumvent this, another strategy is creating a lockfile as a directory. `mkdir` is an atomic operation (no races), has excellent cross-platform support, and works well with network drives. `mkdir` will fail if a directory exists. In this case, the PID could be stored as a file inside of that directory:

```
fs.mkdir('config.lock', function (err) {        Unable
    if (err) return console.error(err);      ←  to create        Indicate which PID
    fs.writeFile('config.lock/'+process.pid, function (err) {  ←  has the lock for
        if (err) return console.error(err);                 directory.   debugging.
    });     ←      Safely modify
});                config.json.
```

Making a lockfile module

So far we've discussed a couple ways to create lockfiles. We also need a mechanism to remove them when we're done. In addition, to be good lockfile citizens, we should remove any lockfiles created whenever our process exits. A lot of this functionality can be wrapped up in a simple module:

```
var fs = require('fs');
var hasLock = false;
var lockDir = 'config.lock';

exports.lock = function (cb) {
  if (hasLock) return cb();

  fs.mkdir(lockDir, function (err) {
    if (err) return cb(err);
    fs.writeFile(lockDir+'/'+process.pid, function (err) {
      if (err) console.error(err);
      hasLock = true;
      return cb();
    });
  });
}

exports.unlock = function (cb) {
  if (!hasLock) return cb();

  fs.unlink(lockDir+'/'+process.pid, function (err) {
    if (err) return cb(err);
    fs.rmdir(lockDir, function (err) {
      if (err) return cb(err);
      hasLock = false;
      cb();
    });
  });
}

process.on('exit', function () {
  if (hasLock) {
    fs.unlinkSync(lockDir+'/'+process.pid);
    fs.rmdirSync(lockDir);
    console.log('removed lock');
  }
});
```

A lock is already obtained.

Write PID in directory for debugging.

Lock created.

No lock to unlock.

Define a method for obtaining a lock.

Unable to create a lock.

If unable to write PID, not the end of the world: log and keep going.

Define a method for releasing a lock.

If we still have a lock, remove it synchronously before exit.

Here's an example usage:

```
var locker = require('./locker');

locker.lock(function (err) {
  if (err) throw err;



  locker.unlock(function () {  });
})
```

Try to attain a lock.

Do modifications here.

Release lock when finished.

For a more full-featured implementation using exclusive mode, check out the lockfile third-party module (https://github.com/isaacs/lockfile).

TECHNIQUE 42 Recursive file operations

Ever need to remove a directory and all subdirectories (akin to `rm -rf`)? Create a directory and any intermediate directories given a path? Search a directory tree for a particular file? Recursive file operations are helpful and hard to get right, especially when done asynchronously. But understanding how to perform them is a good exercise in mastering evented programming with Node. In this technique, we'll dive into recursive file operations by creating a module for searching a directory tree.

PROBLEM

You want to search for a file within a directory tree.

SOLUTION

Use recursion and combine file system primitives.

DISCUSSION

When a task spans multiple directories, things become more interesting, especially in an asynchronous world. You can mimic the command-line functionality of `mkdir` with a single call to `fs.mkdir`, but for fancier things like `mkdir -p` (helpful for creating intermediate directories), you have to think recursively. This means the solution to our problem will depend on "solutions to smaller instances of the same problem" ("Recursion (computer science)": http://en.wikipedia.org/wiki/Recursion_(computer_science)).

In our example we'll write a finder module. Our finder module will recursively look for matching files at a given start path (akin to `find /start/path -name='file-in-question'`) and provide the paths to those files in an array.

Let's say we had the following directory tree:

```
root
├── dir-a
│   ├── dir-b
│   │   ├── dir-c
│   │   │   └── file-e.png
│   │   ├── file-c.js
│   │   └── file-d.txt
│   ├── file-a.js
│   └── file-b.txt
```

A search for the pattern `/file.*/` from the root would give us the following:

```
[ 'dir-a/dir-b/dir-c/file-e.png',
  'dir-a/dir-b/file-c.js',
  'dir-a/dir-b/file-d.txt',
  'dir-a/file-a.js',
  'dir-a/file-b.txt' ]
```

So how do we build this? To start, the `fs` module gives us some primitives we'll need:

- `fs.readdir`/`fs.readdirSync`—List all the files (including directories), given a path.
- `fs.stat`/`fs.statSync`—Give us information about a file at the specified path, including whether the path is a directory.

Our module will expose synchronous (`findSync`) and asynchronous (`find`) implementations. `findSync` will block execution like other `Sync` methods, will be slightly faster than its asynchronous counterpart, and may fail on excessively large directory trees (since JavaScript doesn't have proper tail calls yet: https://people.mozilla.org/~jorendorff/es6-draft.html#sec-tail-position-calls).

> **Why are synchronous functions slightly faster?**
> Synchronous functions aren't deferred until later, even though the asynchronous counterparts happen very quickly. Synchronous functions happen right away while you're already on the CPU and you're guaranteed to wait only exactly as long as necessary for the I/O to complete. But synchronous functions will block other things from happening during the wait period.

On the other hand, `find` will be slightly slower, but won't fail on large trees (since the stack is regularly cleared due to the calls being asynchronous). `find` won't block execution.

Let's take a look at the code for `findSync` first:

```
var fs = require('fs');
var join = require('path').join;

exports.findSync = function (nameRe, startPath) {
  var results = [];

  function finder (path) {
    var files = fs.readdirSync(path);

    for (var i = 0; i < files.length; i++) {
      var fpath = join(path, files[i]);
      var stats = fs.statSync(fpath);

      if (stats.isDirectory()) finder(fpath);
      if (stats.isFile() && nameRe.test(files[i])) results.push(fpath);
    }
  }

  finder(startPath);
  return results;
}
```

Annotations:
- **Takes a regular expression for the file we're searching for and a starting path.**
- **Collection to store matches.**
- **Read a list of files (including directories).**
- **Get path to current file.**
- **Get stats for current file.**
- **If it's a directory, call finder again with the new path.**
- **If it's a file and matches search, add it to results.**
- **Start initial file lookup.**
- **Return results.**

Since everything is synchronous, we can use `return` at the end to get all our results, as it'll never reach there until all the recursion has finished. The first error to occur would throw and could be caught, if desired, in a try/catch block. Let's look at a sample usage:

Success! List files found.

```
var finder = require('./finder');
try {
  var results = finder.findSync(/file.*/, '/path/to/root');
  console.log(results);
} catch (err) {
  console.error(err);
}
```

Oh no! Something bad happened; log error.

Let's switch now and take a look at how to tackle this problem asynchronously with the `find` implementation:

In order to know when we've completed our traversal, we'll need a counter.

Find now takes a third callback parameter.

In order to avoid multiple error calls if we're unsuccessful, we'll track when an error occurs.

Error handler to ensure callback is only called once if multiple errors.

Increment counter before each asynchronous operation.

Need a closure here so we don't lose our file reference later on.

Decrement counter after an asynchronous operation has completed.

If we're back to zero, we're done and had no errors, and can call back with the results.

```
var fs = require('fs');
var join = require('path').join;

exports.find = function (nameRe, startPath, cb) {
  var results = [];
  var asyncOps = 0;
  var errored = false;

  function error (err) {
    if (!errored) cb(err);
    errored = true;
  }

  function finder (path) {
    asyncOps++;
    fs.readdir(path, function (err, files) {
      if (err) return error(err);

      files.forEach(function (file) {
        var fpath = join(path,file);

        asyncOps++;
        fs.stat(fpath, function (err, stats) {
          if (err) return error(err);

          if (stats.isDirectory()) finder(fpath);
          if (stats.isFile() && nameRe.test(file)) results.push(fpath);

          asyncOps--;
          if (asyncOps == 0) cb(null, results);
        })
      })

      asyncOps--;
      if (asyncOps == 0) cb(null, results);
    });
  }

  finder(startPath);
}
```

We can't just return our results, like in the synchronous version; we need to call back with them when we know we're finished. To know that we're finished, we use a counter (asyncOps). We also have to be aware whenever we have callbacks to ensure we have a closure around any variables we expect to have around when any asynchronous call completes (this is why we switched from a standard for loop to a forEach call—more about this at http://mng.bz/rqEA).

Our counter (asyncOps) increments right before we do an asynchronous operation (like fs.readdir or fs.stat). The counter decrements in the callback for the asynchronous operation. Specifically it decrements *after* any other asynchronous calls have been made (otherwise we'll get back to 0 too soon). In a successful scenario, asyncOps will reach 0 when all the recursive asynchronous work has completed, and we can call back with the results (if (asyncOps == 0) cb(null, results)). In a failure scenario, asyncOps will never reach 0, and one of the error handlers would've been triggered and have already called back with the error.

Also, in our example, we can't be sure that fs.stat will be the last thing to be called, since we may have a directory with no files in our chain, so we check at both spots. We also have a simple error wrapper to ensure we never call back with more than one error. If your asynchronous operation returns one value like in our example or one error, it's important to ensure you'll never call the callback more than once, as it leads to hard-to-track bugs later down the road.

> **ALTERNATIVES TO COUNTERS** The counter isn't the only mechanism that can track the completion of a set of asynchronous operations. Depending on the requirements of the application, recursively passing the original callback could work. For an example look at the third-party mkdirp module (https://github.com/substack/node-mkdirp).

Now we have an asynchronous version (find) and can handle the result of that operation with the standard Node-style callback signature:

```
var finder = require('./finder');
finder.find(/file*/, '/path/to/root', function (err, results) {
  if (err) return console.error(err);
  console.log(results);
});
```

> **THIRD-PARTY SOLUTIONS TO PARALLEL OPERATIONS** Parallel operations can be hard to keep track of, and can easily become bug-prone, so you may want to use a third-party library like async (https://github.com/caolan/async) to help. Another alternative is using a promises library like Q (https://github.com/kriskowal/q).

TECHNIQUE 43   Writing a file database

Node's core fs module gives you the tools to build complexity like the recursive operations you saw in the last technique. It also enables you to do other complex tasks such as creating a file database. In this technique we'll write a file database in order to look at other pieces in the fs module, including streaming, working together.

PROBLEM

You want a simple and fast data storage structure with some consistency guarantees.

SOLUTION

Use an in-memory database with append-only journaling.

DISCUSSION

We'll write a simple key/value database module. The database will provide in-memory access to the current state for speed and use an append-only storage format on disk for persistence. Using append-only storage will provide us the following:

- *Efficient disk I/O performance*—We're always writing to the end of the file.
- *Durability*—The previous state of the file is never changed in any way.
- *A simple way to create backups*—We can just copy the file at any point to get the state of the database at that point.

Each line in the file is a record. The record is simply a JSON object with two properties, a key and a value. A key is a string representing a lookup for the value. The value can be anything JSON-serializable, which includes strings and numbers. Let's look at some sample records:

```
{"key":"a","value":23}
{"key":"b","value":["a","list","of","things"]}
{"key":"c","value":{"an":"object"}}
{"key":"d","value":"a string"}
```

If a record is updated, a new version of the record will be found later in the file with the same key:

```
{"key":"d","value":"an updated string"}
```

If a record has been removed, it'll also be found later in the file with a null value:

```
{"key":"b","value":null}
```

When the database is loaded, the journal will be streamed in from top to bottom, building the current state of the database in memory. Remember, data isn't deleted, so it's possible to store the following data:

```
{"key":"c","value":"my first value"}
...
{"key":"c","value":null}
...
{"key":"c","value":{"my":"object"}}
```

In this case, at some point we saved "my first value" as the key c. Later on we deleted the key. Then, most recently, we set the key to be {"my":"object"}. The most recent entry will be loaded in memory, as it represents the current state of the database.

We talked about how data will be persisted to the file system. Let's talk about the API we'll expose next:

Load is triggered when data is loaded into memory.

Load our Database module.

Provide the path to the database file we want to load and/or create.

```
var Database = require('./database');
var client = new Database('./test.db');

client.on('load', function () {
  var foo = client.get('foo');

  client.set('bar', 'my sweet value', function (err) {
    if (err) return console.error(err);
    console.log('write successful');
  });

  client.del('baz');
});
```

Get the value stored at key foo.

Set a value for key bar.

An error occurred when persisting to disk.

Delete key baz; optionally take afterWrite callback.

Let's dive into the code to start putting this together. We'll write a `Database` module to store our logic. It'll inherit from `EventEmitter` so we can emit events back to the consumer (like when the database has loaded all its data and we can start using it):

```
var fs = require('fs')
var EventEmitter = require('events').EventEmitter

var Database = function (path) {
  this.path = path

  this._records = Object.create(null)
  this._writeStream = fs.createWriteStream(this.path, {
    encoding: 'utf8',
    flags: 'a'
  })

  this._load()
}

Database.prototype = Object.create(EventEmitter.prototype)
```

Set the path to the database storage.

Create an internal mapping of all the records in memory.

Create a write stream in append-only mode to handle writes to disk.

Load the database.

Inherit from EventEmitter.

We want to stream the data stored and emit a "load" event when that's completed. Streaming will enable us to handle data as it's being read in. Streaming also is asynchronous, allowing the host application to do other things while the data is being loaded:

```
Database.prototype._load = function () {
  var stream = fs.createReadStream(this.path, { encoding: 'utf8' });
  var database = this;

  var data = '';
  stream.on('readable', function () {
    data += stream.read();
    var records = data.split('\n');
    data = records.pop();
```

Split records on newlines.

Read the available data.

Pop the last record as it may be incomplete.

Otherwise, for all non-null values, store the value for that key.

If the record has a null value, delete the record if stored.

```
      for (var i = 0; i < records.length; i++) {
        try {
          var record = JSON.parse(records[i]);
          if (record.value == null)
            delete database._records[record.key];
          else
            database._records[record.key] = record.value;
        } catch (e) {
          database.emit('error', 'found invalid record:', records[i]);
        }
      }
    });
    stream.on('end', function () {
      database.emit('load');
    });
  }
```

Emit an error if an invalid record was found.

Emit a load event when data is ready to be used.

As we read in data from the file, we find all the complete records that exist.

STRUCTURING OUR WRITES TO STRUCTURE OUR READS   What do we do with the data we just pop()ed the last time a readable event is triggered? The last record turns out to always be an empty string ('') because we end each line with a newline (\n) character.

Once we've loaded the data and emitted the load event, a client can start interacting with the data. Let's look at those methods next, starting with the simplest—the get method:

Return value for key or null if no key exists.

```
Database.prototype.get = function (key) {
  return this._records[key] || null;
}
```

Let's look at storing updates next:

Stringify JSON storage object, and then add newline.

If deleting, remove record from in-memory storage.

Otherwise, set key to value in memory.

```
Database.prototype.set = function (key, value, cb) {
  var toWrite = JSON.stringify({ key: key, value: value }); + '\n'

  if (value == null)
    delete this._records[key];
  else
    this._records[key] = value;

  this._writeStream.write(toWrite, cb);
}
```

Write out record to disk with callback if provided.

Now we add some sugar for deleting a key:

Call set for key with null as its value (storing a delete record).

```
Database.prototype.del = function (key, cb) {
  return this.set(key, null, cb);
}
```

There we have a simple database module. Last thing: we need to export the constructor:

```
module.exports = Database;
```

There are various improvements that could be made on this module, like flushing writes (http://mng.bz/2g19) or retrying on failure. For examples of more full-featured Node-based database modules, check out `node-dirty` (https://github.com/felixge/node-dirty) or `nstore` (https://github.com/creationix/nstore).

TECHNIQUE 44   Watching files and directories

Ever need to process a file when a client adds one to a directory (through FTP, for instance) or reload a web server after a file is modified? You can do both by watching for file changes.

Node has *two* implementations for file watching. We'll talk about both in this technique in order to understand when to use one or the other. But at the core, they enable the same thing: watching files (and directories).

PROBLEM

You want to watch a file or directory and perform an action when a change is made.

SOLUTION

Use `fs.watch` and `fs.watchFile`.

DISCUSSION

It's rare to see multiple implementations for the same purpose in Node core. Node's documentation recommends that you prefer `fs.watch` over `fs.watchFile` if possible, as it's considered more reliable. But `fs.watch` isn't consistent across operating systems, whereas `fs.watchFile` is. Why the madness?

The story about fs.watch

Node's event loop taps into the operating system in order to juggle asynchronous I/O in its single-threaded environment. This also provides a performance benefit, as the OS can let the process know immediately when some new piece of I/O is ready to be handled. Operating systems have different ways of notifying a process about events (that's why we have `libuv`). The culmination of that work for file watching is the `fs.watch` method.

`fs.watch` combines all these different types of event systems into one method with a common API to provide the following:

- A more reliable implementation in terms of file change events always getting fired
- A faster implementation, as notifications get passed to Node immediately when they occur

Let's look at the older method next.

The story about fs.watchFile

There's another, older implementation of file watching called `fs.watchFile`. It doesn't tap into the notification system but instead polls on an interval to see if changes have occurred.

`fs.watchFile` isn't as full-fledged in the changes it can detect, nor as fast. But the advantage of using `fs.watchFile` is that it's *consistent* across platforms and it works more reliably on network file systems (like SMB and NFS).

Which one is right for me?

The preferred is `fs.watch`, but since it's inconsistent across platforms, it's a good idea to test whether it does what you want (and better to have a test suite).

Let's write a program to help us play around file watching and see what each API provides. First, create a file called watcher.js with the following contents:

```
var fs = require('fs');
fs.watch('./watchdir', console.log);
fs.watchFile('./watchdir', console.log);
```

Now create a directory called `watchdir` in the same directory as your watcher.js file:

```
mkdir watchdir
```

Then, open a couple terminals. In the first terminal, run

```
node watcher
```

and in the second terminal, change to `watchdir`:

```
cd watchdir
```

With your two terminals open (preferably side by side), we'll make changes in `watchdir` and see Node pick them up. Let's create a new file:

```
touch file.js
```

We can see the Node output:

```
rename file.js                          ◁——————      A couple of fs.watch events come quickly
change file.js                                        (rename and change). These are the only two
{ dev: 64512,                                         events fs.watch will emit. The second argument,
    mode: 16893,          ◁——————                    file.js, is the file that received the event.
  nlink: 2,
  ... } { dev: 64512,                                The fs.watchFile event comes later and has a
  mode: 16893,                                       different response. It includes two fs.Stats
  nlink: 2,                                          objects for the current and previous state of
  ... }                                              the file. They're the same here because the file
                                                     was just created.
```

All right, so now we have a file created; let's update its modification time with the same command:

```
touch file.js
```

Now when we look at our Node output, we see that only `fs.watch` picked up this change:

```
change file.js
```

So if using `touch` to update a file when watching a directory is important to your application, `fs.watch` has support.

FS.WATCHFILE AND DIRECTORIES   Many updates to files while watching a directory won't be picked up by `fs.watchFile`. If you want to get this behavior with `fs.watchFile`, watch the individual file.

Let's try moving our file:

```
mv file.js moved.js
```

In our Node terminal, we see the following output indicating both APIs picked up the change:

fs.watch reports two rename events from the old to the new name.

```
rename file.js
rename moved.js
{ dev: 64512,
    mode: 16893,
  nlink: 2,
  ... } { dev: 64512,
  mode: 16893,
  nlink: 2,
  ... }
```

fs.watchFile indicates the file was modified.

The main point here is to test the APIs using the exact use case you want to utilize. Hopefully, this API will get more stable in the future. Read the documentation to get the latest development (http://nodejs.org/api/fs.html#fs_fs_watch_filename_options_listener). Here are some tips to help navigate:

- Run your test case, preferring `fs.watch`. Are events getting triggered as you expect them to be?
- If you intend to watch a single file, don't watch the directory it's in; you may end up with more events being triggered.
- If comparing file stats is important between changes, `fs.watchFile` provides that out of the box. Otherwise, you'll need to manage stats manually using `fs.watch`.
- Just because `fs.watch` works on your Mac doesn't mean it will work exactly the same way on your Linux server. Ensure development and production environments are tested for the desired functionality.

Go forth and watch wisely!

6.2   *Summary*

In this chapter we talked through a number of techniques using the `fs` module. We covered asynchronous and synchronous usage while looking at configuration file loading and recursive file handling. We also looked at file descriptors and file locking. Lastly we implemented a file database.

Hopefully this has expanded your understanding of some of the concepts possible with using the `fs` module. Here are a few takeaways:

- Synchronous methods can be a nicer, simpler way to do things over their asynchronous counterparts, but beware of the performance issues, especially if you're writing a server.

- Advisory file locking is a helpful mechanism for resources shared across multiple processes as long as all processes follow the same contract.

- Parallel asynchronous operations that require some sort of response after completion need to be tracked. Although it's helpful to understand how to use counters or recursive techniques, consider using a well-tested third-party module like `async`.

- Look at how you'll use a particular file to determine which course of action to follow. If it's a large file or can be dealt with in chunks, consider using a streaming approach. If it's a smaller file or something you can't use until you have the entire file loaded, consider a bulk method. If you want to change a particular part of a file, you probably want to stick with the POSIX file methods.

In the next chapter we'll look at the other main form of I/O in Node: networking.

Networking: Node's true "Hello, World"

This chapter covers

- Networking concepts and how they relate to Node
- TCP, UDP, and HTTP clients and servers
- DNS
- Network encryption

The Node.js platform itself is billed as a solution for writing fast and scalable network applications. To write network-oriented software, you need to understand how networking technologies and protocols interrelate. Over the course of the next section, we explain how networks have been designed around technology stacks with clear boundaries; and furthermore, how Node implements these protocols and what their APIs look like.

In this chapter you'll learn about how Node's networking modules work. This includes the `dgram`, `dns`, `http`, and `net` modules. If you're unsure about network terminology like *socket*, *packet*, and *protocol*, then don't worry: we also introduce key networking concepts to give you a solid foundation in network programming.

7.1 Networking in Node

This section is an introduction to networking. You'll learn about network layers, packets, sockets—all of the stuff that networks are made of. These ideas are critical to understanding Node's networking APIs.

7.1.1 Networking terminology

Networking jargon can quickly become overwhelming. To get everyone on the same page, we've included table 7.1, which summarizes the main concepts that will form the basis of this chapter.

To understand Node's networking APIs, it's crucial to learn about layers, packets, sockets, and all the other things that networks are made of. If you don't learn about the difference between TCP (Transmission Control Protocol) and UDP (User Datagram Protocol), then it would be difficult for you to know when to use these protocols. In this section we introduce the terms you need to know and then explore the concepts a bit more so you leave the section with a solid foundation.

Table 7.1 Networking concepts

Term	Description
Layer	A slice of related networking protocols that represents a logical group. The application layer, where we work, is the highest level; physical is the lowest.
HTTP	Hypertext Transfer Protocol—An application-layer client-server protocol built on TCP.
TCP	Transmission Control Protocol—Allows communication in both directions from the client to the server, and is built on to create application-layer protocols like HTTP.
UDP	User Datagram Protocol—A lightweight protocol, typically chosen where speed is desired over reliability.
Socket	The combination of an IP address and a port number is generally referred to as a socket.
Packet	TCP packets are also known as *segments*—the combination of a chunk of data along with a header.
Datagram	The UDP equivalent of a packet.
MTU	Maximum Transmission Unit—The largest size of a protocol data unit. Each layer can have an MTU: IPv4 is at least 68 bytes, and Ethernet v2 is 1,500 bytes.

If you're responsible for implementing high-level protocols that run on top of HTTP or even low-latency game code that uses UDP, then you should understand each of these concepts. We break each of these concepts down into more detail over the next few sections.

LAYERS

The stack of protocols and standards that make up the internet and internet technology in general can be modeled as layers. The lowest layers represent physical media—Ethernet, Bluetooth, fiber optics—the world of pins, voltages, and network adapters.

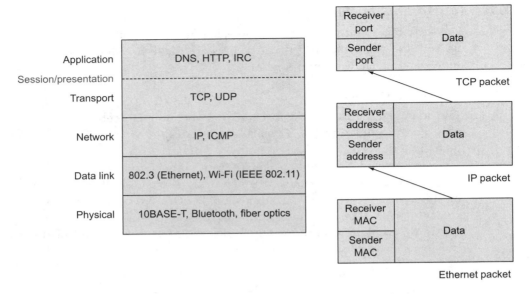

Figure 7.1 **Protocols are grouped into seven logical layers. Packets are wrapped by protocols at consecutive layers.**

As software developers, we work at a higher level than lower-level hardware. When talking to networks with Node, we're concerned with the *application* and *transport* layers of the Internet Protocol (IP) suite.

Layers are best represented visually. Figure 7.1 relates logical network layers to packets. The lower-level physical and data-link layer protocols wrap higher-level protocols.

Packets are wrapped by protocols at consecutive layers. A TCP packet, which could represent part of a series of packets from an HTTP request, is contained in the data section of an IP packet, which in turn is wrapped by an Ethernet packet. Going back to figure 7.1, TCP packets from HTTP requests cut through the transport and application layers: TCP is the transport layer, used to create the higher-level HTTP protocol. The other layers are also involved, but we don't always know which specific protocols are used at each layer: HTTP is always transmitted over TCP/IP, but beyond that, Wi-Fi or Ethernet can be used—your programs won't know the difference.

Figure 7.2 shows how network layers are wrapped by each protocol. Notice that data is never seen to move more than one step between layers—we don't talk about transport layer protocols interacting with the network layer.

When writing Node programs, you should appreciate that HTTP is implemented using TCP because Node's `http` module is built on the underlying TCP implementation found in the `net` module. But you don't need to understand how Ethernet, 10BASE-T, or Bluetooth works.

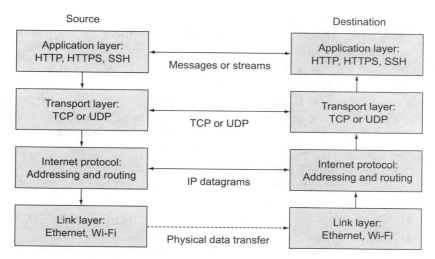

Figure 7.2 Network layer wrapping

TCP/IP

You've probably heard of TCP/IP—this is what we call the *Internet Protocol suite* because the Transmission Control Protocol (TCP) and the Internet Protocol (IP) are the most important and earliest protocols defined by this standard.

In Internet Protocol, a host is identified by an IP address. In IPv4, addresses are 32-bit, which limits the available address space. IP has been at the center of controversy over the last decade because addresses are running out. To fix this, a new version of the protocol known as IPv6 was developed.

You can make TCP connections with Node by using the net module. This allows you to implement application layer protocols that aren't supported by the core modules: IRC, POP, and even FTP could be implemented with Node's core modules. If you find yourself needing to talk to nonstandard TCP protocols, perhaps something used internally in your company, then net.Socket and net.createConnection will make light work of it.

Node supports both IPv4 and IPv6 in several ways: the dns module can query IPv4 and IPv6 records, and the net module can transmit and receive data to hosts on IPv4 and IPv6 networks.

The interesting thing about IP is it doesn't guarantee data integrity or delivery. For reliable communication, we need a transport layer protocol like TCP. There are also times when delivery isn't *always* required, although of course it's preferred—in these situations a lighter protocol is needed, and that's where UDP comes in. The next section examines TCP and UDP in more detail.

UDP AND HOW IT COMPARES TO TCP

Datagrams are the basic unit of communication in UDP. These messages are self-contained, holding a source, destination, and some user data. UDP doesn't guarantee delivery or message order, or offer protection against duplicated data. Most protocols you'll use with Node programs will be built on TCP, but there are times when UDP is useful. If delivery isn't critical, but performance is desired, then UDP may be a better choice. One example is a streaming video service, where occasional glitches are an acceptable trade-off to gain more throughput.

TCP and UDP both use the same network layer—IP. Both provide services to application layer protocols. But they're very different. TCP is a connect-oriented and reliable byte stream service, whereas UDP is based around *datagrams*, and doesn't guarantee the delivery of data.

Contrast this to TCP, which is a full-duplex[1] connection-oriented protocol. In TCP, there are only ever two endpoints for a given connection. The basic unit of information passed between endpoints is known as a *segment*—the combination of a chunk of data along with a header. When you hear the term *packet*, a TCP segment is generally being referred to.

Although UDP packets include checksums that help detect corruption, which can occur as a datagram travels across the internet, there's no automatic retransmission of corrupt packets—it's up to your application to handle this if required. Packets with invalid data will be effectively silently discarded.

Every packet, whether it's TCP or UDP, has an origin and destination address. But the source and destination *programs* are also important. When your Node program connects to a DNS server or accepts incoming HTTP connections, there has to be a way to map between the packets traveling along the network and the programs that generated them. To fully describe a connection, you need an extra piece of information. This is known as a *port number*—the combination of a port number and an address is known as a socket. Read on to learn more about ports and how they relate to sockets.

SOCKETS

The basic unit of a network, from a programmer's perspective, is the socket. A socket is the combination of an IP address and a port number—and there are both TCP and UDP sockets. As you saw in the previous section, a TCP connection is full-duplex— opening a connection to a given host allows communication to flow *to* and *from* that host. Although the term *socket* is correct, historically "socket" meant the Berkeley Sockets API.

> **THE BERKELEY SOCKETS API** Berkeley Sockets, released in 1983, was an API for working with internet sockets. This is the original API for the TCP/IP suite. Although the origins lie in Unix, Microsoft Windows includes a networking stack that closely follows Berkeley Sockets.

There are well-known port numbers for standard TCP/IP services. They include DNS, HTTP, SSH, and more. These port numbers are usually odd numbers due to historical reasons. TCP and UDP ports are distinct so they can overlap. If an application layer

---

[1] Full-duplex: messages can be sent and received in the same connection.

protocol requires both TCP *and* UDP connections, then the convention is to use the same port number for both connections. An example of a protocol that uses both UDP and TCP is DNS.

In Node, you can create TCP sockets with the net module, and UDP is supported by the dgram module. Other networking protocols are also supported—DNS is a good example.

The following sections look at the application layer protocols included in Node's core modules.

7.1.2 *Node's networking modules*

Node has a suite of networking modules that allows you to build web and other server applications. Over the next few sections we'll cover DNS, TCP, HTTP, and encryption.

DNS

The Domain Name System (DNS) is the naming system for addressing resources connected to the internet (or even a private network). Node has a core module called dns for looking up and resolving addresses. Like other core modules, dns has asynchronous APIs. In this case, the implementation is also asynchronous, apart from certain methods that are backed by a thread pool. This means DNS queries in Node are fast, but also have a friendly API that is easy to learn.

You don't often have to use this module, but we've included techniques because it's a powerful API that can come in handy for network programming. Most application layer protocols, HTTP included, accept hostnames rather than IP addresses.

Node also provides modules for networking protocols that we're more familiar with—for example, HTTP.

HTTP

HTTP is important to most Node developers. Whether you're building web applications or calling web services, you're probably interacting with HTTP in some way. Node's http core module is built on the net, stream, buffer, and events modules. It's low-level, but can be used to create simple HTTP servers and clients without too much effort.

Due to the importance of the web to Node development, we've included several techniques that explore Node's http module. Also, when we're working with HTTP we often need to use encryption—Node also supports encryption through the crypto and tls modules.

ENCRYPTION

You should know the term *SSL*—Secure Sockets Layer—because it's how secure web pages are served to web browsers. Not just HTTP traffic gets encrypted, though—other services, like email, encrypt messages as well. Encrypted TCP connections use TLS: Transport Layer Security. Node's tls module is implemented using OpenSSL.

This type of encryption is called *public key cryptography*. Both clients and servers must have private keys. The server can then make its public key available so clients can encrypt messages. To decrypt these messages, access to the server's *private* key is required.

Node supports TLS by allowing TCP servers to be created that support several ciphers. The TCP server itself inherits from net.Server—once you've got your head around TCP clients and servers in Node, encrypted connections are just an extension of these principles.

A solid understanding of TLS is important if you want to deploy web applications with Node. People are increasingly concerned with security and privacy, and unfortunately SSL/TLS is designed in such a way that programmer error can cause security weaknesses.

There's one final aspect of networking in Node that we'd like to introduce before we move on to the techniques for this chapter: how Node is able to give you asynchronous APIs to networking technologies that are sometimes blocking at the system level.

7.1.3   *Non-blocking networking and thread pools*

This section delves into Node's lower-level implementation to explore how networking works under the hood. If you're confused about what exactly "asynchronous" means in the context of networking, then read on for some background information on what makes Node's networking APIs tick.

Remember that in Node, APIs are said to be *asynchronous* when they accept a callback and return immediately. At the operating system level, I/O operations can also be asynchronous, or they can be synchronous and wrapped with threads to appear asynchronous.

Node employs several techniques to provide asynchronous network APIs. The main ones are non-blocking system calls and thread pools to wrap around blocking system calls.

Behind the scenes, most of Node's networking code is written in C and C++—the JavaScript code in Node's source gives you an asynchronous binding to features provided by libuv and c-ares.

Figure 7.3 shows Apple's Instruments tool recording the activity of a Node program that makes 50 HTTP requests. HTTP requests are non-blocking—each takes place using callbacks that are run on the main thread. The BSD sockets library, which is used by libuv, can make non-blocking TCP and UDP connections.

For HTTP and other TCP connections, Node is able to access the network using a system-level non-blocking API.

When writing networking or file system code, the Node code *looks* asynchronous: you pass a function to a method that will execute the function when the I/O operation has reached the desired state. But for file operations, the underlying implementation is not asynchronous: thread pools are used instead.

When dealing with I/O operations, understanding the difference between non-blocking I/O, thread pools, and asynchronous APIs is important if you want to truly understand how Node works.

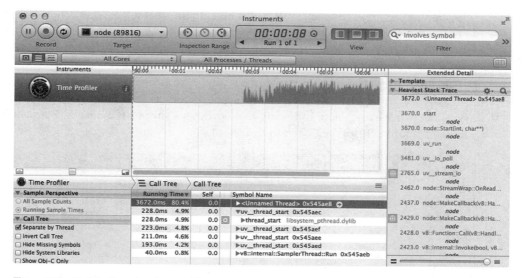

Figure 7.3 Node's threads when making HTTP requests

For those interested in reading more about libuv and networking, the freely available book, *An Introduction to libuv* (http://nikhilm.github.io/uvbook/networking.html#tcp) has a section on networking that covers TCP, DNS, and UDP.

Now on to the first set of networking techniques: TCP clients and servers.

7.2 TCP clients and servers

Node has a simple API for creating TCP connections and servers. Most of the lowest-level classes and methods can be found in the net module. In the next technique, you'll learn how to create a TCP server and track the clients that connect to it. The cool thing about this is that higher-level protocols like HTTP are built on top of the TCP API, so once you've got the hang of TCP clients and servers, you can really start to exploit some of the more subtle features of the HTTP API as well.

TECHNIQUE 45 **Creating a TCP server and tracking clients**

The net module forms the foundation of many of Node's networking features. This technique demonstrates how to create a TCP server.

PROBLEM

You want to start your own TCP server, bind to a port, and send data over the network.

SOLUTION

Use net.createServer to create a server, and then call server.listen to bind it to a port. To connect to the server, either use the command-line tool telnet or create an in-process client connection with its client counterpart, net.connect.

DISCUSSION

The net.createServer method returns an object that can be used to listen on a given TCP port for incoming connections. When a client makes a new connection, the callback passed to `net.createServer` will run. This callback receives a connection object which extends `EventEmitter`.

The server object itself is an instance of `net.Server`, which is just a wrapper around the `net.Socket` class. It's interesting to note that `net.Socket` is implemented using a duplex stream—for more on streams, see chapter 5.

Before going into more theory, let's look at an example that you can run and connect to with `telnet`. The following listing shows a simple TCP server that accepts connections and echoes data back to the client.

Listing 7.1   A simple TCP server

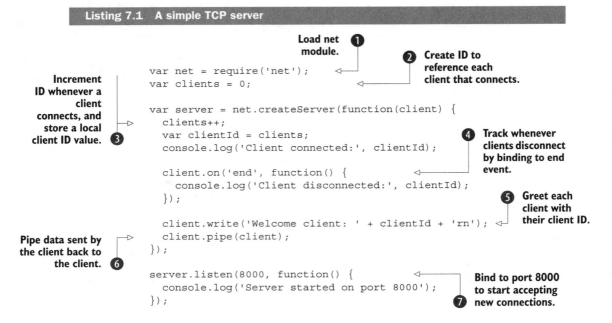

To try out this example, run `node server.js` to start a server, and then run `telnet localhost 8000` to connect to it with `telnet`. You can connect several times to see the ID incremented. If you disconnect, a message should be printed that contains the correct client ID.

Most programs that use TCP clients and servers load the `net` module ❶. Once it has been loaded, TCP servers can be created using `net.createServer`, which is actually just a shortcut for `new net.Server` with a `listener` event listener. After a server has been instantiated, it can be set to listen for connections on a given port using `server.listen` ❼.

To echo back data sent by the client, `pipe` is used ❻. Sockets are streams, so you can use the standard stream API methods with them as you saw in chapter 5.

In this example, we track each client that has connected using a numerical ID by incrementing a "global" value ❷ that tracks the number of clients ❸. The total number of connected clients is stored in the callback's scope by creating a local variable in the connection callback called `clientId`.

This value is displayed whenever a client connects ❺ or disconnects ❹. The client argument passed to the server's callback is actually a socket—you can write to it with `client.write` and data will be sent over the network.

The important thing to note is any event listener added to the socket in the server's callback will share the same scope—it will create closures around any variables inside this callback. That means the client ID is unique to each connection, and you can also store other values that clients might need. This forms a common pattern employed by client-server applications in Node.

The next technique builds on this example by adding client connections in the same process.

TECHNIQUE 46   Testing TCP servers with clients

Node makes creating TCP servers *and* clients in the same process a breeze—it's an approach particularly useful for testing your network programs. In this technique you'll learn how to make TCP clients, and use them to test a server.

PROBLEM
You want to test a TCP server.

SOLUTION
Use `net.connect` to connect to the server's port.

DISCUSSION
Due to how TCP and UDP ports work, it's entirely possible to create multiple servers and clients in the same process. For example, a Node HTTP server could also run a simple TCP server on another port that allows `telnet` connections for remote administration.

In technique 45, we demonstrated a TCP server that can track client connections by issuing each client a unique ID. Let's write a test to ensure this worked correctly.

Listing 7.2 shows how to create client connections to an in-process server, and then run assertions on the data sent over the network by the server. Of course, technically this isn't running over a real network because it all happens in the same process, but it could easily be adapted to work that way; just copy the program to a server and specify its IP address or hostname in the client.

Listing 7.2   Creating TCP clients to test servers

```
var assert = require('assert');
var net = require('net');
var clients = 0;
var expectedAssertions = 2;

var server = net.createServer(function(client) {
  clients++;
  var clientId = clients;
  console.log('Client connected:', clientId);
```

```
      client.on('end', function() {
        console.log('Client disconnected:', clientId);
      });

      client.write('Welcome client: ' + clientId + '\r\n');
      client.pipe(client);
    });

    server.listen(8000, function() {
      console.log('Server started on port 8000');

      runTest(1, function() {
        runTest(2, function() {
          console.log('Tests finished');
          assert.equal(0, expectedAssertions);
          server.close();
        });
      });
    });

    function runTest(expectedId, done) {
      var client = net.connect(8000);

      client.on('data', function(data) {
        var expected = 'Welcome client: ' + expectedId + '\r\n';
        assert.equal(data.toString(), expected);
        expectedAssertions--;
        client.end();
      });

      client.on('end', done);
    }
```

1 runTest function accepts a callback so additional tests can be scheduled.

2 After tests have finished, a counter is checked to see if tests were executed.

3 Once tests and assertions have run, server can be closed.

4 runTest function connects to server, checks that it displays expected client ID, and then disconnects.

5 net.connect is used to connect to server; it returns an EventEmitter object that can be used to listen for events.

6 Client's data event is used to grab the message the server displays after the client connects.

7 Disconnect client when data has been sent.

8 When client has finished sending data, run callback.

This is a long example, but it centers around a relatively simple method: net.connect. This method accepts some optional arguments to describe the remote host. Here we've just specified a port number, but the second argument can be a hostname or IP address—localhost is the default **5**. It also accepts a callback, which can be used to write data to the other end once the client has connected. Remember that TCP servers are full-duplex, so both ends can receive and send data.

The runTest function in this example will run once the server has started listening **1**. It accepts an expected client ID, and a callback called done **4**. The callback will be triggered once the client has connected, received some data by subscribing to the data event **6**, and then disconnected.

Whenever clients are disconnected, the end event will be emitted. We bind the done callback to this event **8**. When the test has finished in the data callback, we call client.end to disconnect the socket manually, but end events will be triggered when servers close connections, as well.

The data event is where the main test is performed ❼. The expected message is passed to assert.equal with the data passed to the event listener. The data is a buffer, so toString is called for the assertion to work. Once the test has finished, and the end event has been triggered ❼, the callback passed to runTest will be executed.

Error handling

If you need to collect errors generated by TCP connections, just subscribe to the error event on the EventEmitter objects returned by net.connect. If you don't, an exception will be raised; this is standard behavior in Node.

Unfortunately, this isn't easy to work with when dealing with sets of distinct network connections. In such cases, a better technique is to use the domain module. Creating a new domain with domain.create() will cause error events to be sent to the domain; you can then handle them in a centralized error handler by subscribing to error events on the domain.

For more about domains, refer to technique 21.

We've used two calls to runTest here by calling one inside the callback. Once both have run, the number of expected assertions is checked ❷, and the server is shut down ❸.

This example highlights two important things: clients and servers can be run together in-process, and Node TCP clients and servers are easy to unit test. If the server in this example were a remote service that we had no control over, then we could create a "mock" server for the express purpose of testing our client code. This forms the basis of how most developers write tests for web applications written with Node.

In the next technique we'll dig deeper into TCP networking by looking at Nagle's algorithm and how it can affect the performance characteristics of network traffic.

TECHNIQUE 47 Improve low-latency applications

Although Node's net module is relatively high-level, it does provide access to some low-level functionality. One example of this is control over the TCP_NODELAY flag, which determines whether Nagle's algorithm is used. This technique explains what Nagle's algorithm is, when you should use it, and how to turn it off for specific sockets.

PROBLEM

You want to improve connection latency in a real-time application.

SOLUTION

Use socket.setNoDelay() to enable TCP_NODELAY.

DISCUSSION

Sometimes it's more efficient to move batches of things together, rather than separately. Every day millions of products are shipped around the globe, but they're not carried one at a time—instead they're grouped together in shipping containers, based

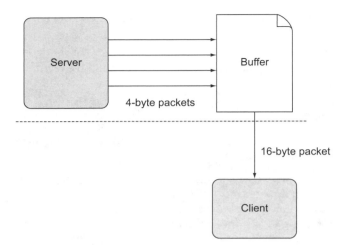

4-byte packets

16-byte packet

Figure 7.4 When Nagle's algorithm is used, smaller packets are collected into a larger payload.

on their final destination. TCP works exactly the same way, and this feature is made possible by Nagle's algorithm.

Nagle's algorithm says that when a connection has data that hasn't yet been acknowledged, small segments should be retained. These small segments will be batched into larger segments that can be transmitted when sufficient data has been acknowledged by the recipient.

In networks where many small packets are transmitted, it can be desirable to reduce congestion by combining small outgoing messages, and sending them together. But sometimes latency is desired over all else, so transmitting small packets is important.

This is particularly true for interactive applications, like ssh, or the X Window System. In these applications, small messages should be delivered without delay to create a sense of real-time feedback. Figure 7.4 illustrates the concept.

Certain classes of Node programs benefit from turning off Nagle's algorithm. For example, you may have created a REPL that transmits a single character at a time as the user types messages, or a game that transmits location data of players. The next listing shows a program that disables Nagle's algorithm.

Listing 7.3 Turning off Nagle's algorithm

```
var net = require('net');
var server = net.createServer(function(c) {
  c.setNoDelay(true);
  c.write('377375042377373001', 'binary');
  console.log('server connected');
  c.on('end', function() {
    console.log('server disconnected');
    server.unref();
  });
  c.on('data', function(data) {
    process.stdout.write(data.toString());
    c.write(data.toString());
```

① Turn off Nagle's algorithm.

② Force client to use character mode.

③ Call unref() so that when last client disconnects, program exits.

④ Print out characters from client to the server's terminal.

```
    });
  });
  server.listen(8000, function() {
    console.log('server bound');
  });
```

To use this example, run the program in a terminal with node `nagle.js`, and then connect to it with `telnet 8000`. The server turns off Nagle's algorithm ❶, and then forces the client to use character mode ❷. Character mode is part of the Telnet Protocol (RFC 854), and will cause the Telnet client to send a packet whenever a key is pressed.

Next, `unref` is used ❸ to cause the program to exit when there are no more client connections. Finally, the `data` event is used to capture characters sent by the client and print them to the server's terminal ❹.

This technique could form the basis for creating low-latency applications where data integrity is important, which therefore excludes UDP. If you really want to get more control over the transmission of data, then read on for some techniques that use UDP.

7.3 UDP clients and servers

Compared to TCP, UDP is a much simpler protocol. That can mean more work for you: rather than being able to rely on data being sent and received, you have to cater to UDP's more volatile nature. UDP is suitable for query-response protocols, which is why it's used for the Domain Name System (DNS). It's also stateless—if you want to transfer data and you value lower latency over data integrity, then UDP is a good choice. That might sound unusual, but there are applications that fit these characteristics: media streaming protocols and online games generally use UDP.

If you wanted to build a video streaming service, you could transfer video over TCP, but each packet would have a lot of overhead for ensuring delivery. With UDP, it would be possible for data to be lost with no simple means of discovery, but with video you don't care about occasional glitches—you just want data as fast as possible. In fact, some video and image formats can survive a small amount of data loss: the JPEG format is resilient to corrupt bytes to a certain extent.

The next technique combines Node's file streams with UDP to create a simple server that can be used to transfer files. Although this can potentially result in data loss, it can be useful when you care about speed over all else.

TECHNIQUE 48 Transferring a file with UDP

This technique is really about sending data from a stream to a UDP server rather than creating a generalized file transfer mechanism. You can use it to learn the basics of Node's datagram API.

PROBLEM

You want to transfer data from a client to a server using datagrams.

SOLUTION

Use the `dgram` module to create datagram sockets, and then send data with `socket.send`.

DISCUSSION

Sending datagrams is similar to using TCP sockets, but the API is slightly different, and datagrams have their own rules that reflect the actual structure of UDP packets. To set up a server, use the following snippet:

```
var dgram = require('dgram');                          ❶ Create UDP
var socket = dgram.createSocket('udp4');                 socket
socket.bind(4000);
                                                       ❷ Bind it to
                                                         a port
```

This example creates a socket that will act as the server ❶, and then binds it to a port ❷. The port can be anything you want, but in both TCP and UDP the first 1,023 ports are privileged.

The client API is different from TCP sockets because UDP is a *stateless* protocol. You must write data a packet at a time, and packets (datagrams) must be relatively small— under 65,507 bytes. The maximum size of a datagram depends on the Maximum Transmission Unit (MTU) of the network. 64 KB is the upper limit, but isn't usually used because large datagrams may be silently dropped by the network.

Creating a client socket is the same as servers—use `dgram.createSocket`. Sending a datagram requires a buffer for the payload, an offset to indicate where in the buffer the message starts, the message length, the server port, the remote IP, and an optional callback that will be triggered when the message has been sent:

```
var message = 'Sample message';
socket.send(new Buffer(message), 0, message.length, port, remoteIP);
```

Listing 7.4 combines a client and a server into a single program. To run it, you must issue two commands: `node udp-client-server.js server` to run the server, and then `node udp-client-server.js client remoteIP` to start a client. The `remoteIP` option can be omitted if you run both locally; we designed this example to be a single file so you can easily copy it to another computer to test sending things over the internet or a local network.

Listing 7.4   A UDP client and server

```
                var dgram = require('dgram');
                var fs = require('fs');
                var port = 41230;
                var defaultSize = 16;                              ❶ Create a
Make a new ❷                                                         readable
datagram         function Client(remoteIP) {                        stream for
socket to          var inStream = fs.createReadStream(__filename);  current file
use as client      var socket = dgram.createSocket('udp4');

                   inStream.on('readable', function() {          ❸ When readable stream
       Use ❹         sendData();                                   is ready, start sending
stream.read(size) to }) ;                                          its data to the server
read chunks of data
                   function sendData() {
                     var message = inStream.read(defaultSize);
```

```
        if (!message) {
          return socket.unref();
        }
```

⑤ When client has finished, call unref to safely close it when no longer needed

Otherwise, send data to server ⑥

```
        socket.send(message, 0, message.length, port, remoteIP,
          function(err, bytes) {
            sendData();
          }
        );
      }
    }
```

When a ⑧ message event is emitted, print data to terminal

```
function Server() {
  var socket = dgram.createSocket('udp4');

  socket.on('message', function(msg, rinfo) {
    process.stdout.write(msg.toString());
  });

  socket.on('listening', function() {
    console.log('Server ready:', socket.address());
  });

  socket.bind(port);
}
```

⑦ Create a socket to use for server

⑨ Indicate server is ready for clients by printing message

Check for ⑩ command-line options to determine if client or server should be run

```
if (process.argv[2] === 'client') {
  new Client(process.argv[3]);
} else {
  new Server();
}
```

⑪ Accept optional setting for connecting to remote IP addresses

When you run this example, it starts by checking the command-line options to see if the client or server is required ⑩. It also accepts an optional argument for clients so you can connect to remote servers ⑪.

If the client was specified, then a new client will be created by making a new datagram socket ②. This involves using a read stream from the `fs` module so we have some data to send to the server ①—we've used `__filename` to make it read the current file, but you could make it send any file.

Before sending any data, we need to make sure the file has been opened and is ready for reading, so the `readable` event is subscribed to ③. The callback for this event executes the `sendData` function. This will be called repeatedly for each chunk of the file—files are read in small chunks at a time using `inStream.read` ④, because UDP packets can be silently dropped if they're too large. The `socket.send` method is used to push the data to the server ⑥. The message object returned when reading the file is an instance of `Buffer`, and it can be passed straight to `socket.send`.

When all of the data has been read, the last chunk is set to `null`. The `socket.unref` ⑤ method is called to cause the program to exit when the socket is no longer required—in this case, once it has sent the last message.

Datagram packet layout and datagram size

UDP packets are comparatively simple. They're composed of a source port, the destination port, datagram length, checksum, and the payload data. The length is the total size of the packet—the header size added to the payload's size. When deciding on your application's buffer size for UDP packets, you should remember that the length passed to `socket.send` is only for the buffer (payload), and the overall packet size must be under the MTU on the network. The structure of a datagram looks like the following.

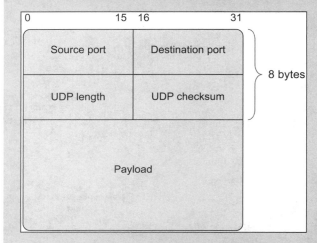

The UDP header is 8 bytes, followed by an optional payload of up to 65,507 bytes for IPv4 and 65,527 bytes for IPv6.

The server is simpler than the client. It sets up a socket in the same way ❼, and then subscribes to two events. The first event is `message`, which is emitted when a datagram is received ❽. The data is written to the terminal by using `process.stdout.write`. This looks better than using `console.log` because it won't automatically add newlines.

The `listening` event is emitted when the server is ready to accept connections ❾. A message is displayed to indicate this so you know it's safe to try connecting a client.

Even though this is a simple example, it's immediately obvious how UDP is different from TCP—you need to pay attention to the size of the messages you send, and realize that it's possible for messages to get lost. Although datagrams have a checksum, lost or damaged packets aren't reported to the application layer, which means data loss is possible. It's generally best to use UDP for sending data where assured integrity is second place to low latency and throughput.

In the next technique you'll see how to build on this example by sending messages back to the client, essentially setting up bidirectional communication channels with UDP.

TECHNIQUE 49 **UDP client server applications**

UDP is often used for query-response protocols, like DNS and DHCP. This technique demonstrates how to send messages back to the client.

PROBLEM

You've created a UDP server that responds to requests, but you want to send messages back to the client.

SOLUTION

Once you've created a server and it has received a message, create a datagram connection *back* to the client based on the `rinfo` argument that's passed to `message` events. Optionally create a unique reference by combining the client port and IP address to send subsequent messages.

DISCUSSION

Chat servers are the classic network programming example for new Node programmers, but this one has a twist—it uses UDP instead of TCP or HTTP.

TCP connections are different from UDP, and this is apparent in the design of Node's networking API. TCP connections are represented as a stream of bidirectional events, so sending a message back to the sender is straightforward—once a client has connected you can write messages to it at any time using `client.write`. UDP, on the other hand, is *connectionless*—messages are received without an active connection to the client.

There are some protocol-level similarities that enable you to respond to messages from clients, however. Both TCP and UDP connections use source and destination ports. Given a suitable network setup, it's possible to open a connection back to the client based on this information. In Node the `rinfo` object that's included with every `message` event contains the relevant details. Figure 7.5 shows how messages flow between two clients using this scheme.

Listing 7.5 presents a client-server program that allows clients to connect to a central server over UDP and message each other. The server keeps details of each client in

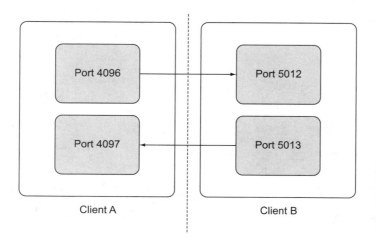

Figure 7.5 Even though UDP isn't full-duplex, it's possible to create connections in two directions given a port number at both sides.

an array, so it can refer to each one uniquely. By storing the client's address and port, you can even run multiple clients on the same machine—it's safe to run this program several times on the same computer.

Listing 7.5   Sending messages back to clients

```
var assert = require('assert');
var dgram = require('dgram');
var fs = require('fs');
var defaultSize = 16;
var port = 41234;

function Client(remoteIP) {                                    ❶ Use readline module
  var socket = dgram.createSocket('udp4');                        to handle user input.
  var readline = require('readline');
  var rl = readline.createInterface(process.stdin, process.stdout);

  socket.send(new Buffer('<JOIN>'), 0, 6, port, remoteIP);

  rl.setPrompt('Message> ');
  rl.prompt();
                                                              ❸ Send messages to server
  rl.on('line', function(line) {                                 when the user types a
    sendData(line);                                              message and presses Return.
  }).on('close', function() {
    process.exit(0);
  });
                                                              ❹ Listen for messages
                                                                 from other users.
  socket.on('message', function(msg, rinfo) {
    console.log('\n<' + rinfo.address + '>', msg.toString());
    rl.prompt();
  });

  function sendData(message) {
    socket.send(new Buffer(message), 0, message.length, port, remoteIP,
      function(err, bytes) {
        console.log('Sent:', message);                      Take user's message and create
        rl.prompt();                                        a new buffer that can then be
      }                                                   ❺ sent as UDP message to server.
    );
  }
}

function Server() {
  var clients = [];
  var server = dgram.createSocket('udp4');                  ❼ Combine client's
                                                               port and address
  server.on('message', function(msg, rinfo) {                  to make a unique
    var clientId = rinfo.address + ':' + rinfo.port;           reference to it.

    msg = msg.toString();                                  ❽ If client hasn't been seen
                                                              before, keep a record of its
    if (!clients[clientId]) {                                 connection details.
      clients[clientId] = rinfo;
```

❷ Whenever a client first joins, send special join message.

❻ Listen for new messages from clients.

```
    }

    if (msg.match(/^</)) {
      console.log('Control message:', msg);
      return;
    }
```

⑨ If message is wrapped in angled brackets, treat it as a control message.

```
    for (var client in clients) {
      if (client !== clientId) {
        client = clients[client];
        server.send(
          new Buffer(msg), 0,
          msg.length, client.port, client.address,
          function(err, bytes) {
            if (err) console.error(err);
            console.log('Bytes sent:', bytes);
          }
        );
      }
    }
  });
```

⑩ Send message to every other client.

```
  server.on('listening', function() {
    console.log('Server ready:', server.address());
  });

  server.bind(port);
}

module.exports = {
  Client: Client,
  Server: Server
};

if (!module.parent) {
  switch (process.argv[2]) {
    case 'client':
      new Client(process.argv[3]);
      break;

    case 'server':
      new Server();
      break;

    default:
      console.log('Unknown option');
  }
}
```

This example builds on technique 48—you can run it in a similar way. Type `node udp-chat.js server` to start a server, and then `node udp-chat.js client` to connect a client. You should run more than one client for it to work; otherwise messages won't get routed anywhere.

The readline module has been used to capture user input in a friendly manner ❶. Like most of the other core modules you've seen, this one is event-based. It'll emit the line event whenever a line of text is entered ❸.

Before messages can be sent by the user, an initial join message is sent ❷. This is just to let the server know it has connected—the server code uses it to store a unique reference to the client ❽.

The Client constructor wraps socket.send inside a function called sendData ❺. This is so messages can be easily sent whenever a line of text is typed. Also, when a client itself receives a message, it'll print it to the console and create a new prompt ❹

Messages received by the server ❻ are used to create a unique reference to the client by combining the port and remote address ❼. We get all of this information from the rinfo object, and it's safe to run multiple clients on the same machine because the port will be the client's port rather than the port the server listens on (which doesn't change). To understand how this is possible, recall that UDP headers include a source and destination port, much like TCP.

Finally, whenever a message is seen that isn't a control message ❾, each client is iterated over and sent the message ❿. The client that has sent the message won't receive a copy. Because we've stored references to each rinfo object in the clients array, messages can be sent back to clients.

Client-server networking is the basis of HTTP. Even though HTTP uses TCP connections, it's slightly different from the type of protocols you've seen so far: it's stateless. That means you need different patterns to model it. The next section has more details on how to make HTTP clients and servers.

7.4   *HTTP clients and servers*

Today most of us work with HTTP—whether we're producing or consuming web services, or building web applications. The HTTP protocol is stateless and built on TCP, and Node's HTTP module is similarly built on top of its TCP module.

You could, of course, use your own protocol built with TCP. After all, HTTP is built on top of TCP. But due to the prevalence of web browsers and tools for working with web-based services, HTTP is a natural fit for many problems that involve communicating between remote systems.

In the next section you'll learn how to write a basic HTTP server using Node's core modules.

TECHNIQUE 50   HTTP servers

In this technique you'll learn how to create HTTP servers with Node's http module. Although this is more work than using a web framework built on top of Node, popular web frameworks generally use the same techniques internally, and the objects they expose are derived from Node's standard classes. Understanding the underlying modules and classes is therefore useful for working extensively with HTTP.

PROBLEM

You want to run HTTP servers and test them.

SOLUTION

Use `http.createServer` and `http.createClient`.

DISCUSSION

The `http.createServer` method is a shortcut for creating a new `http.Server` object that descends from `net.Server`. The HTTP server is extended to handle various elements of the HTTP protocol—parsing headers, dealing with response codes, and setting up various events on sockets. The major focus in Node's HTTP handling code is parsing; a C++ wrapper around Joyent's own C parser library is used. This library can extract header fields and values, Content-Length, request method, response status code, and more.

The following listing shows a small "Hello World" web server that uses the `http` module.

Listing 7.6   A simple HTTP server

Create new HTTP server and pass a callback that will run when there's a new request ❷

Write message back to the client ❹

Make request using http.request ❻

```
var assert = require('assert');
var http = require('http');          ← ❶ Load HTTP module

var server = http.createServer(function(req, res) {
  res.writeHead(200, { 'Content-Type': 'text/plain' });  ←
  res.write('Hello, world.\r\n');
  res.end();                                  Write some sensible
});                                           headers for text-
                                              based response ❸

server.listen(8000, function() {      ←
  console.log('Listening on port 8000');
});                                    Set server to listen
                                     ❺ on port 8000

var req = http.request({
  port: 8000
}, function(res) {
  console.log('HTTP headers:', res.headers);
  res.on('data', function(data) {
    console.log('Body:', data.toString());
    assert.equal('Hello, world.\r\n', data.toString());  ←
    assert.equal(200, res.statusCode);
    server.unref();
  });                                  Add listener to the data event
});                                    and make sure response is
                                            what was expected ❼

req.end();
```

The `http` module contains both Node's client and server HTTP classes ❶. The `http.createServer` creates a new server object and returns it. The argument is a callback that receives `req` and `res` objects—request and response, respectively ❷. You may be familiar with these objects if you've used higher-level Node web frameworks like Express and restify.

The interesting thing about the listener callback passed to `http.createServer` is that it behaves much like the listener passed to `net.createServer`. Indeed, the mechanism is the same—we're creating TCP sockets, but layering HTTP on top. The main conceptual difference between the HTTP protocol and TCP socket communication is a question of state: HTTP is a stateless protocol. It's perfectly acceptable and in fact typical to create and tear down TCP sockets *per request*. This partly explains why Node's underlying HTTP implementation is low-level C++ and C: it needs to be fast and use as little memory as possible.

In listing 7.6, the listener runs for every request. In the TCP example from technique 45, the server kept a connection open as long as the client was connected. Because HTTP connections are just TCP sockets, we can use `res` and `req` like the sockets in listing 7.6: `res.write` will write to the socket ❹, and headers can be written back with `res.writeHead` ❸, which is where the socket connection and HTTP APIs visibly diverge—the underlying socket will be closed as soon as the response has been written.

After the server has been set up, we can set it to listen on a port with `server.listen` ❺.

Now that we can create servers, let's look at creating HTTP requests. The `http.request` method will create new connections ❻, and accepts an `options` argument object and a callback that will be run when a connection is made. This means we still need to attach a `data` listener to the *response* passed to the callback to slurp down any sent data.

The `data` callback ensures the response from the server has the expected format: the body content and status code ❼ are checked. The server is told to stop listening for connections when the last client has disconnected by calling `server.unref`, which means the script exits cleanly. This makes it easy to see if any errors were encountered.

One small feature of the HTTP module is the `http.STATUS_CODES` object. This allows human-readable messages to be generated by looking up the integer status code: `http.STATUS_CODES[302]` will evaluate to `Moved Temporarily`.

Now that you've seen how to create HTTP servers, in the next technique we'll look at the role state plays in HTTP clients—despite HTTP being a stateless protocol—by implementing HTTP redirects.

TECHNIQUE 51 **Following redirects**

Node's `http` module provides a convenient API for handling HTTP requests. But it doesn't follow redirects, and because redirects are so common on the web, it's an important technique to master. You could use a popular third-party module that handles redirection, like the popular *request* module by Mikeal Rogers,[2] but you'll learn much more about Node by looking at how it can be implemented with the core modules.

---

[2] https://npmjs.org/package/request

In this technique we'll look at how to use straightforward JavaScript to maintain state across several requests. This allows a redirect to be followed correctly without creating redirect loops or other issues.

PROBLEM

You want to download pages and follow redirects if necessary.

SOLUTION

Handling redirection is fairly straightforward once the basics of the protocol are understood. The HTTP standard defines status codes that denote when redirection has occurred, and it also states that clients should detect infinite redirect loops. To satisfy these requirements, we'll use a simple prototype class to retain the state of each request, redirecting if needed and detecting redirect loops.

DISCUSSION

In this example we'll use Node's core `http` module to make a GET request to a URL that we know will generate a redirection. To determine if a given response is a redirect, we need to check whether the returned status code begins with a 3. All of the status codes in the 3xx family of responses indicate that a redirect of some kind has occurred.

According to the specification, this is the full set of status codes that we need to deal with:

- *300*—Multiple choices
- *301*—Moved permanently
- *302*—Found
- *303*—See other
- *304*—Not modified
- *305*—See proxy
- *307*—Temporary redirect

Exactly how each of these status codes is handled depends on the application. For example, it might be extremely important for a search engine to identify responses that return a 301, because it means the search engine's list of URLs should be permanently updated. For this technique we simply need to follow redirects, which means a single statement is sufficient to check whether the request is being redirected: `if (response.statusCode >= 300 && response.statusCode < 400)`.

Testing for redirection loops is more involved. A request can no longer exist in isolation—we need to track the state of several requests. The easiest way to model this is by using a class that includes an instance variable for counting how many redirects have occurred. When the counter reaches a limit, an error is raised. Figure 7.6 shows how HTTP redirects are handled.

Before writing any code, it's important to consider what kind of API we need. Since we've already determined a "class" should be used to manage state, then users of our module will need to instantiate an instance of this class. Node's `http` module is asynchronous, and our code should be as well. That means that to get a result back, we'll have to pass a callback to a method.

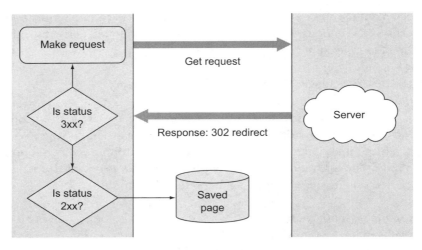

Figure 7.6   Redirection is cyclical, and requests will be made until a 200 status is encountered.

The signature for this callback should use the same format as Node's core modules, where an error variable is the first parameter. Designing the API in this way has the advantage of making error handling straightforward. Making an HTTP request can result in several errors, so it's important to handle them correctly.

The following listing puts all of this together to successfully follow redirects

Listing 7.7   Making an HTTP GET request that follows redirects

```
var http = require('http');
var https = require('https');
var url = require('url');
var request;

function Request() {
  this.maxRedirects = 10;
  this.redirects = 0;
}

Request.prototype.get = function(href, callback) {
  var uri = url.parse(href);
  var options = { host: uri.host, path: uri.path };
  var httpGet = uri.protocol === 'http:' ? http.get : https.get;

  console.log('GET:', href);

  function processResponse(response) {
    if (response.statusCode >= 300 && response.statusCode < 400) {
      if (this.redirects >= this.maxRedirects) {
        this.error = new Error('Too many redirects for: ' + href);
      } else {
        this.redirects++;
        href = url.resolve(options.host, response.headers.location);
```

① **url module has useful methods for parsing URLs**

② **Define constructor to manage request state**

③ **Parse URLs into format used by Node's http module, and determine if HTTPS should be used**

④ **Check to see if statusCode is in the range for HTTP redirects**

⑤ **Increment redirection counter, and use url.resolve to ensure relative URLs are expanded to absolute URLs**

```
        return this.get(href, callback);
      }
    }

    response.url = href;
    response.redirects = this.redirects;

    console.log('Redirected:', href);

    function end() {
      console.log('Connection ended');
      callback(this.error, response);
    }

    response.on('data', function(data) {
      console.log('Got data, length:', data.length);
    });

    response.on('end', end.bind(this));    ◄──────
  }

  httpGet(options, processResponse.bind(this))
    .on('error', function(err) {
      callback(err);
    });
};

request = new Request();    ◄──────
request.get('http://google.com/', function(err, res) {
  if (err) {
    console.error(err);
  } else {
    console.log('Fetched URL:', res.url,
      'with', res.redirects, 'redirects');
    process.exit();
  }
});
```

6 Use Fuction.prototype.bind to bind callback to Request instance so this points to correct object

7 Instantiate Request and fetch a URL

Running this code will display the last-fetched URL, and the number of times the request was redirected. Try it with a few URLs to see what happens: even nonexistent URLs that result in DNS errors should cause error information to be printed to stderr.

After loading the necessary modules ❶, the Request ❷ constructor function is used to create an object that models the lifetime of a request. Using a class in this way keeps implementation details neatly encapsulated from the user. Meanwhile, the Request.prototype.get method does most of the work. It sets up a standard HTTP request, or HTTPS if necessary, and then calls itself recursively whenever a redirect is encountered. Note that the URL has to be parsed ❸ into an object that we use to create the options object that is compatible with Node's http module.

The request protocol (HTTP or HTTPS) is checked to ensure we use the right method from Node's http or https module. Some servers are configured to always redirect HTTP traffic to HTTPS. Without checking for the protocol, this method would repeatedly fetch the original HTTP URL until `maxRedirects` is hit—this is a trivial mistake that's easily avoided.

Once the response has been received, the `statusCode` is checked ❹. The number of redirects is incremented as long as `maxRedirects` hasn't been reached ❺. This process is repeated until there's no longer a status in the 300 range, or too many redirects have been encountered.

When the final request has finished (or the first if there were no redirects), the user-supplied `callback` function is run. The standard Node API signature of `error, result` has been used here to stay consistent with Node's core modules. An error is generated when `maxRedirects` is reached, or when creating the HTTP request by listening for an `error` event.

The user-supplied callback runs after the last request has finished, allowing the callback to access the requested resource. This is handled by running the callback after the `end` event for the last request has been triggered, and by binding the event handler to the current `Request` instance ❻. Binding the event handler means it'll have access to any useful instance variables that the user might need—including errors that are stored in `this.error`.

Lastly, we create an instance of `Request` ❼ to try out the class. You can use it with other URLs if you like.

This technique illustrates an important point: state is important, even though HTTP is technically a stateless protocol. Some misconfigured web applications and servers can create redirect loops, which would cause a client to fetch URLs forever until it's forcibly stopped.

Though listing 7.7 showcases some of Node's HTTP- and URL-handling features, it isn't a complete solution. For a more advanced HTTP API, take a look at Request by Mikeal Rogers (https://github.com/mikeal/request), a widely used simplified Node HTTP API.

In the next technique we'll dissect a simple HTTP proxy. This expands on the client and server techniques discussed here, and could be expanded to create numerous useful applications.

TECHNIQUE 52   HTTP proxies

HTTP proxies are used more often than you might expect—ISPs use transparent proxies to make networks more efficient, corporate systems administrators use caching proxies to reduce bandwidth, and web application DevOps use them to improve the performance of their apps. This technique only scratches the surface of proxies—it catches HTTP requests and responses, and then mirrors them to their intended destinations.

PROBLEM
You want to capture and retransmit HTTP requests.

SOLUTION
Use Node's built-in HTTP module to act as a simple HTTP proxy.

DISCUSSION

A proxy server offers a level of redirection, which facilitates a variety of useful applications: caching, logging, and security-related software. This technique explores how to use the core `http` module to create HTTP proxies. Fundamentally all that's required is an HTTP server that catches requests, and then an HTTP client to clone them.

The `http.createServer` and `http.request` methods can catch and retransmit requests. We'll also need to interpret the original request so we can safely copy it—the `url` core module has an ideal URL-parsing method that can help do this.

The next listing shows how simple it is to create a working proxy in Node.

Listing 7.8   Using the `http` module to create a proxy

```
var http = require('http');
var url = require('url');

http.createServer(function(req, res) {            ◀── ❶ Create standard HTTP
  console.log('start request:', req.url);                server instance
  var options = url.parse(req.url);
  options.headers = req.headers;                  ❷ Create request that copies
  var proxyRequest = http.request(options, function(proxyResponse) {  ◀── the original request
    proxyResponse.on('data', function(chunk) {
      console.log('proxyResponse length:', chunk.length);
      res.write(chunk, 'binary');                 ❸ Listen for data; then
    });                                              write it back to browser

    proxyResponse.on('end', function() {          ◀──
      console.log('proxied request ended');
      res.end();                                  ❹ Track when proxied
    });                                              request has finished

    res.writeHead(proxyResponse.statusCode, proxyResponse.headers);  ◀──
  });
                                                  ❺ Send headers
  req.on('data', function(chunk) {                ◀──  to the browser
    console.log('in request length:', chunk.length);
    proxyRequest.write(chunk, 'binary');
  });                                             ❻ Capture data sent from
                                                     browser to the server
  req.on('end', function() {                      ◀──
    console.log('original request ended');        ❼ Track when original
    proxyRequest.end();                              request ends
  });
}).listen(8080);                                  ◀──
                                                  ❽ Listen for connections
                                                     from local browsers
```

To use this example, your computer will need a bit of configuration. Find your system's internet options, and then look for HTTP proxies. From there you should be able to enter `localhost:8080` as the proxy. Alternatively, add the proxy in a browser's settings if possible. Some browsers don't support this; Google Chrome will open the system proxy dialog.

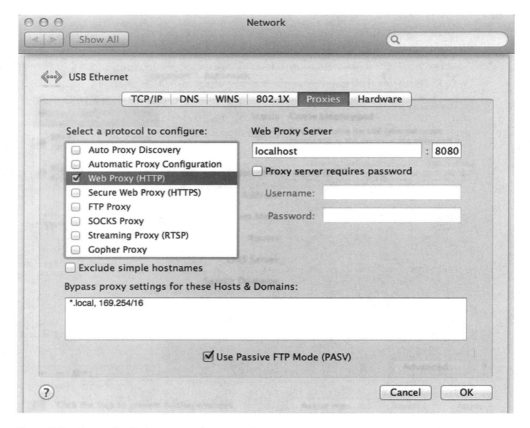

Figure 7.7   To use the Node proxy we've created, set `localhost:8080` **as the Web Proxy Server.**

Figure 7.7 shows how to configure the proxy on a Mac. Make sure you click OK and then Apply in the main *Network* dialog to save the setting. And remember to disable the proxy once you're done!

Once your system is set up to use the proxy, start the Node process up with `node listings/network/proxy.js` in a shell. Now when you visit web pages, you should see the successive requests and responses logged to the console.

This example works by first creating a server ❶ using the `http` module. The callback will be triggered when a browser makes a request. We've used `url.parse` (`url` is another core module) to separate out the URL's various parts so they can be passed as arguments to `http.request`. The parsed URL object is compatible with the arguments that `http.request` expects, so this is convenient ❷.

From within the request's callback, we can subscribe to events that need to be repeated back to the browser. The `data` event is useful because it allows us to capture the response from the server and pass it back to the client with `res.write` ❸. We also respond to the end of the server's connection by closing the connection to the browser ❹. The status code is also written back to the client based on the server's response ❺.

Any data sent by the client is also proxied to the remote server by subscribing to the browser's `data` events ❻. Similarly, the browser's original request is watched for an `end` event so it can be reflected back to the proxied request ❼.

Finally, the HTTP server used as the proxy is set up to listen on port 8080 ❽.

This example creates a special server that sits between the browser and the server the browser wants to talk to. It could be extended to do lots of interesting things. For example, you could cache image files and compress them based on the remote client, sending mobile browsers heavily compressed images. You could even strip out certain content based on rules; some ad-blocking and parental filters work this way.

We've been using the DNS so far without really thinking about it too much. DNS uses TCP *and* UDP for its request/response-based protocol. Fortunately, Node hides this complexity for us with a slick asynchronous DNS module. The next section demonstrates how to make DNS requests using Node's `dns` module.

7.5 *Making DNS requests*

Node's DNS module lives outside of the `net` module, in `dns`. When the `http` or `net` modules are used to connect to remote servers, Node will look up IP addresses using `dns.lookup` internally.

TECHNIQUE 53 **Making a DNS request**

Node has multiple methods for making DNS requests. In this technique you'll learn how and why you should use each to resolve a domain name to an IP address.

When you query a DNS record, the results may include answers for different record types. The DNS is a distributed database, so it isn't used purely for resolving IP addresses—some records like TXT are used to build features off the back of the DNS itself.

Table 7.2 includes a list of each type along with the associated `dns` module method.

Table 7.2 DNS record types

Type	Method	Description
A	`dns.resolve`	An A record stores the IP address. It can have an associated time-to-live (TTL) field to indicate how often the record should be updated.
TXT	`dns.resolveTxt`	Text values that can be used by other services for additional features built on top of DNS.
SRV	`dns.resolveSrv`	Service records define "location" data for a service; this usually includes the port number and hostname.
NS	`dns.resolveNs`	Used for name servers themselves.
CNAME	`dns.resolveCname`	Canonical name records. These are set to domain names rather than IP addresses.

PROBLEM

You want to look up a single or multiple domain names quickly.

SOLUTION

The dns.lookup method can be used to look up either IPv4 or IPv6 addresses. When looking up multiple addresses, it can be faster to use dns.resolve instead.

DISCUSSION

According to Node's documentation, dns.lookup is backed by a thread pool, whereas dns.resolve uses the c-ares library, which is faster. The dns.lookup API is a little friendlier—it uses getaddrinfo, which is more consistent with the other programs on your system. Indeed, the Socket.prototype.connect method, and any of Node's core modules that inherit from the objects in the net module, all use dns.lookup for consistency:

```
var dns = require('dns');                                  ⟵——❶ Load dns module

dns.lookup('www.manning.com', function(err, address) {     ⟵——❷ Look up IP address
                                                                  of the given domain
  if (err) {
    console.error('Error:', err);
  }
  console.log('Addresses:', address);
});
```

This example loads the dns module ❶, and then looks up the IP address using dns.lookup ❷. The API is asynchronous, so we have to pass a callback to receive the IP address and any errors that were raised when looking up the address. Note that the domain name has to be provided, rather than a URL—don't include http:// here.

If everything runs correctly, then you should see 68.180.151.75 printed as the IP address. Conversely, if the previous example is run when you're offline, then a rather interesting error should be printed instead:

```
Error: {
  [Error: getaddrinfo ENOTFOUND]
  code: 'ENOTFOUND',              ⟵——❶ Error code
  errno: 'ENOTFOUND',
  syscall: 'getaddrinfo'          ⟵——  System call where
}                                     ❷ the error originated
```

The error object includes a standard error code ❶ alongside the system call that raised the error ❷. You can use the error code in your programs to detect when this kind of error was raised and handle it appropriately. The syscall property, meanwhile, is useful to us as programmers: it shows that the error was generated by a service outside of our Node code that is provided by the operating system.

Now compare this to the version that uses dns.resolve:

```
var dns = require('dns');
                                                              ❶ Resolve domain name
dns.resolve('www.manning.com', function(err, addresses) {  ⟵——  asynchronously.
  if (err) {
```

```
    console.error(err);
  }

  console.log('Addresses:', addresses);
});
```

The API looks similar to the previous example, apart from `dns.resolve` ❶. You'll still see an error object that includes `ECONNREFUSED` if the DNS server couldn't be reached, but this time the result is different: we receive an array of addresses instead of a single result. In this example you should see [`'68.180.151.75'`], but some servers may return more than one address.

Node's `dns` module is flexible, friendly, and fast. It can scale up well from infrequent single requests to making batches of requests.

The last part of Node's networking suite left to look at is perhaps the hardest to learn, yet paradoxically the most important to get right: encryption. The next section introduces SSL/TLS with the `tls` and `https` modules.

7.6   *Encryption*

Node's encryption module, `tls`, uses OpenSSL Transport Layer Security/Secure Socket Layer (TLS/SSL). This is a public key system, where each client and server both have a private key. The server makes its public key available so clients can encrypt subsequent communications in a way that only that server can decrypt again.

The `tls` module is used as the basis for the `https` module—this allows HTTP servers and clients to communicate over TLS/SSL. Unfortunately, TLS/SSL is a world of potential pitfalls. Node potentially supports different cyphers based on what version of OpenSSL it has been linked against. You can specify what cyphers you want to use when creating servers with `tls.createServer`, but we recommend using the defaults unless you have specific expertise in this area.

In the following technique you'll learn how to start a TCP server that uses SSL and a self-signed certificate. After that, we end the chapter with a technique that shows how encrypting web server communication works in Node.

TECHNIQUE 54   **A TCP server that uses encryption**

TLS can be used to encrypt servers made with `net.createServer`. This technique demonstrates how to do this by first creating the necessary certificates and then starting a client and server.

PROBLEM

You want to encrypt communication sent and received over a TCP connection.

SOLUTION

Use the `tls` module to start a client and server. Set up the required certificate files using OpenSSL.

DISCUSSION

The main thing to master when working with encryption, whether it's web servers, mail servers, or any TCP-based protocol, is how to properly set up the key and certificate files.

Public key cryptography is dependent on public-private key pairs—a pair is required for both clients and servers. But an additional file is needed: the public key of the Certificate Authority (CA).

Our goal in this technique is to create a TLS client and server that both report `authorized` after the TLS handshake. This state is reported when *both* parties have verified each other's identity. When working with web server certificates, your CA will be the well-known organizations that commercially distribute certificates. But for the purposes of testing, you can become your own CA and sign certificates. This is also useful for secure communication between your own systems that don't need publicly verifiable certificates.

That means before you can run any Node examples, you'll need certificates. The OpenSSL command-line tools are required for this. If you don't have them, you should be able to install them with your operating system's package manager, or by visiting www.openssl.org.

The `openssl` tool takes a command as the first argument, and then options as subsequent arguments. For example, `openssl req` is used for X.509 Certificate Signing Request (CSR) management. To make a certificate signed by an authority you control, you'll need to issue the following commands:

- *genrsa*—Generate an RSA certificate; this is our private key.
- *req*—Create a CSR.
- *x509*—Sign the private key with the CSR to produce a public key.

When the process is broken down like this, it's fairly easy to understand: certificates require an authority and must be signed, and we need a public and private key. The process is similar when creating a public and private key signed against a commercial certificate authority, which you'll do if you want to buy certificates to use with public web servers.

The full command list for creating a public and private key is as follows:

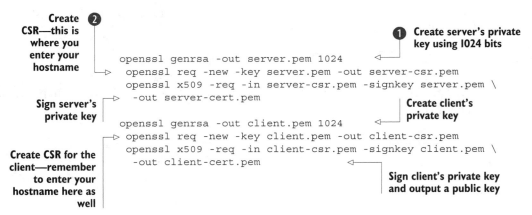

After creating a private key ❶, you'll create a CSR. When prompted for the "Common Name" ❷, enter your computer's hostname, which you can find by typing `hostname` in the terminal on a Unix system. This is important, because when your code sends or receives certificates, it'll check the name value against the `servername` property passed to the `tls.connect` method.

The next listing reads the server's keys and starts a server running using `tls.createServer`.

Listing 7.9   A TCP server that uses TLS for encryption

```
var fs = require('fs');
var tls = require('tls');

var options = {
  key: fs.readFileSync('server.pem'),          ⟵—❶ Private key
  cert: fs.readFileSync('server-cert.pem'),
  ca: [ fs.readFileSync('client-cert.pem') ],  ⟵
  requestCert: true                                 Client as a certificate
};                                              ❸ authority

var server = tls.createServer(options, function(cleartextStream) {
  var authorized = cleartextStream.authorized ?
    'authorized' : 'unauthorized';
  console.log('Connected:', authorized);       ⟵   Whenever a client
  cleartextStream.write('Welcome!\n');              connects, show if
  cleartextStream.setEncoding('utf8');              server was able to
  cleartextStream.pipe(cleartextStream);       ❺ verify the certificates
});

server.listen(8000, function() {
  console.log('Server listening');
});
```

Public key ❷ ⟶ (points to `cert:` line)
Ensure client certificates are always checked ❹ (points to `requestCert: true`)

The network code in listing 7.9 is very similar to the `net.createServer` method—that's because the `tls` module inherits from it. The rest of the code is concerned with managing certificates, and unfortunately this process is left to us to handle and is often the cause of programmer errors, which can compromise security. First we load the private ❶ and public ❷ keys, passing them to `tls.createServer`. We also load the client's public key as a certificate authority ❸—when using a commercially obtained certificate, this stage isn't usually required.

When clients connect, we want to send them some data, but for the purposes of this example we really just want to see if the client was authorized ❺. Client authorization has been forced by setting the `requestCert` option ❹.

This server can be run with `node tls.js`—but there's something missing: a client! The next listing contains a client that can connect to this server.

Listing 7.10   A TCP client that uses TLS

```
var fs = require('fs');
var os = require('os');
var tls = require('tls');

var options = {
```

```
             key: fs.readFileSync('client.pem'),           ◁──1  Load private key
Load public key 2 ▷ cert: fs.readFileSync('client-cert.pem'),
             ca: [ fs.readFileSync('server-cert.pem') ], ◁──   Treat server as a
             servername: os.hostname()                     3   certificate authority
Set hostname    };
as the server
name    4   var cleartextStream = tls.connect(8000, options, function() {
             var authorized = cleartextStream.authorized ?
               'authorized' : 'unauthorized';
             console.log('Connected:', authorized);
             process.stdin.pipe(cleartextStream);          ◁──   Read data from server
           });                                              5    and print it out

           cleartextStream.setEncoding('utf8');

           cleartextStream.on('data', function(data) {
             console.log(data);
           });
```

The client is similar to the server: the private **1** and public keys **2** are loaded, and this time the server is treated as the CA **3**. The server's name is set to the same value as the Common Name in the CSR by using os.hostname **4**—you could type in the name manually if you set it to something else. After that the client connects, displays whether it was able to authorize the certificates, and then reads data sent by the server and pipes it to the standard output **5**.

Testing SSL/TLS

When testing secure certificates, it can be hard to tell whether the problem lies in your code or elsewhere. One way around this is to use the openssl command-line tool to simulate a client or server. The following command will start a client that connects to a server with the given certificate file:

```
openssl s_client -connect 127.0.0.1:8000 \
  ➥ -CAfile ./server-cert.pem
```

The openssl tool will display a lot of extra information about the connection. When we wrote the example in this technique, we used it to figure out that the certificate we'd generated had the wrong value for its Common Name.

An instance of tls.Server is instantiated when you call tls.createServer. This constructor calls net.Server—there's a clear inheritance chain between each networking module. That means the events emitted by net.Server are the same for TLS servers.

In the next technique you'll see how to use HTTPS, and how this is also related to the tls and net modules.

TECHNIQUE 55   Encrypted web servers and clients

Though it's possible to host Node applications behind other web servers like Apache and nginx, there are times when you'll want to run your own HTTPS servers. This technique introduces the https module and shows how it's related to the tls module.

PROBLEM

You want to run a server that supports SSL/TLS.

SOLUTION

Use the `https` module and `https.createServer`.

DISCUSSION

To run the examples in this technique, you'll need to have followed the steps to create suitable self-signed certificates, as found in technique 54. Once you've set up some public and private keys, you'll be able to run the examples.

The following listing shows an HTTPS server.

Listing 7.11 A basic HTTP server that uses TLS for encryption

```
var fs = require('fs');
var https = require('https');

var options = {
  key: fs.readFileSync('server.pem'),            ⬅──❶ Private key
  cert: fs.readFileSync('server-cert.pem'),   Public key ❷ ➤
  ca: [ fs.readFileSync('client-cert.pem') ],
  requestCert: true                              ⬅── Ensure client certificates
};                                                   are always checked

var server = https.createServer(options, function(req, res) {
  var authorized = req.socket.authorized
    ? 'authorized' : 'unauthorized';
  res.writeHead(200);
  res.write('Welcome! You are ' + authorized + '\n');
  res.end();
});

server.listen(8000, function() {
  console.log('Server listening');
});
```

Public key ❷ (annotation pointing to cert line)

When a browser requests a page, show if server was able to verify the certificates (annotation pointing to the authorized block)

The server in listing 7.11 is basically the same as the one in technique 54. Again, the private ❶ and public ❷ keys are loaded and passed to `https.createServer`.

When browsers request a page, we check the `req.socket.authorized` property to see if the request was authorized. This status is returned to the browser. If you want to try this out with a browser, ensure you type `https://` into the address bar; otherwise it won't work. You'll see a warning message because the browser won't be able to verify the server's certificate—that's OK; you know what's going on because you created the server. The server will respond saying that you're *unauthorized* because it won't be able to authorize you, either.

To make a client that can connect to this server, follow the code shown next.

Listing 7.12 An example HTTPS client

```
var fs = require('fs');
var https = require('https');
var os = require('os');
```

```
var options = {
  key: fs.readFileSync('client.pem'),
  cert: fs.readFileSync('client-cert.pem'),
  ca: [ fs.readFileSync('server-cert.pem') ],
  hostname: os.hostname(),
  port: 8000,
  path: '/',
  method: 'GET'
};

var req = https.request(options, function(res) {
  res.on('data', function(d) {
    process.stdout.write(d);
  });
});
req.end();

req.on('error', function(e) {
  console.error(e);
});
```

Load private key ❶

Load public key ❷

Load server's certificate as a CA ❸

Set hostname as the machine's hostname ❹

Make HTTPS request using https.request ❺

This example sets the private ❶ and public ❷ keys for the client, which is what your browser does transparently when making secure requests. It also sets the server as a certificate authority ❸, which wouldn't usually be required. The hostname used for the HTTP request is the machine's current hostname ❹.

Once all of this setup is done, the HTTPS request can be made. This is done using `https.request` ❺. The API is identical to the `http` module. In this example the server will ensure the SSL/TLS authorization procedure was valid, so the server will return text to indicate if the connection was fully authorized.

In real HTTPS code, you probably wouldn't make your own CA. This can be useful if you have internal systems that you want to communicate with using HTTPS—perhaps for testing or for API requests over the internet. When making HTTPS requests against public web servers, Node will be able to verify the server's certificates for you, so you won't need to set the `key`, `cert`, and `ca` options.

The `https` module has some other features—there's an `https.get` convenience method for making `GET` requests more easily. Otherwise, that wraps up our set of techniques on encryption in Node.

Secure pairs

Before moving off encryption for greener pastures, there's one patch of delicious turf left to chew: `SecurePair`. This is a class in the `tls` module that can be used to create a secure pair of streams: one reads and writes encrypted data, and the other reads and writes clear text. This potentially allows you to stream anything to an encrypted output.

There's a convenience method for this: `tls.createSecurePair`. When a `SecurePair` establishes a secure connection, it'll emit a `secure` event, but you'll still need to check for `cleartext.authorized` to ensure the certificates were properly authorized.

7.7   *Summary*

This chapter has been long, but that's because networking in Node is important. Node is built on excellent foundations for network programming; buffers, streams, and asynchronous I/O all contribute to an environment that is perfect for writing the next generation of network-oriented programs.

With this chapter you should be able to appreciate how Node fits into the wider world of network software. Whether you're developing Unix daemons, Windows-based game servers, or the next big web app, you should now know where to start.

It goes without saying that networking and encryption are closely related. With Node's `tls` and `https` modules, you should be able to write network clients and servers that can talk to other systems without fear of eavesdroppers.

The next chapter is the last on Node's core modules, `child_process`, and looks at techniques for interfacing with other command-line programs.

Child processes: Integrating external applications with Node

This chapter covers

- Executing external applications
- Detaching a child process
- Interprocess communication between Node processes
- Making Node programs executable
- Creating job pools
- Synchronous child processes

No platform is an island. Although it would be fun to write everything in JavaScript, we'd miss out on valuable applications that already exist in other platforms. Take GraphicsMagick, for instance (http://www.graphicsmagick.org/): a full-featured image manipulation tool, great for resizing that massively large profile photo that was just uploaded. Or take wkhtmltopdf (http://wkhtmltopdf.org/), a headless webkit PDF generator, perfect for turning that HTML report into a PDF download.

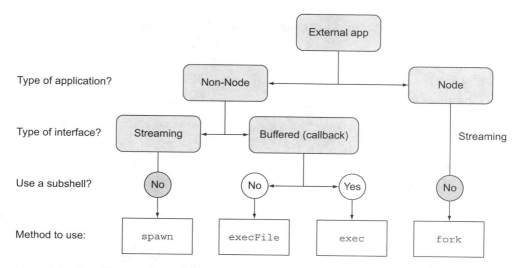

Figure 8.1 Choosing the right method

In Node, the `child_process` module allows us to execute these applications and others (including Node applications) to use with our programs. Thankfully, we don't have to re-invent the wheel.

The `child_process` module provides four different methods for executing external applications. All methods are asynchronous. The right method will depend on what you need, as shown in figure 8.1.

- *execFile*—Execute an external application, given a set of arguments, and callback with the buffered output after the process exits.
- *spawn*—Execute an external application, given a set of arguments, and provide a streaming interface for I/O and events for when the process exits.
- *exec*—Execute one or more commands inside a shell and callback with the buffered output after the process exits.
- *fork*—Execute a Node module as a separate process, given a set of arguments, provide a streaming and evented interface like `spawn`, and also set up an inter-process communication (IPC) channel between the parent and child process.

Throughout this chapter we'll dive into how to get the most out of these methods, giving practical examples of where you'd want to use each. Later on, we'll look into some other techniques to use when working with child processes: detaching processes, interprocess communication, file descriptors, and pooling.

8.1 Executing external applications

In this first section, we will look at all the ways you can work asynchronously with an external program.

Executing external applications

Wouldn't it be great to run some image processing on a user's uploaded photo with ImageMagick, or validate an XML file with xmllint? Node makes it easy to execute external applications.

PROBLEM

You want to execute an external application and get the output.

SOLUTION

Use execFile (see figure 8.2).

DISCUSSION

If you want to run an external application and get the result, using execFile makes it simple and straightforward. It'll buffer the output for you and provide the results and any errors in a callback. Let's say we want to run the echo program given the parameters hello world. With execFile, we would do the following:

```
var cp = require('child_process');

cp.execFile('echo', ['hello', 'world'],
   function (err, stdout, stderr) {
     if (err) console.error(err);
     console.log('stdout', stdout);
     console.log('stderr', stderr);
   });
```

Provide command as first parameter and any command arguments as an array for second parameter

Callback includes any error executing the command and buffered output from stdout and stderr

How does Node know where to find the external application? To answer that, we need to look at how paths work in the underlying operating system.

8.1.1 *Paths and the PATH environment variable*

Windows/UNIX has a PATH environment variable (envvar: http://en.wikipedia.org/wiki/PATH_(variable)). PATH contains a list of directories where executable programs exist. If a program exists in one of the listed directories, it can be located without needing an absolute or relative path to the application.

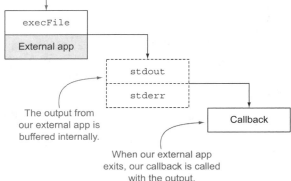

Execute our external app asynchronously.

execFile

External app

stdout

stderr

The output from our external app is buffered internally.

When our external app exits, our callback is called with the output.

Callback

Figure 8.2   The execFile method buffers the result and provides a callback interface.

Node, using execvp behind the scenes, will search for applications using PATH when no absolute or relative location is provided. We can see this in our earlier example, since directories to common system applications like echo usually exist in PATH already.

If the directory containing the application isn't in PATH, you'll need to provide the location explicitly like you would on the command line:

```
cp.execFile('./app-in-this-directory' ...
cp.execFile('/absolute/path/to/app' ...
cp.execFile('../relative/path/to/app' ...
```

To see what directories are listed in PATH, you can run a simple one-liner in the Node REPL:

```
$ node
> console.log(process.env.PATH.split(':').join('\n'))
/usr/local/bin
/usr/bin/bin
...
```

If you want to avoid including the location to external applications not in PATH, one option is to add any new directories to PATH inside your Node application. Just add this line before any execFile calls:

```
process.env.PATH += ':/a/new/path/to/executables';
```

Now any applications in that new directory will be accessible without providing a path to execFile.

8.1.2   *Errors when executing external applications*

If your external application doesn't exist, you'll get an ENOENT error. Often this is due to a typo in the application name or path with the result that Node can't find the application, as shown in figure 8.3.

If the external application does exist but Node can't access it (typically due to insufficient permissions), you'll get an EACCES or EPERM error. This can often be mitigated by either running your Node program as a user with sufficient permissions or changing the external application permissions themselves to allow access.

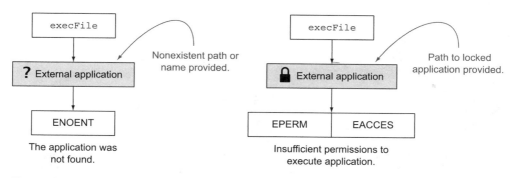

Figure 8.3   Common child process errors

You'll also get an error if the external application has a non-zero exit status (http://mng.bz/MLXP), which is used to indicate that an application couldn't perform the task it was given (on both UNIX and Windows). Node will provide the exit status as part of the error object and will also provide any data that was written to stdout or stderr:

```
var cp = require('child_process');
cp.execFile('ls', ['non-existent-directory-to-list'],
  function (err, stdout, stderr) {
    console.log(err.code);
    console.log(stderr);
});
```

Output exit code, which is 1 in this case, indicating command failed

Output error details stored in stderr

Having execFile is great for when you want to just execute an application and get the output (or discard it), for example, if you want to run an image-processing command with ImageMagick and only care if it succeeds or not. But if an application has a lot of output or you want to do more real-time analysis of the data returned, using streams is a better approach.

TECHNIQUE 57   **Streaming and external applications**

Imagine a web application that uses the output from an external application. As that data is being made available, you can at the same time be pushing it out to the client. Streaming enables you to tap into the data from a child process as it's being output-ted, versus having the data buffered and then provided. This is good if you expect the external application to output large amounts of data. Why? Buffering a large set of data can take up a lot of memory. Also, this enables data to be consumed as it's being made available, which improves responsiveness.

PROBLEM

You want to execute an external application and stream the output.

SOLUTION

Use spawn (see figure 8.4).

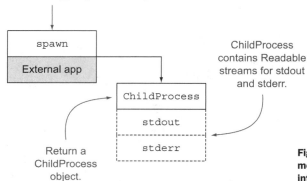

Figure 8.4 The spawn method returns a streaming interface for I/O.

DISCUSSION

The spawn method has a function signature similar to execFile:

```
cp.execFile('echo', ['hello', 'world'], ...);
cp.spawn('echo', ['hello', 'world'], ...);
```

The application is the first argument, and an array of parameters/flags for the application is the second. But instead of taking a callback providing the output already buffered, spawn relies on streams:

> **Spawn method returns a ChildProcess object containing stdin, stdout, and stderr stream objects**

```
var cp = require('child_process');

var child = cp.spawn('echo', ['hello', 'world']);
child.on('error', console.error);
child.stdout.pipe(process.stdout);
child.stderr.pipe(process.stderr);
```

Errors are emitted on error event

Output from stdout and stderr can be read as it's available

Since spawn is stream-based, it's great for handling large outputs or working with data as it's read in. All other benefits of streams apply as well. For example, child.stdin is a Writeable stream, so you can hook that up to any Readable stream to get data. The reverse is true for child.stdout and child.stderr, which are Readable streams that can be hooked into any Writeable stream.

> **API SYMMETRY** The ChildProcess API (child.stdin, child.stdout, child.stderr) share a nice symmetry with the parent process streams (process.stdin, process.stdout, process.stderr).

8.1.3 Stringing external applications together

A large part of UNIX philosophy is building applications that do one thing and do it well, and then communicating between those applications with a common interface (that being plain text).

Let's make a Node program that exemplifies this by taking three simple applications that deal with text streams and sticking them together using spawn. The cat application will read a file and output its contents. The sort application will take in the file as input and provide the lines sorted as output. The uniq application will take the sorted file as input, and output the sorted file with all the duplicate lines removed. This is illustrated in figure 8.5.

Let's look at how we can do this with spawn and streams:

```
var cp = require('child_process');
var cat = cp.spawn('cat', ['messy.txt']);
var sort = cp.spawn('sort');
var uniq = cp.spawn('uniq');

cat.stdout.pipe(sort.stdin);
sort.stdout.pipe(uniq.stdin);
uniq.stdout.pipe(process.stdout);
```

Call spawn for each command we want to chain together

Stream result to the console with process.stdout

Output of each command becomes input for next command

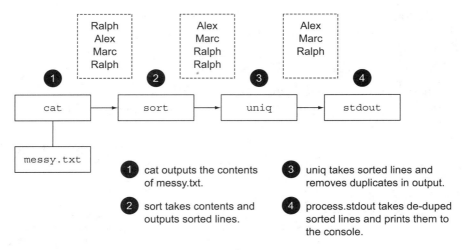

Figure 8.5   Stringing external applications together with `spawn`

Using `spawn`'s streaming interfaces allows a seamless way to work with any stream objects in Node, including stringing external applications together. But sometimes we need the facilities of our underlying shell to do powerful composition of external applications. For that, we can use `exec`.

> **APPLYING WHAT YOU'VE LEARNED**   Can you think of a way to avoid using the `cat` program based on what you learned with the `fs` module and streaming in chapter 6?

TECHNIQUE 58   Executing commands in a shell

Shell programming is a common way to build utility scripts or command-line applications. You could whip up a Bash or Python script, but with Node, you can use JavaScript. Although you could execute a subshell manually using `execFile` or `spawn`, Node provides a convenient, cross-platform method for you.

PROBLEM

You need to use the underlying shell facilities (like pipes, redirects, file blobs) to execute commands and get the output.

SOLUTION

Use `exec` (see figure 8.6).

DISCUSSION

If you need to execute commands in a shell, you can use `exec`. The `exec` method runs the commands with `/bin/sh` or `cmd.exe` (on Windows). Running commands in a shell means you have access to all the functionality provided by your particular shell (like pipes, redirects, and backgrounding).

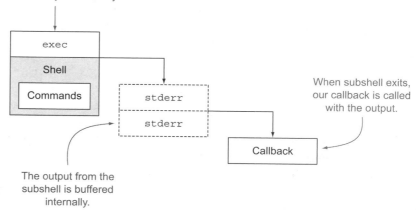

Execute our commands asynchronously in a subshell.

When subshell exits, our callback is called with the output.

The output from the subshell is buffered internally.

Figure 8.6 The `exec` method runs our commands in a subshell.

A SINGLE COMMAND ARGUMENT Unlike `execFile` and `spawn`, the exec method doesn't have a separate argument for command parameters/flags, since you can run more than one command on a shell.

As an example, let's pipe together the same three applications we did in the last technique to generate a sorted, unique list of names. But this time, we'll use common UNIX shell facilities rather than streams:

If successful, stdout will contain sorted, de-duped version of messy.txt

```
cp.exec('cat messy.txt | sort | uniq',
    function (err, stdout, stderr) {
        console.log(stdout);
    });
```

Pipe cat, sort, and uniq together like we would on command line

ABOUT SHELLS UNIX users should keep in mind that Node uses whatever is mapped to `/bin/sh` for execution. This typically will be Bash on most modern operating systems, but you have the option to remap it to another shell of your liking. Windows users who need a piping facility can use streams and spawn as discussed in technique 57.

8.1.4 *Security and shell command execution*

Having access to a shell is powerful and convenient, but it should be used cautiously, especially with a user's input.

Let's say we're using xmllint (http://xmlsoft.org/xmllint.html) to parse and detect errors in a user's uploaded XML file where the user provides a schema to validate against:

```
cp.exec('xmllint --schema '+req.query.schema+' the.xml');
```

If a user provided "http://site.com/schema.xsd," it would be replaced and the following command would run:

```
xmllint --schema http://site.com/schema.xsd the.xml
```

But since the argument has user input, it can easily fall prey to command (or shell) injection attacks (https://golemtechnologies.com/articles/shell-injection)—for example, a malicious user provides "; rm -rf / ;" causing the following comment to run (*please don't run this in your terminal!*):

```
xmllint --schema ; rm -rf / ; the.xml
```

If you haven't guessed already, this says, "Start new command (;), remove forcibly and recursively all files/directories at root of the file system (rm -rf /), and end the command (;) in case something follows it."

   In other words, this injection could potentially delete all the files the Node process has permission to access on the entire operating system! And that's just one of the commands that can be run. Anything your process user has access to (files, commands, and so on) can be exploited.

   If you need to run an application and don't need shell facilities, it's safer (and slightly faster) to use execFile instead:

```
cp.execFile('xmllint', ['--schema', req.query.schema, 'the.xml']);
```

Here this malicious injection attack would fail since it's not run in a shell and the external application likely wouldn't understand the argument and would raise an error.

TECHNIQUE 59   Detaching a child process

Node can be used to kick off external applications and then allow them to run on their own. For example, let's say you have an administrative web application in Node that allows you to kick off a long-running synchronization process with your cloud provider. If that Node application were to crash, your synchronization process would be halted. To avoid this, you detach your external application so it'll be unaffected.

PROBLEM

You have a long-running external application that you want Node to start but then be able to exit with the child process still running.

SOLUTION

Detach a spawned child process (see figure 8.7).

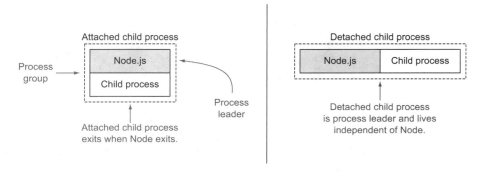

Figure 8.7   Detached child process exists independent of the Node process

DISCUSSION

Normally, any child process will be terminated when the parent Node process is terminated. Child processes are said to be *attached* to the parent process. But the spawn method includes the ability to *detach* a child process and promote it to be a process group leader. In this scenario, if the parent is terminated, the child process will continue until finished.

This scenario is useful when you want Node to set up the execution of a long-running external process and you don't need Node to babysit it after it starts.

This is the detached option, configurable as part of a third options parameter to spawn:

```
var child = cp.spawn('./longrun', [], { detached: true });
```

In this example, longrun will be promoted to a process group leader. If you were to run this Node program and forcibly terminate it (Ctrl-C), longrun would continue executing until finished.

If you didn't forcibly terminate, you'd notice that the parent stays alive until the child has completed. This is because I/O of the child process is connected to the parent. In order to disconnect the I/O, you have to configure the stdio option.

8.1.5 *Handing I/O between the child and parent processes*

The stdio option defines where the I/O from a child process will be redirected. It takes either an array or a string as a value. The string values are simply shorthands that will expand to common array configurations.

The array is structured such that the *indexes* correspond to file descriptors in the child process and the *values* indicate where the I/O for the particular file descriptor (FD) should be redirected.

WHAT ARE FILE DESCRIPTORS? If you're confused about file descriptors, check out technique 40 in chapter 6 for an introduction.

By default, stdio is configured as

```
stdio: 'pipe'
```

which is a shorthand for the following array values:

```
stdio: [ 'pipe', 'pipe', 'pipe' ]
```

This means that file descriptors 0-2 will be made accessible on the ChildProcess object as streams (child.stdio[0], child.stdio[1], child.stdio[2]). But since FDs 0-2 often refer to stdin, stdout, and stderr, they're also made available as the now familiar child.stdin, child.stdout, and child.stderr streams.

The pipe value connects the parent and child processes because these streams stay open, waiting to write or read data. But for this technique, we want to disconnect the two in order to exit the Node process. A brute-force approach would be to simply destroy all the streams created:

```
child.stdin.destroy();
child.stdout.destroy();
child.stderr.destroy();
```

Although this would work, given our intent to not use them, it's better to not create the streams in the first place. Instead, we can assign a file descriptor if we want to direct the I/O elsewhere or use ignore to discard it completely.

Let's look at a solution that uses both options. We want to ignore FD 0 (stdin) since we won't be providing any input to the child process. But let's capture any output from FDs 1 and 2 (stdout, stderr) just in case we need to do some debugging later on. Here's how we can accomplish that:

```
var fs = require('fs');
var cp = require('child_process');                          Open two log files,
                                                            one for stdout and
var outFd = fs.openSync('./longrun.out', 'a');    ◁─┘       one for stderr
var errFd = fs.openSync('./longrun.err', 'a');

var child = cp.spawn('./longrun', [], {            Ignore FD 0; redirect
  detached: true,                                  output from FDs I
  stdio: [ 'ignore', outFd, errFd ]    ◁─┘         and 2 to the log files
});
```

This will disconnect the I/O between the child and parent processes. If we run this application, the output from the child process will end up in the log files.

8.1.6 *Reference counting and child processes*

We're almost there. The child process will live on because it's detached and the I/O is disconnected from the parent. But the parent still has an internal reference to the child process and won't exit until the child process has finished and the reference has been removed.

You can use the child.unref() method to tell Node not to include this child process reference in its count. The following complete application will now exit after spawning the child process:

```
var fs = require('fs');
var cp = require('child_process');

var outFd = fs.openSync('./longrun.out', 'a');
var errFd = fs.openSync('./longrun.err', 'a');

var child = cp.spawn('./longrun', [], {
  detached: true,
  stdio: [ 'ignore', outFd, errFd ]
});
                                          Remove reference of child
child.unref();    ◁─┘                     in the parent process
```

To review, detaching a process requires three things:

- The `detached` option must be set to `true` so the child becomes its own process leader.
- The `stdio` option must be configured so the parent and child are disconnected.
- The reference to the child must be severed in the parent using `child.unref()`.

8.2 Executing Node programs

Any of the prior techniques can be used to execute Node applications. However, in the techniques to follow, we will focus on making the most out of Node child processes.

TECHNIQUE 60 Executing Node programs

When writing shell scripts, utilities, or other command-line applications in Node, it's often handy to make executables out of them for ease of use and portability. If you publish command-line applications to npm, this also comes in handy.

PROBLEM

You want to make a Node program an executable script.

SOLUTION

Set up the file to be executable by your underlying platform.

DISCUSSION

A Node program can be run as a child process with any of the means we've already described by simply using the `node` executable:

```
var cp = require('child_process');
cp.execFile('node', ['myapp.js', 'myarg1', 'myarg2' ], ...
```

But there are many cases where having a standalone executable is more convenient, where you can instead use your app like this:

```
myapp myarg1 myarg2
```

The process for making an executable will vary depending on whether you're on Windows or UNIX.

Executables on Windows

Let's say we have a simple one-liner `hello.js` program that echoes the first argument passed:

```
console.log('hello', process.argv[2]);
```

To run this program, we type

```
$ node hello.js marty
hello marty
```

To make a Windows executable, we can make a simple batch script calling the Node program. For consistency, let's call it `hello.bat`:

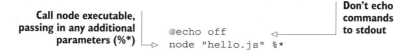

Call node executable, passing in any additional parameters (%*)

```
@echo off
node "hello.js" %*
```

Don't echo commands to stdout

Now we can execute our hello.js program by simply running the following:

```
$ hello tom
hello tom
```

Running it as a child process requires the .bat extension:

```
var cp = require('child_process');
cp.execFile('hello.bat', ['billy'], function (err, stdout) {
  console.log(stdout); // hello billy
});
```

Executables on UNIX

To turn a Node program into an executable script on most UNIX systems, we don't need a separate batch file like in Windows; we simply modify hello.js itself by adding the following to the top of the file:

```
#!/usr/bin/env node                  ←——    Execute node command
console.log('hello', process.argv[2]);      wherever it's found in
                                             user's environment
```

Then to actually make the file executable, we run the following command:

```
$ chmod +x hello.js
```

We can then run the command like this:

```
$ ./hello.js jim
hello jim
```

The file can be renamed as well to look more like a standalone program:

```
$ mv hello.js hello
$ ./hello jane
hello jane
```

Executing this program as a child process will look the same as its command-line counterpart:

```
var cp = require('child_process');
cp.execFile('./hello', ['bono'], function (err, stdout) {
  console.log(stdout); // hello bono
});
```

> **PUBLISHING EXECUTABLE FILES IN NPM**   For publishing packages that contain executable files, use the UNIX conventions, and npm will make the proper adjustments for Windows.

TECHNIQUE 61   Forking Node modules

Web workers (http://mng.bz/UG63) provide the browser and JavaScript an elegant way to run computationally intense tasks off the main thread with a built-in communication stream between the parent and worker. This removes the painful work of breaking up computation into pieces in order to not upset the user experience. In Node, we have the same concept, with a slightly different API with fork. This helps us break out any heavy lifting into a separate process, keeping our event loop running smoothly.

PROBLEM

You want to manage separate Node processes.

SOLUTION

Use fork (see figure 8.8).

DISCUSSION

Sometimes it's useful to have separate Node processes. One such case is computation. Since Node is single-threaded, computational tasks directly affect the performance of the whole process. This may be acceptable for certain jobs, but when it comes to network programming, it'll severely affect performance since requests can't be serviced when the process is tied up. Running these types of tasks in a forked process allows the main application to stay responsive. Another use of forking is for sharing file descriptors, where a child can accept an incoming connection received by the parent process.

Node provides a nice way to communicate between other Node programs. Under the hood, it sets up the following stdio configuration:

```
stdio: [ 0, 1, 2, 'ipc' ]
```

This means that, by default, all output and input are directly inherited from the parent; there's no child.stdin, child.stdout, or child.stderr:

```
var cp = require('child_process');
var child = cp.fork('./myChild');
```

If you want to provide an I/O configuration that behaves like the spawn defaults (meaning you get a child.stdin, and so on), you can use the silent option:

```
var cp = require('child_process');
var child = cp.fork('./myChild', { silent: true });
```

> **INTERNALS OF INTERPROCESS COMMUNICATION**   Although a number of mechanisms exist to provide interprocess communication (IPC; see http://mng.bz/LGKD), Node IPC channels will use either a UNIX domain socket (http://mng.bz/1189) or a Windows named pipe (http://mng.bz/262Q).

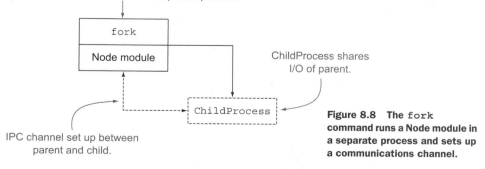

Figure 8.8   The fork command runs a Node module in a separate process and sets up a communications channel.

Communicating with forked Node modules

The fork method opens up an IPC channel that allows message passing between Node processes. On the child side, it exposes process.on('message') and process.send() as mechanisms for receiving and sending messages. On the parent side, it provides child.on('message') and child.send().

Let's make a simple echo module that sends back any message received from the parent:

Send message back to parent

```
process.on('message', function (msg) {
    process.send(msg);
});
```

When child receives a message, this handler will be called

An application can now consume this module using fork:

Log out echoed message

```
var cp = require('child_process');
var child = cp.fork('./child');
child.on('message', function (msg) {
    console.log('got a message from child', msg);
});
child.send('sending a string');
```

When parent receives a message, this handler will be called

Send message to child process

Sending data between the processes maintains the type information, which means you can send any valid JSON value over the wire and it retains the type:

```
child.send(230);
child.send('a string');
child.send(true);
child.send(null);
child.send({ an: 'object' });
```

Disconnecting from forked Node modules

Since we're opening an IPC channel between the parent and child, both stay alive until the child is disconnected (or exits some other way). If you need to disconnect the IPC channel, you can do that explicitly from the parent process:

```
child.disconnect();
```

TECHNIQUE 62   **Running jobs**

When you need to run *routine* computational jobs, forking processes on demand will quickly eat up your CPU resources. It's better to keep a job pool of available Node processes ready for work. This technique takes a look at that.

PROBLEM

You have routine jobs that you don't want to run on the main event loop.

SOLUTION

Use fork and manage a pool of workers.

DISCUSSION

We can use the IPC channel built into fork to create a pattern for handling computationally intensive tasks (or jobs). It builds upon our last technique, but adds an important constraint: when the parent sends a task to the child, it expects to receive exactly one result. Here's how this works in the parent process:

```
function doWork (job, cb) {
  var child = cp.fork('./worker');          Send job to the
  child.send(job);                   ◄────   child process
  child.once('message', function (result) {    ◄─
    cb(null, result);
  });                                             Expect child to respond
}                                                 with exactly one message
                                                  providing the result
```

But receiving a result is only one of the possible outcomes. To build resilience into our doWork function, we'll account for

- The child exiting for any reason
- Unexpected errors (like a closed IPC channel or failure to fork)

Handling those in code will involve a couple more listeners:

```
child.once('error', function (err) {    Unexpected error; kill
  cb(err);                              the process as it's
  child.kill();                  ◄────  likely unusable
});
child.once('exit', function (code, signal) {
  cb(new Error('Child exited with code: ' + code));
});
```

This is a good start, but we run the risk of calling our callback more than once in the case where the worker finished the job but then later exited or had an error. Let's add some state and clean things up a bit:

```
function doWork (job, cb) {
  var child = cp.fork('./worker');      Track if callback
  var cbTriggered = false;        ◄──   was called

  child                    ◄─
    .once('error', function (err) {     Message will never be
      if (!cbTriggered) {               triggered if an error or exit
        cb(err);                        happens, so we don't need
        cbTriggered = true;             cbTriggered check
      }
      child.kill();
    })
    .once('exit', function (code, signal) {
      if (!cbTriggered)
        cb(new Error('Child exited with code: ' + code));
    })
    .once('message', function (result) {
      cb(null, result);
      cbTriggered = true;
    })
    .send(job);
}
```

So far we've only looked at the parent process. The child worker takes in a job, and sends exactly one message back to the parent when completed:

```
process.on('message', function (job) {
  // do work
  process.send(result);
});
```

8.2.1   Job pooling

Currently, our doWork function will spin up a new child process every time we need to do some work. This isn't free, as the Node documentation states:

> *These child Nodes are still whole new instances of V8. Assume at least 30ms startup and 10mb memory for each new Node. That is, you cannot create many thousands of them.*

A performant way to work around this is not to spin off a new process whenever you want to do something computationally expensive, but rather to maintain a pool of long-running processes that can handle the load.

Let's expand our doWork function, creating a module for handling a worker pool. Here are some additional constraints we'll add:

- Only fork up to as many worker processes as CPUs on the machine.
- Ensure new work gets an available worker process and not one that's currently in-process.
- When no worker processes are available, maintain a queue of tasks to execute as processes become available.
- Fork processes on demand.

Let's take a look at the code to implement this:

```
var cp = require('child_process');
var cpus = require('os').cpus().length; )

module.exports = function (workModule) {
  var awaiting = [];
  var readyPool = [];
  var poolSize = 0;

  return function doWork (job, cb) {
    if (!readyPool.length && poolSize > cpus)
      return awaiting.push([ doWork, job, cb ]);

    var child = readyPool.length
      ? readyPool.shift()
      : (poolSize++, cp.fork(workModule));
    var cbTriggered = false;

    child
```

Grab number of CPUs

Keep list of tasks that are queued to run when all processes are in use

Keep list of worker processes that are ready for work

Keep track of how many worker processes exist

If no worker processes are available and we've reached our limit, queue work to be run later

Grab next available child, or fork a new process (incrementing the poolSize)

```
            .removeAllListeners()
            .once('error', function (err) {
              if (!cbTriggered) {
                cb(err);
                cbTriggered = true;
              }
              child.kill();
            })
            .once('exit', function () {
              if (!cbTriggered)
                cb(new Error('Child exited with code: ' + code));
              poolSize--;
              var childIdx = readyPool.indexOf(child);
              if (childIdx > -1) readyPool.splice(childIdx, 1);
            })
            .once('message', function (msg) {
              cb(null, msg);
              cbTriggered = true;
              readyPool.push(child);
              if (awaiting.length) setImmediate.apply(null, awaiting.shift());
            })
            .send(job);
        }
    }
```

Remove any listeners that exist on child, ensuring that a child process will always have only one listener attached for each event at a time

If child exits for any reason, ensure it's removed from the readyPool

Child is ready again; add back to readyPool and run next awaiting task (if any)

APPLYING WHAT YOU'VE LEARNED Other constraints may apply depending on the needs of the pool, for example, retrying jobs on failure or killing long-running jobs. How would you implement a retry or timeout using the preceding example?

8.2.2 Using the pooler module

Let's say we want to run a computationally intensive task based on a user's request to our server. First, let's expand our child worker process to simulate an intensive task:

Actual work happens here; in our case, we'll simply generate a CPU load on the child

Receive task from the parent

Send result of task back to the parent

```
process.on('message', function (job) {
    for (var i = 0; i < 1000000000; i++);
    process.send('finished: ' + job);
});
```

Now that we have a sample child process to run, let's put this all together with a simple application that uses the pooler module and worker modules:

Create job pool around the worker module

Include pooler module to make job pools

Run job on every request to the server, responding with the result

```
var http = require('http');
var makePool = require('./pooler');
var runJob = makePool('./worker');

http.createServer(function (req, res) {
    runJob('some dummy job', function (er, data) {
```

```
        if (er) return res.end('got an error:' + er.message);
        res.end(data);
      });
    }).listen(3000);
```

Pooling saves the overhead of spinning up and destroying child processes. It makes use of the communications channels built into `fork` and allows Node to be used effectively for managing jobs across a set of child processes.

> **GOING FURTHER**   To further investigate job pools, check out the third-party `compute-cluster` module (https://github.com/lloyd/node-compute-cluster).

We've discussed asynchronous child process execution, which is when you need to juggle multiple points of I/O, like servers. But sometimes you just want to execute commands one after another without the overhead. Let's look at that next.

8.3   *Working synchronously*

Non-blocking I/O is important for keeping the event loop humming along without having to wait for an unwieldy child process to finish. However, it has extra coding overhead that isn't pleasant when you want things to block. A good example of this is writing shell scripts. Thankfully, synchronous child processes are also available.

TECHNIQUE 63   Synchronous child processes

Synchronous child process methods are recent additions to the Node scene. They were first introduced in Node 0.12 to address a very real problem in a performant and familiar manner: shell scripting. Before Node 0.12, clever but nonperformant hacks were used to get synchronous-like behavior. Now, synchronous methods are a first-class citizen.

In this technique we'll cover all the synchronous methods available in the child process modules.

PROBLEM
You want to execute commands synchronously.

SOLUTION
Use `execFileSync`, `spawnSync`, and `execFile`.

DISCUSSION
By now, we hope these synchronous methods look extremely familiar. In fact, they're the same in their function signatures and purpose as we've discussed previously in this chapter, with one important distinction—*they block and run to completion* when called.

If you just want to execute a single command and get output synchronously, use `execFileSync`:

```
var ex = require('child_process').execFileSync;      // Extract execFileSync method
var stdout = ex('echo', ['hello']).toString();       // as ex for a shorthand way to
console.log(stdout);                                 // refer to it
```

Outputs "hello" → `console.log(stdout);`

Extract execFileSync method as ex for a shorthand way to refer to it

execFileSync returns a Buffer of the output, which is then converted to a UTF-8 string and assigned to stdout

If you want to execute multiple commands synchronously and programmatically where the input of one depends on the output of another, use `spawnSync`:

Run ps aux and grep node synchronously ⌐→

Extract spawnSync method as sp for a shorthand way to refer to it

```
var sp = require('child_process').spawnSync;  ◄─┘
var ps = sp('ps', ['aux']);
var grep = sp('grep', ['node'], {
  input: ps.stdout,         ◄─
  encoding: 'utf8'
});
console.log(grep);
```

Indicate all resulting stdio should be in UTF-8 ⌐→

Pass stdout Buffer from ps aux as input to grep node

The resulting synchronous child process contains a lot of detail of what happened, which is another advantage of using `spawnSync`:

Signal used to end the process ⌐→

Exit status of the process

Output of all the stdio streams used in the child process; we can see that index 1 (stdout) has data

```
{ status: 0,          ◄─
  signal: null,
  output:          ◄─
    [ null,
      'wavded 4376 ... 9:03PM 0:00.00 (node)\n
       wavded 4400 ... 9:11PM 0:00.10 node spawnSync.js\n',
      '' ],
  pid: 4403,
  stdout: 'wavded ... 9:03PM 0:00.00 (node)\n
   wavded 4400 ... 9:11PM 0:00.10 node spawnSync.js\n',  ◄─
  stderr: '',          ◄─
  envPairs:
    [ 'USER=wavded',
      'EDITOR=vim',
      'NODE_PATH=/Users/wavded/.nvm/v0.11.12/lib/node_modules:',
      ... ],
  options:
    { input: <Buffer 55 53 45 52 20 20 20 ... >,
      encoding: 'utf8',
      file: 'grep',
      args: [ 'grep', 'node' ],
      stdio: [ [Object], [Object], [Object] ] },
  args: [ 'grep', 'node' ],
  file: 'grep' } [          ◄──────  Executable file
```

PID of the process ⌐→

stdout output for the process

stderr output for the process ⌐→

Environment variables present when the process ran

Options used to create the process; we can see our input buffer from ps aux here ⌐→

Arguments used to execute the process ⌐→

Lastly, there's `execSync`, which executes a subshell synchronously and runs the commands given. This can be handy when writing shell scripts in JavaScript:

Extract execSync method as ex for a shorthand way to refer to it ⌐→

```
var ex = require('child_process').execSync;
var stdout = ex('ps aux | grep').toString();  ◄─
console.log(stdout);
```

Execute shell command synchronously and return the output as a string

This will output the following:

```
wavded 4425 29.7 0.2 ... 0:00.10 node execSync.js
wavded 4427 1.5 0.0 ... /bin/sh -c ps aux | grep node
wavded 4429 0.5 0.0 ... grep node
wavded 4376 0.0 0.0 ... (node)
```

Output shows we're executing a subshell with execSync

Error handing with synchronous child process methods

If a non-zero exit status is returned in execSync or execFileSync, an exception will be thrown. The error object will include everything we saw returned using spawnExec. We'll have access to important things like the status code and stderr stream:

```
var ex = require('child-process').execFileSync;
try {
  ex('cd', ['non-existent-dir'], {
    encoding: 'utf8'
  });
} catch (err) {
  console.error('exit status was', err.status);
  console.error('stderr', err.stderr);
}
```

Executing cd on nonexistent directory gives non-zero exit status

Although more verbose than toString(), setting encoding to UTF-8 here will set it for all our stdio streams when we handle the error

This program yields the following output:

```
exit status was 1
stderr /usr/bin/cd: line 4:cd:
  non-existent-dir: No such file or directory
```

We talked errors in execFile and execFileSync. What about spawnSync? Since spawnSync returns everything that happens when running the process, it doesn't throw an exception. Therefore, you're responsible to check the success or failure.

8.4　Summary

In this chapter you learned to integrate different uses of external applications in Node by using the child_process module. Here are some tips in summary:

- Use execFile in cases where you just need to execute an external application. It's fast, simple, and safer when dealing with user input.

- Use spawn when you want to do something more with the I/O of the child process, or when you expect the process to have a large amount of output. It provides a nice streamable interface, and is also safer when dealing with user input.

- Use exec when you want to access your shell's facilities (pipes, redirects, blobs). Many shells allow running multiple applications in one go. Be careful with user input though, as it's never a good idea to put untrusted input into an exec call.

- Use fork when you want to run a Node module as a separate process. This enables computation and file descriptor handling (like an incoming socket) to be handled off the main Node process.

- Detach spawned processes you want to survive after a Node process dies. This allows Node to be used to set up long-running processes and let them live on their own.
- Pool a cluster of Node processes and use the built-in IPC channel to save the overhead of starting and destroying processes on every fork. This is useful for building computational clusters of Node processes.

This concludes our dive into Node fundamentals. We focused on specific core module functionality, focusing on idiomatic Node principals. In the next section, our focus will expand beyond core concepts into real-world development recipes.

Part 2

Real-world recipes

In the first section of this book, we took a deep dive into Node's standard library. Now we'll take a broader look at real-world recipes many Node programs encounter. Node is most famously known for writing fast network-based programs (high-performance HTTP parsing, ease-of-use frameworks like Express), so we devoted a whole chapter to web development.

In addition, there are chapters to help you grasp what a Node program is doing preemptively with tests, and post-mortem with debugging. In closing, we set you up for success when deploying your applications to production environments.

The Web: Build leaner and meaner web applications

This chapter covers

- Using Node for client-side development
- Node in the browser
- Server-side techniques and WebSockets
- Migrating Express 3 applications to Express 4
- Testing web applications
- Full-stack frameworks and real-time services

The purpose of this chapter is to bring together the things you've learned about networking, buffers, streams, and testing to write better web applications with Node. There are practical techniques for browser-based JavaScript, server-side code, and testing.

Node can help you to write better web applications, no matter what your background is. If you're a client-side developer, then you'll find it can help you work more efficiently. You can use it for preprocessing client-side assets and for managing client-side workflows. If you've ever wanted to quickly spin up an HTTP server that builds your CSS or CoffeeScript for a single-page web app, or even just a website, then Node is a great choice.

The previous book in this series, *Node.js in Action*, has a detailed introduction to web development with Connect and Express, and also templating languages like Jade and EJS. In this chapter we'll build on some of these ideas, so if you're completely new to Node, we recommend reading *Node.js in Action* as well. If you're already using Express, then we hope you'll find something new in this chapter; we've included techniques for structuring Express applications to make them easier to scale as your projects grow and mature.

The first section in this chapter has some techniques that focus on the browser. If you're a perplexed front-end developer who's been using Node because your client-side libraries need it, then you should start here. If you're a server-side developer who wants to bring Node to the browser, then skip ahead to technique 66 to see how to use Node modules in the browser.

9.1   Front-end techniques

This section is all about Node and its relationship to client-side technology. You'll see how to use the DOM in Node and Node in the DOM, and run your own local development servers. If you've come to Node from a web design background, then these techniques should help you get into the swing of things before we dive in to deeper server-side examples. But if you're from a server-side background, then you might like to see how Node can help automate front-end chores.

The first technique shows you how to create a quick, static server for simple websites or single-page web applications.

TECHNIQUE 64   Quick servers for static sites

Sometimes you just want to start a web server to work on a static site, or a single-page web application. Node's a good choice for this, because it's easy to get a web server running. It can also neatly encapsulate client-side workflows, making it easier to collaborate with others. Rather than manually running programs over your client-side JavaScript and CSS, you can write Node programs that you can share with other people.

This technique introduces three solutions for starting up a web server: a short Connect script, a command-line web server, and a mini–build system that uses Grunt.

PROBLEM

You want to quickly start a web server so you can develop a static site, or a single-page application.

SOLUTION

Use Connect, a command-line web server, or a client-side workflow tool like Grunt.

DISCUSSION

Plain old HTML, JavaScript, CSS, and images can be viewed in a browser without a server. But because most web development tasks end up with files on a server somewhere, you often need a server just to make a static site. It's a chore, but it doesn't need to be! The power of browsers also means you can create sophisticated web applications by contacting external web APIs: single-page web applications, or so-called *serverless apps.*

In the case of serverless web applications, you can work more efficiently by using build tools to preprocess and package client-side assets. This technique will show you how to start a web server for developing static sites, and also how to use tools like Grunt to get a small project going without too much trouble.

Although you could use Node's built in `http` module to serve static sites, it's a lot of work. You'll need to do things like detect the content type of each file to send the right HTTP headers. While the `http` core module is a solid foundation, you can save time by using a third-party module.

First, let's look at how to start a web server with Connect, the HTTP middleware module used to create the popular Express web framework. The first listing demonstrates just how simple this is.

Listing 9.1 A quick static web server

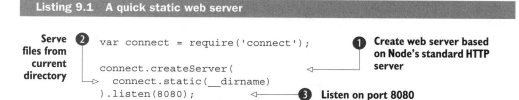

```
var connect = require('connect');

connect.createServer(
    connect.static(__dirname)
).listen(8080);
```

Serve files from current directory **②**

① Create web server based on Node's standard HTTP server

③ Listen on port 8080

To use the example in listing 9.1, you'll need to install Connect. You can do that by running `npm install connect`, but it's a better idea to create a package.json file so it's easier for other people to see how your project works. Even if your project is a simple static site, creating a package.json file will help your project to grow in the future. All you need to do is memorize these commands: `npm init` and `npm install --save connect`. The first command creates a manifest file for the current directory, and the second will install Connect and save it to the list of dependencies in the new package.json file. Learn these and you'll be creating new Node projects in no time.

The `createServer` method **①** is derived from Node's `http.createServer`, but it's wrapped with a few things that Connect adds behind the scenes. The `static` server middleware component **②** is used to serve files from the current directory (`__dirname` with two underscores means "current directory"), but you can change the directory if you like. For example, if you have client-side assets in public/, then you can use `connect.static(__dirname + '/public')` instead.

Finally, the server is set to listen on port 8080 **③**. That means if you run this script and visit http://localhost:8080/file.html in a browser, you should see file.html.

If you've been sent a bunch of HTML files from a designer, and you want to use a server to view them because they make use of paths to images and CSS files with a leading forward slash (/), then you can also use a command-line web server. There are many of these available on npm, and they all support different options. One example is glance by Jesse Keane. You can find it on GitHub at https://github.com/jarofghosts/glance, and on npm as glance.

To use glance on the command line, navigate to a directory where you have some HTML files that you want to look at. Then install glance systemwide with npm install --global glance, and type glance. Now go to http://localhost:61403/file, where *file* is a file you want to look at, and you should see it in your browser.

glance can be configured in various ways—you can change the port from 61403 to something else with --port, and specify the directory to be served with --dir. Type --help to get a list of options. It also has some nice defaults for things like 404s—figure 9.1 shows what a 404 looks like.

The third way of running a web server is to use a task runner like Grunt. This allows you to automate your client-side tasks in a way that others can replicate. Using Grunt is a bit like a combination of the previous two approaches: it requires a web server module like Connect, and a command-line tool.

To use Grunt for a client-side project you'll need to do three things:

1 Install the grunt-cli module.
2 Make a package.json to manage the dependencies for your project.
3 Use a Grunt plugin that runs a web server.

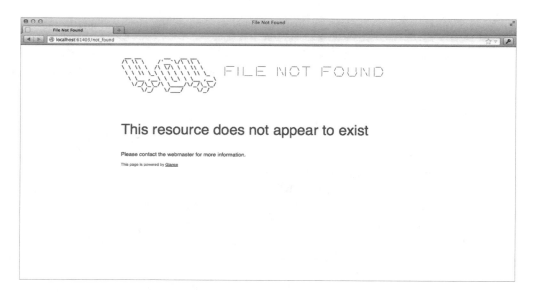

Figure 9.1   Glance has built-in pages for errors.

The first step is easy: install `grunt-cli` as a global module with `npm install -g grunt-cli`. Now you can run Grunt tasks from any project that includes them by typing `grunt`.

Next, make a new directory for your project. Change to this new directory and type `npm init`—you can press Return to accept each of the defaults. Now you need to install a web server module: `npm install --save-dev grunt grunt-contrib-connect` will do the job.

The previous command also installed `grunt` as a development dependency. The reason for this is it locks Grunt to the current version—if you look at package.json you'll see something like `"grunt": "~0.4.2"`, which means Grunt was installed first at `0.4.2`, but newer versions on the `0.4` branch will be used in the future. The popularity of modules like Grunt forced npm to support something known as *peer dependencies*. Peer dependencies allow Grunt plugins to express a dependency on a specific version of Grunt, so the Connect module we'll use actually has a `peerDependencies` property in its package.json file. The benefit of this is you can be sure plugins will work as Grunt changes—otherwise, as Grunt's API changes, plugins might just break with no obvious cause.

> **ALTERNATIVES TO GRUNT**   At the time of writing, Grunt was the most popular build system for Node. But new alternatives have appeared and are rapidly gaining adoption. One example is Gulp (http://gulpjs.com/), which takes advantage of Node's streaming APIs and has a light syntax that is easy to learn.

In case all this is new to you, we've included a screenshot of what your project should look like in figure 9.2.

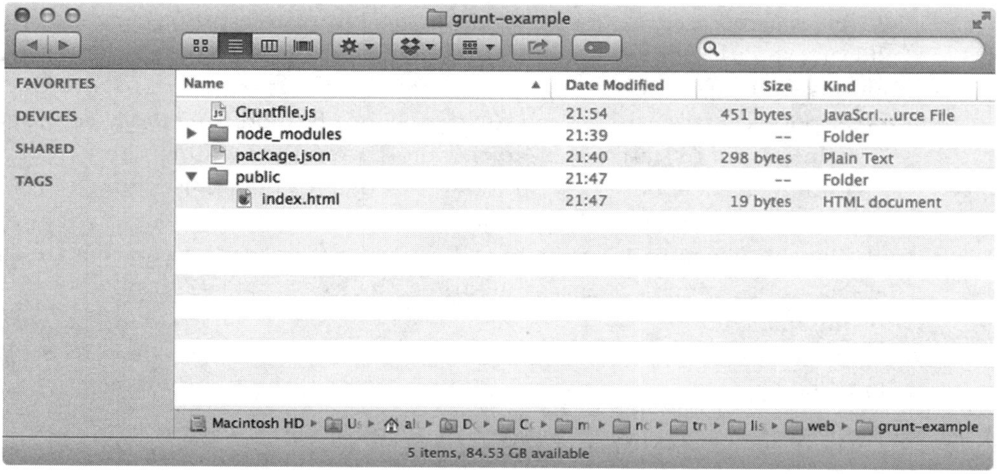

Figure 9.2 Projects that use Grunt typically have a package.json and a Gruntfile.js.

Now that we have a fresh project set up, the final thing to do is create a file called Gruntfile.js. This file contains a list of tasks that `grunt` will run for you. The next listing shows an example that uses the `grunt-contrib-connect` module.

Listing 9.2 A Gruntfile for serving static files

All Gruntfiles export a function ❶

This loads ❷ Connect plugin

The base path ❸ for static files

Default ❹ command is aliased here

```
module.exports = function(grunt) {
    grunt.loadNpmTasks('grunt-contrib-connect');

    grunt.initConfig({
      connect: {
        server: {
          options: {
            port: 8080,
            base: 'public',
            keepalive: true
          }
        }
      }
    });

    grunt.registerTask('default', ['connect:server']);
};
```

You should also create a directory called `public` with an index.html file—the HTML file can contain anything you like. After that, type `grunt connect` from the same directory as your Gruntfile.js, and the server should start. You can also type `grunt` by itself, because we set the default task to `connect:server` ❹.

Gruntfiles use Node's standard module system, and receive an object called `grunt` ❶ that can be used to define tasks. Plugins are loaded with `grunt.loadNpmTasks`, allowing you to reference modules installed with npm ❷. Most plugins have different options, and these are set by passing objects to `grunt.initConfig`—we've defined a server port and base path, which you can change by modifying the `base` property ❸.

Using Grunt to start a web server is more work than writing a tiny Connect script or running `glance`, but if you take a look at Grunt's plugin list (http://gruntjs.com/plugins), you'll see over 2,000 entries that cover everything from building optimized CSS files to Amazon S3 integration. If you've ever needed to concatenate client-side JavaScript or generate image sprites, then chances are there's a plugin that will help you automate it.

In the next technique you'll learn how to reuse client-side code in Node. We'll also show you how to render web content inside Node processes.

TECHNIQUE 65   Using the DOM in Node

With a bit of work, it's possible to simulate a browser in Node. This is useful if you want to make web scrapers—programs that convert web pages into structured content. This is technically rather more complicated than it may seem. Browsers don't just provide JavaScript runtimes; they also have Document Object Model (DOM) APIs that don't exist in Node.

Such a rich collection of libraries has evolved around the DOM that it's sometimes hard to imagine solving problems without them. If only there were a way to run libraries like jQuery inside Node! In this technique you'll learn how to do this by using browser JavaScript in a Node program.

PROBLEM

You want to reuse client-side code that depends on the DOM in Node, or render entire web pages.

SOLUTION

Use a third-party module that provides a DOM layer.

DISCUSSION

The W3C DOM is a well-defined standard. When designers struggle with browser incompatibilities, they're often dealing with the fact that standards require a degree of interpretation, and browser manufacturers have naturally interpreted the standards slightly differently. If your goal is just to run JavaScript that depends on the JavaScript DOM APIs, then you're in luck: these standards can be re-created well enough that you can run popular client-side libraries in Node.

One early solution to this problem was jsdom (https://github.com/tmpvar/jsdom). This module accepts an *environment* specification and then provides a window object. If you install it with npm install -g jsdom, you should be able to run the following example:

```
var jsdom = require('jsdom');                                            HTML you want  ❶
jsdom.env(                                                                  to process
    '<p class="intro">Welcome to Node in Practice</p>',     ◀──
    ['http://code.jquery.com/jquery.js'],
    function(errors, window) {
        console.log('Intro:', window.$('.intro').text());   ◀─┐
    }
);                                                  Access to $() from
                                                    jQuery now possible  ❸
```

External JavaScript libraries jsdom will fetch ❷

This example takes in HTML ❶, fetches some remote scripts ❷, and then gives you a window object that looks a lot like a browser window object ❸. It's good enough that you can use jQuery to manipulate the HTML snippet—jQuery works as if it's running in a browser. This is useful because now you can write scripts that process HTML documents in the way you're probably used to: rather than using a parser, you can query and manipulate HTML using the tools you're familiar with. This is amazing for writing succinct code for tasks like web scraping, which would otherwise be frustrating and tedious.

Others have iterated on jsdom's approach, simplifying the underlying dependencies. If you really just want to process HTML in a jQuery-like way, then you could use cheerio (https://npmjs.org/package/cheerio). This module is more suited to web scraping, so if you're writing something that downloads, processes, and indexes HTML, then cheerio is a good choice.

In the following example, you'll see how to use `cheerio` to process HTML from a real web page. The actual HTML is from manning.com/index.html, but as designs change frequently, we've kept a copy of the page we used in our code samples. You can find it in cheerio-manning/index.html. The following listing opens the HTML file and queries it using a CSS selector, courtesy of `cheerio`.

Listing 9.3 Scraping a web page with `cheerio`

```
                    var cheerio = require('cheerio');
                    var fs = require('fs');

Load HTML   ❶  fs.readFile('./index.html', 'utf8', function(err, html) {
   content         var $ = cheerio.load(html);
                    var releases = $('.Releases a strong');                  ◄┐  Query it using
                                                                             ❷  CSS selector
                    releases.each(function(i) {
                      console.log('New release:', this.text());              ◄┐  Extract
                    });                                                      ❸  the text
                });
```

The HTML is loaded with `fs.readFile`. If you were doing this for real then you'd probably want to download the page using HTTP—feel free to replace `fs.readFile` with `http.get` to fetch Manning's index page over the network. We have a detailed example of `http.get` in chapter 7, technique 51, "Following redirects."

Once the HTML has been fetched, it's passed to `cheerio.load` ❶. Setting the result as a variable called $ is just a convention that will make your code easier to read if you're used to jQuery, but you could name it something else.

Now that everything is set up, you can query the HTML; `$('.Releases a strong')` is used ❷ to query the document for the latest books that have been released. They're in a `div` with a class of `Releases`, as anchor tags.

Each element is iterated over using `releases.each`, just like in jQuery. The callback's context is changed to be the current element, so `this.text()` is called to get the text contained by the node ❸.

Because Node has such a wide collection of third-party modules, you could take this example and make all sorts of amazing things with it. Add Redis for caching and queueing websites to process, then scrape the results and throw it at Elasticsearch, and you've got your own search engine!

Now you've seen how to run JavaScript intended for browsers in Node, but what about the opposite? You might have some Node code that you want to reuse client-side, or you might want to just use Node's module system to organize your client-side code. Much like we can simulate the DOM in Node, we can do the same in the browser. In the next technique you'll learn how to do this by running your Node scripts in browsers.

Using Node modules in the browser

One of Node's selling points for JavaScript is that you can reuse your existing browser programming skills on servers. But what about *reusing* Node code in browsers without any changes? Wouldn't that be cool? Here's an example: you've defined data models in Node that do things like data validation, and you want to reuse them in the browser to automatically display error messages when data is invalid.

This is almost possible, but not quite: unfortunately browsers have quirks that must be ironed out. Also, important features like `require` don't exist in client-side JavaScript. In this technique you'll see how you can take code intended for Node, and convert it to work with most web browsers.

PROBLEM

You want to use `require()` to structure your client-side code, or reuse entire Node modules in the browser.

SOLUTION

Use a program like Browserify that is capable of converting Node JavaScript into browser-friendly code.

DISCUSSION

In this technique we'll use Browserify (http://browserify.org/) to convert Node modules into browser-friendly code. Other solutions also exist, but at this point Browserify is one of the more mature and popular solutions. It doesn't just patch in support for `require()`, though: it can convert code that relies on Node's stream and network APIs. You can even use it to recursively convert modules from npm.

To see how it works, we'll first look at a short self-contained example. To get started, install Browserify with npm: `npm install -g browserify`. Once you've got Browserify installed, you can convert your Node modules into Browser scripts with `browserify index.js -o bundle.js`. Any `require` statements will cause the files to be included in bundle.js, so you shouldn't change this file. Instead, overwrite it whenever your original files have changed.

Listing 9.4 shows a sample Node program that uses `EventEmitter` and `utils.inherit` to make the basis of a small messaging class.

Listing 9.4 Node modules in the browser

```
var EventEmitter = require('events').EventEmitter;        ◁─┐    Load modules with
var util = require('util');                                 │    require() as you
                                                          ❶   usually would.

function MessageBus(options) {
  EventEmitter.call(this, options);
  this.on('message', this.messageReceived.bind(this));
}

util.inherits(MessageBus, EventEmitter);                 ◁─┐    EventEmitter can
                                                            │    be inherited using
MessageBus.prototype.messageReceived = function(message) { ❷  util.inherits.
  console.log('RX:', message);
```

```
};

var messageBus = new MessageBus();
messageBus.emit('message', 'Hello world!');
```

Running Browserify on this script generates a bundle that's about 1,000 lines long! But we can use `require` as we would in any Node program ❶, and the Node modules we know and love will work, as you can see in listing 9.4 by the use of `util.inherits` and `EventEmitter` ❷.

With Browserify, you can also use `require` and `module.exports`, which is better than having to juggle `<script>` tags. The previous example can be extended to do just that. In listing 9.5, Browserify is used to make a client-side script that can load `MessageBus` and jQuery with `require`, and then modify the DOM when messages are emitted.

Listing 9.5   Node modules in the browser

```
var MessageBus = require('./messagebus');
var messageBus = new MessageBus();
var $ = require('jquery')(window);              ◀── ❶ jQuery can be loaded
                                                     with Browserify!

messageBus.on('message', function(msg) {
  $('#messages').append('<p>' + msg + '</p>');
});
                                                ❷ jQuery's DOM ready
$(function() {                              ◀──   function can be used.
  messageBus.emit('message', 'Hello from example 2');
});
```

By creating a package.json file with `jquery` as a dependency, you can load jQuery using Browserify ❶. Here we've used it to attach a `DOMContentLoaded` listener ❷ and append paragraphs to a container element when messages are received.

Source maps

If the JavaScript files you generate with Browserify raise errors, then it can be hard to untangle the line numbers in stack traces, because they refer to line numbers in the monolithic bundle. If you include the `--debug` flag when building the bundle, then Browserify will generate mappings that point to the original files and line numbers.

These mappings require a compatible debugger—you'll also need to tell your browser's debugging tools to use them. In Chrome you'll need to select *Enable source maps*, under the options in Chrome's DevTools.

To make this work, all you need to do is add `module.exports = MessageBus` to the example from listing 9.4, and then generate the bundle with `browserify index.js -o bundle.js`, where index.js is listing 9.5. Browserify will dutifully follow the `require` statements from index.js to pull in jQuery from `./node_modules` and the `MessageBus` class from messagebus.js.

Because people might forget how to build the script, you can add a `scripts` entry to your package.json file, like this: `"build": "browserify index.js -o bundle.js"`. The downloadable code samples for this book include both a sample package.json file and a suitable HTML file for running the entire example in a browser.

There's another way to build bundles with Browserify: by using Browserify as a module in a Node program. To use it, you need to create a `Browserify` instance ❶ and then tell it what files you want to build ❷:

Specify files you ❷
want to bundle

```
var browserify = require('browserify');
var b = browserify();
b.add('./index.js');
b.bundle().pipe(process.stdout);
```

❶ **Create Browserify instance**

You could use this as part of a more complex build process, or put in a Grunt task to automate your build process. Now that you've seen how to use Node modules in the browser and how to simulate the browser in Node, it's time to learn how to improve your server-side web applications.

9.2 Server-side techniques

This section includes general techniques for building web applications. If you're already using Express, then you'll be able to use these techniques to improve how your Express programs are organized. Express aims to be simple, which makes it flexible, but sometimes it's not easy to see how to use it in the best way. The patterns and solutions we've created have come from using Express to build commercial and open source web applications over the last few years. We hope they'll help you to write better web applications.

> **EXPRESS 3 AND 4**   The techniques in this section refer to Express 3. Most will work with Express 4, or may require minor modifications. For more about migrating to Express 4, see technique 75.

TECHNIQUE 67   **Express route separation**

The documentation and popular tutorials for Express usually organize all the code in a single file. In real projects, this eventually becomes unmanageable. This technique uses Node's module system to separate related routes into files, and also includes ways to get around the Express `app` object being in a different file.

PROBLEM

Your main Express application file has become extremely large, and you want a better way to organize all of those routes.

SOLUTION

Use route separation to split related routes into modules.

DISCUSSION

Express is a minimalist framework, so it doesn't hold your hand when it comes to organizing projects. Projects that start simple can become unwieldy if you don't pay attention. The secret to successfully organizing larger projects is to embrace Node's module system.

The first avenue of attack is routes, but you can apply this technique to every facet of development with Express. You can even treat applications as self-contained Node modules, and mount them within other applications.

Here's a typical example of some Express routes:

```
app.get('/notes', function(req, res, next) {              ⟵┐  This route displays
  db.notes.findAll(function(err, notes) {                      a list of notes.
    if (err) return next(err);
    res.send(notes);
  });
});

app.post('/notes', function(req, res, next) {             ⟵┐  This route is used
  db.notes.create(req.body.note, function(err, note) {         to create notes.
    if (err) return next(err);
    res.send(note);
  });
});
```

The full example project can be found in listings/web/route_separation/app_monolithic.js. It contains a set of CRUD routes for creating, finding, and updating notes. An application like this would have other CRUD routes as well: perhaps notes can be organized into notebooks, and there will definitely be some user account management, and extra features like setting reminders. Once you have about four or five of these sets of routes, the application file could be hundreds of lines of code.

If you wrote this project as a single, large file, then it would be prone to many problems. It would be easy to make mistakes where variables are accidentally global instead of local, so dangerous side effects can be encountered under certain conditions. Node has a built-in solution which can be applied to Express and other web frameworks: directories as modules.

To refactor your routes using modules, first create a directory called `routes`, or `controllers` if you prefer. Then create a file called index.js. In our case it'll be a simple three-line file that exports the notes routes:

```
module.exports = {                    ❶  Export each routing
  notes: require('./notes')              module like this
};
```

Here we have just one routing module, which can be loaded with `require` and a relative path ❶. Next, copy and paste the entire set of routes into routes/notes.js. Then delete the route definition part—for example, `app.get('/notes',,` and replace it with an export: `module.exports.index = function(req, res) {`.

The refactored files should look like the next listing.

Listing 9.6 A routing module without the rest of the application

```
var db = require('./../db');

module.exports.index = function(req, res, next) {
  db.notes.findAll(function(err, notes) {
    if (err) return next(err);
    res.send(notes);
  });
};

module.exports.create = function(req, res, next) {
  db.notes.create(req.body.note, function(err, note) {
    if (err) return next(err);
    res.send(note);
  });
};

module.exports.update = function(req, res, next) {
  db.notes.update(req.param('id'), req.body.note, function(err, note) {
    if (err) return next(err);
    res.send(note);
  });
};

module.exports.show = function(req, res, next) {
  db.notes.find(req.param('id'), function(err, note) {
    if (err) return next(err);
    res.send(note);
  });
};
```

❶ Export each routing function with a name that reflects its CRUD operation.

Each routing function is exported with a CRUD-inspired name (index, create, update, show) **❶**. The corresponding app.js file can now be cleared up. The next listing shows just how clean this can look.

Listing 9.7 A refactored app.js file

```
var express = require('express');
var app = express();
var routes = require('./routes');

app.use(express.bodyParser());

app.get('/notes', routes.notes.index);
app.post('/notes', routes.notes.create);
app.patch('/notes/:id', routes.notes.update);
app.get('/notes/:id', routes.notes.show);

module.exports = app;
```

❶ Load all routes at once

❷ Bind them to HTTP verb and partial URL

❸ Export app object

All of the routes can be loaded at once with require('./routes') **❶**. This is convenient and clean, because there are fewer require statements that would otherwise clutter app.js. All you need to do is remove the old route callbacks and add in references to each routing function ❷.

Don't put an `app.listen` call in this file; export app instead ❸. This makes it easier to test the application. Another advantage of exporting the `app` object is that you can easily load the `app.js` module from anywhere within the application. Express allows you to get and set configuration values, so making `app` accessible can be useful if you want to refer to these settings in places outside the routes. Also note that `res.app` is available from within routes, so you don't need to pass the `app` object around too often.

If you want to easily load app.js without creating a server, then name the application file app.js, and have a separate server.js file that calls `app.listen`. You can set up the `server` property in package.json to use `node server.js`, which allows people to start the application with `npm start`—you can also leave out the `server` property, because `node server.js` is the default, but it's better to define it so people know how you intend them to use it.

Directories as modules

This technique puts all of the routes in a directory, and then exports them with an index.js file so they can be loaded in one go with `require('./routes')`.

This pattern can be reused in other places. It's great for organizing middleware, database modules, and configuration files.

For an example of using directories as modules to organize configuration files, see technique 69.

The full example for this technique can be found in listings/web/route-separation, and it includes sample tests in case you want to unit test your own projects.

Properly organizing your Express projects is important, but there are also workflow issues that can slow down development. For example, when you're working on a web application, you'll typically make many small changes and then refresh the browser to see the results. Most Node frameworks require the process to be restarted before seeing the changes take effect, so the next technique explores how this works and how to efficiently solve this problem.

TECHNIQUE 68   Automatically restarting the server

Although Node comes with tools for monitoring changes to files, it can be a lot of work to use them productively. This technique looks at `fs.watch`, and introduces a popular third-party tool for automatically restarting web applications as files are edited.

PROBLEM

You need to restart your Node web application every time you edit files.

SOLUTION

Use a file watcher to restart the application automatically.

DISCUSSION

If you're used to languages like PHP or ASP, Node's in-process server-based model might seem unusual. One of the big differences about Node's model is that you need to restart the process when files change. If you think about how `require` and V8 work, then this makes sense—files are generally loaded and interpreted once.

One way to get around this is to detect when files change, and then restart the application. Node makes good use of non-blocking I/O, and one of the properties of non-blocking file system APIs is that listeners can be used to wait for specific events. To solve this problem, you could set up file system event handlers for all of the files in your project. Then, when files change, your event handler can restart the project.

Node provides an API for this in the `fs` module called `fs.watch`. At the time of writing, this API is unstable—that means it may be changed in subsequent versions of Node. This method has been covered in chapter 6, section 6.1.4. Let's look at how it could be used with a web application. Figure 9.8 shows a program that can watch and reload a simple web server.

Listing 9.8   Reloading a Node process

```
var fs = require('fs');
var exec = require('child_process').exec;

function watch() {
    var child = exec('node server.js');                                    ❶
    var watcher = fs.watch(__dirname + '/server.js', function(event) {
        console.log('File changed, reloading.');
        child.kill();                                                      ❸
        watcher.close();                                                   ❹
        watch();                                                           ❺
    });
}

watch();
```

- ❷ Use fs.watch to watch for changes to file
- ❶ Start web server process
- ❸ When file has changed, kill web server
- ❹ Close watcher
- ❺ Recursively call watcher function to start web server up again

Watching a file for changes with `fs.watch` is slightly convoluted, but you can use `fs.watchFile`, which is based on file polling instead of I/O events. The way listing 9.8 works is to start a child process—in this case `node server.js` ❶—and then watch that file for changes ❷. Starting and stopping processes is managed with the `child_process` core module, and the `kill` method is used to stop the child process ❸.

On Mac OS we found it's best to also stop watching the file with `watcher.close` ❹, although Node's documentation indicates that `fs.watch` should be "persistent." Once all of that is done, the `watch` function is called recursively to launch the web server again ❺.

This example could be run with a server.js file like this:

```
var http = require('http');
var server = http.createServer(function(req, res) {
  res.writeHead(200, { 'Content-Type': 'text/plain' });
```

```
    res.end('This is a super basic web application');
});
```

```
server.listen(8080);
```

This works, but it's not exactly elegant. And it's not complete, either. Most Node web applications consist of multiple files, so the file-watching logic will become more complicated. It's not enough to recurse over the parent directories, because there are lots of files that you don't want to watch—you don't want to watch the files in .git, and if you're writing an Express application you probably don't want to watch view templates, because they're loaded on demand without caching in development mode.

Suddenly automatically restarting Node programs seems less trivial, and that's where third-party modules can help. One of the most widely used modules that solves this problem is Remy Sharp's nodemon (http://nodemon.io/). It works well for watching Express applications out of the box, and you can even use it to automatically restart any kind of program, whether it's written in Node or Python, Ruby, and so on.

To try it out, type npm install -g nodemon, and then navigate to a directory that contains a Node web application. If you want to use a small sample script, you can use our example from listings/web/watch/server.js.

Start running and watching server.js by typing nodemon server.js, and you'll find you can edit the text in res.end and the change will be reflected the next time you load http://localhost:8080/.

You might notice a small delay before changes are visible—that's just Nodemon setting up fs.watch, or fs.watchFile if it's not available on your OS. You can force it to reload by typing rs and pressing Return.

Nodemon has some other features that will help you work on web applications. Typing nodemon --help will show a list of command-line options, but you can get greater, VCS-friendly control by creating a nodemon.json file. This allows you to specify an array of files to ignore, and you can also map file extensions to program names by using the execMap setting. Nodemon's documentation includes a sample file that illustrates each of the features.

The next listing is an example Nodemon configuration that you can adapt for your own projects.

Listing 9.9 Nodemon's configuration file

```
{
  "ignore": [              ◁——❶  A list of paths to ignore
    ".git",
    "node_modulesnode_modules"
  ],                             ❷  Automatically map .js files to
  "execMap": {        ◁————          use node with harmony flag
    "js": "node --harmony"
  },
  "watch": [      ◁——        Specify paths
    "test/fixtures/",   ❸    to watch
```

```
    "test/samples/"
  ],
  "env": {
    "NODE_ENV": "development"
  },
  "ext": "js json"
}
```

List environmental **4** variables

The basic options allow you to ignore specific paths **1**, and list multiple paths to watch **3**. This example uses `execMap` to automatically run `node` with the `--harmony` flag[1] for all JavaScript files **2**. Nodemon can also set environmental variables—just add some values to the `env` property **4**.

Once your workflow is streamlined thanks to Nodemon, the next thing to do is to improve how your project is configured. Most projects need some level of configuration—examples include the database connection details and authorization credentials for remote APIs. The next technique looks at ways to configure your web application so you can easily deploy it to multiple environments, run it in test mode, and even tweak how it behaves during local development.

TECHNIQUE 69   Configuring web applications

This technique looks at the common patterns for configuring Node web applications. We'll include examples for Express, but you can use these patterns with other web frameworks as well.

PROBLEM

You have configuration options that change between development, testing, and production.

SOLUTION

Use JSON configuration files, environmental variables, or a module for managing settings.

DISCUSSION

Most web applications require some configuration values to operate correctly: database connection strings, cache settings, and email server credentials are typical. There are many ways to store application settings, but before you install a third-party module to do it, consider your requirements:

- Is it acceptable to leave database credentials in your version control repository?
- Do you really need configuration files, or can you embed settings into the application?
- How can configuration values be accessed in different parts of the application?
- Does your deployment environment offer a way to store configuration values?

The first point depends on your project or organization's policies. If you're building an open source web application, you don't want to leave database accounts in the public repository, so configuration files might not be the best solution. You want people to

---

[1] `--harmony` is used to enable all of the newer ECMAScript features available to Node.

install your application quickly and easily, but you don't want to accidentally leak your passwords. Similarly, if you work in a large organization with database administrators, they might not be comfortable about letting everyone have direct access to databases.

In such cases, you can set configuration values as part of the deployment environment. Environmental variables are a standard way to configure the behavior of Unix and Windows programs, and you can access them with `process.env`. The basic example of this is switching between deployment environments, using the `NODE_ENV` setting. The following listing shows the pattern Express uses for storing configuration values.

Listing 9.10   Configuring an Express application

This callback will only run if NODE_ENV is set to development. ❷

Use app.get() to access settings. ❹

❶ **Use 3000 if the environmental variable PORT is not set.**

❸ **This callback will only run if NODE_ENV is set to production.**

```
var express = require('express');
var app = express();

app.set('port', process.env.PORT || 3000);

app.configure('development', function() {
  app.set('db', 'localhost/development');
});

app.configure('production', function() {
  app.set('db', 'db.example.com/production');
});

app.listen(app.get('port'), function() {
  console.log('Using database:', app.get('db'));
  console.log('Listening on port:', app.get('port'));
});
```

Express has a small API for setting application configuration values: `app.set`, `app.get` ❹, and `app.configure`. You can also use `app.enable` and `app.disable` to toggle Boolean values, and `app.enabled` and `app.disabled` to query them. The `app.configure` blocks are equivalent to `if (process.env.NODE_ENV === 'development')` ❷ and `if (process.env.NODE_ENV === 'production')` ❸, so you don't really need to use `app.configure` if you don't want to. It will be removed in Express 4. If you're not using Express, you can just query `process.env`.

The `NODE_ENV` environmental variable is controlled by the shell. If you want to run listing 9.10 in production mode, you can type `NODE_ENV=production node config.js`, and you should see it print the production database string. You could also type `export NODE_ENV=production`, which will cause the application to always run in production mode while the current shell is running.

The reason we've used `PORT` ❶ to set the port is because that's the default name Heroku uses. This allows Heroku's internal HTTP routers to override the port your application listens on.

You could use `process.env` throughout your code instead of `app.get`, but using the app object feels cleaner. You don't need to pass `app` around—if you've used the route separation pattern from technique 67, then you'll be able to access it through `res.app`.

If you'd rather use configuration files, the easiest and quickest way is to use the folder as a module technique with JSON files. Create a folder called config/, and then create an index.js file, and a JSON file for each environment. The next listing shows what the index.js file should look like.

Listing 9.11   A JSON configuration file loader

```
var config = {
  development: require('./development.json'),      ◁——   Load a JSON file
  production: require('./production.json'),        ❶     with require()
  test: require('./test.json')
};

module.exports = config[process.env.NODE_ENV || 'development'];   ◁——
```
                                                        Check **NODE_ENV** to
                                                        see which file to use ❷

Node's module system allows you to load a JSON file with require ❶, so you can load each environment's configuration file and then export the relevant one using NODE_ENV ❷. Then whenever you need to access settings, just use var config = require('./config')—you'll get a plain old JavaScript object that contains the settings for the current environment. The next listing shows an example Express application that uses this technique.

Listing 9.12   Loading the configuration directory

```
var express = require('express');
var app = express();
var config = require('./config');        ◁——   Load settings
                                                using require()
app.listen(config.port, function() {
  console.log('Using database:', config.db);
  console.log('Listening on port:', config.port);
});
```

This is so easy it almost feels like cheating! All you have to do is call require ('./config') and you've got your settings. Node's module system should cache the file as well, so once you've called require it shouldn't need to evaluate the JSON files again. You can repeatedly call require('./config') throughout your application.

This technique takes advantage of JavaScript's lightweight syntax for setting and accessing values on objects, as well as Node's module system. It works well for lots of types of projects.

There's one more approach to configuration: using a third-party module. After the last technique, you might think this is overkill, but third-party modules can offer a lot of functionality, including command-line option parsing. It might be that you often need to switch between different options, so overriding application settings with command-line options is attractive.

The web framework Flatiron (http://flatironjs.org/) has an application configuration module called `nconf` (https://npmjs.org/package/nconf) that handles configuration files, environmental variables, and command-line options. Each can be given precedence, so you can make command-line options override configuration files. It's a unifying framework for processing options.

The following listing shows how `nconf` can be used to configure an Express application.

Listing 9.13   Using `nconf` to configure an Express application

```
var express = require('express');
var app = express();
var nconf = require('nconf');
var routes = require('./routes');

nconf                                          ❶ Tell nconf to optionally use
  .argv()                                        configuration file, and override it
  .env()                                         with command-line arguments
  .file({ file: 'config.json' });

nconf.set('db', 'localhost/development');      ❷ Set a default
nconf.set('port', 3000);                          for db setting


app.get('/', routes.index);


app.listen(nconf.get('port'), function() {     ❸ Get the port
  console.log('Using database:', nconf.get('db'));
  console.log('Listening on port:', nconf.get('port'));
});
```

Here we've told `nconf` to prioritize options from the command line, but to also read a configuration file if one is available ❶. You don't need to create a configuration file, and `nconf` can create one for you if you use `nconf.save`. That means you could allow users of your application to change settings and persist them. This works best when `nconf` is set up to use a database to save settings—it comes with built-in Redis support.

Default values can be set with `nconf.set` ❷. If you run this example without any options, it should use port 3000, but if you start it with `node app.js --port 3001`, it'll use whatever you pass with `--port`. Getting settings is as simple as `nconf.get` ❸.

And you don't need to pass the `nconf` object around! Settings are stored in memory. Other files in your project can access settings by loading `nconf` with `require`, and then calling `nconf.get`. The next listing loads `nconf` again, and then tries to access the `db` setting.

Listing 9.14   Loading `nconf` elsewhere in the application

```
var nconf = require('nconf');                  If you load nconf
                                               again, it'll know
module.exports.index = function(req, res) {  ❶ what to do.
  res.send('Using database:', nconf.get('db'));
};
```

Even though it seems like `var nconf = require('nconf')` might return a pristine copy of nconf, it doesn't **❶**.

A well-organized and carefully configured web application can still go wrong. When your application crashes, you'll want logs to help debug the problem. The next technique will help you improve how your application handles errors.

TECHNIQUE 70   **Elegant error handling**

This technique looks at using the `Error` constructor to catch and handle errors in your application.

PROBLEM

You want to centralize error handling to simplify your web applications.

SOLUTION

Inherit from `Error` with error classes that include HTTP status codes, and use a middleware component to handle errors based on content type.

DISCUSSION

JavaScript has an `Error` constructor that you can inherit from to represent specific types of errors. In web development, some errors frequently crop up: incorrect URLs, incorrect parameters for query parameters or form values, and authentication failures. That means you can define errors that include HTTP codes alongside the typical things `Error` provides.

Rather than branching on error conditions in HTTP routers, you should call `next(err)`. The next listing shows how that works.

Listing 9.15   Passing errors to middleware

Make sure the
route handler
signature
includes the
third
parameter,
next. **❷**

If an error was
passed by the
database API,
return early. **❸**

Keep error
objects
organized in **❶**
separate file.

If a note couldn't be found,
create an instance of a
suitable error class. **❹**

```
var db = require('./../db');
var errors = require('./../errors');

module.exports.show = function(req, res, next) {
  db.notes.find(req.param('id'), function(err, note) {
    if (err) return next(err);
    if (!note) {
      return next(new errors.NotFound('That note was not found.'));
    }
    res.send(note);
  });
};
```

In this example, error classes have been defined in a separate file **❶**, which you can find in listing 9.16. The route handler includes a third argument, next **❷**, after the standard req, res arguments that we've used in previous techniques.

Many of your route handlers will load data from a database, whether it's MySQL, PostgreSQL, MongoDB, or Redis, so this example is based around a generic asynchronous database API. If an error was encountered by the database API, then return early and call next, including the error object as the first argument. This will pass the error along to the next middleware component **❸**. This route handler has an additional piece of logic—if a note wasn't found in the database, then an error object is instantiated and passed along using next ❹.

The following listing shows how to inherit from Error.

Listing 9.16   Inheriting errors and including status codes

```
var util = require('util');
                                            ❶ Create generic
function HTTPError() {                         HTTPError class
  Error.call(this, arguments);
}
                                            ❷ Inherit from Error,
util.inherits(HTTPError, Error);               using util.inherits

function NotFound(message) {
  HTTPError.call(this);                              ❸ Optionally capture
  Error.captureStackTrace(this, arguments.callee);      stack trace
  this.statusCode = 404;
  this.message = message;              Set status code that can
  this.name = 'NotFound';          ❹  be passed to browser
}
util.inherits(NotFound, HTTPError);

                                     Additional HTTP
module.exports = {                   errors can inherit
  HTTPError: HTTPError,          ❺  from HTTPError
  NotFound: NotFound
};
```

Here we've opted to create two classes. Instead of just defining NotFound, we've created HTTPError ❶ and inherited from it ❺. This is so it's easier to track if an error is related to HTTP, or if it's something else. The base HTTPError class inherits from Error ❷.

In the NotFound error, we've captured the stack trace to aid with debugging ❸, and set a statusCode property ❹ that can be reported to the browser.

The next listing shows how to create an error-handling middleware component in a typical Express application.

Listing 9.17   Using an error-handling middleware component

```
var errors = require('./errors');
var express = require('express');
var app = express();
var routes = require('./routes');

app.use(express.bodyParser());
                                              ❶ If four arguments are
                                                 used with app.use, then
app.get('/notes/:id', routes.notes.show);        the first argument is
                                                 the error object.
app.use(function(err, req, res, next) {
  if (process.env.NODE_ENV !== 'test') {
    console.error(err.stack);            Print stack traces if you're
  }                                   ❷ not running in the test mode.
```

```
  res.status(err.statusCode || 500);

  res.format({
    text: function() {                    ❸  Respond with errors in
      res.send(err.message);         ⟵┐      the expected format.
    },

    json: function() {
      res.send(err);
    },

    html: function() {
      res.render('errors', { err: err });
    }
  });
});
```

```
module.exports = app;
```

This middleware component is fairly simple, but it has some tweaks that we've found work well in production. To get the error objects passed by next, make sure to use the four-parameter form of app.use's callback ❶. Also note that this middleware component comes at the end of the chain, so you need to put it after all your other middleware and route definitions.

You can conditionally print stack traces so they're not visible when specifically testing expected errors ❷—errors may be triggered as part of testing, and you wouldn't want stack traces cluttering the test output.

Because this centralizes error handling into the main application file, it's a good idea to conditionally return different formats. This is useful if your application provides a JSON API as well as HTML pages. You can use app.format to do this ❸, and it works by checking the MIME type in the request's Accept header. The JSON response might not be needed, but it's possible that your API would return well-formed errors that can be consumed by clients—it can be difficult to deal with APIs that suddenly respond with HTML when you're asking for JSON.

Somewhere in your tests you should check that these errors do what you want. The following snippet shows a Mocha test that makes sure 404s are returned when expected, and in the expected format:

```
describe('Error handling', function() {
  it('should return a 404 for IDs that do not exist', function(done) {
    request(app)
      .get('/notes/999')              ❶  Check that expected
      .expect(404, done);        ⟵┐      status code was returned
  });

  it('should send JSON errors when requested', function(done) {
    request(app)
      .get('/notes/999')                      ❷  Set Accept header
      .set('Accept', 'application/json')  ⟵┐      to get JSON
```

```
        .expect(404, function(err, res) {
          assert.equal(res.body.name, 'NotFound');      ⟵  Check that body was
          done();                                        ❸  in expected format
        });
      });
    });
  });
```

This snippet includes two requests. The first checks that we get an error with a 404 ❶, and the second sets the `Accept` header to make sure we get back JSON ❷. This is implemented with SuperTest, which will give us JSON in responses, so the assertion can check to make sure we get an object in the format we expect ❸. The full source for this example can be found in listings/web/error-handling.

Error email cheat sheet

If you're going to make your application send email notifications when unexpected errors occur, here's a list of things you should include in the email to aid with debugging:

- A string version of the error object
- The contents of `err.stack`—this is a nonstandard property of error objects that Node includes
- The request method and URL
- The Express `req.route` property, if available
- The remote IP, which is `req.ip` in Express
- The request body, which you can convert to a string with `inspect(req.body)`

This error-handling pattern is widely used in Express apps, and it's even built into the restify framework (https://npmjs.org/package/restify). If you remember to pass error objects to `next`, you'll find testing and debugging Express applications easier.

Errors can also be sent as emails with useful transcripts. To make the most out of error emails, include the request and error objects in the email so you can see exactly where things broke. Also, you probably don't want to send details about errors with certain status codes, but that's up to you.

In this technique we mentioned adapting code to work with REST APIs. The next technique delves deeper into the world of REST, and has examples for both Express and restify.

TECHNIQUE 71   **RESTful web applications**

At some stage you might want to add an API to your application. This technique is all about building RESTful APIs. There are examples for both Express and restify, and tips on how to create APIs that use the right HTTP verbs and idiomatic URLs.

PROBLEM

You want to create a RESTful web service in Express, restify, or another web framework.

SOLUTION

Use the right HTTP methods, URLs, and headers to build an intuitive, RESTful API.

DISCUSSION

REST stands for *representational state transfer*,[2] which isn't terribly useful to memorize unless you want to impress someone in a job interview. The way web developers talk about it is usually in contrast to SOAP (Simple Object Access Protocol), which is seen as a more corporate and strict way to create web APIs. In fact, there's such a thing as a strict REST API, but the key distinction is that REST embraces HTTP at a fundamental level—the HTTP methods themselves have semantic meaning.

You should be familiar with using GET and POST requests if you've ever made a basic HTML form. In REST, these HTTP verbs have specific meanings. For example, POST will *create a resource*, and GET means *fetch a resource*.

Node developers typically create APIs that use JSON. JSON is the easiest structured data format to generate and read in Node, but it also works well in client-side JavaScript. But REST doesn't imply JSON—you're free to use any data format. Certain clients and services expect XML, and we've even seen those that work with CSV and spreadsheet formats like Excel.

The desired data format is specified by the request's Accept header. For JSON that should be application/json, and application/xml for XML. There are other useful request headers as well—Accept-Version can be used to request a different version of the API. This allows clients to lock themselves against a supported version, while you're free to improve the server without breaking backward compatibility—you can always update your server faster than people can update their clients.

Express provides a lightweight layer over Node's http core module, but it doesn't include any data persistence functionality outside of in-memory sessions and cookies. You'll have to decide which database and database module to use. The same is true with restify: it doesn't automatically map data from HTTP to be stored offline; you'll need to find a way to do that.

Restify is superficially similar to Express. The difference is that Express has features that help you build web applications, which includes rendering templates. Conversely, restify is focused on building REST APIs, and that brings a different set of requirements. Restify makes it easy to serve multiple versions of an API with semantic versioning using HTTP headers, and has an event-based API for emitting and listening for HTTP-related events and errors. It also supports throttling, so you can control how quickly responses are made.

Figure 9.3 shows a typical RESTful API that allows *page* objects to be created, read, updated, and deleted.

To get started building REST APIs, you should consider what your objects are. Imagine you're building a content management system: it probably has pages, users, and images. If you want to add a button that allows pages to be toggled between "published" and "draft," and if you've already got a REST API and it supports requests to PATCH /pages/:id, you could just tie the button to some client-side JavaScript or a form that posts to /pages/:id with { state: 'published' } or { state: 'draft' }. If

---

[2] For more about REST, see Fielding's dissertation on the subject at http://mng.bz/7Fhj.

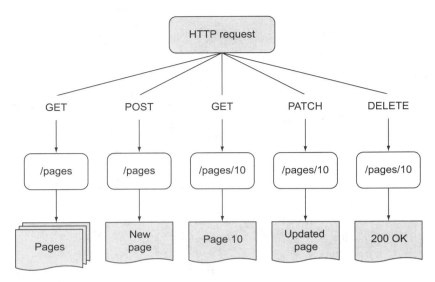

Figure 9.3   Making requests to a REST API

you've been given an Express application that only has PUT /pages/:id, then you could probably derive the code for PATCH from the existing implementation.

Plural or singular?

When you design your API's URI endpoints, you should generally use *plural nouns*. That means /pages and also /pages/1 for a specific page, not /page/1. It'll be easier to use your API if the endpoints are consistent.

You may find there are certain resources that should be singular nouns, because there's only ever one such item. If it makes semantic sense, use a singular noun, but use it consistently. For example, if your API requires that users sign in, and you don't want to expose a unique user ID, then /account might be a sensible endpoint for user account management, if there's only ever one account for a given user.

Table 9.1 shows HTTP verbs alongside the typical response. Note that PUT and PATCH have different but similar meanings—PATCH means modify some of the fields in a resource, while PUT means *replace* the entire resource. It can take some practice to get the hang of building applications this way, but it's pragmatic and easy to test, so it's worth learning properly. If these HTTP terms are new to you, then use table 9.1 when you're designing the API for your application.

In an Express application, these URLs and methods are mapped using routes. Routes specify the HTTP verb and a partial URL. You can map these to any function that you like, but if you use the route separation pattern from technique 67, which is advisable, then you should use the method names that are close to their associated

Table 9.1 Choosing the correct HTTP verbs

Verb	Description	Response
GET /animals	Get a list of animals.	An array of animal objects
GET /animals/:id	Get a single animal.	A single animal object, or an error
POST /animals	Create an animal by sending the properties of a single animal.	The new animal
PUT /animals/:id	Update a single animal record. All properties will be replaced.	The updated animal
PATCH /animals/:id/	Update a single animal record, but only change the fields specified.	The updated animal

HTTP verbs. Listing 9.18 shows the routes for a RESTful resource in Express, and some of the required configuration to make it work.

Listing 9.18   A RESTful resource in Express

```
var app;
var express = require('express');
var routes = require('./routes');

module.exports = app = express();

app.use(express.json());
app.use(express.methodOverride());

app.get('/pages', routes.pages.index);
app.get('/pages/:id', routes.pages.show);
app.post('/pages', routes.pages.create);
app.patch('/pages/:id', routes.pages.patch);
app.put('/pages/:id', routes.pages.update);
app.del('/pages/:id', routes.pages.remove);
```

❶ Use JSON body parser

methodOverride middleware component allows a query parameter to specify extra HTTP methods ❷

❸ The routes for the resource

This example uses some middleware for automatically parsing JSON requests ❶, and overrides the HTTP method POST with the query parameter, _method ❷. That means that the PUT, PATCH, and DELETE HTTP verbs are actually determined by the _method query parameter. This is because most browsers can only send a GET or POST, so _method is a hack used by many web frameworks.

The routes in listing 9.18 define each of the usual RESTful resource methods ❸. Table 9.1 shows how these routes map to actions.

Table 9.2 Mapping routes to responses

Verb, URL	Description
GET /pages	An array of pages.
GET /pages/:id	An object containing the page specified by id.

Table 9.2   Mapping routes to responses *(continued)*

Verb, URL	Description
POST /pages	Create a page.
PATCH /pages/:id	Load the page for id, and change some of the fields.
PUT /pages/:id	Replace the page for id.
DELETE /pages/:id	Remove the page for id.

Listing 9.19 is an example implementation for the route handlers. It has a generic Node database API—a real Redis, MongoDB, MySQL, or PostgreSQL database module wouldn't be too far off, so you should be able to adapt it.

Listing 9.19   RESTful route handlers

```
var db = require('./../db');

module.exports.index = function(req, res, next) {
  db.pages.findAll(function(err, pages) {
    if (err) return next(err);
    res.send(pages);
  });
};

module.exports.create = function(req, res, next) {
  var page = req.body.page;
  db.pages.create(page, function(err, page) {
    if (err) return next(err);
    res.send(page);
  });
};

module.exports.update = function(req, res, next) {
  var id = req.param('id');
  var page = req.body.page;
  db.pages.update(id, page, function(err, page) {
    if (err) return next(err);
    res.send(page);
  });
};

module.exports.show = function(req, res, next) {
  db.pages.find(req.param('id'), function(err, page) {
    if (err) return next(err);
    res.send(page);
  });
};

module.exports.patch = function(req, res, next) {
  var id = req.param('id');
  var page = req.body.page;
```

❶ **Fall through to next middleware component when an error is raised by the database**

❷ **Calling send will automatically return JSON to browser**

```
    db.pages.patch(id, page, function(err, page) {      ◁
      if (err) return next(err);
      res.send(page);
    });
};
```

Most database modules won't
have method named patch,
③ but something similar

```
module.exports.remove = function(req, res, next) {
  var id = req.param('id');
  db.pages.remove(id, function(err) {
    if (err) return next(err);
    res.send(200);
  });
};
```

Although this example is simple, it illustrates something important: you should keep your route handlers lightweight. They deal with HTTP and then let other parts of your code handle the underlying business logic. Another pattern used in this example is the error handling—errors are passed by calling next(err) **①**. Try to keep error-handling code centralizing and generic—technique 70 has more details on this.

To return the JSON to the browser, res.send() is called with a JavaScript object **②**. Express knows how to convert the object to JSON, so that's all you need to do.

All of these route handlers use the same pattern: map the query or body to something the database can use, and then call the corresponding database method. If you're using an ORM or ODM—a more abstracted database layer—then you'll probably have something analogous to PATCH **③**. This could be an API method that allows you to update only the specified fields. Relational databases and MongoDB work that way.

If you download this book's source code, you'll get the other files required to try out the full example. To run it, type npm start. Once the server is running, you can use some of the following Curl commands to communicate with the server.

The first command creates a page:

Method **②**   `curl -H "Content-Type: application/json" \`   ◁   **①** Use JSON as
is POST └─▷ `-X POST -d '{ "page": { "title": "Home" } }' \`   body encoding
                  `http://localhost:3000/pages`   ◁

③ URL for creating
pages is /pages

First we specify the Content-Type using the -H option **①**. Next, the request is set to use POST, and the request body is included as a JSON string **②**. The URL is /pages because we're creating a resource **③**.

Curl is a useful tool for exploring APIs, once you understand the basic options. The ones to remember are -H for setting headers, -X for setting the HTTP method, and -d for the request body.

To see the list of pages, just use curl http://localhost:3000/pages. To change the contents, try PATCH:

```
curl -H "Content-Type: application/json" \
  -X PATCH -d '{ "page": { "title": "The Moon" } }' \
  http://localhost:3000/pages/1
```

Express has a few other tricks up its sleeves for creating RESTful web services. Remember that some REST APIs use other data formats, like XML? What if you want both? You can solve this by using res.format:

```
module.exports.show = function(req, res, next) {
    db.pages.find(req.param('id'), function(err, page) {
        if (err) return next(err);
        res.format({
            json: function() {
                res.send(page);
            },
            xml: function() {
                res.send('<page><title>' + page.title + '</title></page>');
            }
        });
    });
};
```

format method accepts an object ❶

json is shorthand for application/json ❷

Include a function for each content type ❸

To use XML instead of JSON, you have to include the Accept header in the request. With Curl, you can do this:

```
curl -H 'Accept: application/xml' \
  http://localhost:3000/pages/1
```

Just remember that Accept is used to ask the server for a specific format, and Content-Type is used to tell the server what format you're sending it. It sometimes makes sense to include both in a single request!

Now that you've seen how REST APIs in Express work, we can compare them with restify. The patterns used to structure Express applications can be reused for restify projects. The two important patterns are route separation, as described in technique 67, and defining the application in a separate file to the server (for easier testing and internal reuse). Listing 9.20 is the restify equivalent of listing 9.18.

Listing 9.20   A restify application

```
var app;
var restify = require('restify');
var routes = require('./routes');

module.exports = app = restify.createServer({
  name: 'NIP CMS',
});

app.use(restify.bodyParser());

app.get('/pages', routes.pages.index);
app.get('/pages/:id', routes.pages.show);
app.post('/pages', routes.pages.create);
app.patch('/pages/:id', routes.pages.patch);
app.put('/pages/:id', routes.pages.update);
app.del('/pages/:id', routes.pages.remove);
```

❶ **Create restify server instance**

❷ **Use middleware component to parse JSON**

❸ **Set up routes**

Using restify, instances of servers are created with some initial configuration options
❶. You don't have to pass in any options, but here we've specified a name. The
options are actually the same as Node's built-in `http.Server.listen`, so you can pass
in options for SSL/TLS certificates, if you want to use encryption. Restify-specific
options that aren't available in Express include `formatters`, which allows you to set up
functions that `res.send` will use for custom content types.

This example uses `bodyParser` to parse JSON in the request bodies ❷. This is like
the Express middleware component in the previous example.

The route definitions are identical to Express ❸. The actual route callbacks are
slightly different. Listing 9.21 shows a translation of listing 9.19. See if you can spot the
differences.

Listing 9.21   Restify routes

```
var db = require('./../db');

module.exports.index = function(req, res, next) {
  db.pages.findAll(function(err, pages) {
    if (err) return next(err);
    res.send(pages);
  });
};

module.exports.create = function(req, res, next) {
  var page = req.body.page;
  db.pages.create(page, function(err, page) {
    if (err) return next(err);
    res.send(page);
  });
};

module.exports.update = function(req, res, next) {
  var id = req.params.id;
  var page = req.body.page;
  db.pages.update(id, page, function(err, page) {
    if (err) return next(err);
    res.send(page);
  });
};

module.exports.show = function(req, res, next) {
  db.pages.find(req.params.id, function(err, page) {
    if (err) return next(err);
    res.send(page);
  });
};

module.exports.patch = function(req, res, next) {
  var id = req.params.id;
  var page = req.body.page;
  db.pages.patch(id, page, function(err, page) {
    if (err) return next(err);
```

❶ **The callback arguments are similar to Express.**

❷ **Getting URL parameters is slightly different.**

```
      res.send(page);
  });
};

module.exports.remove = function(req, res, next) {
  var id = req.params.id;
  db.pages.remove(id, function(err) {
    if (err) return next(err);
    res.send(200);
  });
};
```

❸ Passing an integer to send() returns the status code.

The first thing to note is the callback arguments for route handlers are the same as Express ❶. In fact, you can almost lift the equivalent code directly from Express applications. There are a few differences though: `req.param()` doesn't exist—you need to use `req.params` instead, and note this is an object rather than a method ❷. Like Express, calling `res.send()` with an integer will return a status code to the client ❸.

Using other HTTP headers

In this technique you've seen how the `Content-Type` and `Accept` headers can be used to deal with different data formats. There are other useful headers that you should take into account when building APIs.

One such header, supported by restify, is `Accept-Version`. When you define a route, you can include an optional first parameter that includes options, instead of the usual string. The `version` property allows your API to respond differently based on the `Accept-Version` header.

For example, using `app.get({ path: '/pages', version: '1.1.8' }, routes.v1.pages);` allows you to bind specific route handlers to version 1.1.8. If you have to change your API in 2.0.0, then you can do this without breaking older clients.

There's nothing to stop you from using this header in an Express application, but it's easier in restify. If you decide to take this approach, you should learn how *major.minor.patch* works in semantic versioning (http://semver.org/).

If you download the full example and run it (listings/web/restify), you can try out some of the Curl commands we described earlier. Create, update, and show should work the same way.

Knowing that Express and restify applications are similar is useful, because you can start to compose applications made from both frameworks. Both are based on Node's `http` module, which means you could technically mount a restify application inside Express using `app.use(restifyApp)`. This works well if the restify application is in its own module—you could install it using npm, or put it in its own directory.

Both Express and restify use middleware, and you'll find well-structured applications have loosely coupled middleware that can be reused across different projects. In the next technique you'll see how to write your own middleware, so you can start decorating applications with useful features like custom logging.

TECHNIQUE 72 **Using custom middleware**

You've seen middleware being used for error handling, and you've also used some of Express's built-in middleware. You can also use middleware to add custom behavior to routes; this might add new functionality, improve logging, or control access based on authentication or permissions.

The benefit of middleware is that it can improve code reuse in your application. This technique will teach you how to write your own middleware, so you can share code between projects, and structure projects in a more readable way.

PROBLEM

You want to add behavior—in a reusable, testable manner—that's triggered when certain routes are accessed.

SOLUTION

Write your own middleware.

DISCUSSION

When you first start using Express, middleware sounds like a complicated concept that other people use for writing plugins that extend Express. But in fact, writing middleware is a fundamental part of using Express, and you should start writing middleware as soon as possible. And if you can write routes, then you can write middleware: it's basically the same API!

In technique 70, you saw how to handle errors with a middleware component. Error handling is a special case—you have to include a fourth parameter to capture the error object: `app.use(function(err, req, res, next) {`. With other middleware, you can just use three arguments, like standard route handlers. This is the simplest middleware component:

```
app.use(function(req, res, next) {      ← ❶ Apply middleware component
  console.log('%s %s', req.method, req.url);    by calling app.use()
  next();      ←
});                   ❷ Call next() to continue execution
                         to next middleware component
```

❶ **Apply middleware component by calling app.use()**

❷ **Call next() to continue execution to next middleware component**

By passing an anonymous callback to `app.use` ❶, the middleware component will always run, unless a previous middleware component fails to call `next`. When your code is finished, you can call `next` ❷ to trigger the next middleware component in the stack. That means two things: asynchronous APIs are supported, and the order in which you add middleware is important.

The following example shows how you can use asynchronous APIs inside middleware. This example is based on the idea of loading a user based on a user ID that has been set in the session:

**If a user ID has
been set in the
session, load
the account.** ❷

**This callback will run
for every request.** ❶

```
app.use(function(req, res, next) {
    if (req.session.user_id) {
        db.users.find(req.session.user_id, function(err, user) {
            if (err) {
                next(err);
            } else if (user) {
                res.locals.user = user;
                next();
            } else {
                next(new Error('Account not found'));
            }
        });
    } else {
        next();
    }
});
```

**If there was an error
loading the user,
pass control to the
error middleware
component.** ❸

**If the user was
loaded, set it
on res.locals so
it can be used
elsewhere.** ❹

This middleware will be triggered for every request ❶. It loads user accounts from a database, but only when the user's ID has been set in the session ❷. The code that loads the user is asynchronous, so next could be called after a short delay. There are several points where next is called: for example, if an error was encountered when loading the user, next will be called with an error ❸.

In this example the loaded user is set as a property of res.locals ❹. By using res.locals, you'll be able to access the user in other middleware, route handlers, and templates.

This isn't necessarily the best way to use middleware. Including an anonymous function this way means it can be hard to test—you can only test middleware by starting up the entire Express application. You might want to write simpler unit tests that don't use HTTP requests, so it would be better to refactor this code into a function. The function would have the same signature, and would be used like this:

```
var middleware = require('./middleware');
app.use(middleware.loadUser);
```

**Loading a module that
contains middleware** ❶

By grouping all the middleware together as modules ❶, you can load the middleware from other locations, whether they're entirely different projects, test code, or inside separated routes. This function has decoupled the middleware to improve how it can be reused.

If you're using the route separation pattern from technique 67, then this makes sense, because middleware can be applied to specific routes that might be defined in different files. Let's say you're using the RESTful API style from technique 71, and your *page* resource can only be updated by signed-in users, but other parts of the application should be accessible to anyone. You can restrict access to the page resource routes like this:

```
var middleware = require('./middleware');

app.get('/pages', routes.pages.index);
app.get('/pages/:id', routes.pages.show);
app.post('/pages', middleware.loadUser, routes.pages.create);
app.patch('/pages/:id', middleware.loadUser, routes.pages.patch);
```

❶ Anyone can view pages.

Only signed-in users can create or update pages. ❷

In this fragment, routes are defined for a resource called pages. Some routes are accessible to anyone ❶, but creating or updating pages is limited to people with accounts on the system ❷. This is done by supplying the loadUser middleware component as the second argument when defining a route. In fact, multiple arguments could be used—you could have a generic user loading route, and then a more specific permission checking route that ensures users are administrators, or have the necessary rights to change pages.

Figure 9.4 shows how requests can pass through several callbacks until the final response is sent back to the client. Sometimes this might cause a response to finish before other middleware has had a chance to run—if an error is encountered and passed to next(err).

You can even apply middleware to batches of routes. It's common to see something like app.all('/admin/*', middleware.loadUser); in Express applications.

If you use modules to manage your middleware, and simplify route handlers by moving shared functionality into separate files, then you'll find that organizing middleware into modules becomes a fundamental architectural tool for organizing applications.

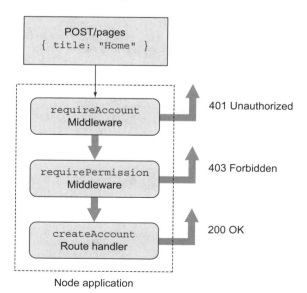

Figure 9.4 Requests can pass through several callbacks until the final response is sent.

If you're designing a new Express application, you should think in terms of middleware. Ask yourself what kinds of HTTP requests you're going to deal with, and what kinds of filtering they might need.

Now it's time to combine all of these ideas into a worked example. Listing 9.22 demonstrates one way of parsing requests that contain XML. Middleware has been used to parse the XML, turning it into plain old JavaScript objects. That means two things: only a small part of your code has to worry about XML, and you could potentially add support for other data formats as well.

Listing 9.22   Three types of middleware

```
var express = require('express');
var app = express();
var Schema = require('validate');
var xml2json = require('xml2json');
var util = require('util');
var Page = new Schema();

Page.path('title').type('string').required();      ◁──┐  ❶ Define some data validation
                                                          to ensure pages have titles

function ValidatorError(errors) {                  ◁──┐
  this.statusCode = 400;                                Inherit from standard error object
  this.message = errors.join(', ');                     so validation errors can be handled
}                                                    ❷  in error middleware component
util.inherits(ValidatorError, Error);

function xmlMiddleware(req, res, next) {           ◁──┐  This function will be used as
  if (!req.is('xml')) return next();               ❸  XML middleware component

  var body = '';
  req.on('data', function(str) {                   ◁──┐
    body += str;                                       Request object will emit data events
  });                                              ❹  when body is read from the client

  req.on('end', function() {
    req.body = xml2json.toJson(body.toString(), {
      object: true,
      sanitize: false
    });
    next();
  });
}

function checkValidXml(req, res, next) {           ◁──┐  ❺ Data-validation
  var page = Page.validate(req.body.page);                middleware component
  if (page.errors.length) {
    next(new ValidatorError(page.errors));         ◁──┐  Passing errors to next() will stop
  } else {                                         ❻  route handler from running
    next();
  }
}

function errorHandler(err, req, res, next) {       ◁──┐  ❼ This is error-handling
                                                          middleware component
```

```
      console.error('errorHandler', err);
      res.send(err.statusCode || 500, err.message);
}

app.use(xmlMiddleware);
```
❽ **Use XML middleware component for all requests**

```
app.post('/pages', checkValidXml, function(req, res) {
      console.log('Valid page:', req.body.page);
      res.send(req.body);
});
```
❾ **Validate XML for specific requests**

```
app.use(errorHandler);
```
❿ **Last middleware component to be added should be error handler**

```
app.listen(3000);
```

In summary, this example defines three middleware components to parse XML, validate it, and then either respond with a JSON object or display an error. We've used an arbitrary data-validation library here ❶—your database module may come with something similar.

The routes deal with *page* resources, and the expected format for pages is XML. It's passed in as request bodies and validated. An error object, ValidatorError ❷, is used to return a 400 error when invalid data is sent to the server. The XML parser ❸ reads in the request body using the standard event-based API ❹. This middleware component is called for every request ❽ because it's passed directly to app.use, but it only runs if the Content-Type is set to XML.

The data-validation middleware component ❺ ensures a page title has been set—this is just an arbitrary example we've chosen to illustrate how this kind of validation works. If the data is invalid, an instance of ValidatorError is passed when next is called ❻. This will trigger the error-handling middleware component ❼.

Data is only validated for certain requests. This is done by passing checkValidXml when the /pages route is defined ❾.

The global error handler is the last middleware component to be added ❿. This should always be the case, because middleware is executed in the order it's defined. Once res.send has been called, then no more processing will occur, so errors won't be triggered.

To try this example out, run node server.js and then try posting XML to the server using curl:

```
curl -H "Content-Type: application/xml" \
  -X POST -d '<page><title>Node in Practice</title></page>' \
  http://localhost:3000/pages
```

You should try leaving out a title to ensure a 400 error is raised!

This approach can be used for XML, JSON, CSV, or any other data formats you like. It works well for minimizing the code that has to deal with XML, but there are other ways you can write decoupled code in Node web applications. In the next technique you'll see how something fundamental to Node—events—can be used as another useful architectural pattern.

TECHNIQUE 73 **Using events to decouple functionality**

In the average Express application, most code is organized into methods and modules. This can make sharing functionality inconvenient in some cases, particularly if you want to neatly separate concerns within your application. This technique uses sending emails as an example of something that doesn't fit neatly into routers, models, or views. Events are used to decouple emails from routers, which keeps email-related code outside of HTTP code.

PROBLEM

You want to do things that aren't related to HTTP, like send emails, but aren't sure how to structure the code so it's neatly decoupled and easy to test.

SOLUTION

Use easily accessible `EventEmitter` objects, like the Express `app` object.

DISCUSSION

Express and restify applications generally follow the Model-View-Controller (MVC) pattern. Models are used to save data, controllers are route handlers, and views are the templates in the views/ directory.

Some code doesn't fit neatly into these categories. For example, where would you keep email-handling code? Email generation clearly doesn't belong in routes, because email isn't related to HTTP. But like route handlers, it does require templates. It also isn't really a model, because it doesn't interact with the database.

What if you did put the email-handling code into models? In that case, given an instance of a `User` model, you want to send an email when a new account is created. You could put the email code in the `User.prototype.registerUser` method. The problem with that is you might not always want to send emails when users are created. It might not be convenient during testing, or some kind of periodic maintenance tasks.

The reason why sending email isn't quite suitable for models or HTTP routes can be understood by thinking about the SOLID principles (http://en.wikipedia.org/wiki/SOLID). There are two principles that are relevant to us: the *single responsibility principle* and the *dependency inversion principle*.

Single responsibility dictates that the class that deals with HTTP routes really shouldn't send emails, because these are different responsibilities that shouldn't be mixed together. Inversion of control is a specific type of dependency inversion, and can be done by removing direct invocation—rather than calling `emails.sendAccount-Creation`, your email-handling class should respond to events.

For Node programmers, events are one of the most important tools available. And fortunately for us, the SOLID principles indicate that we can write better HTTP routers by removing our email code, and replacing it with abstract and generalized events. These events can then be responded to by the relevant classes.

Figure 9.5 shows what our idealized application structure might look like. But how do we achieve this? Take Express applications as an example; they don't typically have a suitable global event object. You could technically create a global variable somewhere

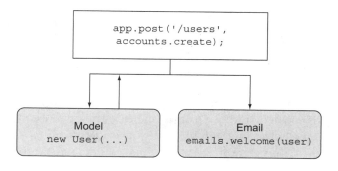

Figure 9.5 Applications can be easier to understand if organized according to the SOLID principles.

central, like the file that calls `express()`, but that would introduce a global shared state, and that would break the principles we described earlier.

Fortunately, Express includes a reference to the `app` object in the request. Route handlers, which accept the `req`, `res` parameters, always have access to `app` in `res.app`. The `app` object inherits from `EventEmitter`, so we can use it to broadcast when things happen. If your route handler creates and saves new users, then it can also call `res.app.emit('user:created', user)`, or something similar—you can use any naming scheme for events as long as it's consistent. Then you can listen for `user:created` events and respond accordingly. This could include sending email notifications, or perhaps even logging useful statistics about users.

The following listing shows how to listen for events on the application object.

Listing 9.23 Using events to structure an application

```
var express = require('express');
var app = express();
var emails = require('./emails');
var routes = require('./routes');

app.use(express.json());

app.post('/users', routes.users.create);        ❶ Set up a route for
                                                    creating users.
app.on('user:created', emails.welcome);

module.exports = app;                            ❷ Listen for user creation
                                                    events, and bind them to
                                                    the email code.
```

In this example a route for registering users is defined ❶, and then an event listener is defined and bound to a method that sends emails ❷.

The route is shown in the next listing.

Listing 9.24 Emitting events

```
var User = require('./../models/user');

module.exports.create = function(req, res, next) {
  var user = new User(req.body);
```

```
user.save(function(err) {
  if (err) return next(err);
  res.app.emit('user:created', user);       Emit user creation events when
  res.send('User created');                 users are successfully registered.
});
};
```

This listing contains an example model for `User` objects. If a user is successfully created, then `user:created` is emitted on the `app` object. The downloadable code for this book includes a more complete example with the code that sends emails, but the basic principle for removing direct invocation and adhering to the single responsibility principle is represented here.

Communication with events inside applications is useful when you need to make the code easier for other developers to understand. There are also times when you need to communicate with client-side code. The next technique shows you how to take advantage of WebSockets in your Node applications, while still being able to access resources like sessions.

TECHNIQUE 74 Using sessions with WebSockets

Node has strong support for the real-time web. Adopting event-oriented, asynchronous APIs means supporting WebSockets is a natural fit. Also, it's trivial to run two servers in the same process: a WebSocket server and a standard Node HTTP server can coexist happily.

This technique shows you how to reuse the Connect and Express middleware that we've been using so far with a WebSocket server. If your application allows users to sign in, and you want to add WebSocket support, then read on to learn how to master sessions in WebSockets.

PROBLEM

You want to add WebSocket support to an existing Express application, but you're not sure how to access session variables, like whether the user is currently signed in.

SOLUTION

Reuse Connect's cookie and session middleware with your WebSocket server.

DISCUSSION

This technique assumes you have a passing familiarity with WebSockets. To recap: HTTP requests are stateless and relatively short-lived. They're great for downloading documents, and requesting a state change for a resource. But what about streaming data to and from a server?

Certain types of events originate from servers. Think about a web mail service. When you create and send a message, you push it to the server, and the server sends it to the recipients. If the recipient is sitting watching their inbox, there's no easy way for their browser to get updated. It could periodically check for new messages using an Ajax request, but this isn't very elegant. The server *knows* it has a new message for the recipient, so it would be much better if it could push that message directly to the user.

Node web application

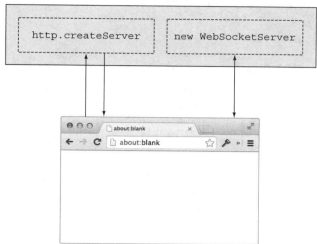

Figure 9.6   A Node web application should support both standard HTTP requests and WebSockets.

That's where WebSockets come in. They're conceptually like the TCP sockets we saw in chapter 7: a bidirectional bridge is set up between the client and server. To do this you need a WebSocket server in addition to your standard Express server, or plain old Node `http` server. Figure 9.6 illustrates how this works in a typical Node web application.

HTTP requests are short-lived, have specific endpoints, and use methods like `POST` and `PUT`. WebSockets are long-lived, don't have specific endpoints, and don't have methods. They're conceptually different, but since they're used to communicate with the same application, they typically need access to the same data.

This presents a problem for sessions. The Express examples we've looked at used middleware to automatically load the session. Connect middleware is based on the HTTP request and response, so how do we map this to WebSockets, which are long-lived and bidirectional? To understand this, we need to look at how WebSockets and sessions work.

Sessions are loaded based on unique identifiers that are included in cookies. Cookies are sent with every HTTP request. WebSockets are initiated with a standard HTTP request that asks to be upgraded to a WebSocket. This means there's a point where you can grab the cookie from the request, and then load the session. For each Web-Socket, you can store a reference to the user's session. Now you can do all the usual things you need to do with a session: verify the user is signed in, set preferences, and so on.

Figure 9.7 extends figure 9.6 to show how sessions can be used with WebSockets, by incorporating the Connect middleware for parsing cookies and loading the session.

Now that you know how the parts fit together, how do you go about building it? The cookie-parsing middleware component can be found in `express.cookieParser`. This is actually a simple method that gets the cookie from the request headers, and then parses the cookie string into separate values. It accepts an argument, `secret`,

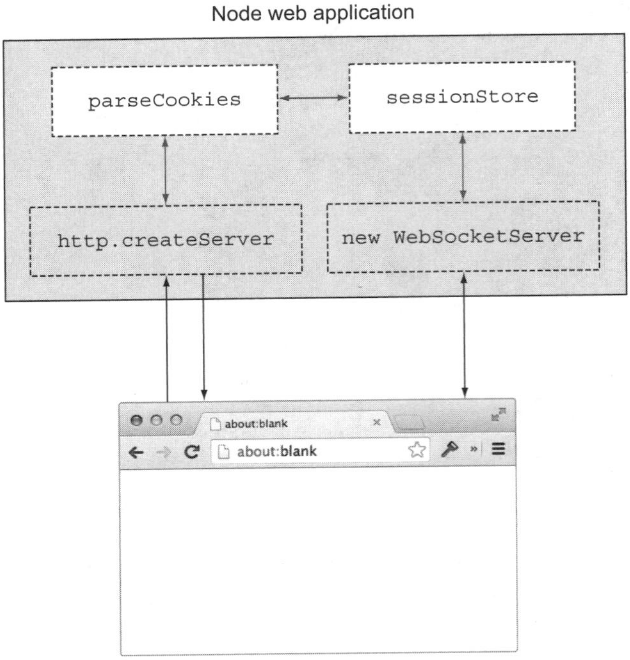

Node web application

Figure 9.7 Accessing
sessions from WebSockets

which is the value used to sign the cookie. Once the cookie is decrypted, you can get the session ID from it and load the session.

Sessions in Express are modeled on an asynchronous API for storing and retrieving values. They can be backed by a database, or you can use the built-in memory-based class. Passing the session ID and a callback to `sessionStore.get` will load the session, if the session ID is correct.

In this technique we'll use the `ws` WebSocket module (https://www.npmjs.org/package/ws). This is a fast-but-minimal implementation that has a very different API than Socket.IO. If you want to learn about Socket.IO, then *Node in Action* has some excellent tutorials. Here we're using a simpler module so you can really see how WebSockets work.

To make `ws` load the session, you need to parse the cookies from the HTTP upgrade request, and then call `sessionStore.get`. A full example that shows how it all works follows.

Listing 9.25 An Express application that uses WebSockets

```
var express = require('express');
var WebSocketServer = require('ws').Server;
var parseCookie = express.cookieParser('some secret');
var MemoryStore = express.session.MemoryStore;
var store = new MemoryStore();
```

Load cookie-parser middleware component and set the secret ❶

❷ **Load desired session store**

```
                         var app = express();
                         var server = app.listen(process.env.PORT || 3000);      Tell Express to use  3
                         var webSocketServer;                                     session store, and
             Create  4                                                           set the secret
             Express      app.use(parseCookie);
          route that      app.use(express.session({ store: store, secret: 'some secret' }));
          will set a      app.use(express.static(__dirname + '/public'));
      session value
        for testing    ⌐▷ app.get('/random', function(req, res) {
                          req.session.random = Math.random().toString();
                          res.send(200);                                      Start up WebSocket  5
                         });                                                  server, and pass it
                                                                             the Express server
                         webSocketServer = new WebSocketServer({ server: server });   ◁

     On connection  ⌐▷ webSocketServer.on('connection', function(ws) {
     events, create       var session;
        WebSocket
       for the client 6    ws.on('message', function(data, flags) {
                           var message = JSON.parse(data);                7  Data sent by the client is
                                                                             assumed to be JSON, and
                           if (message.type === 'getSession') {   ◁━━┘      is parsed here
                             parseCookie(ws.upgradeReq, null, function(err) {
      Get session ID for  ▷  var sid = ws.upgradeReq.signedCookies['connect.sid'];
      WebSocket from the
      HTTP upgrade request 8    store.get(sid, function(err, loadedSession) {  ◁⌐
                                 if (err) console.error(err);                    Get user's
                                 session = loadedSession;                     9  session from
                                 ws.send('session.random: ' + session.random, {   the store
                                   mask: false
                                 });                        Send value from
                               });                          session back through
                             });                        10  the WebSocket
                           } else {
                             ws.send('Unknown command');
                           }
                         });
                       });
```

This example starts by loading and configuring the cookie parser ❶ and the session store ❷. We're using signed cookies, so note that `ws.upgradeReq.signedCookies` is used when loading the session later.

Express is set up to use the session middleware component ❸, and we've created a route that you can use for testing ❹. Just load http://localhost:3000/random in your browser to set a random value in the session, and then visit http://localhost:3000/ to see it printed back.

The `ws` module works by using a plain old constructor, `WebSocketServer`, to handle WebSockets. To use it, you instantiate it with a Node HTTP server object—we've just passed in the Express server here ❺. Once the server is started, it'll emit events when connections are created ❻.

The client code for this example sends JSON to the server, so there's some code to parse the JSON string and check whether it's valid ❼. This wasn't entirely necessary for this example, but we included it to show that ws requires this kind of extra work to be used in most practical situations.

Once the WebSocket server has a connection, the session ID can be accessed through the cookies on the upgrade request ❽. This is similar to what Express does behind the scenes—we just need to manually pass a reference to the upgrade request to the cookie-parser middleware component. Then the session is loaded using the session store's get method ❾. Once the session has been loaded, a message is sent back to the client that contains a value from the session ❿.

The associated client-side implementation that's required to run this example is shown in the following listing.

Listing 9.26   The client-side WebSocket implementation

```
<!DOCTYPE html>
<html>
<head>
<script>
var host = window.document.location.host.replace(/:.*/, '');
var ws = new WebSocket('ws://' + host + ':3000');

setInterval(function() {
  ws.send('{ "type": "getSession" }');        ⟵——  Periodically
}, 1000);                                            send message
                                                     to the server
ws.onmessage = function(event) {
  document.getElementById('message').innerHTML = event.data;
};
</script>
</head>
<body>
  <h1>WebSocket sessions</h1>
  <div id='message'></div><br>
</body>
</html>
```

All it does is periodically send a message to the server. It'll display undefined until you visit http://localhost:3000/random. If you open two windows, one to http://localhost:3000/random and the other to http://localhost:3000/, you'll be able to keep refreshing the random page so the WebSocket view shows new values.

Running this example requires Express 3 and ws 0.4—we've included a package.json with everything you need in the book's full listings.

The next technique has tips for migrating from Express 3 to Express 4.

TECHNIQUE 75   **Migrating Express 3 applications to Express 4**

This book was written before Express 4 was released, so our Express examples are written with version 3 of the framework in mind. We've included this technique to help you migrate, and also so you can see how version 4 differs from the previous versions.

PROBLEM

You have an Express 3 application and want to upgrade it to use Express 4.

SOLUTION

Update your application configuration, install missing middleware, and take advantage of the new routing API.

DISCUSSION

Most of the updates from Express 3 to 4 were a long time coming. Certain changes have been hinted at in Express 3's documentation, so the API changes weren't unexpected or even too dramatic for the most part. You'll probably spend most of your time replacing the middleware that used to ship with Express, because Express 4 no longer has any built-in middleware components, apart from express.static.

The express.static middleware component enables Express to mount your public folder that contains JavaScript, CSS, and image assets. This has been left in because it's convenient, but the rest of the middleware components have gone. That means you'll need to use npm install --save body-parser if you previously used bodyParser, for example. Refer to table 9.1 that has the old middleware names and the newer equivalents. Just remember that you need to npm install --save each one that you need, and then require it in your app.js file.

Table 9.3   Migrating Express middleware components

Express 3	Express 4 npm package	Description
bodyParser	body-parser	Parses URL-encoded and JSON POST bodies
compress	compression	Compresses the server's responses
timeout	connect-timeout	Allows requests to timeout if they take too long
cookieParser	cookie-parser	Parses cookies from HTTP headers, leaving the result in req.cookies
cookieSession	cookie-session	Simple session support using cookies
csrf	csurf	Adds a token to the session that you can use to protect forms from CSRF attacks
error-handler	errorhandler	The default error handler used by Connect
session	express-session	Simple session handler that can be extended with *stores* that write sessions to databases or files
method-override	method-override	Maps new HTTP verbs to the _method request variable
logger	morgan	Log formatting
response-time	response-time	Track response time
favicon	serve-favicon	Send favicons, including a built-in default if you don't have one yet

Table 9.3 Migrating Express middleware components *(continued)*

Express 3	Express 4 npm package	Description
directory	serve-index	Directory listings, similar to Apache's directory indexing
vhost	vhost	Allow routes to match on subdomains

You might not use most of these modules. In my applications I (Alex) usually have only body-parser, cookie-parser, csurf, express-session, and method-override, so migration isn't too difficult. The following listing shows a small application that uses these middleware components.

Listing 9.27 Express 4 middleware

```
var bodyParser = require('body-parser');          Load middleware
var cookieParser = require('cookie-parser');   ❶ modules
var csurf = require('csurf');
var session = require('express-session');
var methodOverride = require('method-override');
var express = require('express');
var app = express();

app.use(cookieParser('secret'));               Configure each piece
app.use(session({ secret: 'secret' }));      ❷ of middleware
app.use(bodyParser());
app.use(methodOverride());
app.use(csurf());

app.get('/', function(req, res) {              Define
  res.send('Hello');                         ❸ a route
});

app.listen(3000);
```

To install Express 4 and the necessary middleware, you should run the following command in a new directory:

```
npm install --save body-parser cookie-parser \
        csurf express-session method-override \
        serve-favicon express
```

This will install all of the required middleware modules along with Express 4, and save them to a package.json file. Once you've loaded the middleware components with require ❶, you can add them to your application's stack with app.use as you did in Express 3 ❷. Route handlers can be added exactly as they were in Express 3 ❸.

> **OFFICIAL MIGRATION GUIDE** The Express authors have written a migration guide that's available in the Express wiki on GitHub.[3] This includes a quick rundown of every change.

---

[3] https://github.com/visionmedia/express/wiki/Migrating-from-3.x-to-4.x

You can't use `app.configure` anymore, but it should be easy to stop using it. If you're using `app.configure` to do only certain things for specific environments, then just use a conditional statement with `process.env.NODE_ENV`. The following example assumes a fictitious middleware component called `logger` that can be set to be noisy, which might not be desirable when the tests are running:

```
if (process.env.NODE_ENV !== 'test') {
  app.use(logger({ verbose: true }));
}
```

The new routing API reinforces the concept of mini-applications that can be mounted on different endpoints. That means your RESTful resources can leave off the resource name from URLs. Instead of writing `app.get('/songs', songs.index)`, you can now write `songs.get('/', index)` and mount `songs` on `/songs` with `app.use`. This fits in well with the route separation pattern in technique 67.

The next listing shows how to use the new router API.

Listing 9.28 Express 4 middleware

```
var express = require('express');
var app = express();

app.get('/', function(req, res) {
  res.send('Hello');
});

var songs = express.Router();          ①  Create new
                                           router

songs.get('/', function(req, res) {
  res.send('A list of songs');         ②  Add route handler to
});                                        this set of routes

songs.get('/:id', function(req, res) {
  res.send('A specific song');
});
                                       ③  Mount router with
app.use('/songs', songs);                  a URL prefix

app.listen(3000);
```

After creating a new router ①, you can add routes the same way you always did, using HTTP verbs like get ②. The cool thing about this is you can also add middleware that will be confined to these routes only: just call `songs.use`. That was previously trickier in older versions of Express.

Once you've set up a router, you can mount it using a URL prefix ③. That means you could do things like mount the same route handler on different URLs to easily alias them.

If you put the routers in their own files and mount them in your main app.js file, then you could even distribute routers as modules on npm. That means you could compose applications from reusable routers.

The final thing we'll mention about Express 4 is the new `router.param` method. This allows you to run asynchronous code when certain route parameters are present. Let's say you have `'/songs/:song_id'`, and `:song_id` should only ever be a valid song that's in the database. With `route.param` you can validate that the value is a number *and* exists in the database, before any route handlers run!

```
router.param('song_id', function(req, res, next, id) {
  Song.find(id, function(err, song) {
    if (err) {
      return next(err);
    } else if (!song) {
      return next(new Error('Song not found'));
    }
    req.song = song;
    next();
  });
});

router.get('/songs/:song_id', function(req, res, next) {
  res.send(req.song);
});
```

In this example, `Song` is assumed to be a class that fetches songs from a database. The actual route handler is now extremely simple, because it only runs if a valid song has been found. Otherwise, `next` will shortcut execution and pass an error to the error-handling middleware.

That wraps up our section on web application development techniques. There's one more important thing before we move on to the next chapter. Like everything else, web applications should be well tested. The next section has some techniques that we've found useful when testing web applications.

9.3   *Testing web applications*

Testing can feel like a chore, but it can also be an indispensable tool for verifying ideas, particularly if you're creating web APIs without user interfaces.

Chapter 10 has an introduction to testing in Node, and technique 84 has an example for testing web applications. In the next technique we extend this example to show you how to test authenticated routes.

TECHNIQUE 76   **Testing authenticated routes**

Test frameworks like Mocha make tests easy to read and write, and SuperTest helps keep HTTP-related tests clean. But authentication support isn't usually built into such modules. In this technique you'll learn one way to handle authentication in tests, and the approach is general enough that it can be reused with other test modules as well.

PROBLEM

You want to test parts of your application that are behind a session-based username and password.

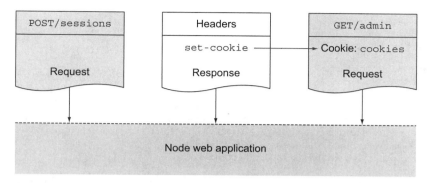

Figure 9.8 You can test authenticated routes by catching cookies.

SOLUTION

Make a request that signs in during the setup phase of the tests, and then reuse the cookies for subsequent tests.

DISCUSSION

Some web frameworks and testing libraries handle sessions for you, so you can test routes without worrying too much about logging in. This isn't true for Mocha and SuperTest, which we've used before in this book, so you'll need to know a bit about how sessions work.

The session handling that Express uses from Connect is based around a cookie. Once the cookie has been set, it can be used to load the user's session. That means that to write a test that accesses a secure part of your application, you'll need to make a request that signs in the user, grabs the cookies, and then use the cookies for subsequent requests. This process is shown in figure 9.8.

To write tests that access authenticated routes, you'll need a test user account, which usually involves creating database fixtures. You'll read about fixtures in chapter 10, technique 87.

Once the data is ready, you can use a library like SuperTest to make a POST to your session-handling endpoint with a username and password. Cookies are transmitted using HTTP headers, so you can read them from res.headers['set-cookie']. You should also make an assertion to ensure the account was signed in.

Now any new requests just need to set the Cookie header with the value from res.headers, and your test user will be signed in. The next listing shows how this works.

Listing 9.29 Testing authenticated requests

```
var app = require('./../app');
var assert = require('assert');
var request = require('supertest');
var administrator = {
  username: 'admin',
  password: 'secret'
};
```

① This is a test user that would usually be loaded from a fixture.

```
describe('authentication', function() {
  var cookies;

  before(function(done) {
    request(app)
      .post('/session')
      .field('username', administrator.username)
      .field('password', administrator.password)
      .end(function(err, res) {
        assert.equal(200, res.statusCode);
        cookies = res.headers['set-cookie'];
        done();
      });
  });

  it('should allow admins to access the admin area', function(done) {
    request(app)
      .get('/admin')
      .set('Cookie', cookies)
      .expect(200, done);
  });
});
```

The session cookie is in the set-cookie header. ③

❷ **Post the username and password.**

This route is behind a login. ④

❺ **Set the Cookie header with the saved session cookie.**

The first part of this test loads the required modules and sets up an example user ❶. This would usually be stored in a database, or set by a fixture. Next, a POST is made with the username and password ❷. The session cookie will be available in the set-cookie header ❸.

To access a route that's behind a login ❹, set the Cookie header with the previously saved cookies ❺. You should find that the request is handled as if the user had signed in normally.

The trick to understanding testing with sessions can be learned by looking at how Connect's session middleware component works. Other middleware isn't as easy to manage during testing, so the next technique introduces the concept of test *seams*, which will allow you to bring middleware under control during testing.

TECHNIQUE 77   Creating seams for middleware injection

Middleware is flexible and composable. This modular approach makes Connect-based applications a joy to work on. But there's a downside to middleware: testability. Some middleware makes routes inherently difficult to test. This technique looks at ways to get around this by creating *seams*.

PROBLEM
You're using middleware that has made your application difficult to test.

SOLUTION
Find seams where middleware can be replaced for the duration of the tests.

DISCUSSION
The term *seam* is a formal way of describing places in code that can be changed without editing the original code. The concept is extended to apply to languages like

JavaScript by Stephen Vance in his book *Quality Code: Software Testing Principles, Practices, and Patterns.*[4]

> *A seam in our code gives us the opportunity to take control of that code and exercise it in a testing context. Any place that we can execute, override, inject, or control the code could be a seam.*

One example of this is the `csrf` middleware component from Connect. It creates a session variable that can be included in forms to avoid cross-site request forgery attacks. Let's say you have a web application that allows registered users to create calendar entries. If your site didn't use CSRF protection, someone could create a web page that tricks a user of your site into deleting items from their calendar. The attack might look like this:

```
<img src="http://calendar.example.com/entry/1?_method=delete">
```

The user's browser will dutifully load the image source that's hosted on an external site. But it references your site in a potentially dangerous way. To prevent this, a random token is generated on each request and inserted into forms. The attacker doesn't have access to the token, so the attack is mitigated.

Unfortunately, simply adding `express.csrf` to routes that render forms isn't entirely testable. Tests can no longer post to route handlers without first loading the form and scraping out the session variable that contains the secret CSRF token.

To get around this, you need to take `express.csrf` under your control. Refactor it to create a seam: place it in a module that contains your other custom middleware, and then change it during tests. You don't need to test `express.csrf` because the authors of Express and Connect have done that for you—instead, change its behavior during tests.

Two other options are available: checking if `process.env.NODE_ENV` is set to `test` and then branching to a test-only version of the CSRF middleware component, or patching `express.csrf`'s internals so you can extract the secret token. There are problems with both of these approaches: the first means you can't get 100% code coverage—your production code has to include test code. The second approach is potentially brittle: it's too sensitive to Connect changing the way CSRF works in the future.

The seam-based concept that we'll use requires that you create a middleware file if you don't already have one. This is just a file that groups all of your middleware together into a module that can be easily loaded. Then you need to create a function that wraps around `express.csrf`, or just returns it. A basic example follows.

Listing 9.30   Taking control of middleware

```
var express = require('express');

module.exports.csrf = express.csrf;
```
 Create a place where other middleware can be injected.

4 https://www.informit.com/store/quality-code-software-testing-principles-practices-9780321832986

All this does is export the original `csrf` middleware component ❶, but now it's much easier to inject different behavior during tests. The next listing shows what such a test might look like.

Listing 9.31   Injecting new behavior during tests

```
var middleware = require('./../middleware');

middleware.csrf = function() {
  return function(req, res, next) {
    req.session._csrf = '';
    next();
  };
};

var app = require('./../app');
var request = require('supertest');

describe('calendar', function() {
  it('should allow us to turn off csrf', function(done) {
    request(app)
      .post('/calendars')
      .expect(200, done);
  });
});
```

❶ Load middleware component first, and replace csrf method.

❷ This stops views from breaking if they expect _csrf to be set.

❸ A 200 should be returned, not a 403!

This test loads our custom middleware module before anything else, and then replaces the `csrf` method ❶. When it loads `app` and fires off a request using Super-Test, Express will use our injected middleware component because `middleware.js` will be cached. The `_csrf` value is set just in case any views expected it ❷, and the request should return a 200 instead of a 403 (forbidden) ❸.

It might not seem like we've done much, but by refactoring how `express.csrf` is loaded, we've been able to run our application in a more testable way. You may prefer to make two requests to ensure the `csrf` middleware component is used normally, but this technique can be used for other things as well. You can bring any middleware under control for testing. If there's something you don't want to run during tests, look for seams that allow you to inject the desired behavior, or try to create a seam using simple JavaScript or Node patterns—you don't need a complex dependency injection framework; you can take advantage of Node's module system.

The next technique builds on some of these ideas to allow tests to interact with simulated versions of remote services. This will make it easier if you're writing tests for an application that accesses remote services, like a payment gateway.

TECHNIQUE 78   **Testing applications that depend on remote services**

Third-party modules can help you integrate your applications with remote services like GitHub, Twitter, and Facebook. But how do you test applications that depend on such remote services? This technique looks at ways to insert stubs for remote dependencies, to make your tests faster and more maintainable.

PROBLEM

You're using a social network for authentication, or a service to accept payments, and you don't want your tests to access these remote dependencies.

SOLUTION

Find the seams between your application, the remote service, and the things you want to test, and then insert your own HTTP servers to simulate parts of the remote dependency.

DISCUSSION

One of the things that most web applications need, yet is easy to get dangerously wrong, is user accounts. Using a Node module that supports the authorization services provided by companies like GitHub, Google, Facebook, and Twitter is both quick and potentially safer than creating a bespoke solution.

It's comparatively easy to adopt one of these services, but how do you test it? In technique 76, you saw how to write tests for authenticated routes. This involved signing in and saving the session cookies so subsequent requests appeared authenticated. You can't use the same approach with remote services, because your tests would have to make requests to real-life production services. You could use a test account, but what if you wanted to run your tests offline?

To get around this, you need to create a seam between your application and the remote service. Whenever your application attempts to communicate with the remote service, you need to slot in a fake version that emits similar responses. In unit tests, mock objects simulate other objects. What you want is to mock a service.

There are two requirements that your application needs to satisfy to make this possible:

- Configurable remote services
- A web server that can stand in for the remote service

The first condition means your application should allow the URLs of remote services to be changed. If it needs to connect to http://auth.example.com/signin, then you'll need to specify http://localhost:3001/signin during testing. The port is entirely up to you—some solutions we've seen use a sequence of port numbers so multiple services can be run at once for the same tests.

The second condition can be handled however you want. If you're using Express, you could start an Express server with a limited set of routes defined—just enough routes and code to simulate the remote service. This server can be kept in its own module, and loaded in the tests that need it.

In practice this doesn't require much code, so once you understand the principle it shouldn't be too difficult to reuse it to handle practically any API. If the API you're attempting to simulate isn't well documented, then you may need to capture real requests to figure out how it works.

Investigating remote APIs

There are times when remote APIs aren't well documented. Once you get beyond the basic API calls, there are bound to be parts that aren't easy to understand. In cases like this, we find it's best to make requests with a command-line tool like `curl`, and watch the requests and responses in an HTTP logging tool.

If you're using Windows, then Fiddler (http://www.telerik.com/fiddler) is absolutely essential. It's described as a HTTP debugging proxy, and it supports HTTPS as well.

```
GET https://github.com/
    ← 200 text/html 5.52kB
GET https://a248.e.akamai.net/assets.github.com/stylesheets/bundles/github2-24f59e3ded11f2a
    1c7ef9ee730882bd8d550cfb8.css
    ← 200 text/css 28.27kB
GET https://a248.e.akamai.net/assets.github.com/images/modules/header/logov7@4x-hover.png?1
    324325424
    ← 200 image/png 6.01kB
GET https://a248.e.akamai.net/assets.github.com/javascripts/bundles/jquery-b2ca07cb3c906cec
    cfd58811b430b8bc25245926.js
    ← 200 application/x-javascript 32.59kB
↻ GET https://a248.e.akamai.net/assets.github.com/stylesheets/bundles/github-cb564c47c51a14
    af1ae265d7ebab59c4e78b92cb.css
    ← 200 text/css 37.09kB
GET https://a248.e.akamai.net/assets.github.com/images/modules/home/logos/facebook.png?1324
    526958
    ← 200 image/png 5.55kB
>> GET https://github.com/twitter

[7]    [i:.*]                                                              ?:help [*:8080]
```

Glance has built-in pages for errors.

For Linux and Mac OS, mitmproxy (http://mitmproxy.org/) is a powerful choice. It allows HTTP traffic to be observed in real time, dumped, saved, and replayed. We've found it perfect for debugging our own Node-powered APIs that support desktop apps, as well as figuring out the quirks of certain popular payment gateways.

In the following three listings, you'll see how to create a *mock server* that a test can use to simulate some of PayPal's behavior. The first listing shows the application itself.

Listing 9.32   A small web store that uses PayPal

```
var express = require('express');
var app = express();
var PayPal = require('./paypal');
var payPal = new PayPal({
  user: 'NIP',
  payPalUrl: 'http://localhost:3001/validate',   ←──① These settings control
                                                         PayPal's behavior.
```

```
    rootUrl: 'http://localhost:3000'
});

app.use(express.bodyParser());

app.post('/buy', function(req, res, next) {        ❷ Get the purchase URL
  var url = payPal.generateUrl(req.body);          ◄─    used by PayPal.

  // Send the user to the PayPal payment page
  res.redirect(url);
});

app.post('/paypal/success', function(req, res, next) {   ❸ Handle payment
  payPal.verify(req.body, function(err) {           ◄─      notifications.
    if (err) next(err);
    app.emit('purchase:accepted', req.body);        ◄─  When a payment is
    res.send(200);                                  ❹  successful, emit an event.
  });
});

module.exports = app;
```

The settings passed to the `PayPal` class near the top of the file ❶ are used to control PayPal's behavior. One of them, `payPalUrl`, could be https://www.sandbox.paypal .com/cgi-bin/webscr for testing against PayPal's staging server. Here we use a local URL, because we're going to run our own mock server.

If this were a real project, you should use a configuration file to store these options. One for each environment would make sense. Then the test configuration could point to a local server, staging could use PayPal sandbox, and live would use Pay-Pal.com. For more on configuration files, see technique 69.

To make a payment, the user is forwarded to PayPal's hosted forms. Our demonstration `PayPal` class has the ability to generate this URL, and it'll use `payPalUrl` ❷. This example also features payment notification handling ❸—known as IPN in Pay-Pal's nomenclature.

An extra feature we've added here is the call to `emit` ❹. This makes it easier to test, because our tests can now listen for `purchase:accepted` events. It's also useful for setting up email handling—see technique 73 for more on that.

Now for the mock PayPal server. All it needs to do is handle IPN requests. It basically needs to say, "Yes, that purchase has been validated." It could also optionally report errors so we can test error handling on our side as well. The next listing shows what the tiny mocked server looks like.

Listing 9.33 Mocking PayPal's IPN requests

```
var express = require('express');
var paypalApp = express();
                                                  ❶ Allow errors
                                                     to be toggled
paypalApp.returnInvalid = false;        ◄─┘
                                                        ❷ Handle IPN
                                                           validation
paypalApp.post('/validate', function(req, res) {   ◄─
```

```
    if (paypalApp.returnInvalid) {
      res.send('INVALID');
    } else {
      res.send('VERIFIED');
    }
});
```

```
module.exports = paypalApp;
```

Real-life PayPal stores receive a POST from PayPal with an order's details, near the end of the sales process. You need to take that order and send it back to PayPal for verification. This prevents attackers from crafting a POST request that tricks your application into thinking a fake purchase was made.

This example includes a toggle so errors can be turned on ❶. We're not going to use it here, but it's useful in real projects because you'll want to test how errors are handled. There will be customers that encounter errors, so ensuring they're handled gracefully is critical.

Once all that's in place, all we need to do is send back the text VERIFIED ❷. That's all PayPal does—it can be frustratingly abstruse at times!

Finally, let's look at a test that puts all of this together. The next listing uses both the mocked PayPal server and our application to make purchases.

Listing 9.34   Testing PayPal

```
var app = require('./../app');
var assert = require('assert');
var request = require('supertest');
var payPalMock = require('./paypalmock');

function makeCustomer() {                        ◁──┐  Customer
  return {                                        ❶  fixture
    address1: '123',
    city: 'Nottingham',
    country: 'GB',
    email: 'user@example.com',
    first_name: 'Paul',
    last_name: 'Smith',
    state: 'Nottinghamshire',
    zip: 'NG10932',
    tax_number: ''
  };
}
                                        ❷  Order
function makeOrder() {                  ◁──┘  fixture
  return {
    id: 1,
    customer: makeCustomer()
  };
}
                                                    ❸  What PayPal
function makePayPalIpn(order) {              ◁──────┘  would send
  // More fields should be used for the real PayPal system
```

```
    return {
      'payment_status': 'Completed',
      'receiver_email': order.customer.email,
      'invoice': order.id
    };
}

describe('buying the book', function() {
  var payPalServer;

  before(function(done) {                                    ④ Before each test, start
    payPalServer = payPalMock.listen(3001, done);              up mock PayPal server
  });
                                              ⑤ After each test, close
  after(function(done) {                        mock PayPal server
    payPalServer.close(done);
  });

  it('should redirect the user to paypal', function(done) {
    var order = makeOrder();

    request(app)
      .post('/buy')
      .send(order)                      ⑥ User should be redirected
      .expect(302, done);                 for valid orders
  });

  it('should handle IPN requests from PayPal', function(done) {
    var order = makeOrder();

    app.once('purchase:accepted', function(details) {
      assert.equal(details.receiver_email, order.customer.email);
    });

    request(app)
      .post('/paypal/success')
      .send(makePayPalIpn(order))       ⑦ 200 OK should be returned
      .expect(200, done);                 for valid orders
  });
});
```

This test sets up a sample order ❷, which requires a customer ❶. We also create an object that has the same fields as a PayPal IPN request—this is what we're going to send to our mock PayPal server for validation. Before ❹ and after ❺ each test, we have to start and stop the mock PayPal server. That's because we don't want servers running when they're not needed—it might cause other tests to behave strangely.

When the user fills out the order form on our site, it will be posted to a route that generates a PayPal URL. The PayPal URL will forward the user's browser to PayPal for payment. Listing 9.34 includes a test for this ❻, and the URL it generates will start with our local test PayPal URL from listing 9.32.

There's also a test for the notification sent by PayPal ❼. This is the one we're focusing on that requires the PayPal mocked server. First we have to POST to our server at /paypal/success with the notification object ❸—this is what PayPal would normally do—and then our application will make an HTTP request to PayPal, which will hit the mocked server, and then return VERIFIED. The test simply ensures a 200 is returned, but it's also able to listen for the purchase:accepted event, which indicates a given purchase is complete.

It might seem like a lot of work, but you'll be able to work more efficiently once your remote services are simulated with mock servers. Your tests run faster, and you can work offline. You can also make your mocked services generate all kinds of unusual responses, which will help you get better test coverage if that's one of your goals.

This is the last web-related technique that we cover in this chapter. The next sections discuss emerging trends in Node web development.

9.4   *Full stack frameworks*

In this chapter you've seen how to build web applications with Node's built-in modules, Connect, and Express. There's an emerging class of new frameworks known as *full stack frameworks*. They provide features that are needed to make rich, browser-based applications with modern tools like data binding, but also handle server-side concerns like modeling business logic and data persistence.

If you're set on using Express, then you can still start working with full stack frameworks today. The *MEAN* solution stack uses MongoDB, Express, AngularJS, and Node. There could be many MEAN implementations out there, but the MEAN Stack from Linnovate (https://github.com/linnovate/mean) is currently the most popular. It comes with Mongoose for data models, Passport for authorization, and Twitter Bootstrap for the user interface. If you're working in a team that's already familiar with Bootstrap, AngularJS, and Mongoose, then this is a great way to get new projects off the ground quickly.

The book *Getting MEAN* [5] introduces full stack development and covers Mongoose models, RESTful API design, and account management with Facebook and Twitter.

Another framework that builds on Express and MongoDB is Derby (http://derbyjs.com/). Instead of Mongoose, Derby uses Racer to implement data models. This allows data from different clients to be synchronized, using operational transformation (OT). OT is specifically designed to support collaborative systems, so Derby is a good choice for developing software inspired by Etherpad (http://etherpad.org/). It also has client-side features like templates and data binding.

If you like Express but want more features, then one option that we haven't covered is Kraken (http://krakenjs.com/) by PayPal. This framework adds more structure to Express projects by adding subdirectories for configuration, controllers, Grunt tasks, and tests. It also supports internationalization out of the box.

Some frameworks are almost entirely focused on the browser, relying on Node only for sensitive operations and data persistence. One popular example is Meteor (https://www.meteor.com/). Like Derby and MEAN Stack, it uses MongoDB, but the creators

---

[5]   *Getting MEAN* by Simon Holmes: http://www.manning.com/sholmes/.

are planning support for other databases. It's based around a pub/sub architecture, where JSON documents are pushed between the client and server. Clients retain an in-memory copy of the documents—servers publish sets of documents, while clients subscribe to them. This means most model-related code in the browser can be written synchronously.

Meteor embraces reactive programming, a paradigm that's currently popular in desktop development circles. This allows *reactive computations* to be bound to methods. If you subscribe a function to such a value, the function will be rerun when the value changes. The overall effect in a real application is streamlined code—there's essentially less pub/sub management and event-handling code.

Hoodie (http://hood.ie/) is a competitor to Meteor. It uses CouchDB, and is suitable for mobile applications because it synchronizes data when possible. Almost everything can happen locally. It comes with built-in account management, which is as simple as `hoodie.account.signUp('alex@example.com', 'pass')`. There's even a global public store, so data can be saved for specific users or made available to everyone using a given application.

There's lots of activity in the Node web framework scene, but there's another aspect to Node web development that we haven't mentioned yet: real-time development.

9.5   *Real-time services*

Node is the natural choice for web-based real-time services. Broadly speaking, this involves three types of applications: statistics servers, collaboration services, and latency-sensitive applications like game servers.

It's not that difficult to start a server with Express and collect data about your other applications, servers, weather sensor data, or dog-feeding robot. Unfortunately, doing this well isn't trivial. If you're logging something every time someone plays your free-to-play iOS game, what happens when there are thousands of events a minute? How do you scale this, or view critical information in real time?

Some companies have this problem on a huge scale, and fortunately some of them have created open source tools that we can reuse. One example is Cube (http://square.github.io/cube/) by Square. Cube allows you to collect timestamped events and then derive metrics on them. It uses MongoDB, so you could feed data out to something that generates graphs. Square has a solution for visualizing the data called Cubism.js (http://square.github.io/cubism/), which renders new values in real-time (see figure 9.9).

The Etherpad project (http://etherpad.org/) is a Node-powered collaborative document editor. It allows users to chat as they make changes to documents, and color-codes the changes so it's easy to see what each person is doing. It's based on some of the modules you've seen in this book: Mikeal Rogers' `request`, Express, and Socket.IO.

WebSockets make these projects possible. Without WebSockets, pushing data to the client would be more cumbersome. Node has a rich set of WebSockets

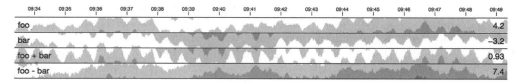

Figure 9.9 Cubism.js shows time series values in real time.

implementations—Socket.IO (http://socket.io/) is the most popular, but there's also `ws` (https://www.npmjs.org/package/ws), which claims to be the fastest WebSocket implementation.

There's a parallel between sockets and streams; SocketStream (http://socketstream .org/) aims to bridge the gap by building web applications entirely around streams. It uses the HTML5 `history.pushState` API with single-page applications, Connect middleware, and code sharing with the browser.

9.6 *Summary*

In this chapter you've seen how Node fits in with modern web development. It can be used to improve client-side tooling—it's now normal for client-side developers to install Node and a Node build tool.

Node is also used for server-side development. Express is the major web framework, but many projects can get off the ground with a subset from Connect. Other frameworks are similar to Express, but have a different focus. Restify is one example, and can be used to make strict RESTful APIs (technique 71).

Writing well-structured Express applications means you should adopt certain patterns and idioms that the Node community has adopted. This includes error handling (technique 70), folders as modules and route separation (technique 67), and decoupling through events (technique 73).

It's also increasingly common to use Node modules in the browser (technique 66), and client-side code in Node (technique 65).

If you want to write better code, you should adopt test-driven development as soon as possible. We've included some techniques that enable you to test things like authentication (technique 76) and mocking remote APIs (technique 78), but the simple act of writing a test to think about new code is one of the best ways to improve your Node web applications. One way you can do this is every time you want to add a new route to a web application, write the test first. Practice using Super-

Test, or a comparable HTTP request library, and use it to plan out new API methods, web pages, and forms.

The next chapter shows you how to write better tests, whether they're simple scripts or database-driven web applications.

10

Tests: The key to confident code

This chapter covers

- Assertions, custom assertions, and automated testing
- Ensuring things fail as expected
- Mocha and TAP
- Testing web applications
- Continuous integration
- Database fixtures

Imagine that you wanted to add a new currency to an online shop. First you'd add a test to define the expected calculations: subtotal, tax, and the total. Then you'd write code to make this test pass. This chapter will help you learn how to write tests by looking at Node's built-in features for testing: the `assert` module and test scripts that you can set in your package.json file. We also introduce two major test frameworks: Mocha and `node-tap`.

> ### Introduction to testing
>
> This chapter assumes you have some experience at writing unit tests. Table 10.1 includes definitions of the terminology used; if you want to know what we mean by assertions, test cases, or test harnesses, you can refer to this table.
>
> For a more detailed introduction to testing, *The Art of Unit Testing, Second Edition* (Roy Osherove, Manning, 2013; http://manning.com/osherove2/) has step-by-step examples for writing maintainable and readable tests. *Test Driven Development: By Example* (Kent Beck, Addison-Wesley, 2002; http://mng.bz/UT12) is another well-known foundational book on the topic.

One of the advantages of working with Node is that the community adopted testing early on, so there's no shortage of modules to help you write fast and readable tests. You might be wondering what's so great about tests and why we write them early on during development. Well, tests are important for exploring ideas before committing to them—you can think of them like small, flexible experiments. They also communicate your *intent*, which means they help document and expand on the ideas in the key parts of the project. Tests can also help reduce maintenance in mature projects by allowing you to check that changes haven't broken existing working features.

The first thing to learn about is Node's `assert` module. This module allows you to define an expectation that will throw an error when it isn't met. Expressing and confirming expectations is the main purpose of tests, so you'll see a lot of assertions in this chapter. Although you don't have to use `assert` to write tests, it's a built-in core module and similar to assertion libraries you might've used before in other languages. The first set of techniques in this chapter is all about assertions.

To get everyone up to speed, the next section includes a list of common terms used when working with tests.

10.1   Introduction to testing with Node

To make it easier for newcomers to automated testing, we've included table 10.1 that defines common terminology. This table also outlines what we mean by specific terms, because some programming communities use the same terms slightly differently.

Table 10.1   Node testing concepts

Term	Description
Assertion	A logical statement that allows you to test expressions. Supported by the `assert` core module; for example: `assert.equal(user.email, 'name@example.com');`.

Test case	One or more assertions that test a particular concept. In Mocha, a test case looks like this:
	
	`it('should calculate the square of a number', function() {`
	`    assert.equal(square(4), 16);`
	`});`

Table 10.1   Node testing concepts *(continued)*

Term	Description
| Test harness | A program that runs tests and collates output. The resulting reports help diagnose problems when tests fail.<br>This builds on the previous example, so with Mocha a test harness looks like this:<br><br>```js
var assert = require('assert');
var square = require('./square');

describe('Squaring numbers', function() {
  it('should calculate the square of a number', function() {
    assert.equal(square(4), 16);
  });

  it('should return 0 for 0', function() {
    assert.equal(square(0), 0);
  });
});
``` |
Fixture	Test data that is usually prepared before tests are run. Let's say you want to test a user accounts system. You could predefine users and their passwords, and then include the passwords in the tests to ensure users can sign in correctly. In Node, JSON is a popular file format for fixtures, but you could use a database, SQL dump, or CSV file. It depends on your application's requirements.
Mock	An object that simulates another object. Mocks are often used to replace I/O operations that are either slow or difficult to run in unit tests; for example, downloading data from a remote web API, or accessing a database.
Stub	A method stub is used to replace functionality for the duration of tests. For example, methods used to communicate with an I/O source like a disk or remote API can be stubbed to return predefined data.
Continuous integration server	A CI server runs automated tests whenever a project is updated through a version control server.

The only feature from table 10.1 that Node directly supports is assertions. The other features are provided through third-party libraries—you'll learn about CI servers in technique 86, and mocks and fixtures in technique 87. You don't have to use all of these things to write tests, you can actually write tests with just the assertion module. The next section introduces the `assert` module so you can start writing basic tests.

10.2   *Writing simple tests with assertions*

So far we've briefly mentioned that assertions are used to test expressions. But what does this involve? Typically assertions are functions that cause an exception to be raised if a condition isn't met. A failing assertion is like your credit card being declined in a store—your program will refuse to run no matter how many times you try. The idea of assertions has been around for a long time; even C has assertions.
```

In C, the standard library includes the `assert()` macro, which is used for verifying expressions. In Node, we have the `assert` core module. There are other assertion modules out there, but `assert` is built-in and easy to use and extend.

COMMONJS UNIT TESTING The `assert` module is based on the CommonJS Unit Testing 1.1 specification (http://wiki.commonjs.org/wiki/Unit_Testing/1.1). So even though it's a built-in core module, you can use other assertion modules as well. The underlying principles are always the same.

This section introduces Node's built-in assertions. By following the first technique, you'll be able to write tests using the `assert` core module by using `assert.equal` to check for equality, and to automate the running of tests by using npm scripts.[1]

TECHNIQUE 79 Writing tests with built-in modules

Have you ever tried to write a quick test for an important feature, but you found yourself lost in test library documentation? It can be hard to get started actually writing tests; it seems like there's a lot to learn. If you just start using the `assert` module, though, you can write tests right now without any special libraries.

This is great when you're writing a small module and don't want to install any dependencies. This technique demonstrates how to write clean, expressive, single-file tests.

PROBLEM

You have a clear idea of the acceptable input and output values for your module, class, or functions, and you want it to be clear when the output values don't match the input.

SOLUTION

Use the `assert` module and npm scripts.

DISCUSSION

Node comes with an assertion module. You can think of this as a toolkit for checking expectations against outcomes. Internally this is done by comparing *actual* values against *expected* values. The `assert.equal` method demonstrates this perfectly: the arguments are `actual`, `expected`. There's also a third optional argument: `message`. Passing a message makes it easier to understand what happened when tests fail.

Let's say you're writing an online shop that calculates order prices, and you've sold three items at $3.99 each. You could ensure the correct price gets calculated with this:

```
assert.equal(
  order.subtotal, 11.97,
  'The price of three items at $3.99 each'
);
```

In methods with only a single required argument, like `assert(value)`, the expected value is `true`, so it uses the same pattern.

---

[1] This is defined by the `scripts` property in a package.json file. See `npm help scripts` for details on this feature.

To see what happens when a test fails, try running the next listing.

Listing 10.1   The `assert` module

```
var assert = require('assert');          Load
var actual = square(2);                  assertion
var expected = 4;                     ❶ module

assert(actual, 'square() should have returned a value');
assert.equal(
  actual,                          assert module is a function
  expected,                              for testing truth ❷
  'square() did not calculate the correct value'
);

function square(number) {               square() function is
  return number * number + 1;        ❹ what we're testing
}
```

assert.equal allows expectations to be set up for shallow equality checks ❸

The first line you'll see in most test files is one that loads the `assert` module ❶. The `assert` variable is also a function aliased from `assert.ok`—which means you can use either `assert()` or `assert.ok()` ❷.

It's easy to forget the order of the arguments for `assert.equal`, so you might find yourself checking Node's documentation a lot. It doesn't really matter how you order the arguments—some people might find it easier to list the expected value first so they can scan the code for values—but you should be consistent. That's why this example is explicit about the naming of `actual` and `expected` ❸.

This test has a function that has an intentional bug ❹. You can run the test with `node assertions.js`, which should display an error with a stack trace:

```
assert.js:92
  throw new assert.AssertionError({
        ^
AssertionError: square() did not calculate the correct value
    at Object.anonymous (listings/testing/assertions.js:7:8)     File and line
     at Module._compile (module.js:456:26)                       number where the
    at Object.Module._extensions..js (module.js:474:10)       ❶ assertion failed
    at Module.load (module.js:356:32)
    at Function.Module._load (module.js:312:12)
    at Function.Module.runMain (module.js:497:10)
    at startup (node.js:119:16)
    at node.js:901:3
```

These stack traces can be hard to read. But because we've included a message with the assertion that failed, we can see a description of what went wrong. We can also see that the assertion failed in the file assertions.js on line 7 ❶.

The `assert` module has lots of other useful methods for testing values. The most significant is `assert.deepEqual`, which can check for equality between two objects. This is important because `assert.equal` can only compare shallow equality. Shallow equality is used for comparing primitive values like strings or numbers, whereas `deepEqual` can compare objects with nested objects and values.

You might find `deepEqual` useful when you're writing tests that return complex objects. Think about the online shop example from earlier. Your shopping cart might look like this: `{ items: [ { name: "Coffee beans", price: 4.95 } ], subtotal: 4.95 }`. It's an object that contains an array of shopping cart items, and a subtotal that is calculated by another object. Now, to check this entire object against one that you've defined in your unit test, you'd use `assert.deepEqual`, because it's able to compare objects rather than just primitive values.

The `deepEqual` method can be seen in the next listing.

Listing 10.2   Testing object equality

```
var assert = require('assert');          ◁———❶  Load the assert module.
var actual = login('Alex');
var expected = new User('Alex');

assert.deepEqual(actual, expected, 'The user state was not correct'); ◁┐

function User(name) {                                       Use deepEqual to
  this.name = name;                                         compare objects.  ❷
  this.permissions = {
    admin: false
  };
}

function login(name) {
  var user = new User(name);          ❸  The login system
  user.permissions.admin = true;  ◁─┘   has a bug!
  return user;
}
```

This example uses the `assert` module ❶ to test objects created by a constructor function, and an imaginary login system. The login system is accidentally loading normal users as if they were administrators ❸.

The `assert.deepEqual` method ❷ will go over each property in the objects to see if any are different. When it runs into `user.permissions.admin` and finds the values differ, an `AssertionError` exception will be raised.

If you take a look at the `assert` module's documentation, you'll see many other useful methods. You can invert logic with `notDeepEqual` and `notEqual`, and even perform strict equality checks just like `===` with `strictEqual` and `notStrictEqual`.

There's another aspect to testing, and that's ensuring that things fail the way we expect. The next technique looks at testing for failures.

TECHNIQUE 80   Testing for errors

Programs will eventually fail, but when they do, we want them to produce useful errors. This technique is about ensuring that expected errors are raised, and about how to cause exceptions to be raised during testing.

PROBLEM

You want to test your error-handling code.

SOLUTION

Use assert.throws and assert.ifError.

DISCUSSION

One of the conventions we use as Node developers is that asynchronous methods should return an error as the first argument. When we design our own modules, we know there are places where errors are likely to occur. Ideally we should test these cases to make sure the correct errors are passed to callbacks.

The following listing shows how to ensure an error hasn't been passed to an asynchronous function.

Listing 10.3   Handling errors from asynchronous APIs

```
var assert = require('assert');
var fs = require('fs');

function readConfigFile(cb) {
  fs.readFile('config.cfg', function(err, data) {
    if (err && err.code === 'ENOENT') {
      cb(null, { database: 'psql://localhost/test' });
    } else if (err) {
      cb(err);
    } else {
      // Do important configuration stuff
      cb(null, data);
    }
  });
}

// Test to make sure non-existent configuration
// files are handled correctly.
readConfigFile(function(err, data) {
  assert.ifError(err);
});
```

❶ The function we want to test takes a callback.

❷ If the error is "file not found," return default values.

❸ Otherwise, pass the error to the callback.

❹ Now ifError will fail if any errors are passed.

Although assert.ifError works synchronously, it makes semantic sense to use it for testing asynchronous functions that pass errors to callbacks. Listing 10.3 uses an asynchronous function called readConfigFile ❶ to read a configuration file. In reality this might be the database configuration for a web application, or something similar. If the file isn't found, then it returns default values ❷. Any other error—and this is the important part—will be passed to the callback ❸.

That means the assert.ifError test ❹ can easily detect whether an unexpected error has occurred. If something changes in the structure of the project that causes an unusual error to be raised, then this test will catch that and warn the developers before they release potentially dangerous code.

Now let's look at raising exceptions during testing. Rather than using try and catch in our tests, we can use assert.throws.

To use assert.throws, you must supply the function to be run and an expected error constructor. Because a function is passed, this works well with asynchronous APIs, so you can use it to test things that depend on I/O operations.

The next listing shows how to use `assert.throws` with a fictitious user account system.

Listing 10.4   Ensuring that exceptions are raised

```
var assert = require('assert');
var util = require('util');
                                              ① The first argument of
assert.throws(                                   assert.throws is the
  function() {                                   function being tested.
    loginAdmin('Alex');
  },
  PermissionError,
  'A PermissionError was expected'            The second argument
);                                          ② is the expected error.

function PermissionError() {                    PermissionError inherits
  Error.call(this, arguments);                  from the standard Error
}                                           ③ constructor.
util.inherits(PermissionError, Error);

function User(name) {
  this.name = name;
  this.permissions = {
    admin: false
  };
}
                                            This is a fake login system that  ④
function loginAdmin(name) {                  only allows administrators to
  var user = new User(name);                                    sign in.
  if (!user.permissions.admin) {
    throw new PermissionError('You are not an administrator');
  }
  return user;
}
```

The assertion ① checks to ensure the expected exception is thrown. The first argument is a function to test, in this case `loginAdmin`, and the second is the expected error ②.

This highlights two things about `assert.throws`: it can be used with asynchronous APIs because you pass it a function, and it expects error objects of some kind. When developing projects with Node, it's a good idea to use `util.inherits` to inherit from the built-in `Error` constructor. This allows people to easily catch your errors, and you can decorate them with extra properties that include useful additional information if required.

In this case we've created `PermissionError` ③, which is a clear name and therefore self-documenting—if someone sees a `PermissionError` in a stack trace, they'll know what went wrong. A `PermissionError` is subsequently thrown in the `loginAdmin` function ④.

This technique delved into error handling with the `assert` module. Combined with the previous techniques, you should have a good understanding of how to test a range of situations with assertions. With `assert.equal` you can quickly compare numbers and strings, and this covers a lot of problems like checking prices in invoices or email addresses in web application account-handling code. A lot of the time, assert.ok— which is aliased as assert()—is enough to get by, because it's a quick and handy way for checking for *truthy* expressions. But there's one last thing to master if you want to really take advantage of the assert module; read on to learn how to create custom assertions.

TECHNIQUE 81   Creating custom assertions

Node's built-in assertions can be extended to support application-specific expressions. Sometimes you find yourself repeatedly using the same code to test things, and it seems like there might be a better way. For example, suppose you're checking for valid email addresses with a regular expression in assert.ok. Writing custom assertions can solve this problem, and is easier than you might think. Learning how to write custom assertions will also help you understand the assertion module from the inside out.

PROBLEM

You're repeating a lot of code in your tests that could be replaced if only you had the right assertion.

SOLUTION

Extend the built-in assert module.

DISCUSSION

The assert module is built around a single function: fail. assert.ok actually calls fail with the logic inverted, so it looks like this: if (!value) fail(value). If you look at how fail works, you'll see that it just throws an assert.AssertionError:

```
function fail(actual, expected, message, operator, stackStartFunction) {
  throw new assert.AssertionError({
    message: message,
    actual: actual,
    expected: expected,
    operator: operator,
    stackStartFunction: stackStartFunction
  });
}
```

The error object is decorated with properties that make it easier for test reporters to break down the location and cause of failures. The people who wrote this module knew that others would like to write their own assertions, so the fail function is exported, which means it can be reused.

Writing a custom assertion involves the following steps:

1 Define a method with a signature similar to the existing assertion library.
2 Call fail when an expectation isn't matched.
3 Test to ensure failure results in an AssertionError.

Listing 10.5 puts these steps together to define a custom assertion that ensures a regular expression is matched.

Listing 10.5 A custom assertion

Execute regular expression match against a string using String.prototype .match ❷

Make sure tests fail ❹

Make sure tests pass ❸

```
var assert = require('assert');          ◀━━❶  Load assert module
assert.match = match;

function match(actual, regex, message) {
▷ if (!actual.match(regex)) {
     assert.fail(actual, regex, message, 'match', assert.match);
   }
}

assert.match('{ name: "Alex" }', /Alex/, 'The name should be "Alex"');  ◀┐
▷ assert.throws(
    function() {
      assert.match('{ name: "Alex" }', /xlex/, 'This should fail');
    },
    assert.AssertionError,
    'A non-matching regex should throw an AssertionError'
);
```

This example loads the assertion module ❶ and then defines a function called `match` that runs `assert.fail` to generate the right exception when the regular expression doesn't match the *actual* value ❷. The key detail to remember is to define the argument list to be consistent with other methods in the assertion module—the example here is based on `assert.equal`.

Listing 10.5 also includes some tests. In reality these would be in a separate file, but here they illustrate how the custom assertion works. First we check to see if it passes a simple test by matching a string against a regular expression ❸, and then `assert.throws` is used to ensure the test really does fail when it's meant to ❹.

> ### Your own domain-specific language
>
> Using custom assertions is but one technique for creating your own testing DSL (domain-specific language). If you find you're duplicating code between test cases, then by all means wrap that code in a function or class.
>
> For example, `setUpUserAccount({ email: 'user@example.com' })` is more readable than three or four lines of setup code, particularly if it's repeated between test cases.

This example might seem simple, but understanding how to write custom assertions improves your knowledge of the underlying module. Custom assertions can help clean up tests where expectations have been made less expressive by squeezing concepts into built-in assertions. If you want to be able to say something like `assert.httpStatusOK`, now you can!

With assertions out of the way, it's time to look at how to organize tests across multiple files. The next technique introduces test harnesses that can be used to organize groups of test files and run them more easily.

10.3   *Test harnesses*

A test harness, or automated test framework, generally refers to a program that sets up the runtime environment and runs tests, and then collects and compares the results. Since it's automated, tests can be run by other systems including continuous integration (CI) servers, covered in technique 86.

Test harnesses are used to execute groups of test files. That means you can easily run lots of tests with a single command. This not only makes it easier for you to run tests, but makes it easier for your collaborators as well. You may even decide to start all projects with a test harness before doing anything else. The next technique shows you how to make your own test harness, and how to save time by adding scripts to your package.json files.

TECHNIQUE 82   **Organizing tests with a test harness**

Suppose you're working on a project and it keeps on growing, and using a single test file is starting to feel messy. It's hard to read and causes confusion that leads to mistakes. So you'd like to use separate files that are related in some way. Perhaps you'd even like to run tests one file at a time to help track down issues when things go wrong.

Test harnesses solve this problem.

PROBLEM

You want to write tests organized into test cases and test suites.

SOLUTION

Use a test harness.

DISCUSSION

First, let's consider what a test harness is. In Node, a test harness is a command-line script that you can run by typing the name of the script. At its most basic, it must run a group of test files and display any errors that occur. We don't need anything particularly special to do that—a failed assertion will cause an exception to be thrown; otherwise the program will exit silently with a return code of 0.

That means a basic test harness is just `node test/*.js`, where test/ is a directory that contains a set of test files. We can go one better than that. All Node projects should have a package.json file. One of the properties in this file is `scripts`, and one of the default scripts is `test`. Any string you set here will be executed like a shell command.

The following listing shows an example package.json file with a test script.

Listing 10.6   A package.json with a test script

```
{
  "name": "testrunner",
  "version": "0.0.0",
  "description": "A test runner",
  "main": "test-runner.js",
  "dependencies": {},
  "devDependencies": {},
  "scripts": {
    "test": "node test-runner.js test.js test2.js"
```

❶ Test script invocation goes here

```
    },
    "author": "",
    "license": "MIT"
}
```

With `node test-runner.js test.js test2.js` set as the `test` script ❶, other developers can now run your tests simply by typing `npm test`. This is much easier than having to remember a project-specific command.

Let's expand this example by looking at how test harnesses work. A test harness is a Node program that runs groups of test files. Therefore, we should be able to give such a program a list of files to test. Whenever a test fails, it should display a stack trace so we can easily track down the source of the failure.

In addition, it should exit with a non-zero return code whenever a test fails. That allows tests to be run in an automated way—other software can easily see if a test failed without having to parse the textual output from the tests. This is how continuous integration (CI) servers work: they automatically run tests whenever code is committed to a version control system like Git.

The next listing shows what a test file for this system should look like.

Listing 10.7 An example test file

```
var assert = require('assert');

it('should run a test', function() {        ❶ The it() function
  assert('a' === 'a');                          represents a test case.
});

it('should allow a test to fail', function() {   ❷ A failing test is included
  assert(true);                                     so we can see what the
  assert.equal('a', 'b', 'Bad test');               results look like.
});

it('should run a test after the failed test', function() {
  assert(true);
});                                          ❸ This last test
                                                should still run.
```

The `it` function ❶ looks strange, but it's a global function that will be provided by our test framework. It gives each test case a name so it's easier to understand the results when the tests are run. A failing test is included ❷ so we can see what happens when tests fail. The last test case ❸ should run even though the second one failed.

Now, the final piece of the puzzle: the next listing includes a program capable of executing this test.

Listing 10.8   Running tests in a prescribed manner

```
var assert = require('assert');
var exitCode = 0;
var filenames = process.argv.slice(2);          ❶ The it() function
                                                    is defined as a
it = function(name, test) {                          global.
  var err;

  try {
    test();                    ⟵    Tests are passed as
  } catch (e) {                      callbacks and run inside
    err = e;                    ❷    a try/catch statement.
  }                                                               ❸ Results are printed
                                                                     based on the presence
  console.log(' - it', name, err ? '[FAIL]' : '[OK]');   ⟵         of an exception.

  if (err) {
    console.error(err);              ❹  A stack trace is printed to
    console.error(err.stack);    ⟵       help track down errors.
    exitCode = 1;
  }
};
                                             ❺  Each file passed on the
filenames.forEach(function(filename) {   ⟵      command-line is run.
  console.log(filename);
  require('./' + filename);                ❻  When the program exits,
});                                             return a non-zero error
                                                code if a test failed.
process.on('exit', function() {      ⟵
  process.exit(exitCode);
});
```

This example can be run by passing test files as arguments: node test-runner.js test.js test2.js test-n.js. The it function is defined as a global ❶, and is called it so the tests and their output read logically. This makes sense when the results are printed ❸.

Because it takes a test case name and a callback, the callback can be run under whatever conditions we desire. In this case we're running it inside a try/catch statement ❷, which means we can catch failed assertions and report errors ❹ to the user.

Tests are loaded by calling require on each of the files passed in as command-line arguments ❺. In a more polished version of this program, the file handling would need to be more sophisticated. Wildcard expressions would need to be supported, for example.

A failed test case causes the exitCode variable to be set to a non-zero value. This is returned to the controlling process with process.exit in the exit handler ❻.

Even though this is a minimal example, it can be run with npm test, gives test cases a little syntax sugar with it, improves the error reporting over a simple file full of assertions, and returns a non-zero exit code when something goes wrong. This is the basis for most popular Node test frameworks like Mocha, which we'll look at in the next section.

10.4 Test frameworks

If you're starting a new project, then you should install a test framework early on. Suppose that you're building an online blogging system, or perhaps a simple content management system. You'd like to allow people to sign in, but only allow specific users to access the administration interface. By using a test framework like Mocha or `node-tap`, you can write tests that address these specific concerns: users signing up for accounts, and administrators signing in to the admin interface. You could create separate test files for these concerns, or bundle them up as groups of test cases under "user accounts tests."

Test frameworks include scripts to run tests and other features that make it easier to write and maintain tests. This section features the Mocha test framework in technique 84 and the Test Anything Protocol (TAP; http://testanything.org/) in technique 85—two popular test frameworks favored by the Node community. Mocha is lightweight: it runs tests, provides three styles for structuring test cases,[2] and expects you to use either Node's `assert` module or another third-party module. Conversely, `node-tap`, which implements TAP, uses an API that includes assertions.

TECHNIQUE 83　　**Writing tests with Mocha**

There are many test frameworks for Node, so it's difficult to choose the right one. Mocha is a popular choice because it's well maintained and has the right balance of features and conventions.

In general, you use a test framework to organize tests for a project. You'd like to use a test framework that other people are familiar with so they can easily navigate and collaborate without learning a new module. Perhaps you're just looking for a way to run tests the same way every time, or trigger them from an automated system.

PROBLEM

You need to organize your tests in a way other developers will be familiar with, and run the tests with a single command.

SOLUTION

Use one of the many open source test frameworks for Node, like Mocha.

DISCUSSION

Mocha must be installed from npm before you can do anything else. The best way to install it is with `npm install --save-dev mocha`. The `--save-dev` option causes npm to install Mocha into `node_modules/` and update your project's package.json file with the latest version from npm. It will be saved as a development dependency.

Listing 10.9 shows an example of a simple test written with Mocha. It uses the `assert` core module to make assertions, and should be invoked using the `mocha` command-line binary. You should add `"./node_modules/mocha/bin/mocha test/*.js"` to

---

[2] Mocha supports API styles based on Behavior Driven Development (BDD), Test Driven Development (TDD), and Node's module system (exports).

Mocha versions

The version of Mocha we use for this chapter is 1.13.x. We prefer to run the tests by installing it locally to the project rather than as a systemwide Node module. That means that tests can be run using `./node_modules/mocha/bin/mocha test/*.js` rather than just typing `mocha`. That allows different projects to have different versions of Mocha, just in case the API changes dramatically between major releases.

An alternative is to install Mocha globally with `npm install --global mocha`, and then run tests for a project by typing `mocha`. It will display an error if it can't find any tests.

---

the `"test"` property in package.json—see technique 82 for more details on how to do that.

Listing 10.9   A simple Mocha test

```
var index = require('./../index');
var assert = require('assert');

describe('Amazing mathematical operations', function() {      ❶ Group related
  it('should square numbers', function() {                        tests with
    assert.equal(index.square(4), 16);                            describe()
  });

  it('should run a callback after a delay', function(done) {   ❷ Include done
    index.randomTimeout(function() {                              argument for
      assert(true);                                               asynchronous tests
      done();         ❸ Call done() when
    });                 asynchronous test
  });                   has finished
});
```

The `describe` and `it` functions are provided by Mocha. The `describe` function can be used to group related test cases together, and `it` contains a collection of assertions that form a test case ❶.

Special handling for asynchronous tests is required. This involves including a `done` argument in the callback for the test case ❷, and then calling `done()` when the test has finished ❸. In this example, a timeout will be triggered after a random interval, which means we need to call `done` in the `index.randomTimeout` method. The corresponding file under test is shown in the next listing.

Listing 10.10   A sample module to test

```
module.exports.square = function(a) {      ❶ Simple synchronous function
  return a * a;                                that squares numbers
};

module.exports.randomTimeout = function(cb) {   ❷ Asynchronous function
  setTimeout(cb, Math.random() * 500);             that will run after a
};                                                 random amount of time
```

CONTROLLING SYNCHRONOUS AND ASYNCHRONOUS BEHAVIOR If done isn't included as an argument to it, then Mocha will run the test synchronously. Internally, Mocha looks at the length property of the callback you pass to it to see if an argument has been included. This is how it switches between asynchronous and synchronous behavior. If you include an argument, then Mocha will wait around for done to be called until a timeout is reached.

This module defines two methods: one for squaring numbers ❶ and another that runs a callback after a random amount of time ❷. It's just enough to demonstrate Mocha's main features in listing 10.9.

To set up a project for Mocha, the index.js file we've used in this example should be in its own directory, and at the same level should be a package.json file with a test subproperty of the scripts property set to "./node_modules/mocha/bin/mocha test/*.js". There should also be a test/ directory that contains example_test.js.[3] With all that in place, you can run the tests with npm test.

When the tests are run, you should notice some dots appearing. These mark a completed test case. When the tests take more than a preset amount of time, they'll change color to denote they ran slower than is acceptable. Since index.randomTimeout prevents the second test from completing for a random amount of time, there will be times when Mocha thinks the tests are running too slowly. You can increase this threshold by passing --slow to Mocha, like this: ./node_modules/mocha/bin/mocha --slow 2000 test/*.js. Now you don't need to feel guilty about seemingly slow tests!

Assertions per test

In listing 10.9, each test case has a single assertion. Some consider this best practice—and it can result in readable tests.

But we prefer the idea of a single concept per test. This style structures test cases around well-defined concepts, using the absolute necessary amount of assertions. This will typically be a small number, but occasionally more than one.

To see all of the command-line options, type node_modules/mocha/bin/mocha --help or visit http://mochajs.org/.

We've included the final package.json file in listing 10.11 in case you have trouble writing your own. You can install Mocha and its dependencies with npm install.

Listing 10.11   The Mocha sample project's JSON file

```
{
  "name": "mocha-example-1",
  "version": "0.0.0",
  "description": "A basic Mocha example",
  "main": "index.js",
```

---

[3] The file can be called anything as long as it's in the test/ directory.

```
  "dependencies": {},
  "devDependencies": {
    "mocha": "~1.13.0"
  },
  "scripts": {
    "test": "./node_modules/mocha/bin/mocha --slow 2000 test/*.js"
  },
  "author": "Alex R. Young",
  "license": "MIT"
}
```

In this technique the `assert` core module has been used, but you could swap it for another assertion library if you prefer. Others are available, like chai (https://npmjs .org/package/chai) and should.js (https://github.com/visionmedia/should.js).

Mocha is often used for testing web applications. In the next technique, you'll see how to use Mocha for testing web applications written with Node.

TECHNIQUE 84   Testing web applications with Mocha

Let's suppose you're building a web application with Node. You'd like to test it by running it in a way that allows you to send requests and receive responses—you want to make HTTP requests to test the web application works as expected.

PROBLEM

You're building a web application and would like to test it with Mocha.

SOLUTION

Write tests with Mocha and the standard `http` module. Consider using an HTTP module designed for testing to simplify your code.

DISCUSSION

The trick to understanding web application testing in Node is to learn to think in terms of HTTP. This technique starts off with a Mocha test and the `http` core module. Once you understand the principles at work and can write tests this way, we'll introduce a third-party HTTP testing module to demonstrate how to simplify such tests. The built-in `http` module is demonstrated first because it's useful to see what goes on behind the scenes and to get a handle on exactly how to construct such tests.

The following listing shows what the test looks like.

Listing 10.12   A Mocha test for a web application

```
var assert = require('assert');
var http = require('http');
var index = require('./../index');

function request(method, url, cb) {          ◁────┐  This function is
  http.request({                                   │  used to make HTTP
    hostname: 'localhost',                        ❶  requests in the tests.
    port: 8000,
    path: url,
    method: method
  }, function(res) {
    res.body = '';
```

```
    res.on('data', function(chunk) {
      res.body += chunk;
    });
```

> After the request has been sent, collect any data that is sent back to the client. ❷

```
    res.on('end', function() {
      cb(res);
    });
  }).end();
}
```

> When the request and response have both finished, run the callback. ❸

```
describe('Example web app', function() {
  it('should square numbers', function(done) {
    request('GET', '/square/4', function(res) {
      assert.equal(res.statusCode, 200);
      assert.equal(res.body, '16');
      done();
    });
  });
```

> Ensure the response is what we expect for the /square method. ❹

```
  it('should return a 500 for invalid square requests', function(done) {
    request('GET', '/square', function(res) {
      assert.equal(res.statusCode, 500);
      done();
    });
  });
});
```

> Ensure the server correctly raises an error for invalid requests. ❺

This example is a test for a web service that can square numbers. It's a simple web service that expects GET requests and responds with plain text. The goal of this test suite is to ensure that it returns the expected results and correctly raises errors when invalid data is sent. The tests aim to simulate browsers—or other HTTP clients, for that matter—and to do so, both the server and client are run in the same process.

To run a web service, all you need to do is create a web server with http.create-Server(). Exactly how this is done is shown in listing 10.13. Before discussing that, let's finish looking at this test.

The test starts by creating a function for making HTTP requests ❶. This is to reduce the amount of duplication that would otherwise be present in the test cases. This function could be its own module, which could be used in other test files. After a request has been sent, it listens for data events on the response object to store any data returned by the server ❷. Then it runs the provided callback ❸, which is passed in from the test cases.

Figure 10.1 shows how Node can run both servers and clients in the same process to make web application testing possible.

An example of this is the test for the /square method that ensures 4 * 4 === 16 ❹. Once that's done, we also make sure invalid HTTP query parameters cause the server to respond with a 500 error ❺.

The standard assertion module is used throughout, and res.statusCode is used to test the expected status codes are returned.

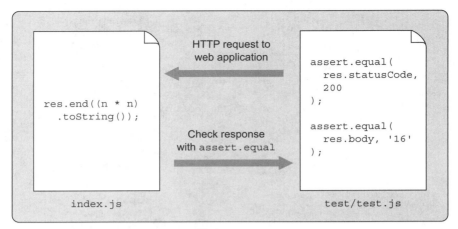

Figure 10.1   **Node can run a web server and requests against it to support web application testing.**

The implementation of the corresponding web service is shown in the next listing.

Listing 10.13   **A web application that can square numbers**

```
var http = require('http');

var server = http.createServer(function(req, res) {          ❶ Parse out number
  if (req.url.match(/^/square/)) {                                parameter from
    var params = req.url.split('/');           ◀─────            the URL
    var number;
    if (params.length > 1 && params[2]) {
      number = parseInt(params[2], 10);
      res.writeHead(200);                     ❷ Perform square
      res.end((number * number).toString());   ◀─┘  calculation
    } else {
      res.writeHead(500);              ◀────
      res.end('Invalid input');           Return a 500 when
    }                                ❸   parameter is invalid
  } else {
    res.writeHead(404);
    res.end('Not found');
  }
})

server.listen(8000);

module.exports = server;
```

Before doing anything else, `http.createServer` is used to create a server. Near the end of the file, `.listen(8000)` is used to make the server start up and listen for connections. Whenever a request with a URL matching /square comes in, the URL is parsed for a numerical parameter ❶ and then the number is squared and sent to the client ❷. When the expected parameter isn't present, a 500 is returned instead ❸.

One part of listing 10.12 that can be improved on is the `request` method. Rather than defining a wrapper around `http.request`, we can use a library designed specifically for testing with web requests.

The module we've chosen is `SuperTest` (https://github.com/visionmedia/supertest) by TJ Holowaychuk, who also wrote Mocha. There are other similar libraries out there. The general idea is to simplify HTTP requests and allow assertions to be made about the request.

You can add SuperTest to the development dependencies for this example by running `npm install --save-dev supertest`.

The following listing shows how the test can be refactored using the `SuperTest` module.

Listing 10.14 The refactored Mocha test that uses SuperTest

```
var assert = require('assert');
var index = require('./../index');
var request = require('supertest');

describe('Example web app', function() {
  it('should square numbers', function(done) {
    request(index)
      .get('/square/4')
      .expect(200)
      .expect(/16/, done);
  });

  it('should return a 500 for invalid square requests', function(done) {
    request(index)
      .get('/square')
      .expect(500, done);
  });
});
```

Pass HTTP server to SuperTest ❶

❷ **Set up an assertion to make sure HTTP status is 200**

❸ **Ensure request body contains the right answer**

❹ **When passing invalid parameters, check a 500 is returned**

Although functionally identical to listing 10.12, this example improves it by removing the boilerplate for making HTTP requests. The `SuperTest` module is easier to understand, and allows assertions to be expressed with less code while still being asynchronous. `SuperTest` expects an instance of an HTTP server ❶, which in this case is the application that we want to test. Once the application has been passed to `SuperTest`'s main function, `request`, we can then make a `GET` request using `request().get`. Other HTTP verbs are also supported, and form parameters can be sent when using `post()` with the `send` method.

`SuperTest`'s methods are chainable, so once a request has been made, we can make an assertion by using `expect`. This method is polymorphic—it checks the type of the argument and acts accordingly. If you pass it a number ❷, it'll ensure that the HTTP status was that number. A regular expression will make it check the response body for a match ❸. These expectations are perfect for the requirements of this test.

Any HTTP status can be checked, so when we actually expect a 500, we can test for it ❹.

Though it's useful to understand how to make simple web applications and test them using the built-in `http` module, we hope you can see how third-party modules like `SuperTest` can simplify your code and make your tests clearer.

Mocha captures the zeitgeist of the current state of testing in Node, but there are other approaches that are just as valid. The next technique introduces TAP and the Test Anything Protocol, due to its endorsement by Node's maintainer and core contributors.

TECHNIQUE 85   The Test Anything Protocol

Test harness output varies based on programming language and test framework. There are initiatives to unify these reports. One such effort that has been adopted by the Node community is the Test Anything Protocol (http://testanything.org). Tests that use TAP will produce lightweight streams of results that can be consumed by compatible tools.

Suppose you need a test harness that's compatible with the Test Anything Protocol, either because you have other tools that use TAP, or because you're already familiar with it from other languages. It could be that you don't like Mocha's API and want an alternative, or are interested in learning about other solutions to testing in Node.

PROBLEM
You want to use a test framework that's designed to interoperate with other systems.

SOLUTION
Use Isaac Z. Schlueter's `tap` module.

DISCUSSION
TAP is unique because it aims to bridge test frameworks and tools by specifying a protocol that implementors can use. The protocol is stream-based, lightweight, and human-readable. In comparison to other, heavier XML-based standards, TAP is easy to implement and use.

It's significant that the `tap` module (https://npmjs.org/package/tap) is written by Node's former maintainer, Isaac Z. Schlueter. This is an important seal of approval by someone highly influential in the Node community.

The example in this technique uses the number squaring and random timeout module used in technique 83 so you can compare how tests look in TAP and Mocha.

The following listing shows what the test looks like. For the corresponding module, see listing 10.10.

Listing 10.15   Testing with TAP

```
var index = require('./../index');          ❶  Load the tap module, and assign
var test = require('tap').test;                 a variable to the test() method.

Define tests
with test().  ❷
             test("Alex's handy mathematics module", function(t) {
               t.test('square', function(t) {
                 t.equal(index.square(4), 16);     ❸  Using tap's built-in assertions.
```

plan() can be used **5** to indicate the expected number of assertions.

4 Call end() to indicate when a test has finished.

6 When plan() has been called there's no need to call end().

```
              t.end();
            });

  t.test('randomTimeout', function(t) {
    t.plan(1);
      index.randomTimeout(function() {
        t.ok(true);
      });
    });

      t.end();
    });
```

This is different from the Mocha example because it doesn't assume there are any global test-related methods like it and describe: a reference to tap.test has to be set up **1** before doing anything else. Tests are then defined with the t.test() method **2**, and can be nested if needed. Nesting allows related concerns to be grouped, so in this case we've created a test case for each method being tested.

The tap module has built-in assertions, and we've used these throughout the test file **3**. Once a test case has finished, t.end() must be called **4**. That's because the tap module assumes tests are asynchronous, so t.end() could be called inside an asynchronous callback.

Another approach is to use t.plan **5**. This method indicates that n assertions are expected. Once the last assertion has been called, the test case will finish running. Unlike the previous test case, the second one can leave off the call to t.end() **6**.

This test can be run with ./node_modules/tap/bin/tap.js test/*_test.js. You can add this line to the test property of scripts in the package.json file to make it run with npm test.

If you run the test with the tap script, you'll see some clean output that consolidates the results of each assertion. This is generated by one of tap's submodules called tap-results. The purpose of the tap-results module is to collect lines from a TAP stream and count up skips, passes, and fails to generate a simplified report;

```
ok test/index_test.js .................................. 3/3
total ............................................. 3/3

ok
```

Due to the design of the tap module, you're free to run the tests with node test/index_test.js. This will print out the TAP stream instead:

```
# Alex's handy mathematics module
# square
ok 1 should be equal
# randomTimeout
ok 2 (unnamed assert)

1..2
# tests 2
# pass  2

# ok
```

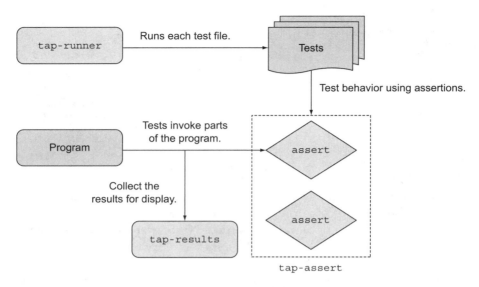

Figure 10.2   `node-tap` **uses several reusable submodules to orchestrate tests.**

Tests written with the `tap` module will still return a non-zero exit code to the shell when tests fail—you can use `echo $?` to see the exit code. Try making the test in listing 10.15 fail on purpose and take a look at `$?`.

The fact that TAP is designed around producing and consuming streams fits in well with Node's design. It's also a fact of life that tests must interact with other automated systems in most projects, whether it's a deployment system or a CI server. Working with this protocol is easier than heavyweight XML standards, so hopefully it will rise in popularity.

Figure 10.2 illustrates how some of `node-tap`'s submodules are used to test a program. Control is transferred from different modules, to your tests, back to your program, and then out through the reporter, which collects and analyzes results. The key thing to realize about this is that `node-tap`'s submodules can be reused and replaced—if you don't like the way results are displayed with `tap-results`, it could be replaced with something else.

Beyond test frameworks, real-world testing depends on several more important tools and techniques. The next section shows you how to use continuous integration servers and database fixtures, and how to mock I/O.

10.5   *Tools for tests*

When you're working in a team, you want to quickly see when someone has committed changes that break the tests. This section will help you to set up a continuous integration server so you can do this. It also has techniques for other project-related issues like using databases with tests and mocking web services.

TECHNIQUE 86   **Continuous integration**

Your tests are running, but what happens when someone makes a change that breaks the project? Continuous integration (CI) servers are used to automatically run tests. Because most test harnesses return a non-zero exit code on failure, they're conceptually simple enough. Their real value comes becomes apparent when they can easily be hooked up to services like GitHub and send out emails or instant messages to team members when tests fail.

PROBLEM

You want to see when members of a team commit broken code so you don't accidentally release it.

SOLUTION

Use a continuous integration server.

DISCUSSION

You're working in a team and want to see when tests start to fail. You're already using a version control system like Git, and want to run tests whenever code is committed to a tracked repository. Or you've written an open source project and want to indicate on the GitHub or Bitbucket page that it's well tested.

There are many popular open source and proprietary continuous integration services. In this technique we'll look at Travis CI (https://travis-ci.org/), because it's free for open source projects and popular in the Node community. If you want an open source CI server that you can install locally, take a look at Jenkins (http://jenkins-ci.org/).

Travis CI provides a link to an image that shows your project's build status. To add a project, sign in with your GitHub account at travis-ci.org, and then go to the profile page at travis-ci.org/profile. You'll see a list of your GitHub projects, and toggling a switch to On will cause the repository to be updated with a service hook that will notify Travis CI whenever you push an update to GitHub.

Once you've done that, you need to add a .travis.yml file to the repository to tell Travis CI about the environment your code depends on. All you need to do is set the Node version.

Let's work through a full example and set up a project on Travis so you can see how it works. You'll need three files: a package.json, a file to test, and the .travis.yml file. The following listing shows the file we'll be testing.

Listing 10.16   A simple test to try with Travis CI

```
var assert = require('assert');

function square(a) {
  return a * a;
}

assert.equal(square(4), 16);
```

❶ This simple test should pass when run with Travis.

This is just a simple test ❶ that we can play with to see what Travis CI does. After running, it should result in an exit code of zero—type `node test.js` and then `echo $?` to see the exit code. Put this file in a new directory so you can set up a Git repository for it later. Before that we'll need to create a package.json file. The next listing is a simple package.json that allows the tests to be run with `npm test`.

Listing 10.17   A basic package.json file

```json
{
  "name": "travis-example",
  "version": "0.0.0",
  "description": "A sample project for setting up Travis CI and Node.",
  "main": "test.js",
  "scripts": {
    "test": "node test.js"
  },
  "author": "Alex R. Young",
  "license": "MIT"
}
```

Finally, you'll need a .travis.yml file. It doesn't need to do much other than tell Travis CI that you're using Node.

Listing 10.18   Travis CI configuration

```yaml
language: node_js
 node_js:
  - "0.10"
```

Now go to GitHub.com and sign in; then click New Repository to create a public repository. We've called ours `travis-example` so people know it's purely educational. Follow the instructions on how to commit and push the project to GitHub—you'll need to run `git init` in the directory where you placed the preceding three code files, and then `git add .` and `git commit -m 'Initial commit'`. Then use `git remote add <url>` with the repository URL GitHub gives you, and push it with `git push -u origin master`.

Go to your profile at travis-ci.org/profile and toggle your new project to On. You might need to tell Travis CI to sync your project list—there's a button near the top of the page.

There's one last step before you can see any tests running on Travis CI. Make a single change in test.js—add another assertion if you like, and then commit and `git push` the change. This will cause GitHub to send an API request to Travis CI that will cause your tests to be run.

Travis CI knows how to run Node tests—it defaults to `npm test`. If you're adapting this technique to an existing project and you use another command (perhaps `make test`), then you can change what Travis CI runs by setting the `script` value in the YML file. Documentation can be found under "Configuring your build" in the documentation (http://about.travis-ci.org/docs/user/build-configuration/#script).

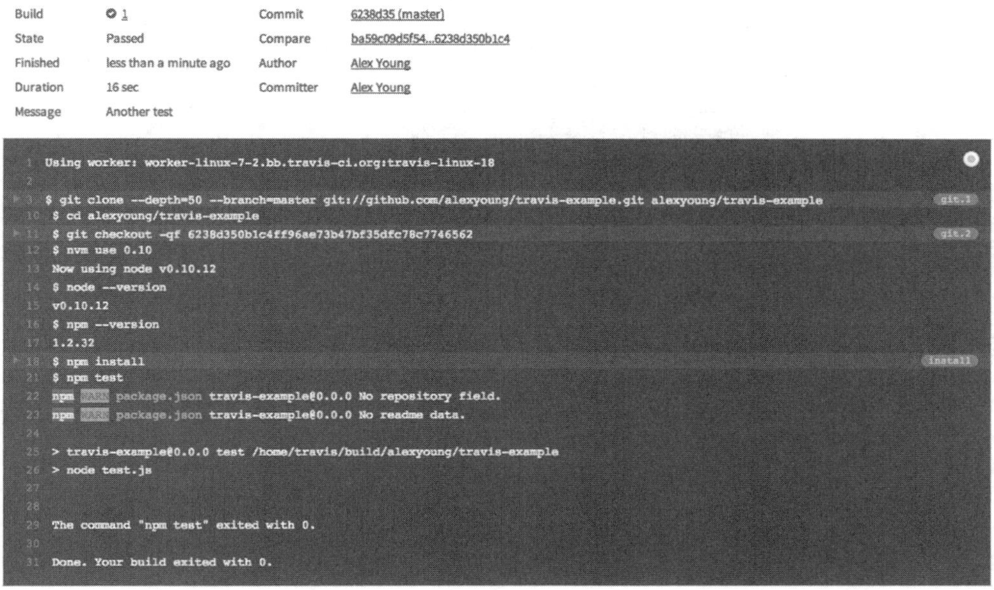

Figure 10.3   Travis CI running tests

If you go to the homepage at Travis CI, you should now see a console log with details on how the tests were run. Figure 10.3 shows what successful tests look like.

Now that you have tests running successfully, you should edit test.js to make the tests fail to see what happens.

Travis can be configured to use most of the things you expect when running tests in real-world projects—databases and other services can be added (http://about .travis-ci.org/docs/user/database-setup/), and even virtual machines.

Getting a database configured with suitable fixtures for your projects is one of the most important parts of testing. The next technique shows how to set up databases for your tests.

TECHNIQUE 87   Database fixtures

Most applications need to persist data in some way, and it's important to test that data is stored correctly. This technique explores three solutions for handling database fixtures in Node: loading database dumps, creating data during tests, and using mocks.

PROBLEM

You need to test code that stores data in a database, or performs some other kind of I/O like sending data over a network. You don't want to access this I/O resource during testing, or you have test data that you want to preload before tests. Either way, your application is highly dependent on an I/O service, and you want to carefully test how your code interacts with it.

SOLUTION

Preload data before the tests, or mock the I/O layer.

DISCUSSION

The mark of well-written code is how testable it is. Code that performs I/O instinctively feels hard to test, but it shouldn't be if the APIs are cleanly decoupled.

For example, if your code performs HTTP requests, then as you've seen in previous techniques, you can run a customized HTTP server within your tests to simulate a remote service. This is known as *mocking*. But sometimes you don't want to mock I/O. You may wish to write tests that result in changes being made against a real database, albeit an instance of the database that tests can safely destroy and re-create. These types of tests are known as *integration tests*—they "integrate" disparate layers of software to deeply test behavior.

This technique presents two ways to handle database fixtures for integration tests; then we'll broaden the scope by demonstrating how to use mocks. First up: preloading data using database dumps.

Database dumps

Using database dumps is the sledgehammer of database fixture techniques. All you need is to be able to run some code before all of your other tests so you can clear out a database and drop in a pristine copy. If this test data is dumped from a database, then you can use your existing database tools for preparing and exporting the data.

Listing 10.19 uses Mocha and MySQL, but you could adapt the same principles to work with other databases and test frameworks. See technique 83 for more on Mocha.

Listing 10.19   The `assert` module

```
var assert = require('assert');
var exec = require('child_process').exec;
var path = require('path');
var ran = 0;                                      ◁——  ❶ ran variable will be used
var db = {                                              to ensure fixtures aren't
  config: {                                             loaded more than once
    username: 'nodeinpractice',
    password: 'password'
  }
};                                                ❷ loadFixture method is
                                                    used to asynchronously
function loadFixture(sqlFile, cb) {          ◁——     prepare database
  sqlFile = path.resolve(sqlFile);
  var command = 'mysql -u ' + db.config.username + ' ';
  command += db.config.database + ' < ' + sqlFile;

  exec(command, function(err, stdout, stderr) {   ◁——
    if (err) {                                           Node's child_process.exec
      console.error(stderr);                             method is used to invoke
      throw err;                                         mysql command-line tool
    } else {                                       ❹    to import data and
      cb();                                              overwrite existing data
    }
  }
```

MySQL command line is prepared for importing database dump ❸

Use assertions ⑥
to ensure
database
import is only
performed
once

Run
database
import ⑧

⑤ **before() callback**
will run prior to
all other tests

```
      });
  }

  before(function(done) {        ⟵   
    ran++;
    assert.equal(1, ran);
    assert.equal(process.env.NODE_ENV, 'test', 'NODE_ENV is not test');   ⟵
    loadFixture(__dirname + '/fixtures/file.sql', function() {
      process.nextTick(done);
    });                                Use assertions to only allow
  });                              import to run in test environment  ⑦
```

The basic principle of this example is to run a database import before the other tests. If you use this approach with your own tests, make sure the import wipes the database first. Relational databases can do this with DROP TABLE IF EXISTS, for example.

To actually run this test, you need to pass the filename to mocha before the other tests, and make sure the test environment is used. For example, if listing 10.19 is called test/init.js, then you could run these commands in the shell: NODE_ENV=test ./node_modules/.bin/mocha test/init.js test/**/*_test.js. Or simply place the commands in your project's package.json file under scripts, test.

The ran variable ❶ is used to ensure the importer is only run once ❻. Mocha's before function is used ❺ to run the importer once, but if test/init.js is accidentally loaded elsewhere (perhaps by running mocha test/**/*.js), then the import would happen twice.

To import the data, the loadFixture function is defined ❷ and run in the before callback ❽. It accepts a filename and a callback, so it's easy to use asynchronously. An additional check is performed to make sure the import is only run in the test environment ❼. The reasoning here is that the database settings would be set by the rest of the application based on NODE_ENV, and you wouldn't want to lose data by overwriting your development or production databases with the test fixtures.

Finally, the shell command to import the data is built up ❸ and run with child_process ❹. This is database-dependent—we've used MySQL as an example, but a similar approach would work with MongoDB, PostgreSQL, or pretty much any database that has command-line tools.

Using dump files for fixtures has some benefits: you can author test data with your favorite database tool (we like Sequel Pro), and it's easy to understand how it all works. If you change your database's schema or the "model" classes that work with the data, then you'll need to update your fixtures.

Creating test data with your ORM

An alternative approach is to create data programmatically. This style requires setup code—run in before callbacks or the equivalent in your test framework—which creates database records using your model classes.

The next listing shows how this works.

Listing 10.20   Preparing test data with an ORM

```
var assert = require('assert');
var crypto = require('crypto');

function User(fields) {                          ❶ A stand-in for
  this.fields = fields;                            a model class
}

User.prototype.save = function(cb) {      ❷ Simulate non-blocking
  process.nextTick(cb);                     database save
};

User.prototype.signIn = function(password) {
  var shasum = crypto.createHash('sha1');
  shasum.update(password);
  return shasum.digest('hex') === this.fields.hashed_password;
};

describe('user model', function() {
  describe('sign in', function() {         ❸ Create user record
    var user = new User({                    to use for this test
      email: 'alex@example.com',
      hashed_password: 'a94a8fe5ccb19ba61c4c0873d391e987982fbbd3'
    });

    before(function(done) {             ❹ Save user before
      user.save(done);                    the test starts
    });

    it('should accept the correct password', function() {
      assert(user.signIn('test'));
    });

    it('should not accept the wrong password', function() {
      assert.equal(user.signIn('wrong'), false);
    });
  });
});
```

This example can be run with Mocha, and although it doesn't use a real database layer, the User class ❶ fakes the kind of behavior you're likely to see with a library for a relational database or even a NoSQL database. A save function is defined that has an asynchronous API ❷ so the tests look close to a real-world test.

In the describe block that groups together each test case, a variable called user is defined ❸. This will be used by some of the following test cases. It's defined above their scope so they can all access it, but also because we want to persist it asynchronously in the before block. This runs prior to the test cases ❹.

Mocking the database

The final approach that will be discussed in this technique is mocking the database API. Although you should always write *some* integration tests, you can also write tests that never touch the database at all. Instead, the database API is abstracted away.

Should I use the ORM for test data?

Like the database dump example in listing 10.19, using an ORM to create test data is useful for integration tests where you really want to talk to a database server. It's more programming effort than using database dumps, but it can be useful if you want to call methods defined above the database in the ORM layer. The downside of this technique is that a database schema change will potentially require changes in multiple test files.

JavaScript allows objects to be modified after they have been defined. That means you can override parts of the database module with your own methods to return test data. There are libraries designed to make this process easier and more expressive. One module that does this exceptionally well is Sinon.JS. The next example uses Sinon.JS along with Mocha to stub the database module.

Listing 10.21 presents an example that stubs a class that uses Redis for a user account database. The goal of the test is to check that password encryption works correctly.

Listing 10.21 Stubbing a database

```
var assert = require('assert');
var sinon = require('sinon');                                  ❶ Mock the database
var db = sinon.mock(require('./../db'));      ◀──┘                module.
var User = require('./../user');

                                                              This hashed password ❷
describe('Users', function() {                                will be used when the
  var fields = {                                                      user signs in.
    name: 'Huxley',
    hashedPassword: 'a94a8fe5ccb19ba61c4c0873d391e987982fbbd3'  ◀──┘
  };
  var user;

  before(function() {
    user = new User(1, fields);            ❸ Stub the Redis
    var stub = sinon                          hmget method.
      .stub(user.db, 'hmget')      ◀──┘
      .callsArgWith(2, null, JSON.stringify(fields));  ◀──┐
  });                                                    Make hmget call the
                                                         passed-in callback,
  it('should allow users to sign in', function(done) {   which is the third
    user.signIn('test', function(err, signedIn) {        argument (index two),
      assert(signedIn);                                  and pass the callback
      done(err);                                      ❹ null and the fields we
    });                                                  want to use.
  });

  it('should require the correct password', function(done) {
    user.signIn('wrong', function(err, signedIn) {
      assert(!signedIn);
      done(err);
```

```
      });
    });
  });
```

This example is part of a large project that includes a package.json file and the User class being tested—it's available in the code samples, under testing/mocha-sinon.

On the third line you'll notice something new: sinon.mock wraps the whole database module ❶. The database module is one we've defined that loads the node-redis module, and then connects to the database. In this test we don't want to connect to a real database, so we call sinon.mock to wrap it instead. This approach can be applied to other projects that use MySQL, PostgreSQL, and so on. As long as you design the project to centralize the database configuration, you can easily swap it for a mock.

Next we set up some fields that we want to use for this user ❷. In an integration test, these fields would be returned by the database. We don't want to do that here, so in the before callback, we use a stub to redefine what Redis hmget does ❸. The stubbing API is chainable, so we chain on the definition of what we want *our* version of hmget to do by using .callsArgWith ❹.

The semantics of .callsArgWith can be confusing, so here's a breakdown of how it works. In the User class, hmget is called like this:

```
this.db.hmget('user:' + this.id, 'fields', function(err, fields) {
  this.fields = JSON.parse(fields);
  cb(err, this);
}.bind(this));
```

As you can see, it takes three arguments: the record key, the hash value to fetch, and then a callback that receives an optional error object and the loaded values. When we stub this, we need to tell Sinon.JS how to respond. Therefore, the first argument to callsArgWith is the index of the callback, which is 2, and then the arguments that the callback should receive. We pass null for the error, and the user's fields serialized as a strong. That gives us callsArgWith(2, null, JSON.stringify(fields)).

This test is useful because the intent of the test is to ensure users can sign in, but only with the correct password. The sign-in code doesn't really require database access, so it's better to pass in predefined values rather than going to the trouble of accessing the database. And, because the code serializes JSON to Redis, we don't need a special library for serializing and decoding JSON—we can use the built-in JSON object.

Now you should know when and how to use integration tests, and mocks and stubs. All of these techniques will help you write better tests, but only if you use them in the correct circumstances. Table 10.2 provides a summary of these techniques and explains when to use each one.

The next time you want to test code that connects to a remote web service, or you need to write tests that run against a database, you should know what to do. If you've found this section interesting and you want to find out more, continue reading for some ideas on what to learn next.

Table 10.2 When to use integration tests, mocks, and stubs

Technique	When to use it
Integration testing	This means testing groups of modules. Here we've used the term to distinguish between tests that access a real database, and tests that somehow replace database access with a compatible API. You should use integration tests to ensure your database behaves the way you expect.
	Integration tests can help verify performance, but this is highly dependent on your test data. It may cause your tests to be more closely coupled to the database, which means that if you change the database or database API, you may need to change your test code as well.
Database dump	This is one way to preload data (before tests) into a test database. It requires a lot of work up front to prepare the data, and the data has to be maintained if you ever change the database schema. The added maintenance work is offset by the simplicity of the approach—you don't need any special tools to create SQL, Mongo, or other data files. You should use this technique when you're writing tests for a project that already has a database. Perhaps you're moving to Node from another programming language or platform, and you're using the existing database. You can take production data—being careful to remove or obscure any personal information, or other sensitive information—and then drop the resulting database export into your project's repository.
ORM fixture	Rather than creating a file to import before the tests are run, you can use your ORM module to create and store data in your test code. This can make it hard to maintain over time—any schema changes mean tests have to be carefully updated.
	You should use this technique for tests where algorithms are closely tied to the underlying data. By keeping the data near the code that uses it, any relating issues can be easier to understand and fix.
Mocks and stubs	Mocks are objects that simulate other objects. In this chapter you saw Sinon.JS, a library for handling mocks and stubs for tests.
	You should use mocks when you don't want to access an I/O resource. For example, if you're writing tests for code that talks to a payment provider like WorldPay or Stripe, then you'd create objects that behave like Stripe's API without actually communicating with Stripe. It's generally safer to ensure tests never need to access the internet, so anything that hits the network should be mocked.

10.6 *Further reading*

Testing is a big topic, and although this chapter has been long, there are still important topics to consider. The Node community continues to explore ways to write better tests, and it has started to bring its ideas to client-side development. One such development is Browserify (http://browserify.org)—this allows Node's module pattern and core modules like `EventEmitter` and `stream.Readable` to be used in the browser.

Some Node developers are taking advantage of Browserify to write better client-side tests. Not only can they take advantage of streams and Node's module pattern for cleaner dependency management, but they can also write Mocha or TAP tests the way they do on the server. James Halliday, the author of Browserify, created Testling, which is a browser automation module for running client-side tests.

Along with continuous integration servers, another useful test-related tool is coverage reports. These analyze code to see how much of a project is hit when the tests are run. There may be functions, methods, or even clauses in `if` statements that never get executed, which means untested and potentially buggy code could be released to the production environment.

10.7　Summary

In this chapter you've learned how to write assertions and extend them, and how to use two popular test frameworks. When writing tests for your Node projects, you should always err on the side of readability—tests should be fast, but if they don't communicate intent, they can cause maintenance issues in the future.

Here's a recap of the main points we covered:

- Master the `assert` module by learning each method and how to ensure errors are correctly handled.
- Use test harnesses like Mocha and `node-tap` to help make tests readable and maintainable.
- Write tests for code that uses a database by loading data or using mocks and stubs.
- Improve mocks and stubs by using third-party modules like Sinon.JS.
- Develop your own domain-specific languages for tests—write functions and classes that help keep test cases lean and succinct.

One aspect of development that we haven't covered yet is debugging Node programs. This can be an important part of writing software, depending on your development style and background. If you're interested in learning the basics of the Node debugger, or want to learn more about it, then read on to dive into debugging with Node.

Debugging: Designing for introspection and resolving issues

This chapter covers

- Handling uncaught exceptions
- Linting Node applications
- Using debugging tools
- Profiling applications and investigating memory leaks
- Using a REPL to investigate a running process
- Tracing system calls

Understanding how errors are generated and handled in any given platform is paramount to building stable applications. Good error introspection and tests that are built-in are the best offense for debugging issues later on. In this chapter we focus on *how to prepare for* and *what to do* when things go south.

Maybe your process keeps crashing or it's using more memory than you expected. Perhaps it's stuck at 100% CPU usage. We'll look at debugging solutions for these and other problems you may encounter in your Node applications.

In the first part we'll cover Node application design for error handling and detection. In the second half we'll look at debugging specific types of problems.

11.1 Designing for introspection

When we design applications, we need to be thinking about how we'll handle errors. Relevant error logging and intervention takes thought. It also takes a good understanding of where errors can occur in order to trap them. Throughout this book, we've covered various forms of errors that can happen in Node applications. Let's cover all the types here.

11.1.1 Explicit exceptions

Explicit exceptions are those *explicitly* triggered by the `throw` keyword. They clearly indicate that something has gone wrong:

```
function formatName (name) {
  if (!name) throw new Error("name is required");
  ...
}
```

Explicit exceptions are handled by a `try`/`catch` block:

```
try {
  formatName();
} catch (err) {
  console.log(err.message, err.stack);
}
```

If you `throw` your own exceptions, keep these guidelines in mind:

- `throw` should be used only in synchronous functions; or in some cases, it makes sense before the asynchronous action has occurred in asynchronous functions (like API misuse).

- Always `throw` an `Error` object or something that inherits from `Error`. Using simple strings (like `throw "Oh no!"`) won't generate a stack trace, so you'll have no information as to where the error occurred.

- Don't `throw` inside Node-style callback functions; nothing exists on the stack to catch it! Instead, deal directly with the error or pass the error off to another function that can properly handle the error.

REGAINING THROW   You can regain the use of `throw` for asynchronous blocks if the structures support it; some notable ones are domains, promises, or generators.

11.1.2 *Implicit exceptions*

Implicit exceptions are any runtime JavaScript errors *not* triggered by the `throw` keyword. Unfortunately, these exceptions can sneak into our code too easily.

One common implicit exception is `ReferenceError`, which is caused when a reference to a variable or property can't be found.

Here, we see an innocent misspelling of `data` causes an exception:

```
function (err, data) {
  res.write(dat); // ReferenceError: dat is not defined
}
```

Another common implicit exception is `SyntaxError`, most famously triggered using `JSON.parse` on invalid JSON data:

```
JSON.parse("undefined"); // SyntaxError: Unexpected token u
```

It's a good idea to wrap `JSON.parse` with a `try/catch` block, especially if you aren't in control of the input JSON data.

> **CATCH IMPLICIT EXCEPTIONS EARLY** A great way to catch implicit exceptions early is to utilize linting tools like JSHint or JSLint. Adding them to your build process helps keep your code in check. We'll talk more on subject this later in the chapter.

11.1.3 *The error event*

The `error` event can be emitted from any `EventEmitter` in Node. If left unhandled, Node *will* throw the error. These events can be the most difficult to debug if not handled, since many times they're triggered during asynchronous operations like streaming data where the call stack is minimal:

```
var EventEmitter = require('events').EventEmitter;
var ee = new EventEmitter();
ee.emit('error', new Error('No handler to catch me'));
```

This will output the following:

```
events.js:72
  throw er; // Unhandled 'error' event
  ^
Error: No handler to catch me
  at Object.<anonymous> (/debugging/domain/ee.js:5:18)
  at Module._compile (module.js:456:26)
  at Object.Module._extensions..js (module.js:474:10)
  at Module.load (module.js:356:32)
  at Function.Module._load (module.js:312:12)
  at Function.Module.runMain (module.js:497:10)
  at startup (node.js:119:16)
  at node.js:902:3
```

Luckily, we know where this error came from; we just wrote the code, after all! But in larger applications, we may have errors triggered at the DNS layer and we have no idea which module utilizing DNS just had a problem.

So, when possible, handle error events:

```
ee.on('error', function (err) {
  console.error(err.message, err.stack);
});
```

When writing your own `EventEmitters`, do yourself and your API consumers a favor and give them context to any errors in your dependencies that you're propagating upward. Also, use `Error` objects over plain strings when emitting errors so a stack trace can be found.

11.1.4 *The error argument*

Errors that occur during an asynchronous operation are provided as the first argument in a callback function. Unlike the previous errors we've talked about, these never cause exceptions *directly*. But they can be the source of many implicit exceptions:

```
fs.readFile('/myfile.txt', function (err, buf) {
  var data = buf.toString();
  ...
});
```

Here, we ignore the error returned from `readFile`, perhaps assuming we'll always have a buffer of the file data to continue working with. Unfortunately, the day comes when we can't read the file and we have a `ReferenceError` because `buf` is not defined.

It's more robust to just handle the asynchronous errors. A lot of times this can mean simply passing the error to another function that can gracefully handle the error:

```
function handleError (err) {
  console.error('Failed:', err.message, err.stack);
}
fs.readFile('/myfile.txt', function (err, buf) {
  if (err) return handleError(err);
  var data = buf.toString();
  ...
});
```

Handling each of these four types of errors effectively will give you much better data to work with when you're debugging issues in the future!

Even with our best efforts and tooling, though, we can still miss exceptions and have a crashed server on our hands. Let's look at designing our applications to handle these situations so we can quickly address and fix uncaught exceptions.

TECHNIQUE 88   **Handling uncaught exceptions**

How do you effectively handle Node crashes? One of the first things you discover when working with Node is that it terminates a process whenever an exception is uncaught. It's important to understand why this behavior exists and how you handle uncaught exceptions in order to build robustness into your programs.

PROBLEM

You have an uncaught exception taking down your process.

SOLUTION

Log the exception, and shut down gracefully.

DISCUSSION

Sometimes exceptions go uncaught. When this happens, Node by default will terminate the process. There's a good reason for this, which we'll come back to, but let's first talk about how we can change this default behavior.

With an uncaughtException handler set on the process object, Node will execute the handler *instead* of terminating your program:

```
process.on('uncaughtException', function (err) {
  console.error(err);
});
```

Yeah! Now your Node application will never crash! Although it's true that exceptions won't take down your process anymore, the drawbacks of leaving the Node program running will most likely outweigh the benefits. If you choose to keep the application running, the application could leak resources and possibly become unstable.

How does that happen? Let's look at an example of an application we intend to run for a long time: a web server. We won't allow Node to terminate the process by adding an uncaughtException handler that just logs the error. What do you think will happen when we have an uncaught exception while we're handling a user's request?

```
var http = require('http');

var server = http.createServer(req, res) {       Throws a ReferenceError
  response.end('hello world');        ◁————        since response is not defined
});
server.listen(3000);

process.on('uncaughtException', function (err) {
  console.error(err);
});
```

When a request comes in, an exception is thrown and then caught by the uncaught-Exception handler. What happens to the request? It is *leaked*, as that connection will remain open until the client times out (we also no longer have access to res to give a response back).

In figure 11.1, you can see an illustration of this leak happening. If we had no exception, we'd be fine, but since we had an exception, we leaked a resource.

Although this example is simplified to be clear, uncaught exceptions are a reality. Most of the time it will be open handles to sockets or files that aren't able to be closed properly. Uncaught exceptions are usually buried much deeper in the code, which makes determining what resources are being leaked even harder.

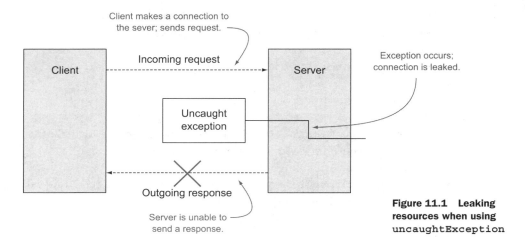

Figure 11.1 Leaking resources when using `uncaughtException`

State can also be affected, since an uncaught exception takes you out of your current context and places you in a completely different context (the uncaughtException handler) where you don't have references to objects in order to clean things up. In our example, we didn't have access to the res object in order to send a response back to the client.

So what good is the uncaughtException handler? It enables your application to log and restart gracefully. It's wise to treat an uncaughtException handler as a last chance to say your goodbyes before going down. Write out the error, perhaps send an email or do some other notification, and then gracefully kill the app:

```
process.on('uncaughtException', function (err) {
    console.error(err);                              ⟵——— Log error
    server.close();
    setTimeout(process.exit, 5000, 1);
});
```

Stop incoming connections

Give any existing connections 5 more seconds and then kill process

The uncaughtException handler is a last defense. Ideally exceptions should be handled closer to the source so action can be taken to prevent leaks and instability. For that, you can use domains.

Using domains for uncaught exceptions

Whereas an uncaughtException casts a net over the entirety of your application code base to catch errors, domains allow you to control the *portions of code* that are monitored by the domain and handle exceptions closer to the source (more on this back in chapter 4). Let's implement the same uncaughtException example from earlier, but using domains instead:

```
var domain = require('domain');
var http = require('http');

var d = domain.create();                ⟵— Set up a new domain.
    d.run(function () {
```

Run the following code inside the domain.

```
                    var server = http.createServer(req, res) {
                      d.on('error', function (er) {           ◄
                        res.statusCode = 500; )
                        res.end('internal server error');
                        server.close();
                        setTimeout(process.exit, 5000, 1);
                      })
                      response.end('hello world');
                    })
                    server.listen(3000);
                  });
```

Respond to the user with an error response. (points to `res.statusCode`...`})` block)

Handle any uncaught exception that occurs in the domain. (points to `d.on('error', function (er) {`)

Using domains allowed us to sandbox our server code and still have access to the `res` object to give the user a response, which is an improvement on the previous example. But even though we're able to give the user a response and close the connection, it's still best practice to close out the process.

If you utilize domains, it's not a bad idea to keep an `uncaughtException` handler as a catchall for those cases where an error slips by one of your domains, or your domain's error handler throws an exception where no other domain is there to catch it.

Let's switch to a helpful way to build introspection into your application and prevent errors before they happen: linting!

TECHNIQUE 89 Linting Node applications

Lint tools can help catch a multitude of application errors when properly tuned. In our previous example, we misspelled `res`, which led to an uncaught exception. Although the code was *valid* JavaScript, we had an undefined variable being accessed. A lint tool would've caught this error.

PROBLEM
You want to catch potential coding errors and exceptions.

SOLUTION
Use a lint tool.

DISCUSSION
Let's talk about setting up an application to use JSHint with Node. JSHint is an actively maintained lint tool that includes a number of customizable options for JavaScript code bases.

First, we assume you already have a package.json file set up (if not: `npm init`) for your project. Next, let's add `jshint` to our development dependencies:

```
npm install jshint --save-dev
```

Now let's configure JSHint so it knows what it's working with. We just throw a .jshintrc file—which takes a JSON configuration—in our project root. Let's look at a basic configuration for Node projects:

```
{
  "node": true,
  "undef": true
}
```

Catch any undefined variable usage. (points to `"undef": true`)

Make JSHint understand it's working with Node. This avoids errors with known global variables and other Node-specific intelligence. (points to `"node": true`)

JSHint has a lot of options (http://jshint.com/docs/options/) that bend rules to match your coding style and intent, but these just shown are some good basic defaults.

To run JSHint, add the following line to the `"scripts"` block in your package.json file (if you don't have a `"scripts"` block, just add one):

```
"scripts": {
  "lint": "jshint *"          ⟵___ Run JSHint against all
}                                   JavaScript files in your project
```

You can then run JSHint from your project root this way:

```
npm run lint
```

JSHint will give you output that tells you what errors it found, and you can either correct or update the options to better fit your coding style and intent. Similarly to tests, it's helpful to have your build tools run the lint tools as you push code, since it's easy to forget to run and can be automated away.

Now that we've looked at ways to prevent and effectively handle application errors, let's switch over to look at tools we can use to debug issues when they occur.

11.2   *Debugging issues*

We have our tests, our logging, and our linting. How do we actually debug and fix issues when they occur? Thankfully, there are a number of tools for a number of different situations. In this section we'll take a look at various and likely unrelated problems you can encounter when running your applications, and techniques to solve them. We'll start with using debuggers and move on to profiling, memory leaks, production debugging, and tracing.

TECHNIQUE 90   **Using Node's built-in debugger**

Whenever you need step-by-step analysis of the state of your application, a debugger can be an invaluable tool, and Node's built-in debugger is no exception. Node's built-in tooling allows you to watch variables, pause execution through breakpoints, step in and out of parts of your application, see backtraces, run an interactive context-aware REPL, and more.

Unfortunately, many shy away from the command-line tool, as it may seem intimidating at first. We want to debunk that and show how powerful it can be by walking you through most of the functionality it has to offer.

PROBLEM

You want to run a debugger to set breakpoints, watch variables, and step through your application.

SOLUTION

Use `node debug`.

DISCUSSION

Let's take a simple program to debug in order to demonstrate some of the features of the debugger:

```
var a = 0;
function changeA () {
  a = 50;
}
function addToA (toAdd) {
  a += toAdd;
}
changeA();
addToA(25);
addToA(25);
```

To run the built-in debugging tool, simply use the `debug` command:

```
node debug myprogram
```

It will start the application with the debugger breaking on the first executable line:

```
< debugger listening on port 5858
connecting... ok
break in start.js:1
  1 var a = 0;
  2
  3 function changeA () {
debug>
```

To view all the available commands and debugging variables, you can type `help`:

```
debug> help
Commands: run (r), cont (c), next (n), step (s), out (o),
backtrace (bt), setBreakpoint (sb), clearBreakpoint (cb),
watch, unwatch, watchers, repl, restart, kill, list, scripts,
breakOnException, breakpoints, version
```

To continue from the default starting breakpoint, just type `cont`, or just `c` for short. Since we don't have any other breakpoints, the application will terminate:

```
debug> cont
program terminated
debug>
```

But we're *still* in the debugger and can restart the application again by using the `run` command (`r` for short):

```
debug> run
< debugger listening on port 5858
connecting... ok
break in start.js:1
  1 var a = 0;
  2
  3 function changeA () {
debug>
```

And we're back in business. We can also restart the application with the `restart` command or manually kill the application with the `kill` command if we need to.

The application is all about the letter *A*, so let's take a peek at how that changes as our application executes by making a `watch` expression for that. The `watch` function takes an expression to watch as an argument:

```
debug> watch('a')
```

We can view the state of all that we're watching using the `watchers` command:

```
debug> watchers
  0: a = undefined
```

Currently we're paused before the assignment to 0 has even been made, so we're `undefined`. Let's step into the next line with `next`(or n for short):

```
debug> next
break in start.js:11
Watchers:
  0: a = 0

  9 }
 10
 11 changeA();
 12 addToA(25);
 13 addToA(25);
debug>
```

Well, that's convenient: the debugger outputs our watchers for us as we step to the next section. If we were to type `watchers` again, we'd see similar output:

```
debug> watchers
  0: a = 0
```

If we ever want to remove a watch expression, we can use the `unwatch` command given the same expression we used to create it.

By default, the debugger will print just a couple lines before and after to give a sense of context. But sometimes we want to see more of what's going on. We can use the `list` command, giving it the number of lines around the current line where we're paused:

```
debug> list(5)
  6
  7 function addToA (toAdd) {
  8   a += toAdd;
  9 }
 10
 11 changeA();
 12 addToA(25);
 13 addToA(25);
 14
 15 });
debug>
```

We're currently at line 11, the changeA function. If we were to type next, we'd move to the next line, which is the addToA function, but let's investigate our changeA function more by stepping into it. To do that we just use the step command (or s for short):

```
debug> step
break in start.js:4
Watchers:
  0: a = 0

  2
  3 function changeA () {
  4   a = 50;
  5 }
  6
debug>
```

Now that we're in this function, we can step out of it at any time using the out command. We'll automatically step out of it once we reach the end, so we can also use next; let's try it:

```
debug> next
break in start.js:5
Watchers:
  0: a = 50

  3 function changeA () {
  4   a = 50;
  5 }
  6
  7 function addToA (toAdd) {
debug>
```

As you can see, our watchers updated to show that *a* is now 50. Let's go to the next line:

```
debug> next
break in start.js:12
Watchers:
  0: a = 50

  10
  11 changeA();
  12 addToA(25);
  13 addToA(25);
  14
debug>
```

Now we're back to the line after our changeA function. Let's step into this next function again. Remember what command that was?

```
debug> step
break in start.js:8
Watchers:
  0: a = 50
```

```
  6
  7 function addToA (toAdd) {
  8   a += toAdd;
  9 }
 10
debug>
```

Let's explore another neat aspect of the debugger: the built-in REPL! We can access it by using the `repl` command:

```
debug> repl
Press Ctrl + C to leave debug repl
>
```

This is a standard REPL that's aware of the context that surrounds it when you used the `repl` command. So we can, for instance, output the value of the `toAdd` argument:

```
> toAdd
25
```

We can also introduce state into the application. Let's create a global b variable:

```
> b = 100100
```

In many ways, this behaves just like the standard Node REPL, so a lot of what you can do there, you can do here.

You can exit the REPL mode at any time with Ctrl-C. Let's do that now. You'll know you've exited because you'll get your debug prompt back:

```
debug>
```

We were in a REPL for a while, so we likely lost context when we were paused. Let's use `list` again to get our bearings:

```
debug> list()
  3 function changeA () {
  4   a = 50;
  5 }
  6
  7 function addToA (toAdd) {
  8 a += toAdd;
  9 }
 10
 11 changeA();
 12 addToA(25);
 13 addToA(25);
```

Ah yes, that's right, we were on line 8. Well, you know what, we really wanted the `changeA` function to assign a to 100. It's such a nice number to accompany such a nice letter! But we forgot to do that when we started the debugger. No problem! We can set a breakpoint here to save our spot by using the `setBreakpoint` function (or `sb` for short):

```
debug> setBreakpoint()
  3 function changeA () {
  4   a = 50;
```

```
  5 }
  6
  7 function addToA (toAdd) {
 *8   a += toAdd;
  9 }
 10
 11 changeA();
 12 addToA(25);
 13 addToA(25);
debug>
```

Note that our line 8 now has a star (*) next to it indicating we have a breakpoint set there. Let's change that function in our code file and save it:

```
function changeA () {
  a = 100;
}
```

Back in our debugger, we can restart the app:

```
debug> restart
program terminated<
debugger listening on port 5858
connecting... ok
Restoring breakpoint debug.js:8
break in start.js:1
  1 var a = 0;
  2
  3 function changeA () {
debug>
```

Looks like our program was restarted and the breakpoint we set is still intact. Did it get our changes? Let's see:

```
debug> list(20)
  1 var a = 0;
  2
  3 function changeA () {
  4   a = 100;
  5 }
  6
  7 function addToA (toAdd) {
  8   a += toAdd;
  9 }
 10
 11 changeA();
 12 addToA(25);
 13 addToA(25);
 14
 15 });
debug>
```

Another way we can set breakpoints right from our application code is to use the debugger keyword:

```
function changeA () {
  debugger;
  a = 100;
}
```

If we restart our application again, we'll always stop on any `debugger` lines. We can clear breakpoints as well using `clearBreakpoint` (or `cb` for short).

Let's look at one more topic: uncaught exceptions. Let's introduce a nasty `ReferenceError` in our `changeA` function:

```
function changeA () {
  a = 100;
  foo = bar;
}
```

If we restart our application using `restart` and then `cont` to skip the initial breakpoint, our application will crash due to an uncaught exception. We can break on these exceptions instead using `breakOnException`:

```
debug> breakOnException
debug>
```

Now, instead of crashing, we'll break first, allowing us to inspect the state of the application and use the REPL before the program terminates.

> **HELPFUL MULTIFILE DEBUGGER COMMANDS** This scenario only looked at a single file that included no other modules. The debugger also has a couple of commands that are helpful when you're within multiple files. Use `backtrace` (or `bt` for short) to get a call stack on whatever line you're currently paused at. You can also use `scripts` to get a list of loaded files and an indicator of what file you're currently in.

The built-in debugger may feel odd at first if you're used to a GUI tool for debugging applications, but it's actually pretty versatile once you get the hang of it! Just throw a quick `debugger` statement where you're working and fire it up.

TECHNIQUE 91 Using Node Inspector

Want to do everything you can with the built-in debugger, but using the Chrome DevTools interface instead? There's a module for that! It's called `node-inspector`. In this technique we'll look at how to set it up and start debugging.

PROBLEM
You want to debug a Node application using Chrome DevTools.

SOLUTION
Use `node-inspector`.

DISCUSSION
Node allows remote debugging by exposing a debugging port that third-party modules and tools can hook into (including the built-in debugger). One popular module is `node-inspector`, which ties in debugging information from Node into the Chrome DevTools interface.

To set up `node-inspector`, simply install it:

```
npm install node-inspector -g
```

Don't forget the `-g` flag to install it globally. Once you have it, you can fire it up by running the following command:

```
node-inspector
```

Now `node-inspector` is ready to roll and will tell you where to reach it:

```
$ node-inspector
Node Inspector v0.7.0-2
  info - socket.io started
Visit http://127.0.0.1:8080/debug?port=5858 to start debugging.
```

You can then visit that URL in any Blink-enabled browser like Chrome or Opera. But we don't have any Node program that has an open debugging port to start debugging, so we receive an error message, as shown in figure 11.2.

Let's leave that running for now and write a little application to debug:

```
var http = require('http');

var server = http.createServer();
server.on('request', function (req, res) {
  res.end('Hello World');
});
server.listen(3000);
```

Now we can run this application exposing the debugging port:

```
$ node --debug test.js
debugger listening on port 5858
```

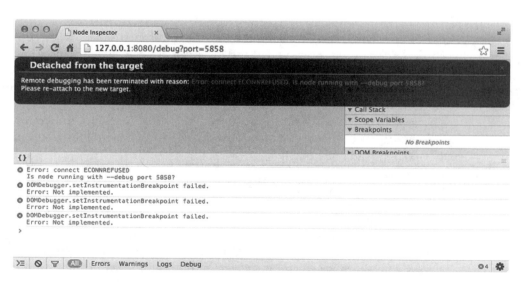

Figure 11.2   Error screen when no debugging agent is found

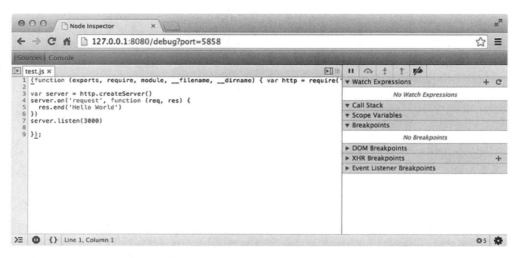

Figure 11.3   Node inspector connected to the debugger

Our application now lets us know that the debugger is listening on port 5858. If we refresh our Node inspector web page, it'll look more interesting, as shown in figure 11.3.

We can use the inspector much like the built-in debugger to set breakpoints and watch expressions. It also includes a console that's similar to the REPL to allow you to poke around at the state of your application while it's paused.

One difference between `node-inspector` and the built-in debugger is that Node doesn't automatically break on the first expression. To enable that, you have to use the `--debug-brk` flag:

```
node --debug-brk test.js
```

This tells the debugger to break on the first line until the inspector can step through or continue execution. If we reload the inspector, we can see it's paused on the first line, as shown in figure 11.4.

`node-inspector` is continually being developed to support more of Chrome Dev-Tools' functionality.

We've looked at two ways to use debugging tools in Node: the command-line debugger and `node-inspector`. Now, let's switch to another tool for resolving performance-related issues: the profiler.

TECHNIQUE 92   Profiling Node applications

Profiling aims to answer this question: *Where is my application spending its time?* For instance, you may have a long-running web server that gets stuck at 100% CPU usage when you hit a particular route. At first glance, you might view the various functions that touch that route to see if anything stands out, or you could run a profiler and let Node tell you where it's stuck. In this technique you'll learn how to use the profiler and interpret the results.

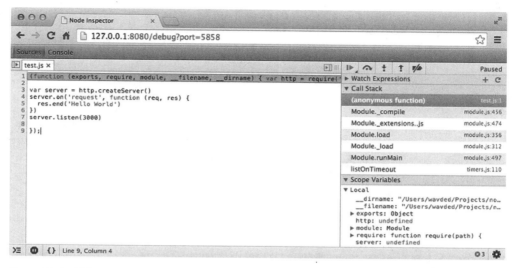

Figure 11.4 Using the `--debug-brk` flag

PROBLEM

You want to find out where your application is spending its time.

SOLUTION

Use `node --prof`.

DISCUSSION

Node taps into the underlying V8 statistical profiler by the use of the `--prof` command-line flag. It's important to understand how it works in order to interpret the data.

Every two milliseconds, the profiler looks at the running application and records the function executing at that moment. The function may be a JavaScript function, but it also can come from C++, shared libraries, or V8 garbage collection. The profiler writes these "ticks" to a file named `v8.log`, where they're then processed by a special V8 tick-processor program.

Let's look at a simple application to see how this works. Here we have an application doing two different things—running a slower computational task every two seconds, and running a quicker I/O task more often:

```
function makeLoad () {
  for (var i=0;i<100000000000;i++);
}
function logSomething () {
  console.log('something');
}

setInterval(makeLoad, 2000);
setInterval(logSomething, 0);
```

We can profile this application like so:

```
node --prof profile-test.js
```

If we let it run for 10 seconds or so and kill it, we'll get a v8.log in that same directory. The log isn't too helpful by itself. Let's process the log by using the V8 tick-processor tools. Those tools require that you build V8 from source on your machine, but there's a handy third-party module that allows you to skip that. Just run the following command to install:

```
npm install tick -g
```

This will install the appropriate tick processor for your operating system in order to view the data. You can then run the following command in the same directory as your v8.log file to get some more helpful output:

```
node-tick-processor
```

You'll get output that looks similar to the following (abbreviated to show structure):

```
Statistical profiling result from v8.log,
  (6404 ticks, 1 unaccounted, 0 excluded).

[Unknown]:
  ticks total nonlib name
     1   0.0%

[Shared libraries]:
  ticks total nonlib name
  4100 64.0%   0.0% /usr/lib/system/libsystem_kernel.dylib
   211  3.3%   0.0% /Users/wavded/.nvm/v0.10.24/bin/node
  ...

[JavaScript]:
  ticks total nonlib name
  1997 31.2%  96.4% LazyCompile: *makeLoad profile-test.js:1
     7  0.1%   0.3% LazyCompile: listOnTimeout timers.js:77
     5  0.1%   0.2% RegExp: %[sdj%]
  ...

[C++]:
  ticks total nonlib name

[GC]:
  ticks total nonlib name
     1   0.0%

[Bottom up (heavy) profile]:
  Note: percentage shows a share of a particular caller in
  the total amount of its parent calls.
  Callers occupying less than 2.0% are not shown.

  ticks parent name
  4100   64.0% /usr/lib/system/libsystem_kernel.dylib

  1997   31.2% LazyCompile: *makeLoad profile-test.js:1
  1997  100.0%   LazyCompile: ~wrapper timers.js:251
  1997  100.0%     LazyCompile: listOnTimeout timers.js:77
```

Let's look at what each section means:

- *Unknown*—For that tick, the profiler couldn't find a meaningful function attached to the pointer. These are noted in the output but aren't much help beyond that and can be safely ignored.
- *Shared libraries*—These are usually underlying C++/C shared libraries; a lot of the I/O stuff happens here as well.
- *JavaScript*—This is typically the most interesting part; it includes your application code as well as Node and V8 internal native JavaScript code.
- *C++*—This is C++ code in V8.
- *GC*—This is the V8 garbage collector.
- *Bottom up (heavy) profile*—This shows a more detailed stack for the highest hitters found by the profiler.

In our case, we can see that *makeLoad is the hottest JavaScript function, with 1997 ticks accounted for:

```
[JavaScript]:
  ticks total nonlib name
  1997 31.2%  96.4% LazyCompile: *makeLoad profile-test.js:1
     7   0.1%   0.3% LazyCompile: listOnTimeout timers.js:77
     5   0.1%   0.2% RegExp: %[sdj%]
```

This makes sense since it has some heavy computation. Another interesting section to note is RegExp: %[sdj%], which is used by util.format, which is used by console.log.

The profiler's job is to show you what functions are running most often. It doesn't necessarily mean that the function is slow, but it does mean either a lot happens in the function or it's called often. The results should serve as clues to help you understand what can be done to improve the performance. In some cases it may be surprising to find out certain functions are running hot; other times it may be expected. Profiling serves as one piece of the puzzle to help solve performance-related issues.

Another potential source of performance-related issues is memory leaks, although, obviously they're *first* a memory concern that may have performance ramifications. Let's look at handling memory leaks next.

TECHNIQUE 93   Debugging memory leaks

Before the days of Ajax and Node, there wasn't much effort put into debugging JavaScript memory leaks, since page views were short-lived. But memory leaks can happen, especially in Node programs where a server process is expected to stay up and running for days, weeks, or months. How do you debug a leaking application? We'll look at a technique that works locally or in production.

PROBLEM

You want to debug a program leaking memory.

SOLUTION

Use heapdump and Chrome DevTools.

DISCUSSION

Let's write a leaky application to demonstrate how to use a couple of tools to debug a memory leak. Let's make a leak.js program:

```
var string = '1 string to rule them all';

var leakyArr = [];
var count = 2;
setInterval(function () {
  leakyArr.push(string.replace(/1/g, count++));
}, 0);
```

Since strings are immutable in JavaScript, we push a unique string every time into the array to intentionally grow memory and not allow the garbage collector to clean.

How do we know this application is growing in memory? We could sit and watch `top` or some other process-monitoring application. We can also test it by logging the memory used. To get an accurate read, let's force a garbage collection before logging out the memory usage. Let's add the following code to our leak.js file:

```
setInterval(function () {
  gc();
  console.log(process.memoryUsage());
}, 10000)
```

In order to use the `gc()` function, we need to expose it by running our application with the `--expose-gc` flag:

```
node --expose-gc leak.js
```

Now we can see some output showing clearly that we're growing in memory usage:

```
{ rss: 15060992, heapTotal: 6163968, heapUsed: 2285608 }
{ rss: 15331328, heapTotal: 6163968, heapUsed: 2428768 }
{ rss: 15495168, heapTotal: 8261120, heapUsed: 2548496 }
{ rss: 15585280, heapTotal: 8261120, heapUsed: 2637936 }
{ rss: 15757312, heapTotal: 8261120, heapUsed: 2723192 }
{ rss: 15835136, heapTotal: 8261120, heapUsed: 2662456 }
{ rss: 15982592, heapTotal: 8261120, heapUsed: 2670824 }
{ rss: 16089088, heapTotal: 8261120, heapUsed: 2814040 }
{ rss: 16220160, heapTotal: 9293056, heapUsed: 2933696 }
{ rss: 16510976, heapTotal: 10324992, heapUsed: 3085112 }
{ rss: 16605184, heapTotal: 10324992, heapUsed: 3179072 }
{ rss: 16699392, heapTotal: 10324992, heapUsed: 3267192 }
{ rss: 16777216, heapTotal: 10324992, heapUsed: 3293760 }
{ rss: 17022976, heapTotal: 10324992, heapUsed: 3528376 }
{ rss: 17117184, heapTotal: 10324992, heapUsed: 3635264 }
{ rss: 17207296, heapTotal: 10324992, heapUsed: 3728544 }
```

Although we know we're growing pretty steadily, we don't really know "what" is leaking from this output. For that we need to take some heap snapshots and compare them to see what's changing in our application. We'll use the third-party `heapdump` module (https://github.com/bnoordhuis/node-heapdump). The `heapdump` module allows us to take snapshots either programmatically or by sending a signal to the process (UNIX only). These snapshots can be processed using the Chrome DevTools.

Let's install the module first:

```
npm install heapdump --save-dev
```

Then include it in our leak.js file and instrument it to output a heap snapshot every 10 seconds:

```
var heapdump = require('heapdump');
var string = '1 string to rule them all';

var leakyArr = [];
var count = 2;
setInterval(function () {
  leakyArr.push(string.replace(/1/g, count++));
}, 0);

setInterval(function () {
  if (heapdump.takeSnapshot()) console.log('wrote snapshot');
}, 10000);
```

Now, every 10 seconds a file is written to the current working directory of the process that contains the snapshot. A garbage collection is automatically performed whenever a snapshot is taken. Let's run our application to write a couple snapshots and then terminate it:

```
$ node leak3.js
wrote snapshot
wrote snapshot
```

Now we can see what was written:

```
$ ls
heapdump-29701132.649984.heapsnapshot
heapdump-29711146.938370.heapsnapshot
```

The files are saved with their respective timestamps. The larger the number, the more recent the snapshot. Now we can load these files into Chrome DevTools. Open Chrome and then the Developer Tools, go to the Profiles tab, and right-click on Profiles to load a snapshot file (see figure 11.5).

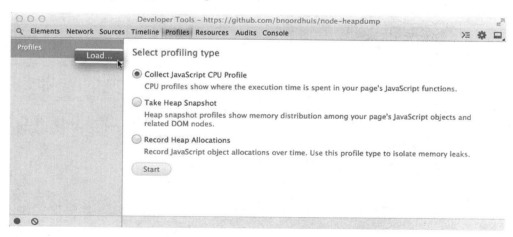

Figure 11.5   Loading a heap snapshot into the Chrome DevTools

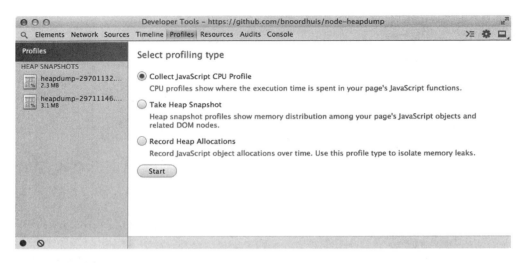

Figure 11.6   Loading a second snapshot for comparison

To compare our two snapshots, let's load them in the order we took them (see figure 11.6).

Now that we have them loaded, we can do some investigation. Let's select the second one and then choose the Comparison option. Chrome will automatically select the previous snapshot to compare to (see figure 11.7).

Now we can see something immediately interesting in our view—a lot of strings are being created and not being garbage collected (see figure 11.8).

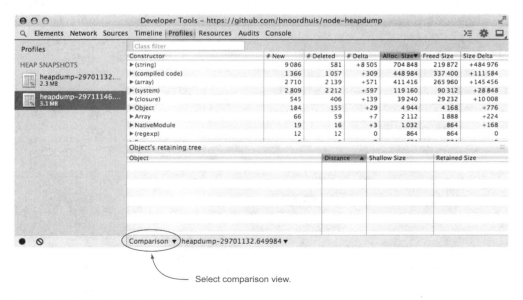

Figure 11.7   Using the comparison view

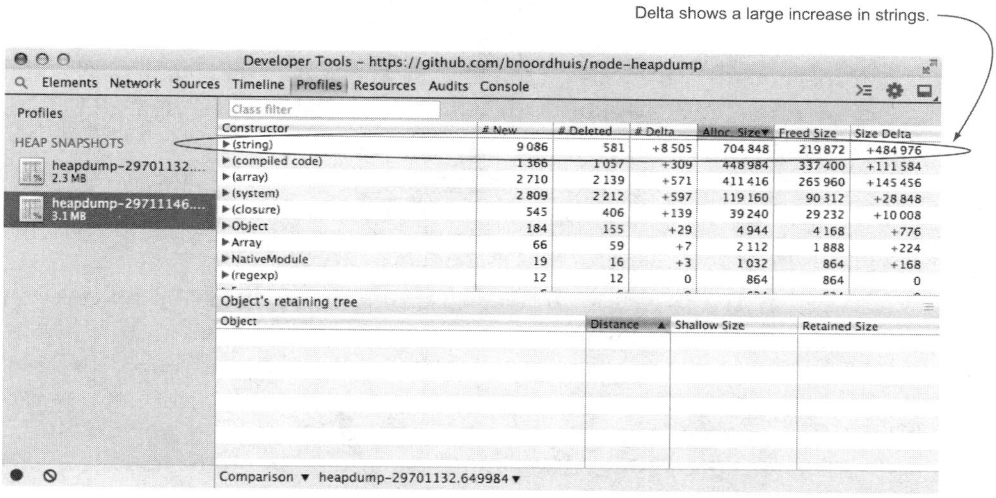

Delta shows a large increase in strings.

Figure 11.8   Examining memory allocations between the snapshots

So we can see that strings could be a problem here. But what strings are getting created? Here we have to do some investigation. Expanding the (string) tree will show us the largest strings first—typically application source code and some larger strings used in Node core and V8. But when we scroll down, we start to see strings generated in our application, and lots of them. By clicking one, we can see the retaining tree, or its relationship to other objects (see figure 11.9).

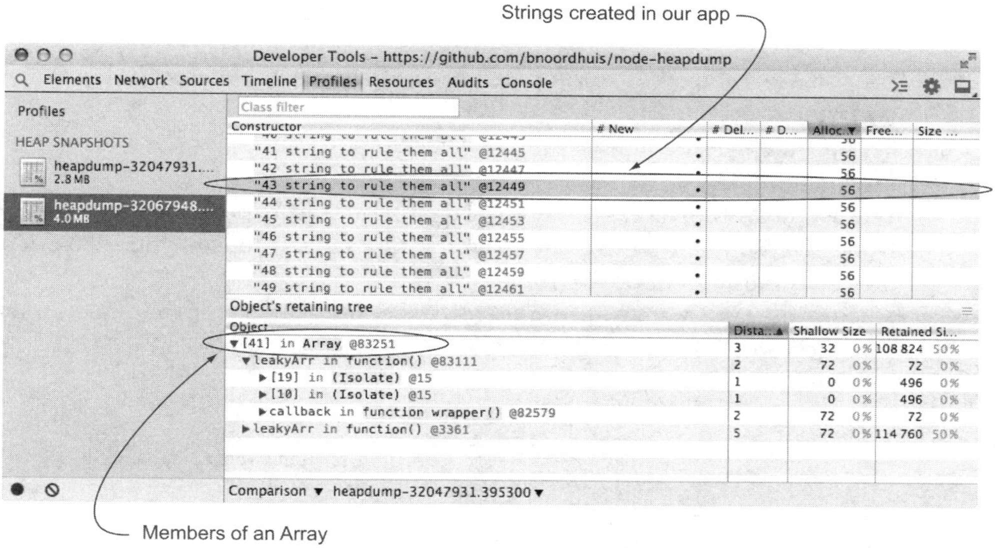

Strings created in our app

Members of an Array

Figure 11.9   Drilling down to the types of data being created in memory

In this exercise, we had a hunch we were going to leak strings stored inside the `leaky-Arr` variable. But this exercise shows the relationship between the code and the tools to inspect memory usage. As a developer, you'll know your source code, and the clues you get inside DevTools will be specific to your code and modules. The Comparison view can give a great snapshot of what's changing.

We only talked about one way of creating snapshots. You can also send a SIGUSR2 (on *NIX systems) to a process with `heapdump` to take a snapshots at will:

```
kill -USR2 1120
```

Just remember that it'll write the snapshot to the CWD of the process and will fail silently if the CWD isn't writable by the process user.

You can also be programmatically clever, depending on your needs. For example, you could set up `heapdump` to take a snapshot after a certain memory threshold is breached, or if it grows faster than some expected limit given an interval.

Taking heap snapshots is something you can do in production for a small performance penalty while the snapshot is being written to disk. Let's turn our attention to another technique you can use in production that has a minimal penalty and lets you poke around at the application state: using a REPL.

TECHNIQUE 94   Inspecting a running program with a REPL

Attaching a debugger to a production process isn't a viable option, as we don't want to be pausing execution or adding a performance tax of running the V8 debugger. So how can we debug live or performance-sensitive issues? We can use a REPL to dive into the process and inspect or change state. In this technique we'll first look at how a REPL works in Node, and how to set up your own REPL server and client. Then we'll turn to inspecting a running process.

PROBLEM
You want to interact with a running process to inspect or change its state.

SOLUTION
Set up a REPL in the process and a REPL client to access.

DISCUSSION
The Node REPL is a great way to play around and experiment with JavaScript and Node. The simplest way to play around with a REPL is to run Node without any arguments, as shown in figure 11.10.

But you can create your own REPLs using the built-in `repl` module. In fact, Node uses the same module when you type `node`. Let's make our own REPL:

```
var repl = require('repl');
repl.start({
  input: process.stdin,
  output: process.stdout
});
```

Use stdin stream as input stream to the REPL

Use stdout stream as output stream from the REPL

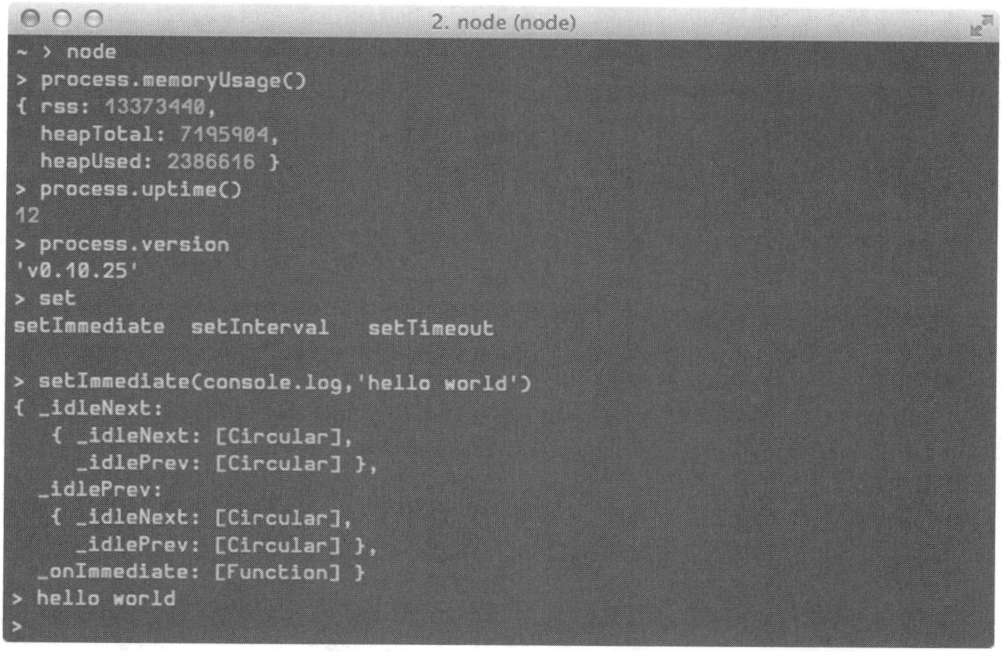

```
○ ○ ○                          2. node (node)

~ > node
> process.memoryUsage()
{ rss: 13373440,
  heapTotal: 7195904,
  heapUsed: 2386616 }
> process.uptime()
12
> process.version
'v0.10.25'
> set
setImmediate   setInterval    setTimeout

> setImmediate(console.log,'hello world')
{ _idleNext:
   { _idleNext: [Circular],
     _idlePrev: [Circular] },
  _idlePrev:
   { _idleNext: [Circular],
     _idlePrev: [Circular] },
  _onImmediate: [Function] }
> hello world
>
```

Figure 11.10 Sample Node REPL session

Executing this program creates a REPL that looks and functions much like node does:

```
$ node repl-basic.js
> 10 + 20
30
>
```

But we don't need to use the process's stdio for input and output; we can use a UNIX or a TCP socket! This allows us to connect to a long-running process from the outside. Let's make a TCP REPL server:

```
var net = require('net');
var repl = require('repl');

net.createServer(function (socket) {         Use incoming socket (a
  var r = repl.start({                       Duplex stream) as the input
    input: socket,                           and output stream for REPL
    output: socket
  });
  r.on('exit', function() {
    socket.end();             When REPL is exited,
  });                         end connection
}).listen(1337);

console.log('node repl listening on 1337');
```

Now if we fire up our REPL server, it'll be listening on port 1337:

```
$ node repl-tcp.js
node repl listening on 1337
```

We can then connect to it with a TCP client like telnet or Netcat. You can do this in a separate terminal window:

```
$ nc localhost 1337
> 10 + 20
30
> exit
$
```

That's cool! But it doesn't behave like our basic REPL (see figure 11.11) or the node command:

- The Tab key doesn't autocomplete available properties and variables.
- We don't have any readline support, so the Up Arrow key doesn't give us any command history.
- No color or bold output.

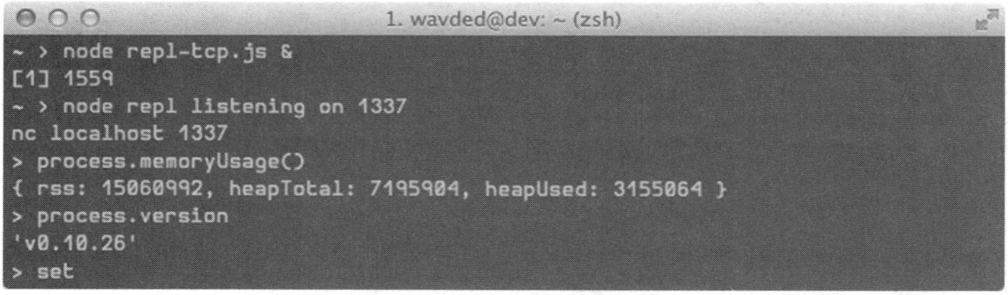

Figure 11.11   Using Netcat against a REPL server

The reasons for this are twofold. First, the repl module can't determine that we're running a TTY (terminal) session, so it provides a minimal interface avoiding the use of ANSI/VT100 escape codes for color and formatting. These escape codes end up being noise to clients like Netcat. Second, our client isn't behaving like a TTY. It isn't sending the proper input codes to get nice perks like autocomplete behavior or history.

In order to change this behavior, we need to modify both the server and client. First, to send proper ANSI/VT100 escape codes for things like color and bold output, we need to add the terminal option to our REPL configuration:

```
var net = require('net');
var repl = require('repl');

net.createServer(function (socket) {
  var r = repl.start({
```

```
    input: socket,
    output: socket,
    terminal: true          ⟵—— Treat output as a TTY stream
  });
  r.on('exit', function() {
    socket.end();
  });
}).listen(1337);

console.log('node repl listening on 1337');
```

Second, to get the input tab completion and readline, we need to create a REPL client that can send the raw TTY input to the server. We can create that using Node:

Treat stdin as a raw TTY input stream. This allows, for example, the Tab key and Up Arrow key to behave as you'd expect in a modern terminal session.

Connect to the REPL TCP server.

Pipe input from stdin to the socket.

Pipe output from the socket to stdout.

When the connection is terminated, destroy the stdin stream, allowing the process to exit.

```
var net = require('net');
var socket = net.connect(1337);

process.stdin.setRawMode(true);
process.stdin.pipe(socket);
socket.pipe(process.stdout);

socket.once('close', function () {
  process.stdin.destroy();
});
```

Now we can start our REPL server with terminal support:

```
$ node repl-tcp-terminal.js
node repl listening on 1337
```

We can connect to the server with our REPL client in another terminal session:

```
$ node repl-client.js
> 10 + 20
30
> .exit
$
```

Now our REPL session behaves as if we were running the node or a basic REPL. We can use autocomplete, access our command history, and get colored output. Sweet!

Inspecting a running process

We've discussed how to use the `repl` module to create connection points and use various clients to access it. We did this to get you comfortable setting up REPL instances on your applications so you can use them to inspect a running process. Now, let's get practical and instrument an existing application with a REPL server, and interact with it using the REPL client we created.

First, let's create a basic HTTP server:

```
var http = require('http');
var server = http.createServer();
server.on('request', function (req, res) {
  res.end('Hello World');
});
server.listen(3000);
console.log('server listening on 3000');
```

This should look familiar. But let's expose this server to our REPL server by adding the following code:

```
var net = require('net');
var repl = require('repl');
net.createServer(function (socket) {
  var r = repl.start({
    input: socket,
    output: socket,
    terminal: true,
    useGlobal: true          ◁──── Allow scripts to be
  });                               executed in global context
  r.on('exit', function () { socket.end() });    versus a separate context
  r.context.server = server;   ◁──
}).listen(1337);                    Expose our server
console.log('repl listening on 1337');    instance to REPL
```

A NOTE ABOUT USEGLOBAL   When enabled, whenever you create a new variable (like var a = 1), it will be put in the global context (global.a === 1). But a now will also be accessible in functions run in a later turn in the event loop.

We exposed the server by setting a property on r.context. We can expose anything we want to the REPL in order to interact with it. It's important to note that we also can *override* anything already existing in the context. This includes all the standard Node global variables like global, process, or Buffer.

Now that we have our server exposed, let's see how we can inspect and debug our HTTP server. First let's fire up our HTTP and REPL servers:

```
$ node repl-app.js
server listening on 3000
repl listening on 1337
```

Now let's use our REPL client to tap into the server:

```
$ node repl-client.js
>
```

We can tap into useful bits of information right away. For instance, we can see how long our process has been running, or how its memory usage is:

```
> process.uptime()
115                     ◁──────── Uptime in seconds
 > process.memoryUsage()
{ rss: 17399808,        ◁──────── Memory in bytes
  heapTotal: 7195904,
  heapUsed: 4146840 }
```

We also exposed the `server` object, and we can access that by just typing `server`:

```
> server
{ domain: null,
  _events:
  ...
  _connectionKey: '4:0.0.0.0:3000' }
```

Let's see how many connections are currently active:

```
> server.connections
0
```

Clearly this would be more interesting in a production context, since we are the only ones using the server and we haven't made a connection yet! Let's hit http://local-host:3000 in our browser and inspect the connections again and see if they've changed:

```
> server.connections
6
```
⟵ **Connections vary on browser/client**

That works. Let's instrument something more complex. Can you think of a way to start tallying the number of requests coming in to our server using the REPL?

ADDING INSTRUMENTATION   One powerful aspect of a REPL is the ability to add instrumentation to help us understand behavior in our application as it's happening. This is especially handy for tricky problems where restarting the application loses our precious state and we have no idea how to duplicate the issue except to wait for it to happen again.

Since our HTTP server is an `EventEmitter`, we can add another request handler that will be called on every request to instrument it with the behavior we want using the REPL:

```
> var numReqs = 0        ⟵  Create variable to store
undefined                    the number of requests
> function trackReqs (req, res) {    ⟵  Create handler function
..... numReqs++                          for incoming requests that
..... }                                  increments the request count
undefined
> server.on('request', trackReqs)    ⟵
{ domain: null,
  _events:                           Add handler to
  ...                                the request event
  _connectionKey: '4:0.0.0.0:3000' }
>
```

Now we're tracking incoming requests. Let's hit Refresh a few times on our browser and see if it worked:

```
> numReqs
8
```

Excellent. Since we have access to the request objects, we can inspect any information about requests available to us: IP addresses, headers, paths, and so on. In this example we exposed an HTTP server, but any objects can be put on the context where it makes sense in your application. You may even consider writing a module exposing commonly used methods in the REPL.

Some issues can't be resolved at an application level and need deeper system introspection. One way to gain deeper understanding is by tracing.

TECHNIQUE 95   Tracing system calls

Understanding how the underlying system calls work can really help you understand a platform. For example, Python and Node both have functionality to perform DNS lookups, but they go about it differently at a lower level. And if you're wondering why one is behaving differently than the other, tracing tools will show you that!

At their core, tracing tools monitor underlying system calls (typically C function names, arguments, and return values) that an application or multiple applications are making, and do interesting things with the data (like logging or statistics).

Tracing helps in production. If you have a process stuck at 100% and are unsure why, a tracer can help expose the underlying state at the system level. For example, you may discover in this instance that you exceeded the allowed open files for a process, and all I/O attempts are being rejected, causing the problem. Since tracing tools aren't performance intrusive like a profiler, they can be valuable assets.

PROBLEM
You want to understand what's happening in your application at the system level.

SOLUTION
Use tracing tools specific to the operating system to gain introspection.

DISCUSSION
All the techniques we've discussed so far have been system-agnostic. This one is OS-specific. There are a lot of different tools, but most are unique to an operating system. For our example, we'll use the Linux-specific tool called `strace`. Similar tools exists for Mac OS X/Solaris (`dtruss`) and Windows (`ProcessMonitor`: http://technet .microsoft.com/en-us/sysinternals/bb896645.aspx).

A tracing program is essentially a dump of system calls as they happen in a process. If you're unfamiliar with the underlying OS, prepare to learn! We'll walk through tracing a simple application to see what's happening at the OS level when we run it to learn how to read trace logs.

Let's write an extremely simple program to trace:

```
console.log('hello world');
```

This seems innocent enough. To see what's going on behind the scenes, let's trace this:

```
sudo strace -o trace.out node hello
```

You'll see the program output "hello world" and exit as expected. But we also got a dump of every system call in trace.out. Let's examine that file.

Right at the top we can see our first call, which makes sense. We're executing /usr/bin/node, passing it the arguments node and hello:

```
execve("/usr/bin/node", ["node", "hello"], [/* 24 vars */]) = 0
```

If you ever wondered why process.argv[0] is node and process.argv[1] is the path to our Node program, now you can see how the underlying call is being made! The strace output tells us the arguments passed and the return value.

To find more information about what execve is (and any other system call), we can just look at the man pages on the host if available (best option), or if not, look online:

```
man execve
```

MORE ON MAN COMMAND Manual pages also include error codes that are helpful to get more details on, for example, what ENOENT or EPERM mean on an operating system. Many of these error codes can be found in the openman page.

Let's examine more of this file. Many of the initial calls are loading the shared libraries libuv needs. Then we get to our application:

```
getcwd("/home/wavded", 4096) = 13
...
stat("/home/wavded/hello", 0x7fff082fda08) = -1
  ENOENT (No such file or directory)
stat("/home/wavded/hello.js",
  {st_mode=S_IFREG|0664, st_size=27, ...}) = 0
```

We can see Node grabbing the current working directory and then looking up our file to run. Note that we executed our application *without* the .js extension, so Node first looks for a program called "hello" and doesn't find it, and then looks for hello.js and is successful. If we were to run it with the .js extension, you wouldn't see the first stat call.

Let's look at the next interesting bit:

```
open("/home/wavded/hello.js", O_RDONLY) = 9
fstat(9, {st_mode=S_IFREG|0664, st_size=27, ...}) = 0
...
read(9, "console.log('hello world')\n", 27) = 27
close(9) = 0
```

Here we open the hello.js file in read-only mode and get assigned a file descriptor. File descriptors are just integers assigned by the OS. But to understand the subsequent calls, we should take note that 9 is the number assigned for hello.js until we see a subsequent close call.

After open, we then see an fstat to get the file's size. Then we read the contents of the file in the read line. The strace output also shows us the contents of the buffer we used to store the file. We then close the file descriptor.

A trace output file won't show us any application code being run. We just see the system *effects* of what's being run. That is, we won't see V8 parsing or executing our console.log but we'll see the underlying write out to stdout. Let's look at that next:

```
write(1, "hello world\n", 12) = 12
```

Recall from chapter 6 that every process has three file descriptors automatically assigned for stdin (0), stdout (1), and stderr (2). We can see that this `write` call uses stdout (1) to write out `hello world`. We also see that `console.log` appends a newline for us.

Our program eventually exits on the last line of `trace.out`:

```
exit_group(0)
```

The zero (0) here represents the process exit code. In this case it's successful. If we were to exit with `process.exit(1)` or some other status, we'd see that number reflected here.

Tracing a running process

So far we've used `strace` to start and trace a program till it exits. How about tapping into a running process?

Here we can just grab the PID for the process:

```
ps ax | grep node
```

The first number in the row is our PID:

```
32476 ? Ssl 0:08 /usr/bin/node long-running.js
```

Once we have our PID, we can run `strace` against it:

```
sudo strace -p 32476
```

All the currently running system calls will output to the console.

This can be a great first line of defense when debugging live issues where CPU is pegged. For example, if we've exceeded our `ulimit` for a process, this will typically peg our CPU, since `open` system calls continually will fail. Running `strace` on the process would quickly show a bunch of `ENFILE` errors occurring. And from the `openman` page, we can see a nice entry for the error:

```
ENFILE The system limit on the total number of
open files has been reached.
```

> **LISTING OPEN FILES** In this case, we can use another handy Linux tool called `lsof` to get a list of open files for a process given a PID to further investigate what we have open right now.

We can also get a CPU pegged at 100% and open up `strace` and see just the following repeating over and over:

```
futex(0x7ffbe00008c8, FUTEX_WAKE_PRIVATE, 1) = 1
```

This, for the most part, is just event loop noise, and it's likely that your application code is stuck in an infinite loop somewhere. Tools like `node --prof` would help at this point.

About other operating system tools

The actual system calls we looked at will be different on other operating systems. For example, you'll see epoll calls being made on Linux that you won't ever see on Mac OS X because libuv uses kqueue for Mac. Although most OSes have POSIX methods like open, the function signatures and error codes can vary. Get to understand the machines you host and develop your Node applications on to make best use of the tracing tools!

> **HOMEWORK!** Make a simple HTTP server and trace it. Can you find out where the port is being bound, where connections are being accepted, and where responses are being written back to the client?

11.3 Summary

In this chapter we looked at debugging Node applications. First, we focused on error handling and prevention:

- How do you handle errors that your application generates?
- How are you notified about crashes? Do you have domains set up or an uncaughtException handler?
- Are you using a lint tool to help prevent exceptions?

Then, we focused on debugging specific problems. We used various tools available in Node and third-party modules. The big thing to take away is knowing the right tool for the job, so when a problem arises, you can assess it and gain useful information:

- Do you need to be able to set breakpoints, watch expressions, and step through your code? Use the built-in debug command or node-inspector.
- Do you need to see where your application is spending its time? Use the Node built-in profiler (node --prof).
- Is your application using more memory than expected? Take heap snapshots and inspect the results.
- Do you want to investigate a running process without pausing it or incurring a performance penalty? Set up and use a REPL server.
- Do you want to see what underlying system calls are being made? Use your operating system's tracing tools.

In the next chapter we'll dive into writing web applications with Node!

Node in production: Deploying applications safely

This chapter covers

- Deploying Node applications to your own server
- Deploying Node applications to cloud providers
- Managing packages for production
- Logging
- Scaling with proxies and cluster

Once you've built and tested a Node application, you'll want to release it. Popular PaaS (platform as a service) providers like Heroku and Nodejitsu make deployment simple, but you can also deploy to private servers. Once your code is out there, you'll need to cope with unexpected errors, service outages, and bugs, and monitor performance.

This chapter shows you how to safely release and maintain Node programs. It covers privately hosted servers that use Apache and nginx, WebSockets, horizontal scaling, automated deployment, logging, and ways to boost performance.

12.1 Deployment

In this section you'll learn how to deploy Node applications to popular cloud providers and your own private servers. It's likely that you'll only typically use one of these approaches, depending on the requirements of your application or employer, but being familiar with both is instructive. For example, the Git-based workflow employed by Heroku has influenced how people deploy applications to servers they control, and with a bit of knowledge you can set up a server without having to call for help from a DevOps specialist.

The first technique we cover is based on Windows Azure, Heroku, and Nodejitsu. This is probably the easiest way to deploy web applications today, and cloud providers have free plans that make it cheap and painless to share your work.

TECHNIQUE 96 **Deploying Node applications to the cloud**

This technique outlines how to use Node with PaaS providers, and has tips on how to configure and maintain applications in production. The focus is on the practical aspects of deployment and maintenance, rather than pricing or business models.

You can try out Heroku and Azure for free, so follow along if you've ever wanted to run a Node application in the cloud.

PROBLEM

You've built a Node web application and want to run it on servers so people can use it.

SOLUTION

Use a PaaS provider like Heroku or Nodejitsu.

DISCUSSION

We'll look at three options for cloud deployment: Nodejitsu, Heroku, and Windows Azure. All of these services allow you to deploy Node web applications, but they all handle things slightly differently. The methods for uploading an application and configuring it vary, even though the fundamental concepts are the same.

Nodejitsu is an interesting case because it's dedicated to Node. On the other hand, Windows Azure supports Microsoft's software development tools, programming languages, and databases. Azure even has features beyond web application hosting, like databases and Active Directory integration. Heroku draws on a rich community of partners that offers add-ons, whereas Azure is more of a full-service offering.

If you look in the source code provided with this book, you should find a small Express application in production/inky. This is the application we used to research this technique, and you can use it as a sample application to try each service provider. Nodejitsu and Azure's documentation includes examples based on Node's http module, but you really need something with a package.json to see how things work for typical Node applications.

The first service provider we'll look at is Nodejitsu (https://www.nodejitsu.com/). Nodejitsu is based in New York, and has data centers in North America and Western Europe. Nodejitsu was founded in 2010, and has funding from the Bloomberg Beta fund.

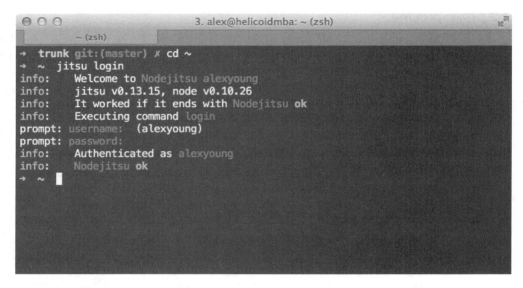

Figure 12.1   The `jitsu` **command-line client allows you to sign in.**

To get started with Nodejitsu, you'll need to register an account. Go to Nodejitsu.com and sign up. You can sign up without selecting a pricing plan if you intend to release an open source project through Nodejitsu.

Nodejitsu has a command-line client called `jitsu`. You can install it with `npm install -g jitsu`. Once npm has finished, you'll need to sign in—type `jitsu login` and enter your username and password. This will save an API token to a file called ~/.jitsuconf, so your password won't be stored locally. Figure 12.1 shows what this process looks like in the terminal.

To deploy an application, type `jitsu deploy`. The `jitsu` command will prompt with questions about your application, and then set it up to run on a temporary subdomain. If you're using an Express application, it'll automatically set `NODE_ENV` to production, but you can edit this setting along with other environmental variables in the web interface. In fact, the web interface can do most of the things the `jitsu` command does, which means you don't necessarily need a developer on hand to do basic maintenance chores like restarting applications.

Figure 12.2 shows a preview of Nodejitsu's web interface, which is called *WebOps*. It allows you to stop and start applications, manage environmental variables, roll back to earlier versions of your application, and even stream logs in real time.

Unsurprisingly Nodejitsu is heavily tailored toward Node applications, and the deployment process is heavily influenced by npm. If you have a strong grasp of npm and package.json files, and your projects are all Node applications, then you'll feel at home with Nodejitsu.

Another PaaS solution that's popular with Node developers is Heroku. Heroku supports several programming languages and platforms, including Node, and was

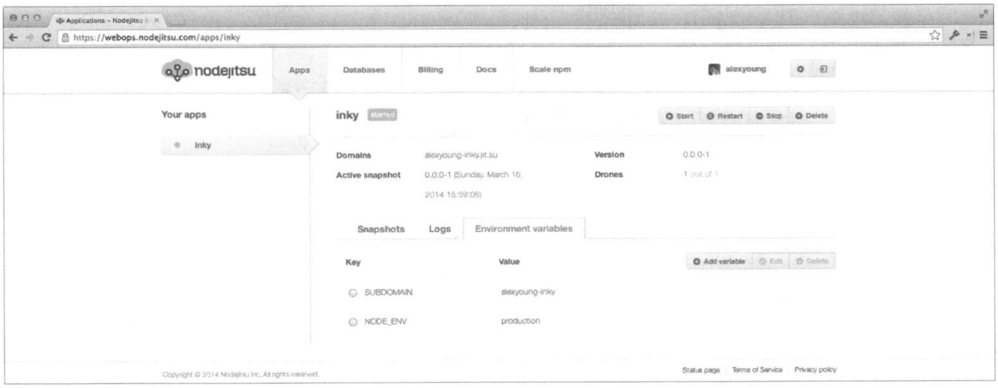

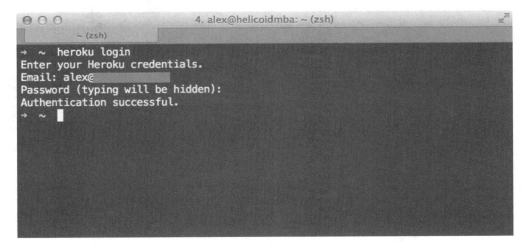

Figure 12.2   The WebOps management interface

founded in 2007. It has since been acquired by Salesforce.com, and uses a virtualized solution based on Ubuntu servers. To use Heroku, you'll need to sign up at heroku .com. It's easy to create a free account, and you can even run production applications on the free tier. Essential features like domain aliases and SSL are paid, so it doesn't take many requirements to hit around $20 a month, but if you don't mind using a Heroku subdomain, you can keep things running for free.

Once you've created an account, you'll need to install the Heroku Toolbelt from toolbelt.heroku.com. There are installers for Linux, Mac OS X, and Windows. Once you've installed it, you'll have a command-line client called `heroku` that can be used to create and manage applications. Before you can use it, you'll have to sign in; `heroku login` can be used to do this, and functions in much the same way as Nodejitsu's `jitsu` command. You only need to log in once because it stores a token that will be used for subsequent requests. Figure 12.3 shows what this should look like.

Figure 12.3   Signing in with Heroku

The next step with a Heroku deploy is to prepare your repository. You'll need to `git init` and commit your project. If you're using our code samples and have checked them out of Git, then you should copy the specific project that you want to deploy out of our working tree. The full steps are as follows:

1 `git init`
2 `git add .`
3 `git commit -m 'Create new project'`
4 `heroku create`
5 `git push heroku master`

The `heroku create` command sets up a remote repository called `heroku`, and the first `git push` to it will trigger the creation of a temporary `herokuapp.com` subdomain.

If your application can be started with `npm start`, it should just work. If not, you might need to add a file called Procfile to your application that contains `web: node yourapp.js`. This file lists the processes that your application needs to run—it could include background workers as well.

If you're using an Express application that expects `NODE_ENV` to be set, then you'll need to do this manually with Heroku. The command is just `heroku config:set NODE_ENV=production`, but notice that this is automatic with Nodejitsu.

The last PaaS provider we'll discuss is Windows Azure. Microsoft's Azure platform can be used entirely through the web interface, but there's also a command-line interface that you can install with `npm install -g azure-cli`. Figure 12.4 shows what the command-line tool looks like.

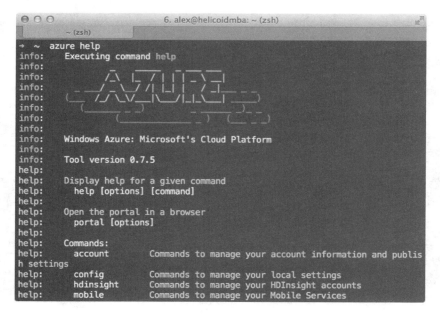

Figure 12.4   The Azure CLI tool

Azure also has an SDK that you can download for Linux, Mac OS X, and Windows. The downloads are available at www.windowsazure.com/en-us/downloads/.

To start using Azure, you'll need to sign in to www.windowsazure.com with a Microsoft account. This is the same account that you can use for other Microsoft services, so if you already have an email account with Microsoft, you should be able to sign in. Azure's registration process has extra security steps: a credit card and phone number are used to validate your account, so it's a bit more tedious than Heroku or Nodejitsu.

Once you've created your Windows Azure account, you'll want to go to the Portal page. Next go to *Compute, Web Site,* and then *Quick Create.* Just keep in mind that you're creating a "Web Site" and you should be fine—Microsoft supports a wide range of services that are partly tailored to .NET development with their existing tools like Visual Studio, so it can be bewildering for Mac and Unix developers.

Once your application has been created, you'll need to tie it to a source control repository. Don't worry, you can use GitHub! Before we go any further, check that you're looking at a page like the one in figure 12.5.

Cloud configuration

PaaS providers all seem to have their own approaches to application configuration. You can, of course, keep configuration settings in your code, or JSON files, but there are times when it's useful to store them outside of your repository.

For example, we build open source web applications that we also run on Heroku, so we keep our database passwords outside of our open source repository and use `heroku config:set` instead.

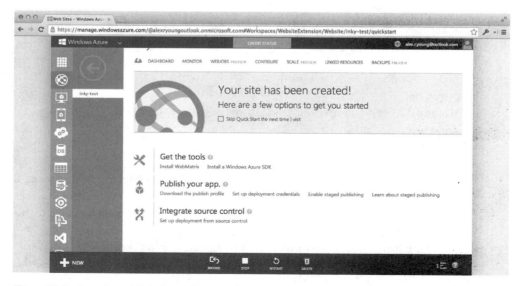

Figure 12.5 Azure's web interface after creating a website

Click your application's name, select *Set up deployment from source control*, and then look for *site URL* on the right side. From here you'll be able to choose from a huge range of repositories and service providers, but we tested our application with GitHub. Azure fetched the code and set up a Node application—it was the same Express code that we used for Heroku (listings/production/inky), and worked the first time.

Table 12.1 shows how to get and set configuration values on each of the cloud providers we've discussed here.

Table 12.1   Setting environmental variables

Provider	Set	Remove	List
Nodejitsu	`jitsu env set name value`	`jitsu env delete name`	`jitsu env list`
Heroku	`heroku config:set name=value`	`heroku config:unset name`	`heroku config`
Azure	`azure site appsetting add name=value`	`azure site appsetting delete name`	`azure site appsetting list`

Although Azure's registration requirements might seem less convenient than Heroku and Nodejitsu, it does have several benefits: if you're working with .NET, then you can use your existing tools. Also, Microsoft's documentation is excellent, and includes guides on setup and deploying for Linux and Mac OS X (http://www.windowsazure .com/en-us/documentation/articles/web-sites-nodejs-develop-deploy-mac/).

Your own servers, rented servers, or cheap virtual hosts all have their own advantages. If you want complete control over your server, or if your business already has its own servers or data centers, then read on to learn how to deploy Node to your own servers.

TECHNIQUE 97   Using Node with Apache and nginx

Deploying Node to private servers running Apache or nginx is entirely possible, and recommended for certain situations. This technique demonstrates how to run a Node program behind Apache and nginx.

PROBLEM
You want to run a Node web application on your own server.

SOLUTION
Use Apache or nginx proxying and a service supervisor like runit.

DISCUSSION
While PaaS solutions are easy to use, there are times when you have to use dedicated hardware, or virtual machines that you have full control over. Larger businesses often have investments in their own data centers, so it doesn't make sense to switch to an external service provider.

Virtualization has transformed web hosting. Linux virtual machines have been a key solution for hosting web applications for several years, and services like Amazon Elastic Compute Cloud make it easy to create and destroy services on demand.

It's therefore likely that at some point you'll be faced with deploying Node applications to servers that need configuration and maintenance. If you're already experienced with basic systems administration tasks, then you can reuse your existing skills and software. Otherwise, you'll have to become familiar with web server daemons and the tools used to keep Node programs running and recovering from errors.

This technique presents examples for Apache and nginx. They're both web servers, but their configuration formats are very different, and they're built in different ways. Figure 12.6 shows the basic server architecture that we'll create in this section.

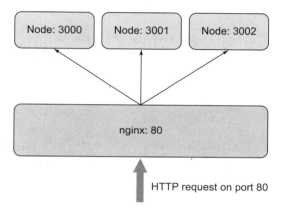

It's not actually necessary to run a web server—there are ways to make Node programs safely access port 80. But we assume that you're deploying to a server that has existing websites. Also, some people prefer to serve static assets from Apache or nginx.

The same technique is used for both servers: proxying. The following listing shows how to do this with Apache.

Figure 12.6 A Node program running alongside Apache or nginx

Listing 12.1 Proxying requests to a Node application with Apache

❶ **Proxy requests starting at / to localhost:3000**

```
ProxyPass / http://localhost:3000/
LoadModule proxy_module /lib/apache2/modules/mod_proxy.so
LoadModule proxy_http_module /lib/apache2/modules/mod_proxy_http.so
```

Load proxy module ❷

Load HTTP proxy module ❸

The directives in listing 12.1 should be added to your Apache configuration file. To find the right file, type apache2 -V on your server, and look for the HTTPD_ROOT and SERVER_CONFIG_FILE values—joining them will give you the right path and file. It's likely that you won't want to redirect *all* requests to your Node application, so you can add the proxy settings to a VirtualHost block.

With these three lines, requests to / will now be proxied to a process listening on port 3000 ❶. In this case, the process is assumed to be a Node program that you've run with node server.js or npm start, but it could technically be any HTTP server. The LoadModule directives tell Apache to use the proxy ❷ and HTTP proxying ❸ modules.

If you forget to start the Node process, or quit it, then Apache will return a 503 error. To avoid errors like this, you need a way to keep the Node process running, and to also run it when the server boots. One way to do this is with runit (http://smarden.org/runit/).

If you're using Debian or Ubuntu, you can install runit with `apt-get install runit`. Once it's ready, create a shell script that can start your Node process. First, create a directory for your project: sudo mkdir /etc/service/nodeapp. Next, create a file that will be used for the script: sudo touch /etc/service/nodeapp/run. Then edit the file to make it look like the next listing.

Listing 12.2   Running a program with `runit`

```
#!/bin/sh
export PATH=$PATH:/home/vagrant/.nvm/v0.10.26/bin
cd /home/vagrant/inky
exec npm start
```

❶ Set PATH so the shell can find your Node installation

❷ Change directory to location of your Node project

Our server was using nvm (https://github.com/creationix/nvm) to manage the installed versions of Node, so we added its location to `$PATH` ❶; otherwise the shell couldn't find where `node` and `npm` were installed. You may have to modify this based on the output of `which node`, or remove it entirely. The last two lines ❷ just change the directory to the location of your Node project, and then start it with `npm start`.

The application can be started with `sudo sv start /etc/service/nodeapp` and stopped with `sudo sv stop /etc/service/nodeapp`. Once the Node process is running, you can test it by killing it, and then checking to see that it automatically gets restarted by runit.

Now that you know how Apache handles proxies, and how to keep a process running, let's look at nginx. Nginx is often used as a web server, but it's technically a reverse proxy server that supports HTTP, HTTPS, and email. To make nginx proxy connections to Node applications, you can use the `Proxy` module, which uses a `proxy_pass` directive in a way similar to Apache.

Listing 12.3 has the settings needed by nginx. Like Apache, you could also put the `server` block in a virtual host file.

Listing 12.3   Proxying requests to a Node application with nginx

```
http {
  server {
    listen 80;

    location / {
      proxy_pass http://localhost:3000;
      proxy_http_version 1.1;
    }
  }
}
```

❶ This proxies to port 3000, so you can change it to other ports if you use multiple applications.

If you have multiple applications on the same server, then you can use a different port, but we've used 3000 here ❶. This example is basically the same as Apache—you tell the server what location to proxy, and then the port. And of course, this example could be combined with runit.

If you don't want to run Apache or nginx, you can run Node web applications without a web server. Read on to learn how to do this using firewall rules and other techniques.

TECHNIQUE 98   Safely running Node on port 80

You can still run Node without a web server daemon like Apache. To do this, you basically need to forward the external port 80 to an internal, unprivileged port. This technique presents some ways to do this in Linux.

PROBLEM

You don't want to use Apache or nginx.

SOLUTION

Use firewall rules to redirect port 80 to another, unprivileged port.

DISCUSSION

In most operating systems, binding to port 80 requires special privileges. That means that if you try to use app.listen(80) instead of port 3000 as we've used in most of our examples, you'll see Error: listen EACCES. This happens because your current user account doesn't have permission to bind to port 80.

You could get around this restriction by running sudo npm start, but this is dangerous. Ideally you want your Node program to run as a nonroot user.

In Linux, traffic can be redirected from port 80 to a higher port number by using iptables. Linux uses iptables to manage firewall rules, so you just need a rule that maps from port 80 to 3000:

```
iptables -t nat -I PREROUTING -p tcp --dport\
   80 -j REDIRECT --to-port 3000
```

To make this change permanent, you'll need to save the rules to a file that gets run whenever the network interface is set up. The general approach is to save the rules to a file, like /etc/iptables.up.rules, and then edit /etc/network/interfaces to use it:

```
auto eth0
iface eth0 inet dhcp
  pre-up iptables-restore < /etc/iptables.up.rules
  post-down iptables-restore < /etc/iptables.down.rules
```

This is highly dependent on your operating system; these rules are adapted from Debian and Ubuntu's documentation, but it may be different in other Linux distributions.

One downside of this technique is that it maps traffic to *any* process that's listening to that port. An alternative solution is to grant the Node binary extra capabilities. You can do this by installing libcap2.

In Debian and Ubuntu, you can use sudo apt-get install libcap2-bin. Then you just need to grant the Node binary the capabilities for accessing privileged ports:

```
sudo setcap cap_net_bind_service=+ep /usr/local/bin/node
```

You may need to change the path to Node—check the output of which node if you're not sure where it is. The downside of using capabilities for this is that now the node binary can bind to all ports from 1–1024, so it's not as specific as restricting it to port 80.

Once you've applied a capability to a binary, it will be fixed until the file changes. That means that you'll need to run this command again if you upgrade Node.

Now that your application is running on a server, you'll want to ensure that it runs forever. There are many different ways to do this; the next technique outlines runit and the `forever` module.

TECHNIQUE 99   Keeping Node processes running

Programs inevitably crash, and it's unfortunate when this happens. What matters is how well you handle failure—users should be informed, and programs should recover elegantly. This technique is all about keeping Node programs running, no matter what.

PROBLEM

Your program crashed in the middle of the night, and customers were unable to use the service until you restarted it.

SOLUTION

Use a process monitor to automatically restart the Node program.

DISCUSSION

There are two main ways to keep a Node program running: service supervision or a Node program that manages other Node programs. The first method is a generic, operating system–specific technique. You've already seen runit in technique 97. Runit supports service supervision, which means it detects when a process stops running and tries to restart it.

Another daemon manager is Upstart (http://upstart.ubuntu.com/). You may have seen Upstart if you use Ubuntu. To use it, you'll need a configuration file that describes how the Node program is managed. Listing 12.4 contains an example that you can modify for your server—it should be saved in /etc/init/nodeapp.conf, where nodeapp is the name of your application.

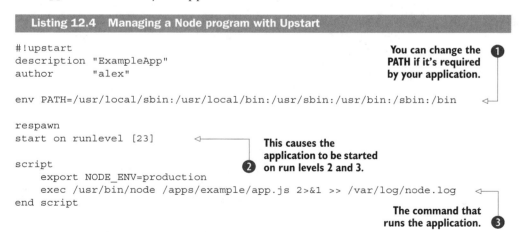

Listing 12.4   Managing a Node program with Upstart

```
#!upstart                                          You can change the  ❶
description "ExampleApp"                            PATH if it's required
author    "alex"                                   by your application.

env PATH=/usr/local/sbin:/usr/local/bin:/usr/sbin:/usr/bin:/sbin:/bin

respawn
start on runlevel [23]                 ◁──    This causes the
                                              application to be started
script                                 ❷     on run levels 2 and 3.
    export NODE_ENV=production
    exec /usr/bin/node /apps/example/app.js 2>&1 >> /var/log/node.log  ◁──
end script
                                              The command that
                                              runs the application.  ❸
```

This configuration file tells Upstart to respawn the application (http://upstart .ubuntu.com/wiki/Stanzas#respawn) if it dies for any reason. It sets up a PATH ❶ that's similar to the one you'll see in your terminal if you type `echo $PATH`. Then it states the program should be run on run levels 2 and 3 ❷—run level 2 is usually when networking daemons are started.

> **RUN LEVELS** Unix systems handle run levels differently depending on the vendor. The Linux Standard Base specification describes run level 2 as multi-user mode, and 3 as multi-user mode with networking. In Debian, 2–5 are grouped as multi-user mode with console logins and the display manager. However, Ubuntu treats run level 2 as graphical multi-user with networking, so you should check how your system implements run levels before using Upstart.

The Upstart `script` stanza allows you to include a short script, so this means you can do things like set `NODE_ENV` to `production`. The application itself is launched with the `exec` instruction. We've included some logging support by redirecting standard out and standard error to a log file ❸.

Upstart can be more work to set up than runit, but we've used it in production for three years now without any issues. Both are easier to set up and maintain than traditional stop/start init scripts, but there's another technique you can use: Node programs that monitor other Node programs.

Node process managers work by using a small program that ensures another program runs continuously. This program is simple and therefore less likely to crash than a more complex web application. One of the most popular modules for this is `forever` (https://www.npmjs.org/package/forever), which can be used as a command-line program or programmatically.

Most people use it through the command-line interface. The basic usage is `forever start app.js`, where app.js is your web application. It has lots of options beyond this, though: it can manage log files and even wrap your program so it behaves like a daemon.

To start your program as a daemon, use the following options:

```
forever start -l forever.log -o out.log -e err.log app.js
```

This will start app.js, creating some additional files: one to store the current PID of the active process, a log file, and an error log file. Once the program is running, you can stop it gracefully like this:

```
forever stop app.js
```

Forever can be used with any Node program, but it's generally seen as a tool for keeping web applications running for a long time. The command-line interface makes it easy to use alongside other Unix programs.

Deploying applications that use WebSockets can bring a set of unique requirements. It can be more difficult with PaaS providers, because they can kill requests that last for more than a certain number of seconds. If you're using WebSockets, look through the next technique to make sure your setup will work in production.

TECHNIQUE 100   **Using WebSockets in production**

Node is great for WebSockets—the same process can serve both standard HTTP requests and the newer WebSocket protocol. But how exactly do you deploy programs that use WebSockets in production? Read on to find out how to do this with web servers and cloud providers.

PROBLEM

You want to use WebSockets in production.

SOLUTION

Make sure the service provider or proxy you're using supports HTTP Upgrade headers.

DISCUSSION

WebSockets are amazing, but are still treated almost like second-class citizens by hosting providers. Nodejitsu was the first PaaS provider to support WebSockets, and it uses node-http-proxy (https://github.com/nodejitsu/node-http-proxy) to do this. Almost all solutions involve a proxy. To understand why, you need to look at how WebSockets work.

HTTP is essentially a stateless protocol, which means all interactions between a server and a client can be modeled with requests and responses that hold all of the required state. This level of encapsulation has led to the design of modern client/server web applications.

The downside of this is that the underlying protocol doesn't support long-running full-duplex connections. There's a wide class of applications that are built on TCP connections of this type; video streaming and conferencing, real-time messaging, and games are prominent examples. As web browsers have evolved to support richer, more sophisticated applications, we're naturally left trying to simulate these types of applications using HTTP.

The WebSocket protocol was developed to support long-lived TCP-like connections. It works by using a standard HTTP handshake where the client establishes whether the server supports WebSockets. The mechanism for this is a new header called Upgrade. As HTTP clients and servers are typically bombarded with a variety of nonstandard headers, servers that don't support Upgrade should be fine—the client will just have to fall back to old-fashioned HTTP polling.

Because servers have to handle WebSocket connections so differently, it makes sense to effectively run two servers. In a Node program, we typically have an http.listen for our standard HTTP requests, and another "internal" WebSocket server.

In technique 97, you saw how to use nginx with Node. The example used proxies to pass requests from nginx to your Node process, which meant the Node process could bind to a different port to 80. By using the same technique, you can make nginx support WebSockets. A typical nginx.conf would look like the next listing.

Listing 12.5   Adding WebSocket support to nginx

```
http {
  server {
    listen 80;
```

```
    server_name example.com;

    location / {
      proxy_pass http://localhost:3000;
      proxy_http_version 1.1;
      proxy_set_header Upgrade $http_upgrade;
      proxy_set_header Connection 'upgrade';
      proxy_set_header Host $host;
      proxy_cache_bypass $http_upgrade;
    }
  }
}
```

❶ **Support Upgrade header**

Adding `proxy_http_version 1.1` and `proxy_set_header Upgrade` ❶ enables nginx to filter WebSocket requests through to your Node process. This example will also skip caching for WebSocket requests.

Since we mentioned Nodejitsu supports WebSockets, what about Heroku? Well, you currently need to enable it as an add-on, which means you need to run a `heroku` command:

```
heroku labs:enable websockets
```

Heroku's web servers usually kill requests that take longer than around 75 seconds, but enabling this add-on means requests that originate with an `Upgrade` header should keep running for as long as the network allows.

There are times when you might not be able to use WebSockets easily. One example is older versions of Apache, where the proxy module doesn't support them. In cases like this, it can be better to use a proxy server that runs *before* everything else.

HAProxy (http://haproxy.1wt.eu/) is a flexible proxy server. The usage is similar to nginx, and it's also event-based, so it has been widely adopted in the Node community. If you're using an old version of Apache, you can proxy web requests to Apache or Node, depending on various options like URL or headers.

If you want to install HAProxy in Debian or Ubuntu, you can do so with `sudo apt-get install haproxy`. Once it's set up, you'll need to edit /etc/default/haproxy and set `ENABLED=1`—this is just because it ships with a default configuration, so it's disabled by default. Listing 12.6 is a sample configuration that's capable of routing requests to a Node web application that runs on port 3000, but will be accessible using port 80 externally.

Listing 12.6   Using HAProxy with a Node application

```
frontend http-in
  mode http
  bind *:80
  timeout client 999s
  default_backend node_backend

backend node_backend
  mode http
```

Allow WebSocket ❶
connections a very
long time to live.

All HTTP requests will be routed to your Node application.

```
timeout server 86400000
timeout connect 5000
server io_test localhost:3000
```

This should work with WebSockets, and we've used a long timeout so HAProxy doesn't close WebSockets connections, which are typically long-lived ❶. If you run a Node program that listens on port 3000, then after restarting HAProxy with sudo /etc/init.d/haproxy restart, your application should be accessible on port 80.

You can use table 12.2 to find the web server that's right for your application.

Table 12.2 **Comparing server options**

Server	Features	Best for
Apache	■ Fast asset serving ■ Works well with established web platforms (PHP, Ruby) ■ Lots of modules for things like proxying, URL rewriting ■ Virtual hosts	May already be on servers
nginx	■ Event-based architecture, very fast ■ Easy to configure ■ Proxy module works well with Node and WebSockets ■ Virtual hosts	Hosting Node applications when you also want to host static websites, but don't yet have Apache or a legacy server set up
HAProxy	■ Event-based and fast ■ Can route to other web servers on the same machine ■ Works well with WebSockets.	Scaling up to a cluster for high-traffic sites, or complex heterogeneous setups
Native Node proxy	■ Reuse your Node programming knowledge ■ Flexible	Useful if you want to scale and have a team with excellent Node skills

Which server is right for me?

This chapter doesn't cover *every* server choice out there—we've mainly focused on Apache and nginx for Unix servers. Even so, it can be difficult to pick between these options. We've included table 12.2 so you can quickly compare each option.

Your HAProxy setup can be made aware of multiple "back ends" by naming them with the backend instruction. In listing 12.7 we only have one—node_backend . It would be possible to also run Apache, and route certain requests to it based on the domain name:

```
frontend http-in
  mode http
  bind *:80
  acl static_assets hdr_end(host) -i static.manning.com
```

```
backend static_assets
  mode http
  server www_static localhost:8080
```

This works well if you have an existing set of Apache virtual hosts—perhaps serving things like static assets, blogs, and websites—and you want to add Node to the same server. Apache can be set up to listen on a different port so HAProxy can sit in front of it, and then route requests to Express on port 3000 and the existing Apache sites on port 8080. Apache allows you to change the port by using the `Listen 8080` directive.

You can use the same `acl` option to route WebSockets based on URL. Let's say you've mounted your WebSocket server on /chat in your Node application. You could have a specific instance of your server that just handles WebSockets, and route conditionally using HAProxy by using `path_beg`. The following listing shows how this works.

Listing 12.7 Using HAProxy with WebSockets

```
frontend http-in
  mode http
  bind *:80
  acl is_websocket hdr(Upgrade) -i WebSocket          ❶ Check WebSocket
                                                         header

  acl is_websocket path_beg -i /chat                  ❷ Check if path for
                                                         WebSockets was used
  use_backend ws if is_websocket
  default_backend node_backend

backend node_backend
  mode http
  server www_static localhost:3000

backend ws
  timeout server 600s
  server ws1 localhost:3001
```

HAProxy can match requests based on lots of parameters. Here we've used `hdr(Upgrade) -i WebSocket` to test if an `Upgrade` header has been used ❶. As you've already seen, that denotes a WebSocket handshake.

By using `path_beg` and marking matching routes with `acl is_websocket` ❷, you can now route requests based on the prefix expression `if is_websocket`.

All of these HAProxy options can be combined to route requests to your Node application, Apache server, and WebSocket-specific Node server. That means you can run your WebSockets off an entirely different process, or even another internal web server. HAProxy is a great choice for scaling up Node programs—you could run multiple instances of your application on multiple servers.

HAProxy provides a `weight` option that allows you to implement *round-robin* load balancing by adding `balance roundrobin` to a `backend`.

You can initially deploy your application without nginx or HAProxy in front of it, but when you're ready, you can scale up by using a proxy. If you don't have performance issues right now, then it's worth just being aware that proxies can do things like route WebSockets to different servers and handle round-robin load balancing. If you already have a server using Apache 2.2.x that isn't compatible with proxying WebSockets, then you can drop HAProxy in front of Apache.

If you're using HAProxy, you'll still have to manage your Node processes with a monitoring daemon like runit or Upstart, but it has proven to be an incredibly flexible solution.

Another approach that we haven't discussed yet is to put your Node applications behind a lightweight Node program that acts as a proxy itself. This is actually used behind the scenes by PaaS providers like Nodejitsu.

Selecting the right server architecture is just the first step to successfully deploying a Node application. You should also consider performance and scalability. The next three techniques include advice on caching and running clusters of Node programs.

12.2   *Caching and scaling*

This section is mainly about running multiple copies of Node applications at once, but we've also included a technique to give you details on caching. If you can make the client do more work, then why not?

TECHNIQUE 101   HTTP caching

Even though Node is known for high-performance web applications, there are ways you can speed things up. Caching is the major technique, and you should consider caching before deploying your application. This technique introduces the concepts behind HTTP caching.

PROBLEM

You want to reduce how long it takes to make requests to your application.

SOLUTION

Check to ensure that you're using HTTP caching correctly.

DISCUSSION

Modern web applications can be huge: image assets, fonts, CSS, JavaScript, and HTML all add up to a formidable payload that's spread across several HTTP requests. Even with the best minimizers and compression, downloads can still run into megabytes. To avoid requiring users to wait for every action they perform on your site, the best strategy can be to remove the need to download anything at all.

Browsers cache content locally, and can look at the cache to determine if a resource needs to be downloaded. This process is controlled by *HTTP cache headers* and conditional requests. In this technique we'll introduce cache headers and explain how they work, so when you watch your application serving responses in a debugging tool like WebKit Inspector, you'll know what caching headers to expect.

The main two headers are `Cache-Control` and `Expires`. The `Cache-Control` header allows the server to specify a directive that controls how a resource is cached. The basic directives are as follows:

- *public*—Allow caching in the browser and any intermediate proxies between the browser and server.
- *private*—Only allow the browser to cache the resource.
- *no-store*—Don't cache the resource (but some clients still cache under certain conditions).

For a full list of `Cache-Control` directives, refer to the Hypertext Transfer Protocol 1.1 specification (http://www.w3.org/Protocols/rfc2616/rfc2616.html).

The `Expires` header tells the browser when to replace the local resource. The date should be in the RFC 1123 format: `Fri, 03 Apr 2014 19:06 BST`. The HTTP/1.1 specification notes that dates over a year shouldn't be used, so don't set dates too far into the future because the behavior is undefined.

These two headers allow the server to tell clients *when* a resource should be cached. Most Node frameworks like Express will set these headers for you—the static serving middleware that's part of Connect, for example, will set `maxAge` to 0 to indicate cache revalidation should occur. If you watch the Network console in your browser's debugging tools, you should see Express serving static assets with `Cache-Control: public, max-age=0`, and a `Last-Modified` dates based on the file date.

Connect's `static` middleware, which is found in the `send` module, does this by using `stat.mtime.toUTCString` to get the date of the last file modification. The browser will make a standard HTTP `GET` request for the resource with two additional request headers: `If-Modified-Since` and `If-None-Match`. Connect will then check `If-Modified-Since` against the file modification date, and respond with an HTTP 304, depending on the modification date. A 304 response like this will have no body, so the browser can conditionally use local content instead of downloading the resource again.

Figure 12.7 shows a high-level overview of HTTP caching, from the browser's perspective.

Conditional caching is great for large assets that may change, like images, because it's much cheaper to make a `GET` request to find out if a resource should be downloaded again. This is known as a *time-based conditional request*. There are also *content-based conditional* requests, where a digest of the resource is used to see if a resource has changed.

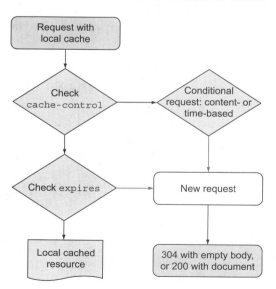

Figure 12.7   Browsers either use the local cache or make a conditional request, based on the previous request's headers.

Content-based conditional requests work using ETags. *ETag* is short for *entity tag*, and allows servers to validate resources in a cache based on their content. Connect's static middleware generates ETags like this:

```
exports.etag = function(stat) {
  return '"' + stat.size + '-' + Number(stat.mtime) + '"';
};
```

Now contrast this to how Express generates ETags for dynamic content—this is usually content sent with res.send, like a JavaScript object or a string:

```
exports.etag = function(body){
  return '"' + crc32.signed(body) + '"';
};
```

The first example uses the file modification time and size to create a hash. The second uses a hashing function based on the content. Both techniques send the browser tags that are based on the content, but they've been optimized for performance based on the resource type.

There's pressure on developers of static servers to make them as fast as possible. If you were to use Node's built-in http module, you'd have to take all of these caching headers into account, and then optimize things like ETag generation. That's why it's advisable to use a module like Express—it'll handle the details of the required headers based on sensible default behavior, so you can focus on developing your application.

Caching is an elegant way of improving performance because it effectively allows you to reduce traffic by making clients do a bit more work. Another option is to use a Node-based HTTP proxy to route between a cluster of processes or servers. Read on to learn how to do this, or skip to technique 103 to see how to use Node's cluster module to manage multiple Node processes.

TECHNIQUE 102   Using a Node proxy for routing and scaling

Local development is simple because you generally run one Node application at a time. But a production server can host multiple applications, and run the same application on multiple CPU cores to improve performance. So far we've talked about web and proxy servers, but this technique focuses on pure Node servers.

PROBLEM

You want to use a pure Node solution to host multiple applications, or scale an application.

SOLUTION

Use a proxy server module like Nodejitsu's http-proxy.

DISCUSSION

This technique demonstrates how to use Node programs to route traffic. It's similar to the proxy server examples in technique 100, so you can reapply these ideas to HAProxy or nginx. But there are times when it might be easier to express routing logic in code rather than using settings files.

Also, as you've seen before in this book, Node programs run as a single process, which doesn't usually take advantage of a modern server that may have multiple CPUs and CPU cores. Therefore, you can use the techniques here to route traffic based on your production needs, but also to run multiple instances of your application so it can better take advantage of your server's resources, reducing response latency and hopefully keeping your customers happy.

Nodejitsu's `http-proxy` (https://www.npmjs.org/package/http-proxy) is a lightweight wrapper around Node's built-in `http` core module that makes it easier to define proxies with code. The basic usage should be familiar to you if you've followed our chapter on Node web development. The following listing is a simple proxy that redirects traffic to another port.

Listing 12.8   Redirecting traffic to another port with `http-proxy`

```
var httpProxy = require('http-proxy');
var proxy = httpProxy.createProxyServer({          ❶ Redirect traffic
  target: 'http://localhost:3000'                     to port 3000
});

proxy.on('error', function(err) {                  ❷ Catch errors
  console.error('Error:', err);                       and log them
});
                                                   ❸ Set this server to
proxy.listen(9000);                                   listen on port 9000
```

This example redirects traffic to port 3000 by using `http-proxy`'s `target` option ❶. This module is event-based, so errors can be handled by setting up an error listener ❷. The proxy server itself is set to listen on port 9000 ❸, but we've just used that so you can run it easily—port 80 would be used in production.

The options passed to `createProxyServer` can define other routing logic. If `ws: true` is set, then WebSockets will be routed separately. That means you can create a proxy server that routes WebSockets to one application, and standard requests elsewhere. Let's look at that in a more detailed example. The next listing shows you how to route WebSocket requests to a separate application.

Listing 12.9   Routing WebSocket connections separately

```
var http = require('http');
var httpProxy = require('http-proxy');

var proxy = new httpProxy.createProxyServer({
  target: 'http://localhost:3000'
});

var wsProxy = new httpProxy.createProxyServer({    ❶ Create another proxy
  target: 'http://localhost:3001'                     server for WebSockets
});

var proxyServer = http.createServer(function(req, res) {
```

```
    proxy.web(req, res);
});

proxyServer.on('upgrade', function(req, socket, head) {
  wsProxy.ws(req, socket, head);
});

proxyServer.listen(9000);
```

> **Listen for upgrade event; then use WebSocket proxy instead of the standard ❷ web request proxy**

This example creates two proxy servers: one for web requests and the other for Web-Sockets ❶. The main web-facing server emits `upgrade` events when a WebSocket is initiated, and this is intercepted so requests can be routed elsewhere ❷.

This technique can be extended to route traffic according to any rules you like—if you can infer something from a `request` object, you can route traffic accordingly. The same idea can also be used to map traffic to multiple machines. This allows you to create a cluster of servers, which can help you scale up an application. The following listing could be used to proxy to several servers.

Listing 12.10   Scaling using multiple instances of a server

```
var http = require('http');
var httpProxy = require('http-proxy');

var targets = [
  { target: 'http://localhost:3000' },
  { target: 'http://localhost:3001' },
  { target: 'http://localhost:3002' }
];

var proxies = targets.map(function(options, i) {
  var proxy = new httpProxy.createProxyServer(options);
  proxy.on('error', function(err) {
    console.error('Proxy error:', err);
    console.error('Server:', i);
  });
  return proxy;
});

var i = 0;
http.createServer(function(req, res) {
  proxies[i].web(req, res);
  i = (i + 1) % proxies.length;
}).listen(9000);
```

> ❶ **Create a proxy for each instance of application**

> ❷ **Proxy requests using round-robin**

This example uses an array that contains the options for each proxy server, and then creates an instance of proxy server for each one ❶. Then all you need to do is create a standard HTTP server and map requests to each server ❷. This example uses a basic round-robin implementation—after each request a counter is incremented, so the next request will be mapped to a different server. You could easily take this example and reconfigure it to map to any number of servers.

Mapping requests like this can be useful on a single server with multiple CPUs and CPU cores. If you run your application multiple times and set each instance to listen on a different port, then your operating system should run each Node process on a different CPU core. This example uses `localhost`, but you could use another server, thereby clustering the application across several servers.

In contrast to this technique's use of additional servers for scaling, the next technique uses Node's built-in features to manage multiple copies of the same Node program.

<hr>

TECHNIQUE 103   **Scaling and resiliency with cluster**

JavaScript programs are considered *single-threaded*. Whether they actually use a single thread or not is dependent on the platform, but conceptually they execute as a single thread. That means you may have to do additional work to scale your application to take advantage of multiple CPUs and cores.

This technique demonstrates the core module `cluster`, and shows how it relates to scalability, resiliency, and your Node applications.

PROBLEM

You want to improve your application's response time, or increase its resiliency.

SOLUTION

Use the `cluster` module.

DISCUSSION

In technique 102, we mentioned running multiple Node processes behind a proxy. In this technique we'll explain how this works purely on the Node side. You can use the ideas in this technique with or without a proxy server to load balance. Either way, the goal is the same: to make better use of available processor resources.

Figure 12.8 shows a system with two CPUs with four cores each. A Node program is running on the system, but only fully utilizing a single core.

There are reasons why figure 12.8 isn't entirely accurate. Depending on the operating system, the process might be moved around cores, and although it's accurate to say a Node program is a single process, it still uses several threads. Let's say you start up an Express application that uses a MySQL database, static file serving, user sessions, and so on. Even though it will run as a single process, it'll still have eight separate threads.

We're trained to think of Node programs as single-threaded because JavaScript platforms are conceptually single-threaded, but behind the scenes, Node's libraries like `libuv` will use threads to provide asynchronous APIs. That gives us the event-based programming style without having to worry about the complexity of threads.

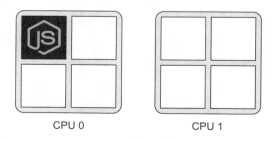

Figure 12.8   A Node process running on a single core

If you're deploying Node applications and want to get more performance out of your multicore, multi-CPU system, then you need to start thinking more about how Node works at this level. If you're running a single application on a multicore system, you want something like the illustration in figure 12.9.

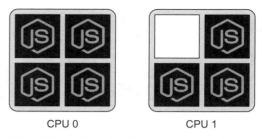

CPU 0   CPU 1

Figure 12.9   Take advantage of more cores by running multiple processes.

Here we're running a Node program on all but one core, the idea being that a core is left free for the system. You can get the number of cores for a system with the os core module. On our system, running require('os').cpus().length returns 4—that's the number of cores we have, rather than CPUs—Node's API cpus method returns an array of objects that represent each core:

```
[{ model: 'Intel(R) Core(TM) i7-4650U CPU @ 1.70GHz',
   speed: 1700,
   times:
   { user: 11299970, nice: 0, sys: 8459650, idle: 93736040, irq: 0 } },
 { model: 'Intel(R) Core(TM) i7-4650U CPU @ 1.70GHz',
   speed: 1700,
   times:
   { user: 5410120, nice: 0, sys: 2514770, idle: 105568320, irq: 0 } },
 { model: 'Intel(R) Core(TM) i7-4650U CPU @ 1.70GHz',
   speed: 1700,
   times:
   { user: 10825170, nice: 0, sys: 6760890, idle: 95907170, irq: 0 } },
 { model: 'Intel(R) Core(TM) i7-4650U CPU @ 1.70GHz',
   speed: 1700,
   times:
   { user: 5431950, nice: 0, sys: 2498340, idle: 105562910, irq: 0 } } ]
```

With this information, we can automatically tailor an application to scale to the target server. Next, we need a way of forking our application so it can run as multiple processes. Let's say you have an Express web application: how do you safely scale it up without completely rewriting it? The main issue is communication: once you start running multiple instances of an application, how does it safely access shared resources like databases? There are platform-agnostic solutions to this that would require a big project rewrite—pub/sub servers, object brokers, distributed systems—but we'll use Node's cluster module.

The cluster module provides a way of running multiple worker processes that share access to underlying file handles and sockets. That means you can wrap a Node application with a master process that works workers. Workers don't need access to shared state if you're doing things like accessing user sessions in a database; all the workers will have access to the database connection, so you shouldn't need to set up any communication between workers.

Listing 12.11 is a basic example of using clustering with an Express application. We've just included the server.js file that loads the main Express application in app.js. This is our preferred method of structuring Node web applications—the part that sets up the server using `.listen(port)` is in a different file than the application itself. In this case, separating the server and application has the additional benefit of making it easier to add clustering to the project.

Listing 12.11 Clustering a Node web application

```
var app = require('./app');
var cluster = require('cluster');        ◁———❶  Load the cluster core module.

if (cluster.isMaster) {
  var totalWorkers = require('os').cpus().length - 1;   ◁
                                                            Determine how many
  console.log('Running %d total workers', totalWorkers);  ❷ processes should be
                                                            started.
  for (var i = 0; i < totalWorkers; i += 1) {
    cluster.fork();                        ◁              Fork the process to
  }                                               ❸       create a worker.
} else {
  console.log('Worker PID:', process.pid);    ◁           Workers will hit this
  app.listen(process.env.PORT || 3000);                   branch, and the PID
}                                               ❹         is displayed.
```

The basic pattern is to load the `cluster` core module ❶, and then determine how many cores should be used ❷. The `cluster.isMaster` allows the code to branch if this is the first (or *master*) process, and then fork workers as needed with `cluster.fork` ❸.

Each worker will rerun this code, so when a worker hits the `else` branch, the server can run the code particular to the worker ❹. In this example workers start listening for HTTP connections, thereby starting the Express application.

There's a full example that includes this code in this book's code samples, which can be found in production/inky-cluster.

If you're a Unix hacker, this should all look suspiciously familiar. The semantics of `fork()` are well known to C programmers. The way it works is whenever the system call `fork()` is used, the current process is cloned. Child processes have access to open files, network connections, and data structures in memory. To avoid performance issues, a system called *copy on write* is used. This allows the same memory locations to be used until a write is attempted, at which point each forked process receives a copy of the original. After the processes are forked, they're isolated.

There's an additional step to properly dealing with clustered applications: worker exit recovery. If one of your workers encounters an error and the process ends, then you'll want to restart it. The cool thing about this is any other active workers can still serve requests, so clustering will not only improve request latency but also potentially uptime as well. The next listing is a modification of listing 12.11, to recover from workers exiting.

Listing 12.12   Recovering from untimely worker death

```
var app = require('./app');
var cluster = require('cluster');

if (cluster.isMaster) {
  var totalWorkers = require('os').cpus().length - 1;

  console.log('Running %d total workers', totalWorkers);

  for (var i = 0; i < totalWorkers; i += 1) {
    cluster.fork();
  }

  cluster.on('exit', function(worker) {        ◁——  ❶ cluster module
    console.log('Worker %d died', worker.id);           is event-based
    cluster.fork();                            ◁——  ❷ Fork again after
  });                                                   worker dies
} else {
  console.log('Worker PID:', process.pid);
  app.listen(process.env.PORT || 3000);
}
```

The cluster module is event-based, so the master can listen for events like exit ❶, which denotes the worker died. The callback for this event gets a worker object, so you can get a limited amount of information about the worker. After that all you need to do is fork again ❷, and you'll be back to the full complement of workers.

Recovering from a crash in the master process

You might be wondering what happens when the master process itself dies. Even though the master should be kept simple to make this unlikely, a crash is still of course possible. To minimize downtime, you should still manage your clustered applications with a process manager like the forever module or Upstart. Both of these solutions are explored in technique 99.

You can run this example with an Express application, and then use kill to force workers to quit. The transcript of such a session should look something like this:

```
Running 3 total workers
    Worker PID: 58733
    Worker PID: 58732
    Worker PID: 58734
    Worker 1 died
    Worker PID: 58737
```

Three workers were running until kill 58734 was issued, and then a new worker was forked and 58737 started.

Once you've got clustering set up, there's one more thing to do: benchmark. We'll use ab (http://httpd.apache.org/docs/2.0/programs/ab.html), the Apache benchmarking tool. It's used like this:

```
ab -n 10000 -c 100 http://localhost:3000/
```

This makes 10,000 requests with 100 concurrent requests at any one time. Using three workers on our system gave 260 requests per second, whereas a single process version resulted in 171 requests per second. The cluster was definitely faster, but is this really working as well as our round-robin example with HAProxy or nginx?

The advantage of the cluster module is that you can script it with Node. That means your developers should be able to understand it rather than having to learn how HAProxy or nginx works for load balancing. Load balancing with an additional proxy server doesn't have the same kind of interprocess communication options that cluster has—you can use process.send and cluster.workers[id].on('message', fn) to communicate between workers.

But proxies with dedicated load-balancing features have a wider choice of load-balancing algorithms. Like all things, it would be wise to invest time in testing HAProxy, nginx, and Node's clustering module to see which works best for your application and your team.

Also, dedicated load-balancing servers can proxy requests to multiple servers—you could technically proxy from a central server to multiple Node application servers, each of which uses the cluster core module to take advantage of the server's multi-core CPU.

With heterogeneous setups like this, you'll need to keep track of what instances of your application are doing. The next section is dedicated to maintaining production Node programs.

12.3 *Maintenance*

No matter how solid your server architecture is, you're still going to have to maintain your production system. The techniques in this section are all about maintaining your Node program; first, package optimization with npm.

TECHNIQUE 104 **Package optimization**

This technique is all about npm and how it can make deployments more efficient. If you feel like your module folder might be getting a bit large, then read on for some ideas on how to fix it.

PROBLEM

Your application seems larger than expected when it's released to production.

SOLUTION

Try out some of npm's maintenance features, like npm prune and npm shrinkwrap.

DISCUSSION

Heroku makes your application's size clear when you deploy: each release displays a *slug size* in megabytes, and the maximum size on Heroku is 300 MB. Slug size is closely related to dependencies, so as your application grows and new dependencies are added, you'll notice that it can increase dramatically.

Even if you're not using Heroku, you should be aware of your application's size. It will impact how quickly you can release new code, and releasing new code should be as fast as possible. When deployment is fast, then releasing bug fixes and new features becomes less of a chore and less risky.

Once you've gone through your dependencies in package.json and weeded out any that aren't necessary, there are some other tricks you can use to reduce your application's size. The `npm prune` command removes packages that are no longer listed in your package.json, but it also applies to the dependencies themselves, so it can sometimes dramatically reduce your application's storage footprint.

You should also consider using `npm prune --production` to remove devDependencies from production releases. We've found test frameworks in our production releases that didn't need to be there. If you have `./node_modules` checked into git, then Heroku will run `npm prune` for you, but it doesn't currently run `npm prune --production`.

> **Why check in ./node_modules?**
>
> It might be tempting to add `./node_modules` to `.gitignore`, but don't! When you're working on an application that will be deployed, then you should keep `./node_modules` in your repository. This will help other people to run your application, and make it easier to reproduce your local setup that passes tests and everything else on a production environment.
>
> Do not do this for modules you release through *npm*. Open source libraries should use *npm* to manage dependencies during installation.

Another command you can use to potentially improve deployment is `npm shrinkwrap`. This will create a file called npm-shrinkwrap.json that specifies the exact version of each of your dependencies, but it doesn't stop there—it continues recursively to capture the version of each submodule as well. The npm-shrinkwrap.json file can be checked into your repository, and npm will use it during deployment to get the exact version of each package.

`shrinkwrap` is also useful for collaboration, because it means people can duplicate the modules you've had living on your computer during development. This helps when someone joins a project after you've been working solo for a few months.

Some PaaS providers have features for excluding files from deployment as well. For example, Heroku can accept a .slugignore file, which works like .gitignore—you could create one like this to ignore tests and local seed data:

```
/test
/seed-data
/docs
```

By taking advantage of npm's built-in features, you can create solid and maintainable packages, reduce deployment time, and improve deployment reliability.

Even with a well-configured, scalable, and carefully deployed application, you'll still run into issues. When things go wrong, you need logs. Read on for techniques when dealing with log files and logging services.

TECHNIQUE 105   **Logging and logging services**

When things break—not if, but when—you'll need logs to uncover what happened. On a typical server, logs are text files. But what about PaaS providers, like Heroku and Nodejitsu? For these platforms you'll need logging services.

PROBLEM

You want to log messages from a Node application on your own server, or on a PaaS provider.

SOLUTION

Either redirect logs to files and use `logrotate`, or use a third-party logging service.

DISCUSSION

In Unix, everything is a file, and that partly dictates the way systems administrators and DevOps experts think about log files. Logs are just files: programs stream data into them, and we stream data out. This kind of setup is convenient for those of us that live in the command line—piping files through commands like `grep`, `sed`, and `awk` makes light work of even gigabyte-sized logs.

Therefore, whatever you do, you'll want to correctly use `console.log` and `console.error`. It also doesn't hurt to be aware of `err.stack`—instances of `Error` in Node get a `stack` property when they're defined, which can be extremely helpful for debugging problems in production. For more on writing logs, take a look at technique 6 in chapter 2.

The benefit of using `console.error` and `console.log` is that you can pipe output to different locations. The following command will redirect data from standard out (`console.log`) to `application.log`, and standard error (`console.error`) to `errors.log`:

```
npm start 1> application.log 2> errors.log
```

All you need to remember is the greater-than symbol redirects output, and using a number specifies the output stream: 1 is standard out, and 2 is standard error.

After a while, your log files will get too large. Fortunately, modern Unix systems usually come with a log rotation package. This will split files up over time and optionally compress them. The `logrotate` package can be installed in Debian or Ubuntu with `apt-get install logrotate`. Once you've installed it, you'll need a configuration file for each set of log files you want to rotate. The following listing shows an example configuration that you can tailor for your application.

Listing 12.13   `logrotate` configuration

Run every ❶ `"/var/www/nodeapp/logs/application.log"`
day `"/var/www/nodeapp/logs/application.err" {`
    `daily`
    `rotate 20` ◁— ❷ **Keep 20 files**
Compress `compress`
rotated files ❸ `copytruncate` ◁— ❹ **Truncate current log file**
`}`

After listing the log files you want to rotate, you can list the options you want to use. `logrotate` has many options, and they're documented in `man logrotate`. The first one here, `daily` ❶, just states that we want to rotate files every day. The next line makes `logrotate` keep 20 files; after that files will be removed ❷. The third option will make sure old log files are compressed so they don't use up too much space ❸.

The fourth option, `copytruncate` ❹, is more important for an application that uses simple standard I/O-based logging. It makes `logrotate` copy and then truncate the current log file. That means that your application doesn't need to close and re-open standard out—it should just work without any special configuration.

Using standard I/O and `logrotate` works well for a single server and a simple application, but if you're running an application in a cluster, you might find it difficult to manage logging. There are Node modules that are dedicated to logging and provide cluster-specific options. Some people even prefer to use these modules because they generate output in standard log file formats.

Using the `log4node` module (https://github.com/bpaquet/log4node) is similar to using `console.log`, but has features that make it easier for use in a cluster. It creates one log file for all workers, and listens for a USR2 signal to determine when to re-open files. It supports configuration options, including log level and message prefix, so you can keep logs quiet during tests or increase the verbosity for critical production systems.

`winston` (https://github.com/flatiron/winston) is a logging module that supports multiple transports, including Cassandra, which allows you to cluster your log writes. That means that if you have an application that writes millions of log entries an hour, then you can use multiple servers to capture the logs in a more reliable manner.

`winston` supports remote log services, including commercial ones like Papertrail. Papertrail and Loggly (see figure 12.10) are commercial services that you can pipe your logs to, typically using the syslogd protocol. They will also index logs, so searching gigabytes of logs is extremely fast, depending on the query.

A service like Loggly is absolutely critical for Heroku. Heroku only stores the last 5,000 log entries, which can be flooded off within minutes of running a typical application. If you've deployed a Node application to Heroku that uses `console.log`, `log4node`, or `winston`, then you'll be able to redirect your logs just by enabling the add-on.

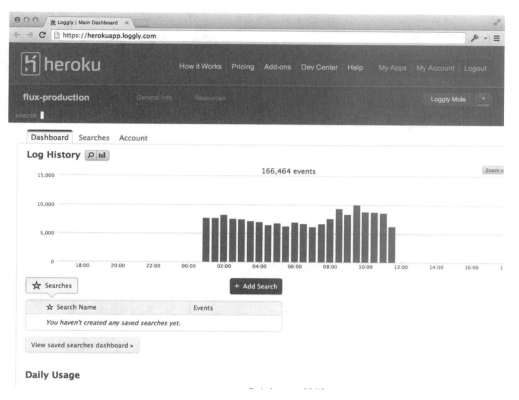

Figure 12.10 Loggly's dashboard

With Heroku, Loggly can be configured by selecting a plan name and running `heroku addons:add Loggly:PlanName` from your project's directory. Typing `heroku addons:open loggly` will open the Loggly web interface, but there's also a link in Heroku's administration panel under *Resources*. Any logging you've done with standard I/O should be sent straight to Loggly.

If you're using `winston`, then there are transports available for Loggly. One is `winston-loggly` (https://github.com/indexzero/winston-loggly), which can be used for easy access to Loggly with non-Heroku services, or your own private servers.

Because Winston transports can be changed by using `winston.add(winston.transports.Loggly, options)`, you don't need to do anything special to support Loggly if you're already using `winston`.

There's a standard for logging that you can use with your applications: The Syslog Protocol (RFC 5424). Syslog message packets have a standard format, so you won't usually generate them by hand. Modules like `winston` typically support syslog, so you can use it with your Node application, but there are two main benefits to using it. The first is that messages have standardized log levels, so filtering logs is easier. Some examples include level 0, known as *Emergency*, and level 4, which is *Warning*. The second is that the protocol defines how messages are sent over the network, which means you can make your Node application talk to a syslog daemon that runs on a remote server.

Some log services like Loggly and Splunk can act as syslog servers; or, you could run your own daemon on dedicated hardware or a virtual machine. By using a standardized protocol like syslog, you can switch between log providers as your requirements change.

That's the last technique on Node-specific production concerns. The next section outlines some additional issues relating to scaling and resiliency.

12.4 *Further notes on scaling and resiliency*

In this chapter we've demonstrated how to use proxies and the `cluster` module to scale Node programs. One of the advantages we cited in `cluster`'s favor is easier inter-process communication. If you're running an application on *separate servers*, how can Node processes communicate?

One simple answer might be HTTP—you could build an internal REST API for communication. You could even use WebSockets if messages need faster responses. When we were faced with this problem, we used RabbitMQ (https://www.rabbitmq.com/). This allowed instances of our Node application to message each other using a shared message bus, thereby distributing work throughout a cluster.

The project was a search engine that used Node programs to download and scrape content. Work was classified into spidering, downloading, and scraping. Swarms of Node processes would take work from queues, and then push new jobs back to queues as well.

There are several implementations of RabbitMQ clients on npm—we used amqplib (https://www.npmjs.org/package/amqplib). There are also competitors to RabbitMQ—zeromq (http://zeromq.org/) is a highly focused and simple alternative.

Another option is to use a hosted publish/subscribe service. One example of this is Pusher (http://pusher.com/), which uses WebSockets to help scale applications. The advantage of this approach is that Pusher can message anything, including mobile clients. Rather than restricting messaging to your Node programs, you can create message channels that web, mobile, and even desktop clients can subscribe to.

Finally, if you're using private servers, you'll need to monitor resource usage. StrongLoop (http://strongloop.com/) offers monitoring and clustering tools for Node, and New Relic (New Relic) also now has Node-specific features. New Relic can help you break down where time is being spent in a live application, so you can use it to discover bottlenecks in database access, view rendering, and application logic.

With service providers like Heroku, Nodejitsu, and Microsoft, and the tools provided by StrongLoop and New Relic, running Node software in production has rapidly matured and become entirely feasible.

12.5 Summary

In this chapter you've seen how to run Node on PaaS providers, including Heroku, Nodejitsu, and Windows Azure. You've also learned about the issues of running Node on private servers: safely accessing port 80 (technique 98), and how WebSockets relate to production requirements (technique 100).

No matter how fast your code is, if your application is popular, then you may run into performance issues. In our section on scaling, you've learned all about caching (technique 101), proxies (technique 102), and scaling with `cluster` (technique 103).

To keep your application running solidly, we've included maintenance-related techniques on npm in production (technique 104) and logging (technique 105). Now if anything goes wrong, you should have enough information to solve the problem.

Now you should know how to build Node web applications and release them in a maintainable and scalable state.

Part 3

Writing modules

As we dove deep into Node's core libraries and looked into real-world recipes, we've been building a narrative that leads to the biggest part of the Node ecosystem: community-driven innovation through third-party module development. As the core provides the Legos with which we build, and the recipes provide the tooling and insight to build confidently, what we ultimately build is up to us!

We have one last chapter that will take you through the ins and outs of building a module and contributing it back to the community.

13

Writing modules: Mastering what Node is all about

The Node package manager (npm) is arguably the *best* package manager any platform has seen to date. npm at its core is a set of tools for installing, managing, and creating Node modules. The barrier to entry is low and uncluttered with ceremony. Things "just work" and work well. If you aren't convinced yet, we hope this chapter will encourage you to take another look.

The subtitle for this chapter is "Mastering what Node is all about." We chose this because user-contributed modules *make up the vast majority of the Node ecosystem*. The core team decided early on that Node would have a *small* standard library, containing just enough core functionality to build great modules upon. We knew understanding this core functionality was paramount to building modules, so we saved this chapter for the end. In Node, you may find 5 or 10 different implementations for a particular protocol or client, and we're *OK* with that because it allows experimentation to drive innovation in the space.

One thing we've learned through our experimentation is that *smaller modules matter.* Larger modules tend to be hard to maintain and test. Node enables smaller modules to be stuck together simply to solve more and more complex problems.

Node's require system (based on CommonJS; http://wiki.commonjs.org/wiki/Modules/1.1) manages those dependencies in a way that avoids dependency hell. It's perfectly fine for modules to depend on different versions of the same module, as shown in figure 13.1.

In addition to standard dependencies, you can specify development and peer dependencies (more on that later) and have npm keep those in check for you.

> **DEPENDENCY GRAPHS** If you ever want to see a dependency graph for your project, just type `npm ls` at the project root to get a listing.

Another difference that was decided early on in the history of npm was to manage dependencies at a *local level by default* as popularized by the bundler Ruby gem. This bundles modules *inside* your project (sitting in the node_modules folder), making dependency hell a non-issue across multiple projects since there's no globally shared module state.

> **INSTALLING GLOBAL MODULES** You can still install global modules if you want with `npm install -g module-name`, which can be useful when you need a system-wide executable, for instance.

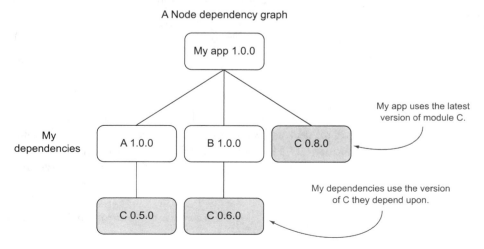

Figure 13.1   Node avoids dependency hell

Hopefully we've whetted your appetite for exploring a range of module-authoring techniques! In this chapter we'll focus on a variety of techniques that center around

- Effectively making the most of the package.json file
- Using npm for various module-authoring tasks
- Best practices for developing modules

Our techniques will follow a logical order from an empty project directory to a completed and published npm module. Although we tried to stuff as many concepts as possible into one module, you may find your module may only need a handful of these steps. When we can't fit a concept into the module, we'll focus on an isolated use case to illustrate the point.

13.1   Brainstorming

What kind of API do we want to build? How should someone consume it? Does it have a clear purpose? These are some of the questions we need to ask as we begin to write a module. In this section we'll walk through researching and proving out a module idea. But first, let's introduce a problem we want to solve, which will provide a context as we progress.

13.1.1   A faster Fibonacci module

One of the most famous Node critiques (although arguably misguided) early on in its history was "Node.js is Cancer" (http://pages.citebite.com/b2x0j8q1megb), where the author argued that a CPU-bound task on a running web server was miserably handled in Node's single-threaded system.

The implementation was a common recursive approach to calculating a Fibonacci sequence (http://en.wikipedia.org/wiki/Fibonacci_number), which could be implemented as follows:

```
function fibonacci (n) {
  if (n === 0) return 0;         ◁——— This line was added to the
  if (n === 1) return 1;               original implementation, since
  return fibonacci(n-1) + fibonacci(n-2);   the original didn't return a
}                                    proper sequence number for 0.
```

This implementation is slow in V8, and since proper tail calls don't yet exist in JavaScript, it wouldn't be able to calculate very high numbers due to a stack overflow.

Let's write a module to help rid the world of slow Fibonacci calculations in order to learn about module development from start to finish.

TECHNIQUE 106   **Planning for our module**

So we want to start writing a module. How should we approach it? Is there anything we can do before we even start writing a line of code? It turns out that planning ahead of time can be extremely helpful and save pain down the road. Let's take a peek on how to do that well.

PROBLEM

You want to write a module. What steps should you take in planning?

SOLUTION

Research what already exists, and ensure that your module does just one thing.

DISCUSSION

It's important to clearly articulate the purpose of your module. If you can't boil it down to one sentence, it may be doing too much. Here's where an important aspect of the Unix philosophy comes in: *make each program do one thing well.*

Surveying the landscape

First, it's good to know what exists already. Has someone else implemented a solution to my problem? Can I contribute there? How did others approach this? A great way to do that is searching on npmjs.org or doing a search from the command line:

```
npm search fibonacci
```

If this is your first time running
npm search, it will take a while
to update the local cache before
you get any results.

Let's look at some of the more interesting results:

```
fibonacci Calculates fibonacci numbers for one or endless iterations.…
   =franklin 2013-05-01 1.2.3 fibonacci math bignum endless

fibonacci-async So, you want to benchmark node.js with fibonacci once…
   =gottox 2012-10-29 0.0.2

fibonacci-native A C++ addon to compute the nth fibonacci number.
   =avianflu 2012-03-21 0.0.0
```

Here we can see the names and descriptions of three different implementations. We also see what version was released last and on what date. It looks like a couple are older and have a lower version number, which may mean the API is in flux or still in progress. But the top result looks pretty mature at version 1.2.3 and has been updated most recently. Let's get more information on that by running the following:

```
npm docs fibonacci
```

The npm docs command will load the module's homepage if specified, or the npmjs search result, which looks like figure 13.2.

The npmjs result page helps give you an overall picture for a module. We can see this module depends on the bignum module and was updated a year ago, and we can view its readme to get a sense of the API.

Although this module looks pretty good, let's create a module as an experiment to try out some other ideas for handling Fibonacci sequences. In our case, let's create a module where we'll experiment with different implementations and benchmark our results using straight JavaScript with no required bignum dependency.

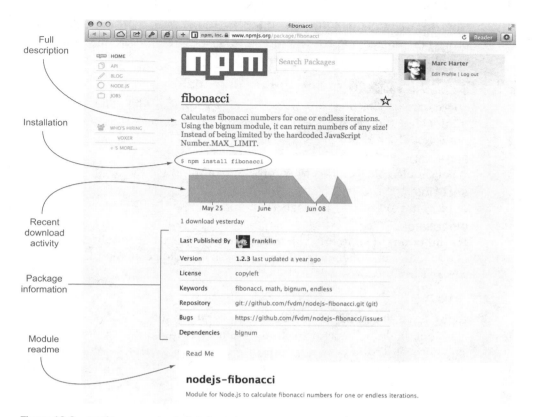

Figure 13.2 npmjs.com package details page

Embrace doing one thing well

A module should be simple and pluggable. In this case, let's try to define our module's purpose in one phrase:

Calculates a Fibonacci number as quickly as possible with only JavaScript

That's a pretty good start: it's clear and succinct. When that concept doesn't ring true anymore, we've blown our scope, and it may be time to write another module that extends this one rather than adding more to it. For this project, adding a web server endpoint that returns the result of this function may be better served in a new module that depends on this one.

Of course, this isn't a rigid requirement, but it helps us clarify the module's purpose and makes it clear for our end users. This statement will be great to add to our package.json (which we'll look at later) and to the top of our readme file.

We'll eventually need a module name, which isn't vital at the start, but in order to refer to it in future techniques, let's call ours `fastfib`. Go ahead and make a fastfib directory that will serve as our project directory:

```
mkdir fastfib && cd fastfib
```

Now that we've defined our "one thing" we want our module to do and have our bare project directory, let's prove out our module idea in the next technique to see if it will actually work.

So we have a focus now; what next? Time to prove our idea. This is the step where we think about the API surface of our module. Is it usable? Does it accomplish its purpose? Let's look at this next.

PROBLEM

What should you code first when proving out your module idea?

SOLUTION

Look at the API surface through TDD.

DISCUSSION

It's important to know how you want your module to function. In `fastfib`, we'll calculate a Fibonacci sequence synchronously. What would be the simplest and easiest-to-use API we can think of?

```
fastfib(3) // => 2
```

Right, just a simple function call that returns the result.

When building an asynchronous API, it's recommended to use the Node callback signature, as it will work well with pretty much any control flow library. If our module were asynchronous, it would look like this:

```
fastfib(3, function (err, result) {
  console.log(result); // => 2
});
```

We have our synchronous API. In the beginning of this chapter, we showed you an implementation that we wanted to improve on. Since we want a baseline to compare other implementations, let's bring that recursive implementation into our project by creating a lib folder with a file called recurse.js with the following content:

```
module.exports = recurse;           ◁──┐ Exporting a single function
                                        │ to match our API design
function recurse (n) {
  if (n === 0) return 0;
  if (n === 1) return 1;
  return recurse(n-1) + recurse(n-2);
}
```

Defining an entry point

Every module has an *entry point*: the object/function/constructor that we get when it's required elsewhere using the `require` keyword. Since we know that we'll be trying different implementations inside our lib directory, we don't want lib/recurse.js to be the entry point, as it may change.

Usually index.js in the project root makes the most sense as an entry point. Many times it makes sense to have the entry point be minimal in nature and just tie together the parts needed to provide the API to the end user. Let's create that file now:

```
module.exports = require('./lib/recurse');
```

Now when a consumer of the module does a `require('fastfib')`, they will get this file and in turn get our recursive implementation. We can then just switch this file whenever we need to change the exposed implementation.

Testing our implementation

Now that we have our first implementation of `fastfib`, let's ensure that we actually have a legit Fibonacci implementation. For that, let's make a folder called test with a single index.js file inside:

```
var assert = require('assert');
var fastfib = require ('../');

assert.equal(fastfib(0), 0);
assert.equal(fastfib(1), 1);
assert.equal(fastfib(2), 1);
assert.equal(fastfib(3), 2);
assert.equal(fastfib(4), 3);
assert.equal(fastfib(5), 5);
assert.equal(fastfib(6), 8);
assert.equal(fastfib(7), 13);
assert.equal(fastfib(8), 21);
assert.equal(fastfib(9), 34);
assert.equal(fastfib(10), 55);
assert.equal(fastfib(11), 89);
assert.equal(fastfib(12), 144);

// if we get this far we can assume we are on the right track
```

Now we can run our test suite to see if we're on track:

```
node test
```

We didn't get any errors thrown, so it looks like we're at least accurate in our implementation.

Benchmarking our implementation

Now that we have a well-defined API and tests around our implementation of `fastfib`, how do we determine how fast it is? For this we'll use a reliable JavaScript benchmarking tool behind the jsperf.com project called Benchmark.js (http://benchmarkjs .com/). Let's include it in our project:

```
npm install benchmark
```

Let's create another folder called benchmark and add an index.js file inside of it with the following code:

```
var assert = require('assert');
var recurse = require('../lib/recurse');    ◄——————  Include our recursive
var suite = new (require('benchmark')).Suite;          implementation to test.
```

Set up a new benchmark suite.

After the tests complete, aggregate the results.

Assert that recurse was the fastest implementation; given it's the only implementation so far, that should be easy!

Add a test for the recurse function, calculating the 20th number in the Fibonacci sequence.

Output the test name, with the amount of iterations it was able to do in the elapsed time.

```
suite
  .add('recurse', function () { recurse(20); })
  .on('complete', function () {
    console.log('results: ') ;
    this.forEach(function (result) {
      console.log(result.name, result.count, result.times.elapsed);
    });
    assert.equal(
      this.filter('fastest').pluck('name')[0],
      'recurse',
      'expect recurse to be the fastest'
    );
  })
  .run();
```

Let's run our benchmark now from the root module directory:

```
$ node benchmark
  results:
  recurse 392 5.491
```

Looks like we were able to calculate `recurse(20)` 392 times in ~5.5 seconds. Let's see if we can improve on that. The original recursive implementation wasn't tail call optimized, so we should be able to get a boost there. Let's add another implementation to the lib folder called tail.js with the following content:

This recursive fibonacci function takes the next index n, the current sequence number, and the next sequence number.

If we've reached the end, return the current sequence number.

In order to expose the same API as recurse, we add this function to set up our default values.

```
module.exports = tail;

function tail (n) { return fib(n, 0, 1); }
function fib (n, current, next) {
  if (n === 0) return current;
  return fib(n -?1, next, current + next);
}
```

Calculate the next call. This is in tail position because the calculations happen before the recursive function call and therefore are able to be optimized by the compiler.

Now, add the test to our benchmark/index.js file and see if we did any better by adding the implementation to the top of the file:

```
var recurse = require('../lib/recurse');
var tail = require('../lib/tail');
---
  .add('recurse', function () { recurse(20); })
  .add('tail', function () { tail(20); })
```

Require tail implementation after the recurse require

Add tail test after the recurse test

Let's see how we did:

```
$ node benchmark
results:
recurse 391 5.501
tail 269702 5.469
```

Putting our recursive function into tail position led to a 689x speedup!

```
assert.js:92
  throw new assert.AssertionError({
  ^
AssertionError: expect recurse to be the fastest
```

Our assertion failed, as recurse is no longer the fastest implementation.

Wow! Tail position really helped speed up our Fibonacci calculation. So let's switch that to be our default implementation in our main index.js file:

```
module.exports = require('lib/tail');
```

And make sure our tests pass:

```
node test
```

No errors; it looks like we're still good. As noted earlier, a proper tail call implementation will still blow our stack when it gets too large, due to it not being supported yet in JavaScript. So let's try one more implementation and see if we can get any better. To avoid a stack overflow on larger sequences of numbers, let's make an iterative implementation and create it at lib/iter.js:

Set up current and next defaults

```
module.exports = iter;

function iter (n) {
  var current = 0, next;
  for (var i = 0; i < n; i++) {
    swap = current, current = next;
    next = swap + next;
  }
  return current;
}
```

Iterate through index n, swapping next and current values and incrementing the next value

Return final current value

Let's add this implementation to the benchmark/index.js file:

Require iterative implementation after the tail require

```
var tail = require('../lib/tail');
var iter = require('../lib/iter');
---
  .add('tail', function () { tail(20) })
  .add('iter', function () { iter(20) })
```

Add iterative test after the tail test

Let's see how we did:

```
$ node benchmark
  results:
  recurse 392 5.456
  tail 266836 5.455
  iter 1109532 5.474
```

An iterative approach turns out to be 4x faster than the tail version, and 2830x faster than the original function. Looks like we have a `fastfib` indeed, and have proven our implementation. Let's update our benchmark/index.js file to assert that `iter` should be the fastest now:

```
assert.equal(
  this.filter('fastest').pluck('name')[0],
  'iter',
  'expect iter to be the fastest'
);
```

Then update our main index.js to point to our fastest version:

```
module.exports = require('./lib/iter');
```

And test that our implementation is still correct:

```
node test
```

No errors still, so we're good! If we later find that V8 optimizes tail call flows to be even faster than our iterative approach, our benchmark test will fail and we can switch implementations. Let's review our overall module structure at this point:

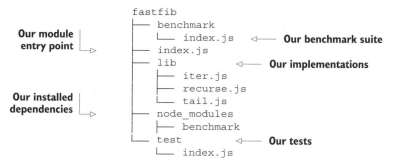

Looks like we've proved our idea. What's important to take away is to experiment! Try different implementations! You likely won't get it right initially, so take this time to experiment until you're satisfied. In this particular technique, we tried three different implementations until we landed one.

Time to look at the next step in module development: setting up a package.json file.

13.2   *Building out the package.json file*

Now we have an idea we like and we've proven that our idea does what we intend it to do, we'll turn to describing that module though a package.json file.

TECHNIQUE 108   **Setting up a package.json file**

A package.json is the central file for managing core data about your module, common scripts, and dependencies. Whether you ultimately publish your module or simply use it to manage your internal projects, setting up a package.json will help drive your development. In this technique we'll talk about how to get a package.json set up and how to populate your package.json using npm.

PROBLEM

You need to create a package.json file.

SOLUTION

Use the built-in npm tools.

DISCUSSION

The `npm init` command provides a nice step-by-step interface for setting up a package.json. Let's run this command on our `fastfib` project directory:

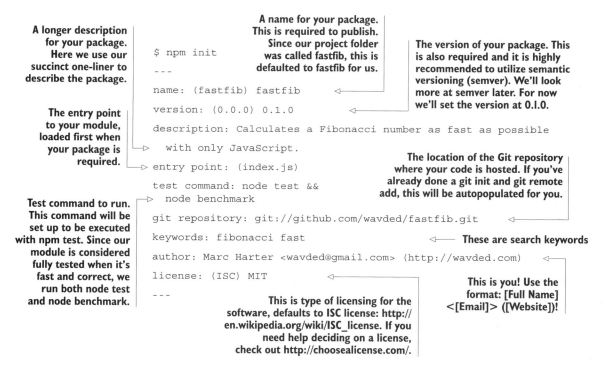

PACKAGE OPTIONS For extensive detail on each package option, view the official documentation (https://www.npmjs.org/doc/json.html) by running `npm help json`.

Running `npm init` gets even simpler when you set up your user config ($HOME/.npmrc) to prepopulate the values for you. Here are all the options you can set:

```
npm config set init.author.name "Marc Harter"
npm config set init.author.email "wavded@gmail.com"
npm config set init.author.url "http://wavded.com"
npm config set init.license "MIT"
```

With these options, `npm init` won't ask you for an author, but instead autopopulate the values. It will also default the license to `MIT`.

A NOTE ABOUT EXISTING MODULES   If you already have modules that you installed prior to setting up your package.json file, `npm init` is smart enough to add them to package.json with the correct versions!

Once you've finished initializing, you'll have a nice package.json file in your directory that looks something like this:

```
{
  "name": "fastfib",
  "version": "0.1.0",
  "description": "Calculates a Fibonacci number as fast
      as possible with only JavaScript.",
  "main": "index.js",
  "bin": {
    "fastfib": "index.js"
  },
  "directories": {
    "test": "test"
  },
  "dependencies": {
    "benchmark": "^1.0.0"
  },
  "devDependencies": {},
  "scripts": {
    "test": "node test && node benchmark"
  },
  "repository": {
    "type": "git",
    "url": "git://github.com/wavded/fastfib.git"
  },
  "keywords": [
    "fibonacci",
    "fast"
  ],
  "author": "Marc Harter <wavded@gmail.com> (http://wavded.com)",
  "license": "MIT",
  "bugs": {
    "url": "https://github.com/wavded/fastfib/issues"
  },
  "homepage": "https://github.com/wavded/fastfib"
}
```

Dependencies your module depends upon. Note how npm init discovered that we already were using the benchmark module and added it for us.

Additional dependencies only used for development. These are by default not included when someone installs your module.

Used by npm bugs to launch a browser at the location where issues can be reported. Since we're using a GitHub repository, npm init autopopulated this property for us.

The location of the project's homepage. Defaulted to GitHub since we entered a GitHub repository URL. This is used by npm docs to launch a browser at the project's homepage.

Now that we have a good start on a package.json file, we can add more properties by either directly modifying the JSON file or using other npm commands that modify different parts of the file for you. The `npm init` command just scratches the surface on what we can do with a package.json file. We'll look at more things we can add as we continue.

In order to look at more package.json configuration and other aspects of module development, let's head to the next technique.

TECHNIQUE 109   **Working with dependencies**

Node has over 80,000 published modules on npm. In our `fastfib` module, we've already tapped into one of those: the `benchmark` module. Having dependencies well defined in our package.json file helps maintain the integrity of our module when it's installed and worked on by ourselves and others. A package.json file tells npm what to fetch and *at what version* to fetch our dependencies when using npm `install`. Failing to include dependencies inside our package.json file will result in errors.

PROBLEM

How do you effectively manage dependencies?

SOLUTION

Keep the package.json file in sync with your module requirements using npm.

DISCUSSION

The package.json file allows you to define four types of dependency objects, shown in figure 13.3.

The types of dependencies are as listed here:

- *dependencies*—Required for your module to function properly
- *devDependencies*—Required solely for development, like testing, benchmarking, and server reloading tools
- *optionalDependencies*—Not required for your module to work, but may enhance the functionality in some way
- *peerDependencies*—Requires another module to be installed in order to run properly

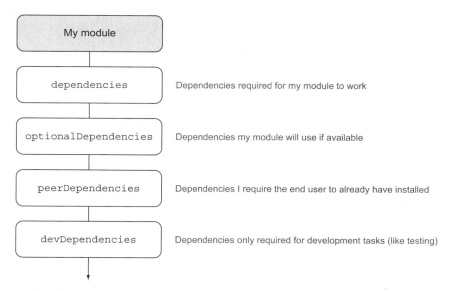

Figure 13.3   The different types of dependencies

Let's look at these in turn with our project and talk about adding and removing within your package.json file as we go.

Main and development dependencies

Currently the package.json file that was generated with `npm init` has `benchmark` listed in the `dependencies` object. If we look at our list, that doesn't hold true for a couple reasons. The first is because our main entry point (index.js) will never require `benchmark` in its require chain, so an end user has no need for it:

```
index.js requires ./lib/iter.js which requires nothing
```

The second reason is because benchmarking is typically a development-only thing for those who work on our module. To remove that out of our dependencies, we can use npm `remove` and have it removed from our package.json file using the `--save` flag:

```
$ npm remove benchmark --save
  unbuild benchmark@1.0.0
```

Then we can install it into our development dependencies using `npm install` with the `--save-dev` flag:

```
$ npm install benchmark --save-dev
  benchmark@1.0.0 node_modules/benchmark
```

Now if we look at our package.json file, we'll see that `benchmark` is now a part of the `devDependencies` object:

```
"devDependencies": {
    "benchmark": "^1.0.0"
},
```

This was somewhat of a brute force way to show you the commands to remove and install with npm. We could have also just moved `benchmark` inside the package.json file in our text editor, avoiding the uninstall and re-install.

Now we have `benchmark` in the right spot, so it won't be installed when others want to use our module.

Optional dependencies

Optional dependencies aren't required for a project to run, but they will be installed along with the regular dependencies. The only difference from normal dependencies is that if an optional dependency *fails* to install, it will be ignored and the module should continue to install properly.

This typically plays out for modules that can get a boost by including a native add-on. For example, `hiredis` is a native C add-on to boost performance for the `redis` module. But it can't be installed everywhere, so it *attempts* to install, but if it fails, the `redis` module falls back to a JavaScript implementation. A typical pattern to check for the dependency in the parent module is this:

```
try {
  var client = require('hiredis'); // super fast!   ◁─┐  Attempt to load the
}                                                      │  optional dependency.
```

```
catch (e) {
  var client = require('./lib/redis'); // fast
}

module.exports = client;
```

If that fails, continue without the dependency, perhaps shimming with another implementation.

Expose a common interface entry point anyone can use regardless of whether they got the optional dependency.

Let's say we wanted to support a larger set of sequence numbers for our `fastfib`. We could add the `bignum` native add-on to enable that functionality by running

```
npm install bignum --save-optional
```

Then we could optionally use that iteration instead if we detect the `bignum` module was able to be installed in our index.js file:

```
try {
    var fastfib = require('./lib/bigiter');
}
catch (er) {
    var fastfib = require('./lib/iter');
}

module.exports = fastfib;
```

Try to include bignum implementation of fastfib.

If that fails, include iterative implementation.

Unfortunately, the `bignum` implementation would be much slower, as it can't be optimized by the V8 compiler. We'd be violating our goal of having the fastest Fibonacci if we included that optional dependency and implementation, so we'll scratch it out for now. But this illustrates how you may want to use optional dependencies (for example, if you wanted to support the highest possible Fibonacci numbers as your goal).

> **HOMEWORK** The code and tests were intentionally left out for the `bignum` implementation; try implementing a version that uses `bignum` and see what performance benchmarks you get from our test suite.

Peer dependencies

Peer dependencies (http://blog.nodejs.org/2013/02/07/peer-dependencies/) are the newest to the dependency scene. Peer dependencies say to someone installing your module: *I expect this module to exist in your project and to be at this version in order for my module to work.* The most common type of this dependency is a plugin.

Some popular modules that have plugins are

- Grunt
- Connect
- winston
- Mongoose

Let's say we *really* wanted to add a Connect middleware component that calculates a Fibonacci number on each request; who wouldn't, right? In order for that to work, we need to make sure the API we write will work against the right version of Connect. For example, we may trust that for Connect 2 we can reliably say our module will work, but we can't speak for Connect 1 or 3. To do this we can add the following to our package.json file:

```
"peerDependencies": {
  "connect": "2.x"
 }
```

Only allow module to be installed if Connect 2.x is also installed.

In this technique we looked at the four types of dependencies you can define in your package.json file. If you're wondering what ^1.0.0 or 2.x means, we'll cover that in depth in the next technique, but let's first talk about updating existing dependencies.

Keeping dependencies up to date

Keeping a module healthy also means keeping your dependencies up to date. Thankfully there are tools to help with that. One built-in tool is npm outdated, which will strictly match your package.json file as well as all the package.json files in your dependencies, to see if any newer versions match.

Let's purposely change our package.json file to make the benchmark module out of date, since npm install gave us the latest version:

```
"devDependencies": {
  "benchmark": "^0.2.0"
 },
```

Roll benchmark back to earlier version.

Then let's run npm outdated and see what we get:

```
$ npm outdated
  Package    Current  Wanted  Latest   Location
  benchmark  1.0.0    0.2.2   1.0.0    benchmark
```

Looks like we have 1.0.0 currently installed, but according to our package.json we just changed, we want the latest package matching ^0.2.0, which will give us version 0.2.2. We also see the latest package available is 1.0.0. The location line will tell us where it found the outdated dependencies.

> **OUTDATED DEPENDENCIES THAT YOU DIRECTLY REQUIRE** Often it's nice to see just your outdated dependencies, not your subdependencies (which can get very large on bigger projects). You can do that by running npm outdated --depth 0.

If we want to update to the wanted version, we can run

```
npm update benchmark --save-dev
```

This will install 0.2.2 and update our package.json file to ^0.2.2.

Let's run npm outdated again:

```
$ npm outdated
  Package Current Wanted Latest Location
  benchmark 0.2.2  0.2.2  1.0.0 benchmark
```

Looks like our current and our desired versions match now. What if we wanted to update to the latest? That's easy: we can install just the latest and save it to our package.json by running

```
npm install benchmark@latest --save-dev
```

> **VERSION TAGS AND RANGES** Note the use of the `@latest` tag in order to get the latest published version of a module. npm also supports the ability to specify versions and version ranges, too! (https://www.npmjs.org/doc/cli/npm-install.html)

We've talked a little about version numbers so far, but they really need a technique unto their own, as it's important to understand what they mean and how to use them effectively. Understanding semantic versioning will help you define versions better for your module and for your dependencies.

TECHNIQUE 110 Semantic versioning

If you're not familiar with semantic versioning, you can read up on it at http://semver.org. Figure 13.4 captures the major points.

Here is how it's described in the official documentation:[1]

Given a version number MAJOR.MINOR.PATCH, increment the:

1 *MAJOR version when you make incompatible API changes,*
2 *MINOR version when you add functionality in a backwards-compatible manner, and*
3 *PATCH version when you make backwards-compatible bug fixes.*

In practice, these rules can be ignored or loosely followed, since, after all, *nobody is mandating* your version numbers. Also, many authors like to play around with their API in the early stages and would prefer not to be at version 24.0.0 right away! But semver can give you, as a module author and as a module consumer, clues within the version number itself as to what may have happened since the last release.

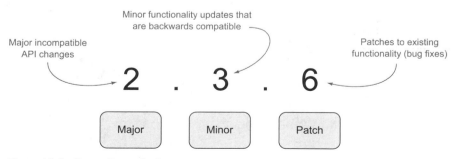

Figure 13.4 Semantic versioning

---

[1] From http://semver.org/.

In this technique we'll look at how to use semver effectively within our `fastfib` library.

PROBLEM

You want to use semver effectively in your module and when including dependencies.

SOLUTION

Understand your underlying projects in order to have a safe upgrade path, and clearly communicate the intent of your module version.

DISCUSSION

We currently have one development dependency in our project, which looks like this in the package.json file:

```
"devDependencies": {
    "benchmark": "^1.0.0"
},
```

This is how npm, by default, will include the version inside the package.json file. This plays nice for how most modules authors behave:

- If the version is less than 1.0.0, like ^0.2.0, then allow any greater PATCH version to be installed. In the previous technique, we saw this ended up being 0.2.2 for the benchmark module.
- If the version is 1.0.0 or greater, like ^1.0.0, then allow any greater MINOR version to be installed. Typically 1.0.0 is considered stable and MINOR versions aren't breaking in nature.

This means that when another user installs your module dependencies, they'll get the latest version that's allowed in your version range. For example, if Benchmark.js released version 1.1.0 tomorrow, although you currently have 1.0.0 on your machine, they would get version 1.1.0, since it still matches the version range.

> **VERSION OPERATORS**   Node supports a whole host of special operators to customize multiple versions or version ranges. You can view them in the semver documentation (https://www.npmjs.org/doc/misc/semver.html).

Versioning dependencies

When writing modules, it can increase the confidence in your dependencies to use a specific version number a user will install along with your module. This way, you know what you've tested will run the same down the dependency chain. Since we know our test suite works with benchmark 1.0.0, let's lock it in to be only that version by running the following:

```
npm install benchmark --save-dev --save-exact
```
Save exact same version installed to the package.json file.

We could've so updated our package.json manually. Let's take a look at what it looks like now:

```
"devDependencies": {
  "benchmark": "1.0.0"
},
```
Exact versions have no special identifiers.

Now that we've locked in our dependency, we can always use npm outdated to see if a new version exists and then npm install using the --save-exact flag to update our package.json!

Versioning the module

As already noted, many module authors use versions less than 1.0.0 to indicate that the API hasn't been fully implemented yet and may change in subsequent versions. Typically, when the version number hits 1.0.0, there's some good stability to the module, and although the API surface may grow, existing functionality shouldn't change that much. This matches how npm behaves when a module is saved to the package.json file.

Currently we have our fastfib module at version 0.1.0 in the package.json file. It's pretty stable, but there may be other changes we want to make before we give it the 1.0.0 status, so we'll leave it at 0.1.0.

The change log

It's also helpful for module authors to have a change log summarizing anything users should be aware of when new releases happen. Here's one such format:

```
Version 0.5.0?--?2014-04-03
---
added; feature x
removed; feature y [breaking change!]
updated; feature z
fixed; bug xx

Version 0.4.3?--?2014-03-25
---
```

Breaking changes, especially in a minor version, should be noted clearly in the change log so users know how to prepare for the update. Some authors like to keep a change log inside their main readme or have a separate change log file.

We've covered some understanding and tooling around versioning our dependencies and our module; let's look at what else we can expose to the consumers of our modules.

13.3   The end user experience

Before we push our module out for consumption, it would be nice to test that it actually works. Of course, we already have a test suite, so we know our logic is sound, but what is the experience of an end user installing the module? How do we expose executable scripts to a user in addition to an API? What versions of Node can we support? In this section we'll take a look at those questions, starting with adding executable scripts.

TECHNIQUE 111   Adding executable scripts

Want to expose an executable when your module is installed? Express, for example, includes an express executable you can run from the command line to help initialize new projects:

```
$ npm install express -g
$ express
```

Installs express module globally making the executable accessible from anywhere

npm itself is an installable module with an npm executable, which we've been using all over in this chapter.

Executables can help end users use your module in different ways. In this technique we'll look at adding an executable script to `fastfib` and include it in our package.json to be installed along with our module.

PROBLEM

How do you add an executable script?

SOLUTION

How do you add command-line tools and scripts for a package and link it inside the package.json file?

DISCUSSION

We have our `fastfib` module built, but what if we wanted to expose a `fastfib` executable to the end user where they could run a command like `fastfib 40` and get the 40th Fibonacci number printed out? This would allow our module to be used on the command line as well as programmatically.

In order to do this, let's create a bin directory with an index.js file inside containing the following:

Require fastfib module

Get sequence number argument

Indicate operating system should look for a node executable to run following code

If we didn't get valid number, exit early and give error message with instructions

```
#!/usr/bin/env node
var fastfib = require('../');
var seqNo = Number(process.argv[2]);

if (isNaN(seqNo)) {
    return console.error('\nInvalid sequence number provided,
    try:\n  fastfib 30\n');
}

console.log(fastfib(seqNo));
```

Output result

Now that we have our application executable, how do we expose it as the `fastfib` command when someone installs our module? For that, we need to update our package.json file. Add the following lines underneath `main`:

```
"main": "index.js",
"bin": {
  "fastfib": "./bin/index.js"
},
```

Alias executable as fastfib and have it run ./bin/index.js

Testing executables with npm link

We can test our executable by using `npm link`. The `link` command will create a global symbolic link to our live module, simulating installing the package globally, as a user would if they installed the module globally.

Let's run `npm link` from our `fastfib` directory:

```
$ npm link
/usr/bin/fastfib
  -> /usr/lib/node_modules/fastfib/bin/index.js
/usr/lib/node_modules/fastfib
  -> /Users/wavded/Dev/fastfib
```

Link fastfib executable to the ./bin/index.js file

Link fastfib module to our working directory code

Now that we've globally linked up our executable, let's try it out:

```
$ fastfib 40
  102334155
```

Since these links are in place now, any edits will be reflected globally. Let's update the last line of our bin/index.js file to announce our result:

```
console.log('The result is', fastfib(seqNo));
```

If we run the `fastfib` executable again, we get our update immediately:

```
$ fastfib 40
  The result is 102334155
```

We've added a `fastfib` executable to our module. It's important to note that everything discussed in this technique is completely cross-platform compatible. Windows doesn't have symbolic links or #! statements, but npm wraps the executable with additional code to get the same behavior when you run `npm link` or `npm install`.

Linking is such a powerful tool, we've devoted the next technique to it!

TECHNIQUE 112   Trying out a module

Besides using `npm link` to test our executables globally, we can use `npm link` to try out our module elsewhere. Say we wanted to try out our shiny new module in another project and see if it'll work out. Instead of publishing our module and installing it, we can just link to it and play around with the module as we see it used in the context of another project.

PROBLEM

You want to try out your module before publishing it *or* you want to make changes to your module and test them in another project without having to republish first.

SOLUTION

Use `npm link`

DISCUSSION

In the previous technique we showed how to use `npm link` to test an executable script's behavior. This showed that we can test our executables while we're developing, but now we want to simulate a local install of our module, not a global one.

Let's start by setting up another project. Since we started this chapter with our cancerous implementation of a Fibonacci web server, let's go full circle and make a little project that exposes `fastfib` as a web service.

Create a new project called `fastfibserver` and put a single server.js file inside with the following content:

```
var fastfib = require('fastfib');          ⟵  Require fastfib
var http = require('http');                    module

http.createServer(function (req, res) {
  res.end(fastfib(40));                     ⟵  Respond with 40th Fibonacci
}).listen(3000);                               number on every request

console.log('fastfibber running on port 3000');
```

We have our server set up, but if we were to run `node server`, it wouldn't work yet because we haven't installed the `fastfib` module in this project yet. To do that we use `npm link`:

```
$ npm link ../fastfib                      ⟵  Pass in path to
  /usr/bin/fastfib                             fastfib module
    -> /usr/lib/node_modules/fastfib/bin/index.js   ⟵  Links are created
  /usr/lib/node_modules/fastfib                         globally first
    -> /Users/wavded/Dev/fastfib
  /Users/wavded/Projects/Dev/fastfibserver/node_modules/fastfib   ⟵
    -> /usr/lib/node_modules/fastfib
    -> /Users/wavded/Dev/fastfib            A final link is set up
                                              in fastwebserver
                                                      project
```

Now if we run our web server, it will run successfully:

```
$ node server
  fastfibber running on port 3000
```

And a visit to our site will give us the 40th Fibonacci number, as shown in figure 13.5.

ANOTHER WAY TO LINK　Since we already linked our module globally in the previous technique running `npm link` inside the `fastfib` project, we could've also run `npm link fastfib` in our `fastfibserver` project to set up the link.

Using `npm link` also helps a lot in debugging your module in the context of another module. Edge cases come up that can best be debugged while running the project that's requiring your module. Once you `npm link` the module, any changes will take

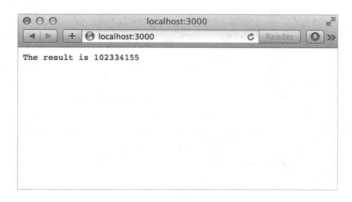

Figure 13.5　Sample output from fastfibserver

effect immediately without the need to republish and re-install. This allows you to fix the problem in your module's code base as you debug.

So far we've defined and implemented our module with tests, set up our dependencies, locked our versions down for our dependencies and our module, added a command-line executable, and practiced using our module. Next we'll look at another aspect of the package.json file—the engines section, and testing our module across multiple versions of Node.

TECHNIQUE 113 Testing across multiple Node versions

Unfortunately, not everybody is able to upgrade to the latest and greatest Node version when it comes on the scene. It takes time for companies to adapt all their code to newer versions, and some may never update. It's important that we know what versions of Node our module can run on so npm knows who can install and run it.

PROBLEM

You want to test your module across multiple versions of Node, and you want your application to be installed only for those versions.

SOLUTION

Keep the `engines` object accurate in the package.json file by running tests across multiple versions of Node.

DISCUSSION

The `npm init` script we ran when first setting up our package.json doesn't include an `engines` section, which means that npm will install it on *any* version of Node. At first glance, we may think that's OK, since we're running pretty vanilla JavaScript code. But we don't really know that without actually testing it.

Typically patch version updates (Node 0.10.2 to 0.10.3, for instance) shouldn't break your modules. But it's a good idea at a minimum to test your modules across minor and major version updates, as V8 receives a decent upgrade and Node's APIs can change. Currently, we've been working off 0.10 branch of Node and things have been working well. So let's start with that. Let's add the following to the end of our package.json file:

```
"homepage": "https://github.com/wavded/fastfib",
  "engines": {
    "node": "0.10.x"        ◁──── Indicate that our module
  }                                can run on any patch
}                                  version of Node 0.10.
```

That's a start, but it really seems like we should be able to support earlier versions of Node. How do we test for that?

A variety of popular options are available:

- Install multiple versions of Node on your machine
- Use Travis CI's multi-Node version support (https://travis-ci.org/)
- Use a third-party multiversion test module that works for your environment (like dnt—https://github.com/rvagg/dnt)

ABOUT NODE VERSIONS   In Node, all odd-numbered minor versions are considered unstable. So 0.11.0 is the unstable version for 0.12.0, and so on. You shouldn't need to test any existing unstable releases. Typically, module authors will only test the latest unstable release as it nears completion.

For our technique we'll focus on installing multiple versions of Node, as that can come in handy for testing new features in upcoming versions of Node, as well as for testing our module.

The tool we'll use is nvm (https://github.com/creationix/nvm; the Windows counterpart is nvmw: https://github.com/hakobera/nvmw). The following instructions will be for nvm, but the commands will be similar in nvmw once installed.

To install, run

```
curl https://raw.github.com/creationix/nvm/v0.5.0/install.sh | sh
source ~/.nvm/nvm.sh        ⟵
```

> We source it right away so we don't have to reload our session. This is done automatically in future sessions.

Now that we have it installed, let's go ahead and test Node version 0.8 of our `fastfib` module. First let's install Node 0.8:

```
$ nvm install 0.8
 ######################################################## 100.0%
 Now using node v0.8.26
```

nvm went out and grabbed the latest version of the 0.8 branch to test against. We could have specified a patch if we wanted, but this will work for now. Note how we're also using this version. We can validate that by running

```
$ node -v
 v0.8.26
```

Now, all Node and npm interaction happens within an isolated environment just for Node 0.8.26. If we were to install more versions, they would be in their own isolated environments. We use `nvm use` to switch between them. For example, if you wanted to go back to your system install of Node, you could do the following:

```
nvm use system
```

And to go back to Node version 0.8.26:

```
nvm use 0.8
```

Let's run our test suite in 0.8.26 and see how we do:

```
$ npm test

  > fastfib@0.1.0 test /Users/wavded/Dev/fastfib
  > node test && node benchmark

  results:
  recurse 432 5.48
  tail 300770 5.361
  iter 1109759 5.428
```

Looks good! Let's update our package.json to include 0.8 versions:

```
"engines": {
  "node": ">=0.8.0 <0.11.0"
}
```

◁─┐ **Include any version
from 0.8.0 up to but
not including 0.11.0.**

WHAT IF MY MODULE LOSES SUPPORT FOR A PARTICULAR NODE VERSION? That's totally fine. Users of an older version of Node will get the last-published package that's supported for their version.

We've tested Node version 0.10 and 0.8; try testing a few other versions on your own. When you're done, switch back to the system Node version.

Now that we've looked through a variety of steps to get our module into a usable state for others, let's publish it!

13.4 Publishing

As we wrap up this chapter, we'll turn our focus on module distribution by looking at publishing modules publicly on npm or privately for internal use.

TECHNIQUE 114   Publishing modules

Whew! We've gone through a lot of different techniques getting our module ready to publish. We know there will likely be changes, but we're ready to release our first version out in the wild to be required in other projects. This technique explores the various aspects of publishing.

PROBLEM

You want to get your module published publicly.

SOLUTION

Register with npm if you haven't and `npm publish`.

DISCUSSION

If it's your first time publishing a module, you'll need to register yourself with npm. Thankfully, it couldn't be any easier. Run the following command and follow the prompts:

```
npm adduser
```

Once finished, npm will save your credentials to the .npmrc file.

CHANGING EXISTING ACCOUNT DETAILS The `adduser` command can also be used to change account details (except username) and register a fresh install with an existing account.

Once registered, publishing a module is just as simple as adding a user. But before we get to that, let's cover some good practices when publishing modules.

Before you publish

One of the biggest things before publishing is to review technique 110 about semantic versioning:

- Does your version number accurately reflect the changes since the last push? If this is your first push, this doesn't matter as much.
- Do you do a changelog update with your release? Although not required, it can be extremely helpful to those who depend on your project to get a high-level view of what they can expect in this release.

Also, check whether your tests pass to avoid publishing broken code.

Publishing to npm

Once you're ready to publish, it's as simple as running the following command from the project root directory:

```
npm publish
```

npm will respond with the success or failure of the publish. If successful, it will indicate the version that was pushed to the public registry.

Can you tell that npm wants you to get your modules out there as painlessly as possible?

Undoing a publish

Although we want a publish to go well, sometimes we miss things we wanted to release, or have some things we realize are broken after the fact. It's recommended you don't unpublish modules (although the ability exists). The reason is that people who are depending on that module and/or version can no longer get it.

Typically, make the fix, increase the PATCH version, and npm publish again. A simple way to do that is by running the following commands:

```
// make fixes
$ npm version patch
  v0.1.1
$ npm publish
```

The npm version command (https://www.npmjs.org/doc/cli/npm-version.html) will update your package.json based on the arguments passed. Here we used patch to tell it to increment the patch version.

npm *does not* allow you to publish over an existing version, since that also would affect people who have already downloaded that particular version.

There are some cases where you really want to discourage users from using a particular version. For example, maybe a severe security flaw was fixed in versions 0.2.5 and above, yet you have users depending on versions earlier than that. npm can help you get the word out by using npm deprecate.

Let's say in the future, we find a critical bug in fastfib version 0.2.5 and below, and we wanted to warn users who are using those modules. We could run the following:

```
npm deprecate fastfib@"<= 0.2.5"
  "major security issue was fixed in v0.2.6"
```

Deprecate module name followed by version range affected and message NPM should display

Now if any user installs fastfib 0.2.5 or less, they'll receive the specified warning from npm.

Keeping modules private

Although open source can be a fun and collaborative environment, there are times when you want your project to remain private. This is especially true for work done for clients. It can also be handy to bake a module first internally before deciding whether to publish. npm can safeguard your module and keep it private for you. In this technique we'll talk about configuring your module to stay private and including private modules in your projects.

PROBLEM

You want to keep your module private and use it internally.

SOLUTION

Configure `private` in your package.json file and share it internally.

DISCUSSION

Let's say we want to let `fastfib` to only be used internally. To ensure it doesn't get accidentally published, we add the following to our package.json file:

```
"private": true
```

This tells npm to refuse to publish your package with `npm publish`.

This setting works well for client-specific projects. But what if you have a core set of internal modules you want to share across projects within your development team? For that there are a few different options.

Sharing private modules with Git

npm supports a couple of ways you can share your internal modules that are minimal to set up out of the box. If you're using a Git repository, npm makes this incredibly simple to do.

Let's use GitHub as an example (although it can be *any* Git remote). Let's say we had our private repo at

```
git@github.com:mycompany/fastfib.git
```

We can then include it in our package.json dependencies with `npm install` (or modify the package.json directly):

```
npm install git+ssh://git@github.com:mycompany/fastfib.git --save
```

Pretty sweet! This by default will pull the contents of the `master` branch. If we wanted to specify a particular commit-ish (tag, branch, or SHA-1—http://git-scm.com/book/en/Git-Internals-Git-Objects), we can do that too! Here are some examples within a package.json file:

```
"dependencies": {
  "a": "git+ssh://git@github.com:mycompany/a.git#0.1.0",
  "b": "git+ssh://git@github.com:mycompany/b.git#develop",
  "c": "git+ssh://git@github.com:mycompany/c.git#dacc525c"
}
```

Specifying by tag

Specifying by branch name

Specifying by commit SHA-I (typically you won't need the whole SHA-I)

INCLUDING PUBLIC REPOSITORIES   You may have guessed it, but you can also use `public` Git repositories as well. This can be helpful if you really need a feature or fix that hasn't been published on npm yet. For more examples, see the package.json documentation (https://www.npmjs.org/doc/json.html#Git-URLs-as-Dependencies).

Sharing private modules as a URL

If you aren't using Git or prefer to have your build system spit out packages, you can specify a URL endpoint where npm can find a tarball. To package up your module, you can use the `tar` command like the following:

> We tell tar to make a new archive (c), compress the archive using gzip (z), and store it in the file (f) fastfib.tar.gz, giving it the contents of the fastfib directory.

```
tar -czf fastfib.tar.gz fastfib
```

From here, we can throw that file on a web server and install it using the following:

```
npm install http://internal-server.com/fastfib.tar.gz --save
```

A NOTE ABOUT PUBLIC ENDPOINTS   Although typically not used often, tarballs of packages can be used with public endpoints too; it's usually better and easier to publish to npm instead.

Sharing modules with a private npm registry

Another option for private repositories is hosting your own private npm registry and having `npm publish` push to that repository. For the complete functionality of npm, this will require an installation of a recent version of CouchDB, which, in turn, requires Erlang.

Since this involves a variety of tricks/headaches depending on your operating system, we won't cover setting up an instance here. Hopefully, the process will get streamlined soon. If you want to experiment, check out the `npm-registry-couchapp` project (https://github.com/npm/npm-registry-couchapp).

13.5   *Summary*

Third-party modules are where innovation happens. npm makes this trivial and fun! With the rise of social coding sites like GitHub, collaboration on modules is also easy to do. In this chapter we looked at many different aspects of module development. Let's summarize what we learned.

When starting to work on a module, consider the following:

- Define your module idea. Can you summarize it in one sentence?
- Check your module idea. Is there another module out there doing what you want to do? Search it out with `npm search` or npmjs.org.

Once you've landed on an idea, prove it out. Start with a simple API you'd like to work with. Write an implementation and tests installing any dependencies you need along the way.

After you've proven your idea (or perhaps during), think about these things:

- Have you initialized your package.json file? Run `npm init` to get a skeleton representing the state of the current project.
- Work with your dependencies. Are some optional, development-only? Make sure that's indicated in your package.json file.
- Check your semver ranges in package.json. Do you trust the version ranges specified in your package.json file? Check for updates with `npm outdated`.
- What versions of Node will your code run on? Check it out by using nvm or a build system like Travis CI. Specify the version range in your package.json file.
- Try out your module using `npm link` in another project.

When you're ready to publish, it's as simple as `npm publish`. Consider keeping a changelog for your users and try to follow semantic versioning, so users have a reasonable idea of what to expect from version to version.

And that's a wrap for this book! We hope at this point you were able to grasp the core foundations of Node, understand how to apply those foundations in real-world scenarios, and how to go beyond standard development by writing your own Node modules (which we hope to see on npm!).

A growing Node community is available to help you continue to level up on your journey. Please check out the appendix to make the most of that community. If you have specific questions for us, please visit the #nodejsinpractice Google group (https://groups.google.com/forum/#!forum/nodejsinpractice), and thanks for reading!

appendix
Community

This section will help you to make the most of the growing Node community. Programming communities can help you get answers to problems that aren't directly answered by the documentation. You can learn more effectively just by hanging out with like-minded people—whether online or in person.

A.1 Asking questions

Sometimes you just want to know how to do something that seems like it should be easy, but isn't. Other times you think you might have found a serious bug in Node. Whatever the situation, when you need help that isn't satisfied by Node's API documentation, there are several official channels you can use.

The first is the Node mailing list, which is the nodejs Google Group (http://groups.google.com/group/nodejs). You can subscribe by email or use Google's web interface. The web interface allows posts to be searched, so you can see if someone has asked your question before.

The group has contributions from prominent community members, including Isaac Schlueter, Mikeal Rogers, and Tim Caswell, so it's a good place to get help and learn about Node in general.

There's also an official IRC chat room: #node.js on irc.freenode.net. It's extremely busy though, so be prepared for a lot of messages. Informative discussions do happen in #node.js, so some patience may be rewarded!

If you're a fan of the Stack Exchange network, you can post questions using the node.js tag (http://stackoverflow.com/questions/tagged/node.js).

If you prefer social networks, the Node users group (https://github.com/joyent/node/wiki/Node-Users) in the Node wiki lists hundreds of Twitter accounts alongside the developer's time zone, so you could look for people to talk to that way. Hint: the authors of this book are listed!

Finally, if your question is about a specific module, you should check that module's documentation for community information. For example, the Express web framework has its own express-js Google Group (https://groups.google.com/group/express-js).

A.2 *Hanging out*

Your city may have an active Node meet-up group. Examples include the London Node.js User Group (http://lnug.org/), the Melbourne Node.JS Meetup Group (http://www.meetup.com/MelbNodeJS/), and BayNode (http://meetup.com/BayNode/) in Mountain View, California.

There are also major Node conferences, including NodeConf (http://nodeconf.com/) and NodeConf EU (http://nodeconfeu.com/).

To help you find more meet-up groups and conferences, the Node.js Meatspace page at https://github.com/knode/node-meatspace is frequently updated. You can, of course, try searching at meetup.com as well.

A.3 *Reading*

If you're looking for something to read, you'll find some great community publications. Naturally reddit.com/r/node collects some great posts, but there are also collections on Medium, including medium.com/node-js-javascript.

Noted Node developers have blogs you can check as well. Isaac Z. Schlueter (http://blog.izs.me/), James Halliday (http://substack.net/; see figure A.1), and Tim Caswell all have personal blogs where they write about Node. Tim's howtonode.org has material suitable for beginners, but will also help you keep track of new developments.

There are also commercial blogs that have some contributions from talented Node developers. Joyent's blog at joyent.com/blog often has interesting posts relating to deploying Node, and StrongLoop's blog, "In the Loop," at strongloop.com/strongblog, does as well.

Nodejitsu's blog at blog.nodejitsu.com has advice on deployment, and also features module authors talking about their work.

Figure A.1 James Halliday's blog about Node and testing

A.4 Training by the community, for the community

One interesting development in teaching Node is NodeSchool (http://nodeschool.io/; see figure A.2). You can install lessons yourself, but there are also community-run in-person training events. NodeSchool provides the materials to set up training events, so they're proliferating rapidly around the world. The site has more details on upcoming events.

**Figure A.2
Learn Node with
NodeSchool.**

A.5 Marketing your open source projects

If you're going to take part in the Node community, one of the best ways to it is to share your work. But npm is now so popular that it's hard to get your module noticed.

To really make an impact, you should consider marketing your open source projects. If prominent Node bloggers have contact forms or Twitter accounts, it won't hurt to tell them about what you've made. As long as you're polite, and give your work some context so it's easy to understand, then it can really help you get feedback and improve your skills.

index